Communications
in Computer and Information Science 2375

Series Editors

Gang Li ⓘ, *School of Information Technology, Deakin University, Burwood, VIC,
Australia*
Joaquim Filipe ⓘ, *Polytechnic Institute of Setúbal, Setúbal, Portugal*
Zhiwei Xu, *Chinese Academy of Sciences, Beijing, China*

Rationale
The CCIS series is devoted to the publication of proceedings of computer science conferences. Its aim is to efficiently disseminate original research results in informatics in printed and electronic form. While the focus is on publication of peer-reviewed full papers presenting mature work, inclusion of reviewed short papers reporting on work in progress is welcome, too. Besides globally relevant meetings with internationally representative program committees guaranteeing a strict peer-reviewing and paper selection process, conferences run by societies or of high regional or national relevance are also considered for publication.

Topics
The topical scope of CCIS spans the entire spectrum of informatics ranging from foundational topics in the theory of computing to information and communications science and technology and a broad variety of interdisciplinary application fields.

Information for Volume Editors and Authors
Publication in CCIS is free of charge. No royalties are paid, however, we offer registered conference participants temporary free access to the online version of the conference proceedings on SpringerLink (http://link.springer.com) by means of an http referrer from the conference website and/or a number of complimentary printed copies, as specified in the official acceptance email of the event.

CCIS proceedings can be published in time for distribution at conferences or as post-proceedings, and delivered in the form of printed books and/or electronically as USBs and/or e-content licenses for accessing proceedings at SpringerLink. Furthermore, CCIS proceedings are included in the CCIS electronic book series hosted in the SpringerLink digital library at http://link.springer.com/bookseries/7899. Conferences publishing in CCIS are allowed to use Online Conference Service (OCS) for managing the whole proceedings lifecycle (from submission and reviewing to preparing for publication) free of charge.

Publication process
The language of publication is exclusively English. Authors publishing in CCIS have to sign the Springer CCIS copyright transfer form, however, they are free to use their material published in CCIS for substantially changed, more elaborate subsequent publications elsewhere. For the preparation of the camera-ready papers/files, authors have to strictly adhere to the Springer CCIS Authors' Instructions and are strongly encouraged to use the CCIS LaTeX style files or templates.

Abstracting/Indexing
CCIS is abstracted/indexed in DBLP, Google Scholar, EI-Compendex, Mathematical Reviews, SCImago, Scopus. CCIS volumes are also submitted for the inclusion in ISI Proceedings.

How to start
To start the evaluation of your proposal for inclusion in the CCIS series, please send an e-mail to ccis@springer.com.

Nadia Magnenat Thalmann · Xinrong Hu ·
Bin Sheng · Daniel Thalmann · Tao Peng ·
Weiliang Meng · Jin Huang · Lei Zhu · Xiong Wei
Editors

Computer Animation and Social Agents

37th International Conference, CASA 2024
Wuhan, China, June 5–7, 2024
Revised Selected Papers, Part II

Editors
Nadia Magnenat Thalmann
MIRALab-University of Geneva
Geneva, Switzerland

Bin Sheng
Shanghai Jiao Tong University
Shanghai, China

Tao Peng
Wuhan Textile University
Wuhan, China

Jin Huang
Wuhan Textile University
Wuhan, China

Xiong Wei
Wuhan Textile University
Wuhan, China

Xinrong Hu
Wuhan Textile University
Wuhan, China

Daniel Thalmann
Swiss Federal Institute of Technology
Lausanne, Switzerland

Weiliang Meng
University of Chinese Academy of Sciences
Beijing, China

Lei Zhu
The Hong Kong University of Science
and Technology
Guangzhou, China

ISSN 1865-0929 ISSN 1865-0937 (electronic)
Communications in Computer and Information Science
ISBN 978-981-96-2683-0 ISBN 978-981-96-2684-7 (eBook)
https://doi.org/10.1007/978-981-96-2684-7

© The Editor(s) (if applicable) and The Author(s), under exclusive license
to Springer Nature Singapore Pte Ltd. 2025

This work is subject to copyright. All rights are solely and exclusively licensed by the Publisher, whether the whole or part of the material is concerned, specifically the rights of translation, reprinting, reuse of illustrations, recitation, broadcasting, reproduction on microfilms or in any other physical way, and transmission or information storage and retrieval, electronic adaptation, computer software, or by similar or dissimilar methodology now known or hereafter developed.
The use of general descriptive names, registered names, trademarks, service marks, etc. in this publication does not imply, even in the absence of a specific statement, that such names are exempt from the relevant protective laws and regulations and therefore free for general use.
The publisher, the authors and the editors are safe to assume that the advice and information in this book are believed to be true and accurate at the date of publication. Neither the publisher nor the authors or the editors give a warranty, expressed or implied, with respect to the material contained herein or for any errors or omissions that may have been made. The publisher remains neutral with regard to jurisdictional claims in published maps and institutional affiliations.

This Springer imprint is published by the registered company Springer Nature Singapore Pte Ltd.
The registered company address is: 152 Beach Road, #21-01/04 Gateway East, Singapore 189721, Singapore

If disposing of this product, please recycle the paper.

Preface

CASA is the oldest international conference on computer animation and social agents in the world. It was founded in Geneva in 1988 under the name of Computer Animation (CA) by the Computer Graphics Society (CGS). In the past few years, CASA was held in Europe (Belgium, Netherlands, France, Switzerland, UK, etc.), Asia (South Korea, China, Singapore) and the USA. CASA 2024 provided a great opportunity to interact with leading experts, share your own work, and educate yourself through exposure to the research of your peers from around the world.

The 37th International Conference on Computer Animation and Social Agents (CASA 2024) was held on June 5–7, 2024, in Wuhan, China. The conference was organized by the Wuhan Textile University (WTU), Shanghai Jiao Tong University (SJTU), State Key Laboratory of Computer Science, Institute of Software, Chinese Academy of Sciences and State Key Laboratory of Multimodal Artificial Intelligence Systems/National Laboratory of Pattern Recognition, Institute of Automation, Chinese Academy of Sciences.

These CASA 2024 CCIS proceedings are composed of 60 papers from a total of 208 submissions. To ensure the high quality of the publications, each paper was reviewed by at least two experts in the field and authors of accepted papers were asked to revise their paper according to the review comments prior to publication.

We would like to express our deepest gratitude to all the PC members and external reviewers who provided timely high-quality reviews. We would also like to thank all the authors for contributing to the conference by submitting their work.

November 2024

Nadia Magnenat Thalmann
Xinrong Hu
Bin Sheng
Daniel Thalmann
Tao Peng
Weiliang Meng
Jin Huang
Lei Zhu
Xiong Wei

Organization

Honorary Conference Co-chairs

Weilin Xu	Wuhan Textile University, China
Enhua Wu	Chinese Academy of Sciences and University of Macao, China
Dagan Feng	University of Sydney, Australia

Conference Co-chairs

Minghua Jiang	Wuhan Textile University, China
Nadia Magnenat Thalmann	Nanyang Technological University, Singapore
Bin Sheng	Shanghai Jiao Tong University, China

Program Co-chairs

Jun Feng	Wuhan Textile University, China
Daniel Thalmann	École Polytechnique Fédérale de Lausanne, Switzerland
Weiliang Meng	Inst. of Automation, Chinese Academy of Sciences, China
Xuequan Lu	La Trobe University, Australia

Organization Co-chairs

Xinrong Hu	Wuhan Textile University, China
Ping Li	Hong Kong Polytechnic University, China
Sheng Li	Peking University, China
Jin Huang	Wuhan Textile University, China
Lei Zhu	Hong Kong University of Science and Technology, China

Publication Co-chairs

Yongtian Wang — Beijing Institute of Technology, China
Jian Zhu — Guangdong University of Technology, China
Xiao Lin — Shanghai Normal University, China
Chunwei Tian — Northwestern Polytechnical University, China

Publicity Co-chairs

Tao Peng — Wuhan Textile University, China
Xiong Wei — Wuhan Textile University, China
Anton Bardera — University of Girona, Spain
Jun Tie — South-Central Minzu University, China
Kai Zhang — Wuhan University of Science and Technology, China
Zhiwei Ye — Hubei University of Technology, China
Tao Lu — Wuhan Institute of Technology, China
Jinxing Liang — Wuhan Textile University, China
Feng Yu — Wuhan Textile University, China
Bangchao Wang — Wuhan Textile University, China

Technical Chair

Kunfang Song — Wuhan Textile University, China

Workshop Co-chairs

Guangzheng Fei — Communication University of China, China
Ye Pan — Shanghai Jiao Tong University, China
Zixin Huang — Wuhan Institute of Technology, China
Ruhan He — Wuhan Textile University, China

Poster Co-chairs

Jia Chen — Wuhan Textile University, China
Li Li — Wuhan Textile University, China

Zixin Huang   Wuhan Institute of Technology, China
Peng Ye   Wuhan Textile University, China

Program Committee

Weilin Xu	Wuhan Textile University; Chinese Academy of Engineering, China
Nadia Magnenat Thalmann	University of Geneva, Switzerland
Enhua Wu	Chinese Academy of Sciences and University of Macau, China
Daniel Thalmann	École Polytechnique Fédérale de Lausanne, Switzerland
Xinrong Hu	Wuhan Textile University, China
Sheng Li	Peking University, China
Bin Sheng	Shanghai Jiao Tong University, China
Weiliang Meng	Chinese Academy of Sciences, China
Ping Li	Hong Kong Polytechnic University, China
Ruhan He	Wuhan Textile University, China
Jian Zhu	Guangdong University of Technology, China
Tao Peng	Wuhan Textile University, China
Xiao Lin	Shanghai Normal University, China
Feng Yu	Wuhan Textile University, China
Guangzheng Fei	Communication University of China, China
Min Li	Wuhan Textile University, China
Ye Pan	Shanghai Jiao Tong University, China
Jinxing Liang	Wuhan Textile University, China
Ran Yi	Shanghai Jiao Tong University, China
Junping Liu	Wuhan Textile University, China
Youquan Liu	Chang'an University, China
Jia Chen	Wuhan Textile University, China
Andrea Bönsch	RWTH Aachen University, Germany
Carlo Harvey	Birmingham City University, UK
Changhe Tu	Shandong University, China
Jin Huang	Wuhan Textile University, China
Dominik Michels	KAUST, Saudi Arabia
Edmond S. L. Ho	University of Glasgow, UK
Etienne Vouga	University of Texas at Austin, USA
Hui Chen	Institute of Software, Chinese Academy of Sciences, China
James Hahn	George Washington University, USA
Jason Peng	Simon Fraser University, Canada

Li Li	Wuhan Textile University, China
Jian Chang	Bournemouth University, UK
Jianmin Zheng	Nanyang Technological University, Singapore
Libin Liu	Peking University, China
Marcelo Kallmann	University of California Merced, USA
Nadine Aburumman	Brunel University London, UK
Qiong Zeng	Shandong University, China
Sehoon Ha	Georgia Institute of Technology, USA
Shihui Guo	Xiamen University, China
Xiong Pan	Wuhan Textile University, China
Shinjiro Sueda	Texas A&M University, USA
Taesoo Kwon	Hanyang University, South Korea
Taku Komura	Hong Kong University, China
Xiaokun Wang	University of Science and Technology Beijing, China
Yi Zhang	Sichuan University, China
Yoonsang Lee	Hanyang University, South Korea
Xiao Zhang	South-Central Minzu University, China
Ximing Yang	South-Central Minzu University, China
Bo Meng	South-Central Minzu University, China
Shihua Zhang	South-Central Minzu University, China
Wan Tang	South-Central Minzu University, China
Zheng Ye	South-Central Minzu University, China
Shengzhou Xu	South-Central Minzu University, China
Pan Lai	South-Central Minzu University, China
Dejun Wang	South-Central Minzu University, China
Jun Wang	South-Central Minzu University, China
Lingyun Zhou	South-Central Minzu University, China
Yuanai Xie	South-Central Minzu University, China
Ke Xu	South-Central Minzu University, China
Tongzhou Zhao	Wuhan Institute of Technology, China
Tongwei Lu	Wuhan Institute of Technology, China
Hui Li	Wuhan Institute of Technology, China
Bin Zhang	Wuhan Institute of Technology, China
Juan Li	Wuhan Institute of Technology, China
Xin Nie	Wuhan Institute of Technology, China
Tao Lu	Wuhan Institute of Technology, China
Wei Liu	Wuhan Institute of Technology, China
Yanan Li	Wuhan Institute of Technology, China
Jun Liu	Wuhan Institute of Technology, China
Xin Xu	Wuhan University of Science and Technology, China

Bo Li	Wuhan University of Science and Technology, China
He Deng	Wuhan University of Science and Technology, China
Peng Li	Wuhan University of Science and Technology, China
Jianfeng Lu	Wuhan University of Science and Technology, China
Ling Zhang	Wuhan University of Science and Technology, China
Jun Pang	Wuhan University of Science and Technology, China
Jianfeng Lu	Wuhan University of Science and Technology, China
Xiaoming Liu	Wuhan University of Science and Technology, China
Jinguang Gu	Wuhan University of Science and Technology, China
Maofu Liu	Wuhan University of Science and Technology, China
Feng Gao	Wuhan University of Science and Technology, China
Mingwei Wang	Hubei University of Technology, China
Jinshan Cao	Hubei University of Technology, China
Ran Zhou	Hubei University of Technology, China
Guangqi Xie	Hubei University of Technology, China
Yepei Chen	Hubei University of Technology, China
Zhina Song	Hubei University of Technology, China
Teng Xiao	Hubei University of Technology, China

Contents – Part II

Augmented Knowledge Distillation via Contrastive Learning 1
    Jianhua Xu, Lin Li, Jianping Gou, Lan Du, and Yibing Zhan

Near-Eye Gaze Estimation in Virtual Reality Based on Deep Learning 13
    Zian Sun, Yang Liu, and Shiwei Cheng

N-Sand Table: A Multi-user Interactive Virtual Sand Table Based on NeRF
Technology 28
    *Xinlei Zhang, Jiahui Yu, Chenchen Gong, Danming Huang,
Yuxiang Sun, and Xianzhong Zhou*

A Weakly Supervised Crowd Counting Method Based on Contrastive
Deep Supervision 46
    Guohang Huang, Bo Yang, Jianlin Zhu, and Yong Zhang

The Detection and Rectification for Identity-Switch Based
on the Unfalsified Control 61
    Junchao Huang, Xiaoqi He, Yebo Wu, and Sheng Zhao

LDSBC: Lightweight Detection Network for Student Behavior
in Classroom Scenario 74
    Minghua Jiang, Cheng Wang, Xingwei Zheng, Li Liu, and Feng Yu

YOLO-DPW: An Efficient Real-Time Fabric Defect Detection Model 89
    Wentao Hu, Xinrong Hu, Rui Yang, Li Li, and Xiaoyun Yan

Quadrotor Unmanned Aerial Vehicle Trajectory Tracking Under
Event-Triggered Sliding Mode Control 101
    *Han Jiang, Ruhui Yin, Zilin Shu, Ziang Ren, Hongyu Zhu,
and Zixin Huang*

Emotion Loss Attacking: Adversarial Attack Perception for Skeleton
Based on Multi-dimensional Features 112
    Feng Liu, Qing Xu, and Qijian Zheng

Method of Ionospheric Delay Positioning Error Correction Based
on Transformer Model Prediction 123
    *Hongteng Ma, Mengying Lin, Die Zou, Ziang Wei, Zhengke Wen,
and Zixin Huang*

RFBR-IR:Regularized Frequency BRDF Reconstruction Inverse Rendering 134
  Xiuyuan zheng, Weibing Wan, Zhijun Fang, and Dezhi Liu

A Lightweight Camouflaged Object Detection Model Based on Improved
Attention Mechanism 150
  Jinyu Song, Xianzhi Luo, Li Jiang, Yan Zhang, and Chun Liu

A Fabric Defect Detection Method Based on Improved YOLOv5 165
  *Chi Zhang, Cancan Rao, Hongjun Li, Chengjun Chang, Jun Wang,
  Aijie Yin, and Zixuan Wang*

UBAViz: User Behavior Analyzing in Literature Resources by Modeling
User Behavior Sequences 181
  Junxiang Cao, Xiaoju Dong, Zhiyuan Wu, and Xuefei Tian

ACDiff: Angle Craft Diffusion Model for Novel View Synthesis 197
  Huangqianyu Luo

A Training and Evaluation System for Magnetic-Actuated Virtual Vessel
Interventional Surgery 215
  Bosi Cai, Jianhui Zhao, Zhiyong Yuan, Tingbao Zhang, and Yu Feng

Self-Adapting NeRF: Non-ideal Video Based NeRF for High-Quality
Novel View Synthesis 233
  Tao Huang, Dengming Zhu, Min Shi, and Zhaoqi Wang

AnisoVector: Separable Anisotropic Set Abstraction and Group Vector
Attention for Efficient Point Cloud Analysis 249
  Zhicheng Wen and Lei Wang

Automatic Code Generation from GUI Screenshots with Vision-Language
Models 267
  Jingbin Liang, Jing Liang, and Shuang Li

SymMoment: A Symbol Recognition System Using Multiple Moments
and Multicore Computing 280
  Zili Zhang, Tao Peng, Xinrong Hu, and Jun Zhang

DBFF-PCGC: Dual-Branch Feature Fusion for Point Cloud Geometry
Compression 302
  Shiyu Lu, Cheng Han, Huamin Yang, and Fudong Yu

Camouflaged Object Detection Based on Edge-Feature Interation 316
  Aiqing Zhu, Xiaomei Kuang, Junbin Yuan, and Qingzhen Xu

EyeGlove: Enhancing Smart Glove with Visual Information to Assist Students in Conducting Chemistry Experiments in Mixed Reality Laboratory 330
   Hong Cui, Dehui Kong, and Zhiquan Feng

Multilevel Topology Structure-Aware Network for 3D Hand Pose Estimation 342
   Yanjun Liu, Wanshu Fan, Xiaopeng Wei, and Dongsheng Zhou

Research on Garment Image Retrieval Method Based on Transformer and Multi-layer Feature Fusion 357
   Guangjian Sheng, Wei Ye, Lei Zhang, and Zhiran Yu

Hybrid Attention Mechanism for 3D LIDAR Point Clouds Semantic Segmentation 370
   Yujie Miao, Xiaodong Yi, Naiyang Guan, and Hailun Lu

Think Twice Before Acting: Efficient Knowledge Distillation for 6-DOF Camera Relocalization 385
   Zhendong Xiao, Junqi Wu, and Wu Wei

A Spatially Enhanced CNN and Multiscale Transformer Fusion Approach for Chest Radiograph Registration 397
   Jia Chen, Zeping Lin, Fei Fang, Huanrong Jiang, Yajie Meng, and Jinlong Qin

The Phantom Dance: Personalized Anatomical Skeleton Inference from Monocular Views 409
   Boyuan Cheng, Yingjie Xi, Jingyao Cai, Rupert Page, Jian Jun Zhang, and Xiaosong Yang

Research on Human-Robot Collaboration Safety Model and Key Algorithms in Assembly Systems 424
   Weina Li, Zhiquan Feng, Dehui Kong, and Zishuo Xia

Seam Carving Empowered by Reinforcement Learning for Optimal Content Preservation 441
   Muhammad Mujahid, Md. Shamim Hossain, Asad Khan, and Zhangjin Huang

Robust Mesh Denoising Based on Weighted Least Squares 456
   Xi Lan, Saishang Zhong, Jia Chen, Zheng Liu, and Xiong Pan

Author Index 471

Contents – Part I

YOLOv8_ODY: An Object Detection Model for Traffic Signs 1
   JiaHui Lv and Xiang Li

Mask-Based Matching Enhancement for Unsupervised Point Cloud
Registration 13
   Minghua Jiang, Liyu Ren, Zhaoxiang Chen, Li Liu, and Feng Yu

Driver Action Recognition Based on Dynamic Adaptive Transformer 28
   Wei Xu, Yu Mao, Junqi Li, Tao Peng, Cuilan Li, and Yalan Fang

SimNET: A Deep Learning Macroscopic Traffic Simulation Model
for Signal Controlled Urban Road Network 39
   Jingyao Liu, Tianlu Mao, Zhaoqi Wang, and Huikun Bi

UAV-LMDN: Lightweight Multi-scale Small Object Detection Network
for Unmanned Aerial Vehicle Perspective 57
   Li Liu, Long Chen, Feng Yu, Tao Peng, Xinrong Hu, and Minghua Jiang

LRDN: Lightweight Risk Detection Network for Power System Operations 72
   Li Liu, Yukun Chen, Feng Yu, Tao Peng, Xinrong Hu, and Minghua Jiang

Personalized Federated Learning by Model Pruning via Batch
Normalization Layers 86
   Annan Wang and Bencan Gong

IT-HMDM: Invertible Transformer for Human Motion Diffusion Model 105
   Jiashuang Zhou and Xiaoqin Du

Fashion Image Retrieval Based on Multimodal Features Enhancement
and Fusion 118
   Yingjin Li, Shufan He, Zhaojing Wang, Jin Huang, Xinrong Hu, and Li Li

Syntactic Enhanced Multi-channel Graph Convolutional Networks
for Aspect-Based Sentiment Analysis 132
   Yuhang Ding and Jianyu Gao

Intelligent Helmet with Hazardous Area Detection Based on Digital Twin
Technology 146
   Jiajie Liu, Feng Yu, Li Liu, and Minghua Jiang

An Evaluation of a Simulation System for Visitors in Exhibit Halls 160
   Cheng-Hao Hung, Sai-Keung Wong, Shu-Chi Yang, and I-Cheng Yeh

Foley Agent: Automatic Sound Design and Mixing Agent for Silent
Videos Driven by LLMs 177
   Kun Lin and Shiguang Liu

Deep Metric Learning with Feature Aggregation for Generalizable Person
Re-identification 193
   Mingfu Xiong, Yang Xu, Xiangguo Huang, Yi Wen, Tao Peng, and Xinrong Hu

Diverse 3D Human Pose Generation in Scenes Based on Decoupled
Structure 207
   Bowen Dang and Xi Zhao

A Combination Simulation Method for Low Orbit Large Scale Satellites
via STK and NS2 224
   Maolin Xiong, Haowen Wu, Yong Wang, Yan Zhang, and Wei Ren

Semantic-Guided Prompt Learning Network for Generalized Zero-Shot
Learning 241
   Yongli Hu, Lincong Feng, Huajie Jiang, Mengting Liu, and Baocai Yin

MiT-Unet: Mixed Transformer Unet for Transmission Line Segmentation
in UAV Images 254
   Jianwei Chen, Yuan Liu, Lifang Li, Shuifa Sun, and Ning Wei

Semantic-Driven Multi-character Multi-motion 3D Animation Generation 268
   Hui Liang, Fan Xu, Junjun Pan, and Zhaolin Zhang

MSAR: A Mask Branch Module Integrating Multi-scale Attention
and RefineNet 281
   Ping Han, Zhicheng Liu, and Huahong Zuo

Multi-level Knowledge Distillation for Class Incremental Learning 290
   Yongli Hu, Mengting Liu, Huajie Jiang, Lincong Feng, and Baocai Yin

Research on the Algorithm of Helmet-Wearing Detection Based
on the Optimized Mobilevit and Centernet 306
   Min Li, Chun Wang, Peng Luo, and Menghan Ai

Better Sampling, Towards Better End-to-End Small Object Detection 319
   Zile Huang, Chong Zhang, Mingyu Jin, Fangyu Wu, Chengzhi Liu, and Xiaobo Jin

Stealthily Launch Backdoor Attacks Against Deep Neural Network
Models via Steganography 336
  *Aolin Che, Miaoxia Chen, Abdul Samad Shibghatullah, Cai Guo,
  and Ping Li*

Seat Belt Wearing Detection Based on EfficientDet_Ad 350
  Min Li, Menghan Ai, Peng Luo, and Chun Wang

DHNet: A Depthwise Separable Convolution-Based High-Resolution Full
Projector Compensation Network 366
  Yuqiang Zhang, Huamin Yang, Cheng Han, and Chao Zhang

Denoising Implicit Feedback for Extractive Question Answering 375
  Xinrong Hu, Jingxue Chen, Zijian Huang, Xun Yao, and Jie Yang

Iterative Consistent Attentional Diffusion Model for Multi-Contrast MRI
Super-Resolution 388
  *Jia Chen, Tong Zhang, Fei Fang, Huanrong Jiang, Yajie Meng,
  and Jinlong Qin*

Author Index 403

Augmented Knowledge Distillation via Contrastive Learning

Jianhua Xu[1], Lin Li[1], Jianping Gou[2(✉)], Lan Du[3], and Yibing Zhan[4]

[1] Jiangsu University, Zhenjiang, China
{2212208043,2112208002}@stmail.ujs.edu.cn
[2] Southwest University, Chongqing, China
cherish.gjp@gmail.com
[3] Monash University, Clayton, VIC, Australia
lan.du@monash.edu
[4] JD Explore Academy, Beijing, China
zhanyibing@jd.com

Abstract. Deploying computer animation and social agent models on devices with limited computing resources presents a significant challenge. Knowledge distillation (KD) emerges as an effective model compression technique, harnessing the extensive knowledge of a large teacher model to facilitate the training of a smaller student model. However, existing KD methodologies predominantly concentrate on transferring task-specific knowledge from supervised tasks, such as logit and feature, overlooking the valuable insights into cross-sample discrepancy inherent in teacher and student models. In response, we propose a novel KD approach, termed augmented knowledge distillation via contrastive learning (CAKD). Initially, in the supervision task, we enhance vanilla KD by integrating logit and feature outputs derived from both the original and the augmented data. Subsequently, in the self-supervision task, we identify pivotal sample pairs and delineate the inter-sample multi-discrepancy relationships using the intrinsic data structure, thus obviating the need for external labels or supervision. This enables knowledge transfer through contrastive learning. The fusion of knowledge from both tasks synergistically enhances student performance. Experimental assessments conducted on two publicly available datasets demonstrate that CAKD surpasses state-of-the-art knowledge distillation methodologies.

Keywords: Model compression · knowledge distillation · contrastive learning · vision recognition

1 Introduction

The rapid evolution of deep neural networks has spurred innovation in the realms of computer animation and social agents. Remarkable progress have been achieved in fields like Machine Learning for Animation, AI-based Animation, and Social Robots, furnishing artists, the entertainment industry, and virtual interaction platforms with more potent tools. Consequently, user experience and creative efficiency have been augmented. However, these sophisticated applications rely on intricate artificial intelligence algorithms and models. The deployment of these large deep models on edge devices encounters challenges stemming from computational and memory constraints. Knowledge distillation (KD) [1], a widely adopted model compression technique, facilitates the training of lightweight models by distilling pertinent knowledge from larger teacher models. KD has exhibited promising outcomes across diverse domains, including computer vision [2,3] and natural language processing [4,5].

KD guides student training by generating a soft target through incrementing the final softmax temperature. The "dark knowledge" encapsulated within this soft target provides the student with additional information. Subsequent research endeavors have proposed the transfer of feature maps [6,7] or their refined information [8] between intermediate layers of teachers and students to provide more nuanced insights. However, these forms of knowledge are tailored to supervised classification tasks, potentially limiting the exploration of richer feature representations by the network. To address this limitation and mine knowledge that is not task-specific as a complement to supervised classification knowledge, [9] pioneers the combination of self-supervision with KD for the first time, attaching lightweight modules to a teacher's backbone. Additionally, [10] contrasts similar and dissimilar data pairs to extract non-task-specific visual representations. Moreover, [11] employs rotation-based self-supervision and auxiliary branching for knowledge transfer, while [12] models relationships and transfers knowledge by aligning graphs.

While these approaches have yielded commendable results in integrating self-supervision tasks into KD, they overlook the potential of leveraging the cross-sample discrepancy relationship between the teacher and the student to learn a better student model. Furthermore, they have not explored the potential impact of this discrepancy strength on KD. To address these oversights, we propose CAKD, wherein, unlike vanilla KD, students mimic teachers not only from normal data based on a supervision task but also from a broader scope encompassing imitated augmented data and self-supervision tasks.

In summary, our main contributions are as follows: 1) We enhance vanilla KD by merging logit and feature outputs generated from both the original and the augmented data. 2) We introduce multi-discrepancy contrastive distillation as a self-supervision task. Here, we identify key sample pairs and delineate the cross-sample multi-discrepancy relationships using the intrinsic structure of the data, without relying on external labels or supervision. This enables knowledge transfer through contrastive learning.

2 Augmented KD via Contrastive Learning

We enhance vanilla knowledge distillation by employing data splicing techniques and subsequently extract cross-sample discrepancy knowledge through contrastive learning. The framework is illustrated in Fig. 1.

2.1 Knowledge Fusion: Logit and Feature

As our CAKD incorporates contrastive learning, necessitating two transformed datasets, we have enhanced Vanilla KD [13] by amalgamating the logit and feature outputs generated from both original and augmented data. This amalgamation serves as a supervised task, aiding students in comprehending and accommodating the diversity inherent in various datasets. This process is illustrated in Fig. 2.

Given the original data $\{x\}$, the corresponding augmented datasets $\{\tilde{x}_1, \tilde{x}_2\}$ can be obtained through data augmentation techniques, as described in [14]. We apply random data augmentation methods to the images, including color dithering, grayscale conversion, and Gaussian blur. The combined set $\{x, \tilde{x}_1, \tilde{x}_2\}$ is then input into the network. Features $\{F, \tilde{F}_1, \tilde{F}_2\} \in \mathbb{R}^{b \times c \times h \times w}$ are extracted at the middle layer, and logits $\{Z, \tilde{Z}_1, \tilde{Z}_2\} \in \mathbb{R}^{1 \times C}$ are obtained at the output layer of the network. Here, c represents the channel dimension, while h and w denote the spatial dimensions, b indicates the batch size, and C is the number of classes.

Logit Fusion: We merge the logits $\{Z\}$ derived from the original data with the logits $\{\tilde{Z}_1, \tilde{Z}_2\}$ from the augmented data to obtain a fused logit $\{\tilde{Z}\}$. Subsequently, we compute the predictive probability vector $\tilde{P}_T$ with the softmax function. Finally, the logit fusion KD loss is defined as follows:

$$L_{LSKD} = \lambda_{ce} L_{ce} + \lambda_{kld} L_{kld} \\ = \lambda_{ce} CE(P^s_{T=1}, y) + \lambda_{kld} T^2 KLD\left(\tilde{P}^s_T, \tilde{P}^t_T\right), \quad (1)$$

where $\tilde{P}^s_T$ and $\tilde{P}^t_T$ represent predictive probability vectors corresponding to the fused logits from the student and the teacher, respectively. T is the hyperparameter temperature serving as label softening. $P^s_{T=1}$ is the predictive probability vector generated by the student for the original data sample with $T = 1$. $CE(\cdot)$ denotes the cross-entropy loss, and $KLD(\cdot)$ denotes the KL-Divergence loss. λ_{ce} and λ_{kld} are hyper-parameters.

Feature Fusion: We combine the feature vector $\{F\}$ with those feature vectors $\{\tilde{F}_1, \tilde{F}_2\}$ derived on $\{\tilde{x}_1, \tilde{x}_2\}$ to create a fused feature vector, $\{\tilde{F}\}$. $\tilde{F}^t_l$ and $\tilde{F}^s_l$ represent the fused feature vectors from the l-th layer of the teacher and the student, respectively. Multiplying them with their own transposed matrices yields the $3b \times 3b$ similarity matrices A^t_l and A^s_l:

$$A^s_l = R(\tilde{F}^s_l) \cdot R(\tilde{F}^s_l)^T \quad A^t_l = R(\tilde{F}^t_l) \cdot R(\tilde{F}^t_l)^T, \quad (2)$$

where $R(\cdot) : \mathbb{R}^{3b \times c_1 \times h_1 \times w_1} \mapsto \mathbb{R}^{3b \times c_2 \times h_2 \times w_2}$ denotes feature reshaping, and $(\cdot)^T$ denotes matrix transpose.

Inspired by the self-attention framework [15], we project the similarity matrices A^s_l and A^t_l into two subspaces using multilayer perceptrons (MLP), incorporating "Linear-ReLU-Linear-Normalization" to generate the query vector Q^s_l and

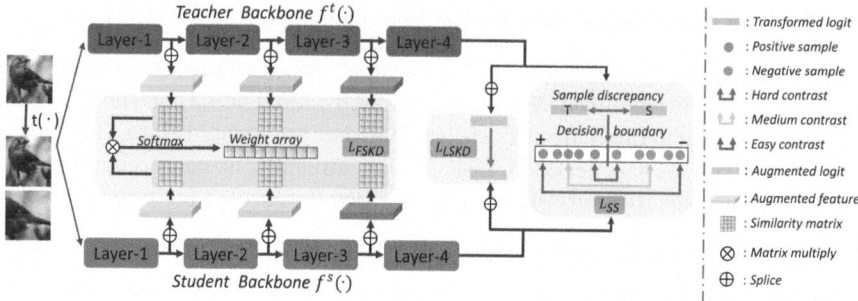

Fig. 1. The overview of proposed CAKD. CAKD includes two components: (1) Data Splicing KD Loss ($L_{LSKD} + L_{FSKD}$). (2) Multi-Discrepancies Contrastive Distillation Loss (L_{SS}).

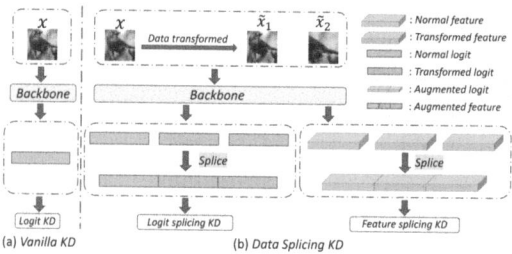

Fig. 2. Difference between (a) vanilla KD and (b) data splicing KD that we propose.

key vectors K_l^t. For the i-th sample:

$$Q_l^s[i] = MLP_Q(A_l^s[i]) \quad K_l^t[i] = MLP_K(A_l^t[i]), \tag{3}$$

where the parameters of MLP_Q and MLP_K are learned during training and shared across all instances.

Then, we employ the softmax function $\mathcal{F}$ to compute the attention weight $\gamma(l', l'')$ between a student's layer l' and a teacher's layer l''. Attention-based allocation can mitigate the adverse impacts stemming from layer mismatch while integrating beneficial guidance from multiple target layers. $\gamma(l', l'')$ is calculated as follows:

$$\gamma(l', l'')[i] = \mathcal{F}(Q_{l'}^s[i] \cdot K_{l''}^t[i]) = \frac{\exp(Q_{l'}^s[i] \cdot K_{l''}^t[i]^T)}{\sum_j \exp(Q_{l'}^s[i] \cdot K_j^t[i]^T)}, \tag{4}$$

With $MSE(\cdot)$ denoting mean squared error loss, the KD loss based on the fused features is computed as:

$$L_{FSKD} = \sum_{i=1}^{b}\sum_{l'=1}^{L'}\sum_{l''=1}^{L''} \gamma(l', l'')[i] \cdot MSE\left(\tilde{F}_{l''}^t[i], \tilde{F}_{l'}^s[i]\right) \tag{5}$$

2.2 Multi-discrepancies Contrastive Distillation

We introduce a self-supervision task aimed at enabling the model to acquire cross-sample multi-discrepancy knowledge, complementing its supervised classification knowledge. The primary process is depicted in Fig. 3: (1) Division into positive and negative sets: Utilizing the sample discrepancy between the teacher and the student as a decision boundary without relying on labels. (2) Multi-mining: Selectively identifying key sample pairs exhibiting diverse discrepancy strengths. (3) Template strategy: Adjusting weights assigned to each sample to facilitate balanced training. (4) Cosine decay strategy: Optimizing the training process by dynamically adapting sample proportions with varying discrepancy strengths.

Divide Positive and Negative Set: The input image x is forwarded through the teacher network $f^t(\cdot)$ and the student network $f^s(\cdot)$ to obtain the teacher feature $f^t(x_i)$ and the student feature $f^s(x_i)$. In each batch, for the teacher, we designate image x_i as an anchor and select another image x_a. If images x_i and x_a belong to the same category, their distance $D\left(f^t(x_i), f^t(x_a)\right)$ is expected to be small, if not approaching zero; and vice versa. Here, $D(\cdot)$ represents the Euclidean distance. For x_i, the distance $D\left(f^t(x_i), f^s(x_i)\right)$ between teacher and student features should neither be excessively large nor too small compared to the distance $D\left(f^t(x_i), f^t(x_a)\right)$, but rather lie within a moderate range. So we utilize $D\left(f^t(x_i), f^s(x_i)\right)$ as the decision boundary to classify (x_i, x_a) into positive or negative sets. If $D\left(f^t(x_i), f^t(x_a)\right)$ is smaller than the decision boundary, it indicates that (x_i, x_a) is similar enough to be classified as a positive pair; otherwise, it is classified as a negative pair [16]. Based on this criterion, we define the positive set S_i^p and the negative set S_i^n as follows:

$$\begin{cases} S_i^p = \{(x_i, x_a) \mid D\left(f^t(x_i), f^t(x_a)\right) < D\left(f^t(x_i), f^s(x_i)\right)\} \\ S_i^n = \{(x_i, x_a) \mid D\left(f^t(x_i), f^t(x_a)\right) \geq D\left(f^t(x_i), f^s(x_i)\right)\} \end{cases} \quad (6)$$

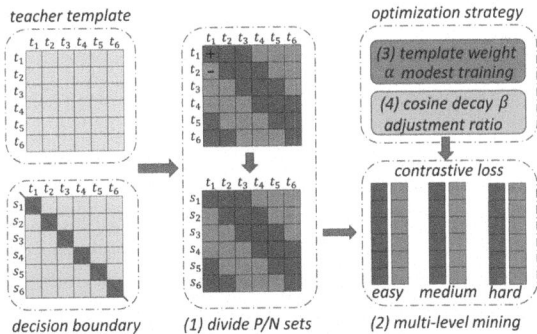

Fig. 3. Multi-discrepancies contrastive distillation.

For each sample x_i, we aim to bring the features $f^t(x_i)$ and $f^s(x_j)$ closer together, while pushing $f^t(x_i)$ and $f^s(x_k)$ apart, where $(x_i, x_j) \in S_i^p$ and $(x_i, x_k) \in S_i^n$. To simplify, we denote $d_{ij}^p = D\left(f^t(x_i), f^s(x_j)\right)$ and $d_{ik}^n = D\left(f^t(x_i), f^s(x_k)\right)$. The relationship between d_{ij}^p and d_{ik}^n is termed **cross-sample discrepancy**. The objective is to enhance the representation of similar samples by increasing positive pair probabilities and improve the separability of dissimilar samples by reducing negative pair probabilities, thereby enhancing overall feature discriminability. To achieve this, we utilize an Info-NCE-like loss [17] to transfer cross-sample discrepancy knowledge:

$$L = -\log \frac{\sum_{k=1}^{K} \exp\left(d_{ik}^n/\tau\right)}{\sum_{k=1}^{K} \exp\left(d_{ik}^n/\tau\right) + \sum_{j=1}^{J} \exp\left(d_{ij}^p/\tau\right)}, \qquad (7)$$

where τ is a hyper-parameter. K and J represent the number of sample pairs in S_i^p and S_i^n.

2) Multi-mining: However, optimizing the above objective in Eq. (7) for all sample pairs within a batch is computationally expensive. Drawing inspiration from hard example mining techniques [18], we introduce multi-mining to address this challenge. Instead of optimizing over all sample pairs, we focus on a select few key pairs $\{d_i^p, d_i^n\}$ in each batch, where $d_i^p = \{d_i^{hp}, d_i^{mp}, d_i^{ep}\}$ denotes the key positive sample pairs and $d_i^n = \{d_i^{hn}, d_i^{mn}, d_i^{en}\}$ represents the key negative sample pairs.

For positive pairs $(x_i, x_j) \in S_i^p$, a large d_{ij}^p indicates a significant discrepancy between x_i and x_j, suggesting that d_{ij}^p is close to the decision boundary, making it more challenging to distinguish between positive and negative pairs. Conversely, a small d_{ij}^p signifies an easy classification as a positive pair. The situation is reversed for negative pairs.

For each teacher feature $f^t(x_i)$, we categorize sample pairs based on their difficulty: easy (d_i^{ep}, d_i^{en}), medium (d_i^{mp}, d_i^{mn}), and hard (d_i^{hp}, d_i^{hn}) pairs from the positive set S_i^n and negative set S_i^n of the student. The mining process is as follows:

$$\begin{aligned}
d_i^{hp} &= \max_{j \in S_i^p}\left(d_{ij}^p\right), & d_i^{hn} &= \min_{k \in S_i^n}\left(d_{ik}^n\right), \\
d_i^{mp} &= \underset{j \in S_i^p}{\text{median}}\left(d_{ij}^p\right), & d_i^{mn} &= \underset{k \in S_i^n}{\text{median}}\left(d_{ik}^n\right), \\
d_i^{ep} &= \min_{j \in S_i^p}\left(d_{ij}^p\right), & d_i^{en} &= \max_{k \in S_i^n}\left(d_{ik}^n\right),
\end{aligned} \qquad (8)$$

where $max(\cdot)$ and $min(\cdot)$ represent the maximum and minimum values of the set, and $median(\cdot)$ denotes the median of the selected set.

To emphasize the influence of a few key samples on the loss, we adjust Eq. (7) to ensure that the denominator includes only one positive and one negative pair. Specifically, we pull the key positive sample pair d_i^p closer while pushing the key negative sample pair d_i^n farther away. The revised equation is as follows:

$$L = -\log \frac{\exp\left(d_i^n/\tau\right)}{\exp\left(d_i^n/\tau\right) + \exp\left(d_i^p/\tau\right)}, \qquad (9)$$

3) Template Strategy: Optimizing Eq. (9) primarily on key sample pairs reduces computational costs, but there's a risk of the model overfitting to these samples, potentially rendering it sensitive to minor variations in them [19]. To mitigate this, we refine Eq. (9) with a template strategy, which redistributes weights for d_i^p and d_i^n throughout the optimization process.

Consider sample x_i with key positive and negative pairs (x_i, x_j) and (x_i, x_k) that we've identified. We compute the distances $D\left(f^t(x_i), f^t(x_j)\right)$ and $D\left(f^t(x_i), f^t(x_k)\right)$ as primary guides for optimizing d_i^p and d_i^n. We define non-negative weight factors α_i^p and α_i^n in a teacher-guided self-supervision manner as follows:

$$\begin{cases} \alpha_i^p = [d_i^p - D\left(f^t(x_i), f^t(x_j)\right)]_+ \\ \alpha_i^n = [D\left(f^t(x_i), f^t(x_k)\right) - d_i^n]_+ \end{cases} \quad (10)$$

where $D\left(f^t(x_i), f^t(x_j)\right)$ and $D\left(f^t(x_i), f^t(x_k)\right)$ define the template relation. The $[]_+$ denotes a "zero cutoff" operation to ensure α_i^p and α_i^n are non-negative. Please note that for d_i^p, when it represents the distance $D\left(f^t(x_i), f^s(x_{j=i})\right)$, serving as the decision boundary, α_i^p must be greater than 0. In other cases, when it represents the distance $D\left(f^t(x_i), f^s(x_{j\neq i})\right)$, the sign of a may vary. The situation is reversed for d_i^n. The student is optimized towards the teacher's template relation, aiming for d_i^p and d_i^n to surpass the template relation. This approach fosters modest training objectives and enhances generalization.

4) Cosine Decay Strategy: We conduct an ablation analysis on samples with varying discrepancy strengths. Inspired by the analysis results and the concept of curriculum temperature [5], we introduce a cosine decay strategy to optimize sample pairs. This strategy aims to mitigate overfitting to difficult samples and prevent performance degradation resulting from neglecting effective samples.

The results are presented in Table 4. The cosine decay formula is as follows:

$$\begin{cases} \beta[j] = \frac{3}{2}\left(1 + \cos\frac{\pi E_n}{k E_{\text{loops}}}\right), & j = 1, 2 \\ \beta[3] = 3 - \beta[1] - \beta[2] \end{cases} \quad (11)$$

Here, the weight factors $\beta[1]$, $\beta[2]$, and $\beta[3]$ regulate the weights of easy, medium, and hard sample pairs. E_{loops} is the total number of epochs, and E_n represents the current epoch. Parameter k controls the decay rate, with $k = 0.5$ for $\beta[1]$ and $k = 1.0$ for $\beta[2]$.

We incorporate the template parameters and cosine decay strategy into Eq. 9. The self-supervision loss obtained is as follows:

$$L_{SS} = \sum_{j=1}^{3} -\log \frac{\exp\left(\alpha_i^n d_i^n / \tau\right)}{\exp\left(\alpha_i^n d_i^n / \tau\right) + \exp\left(\alpha_i^p d_i^p / \tau\right)} \cdot \beta[j] \quad (12)$$

2.3 The Total Loss

Consequently, the total loss L_{total} of our CAKD consists of three components: the fused logit loss L_{LSKD}, the fused feature loss L_{FSKD} and the SS task loss L_{SS}:

$$L_{total} = L_{LSKD} + \lambda_1 L_{FSKD} + \lambda_2 L_{SS} \quad (13)$$

where λ_1 and λ_2 are hyperparameters.

Table 1. Top-1 accuracy (%) on **CIFAR100**.↑ indicates improvement over baseline.

Teacher Student	WRN-40-2 WRN-16-2	ResNet32×4 ResNet8×4	VGG13 VGG8	ResNet32×4 ShuffleNetV2	VGG13 MobileNetV2
Teacher	75.61	79.42	75.38	79.42	75.38
Student	73.26	70.07	70.68	73.12	65.79
KD [13]	74.97 (↑ 1.71)	73.38 (↑ 3.31)	73.41 (↑ 2.73)	75.20 (↑ 2.08)	66.63 (↑ 0.84)
VID [8]	74.90 (↑ 1.64)	73.37 (↑ 3.30)	73.72 (↑ 3.04)	75.40 (↑ 2.28)	67.97 (↑ 2.18)
SSKD [9]	75.77 (↑ 2.51)	76.14 (↑ 6.07)	74.64 (↑ 3.96)	78.63 (↑ 5.51)	70.95 (↑ 5.16)
SRRL [20]	75.63 (↑ 2.37)	74.58 (↑ 4.51)	74.32 (↑ 3.62)	75.68 (↑ 2.56)	69.53 (↑ 3.74)
DKD [21]	75.82 (↑ 2.56)	74.91 (↑ 4.84)	74.27 (↑ 3.59)	76.07 (↑ 2.95)	68.87 (↑ 3.08)
CAT-KD [22]	75.85 (↑ 2.59)	76.81 (↑ 6.74)	74.65 (↑ 3.97)	78.21 (↑ 5.09)	68.80 (↑ 3.01)
CAKD (Ours)	**76.26 (↑ 3.00)**	**77.83 (↑ 7.76)**	**75.57 (↑ 4.89)**	**79.62 (↑ 6.50)**	**71.34 (↑ 5.55)**

Table 2. Top-1 accuracy (%) on **Tiny ImageNet**. ↑ indicates improvement over baseline.

Teacher Student	ResNet34 ResNet18	ResNet50 ResNet18	ResNet101 ResNet34	ResNet34 MobileNetV2	ResNet50 MobileNetV2
Teacher	67.71	68.88	70.39	67.71	68.88
Student	65.95	65.95	67.71	57.34	57.34
KD [13]	67.45 (↑ 1.50)	67.92 (↑ 1.97)	71.31 (↑ 3.60)	57.61 (↑ 0.27)	58.75 (↑ 1.41)
VID [8]	68.41 (↑ 2.46)	69.55 (↑ 3.60)	70.89 (↑ 3.18)	57.55 (↑ 0.21)	58.30 (↑ 0.96)
SSKD [9]	68.63 (↑ 2.68)	69.73 (↑ 3.78)	70.98 (↑ 3.27)	57.49 (↑ 0.15)	59.02 (↑ 1.68)
SRRL [20]	68.73 (↑ 2.78)	69.56 (↑ 3.61)	71.21 (↑ 3.50)	58.39 (↑ 1.05)	59.47 (↑ 2.13)
DKD [21]	68.52 (↑ 2.57)	69.47 (↑ 3.52)	71.56 (↑ 3.85)	60.34 (↑ 3.00)	61.51 (↑ 4.17)
CAT-KD [22]	68.14 (↑ 2.19)	69.20 (↑ 3.25)	70.58 (↑ 2.87)	58.84 (↑ 1.50)	59.16 (↑ 1.82)
CAKD (Ours)	**69.50 (↑ 3.55)**	**70.01 (↑ 4.12)**	**71.69 (↑ 3.98)**	**62.25 (↑ 4.91)**	**63.40 (↑ 6.06)**

3 Experiments

3.1 Datasets

We studied CAKD's classification performance on two benchmarking datasets:

CIFAR-100. [23] is a widely recognized image classification dataset, comprising 32×32 images spanning 100 categories. The training and validation sets consist of 50,000 and 10,000 images respectively.

Tiny ImageNet. [24] is a subset of ImageNet, featuring 200 categories with 500 training images per category. The images are sized at 64 × 64 pixels, making it suitable for small-scale image classification tasks and enabling swift validation of algorithm performance.

Table 3. Ablation study on CIFAR-100.

Cases	Method		L_{SS}	ResNet32×4
	$(L_{LKD},Splice\ )$	$(L_{FKD},Splice)$		ResNet8×4
(1)	(✗, ✗)	(✗, ✗)	✗	70.07
(2)	(✓, ✗)	(✗, ✗)	✗	73.38 (↑ 3.31)
(3)	(✓, ✗)	(✓, ✗)	✗	73.80 (↑ 3.73)
(4)	(✓, ✓)	(✗, ✗)	✗	76.06 (↑ 5.99)
(5)	(✓, ✓)	(✓, ✓)	✗	76.38 (↑ 6.31)
(6)	(✓, ✓)	(✓, ✓)	✓	**77.83 (↑ 7.76)**

Table 4. Sample with different discrepancies.

Teacher	ResNet32×4	ResNet32×4
Student	ResNet8×4	ShuffleNetV2
Teacher	79.42	79.42
Student	70.07	73.12
E	77.10 (↑ 7.03)	78.55 (↑ 5.43)
M	77.19 (↑ 7.12)	78.75 (↑ 5.63)
H	77.20 (↑ 7.13)	79.01 (↑ 5.89)
$E+M+H$ (1 : 1 : 1)	77.25 (↑ 7.18)	78.88 (↑ 5.76)
$E+M+H$ (cosine decay)	**77.83 (↑ 7.76)**	**79.62 (↑ 6.50)**

3.2 Experimental Results

Results on CIFAR100. In Table 1, we present results from five groups of teacher-student pairs utilizing both identical and differing architectures. Our proposed CAKD method yielded significant improvements, outperforming other techniques. Specifically, for the (ResNet32×4, ShuffleNetV2) teacher-student pairs, CAKD showcased a 6.50% enhancement over the baseline, while CAT-KD [22] and SSKD [9] achieved improvements of 5.09% and 5.51% respectively. Notably, SSKD [9], which leverages self-supervision contrastive relations following the approach of Chen et al. [14], achieved superior results compared to CAT-KD [22] and DKD [21]. In contrast to SSKD [9], our CAKD method focuses on optimizing key sample pairs to extract cross-sample multi-discrepancy relationships. This highlights the potential simplicity and effectiveness of optimizing only a few key samples.

Results on Tiny ImageNet. In Table 2, we present the results of five sets of teacher-student pairs, derived on the Tiny ImageNet dataset. Our proposed CAKD method demonstrates significant improvements, surpassing other techniques. Specifically, in the (ResNet50, MobileNetV2) pair, CAKD showcased a notable 6.06% improvement, outperforming DKD [21] by 4.17% and SRRL [20] by 2.13%. It is noteworthy that while our CAKD achieves the best results on networks with the same architecture, the improvement is not as pronounced as on different network architectures. This phenomenon can be attributed to CAKD's ability to fuse logits and features generated from both normal and transformed data, enabling students to better comprehend and adapt to the diversity of different data. This mitigation strategy helps alleviate the impact of varying network architectures on KD.

3.3 Ablation Studies

Loss Function: In Table 3, we evaluated different loss functions. Employing L_{LSKD} alone led to an improvement of 3.73%. Combining L_{LSKD} with L_{FSKD} resulted in a further improvement of 6.31%. Notably, the addition of the self-supervision task loss yielded a significant improvement of 7.76%. These results underscore the effectiveness of our proposed splice logit loss, splice feature loss, and self-supervision task loss.

Sample Difficulty Analysis: In Table 4, we analyze samples with varying discrepancy strengths, categorized as easy (E), medium (M), and hard (H). Sometimes training with all three types of samples together is beneficial, while at other times, focusing solely on difficult samples yields better results. To strike a balance, we employ a cosine decay strategy, which prioritizes the training of hard samples without neglecting the easier ones. This approach leads to superior outcomes.

4 Conclusions

In this paper, we introduced a novel Knowledge Distillation (KD) method termed CAKD. Initially, in the supervision task, we enhanced the conventional KD framework by merging logit and feature information derived from both original and augmented data. Subsequently, in the self-supervision task, we identified key sample pairs and established a cross-sample multi-discrepancy relationship based on the intrinsic data structure, eliminating the need for external labels or supervision. This facilitates knowledge transfer through contrastive learning. The synergistic integration of knowledge from both tasks enhances student performance. Experiments validate CAKD as a promising KD approach. Our method reduces computational resource demands while preserving the high performance of computer animation and social agent models, rendering them more adaptable across diverse environments and devices.

References

1. Gou, J., Yu, B., Maybank, S.J., Tao, D.: Knowledge distillation: a survey. Int. J. Comput. Vis. **129**, 1789–1819 (2021)
2. Lan, Q., Tian, Q.: Gradient-guided knowledge distillation for object detectors. In: Proceedings of the IEEE/CVF Winter Conference on Applications of Computer Vision, pp. 424–433 (2024)
3. Zheng, H., et al.: Distilling temporal knowledge with masked feature reconstruction for 3D object detection. arXiv preprint arXiv:2401.01918 (2024)
4. Wan, Y., Zhang, W., Li, Z., Zhang, H., Li, Y.: Dual knowledge distillation for neural machine translation. Comput. Speech Lang. **84**, 101583 (2024)
5. Li, Z., et al.: Curriculum temperature for knowledge distillation. In: Proceedings of the AAAI Conference on Artificial Intelligence, pp. 1504–1512 (2023)
6. Xu, Q., Li, Y., Shen, J., Liu, J.K., Tang, H., Pan, G.: Constructing deep spiking neural networks from artificial neural networks with knowledge distillation. In: Proceedings of the IEEE/CVF Conference on Computer Vision and Pattern Recognition, pp. 7886–7895 (2023)
7. Gou, J., Sun, L., Baosheng, Yu., Wan, S., Weihua, O., Yi, Z.: Multilevel attention-based sample correlations for knowledge distillation. IEEE Trans. Industr. Inf. **19**, 7099–7109 (2022)
8. Ahn, S., Hu, S.X., Damianou, A., Lawrence, N.D., Dai, Z.: Variational information distillation for knowledge transfer. In: Proceedings of the IEEE/CVF Conference on Computer Vision and Pattern Recognition, pp. 9163–9171 (2019)
9. Xu, G., Liu, Z., Li, X., Loy, C.C.: Knowledge distillation meets self-supervision. In: European Conference on Computer Vision, pp. 588–604 (2020)
10. Bhat, P., Arani, E., Zonooz, B.: Distill on the go: online knowledge distillation in self-supervised learning. In: Proceedings of the IEEE/CVF Conference on Computer Vision and Pattern Recognition, pp. 2678–2687 (2021)
11. Yang, C., An, Z., Cai, L., Yongjun, X.: Knowledge distillation using hierarchical self-supervision augmented distribution. IEEE Trans. Neural Netw. Learn. Syst. **35**, 2094–2108 (2024)
12. Ma, Y., Chen, Y., Akata, Z.: Distilling knowledge from self-supervised teacher by embedding graph alignment. arXiv preprint arXiv:2211.13264 (2022)
13. Hinton, G., Vinyals, O., Dean, J.: Distilling the knowledge in a neural network. arXiv preprint arXiv:1503.02531 (2015)
14. Chen, T., Kornblith, S., Norouzi, M., Hinton, G.: A simple framework for contrastive learning of visual representations. In: International Conference on Machine Learning, pp. 1597–1607 (2020)
15. Vaswani, A., et al.: Attention is all you need. In: Advances in Neural Information Processing Systems, vol. 30, pp. 1–11 (2017)
16. Ye, M., Li, H., Du, B., Shen, J., Shao, L., Hoi, S.C.H.: Collaborative refining for person re-identification with label noise. IEEE Trans. Image Process. **31**, 379–391 (2021)
17. van den Oord, A., Li, Y., Vinyals, O.: Representation learning with contrastive predictive coding. arXiv preprint arXiv:1807.03748 (2018)

18. Shrivastava, A., Gupta, A., Girshick, R.: Training region-based object detectors with online hard example mining. In: Proceedings of the IEEE Conference on Computer Vision and Pattern Recognition, pp. 761–769 (2016)
19. Hawkins, D.M.: The problem of overfitting. J. Chem. Inf. Comput. Sci. **44**, 1–12 (2004)
20. Yang, J., Martinez, B., Bulat, A., Tzimiropoulos, G.: Knowledge distillation via softmax regression representation learning. In: International Conference on Learning Representations, pp. 1–13 (2021)
21. Zhao, B., Cui, Q., Song, R., Qiu, Y., Liang, J.: Decoupled knowledge distillation. In: Proceedings of the IEEE/CVF Conference on Computer Vision and Pattern Recognition, pp. 11953–11962 (2022)
22. Guo, Z., Yan, H., Li, H., Lin, X.: Class attention transfer based knowledge distillation. In: Proceedings of the IEEE/CVF Conference on Computer Vision and Pattern Recognition, pp. 11868–11877 (2023)
23. Krizhevsky, A., Hinton, G.: Learning multiple layers of features from tiny images. Technical Report, pp. 1–60 (2009)
24. Deng, J., Dong, W., Socher, R., Li, L.J., Li, K., Fei-Fei, L.: Imagenet: a large-scale hierarchical image database. In: IEEE Conference on Computer Vision and Pattern Recognition, pp. 248–255 (2009)

Near-Eye Gaze Estimation in Virtual Reality Based on Deep Learning

Zian Sun, Yang Liu, and Shiwei Cheng(✉)

College of Computer Science, Zhejiang University of Technology, Hangzhou 310023, China
249401866@qq.com

Abstract. With the development of immersive and interactive virtual environments, accurately estimating the users' gazes could enhance the evaluation of visual design or gaze-driven interaction, so the precise estimation of gaze fixation has become increasingly crucial. This paper proposes a near-eye gaze estimation method inspired by the Res-Net network and incorporates eye appearance features and bottle-net attention module (BAM) to calculate 2D gaze fixation coordinates. We build a homemade cardboard box-based VR headset by using a mobile phone along with two infrared cameras. Finally, we conducted a user study, and the results show that the proposed method reduces gaze point coordinates' error to 15.3 pixels and visual angle error to 3.54°. The results outperform existing methods and will leverage gaze point interaction in virtual reality applications.

Keywords: human-computer interaction · gaze estimation · mobile computing · deep learning

1 Introduction

The Metaverse is a virtual realm that intertwines multiple technologies, including Virtual Reality (VR) and Augmented Reality (AR) [1, 2]. This concept expands the boundaries of traditional virtual reality and skillfully integrates virtual and reality to build a new interactive virtual environment.

Commercially available virtual reality devices include the Oculus Quest all-in-one, HTC Vive headset, PlayStation VR, and Valve Index [3]. These devices are equipped with interactive tools such as mice, keyboards, and handles. They also include features like eye tracking, gesture recognition, and voice recognition. However, the high cost of virtual reality technology has hindered its widespread adoption, resulting in a limited user base. Since the release of Google Cardboard [4] in 2014, VR headsets that utilize smartphones have gained popularity [5]. These devices allow users to transform their existing smartphones into powerful VR headsets, utilizing the phone's sensing and rendering capabilities to provide rich VR experiences without the expense and complexity of a dedicated VR headset.

Low-cost mobile VR headsets are an inexpensive and widely available option for immersive experiences. However, interaction input methods in mobile VR have been generally limited to less comfortable head tracking [6], sometimes through the use of an aside button on the device's casing. The use of gaze estimation as interactive input in head-mounted displays has been shown to be effective in previous studies. In mobile VR, lighting is emitted only from the smartphone screen, and eye illumination and tracking depend on the displayed content. Accurate eye tracking on mobile VR headsets is challenging due to reflections on the lens of the helmet caused by strong lighting and the loss of the eye picture when the light is too weak [7]. This paper aims to enhance users' eye-tracking experience on low-cost VR devices. An appearance-based gaze estimation method is proposed. This method uses two infrared cameras hidden in the VR headset to obtain a large number of binocular gaze images and uses them for model training. Based on this model, a gaze estimation interaction system under VR was designed. The system predicts the user's gaze point, making the user's interactive experience in VR more immersive and convenient. Compared with previous methods, our method performs significantly better.

2 Related Work

Gaze estimation, as a fundamental skill, plays a pivotal role across various domains such as interface design, advertising evaluation, medical diagnosis, and psychological research [8, 9]. In the realm of virtual reality, gaze estimation takes on an even more significant role [10]. Accurate gaze estimation in VR environments can improve user interaction and enable advanced features such as user behavior recognition and user intent prediction. To this end, we delve into two prevalent gaze estimation algorithms based on prior research: appearance-based and model-based algorithms [11-13]. The appearance-based algorithms focus on detecting physical eye features like pupil centre or corneal reflections, whereas the model-based algorithms involve building the model of the eye.

2.1 The Model-Based Algorithms

Model-based gaze estimation refers to estimating the gaze direction or gaze point of the human eye using an eyeball model constructed based on the physiological structure of the eye and the geometric relationships between facial key points, pupil centre, depth information, and eye corner positions. The method based on corneal reflection uses the canthus point as the reference point of eye movement and achieves line-of-sight estimation by analyzing the mapping relationship between the vector from the reference point to the pupil centre position and the line-of-sight vector. Hennessy et al. [14] proposed an eye model that, after calibration, achieves camera line of sight estimation within the head's field of view, allowing for free head movement. Zhou et al. [15] proposed a method for positioning the iris centre based on gradient characteristics. They approximated the gaze direction as the direction from the iris centre to the gaze point. The final gaze estimation result was obtained by averaging the gaze directions estimated by both eyes. The cross-ratio method is another approach that relies on the inconsistency of the cross-ratio under projective transformation. Coutinho et al. [16] proposed a cross-ratio feature planarization method that uses a weak perspective camera model and an eye model composed of the cornea centre and iris plane to compensate for errors caused by head movement. Arar et al. [17] proposed a multi-camera gaze estimation system based on cross-ratio. The system enables accurate gaze estimation by utilizing multiple independent cameras and adaptively fusing the gaze point estimation results obtained from each camera, even when the experimental subject's head is freely moving.

2.2 The Appearance-Based Algorithms

Current work mainly relies on feature learning to achieve gaze estimation with the rapid development of camera sensors, computer vision, image processing, machine learning, and deep learning technologies. According to different types of features, related methods can be further divided into geometric features and appearance. Huang et al. [18] used support vector machines and random forest regression models to estimate the line of sight based on 6 distance values between head posture and eye area key points as geometric features. Zhang et al. [19] defined the pupil-canthus distance ratio using the pupil center and inner corner of the eye. They then mapped the distance ratio to the horizontal direction of the line of sight using a Gaussian regression model. Deep learning models, specifically convolutional neural networks, have become increasingly popular in appearance-based methods due to the availability of numerous open-source datasets. In their study, Yu et al. [20] identified 17 key points in the eye area to determine the gaze direction. The proposed constrained key point-line of sight model constructs the relationship between heading angle, pitch angle, and the position of the key point in the eye area with the direction of the line of sight. The model parameters are then used to obtain the final results.

In the realm of virtual reality, accurate gaze estimation is confronted with challenges such as diminished visibility and the presence of specular reflections, making the trade-off between performance and precision paramount. In response to these challenges, our proposed method draws inspiration from the appearance-based approach and employs a deep learning framework to conduct visual regression analysis on images of both eyes, aiming to accurately predict the fixation point location. To tackle the identified issues, our initial step involved collecting a comprehensive dataset of binocular images, each annotated with corresponding user gaze and fixation points. Subsequently, we developed an advanced deep learning model specifically, a residual network (ResNet) architecture designed to process binocular images. This model was further enhanced by integrating various attention mechanisms to refine its predictive capabilities. The culmination of our efforts resulted in the creation of the NE-Net network. We conducted a series of experiments to evaluate the network's performance, focusing on comparing its pixel or angular error rates against those reported in existing literature, and assessing its robustness and latency. These experiments underscored the efficacy and reliability of our model in real-world applications.

3 Gaze Estimation Method

The gaze estimation approach detailed in this study involves a three-step process: initially, it captures images of both eyes; subsequently, these images are fed into a near-eye gaze estimation model; and ultimately, it determines the gaze point location on the screen, as shown in Fig. 1. Accordingly, this article is dedicated to discussing the input device, the modeling approach, and the method's accuracy.

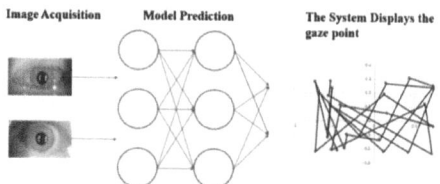

Fig. 1. Overview of the proposed method.

3.1 Input Device

In terms of the input device, the iPhone SE2 was selected as the VR head-mounted display, featuring a 4.7-inch screen with a resolution of 1334x750 pixels and a 60 Hz refresh rate. The infrared camera measures $3 \times 3 \times 2.5$ cm, with two lenses, a 1280x720 pixel resolution, a 30 fps frame rate, and 6 infrared lights providing illumination for the eyes. The computer used has a Windows 10 operating system, an Intel i7 CPU, and an NVIDIA 3070Ti GPU. As shown in Fig. 2, to assemble the system, the mobile phone is installed in a homemade VR box. Two infrared cameras are located under the mobile phone, about 50–80 mm away from the user's eyes, with a field of view (FOV) of 90–100 degrees.

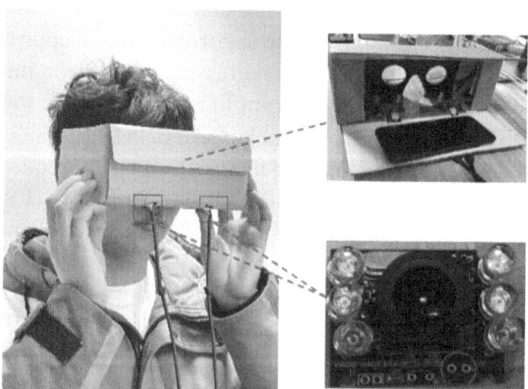

Fig. 2. Input device with iPhone SE2 and two IR cameras.

3.2 NE-Net Model

The proposed method is based on the classical ResNet50 architecture [21] with innovative improvements and optimizations for the complex task of accurate binocular gaze point prediction. As shown in Fig. 3. The initial layer of the model uses a 7 ∗ 7 convolutional kernel, implemented as $Conv2d(Cin, 7, 2, 3)$, which is designed to maximize the capture of the basic features of the image and to cover a wider range of pixel regions by expanding the sensory field, thus providing a solid foundation for the subsequent extraction of deeper features. The output is 64 channels, with *MaxPool* being the pooling layer, and region maxima are downsampled. Then, to reduce the computational load of the model while preserving important feature information and increasing sensitivity to small positional changes, the model performs a feature dimensionality reduction using a 3 ∗ 3 maximum pooling layer $MaxPool(Cout, 3, 2)$.

In this study, within the core part of the model, i.e., the residual block, we introduce the depth-separable convolution technique. The first residual has 64 input channels and 256 output channels and is down-sampled $stride = [1, 1, 1, 1] \rightarrow [1, 2, 1, 2]$. The other two residuals have 256 input/output channels. The structure of these three residual layers is similar to the first except for the number of channels and some details.

Next, AvgPool performs global pooling on each feature map to reduce the size of the feature maps to 1 ∗ 1. The left and right eyes are spliced into a tensor using the torch.cat function, and then the shape is changed for subsequent inputs.

Finally, the output layer FC is defined. This layer contains a fully connected layer with an input vector of size 20, added by the left and right feature vectors of size 10, and an output neuron count of 2, representing the prediction in two consecutives (x, y) coordinates. At the end of the network structure, the traditional fully connected layer is replaced by a more efficient 1 ∗ 1 convolutional layer $Conv2d(Cin, 1, 1, 0)$ to reduce the model parameters while maintaining its ability to handle high-dimensional features.

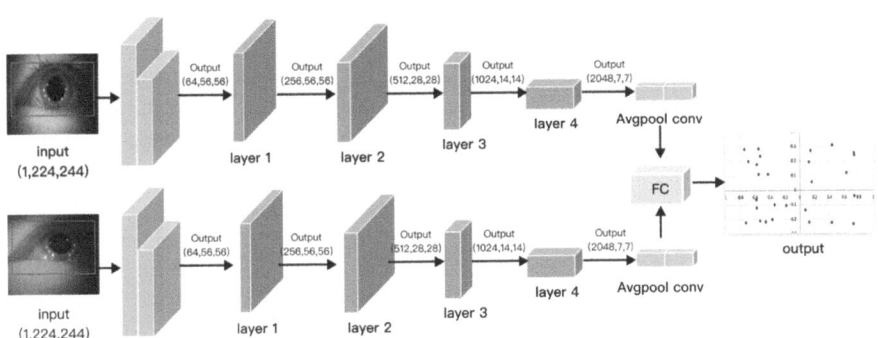

Fig. 3. NE-Net model structure.

Furthermore, it uses independent feature extraction channels for each eye, efficiently merging the extracted features into an overall integrated feature representation. This design not only enhances the model's ability to capture the unique features of each eye but also enables the model to comprehensively utilize binocular data, providing a richer and more accurate information base for accurate gaze point prediction.

In our algorithm (1), we employ several key techniques to optimize the model's performance, namely Mean Squared Error Loss (MSELoss), Adam Optimizer, and Cosine Annealing Learning Rate Scheduler. Mean Squared Error Loss, or MSELoss, is a widely used loss function for regression tasks. It is defined as the average of the squared differences between the predicted and actual values.

$$\mathrm{MSE}(Y, \widehat{Y}) = \frac{1}{N}\sum_{i=1}^{N}(y_i - \widehat{y_i})^2 \quad (1)$$

where $Y = \{y_1, y_2, \ldots, y_N\}$ represents the true values, $\widehat{Y} = \{\widehat{y_1}, \widehat{y_2}, \ldots, \widehat{y_N}\}$ are the predicted values by the model, and N is the number of samples. We choose MSELoss due to its effectiveness in quantifying the variance between the model predictions and the actual observations.

Adam Optimizer (2) is an adaptive learning rate optimization algorithm. It is particularly.

efficient for large-scale and high-dimensional optimization problems. The update rule for Adam is given by:

$$\theta_{t+1} = \theta_t - \frac{\eta}{\sqrt{\widehat{v_t}+\epsilon}}\widehat{m_t} \quad (2)$$

where θ represents the parameters of the model, η is the learning rate, $\widehat{m_t}$ and $\widehat{v_t}$ are estimates of the first and second moments of the gradients, respectively, and ϵ is a small constant added for numerical stability. Adam is chosen for its efficiency in converging and its robustness in handling sparse gradients.

To enhance the training process, we implement the Cosine Annealing Learning Rate Scheduler. This scheduler adjusts the learning rate following a cosine decay in Eq. (3).

$$\eta_t = \eta_{\min} + \frac{1}{2}(\eta_{\max} - \eta_{\min})\left(1 + \cos\left(\frac{T_{\mathrm{cur}}}{T_{\max}}\pi\right)\right) \quad (3)$$

where η_t is the learning rate at epoch t, $\eta_{\min}$ and $\eta_{\max}$ are the minimum and maximum learning rates, respectively, T_{cur} is the current epoch, and $T_{\max}$ is the maximum number of epochs. This approach helps in avoiding local minima and facilitates better convergence.

4 Experimental Evaluation

4.1 Dataset

For the dataset, we recruited 20 participants. There were 9 people with normal vision and 11 people with corrected vision. Between the ages of 22 and 26, the average age is 23.5. Firstly, the mobile phone is connected to the computer, and then the user takes the VR box to detect the pupil. The collection gaze point design is shown in Fig. 4. The collection point can cover most of the content area of the mobile device, the content covered by the VR border has no actual content and is not added to the collection area. There are 14 coordinate points on the X-axis and 15 coordinate points on the Y-axis. A total of 210 coordinate points. The display point will be activated in blue for three seconds and will not be the same as the last activation position. Each point will be activated repeatedly 10 times. A total of 2100 gaze point binocular images and position labels were collected each time.

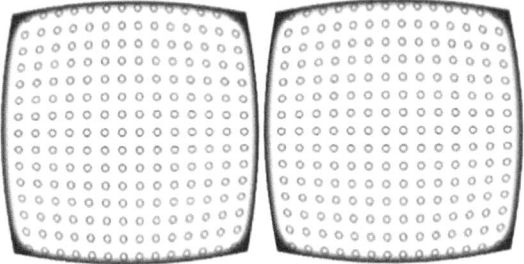

Fig. 4. Distribution of collection points in VR.

After the dataset collection, we filtered the acquired binocular images to remove non-compliant images such as closed eyes and squinting. The image is balanced, the edge information of the eyes is highlighted to improve the image quality, the image is denoised, and the lens reflection under the corrected vision is removed to improve the purity and clarity of the image.

4.2 Experimental Result

After training the model for 100 epochs, the results of the dataset are as follows. We initially compared the error between the predicted and true values on the x- and y-axes, respectively. Figure 5 shows two Q-Q (Quantile-Quantile Plot) plots corresponding to the normality test of the residuals of the Gaze X and Gaze Y axes, respectively. The Q-Q plot on the left side displays the distribution of the residuals of Gaze X, which are normally distributed. The residuals are distributed normally, and the points in the plots align closely with a straight line (the red line in the figure). The Q-Q plot on the right side displays the distribution of the Gaze Y residuals, which confirms that the residuals also follow a normal distribution. This indicates the model's accuracy and reliability.

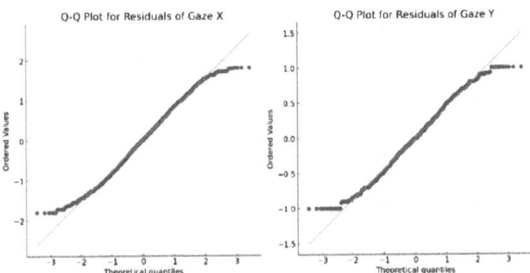

Fig. 5. Quantile-Quantile plot for residuals of gaze X/Y.

As shown in Fig. 6, the histograms of the residuals between the true and predicted values on the x-axis and y-axis are shown to visualize the distribution of the errors, the two residual plots correspond to the distribution of the residuals between the true and predicted values on the x-axis and y-axis, respectively, and the distribution of the residuals between the true and predicted values on the Gaze X residuals on the left-hand side shows that the vast majority of the predictions and the true values have the difference between them in the range of 0.5 and that the maximum number of the predicted numbers on the Gaze Y-axis are in the center 0 interval. The greatest number of predictions on the Gaze Y-axis are in the center of the 0 interval, indicating that the model performs better on the Y-axis.

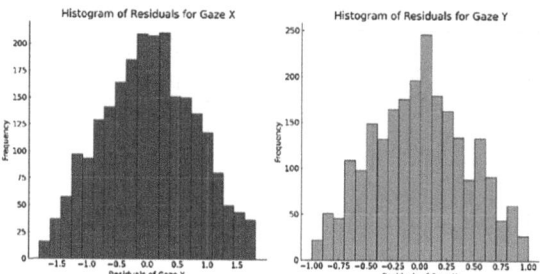

Fig. 6. Histogram of residuals for gaze X/Y (Color figure online).

In addition to the difference in the corresponding coordinate axes, the error between the true value and the predicted value within the two-dimensional coordinate range can be analyzed by dividing the two-dimensional plane into 16 regions and analyzing the accuracy of the regional gaze points by the gaze errors in different regions, as shown in Fig. 7. This figure shows the average error between the true and predicted values in the 16 regions into which the true coordinate range is divided in the two-dimensional coordinate space. The color depth of each region represents the size of the error, with darker colors indicating larger errors and lighter colors indicating smaller errors. In this way, it is possible to visualize in which regions the difference between the predicted and the true value is larger so that the training of the model can be adjusted.

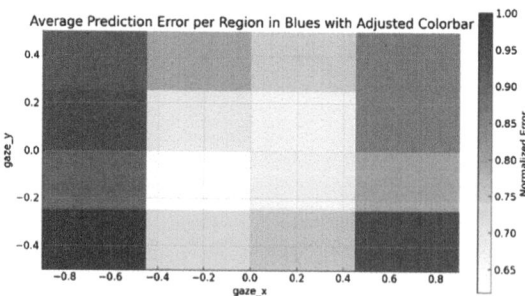

Fig. 7. Average prediction error per region in blues with adjusted colorbar.

From Fig. 7, it can be seen that the error in the center of the coordinates is smaller or close to 0, while the closer to the coordinate boundary, the larger the error, this is because when both eyes are looking at the boundary, due to the angle of the camera, the captured image is not as obvious as the difference between the image looking at the center, and it is easy to be affected by the human eye's reasons, and it is impossible to keep looking at the extreme visual boundary stably all the time, so there is a certain effect on the acquisition of the training data as well.

4.3 Comparison with Other Methods

To compare angular errors in this paper, we need to estimate the pixel size of the iPhone to be $\frac{0.0254}{326}$ m. This is because the iPhone SE display has a resolution of 326 ppi. The width of the screen is approximately 67.78 mm $\left(\frac{1334\,\text{px}}{326\,\text{ppi}} \times mm/inch\right)$, and the height is approximately 37.45 mm $\left(\frac{750\,\text{px}}{326\,\text{ppi}} \times mm/inch\right)$. Use the standard formula. $visual angle = 2 * arctan$. The overall calculation formula is (4).

$$\text{VisualAngle} = 2 \times \arctan\left(\frac{\text{\# pixels} \times \text{pixelSize}}{2 \times \text{distanceToScreen}}\right) \qquad (4)$$

We first experiment to compare the performance of the proposed method with another appearance-based method of Kim et al. [22]. The experiment is conducted in our dataset. We both apply the leave-one-person-out strategy to obtain robust results. The average angular error of Ne-Net on the dataset is between 2.0–2.3° compared to Kim is improved by about 20%. We also compared the angular error concerning other methods, such as the EyeSpyVR by KARAN et al. [22] and the LiGaze by Li et al. [12] The comparative data for angular error is in Table 1, where A.A.E indicates the average angular error.

Table 1. Results of comparison with other methods.

Name	Method	Input	A.A.E. (°)
Kim	Appearance-Based	Dual Infrared Cameras	4.35
EyeSpyVR	Feature-Based	Front-Facing Smartphone Camera	10.8
LiGaze	Light-Based	Light Sensor	3.60
Ours	Appearance-Based	Dual Infrared Cameras	**3.54**

4.4 Ablation Experiments

In this paper, different input conditions are used under the same conditions, the results of single-eye image input and two-eye image input are compared, and the influence of different attention mechanisms on model input is compared. Table 2 shows that training with only one eye resulted in the worst performance due to the variability of binocular features. The pixel errors were 30.2 px and the baseline NE-Net model was 25.5 px. After comparing the three attentional mechanisms using the same training parameters and number of rounds, it was found that the BAM had the smallest error at 15.3 px. The other two methods are slightly less effective, SENet: 18.5 px and CBAM: 17.6px.

Table 2. Comparison of MAE (pixel error) for different attention mechanisms integrated into NE-Net.

Model Method	MAE (pixel error)
NE-Net	25.5
NE-Net (one eye)	30.2
NE-Net + SENet	18.5
NE-Net + CBAM	17.6
NE-Net + BAM	15.3

5 User Study

To validate the model, we applied the NE-Net model to a VR scene. We designed a virtual scene where the user can gaze at a flat poster and select it by obtaining the gaze point through a gaze estimation algorithm. Finally, we verified the effectiveness of the model in VR interactions by comparing user task time and subjective evaluation.

5.1 User Recruitment and Study Design

For the user study, we recruited 15 voluntary participants (12 males, 3 females), all of whom are university students with normal or corrected vision and no other ophthalmological diseases. The participants' ages ranged from 22 to 26 (mean = 23). The majority of the participants had prior experience with VR technologies, reflecting a sample with a good understanding of VR environments and interfaces. All participants were fully informed about the study's objectives, procedures, potential risks, and benefits and provided their written informed consent.

Users viewed the movie posters individually in a VR scene using a VR head-mounted display. As shown in Fig. 8. Participants view the details of a relevant film in a scene and could choose any poster to view. After viewing all three posters, the task ended. The experiment presented three conditions for comparison: gaze point interaction, gyroscope sensing interaction, and handle interaction. The final time taken to read all the posters was used as the evaluation criterion. Each user completed the three conditions in a randomly specified order.

Fig. 8. The images, from left to right, depict the VR scene on the computer, the VR view on the cell phone, and the user wearing the VR headset.

5.2 Study Results and Analysis

The data collected from the experiment was analysed using a one-way analysis of variance (ANOVA) to calculate significant differences. The results indicated a significant difference between the three conditions ($p < 0.001$), as shown in Fig. 9. The completion times for the tasks using gaze point ($M = 24.32$ s, $SD = 3.25$ s), gyroscope sensing ($M = 30.59$ s, $SD = 2.60$ s), and handle interaction ($M = 25.00$ s, $SD = 0.81$ s) were not significantly different from the traditional interaction method but were slightly longer. This indicates that the gaze point interaction method is effective. The gyroscope sensing interaction took significantly longer for the user to use compared to the gaze point and mouse interaction and was 1.25 times longer than the gaze point interaction. This is because the gyroscope interaction approach requires the user to constantly perform behaviours such as head rotation, head tilting, or looking down.

To investigate user preferences for interaction methods, we selectively included 5 out of the 10 users who were more familiar with the VR environment and had shown better performance in the initial task completion compared to the other five, to repeat the experiment under the three conditions. The primary evaluation criterion remained the completion time for reviewing the poster. To ensure a thorough familiarity with each interaction mode and to minimize errors due to unfamiliarity, each participant experimented three times for each mode. This approach also facilitated a deeper understanding of which interaction mode was perceived as more convenient and efficient by users once they became accustomed to it.

To assess any significant differences among the interaction methods, we applied the same one-way (ANOVA). Figure 10 illustrates the experimental outcomes, Notably, there were significant differences across the three conditions for each user. For example, User A experienced a notable reduction in task completion time using the gaze point method, from 25.32 s to 20.55 s over three trials, with a mean (M) of 22.63 s and a standard deviation (SD) of 1.99 s. In contrast, the handle mode did not show a significant time reduction, with times decreasing from 25.42 s to 24.20 s ($M = 24.82$ s, $SD = 0.49$ s). Moreover, the gyroscope mode resulted in the longest completion times among the users ($M = 28$ s, $SD = 1.27$ s). The significant disparity between the gaze point and handle modes aligns with the findings presented in Fig. 10.

The analysis reveals that all participants proficiently completed the tasks across all interaction methods, indicating a universal competence with each mode. Notably, there was a consistent trend of decreasing completion times, suggesting improvements in efficiency over repeated trials. A significant observation from the data is the more substantial reduction in task completion time achieved with the gaze point interaction method compared to that with the handle interaction method. This difference underscores the gaze point method's enhanced convenience and user-friendliness. Furthermore, such outcomes hint at a user preference for the gaze point interaction over other forms, reflecting its potential for a more intuitive and efficient user experience.

User feedback: After each task, this paper asked users to fill out a questionnaire to assess their subjective true feelings in different interactions. Users were asked to answer their satisfaction with the three modes of interaction on a scale from 5 (strongly agree) to 1 (strongly disagree).

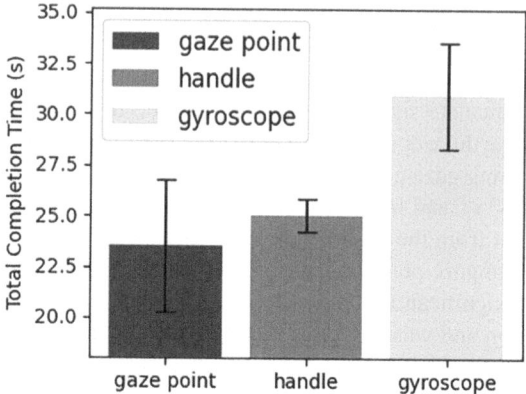

Fig. 9. Time for 15 users to complete a task under different conditions (three horizontal lines indicate significant differences).

Figure 11 illustrates that utilizing the phone's gyroscope as the sole interaction method for task execution led to generally lower satisfaction ratings, primarily due to the physical exertion required. Specifically, four users awarded a score of 3, three users score of 2, and three users a lower score of 1, as evidenced by the median score of 2, attributing this to the physical strain experienced, which was particularly challenging. This difficulty may stem from their limited exposure to VR gaming and the associated sensation of dizziness. In contrast, when employing the gaze point and handle methods, most participants reported ease in task completion, with the majority assigning a perfect score of 5 out of 5, and a few giving a score of 4. User 2, in particular, voiced appreciation for the innovative nature of the gaze point interaction. Additionally, Users 5 and 7 highlighted a favourable aspect of the gaze point method, emphasizing the convenience of directly selecting items without the need to sequentially navigate through them, as required by the handle method.

Feedback collected from participants also revealed that the handle interaction's frustration stemmed from its monotonous and repetitive operation, culminating in feelings of fatigue ($MD = 4$). Furthermore, User 4 specifically highlighted the challenge of managing the tapping speed, indicating that moving too swiftly often led to overshooting the intended targets.

All users rated the gaze interaction's response with a score of 4–5 ($MD = 5$, 7 people rated 5, 3 people rated 4), indicating the accuracy of the model and its ability to meet real-time requirements.

Additionally, this paper analyses the gaze area of users who utilize the gaze mode during the experiment. Figure 12 shows that the users' gaze direction primarily focuses on the centre of the target poster. When comparing the gaze points of handle control, it is observed that the gaze points are more dispersed and susceptible to operational disturbances. This demonstrates that when using VR, users tend to concentrate on the virtual world rather than external distractions and aim to achieve a more authentic experience. The user data using gravity sensing changes direction due to frequent head movements,

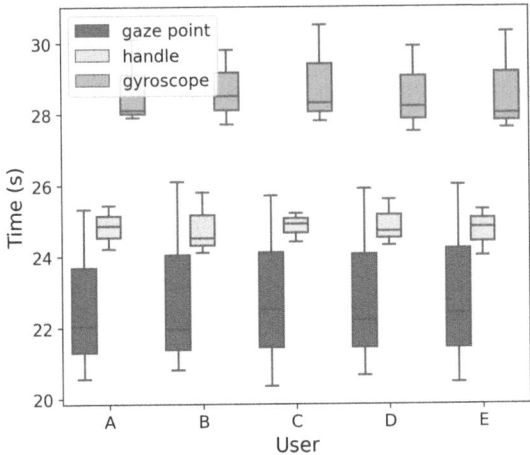

Fig. 10. Completion time of five users under different conditions.

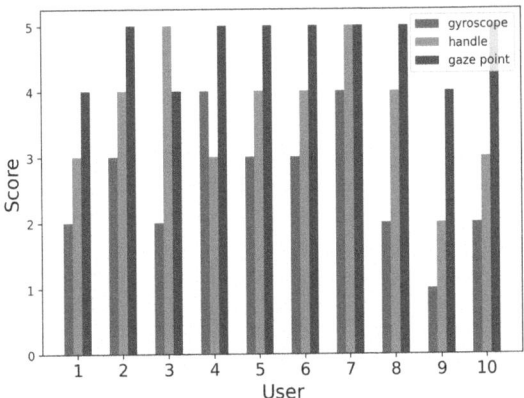

Fig. 11. User subjective scores.

and the line of sight is mainly concentrated in the middle of the screen. It cannot be directly displayed on a flat poster, so it is not included in the comparison.

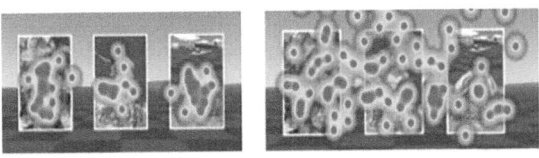

Fig. 12. The left is the Hot zone map of gaze interaction. The right is the hot zone map of handle interaction.

6 Conclusion

In this paper, we propose an appearance-based near-eye gaze estimation method and design a low-cost VR head-mounted display equipped with two infrared cameras and a mobile phone. Compared to previous research, our method shows significant improvement. User studies demonstrate that our method provides a better and faster human-computer interaction experience. The research indicates that the proposed method can effectively enhance the potential of VR interaction. Despite these positive results, there are still limitations. Future research directions include applying more human-computer interaction methods to VR headsets, optimizing algorithm performance, and exploring a wider range of application scenarios, all of which are expected to further advance the development of VR technology.

Acknowledgments. We thank all the volunteers who participated in the experiments. This research work was supported in part by Zhejiang Provincial Key Research and Development Program under Grant No. 2023C01045, Zhejiang Provincial Natural Science Foundation of China under Grant No. LR22F020003, and National Natural Science Foundation of China under Grant No. 62172368, 61772468.

References

1. Mystakidis, S.: Metaverse. Encyclopedia **2**, 486–497 (2022)
2. Wang, Y., et al.: A survey on metaverse: fundamentals, security, and privacy. IEEE Communications Surveys & Tutorials **25**(1), 319–352 (2022)
3. Cipresso, P., et al.: The past, present, and future of virtual and augmented reality research: a network and cluster analysis of the literature. Frontiers in Psychology **9**, 309500 (2018)
4. Powell, W., et al.: Getting around in google cardboard–exploring navigation preferences with low-cost mobile VR. In: 2016 IEEE 2nd Workshop on Everyday Virtual Reality (WEVR). IEEE (2016)
5. Boel, C., et al.: Six years after google cardboard: what has happened in the classroom? a scoping review of empirical research on the use of immersive virtual reality in secondary education. In: 13th International Conference on Education and New Learning Technologies. IATED (2021)
6. Drakopoulos, P., Koulieris, G.-A., Mania, K.: Eye tracking interaction on unmodified mobile VR headsets using the selfie camera. ACM Transactions on Applied Perception (TAP) **18**(3), 1–20 (2021)
7. Hansen, D.W., Ji, Q.: In the eye of the beholder: A survey of models for eyes and gaze. IEEE Transactions on Pattern Analysis and Machine Intelligence **32**(3), 478–500 (2009)
8. Klaib, A.F., et al.: Eye tracking algorithms, techniques, tools, and applications with an emphasis on machine learning and Internet of Things technologies. Expert Systems with Applications **166**, 114037 (2021)
9. Clay, V., Peter, K., Sabine, K.: Eye tracking in virtual reality. J. eye Movement Res. **12**(1) (2019)
10. Ying, Z., Kang, W., Fei-Yue, W.: Research advances and prospects of eye tracking. Acta Automatica Sinica **48**(5), 1173–1192 (2022)
11. Cheng, Y., et al.: Appearance-based gaze estimation with deep learning: A review and benchmark. IEEE Transactions on Pattern Analysis and Machine Intelligence (2024)

12. Li, D., David, W., Parkhurst, D.J.: Starburst: A hybrid algorithm for video-based eye tracking combining feature-based and model-based approaches. In: 2005 IEEE Computer Society Conference on Computer Vision and Pattern Recognition (CVPR'05)-Workshops. IEEE (2005)
13. Wang, K., Ji, Q.: 3D gaze estimation without explicit personal calibration. Pattern Recogn. **79**, 216–227 (2018)
14. Hennessey, C., Borna, N., Peter, L.: A single camera eye-gaze tracking system with free head motion. Proceedings of the 2006 Symposium on Eye Tracking Research & Applications 2006
15. Zhou, X., et al.: Two-eye model-based gaze estimation from a Kinect sensor. In: 2017 IEEE International Conference on Robotics and Automation (ICRA). IEEE (2017)
16. Coutinho, F.L., Morimoto, C.H.: Improving head movement tolerance of cross-ratio based eye trackers. Int. J. Comput. Vision **101**, 459–481 (2013)
17. Arar, N.M., Gao, H., Thiran, J.-P.: Robust gaze estimation based on adaptive fusion of multiple cameras. In: 2015 11th IEEE International Conference and Workshops on Automatic Face and Gesture Recognition (FG). Vol. 1. IEEE (2015)
18. Huang, M.X., et al.: Building a self-learning eye gaze model from user interaction data. Proceedings of the 22nd ACM International Conference on Multimedia (2014)
19. Zhang, Y., Bulling, A., Gellersen, H.: Pupil-canthi-ratio: a calibration-free method for tracking horizontal gaze direction. Proceedings of the 2014 International Working Conference on Advanced Visual Interfaces (2014)
20. Yu, Y., Liu, G., Odobez, J.-M.: Deep multitask gaze estimation with a constrained landmark-gaze model. Proceedings of the European Conference on Computer Vision (ECCV) Workshops (2018)
21. Russakovsky, O., et al.: Imagenet large scale visual recognition challenge. International Journal of Computer Vision **115**, 211–252 (2015)
22. Ahuja, K., et al.: Eyespyvr: Interactive eye sensing using off-the-shelf, smartphone-based vr headsets. Proceedings of the ACM on Interactive, Mobile, Wearable and Ubiquitous Technologies **2**(2), 1–10 (2018)

N-Sand Table: A Multi-user Interactive Virtual Sand Table Based on NeRF Technology

Xinlei Zhang[1], Jiahui Yu[1], Chenchen Gong[2], Danming Huang[1], Yuxiang Sun[1], and Xianzhong Zhou[1](✉)

[1] Department of Control and Systems Engineering, School of Management and Engineering, Nanjing University, Nanjing, China
`{602023150020,mg1815007,502022150003}@smail.nju.edu.cn,`
`{sunyuxiang,zhouxz}@nju.edu.cn`
[2] ShangYu Personnel Bureau, Shaoxing, China

Abstract. The N-Sand Table, a multi-user interactive virtual sand table system based on Neural Radiance Fields (NeRF) technology, is proposed to address the issues of weak interactivity, severe standalone operation, difficulty in constructing map models, and challenges in meeting multi-user remote planning needs prevalent in traditional virtual sand tables. Utilizing NeRF technology with real-world image data, this system creates highly realistic virtual sand tables and employs intelligent algorithms to dynamically adjust the terrain, achieving a high degree of user customization and interactivity. Moreover, the system enhances user interaction convenience by supporting multi-channel interactions through gestures and voice, and facilitates real-time remote interaction among multiple users. Experimental results demonstrate the system's excellent performance in terms of interaction real-time and stability, effectively supporting multi-user remote collaborative planning.

Keywords: Virtual Reality · NeRF · Multi-user Interaction · Virtual Sand Table

1 Introduction

Sand tables are a three-dimensional graphical tool capable of presenting geographic information and showcasing the three-dimensional characteristics of terrain. Traditional physical sand tables are models made from materials such as sand, shaped according to a specific scale of topographic maps. They offer a strong sense of dimensionality, displaying more complex information than two-dimensional maps. Sand tables support multi-user observation from different perspectives through direct interaction with the model and terrain adjustments, enhancing information visualization and interactivity. Despite their limited interactivity and the complexity of construction, physical sand tables have been widely applied in military command and strategic planning due to their alignment with human physiological and psychological habits [1].

However, as the demand for information presentation becomes more complex, traditional physical sand tables can no longer meet these needs. The emergence of new situational information and cutting-edge technologies has expanded the form and application areas of sand tables. With the development of three-dimensional animation and computer remote control technologies, multimedia sand tables that combine physical sand tables with multimedia audio and video technology have been extensively used in museums and science centers [2–4]. However, due to their poor portability and reliance on specific sand tables, multimedia sand tables also face challenges in widespread application.

Entering the digital era, the application of three-dimensional modeling technology has freed sand tables from the constraints of physical models, allowing electronic sand tables to simulate and display terrain information on digital display devices. In recent years, with the advancement of virtual reality, computer graphics, and human-machine interaction technologies, interactive virtual sand tables based on data modeling have gradually emerged and been promoted in military training, psychological counseling, and urban planning [5–7].

Currently, with the integration of cutting-edge technologies such as virtual reality, augmented reality, multiplayer interaction, and blockchain, the concept of the metaverse has been proposed, providing a new direction for the further innovation of sand table technology. The foundation of the metaverse is to allow users to create their content beyond the limits of physical space and experience things in virtual scenes that are difficult or impossible to obtain in real life [8, 9]. This aligns with the application method of virtual sand tables, which detach from real-world scenarios and build required scenes in virtual spaces based on data, even constructing scenarios beyond reality based on predictive data.

Besides linking virtual environments with real-life and economic activities, the metaverse concept also necessitates more natural ways of human-machine interaction and involves interactions among multiple users [10]. This interaction is not limited to exchanging information through communication but also involves users affecting others by interacting with objects in the virtual environment. This new mode of interaction and communication among multiple users lays the foundation for the future development of virtual sand tables.

However, current applications of virtual sand tables primarily utilize touch-based interfaces [11–13], despite research efforts to improve user interaction experiences through the introduction of gesture and voice interactions. Yet, most virtual sand table systems still operate independently, lacking support for interactive functionalities among multiple users [14–18]. Furthermore, virtual sand tables face challenges in terrain construction, with high thresholds for application. Traditional methods are time-consuming and often fail to achieve the desired precision and detail level, limiting the further development of virtual sand table technology [19, 20].

To address the issues of weak interactivity, severe standalone operation, difficulty in map model construction, and the inability to meet the needs of multi-user remote planning faced by current virtual Sand tables, this study designed N-Sand Table: an innovative, NeRF technology-based, multi-user interactive virtual Sand table system. The contributions of this paper can be summarized as follows:

- Design of a virtual Sand table based on NeRF: Utilizing NeRF technology and based on real-world image data, a highly realistic virtual Sand table is constructed, allowing users to experience terrain similar to the real world in a virtual environment. Additionally, through intelligent algorithms, the system dynamically adjusts the virtual

Sand table's terrain according to users' needs and behaviors, achieving a high degree of user customization and interactivity.
- Implementation of multi-channel interaction: To enhance users' interaction experience, the system supports multi-channel interactions through gestures and voice, achieving hand grabbing, gesture recognition, and voice recognition. This interaction method increases user convenience and enables the system to be applied in a wider range of scenarios.
- Multi-user collaboration mechanism: To meet the needs of multi-user remote collaborative planning, the system implements a real-time interaction function among multiple users at different locations. Experimental results show that the system performs excellently in terms of interaction real-time and stability, with an average packet loss rate of only 0.34% and a delay of 15.21 ms.

The rest of the paper is organized as follows: Sect. 2 introduces the overall design of the virtual Sand table; Sect. 3 describes the key technological implementations of the Sand table system; Sect. 4 demonstrates the multi-user interactive virtual Sand table system; Sect. 5 discusses the experimental results; and finally, Sect. 6 concludes the study and points out future research directions.

2 Overall Design

2.1 System Technical Specifications

This paper summarizes the technical specifications required by combining virtual reality interaction technology with the specific application of the virtual Sand table system, as shown in Fig. 1.

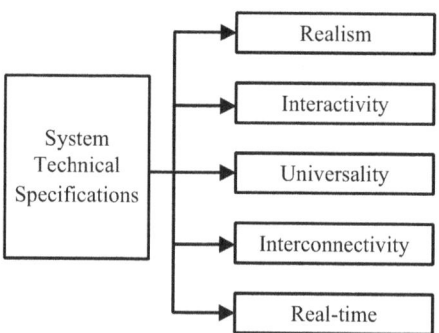

Fig. 1. System Technical Specifications

(1) Realism. The design principle of the Sand table system is to accurately map the real world, hence, the construction of the model must reflect true attributes. Considering that a detailed reproduction of all attributes may be too cumbersome, this system employs NeRF technology to make the constructed model approach real standards.

(2) Interactivity. Real Sand tables often involve hand grabbing, verbal communication, etc., so the virtual Sand table system should include gesture interactions, voice communication, etc., and further enhance the convenience of user operations by integrating new human-machine interaction technologies.
(3) Universality. The Sand table system built should not only be suitable for a single scenario. For Sand table scenes, there should be a variety of types of Sand tables to choose from, and the equipment models established should be portable.
(4) Interconnectivity. Sand table systems often involve interactions among multiple users. For objects in the same virtual scene, it is necessary to maintain the unity of their interactions among multiple users and avoid conflicts in object manipulation by multiple users.
(5) Real-time. The virtual reality scene should be updated in real-time, quickly rendering objects in the field of view, and ensuring fast data transmission among multiple users to maintain real-time synchronization.

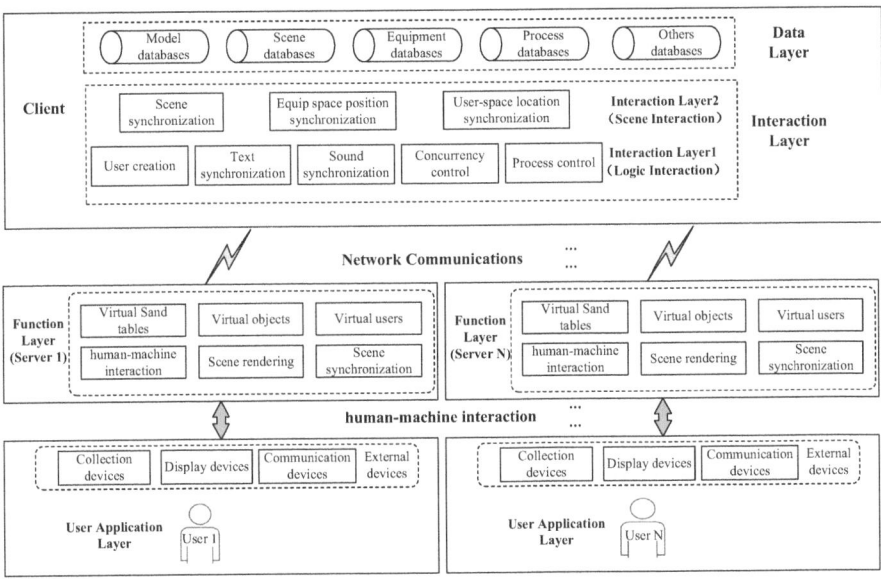

Fig. 2. The framework of the multi-user virtual Sand table system

2.2 System Overall Framework

The framework of the multi-user virtual Sand table system is shown in Fig. 2, briefly divided into four layers: Data Layer, Interaction Layer, Function Layer, and User Application Layer. Based on the system database, various planning information is concretely processed, and information is effectively transmitted through interfaces between layers, with user data transmitted to the server via human-machine interaction and network communication. After server processing, it is issued to each client, forming a closed loop of data transmission and information interaction.

Data Layer: This layer is the foundation of the system, covering model databases, scene databases, equipment databases, process databases, etc., modularizing and categorizing the data and algorithms in the system. Through this method, the system can operate data efficiently while ensuring good portability.

Interaction Layer: Divided into Scene Interaction and Logic Interaction sub-layers. The Scene Interaction Layer is mainly responsible for synchronizing the Sand table scenes and the spatial positions of equipment and users across clients on the server, while the Logic Interaction Layer conducts logical checks based on changes and operations in user information, completing the information exchange between server and clients.

Function Layer: Integrates elements such as virtual Sand tables, virtual objects, and virtual users, and is responsible for key tasks such as human-machine interaction, scene rendering and synchronization. This layer ensures that each client can perform interface display, interaction implementation, and synchronization of virtual scenes. Its goal is to provide functions such as real-time rendering, action simulation synchronization, and user interaction display, enabling clients to synchronize scene rendering and interaction information within the viewpoint range.

User Application Layer: Constitutes the direct contact point between the system and users, including external devices and the users themselves. External devices are divided into collection devices, display devices, and communication devices, where display devices are responsible for generating the interactive interface and synchronizing virtual scenes, collection devices collect user interaction information, and communication devices are responsible for transmitting information between clients and the server.

3 Key Technology Implementation

3.1 Virtual Scene Construction

The key to the virtual sand table system is the establishment of interactive models within the virtual scene. Thus, the initial intention of system development is to achieve good visual effects and a variety of interaction modes. To make the designed sand table more realistic, Unity3D, integrated with the PhysX physics engine, is used as the development platform.

The model creation process encompasses the comprehensive application of 3D-Max, Photoshop, and Unity3D to ensure the accuracy and visual appeal of the models. Initially, 3D-Max is responsible for constructing three-dimensional models of user models, action scripts, and equipment information, which are then imported into Unity3D and converted into components. Photoshop plays the role of drawing appearance images for models during this process; these images are later imported into Unity to expand the material properties of objects. Subsequently, in Unity3D, corresponding components are assigned appropriate materials and baked to build the model library. Finally, models in the model library are connected to the database through C# coding, thus retrieving corresponding model data and implementing control logic (Fig. 3).

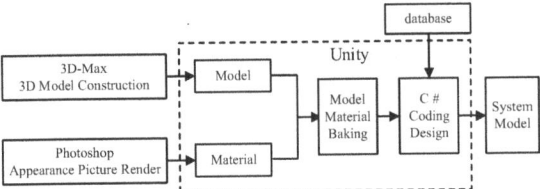

Fig. 3. Model Construction Process

In terms of environmental rendering, the system adopts the dynamic Level Of Detail (LOD) algorithm [21] to adjust the rendering detail level based on the relative distance between objects and the observation point, optimizing the allocation of rendering resources. Objects closer to the observation point or occupying more pixels are given richer details, while objects further from the observation point or with fewer pixels simplify their models. This aims to reduce scene complexity without sacrificing visual experience, thereby improving rendering efficiency. Compared to static Level Of Detail algorithms, the dynamic LOD algorithm is more suitable for virtual sand table scenes. It can automatically update the scene as the user's viewpoint changes, avoiding the visual discontinuity caused by rapid viewpoint movements, thus ensuring a smooth and coherent visual experience.

3.2 NeRF-Based Interactive Sand Table Construction

Neural Radiance Fields (NeRF) [22] is a revolutionary 3D reconstruction method that can predict a scene's continuous volumetric representation from sparse viewpoints through deep learning. NeRF trains a deep neural network to learn the color and density information of a scene, which can then be used to render high-quality images from new viewpoints. The core idea utilizes images from multiple camera angles, learning the color and transparency of each point in space through the network, thus achieving 3D reconstruction of the entire scene.

To lower the barrier to three-dimensional terrain construction and enhance the realism of sand table terrain, this paper employs a method combining terrain top-down views with pixelNeRF for terrain construction. PixelNeRF [23] can predict a continuous neural scene representation based on one or several input images. This method is particularly suited for 3D reconstruction from limited viewpoint information, making it an ideal choice for precise 3D model reconstruction from a single or a few images (Fig. 4).

The process begins with extracting grayscale height maps from terrain top-down views, further extracting the basic contours and key features of the terrain to obtain a corresponding basic contour model. Simultaneously, pixelNeRF technology is used to simulate new viewpoint synthesis of the terrain surface to accommodate changes in lighting and spatial details, achieving a reconstructed terrain with rendering effects. Finally, the two models are overlaid and fitted together to achieve a refined reconstruction of three-dimensional terrain.

With NeRF technology, the system can simulate the texture and subtle details of the terrain surface, such as rock cracks, river directions, and vegetation distribution, with high precision, achieving extremely realistic visual effects.

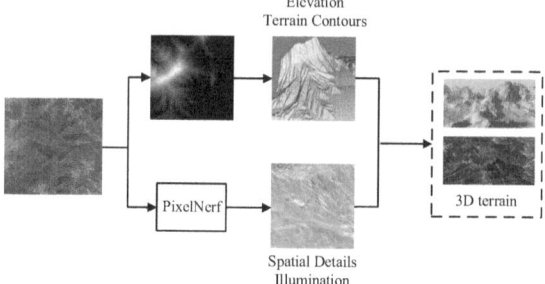

Fig. 4. Sand Table Construction Diagram

To avoid terrain noise issues in terrain generated by NeRF during data preprocessing and format conversion, such as terrain abrupt changes due to precision or overly smooth problems, making the generated terrain unrealistic or even contradictory to actual situations, the system designed a terrain fine-tuning feature. Initially, the map is coarsely processed using two-dimensional Perlin noise to avoid overly smooth map problems, then based on two-dimensional Perlin noise, a terrain brush is built, allowing users to adjust the terrain themselves, enhancing system interactivity [22].

The Perlin noise function is composed of many different noise functions overlaid, where the terrain brush uses noise overlays at different scales to construct the fractal Perlin noise function, set $Noise(\ )$ as a two-dimensional smooth noise function, then the Perlin noise function can be expressed as

$$PerlinNoise(\boldsymbol{p}) = \sum_{i=1}^{octaves} A_i Noise(\boldsymbol{p}f_i) \quad (1)$$

where: $\boldsymbol{p}$ is the designated sampling point; $octaves$ is the number of fractal iterations, reflecting the level of detail; A_i is a weighting coefficient, its size determines the amplitude of the fractal surface; f_i is the frequency of the nth overlaid noise function.

The terrain brush's height calculation formula is:

$$H = H_0(\boldsymbol{p}) + ab_n PerlinNoise(\boldsymbol{p})w \quad (2)$$

where: $H_0(\boldsymbol{p})$ is the original height value of point $\boldsymbol{p}$; H is the modified height value of point $\boldsymbol{p}$; $b_n PerlinNoise(\boldsymbol{p})w$ represents the strength of disturbance, where b_n is a scale parameter, a is the terrain brush type, 1 for enhancement, -1 for weakening; w ($0 \le w \le 1$) is the weight coefficient radiating from point $\boldsymbol{p}$, its calculation formula is:

$$w = \begin{cases} 1 - (\boldsymbol{p} - \boldsymbol{c})^2/r^2, & 0 \le \|\boldsymbol{p} - \boldsymbol{c}\| < r \\ 1, & r \le \|\boldsymbol{p} - \boldsymbol{c}\| \end{cases} \quad (3)$$

The key to the virtual sand table system is the establishment of interactive models within the virtual scene. Thus, the initial intention of system development is to achieve good visual effects and a variety of interaction modes. To make the designed sand table more realistic, Unity3D, integrated with the PhysX physics engine, is used as the development platform.

3.3 Design of Human-Machine Interaction

Sand table simulations typically rely on the grabbing and placing of physical objects for interaction. In this study, real-time hand tracking technology is employed, enabling interaction within the virtual environment through the construction of a virtual hand model. We use Leap Motion technology to capture information on 21 skeletal points of the hand, which is then mapped to generate a virtual hand model. By simulating physical collision detection between the virtual hand and virtual objects, precise virtual interaction operations are achieved.

Since Leap Motion cannot provide tactile feedback in real scenarios, to better reflect the interaction between the virtual hand and virtual objects, visual and auditory feedback are used to enhance the realism of the interaction. The relative distance L between the fingertips and the edges of objects in the virtual scene is used as a criterion. Based on changes in L, virtual objects visually transition, including changes in color and size, to simulate the interaction between objects and hands in the real world. The pseudocode is as follows:

```
Algorithm: Hand-Based Virtual Object Interaction
Input: Leap Motion data
Output: Virtual object interaction feedback
1: finger_position
2: object_edge_position
3: CALCULATE_DISTANCE (finger_position,
   object_edge_position)
4: L1 ← 0.2, L2 ← 0.1
5: IF distance > L1 THEN
       SET_OBJECT_STYLE('original')
6: ELSE IF distance > L2 THEN
       SET_OBJECT_STYLE('change')
7: ELSE
       SET_OBJECT_STYLE('attached')
       PLAY_SOUND('click')
```

As specifically shown in Fig. 5, when the virtual hand approaches a virtual cube, the cube turns yellow and increases in size, thereafter being attracted to the hand to complete the grab.

Fig. 5. Example of Real-Time Hand Interaction

Related research shows [24–26] that fully utilizing the complementary characteristics of more than one sensory and action channel (such as voice, gestures, etc.) to capture users' intentions can compensate for the low accuracy and efficiency of single-channel recognition, enabling better human-computer communication. Therefore, to allow virtual sand table users to operate in an immersive human-machine interaction mode, two new interaction channels, devices, and related interaction technologies, voice and gestures, are adopted to establish a multi-channel collaborative intelligent interaction model, achieving multi-channel integration with traditional interaction devices such as mouse and keyboard.

This model includes two key stages: database construction and behavior matching. Firstly, by extracting gesture and voice signals as well as keyboard and mouse input information, a comprehensive semantic behavior table and semantic library are constructed. Then, system executable tasks are subdivided and constructed into a task library, establishing matching rules between tasks and channels, thereby realizing rule-based mapping from behavior to tasks, ensuring users can control and complete tasks through various channels.

To further refine control, in this system, multi-channel interaction is used to control the displacement of virtual humans, where hand grabbing and mouse can be used to move other objects in the virtual scene.

3.4 Multi-user Real-Time Interaction

To enhance the application security of the virtual sand table system, especially in critical fields such as military command, this system adopts a Client/Server (C/S) mode for network communication. In this mode, the user creating the sand table environment acts as the server side, while users joining the environment play the role of clients. The advantage of the C/S architecture is its effective utilization of client computational resources, significantly reducing server-side operational load by decomposing tasks and distributing them among clients for execution [27].

In choosing network protocols, although TCP and UDP are the current mainstream protocols, TCP is known for its high transmission accuracy and stability but lacks in security and transmission speed; conversely, UDP, while offering improvements in transmission speed and security, falls slightly short in accuracy and stability. Given the characteristics of multi-user real-time interaction and the high requirements for security and stability of the virtual sand table system, this system selects the KCP protocol as the communication protocol. KCP [28] is a fast and reliable network transmission protocol based on UDP, which, while maintaining UDP's speed, provides more reliable data transmission services, making application layer usage simpler and effectively solving TCP's problems of slow transmission speed and low security under network congestion conditions.

3.5 Conflict Resolution Mechanism

In a multi-user virtual sand table system, when multiple users perform multiple operations due to differences in user cognition, overall collaboration is difficult to achieve. To address this collaboration conflict issue, a control allocation mechanism based on user intention inference is designed, aiming to optimize the distribution of control rights by predicting users' operational intentions, thereby avoiding operational conflicts. The specific steps are as follows:

Object Segmentation and Classification: The system first segments objects in the sand table environment into basic components and classifies these components based on their operability into non-operable components N, user-designated operable components S, and jointly operable components C.

Control Candidate Filtering: For objects classified as jointly operable components C, the system sets a control radius R_c, marking users within radius R_c as primary control candidates based on their position P_u and viewpoint direction D_u. Then, the system filters for secondary control candidates by calculating the visual offset angle θ between candidates and components, selecting users who meet $\theta < \Theta$, where Θ is the preset visual offset angle threshold.

Control Rights Allocation: When multiple secondary control candidates exist, the system distributes control rights based on operational intent weight W, calculated by analyzing users' behavior history and current operation context. The specific formula is:

$$W_i = f(H_u, C_u) \qquad (4)$$

where H_u represents the user's behavior history, C_u represents the current operation context, and f is the weight calculation function. The system decides the distribution of control rights based on the size of W, giving priority to the user with the highest weight.

To reduce the risk of frequent switching and misallocation of control rights, a delayed authorization and permission exchange strategy is introduced, aimed at improving the stability and flexibility of control rights. Delayed authorization is implemented by setting a time threshold T_d, officially allocating control rights only when a user's continuous operational intent is clear and exceeds T_d. The permission exchange strategy allows users to actively exchange control rights under certain conditions to accommodate dynamically changing collaboration needs.

4 System Demonstration

4.1 System Composition

The system uses Leap Motion, voice devices (such as headphones), and traditional mouse and keyboard as interaction devices, and selects Unity3D as the simulation platform to implement a multi-user virtual sand table system based on multi-channel operations. Taking a sand table system commonly used in command and control as a prototype, a multi-user interactive virtual sand table based on NeRF technology has been realized. This system generates terrain through NeRF technology from typical real satellite terrain top-down views.

To avoid the potential weight burden, rendering desynchronization, and dizziness issues caused by head-mounted displays, the system provides two types of scene display modes: desktop and immersive. Operators can view the virtual scene rendered by Unity3D through a computer monitor or VR display. Through controllers like Leap Motion and voice devices, the system is capable of tracking human operation data to control the movement of equipment and user space positions in the virtual environment.

Additionally, the system supports real-time communication between users through voice and text, achieving sand table interaction among multiple users (Figs. 6 and 7).

Fig. 6. Sand Table System Display(1)

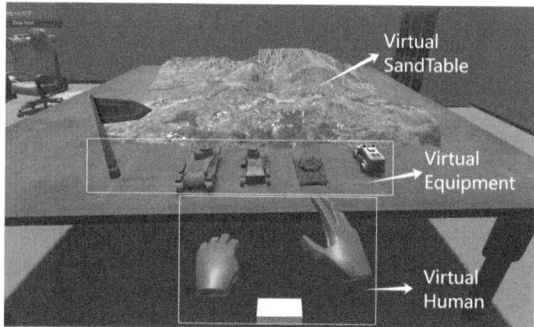

Fig. 7. Sand Table System Display(2)

To provide a realistic user interaction experience, the system adopts a first-person perspective and real-time tracks the user's hand movements to construct a virtual hand at the bottom of the field of view. Users can view the virtual scene rendered by Unity3D through a computer monitor or VR display device and use controllers like Leap Motion and voice devices to manipulate devices and spatial positions in the virtual environment. Moreover, the system supports real-time communication between users through voice and text to facilitate sand table interaction among multiple users. Notably, interactions between users are not limited to communication but focus more on users' manipulation of environmental objects and their synchronous impact on other users, such as changes in user positions, adjustments of item locations, and alterations of the sand table terrain.

4.2 Single User Interaction Demonstration

As shown in Fig. 8-a, a user can place the mouse or virtual hand over equipment, and the system will display the equipment name above it and show detailed information about the equipment on the user interface; as shown in Fig. 8-b, a user can use the virtual hand to grasp the corresponding equipment and move it to any position on the virtual sand table through user movement; Fig. 8-c and d show the effects before and after a user makes fine adjustments to the terrain according to their requirements.

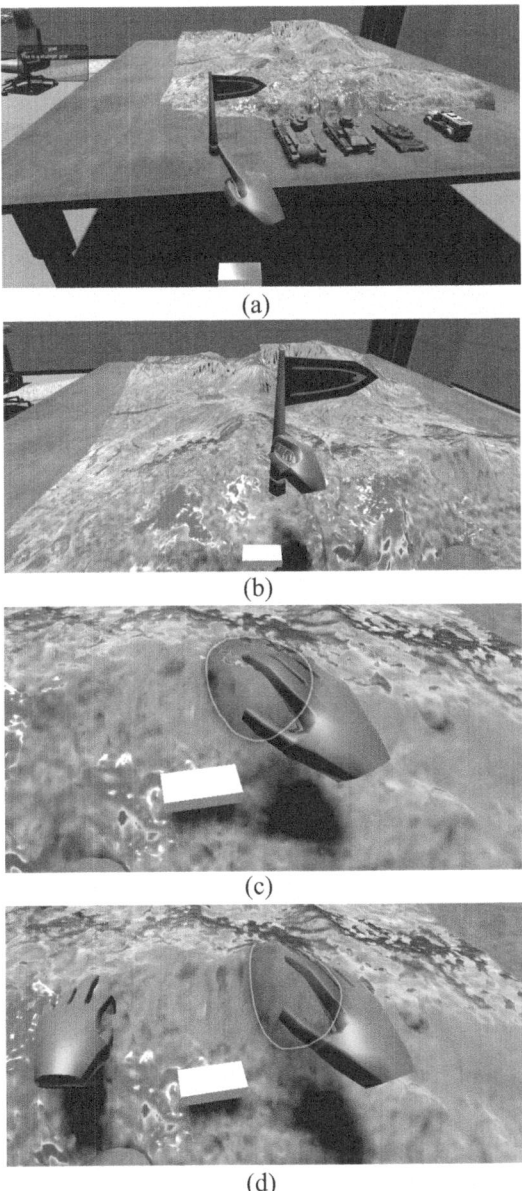

Fig. 8. a: Equipment Details Display. b. Equipment Grasping. c. Before Terrain Change. d. After Terrain Change

4.3 Multi-user Interaction Demonstration

Interactions between users mainly include user movement, object manipulation, text communication between users, and voice communication. Figure 9 demonstrates part of the multi-user interaction process.

Fig. 9. a. Synchronization of User and Object Positions. b. Multi-User Interaction Demonstration. c. Exchange of Equipment Control Rights Figure

Figure 9-a shows the perspectives of two users in the same virtual sand table environment, where users can update the positions and hand movements of other users within their field of view in real-time, as well as the positions of controlled objects; in Fig. 9-b, User A says to User B, "Put it in the corresponding position", facilitating communication between users; Fig. 9-c shows the change in control rights between users, where the system's control allocation mechanism successfully transfers the control rights of equipment from User A to User B. It is observable that after the change of ownership, the color of the corresponding object also changes.

5 System Testing

5.1 Test Details

To evaluate the multi-user virtual sand table system, we conducted system tests based on two key indicators: synchronization effects and interaction experience. A total of 20 participants (including 11 females, aged between 19 to 33 years, with an average age of 23 years and a standard deviation of 3.89) took part in the test. Among them, 5 were proficient users of virtual systems (referred to as "veterans"), while the remaining 15 had little to no experience with virtual system interactions (referred to as "novices"). The test was divided into three rounds: novice group, novice-veteran mixed group, and veteran group, with each round consisting of pairs of two, totaling 15 tests. All participants used interaction devices and laptops in a local area network environment, with 2 min allocated before the test to familiarize themselves with the system. The test grouping details are as follows:

- Novice Group: 5 groups, 10 novices in total, paired in twos
- Novice-Veteran Group: 5 groups, 5 novices from outside the novice group paired with 5 veterans
- Veteran Group: 5 groups, 5 veterans paired in non-repeating pairs

During the test, we used Wireshark software to collect network communication data, and after the test concluded, we gathered feedback from participants through a questionnaire survey to understand the specifics of the interaction effect.

5.2 Synchronization Effect

The synchronization between multiple users requires low network latency to meet the real-time requirements of synchronization, and to maintain the consistency of synchronization, a low packet loss rate is needed. According to related literature [29], latency should be less than 50ms for good communication strength, and a packet loss rate greater than 1% can easily cause network congestion and increased delay. Based on data collected by Wire Shark software, the following results were obtained.

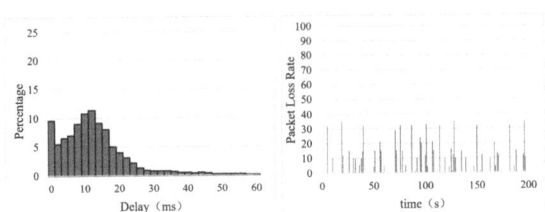

Fig. 10. Network Latency Distribution and Network Packet Loss Rate

Figure 10a shows the network latency distribution of the system, which is long-tailed, with an average network latency of 15.21 ms, less than 30 ms, classified as extremely fast, and delays over 50 ms only accounting for 1.1%. Figure 10b shows the average packet loss rate during data transmission between servers and clients, with an average system packet loss rate of 0.34%, meeting the requirement of less than 1%, and with an average packet loss duration of 191 ms over a 10 s period, the system did not experience packet loss for 98.19% of the time. These results indicate that the system has low network latency and rarely experiences packet loss, providing good network synchronization effects suitable for transmission synchronization between multiple users.

5.3 Interaction Experience

To evaluate the interaction experience of the multi-user virtual sand table system, we used a questionnaire survey, assessing users' subjective feelings through the NASA Task Load Index (NASA TLX) [30], and also evaluating the system interaction smoothness and subjective interaction accuracy. After completing tasks, users rated these aspects using a 7-point Likert scale (Fig. 11).

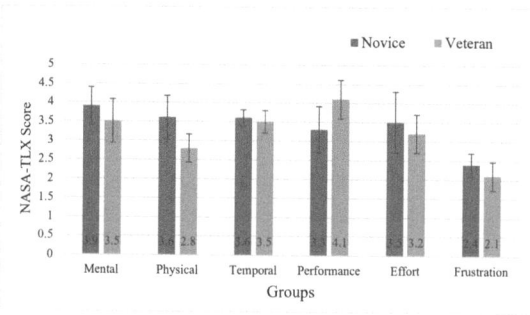

Fig. 11. Results of NASA TLX

Through the analysis of the NASA TLX questionnaire results, we found that veterans achieve more efficient interaction effects compared to novices. Novices scored higher in terms of mental and physical workload, a phenomenon primarily due to their unfamiliarity with the system's mode of interaction. This also led to increased effort and frustration, consistent with habitual cognitive patterns (Fig. 12).

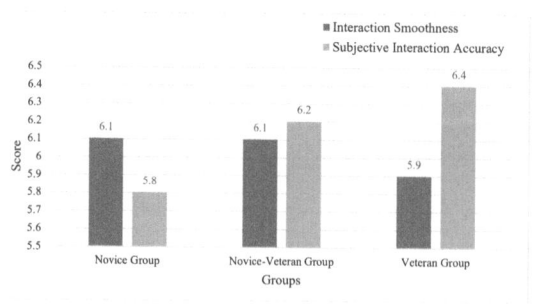

Fig. 12. Results of interactive Experience Questionnaire

The NASA TLX questionnaire revealed differences between novices and veterans in their perceptions of the system. To more accurately reflect the interaction experience, this study conducted a comprehensive analysis of the ratings for system interaction smoothness and subjective interaction accuracy given by novices and veterans. We averaged the scores of the novice and veteran groups and applied a 7:3 weighted average method for the mixed group of novices and veterans, assigning 70% of the weight to the opinions of novices to minimize bias that might be introduced by the veterans' familiarity.

The results showed that the scores for system interaction smoothness were quite close, around 6 points, indicating that the system's smoothness meets the needs of most users. In terms of interaction accuracy, novices scored 5.8 points, while veterans scored 6.4 points. Some novices reported that although they did not use all interaction methods, they were still able to complete tasks, indicating the system is novice-friendly. The novice-veteran group scored 6.2 points, showing a significant improvement in novices' adaptability under the guidance of veterans compared to the novice group. In summary, the system's interaction experience generally meets requirements and is friendly to novices, with a low barrier to entry.

6 Conclusion

Addressing the critical issues of severe standalone operation, weak interactivity, and difficulty in constructing map models in current virtual sand tables, this paper presents the development of the N-Sand Table system. The research and development of the N-Sand Table system mark a significant extension of virtual sand table technology towards higher realism, enhanced interactivity, and broader application fields. By incorporating NeRF technology and a multi-channel interaction design, the system not only improves the realism and interaction experience of virtual sand tables but also successfully enables real-time collaboration and communication among multiple users. With the emergence of the metaverse concept and the development of cutting-edge technologies, the innovation and application of virtual sand table technology are set to explore more possibilities, offering users richer, more realistic, and interactive virtual experiences.

The paper primarily showcases the system's design process and outcomes, with future research aimed at exploring more efficient data processing methods, advanced interaction technologies, and broader application scenarios to further refine interaction methods and collaborative approaches in the virtual environment, thereby optimizing system performance and expanding its application scope.

Acknowledgements. This work is supported by the National Natural Science Foundation of China(72394363、62306135), Youth Fund of Science Foundation of Ministry of Education of China(23YJC630156), Jiangsu Province Science Foundation for Youths(BK20230783), the Postgradu-ate Research Practice Innovation Program of Jiangsu Province (KYCX23_0062).

References

1. Lv, X., Cai, M., Chen, B.: Frontiers and development trend of tabletop exercise technology. Bull. Natl. Nat. Sci. Found. China **35**(05), 742–751 (2021)
2. Quarantelli, E.L.: Problematical aspects of the information/communication revolution for disaster planning and research: ten non-technical issues and questions. Disaster Prev Manag. **6**(2), 94–106 (1997)
3. Haihan, C., Zhitang, L.: Reasearch on the technology of electronic sand table based on GIS. In: International Conference on Information Science and Engineering, pp. 3881–3884. IEEE (2011)

4. Attorre, F., De Sanctis, M., Francesconi, F., et al.: Research on the technology of electronic sand table based on GIS. Annali di Botanica, 37–47(11) (2004)
5. Schlager, B., Stoll, D., Krosl, K., et al.: Tactical and strategical analysis in virtual geographical environments. In: 2021 IEEE Conference on Virtual Reality and 3D User Interfaces Abstracts and Workshops, pp. 621–622. IEEE Computer Society Press, Los Alamitos (2021)
6. Roesler, C.: Sandplay therapy: an overview of theory, applications and evidence base. Arts Psychother. **64**, 84–94 (2019)
7. Shan, P., Sun, W.: Research on 3D urban landscape design and evaluation based on geographic information system. Environ. Earth Sci. **80**(17), 1–15 (2021)
8. Park, S.M., Kim, Y.G.: A Metaverse: Taxonomy, components, applications, and open challenges. IEEE Access **10**, 4209–4251 (2022)
9. Zhao, Y.H., Jiang, J.J., Chen, Y., et al.: Metaverse: Perspectives from graphics, interactions and visualization. Vis. Inform. **6**(1), 56–67 (2022)
10. Rauschnabel, P.A., Babin, B.J., Tom, D.M., et al.: What is augmented reality marketing? Its definition, complexity, and future. J. Bus. Res. **142**, 1140–1150 (2022)
11. Huang, G., Guo, R.C.: Intelligent manor sand table demo system based on Internet of things and virtual reality technology. In: Proceedings of 2017 IEEE 3rd Information Technology and Mechatronics Engineering Conference, pp. 597–601. IEEE Computer Society Press, Los Alamitos (2017)
12. Liu, X., Shiotani, S.: A virtual globe-based visualization and interactive framework for a small craft navigation assistance system in the near sea. J. Traff. Transp. Eng. (Engl. Ed.) **4**(06), 68–79 (2017)
13. Ou, P., Chen, M., Yu, Q.: Landscape sand table system based on deep learning and augmented reality technology. Adv. Intell. Syst. Comput. **1117**, 565–570 (2020)
14. O'Banion, M.S., Lewis, N.S., Boyce, M.W., et al.: Use of an augmented reality sand table for satellite remote sensing education. J. Geogr. High. Educ. **47**(4), 685–696 (2023)
15. Heng, L., Zhaonian, H., Chen, G.: An interactive method with gestures oriented toward the augmented reality electronic sand table. In: International Conference on Electronic Information Engineering and Computer Science (EIECS 2022), pp. 84–90 (2023)
16. Wu, D., Gong, J.H., Li, Y.: Interaction technology based on 3D printing topographic sand table for Emergency Management. In: Proceedings of the 2nd International Conference on Big Data and Internet of Things, pp. 100–104. ACM Press, New York (2018)
17. Li, Q., Liu, H., Wu, Z.: A situation visualization system based on 2D&3D electronic sand table. In: Proceedings of the IEEE Advanced Information Technology, Electronic and Automation Control Conference, pp. 2057–2060. IEEE Computer Society Press, Los Alamitos (2018)
18. Lee, A., Chang, Y.S., Jang, I.: Planetary-scale geospatial open platform based on the Unity 3D environment. Sensors **20**(20), 1–19 (2020)
19. Liu, X., Tian, R.J.: RiverGAN: fluvial landform generation based on physical simulations and generative adversarial network. J. Digit. Landsc. Archit. **202**(7), 105–111 (2022)
20. Liu, H., Zhao, W.J., Duan, F.Z., et al.: Interactive terrain modification technology for earthquake disaster scene modeling. J. Jilin Univ. Earth Sci. Ed. **43**(05), 1687–1696 (2013). (in Chinese)
21. Wu, P.L., Chen, S.Y.: Innovation in optimization of virtual space experience using interactive engine and device—example of a song dynasty landscape painting. Sens. Mater. **32**(10), 3419–3428 (2020)
22. Mildenhall, B., Srinivasan, P.P., Tancik, M., et al.: NERF: representing scenes as neural radiance fields for view synthesis. In: European Conference on Computer Vision, pp. 405–421. Springer, Cham (2020)
23. Yu, A., Ye, V., Tancik, M., Kanazawa, A.: pixelNeRF: neural radiance fields from one or few images. In: 2021 IEEE/CVF Conference on Computer Vision and Pattern Recognition (CVPR), Nashville, TN, USA, pp. 4576–4585 (2021)

24. Jiang, R.M., Sadka, A.H., Crookes, D.: Multimodal biometric human recognition for perceptual human-computer interaction. IEEE Trans. Syst. Man Cybern. Part C **40**(6), 676–681 (2010)
25. Pradeep, K.A., Anwar, H., Abdulmotaleb, E.S., et al.: Multimodal fusion for multimedia analysis: a survey. Multimedia Syst. **16**(6), 345–379 (2010)
26. Saima, M., Khalil, T.S., Muhammad, A., et al.: Move to smart learning environment: exploratory research of challenges in computer laboratory and design intelligent virtual laboratory for eLearning technology. Eurasia J. Math. Sci. Technol. Educ. **14**(5), 1645–1662 (2018)
27. Jaenicke, S., Albaum, S.P., Blumenkamp, P., et al.: Flexible metagenome analysis using the MGX framework. Microbiome **6**(1), 76 (2018)
28. Zhou, Y.C.: Design and Implementation of Real-Time Video Transmission Scheme Based on KCP. Chongqing University of Posts and Telecommunications, Chongqing (2020)
29. Zhang, R.: Research and implementation of multi-user virtual training system based on unity3D. South-West University of Science and Technology, Mianyang (2021)
30. Hart, S.G.: NASA-task load index (NASA-TLX); 20 years later. In: Proceedings of the Human Factors and Ergonomics Society Annual Meeting, vol. 50, pp. 904–908 (2006)

A Weakly Supervised Crowd Counting Method Based on Contrastive Deep Supervision

Guohang Huang, Bo Yang[✉], Jianlin Zhu, and Yong Zhang

College of Computer Science and Key Laboratory of Information Physics Fusion and Intelligent Computing of the National Ethnic Affairs Commission, South-Central Minzu University, Wuhan 430074, China
yangbo@mail.scuec.edu.cn

Abstract. Crowd counting is a challenging task with important applications in public safety, traffic control and planning. Weakly supervised crowd counting models, in contrast to fully supervised models, do not require object-level annotations during training, which can reduce the cost of manual labeling. However, the lack of object-level constraints often leads to poor performance. To address this, we propose a weakly supervised crowd counting method that combines contrastive deep supervision and feature fusion. During training, we project intermediate feature maps from different stages and perform contrastive deep supervision, which strengthens the model's understanding of crowd features. The model also introduces feature fusion to allow the regression layer to fully utilize feature information from both deep and shallow layers for regression counting. Additionally, we introduce an attention mechanism in the forward process to enhance the weights of important crowd features. Experimental results show that our method achieves good performance on multiple crowd datasets, even better than some fully supervised methods.

Keywords: crowd counting · weak supervision · contrastive deep supervision · feature fusion · attention mechanism

1 Introduction

Crowd counting, the task of estimating the number of individuals in an image, is of paramount importance in various domains, including social security management, abnormal situation warning, and traffic control. In crowded scenes, accurate crowd counting assumes a pivotal role in the reduction of potential hazards and the assurance of public safety [1].

Early crowd counting methods predominantly relied on traditional machine learning approaches, such as detection-based and regression-based methods. However, these methods faced significant limitations in real-world applications due to factors such as uneven crowd density distribution, large variations in crowd scale, and cross-scene variability. In recent years, the emergence of CNNs and vision transformers (ViTs) has led to significant advancements in crowd counting. These deep learning models have demonstrated superior performance in addressing the aforementioned challenges, leading to improved counting accuracy and robustness.

The majority of existing crowd counting models are fully supervised networks that require ground truth with location information for training. However, the cost of manual annotation for such fine-grained information is prohibitive, especially for images containing a large number of individuals. In contrast, weakly supervised crowd counting models require only count-level labels, eliminating the need for labor-intensive location annotations for each individual in the image, which can greatly reduce the training cost of crowd counting models and is conducive to reducing the difficulty of data collection and annotation for real-world deployment of crowd counting models.

However, weakly supervised crowd counting models are limited by the weak supervision signals that contain less information, and the accuracy and stability of the model's counting are difficult to match those of fully supervised models. Most of the current high-performance weakly supervised crowd counting models are based on ViT. Such ViT-based crowd counting models have high hardware computing power requirements, which increases the cost of deploying the model to real-world applications.

Contrastive deep supervision (CDS) [2] offers a promising approach for improving the performance of weakly supervised crowd counting models. By incorporating CDS into the intermediate layers of a CNN, the model is able to learn discriminative features from different augmented samples, enhancing its understanding of low-level semantic information such as crowd characteristics. This strategy effectively addresses the challenge of optimizing intermediate layers with weak supervision signals. To this end, we propose a novel weakly supervised crowd counting model that leverages a CNN architecture and integrates CDS, multi-level feature fusion, and multiple attention mechanisms. The proposed model has been extensively evaluated on multiple benchmark datasets. Notably, the CDS module is only employed during the training phase and can be completely discarded during inference, significantly reducing the computational complexity and facilitating real-world deployment.

2 Related Work

Over the past decade, a large number of researchers have studied crowd counting models trained in a fully supervised manner. Zhang et al. [3] improved the performance of crowd counting across scenes by alternating the crowd density and crowd counting as the learning target of a deep convolutional neural network. The MCNN [4] method uses a multi-branch convolutional neural network structure and introduces a geometrically adaptive kernel to generate a more reasonable crowd density map. CSRNet proposed by Li et al. [5] is a crowd counting method with a pure convolutional structure, which uses dilated convolutions instead of pooling operations. To address the challenges posed by diverse camera viewpoints, Liu et al. [6] proposed a method that utilizes features extracted with different receptive field sizes. Wang et al. [7] proposed the DM-Count method, which leverages a distribution matching approach for crowd counting and achieves improved counting accuracy. Song et al. [8] argued that predicting density maps is counterintuitive for crowd counting models, and proposed the P2PNet method that directly predicts crowd point locations, achieving promising counting performance. STNet [9] utilizes a tree structure to handle the multi-scale problem and achieves significant performance improvements. Yang et al. [10] proposed CrowdFormer, which utilizes a ViT architecture and proposes a density kernel fusion framework for more accurate density map estimation and generation.

Fully supervised crowd counting models require a large amount of location-level information annotation, while weakly supervised crowd counting models aim to reduce the cost of such annotation. Lei et al. [11] proposed the MATT method, which uses a multi-task training strategy. The method uses mostly count-level labels for training, but they still use a small number of position-level annotations. Yang et al. [12] tried to only use count-level labels for training. They designed a network that performs both a ranking task and a regression counting task, and let the ranking and regression counting mutually optimize each other. Weakly supervised models have difficulty training a high-performance crowd counting model with only one count-level supervision signal because they lack supervision of position-level information. Recently, weakly supervised crowd counting models based on ViT have been proposed, such as TransCrowd proposed by Liang et al. [13], which achieved excellent counting performance. Hu et al. [14] proposed a unified model based on visual transformer for both density classification and crowd counting tasks, and achieved good counting accuracy.

Due to the high computational cost of crowd counting models based on ViT architecture, this paper introduces a contrastive deep supervision architecture into CNN models and constructs a high-performance weakly supervised crowd counting model by combining feature fusion and attention mechanisms.

3 Methodology

3.1 Architecture Overview

The proposed network architecture consists of two major components: a feature extraction backbone and a regression counting head for estimating the crowd count. The overall structure is illustrated in Fig. 1.

The backbone utilizes VGG19 [15] as the underlying architecture for feature extraction. The fully connected layers and the final max pooling layer of VGG19 are discarded, while all convolutional layers are retained. To facilitate deep supervision, a normalized projection head branch with varying complexities is incorporated before each max pooling layer, starting from two stacked Conv3-128 modules. These branches project intermediate feature maps from different layers and compute contrastive losses for enhanced learning. A Coordinate Attention (CA) module [16] is integrated after the four Conv3-256 convolutional layers, and a Squeeze and Excitation (SE) attention module [17] is employed after the first four Conv3-512 convolutional layers. The final feature map of the backbone is up-sampled and fused with the outputs of the first four Conv3-512 convolutional layers before being fed into the regression counting head.

In the regression counting head, two convolutional layers are initially employed to reduce the channel dimensionality of the feature map to 128, followed by processing through the SE attention module. Subsequently, a convolutional layer is utilized to transform the feature map into a single channel, and the predicted result is obtained by summing the values at all locations within the feature map.

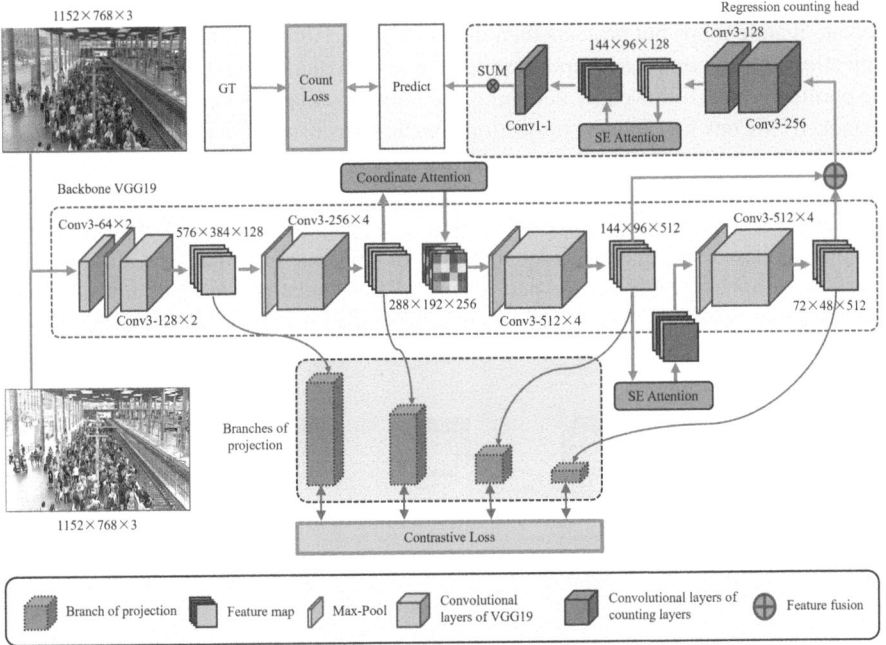

Fig. 1. The overall structure of the proposed method

3.2 Contrastive Deep Supervision Setting

During the training phase, weakly supervised models, which rely only on count-level labels, suffer from the challenge of exploring an intractable search space for parameter optimization. In contrast, fully supervised models benefit from both count and pixel-level location constraints. However, weakly supervised models cannot learn crowd location information from count labels. This deficiency in supervision signals is further amplified during propagation from deep to shallow layers, ultimately hindering the overall performance of the model. To address this issue, we incorporate a contrastive deep supervision architecture into the model.

Since simple image transformations do not affect the actual number of people, the intermediate feature maps generated by the model for two such transformed images should exhibit certain similarities, as the underlying crowd structure remains unchanged. To leverage this property, we apply data augmentation twice to the same image (detailed in Sect. 4.3) to obtain two images with the same count label and essentially identical content. These augmented images are then fed into the model, and feature maps are extracted and projected at different stages. Contrastive losses are calculated based on these projected feature maps and backpropagated for model learning.

Notably, the contrastive deep supervision framework in this paper prioritizes identifying similarities in the intermediate feature maps of two images that are conducive to inference, rather than striving for completely identical intermediate feature maps from different inputs. Consequently, the proposed method does not directly compare the intermediate feature maps but projects them before comparison. As illustrated in Fig. 2, the projection branch comprises depthwise separable convolution (DSConv) [18] and average pooling layers, followed by flattening and normalization. By controlling the number of stacked DSConv layers in the projection branch, we construct four projection branches with varying complexities for the intermediate feature maps of four different layers with varying depths. The shallow layers utilize more complex projection branches, whereas the deep layers utilize simpler ones. This design is primarily motivated by the observation that shallow features encapsulate a wealth of semantic information. Our work lays significant emphasis on crowd-related features. Consequently, a more complex projection is required to enable the model to learn these features from the disparities during backpropagation.

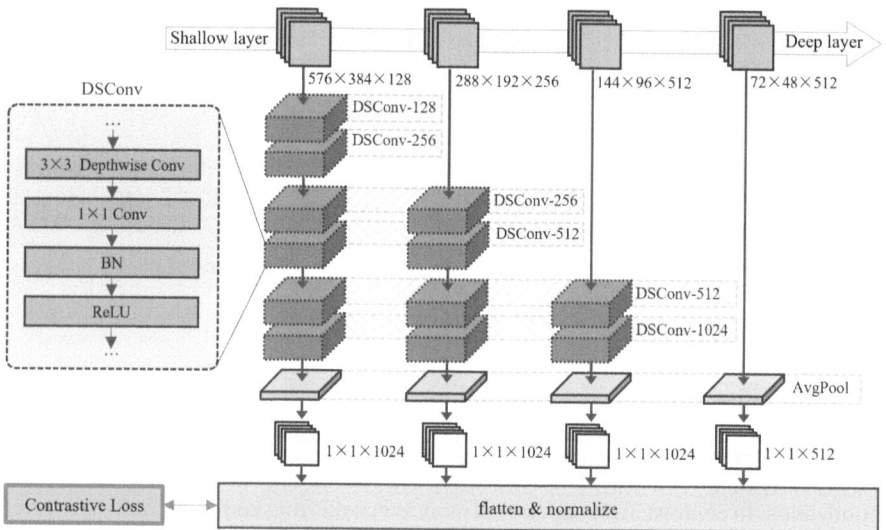

Fig. 2. Projection branches of contrastive deep supervision

3.3 Attention Mechanism and Feature Fusion

To enhance the model's utilization of critical features, this paper incorporates different attention mechanisms at various stages of the model. The CA attention mechanism can attend to the feature importance at different locations. In the backbone, the shallow feature maps retain relatively large sizes, and the location information embedded within them could be beneficial for the performance of the counting results. Therefore, a CA attention mechanism is added after the shallow convolutional layers to fully exploit the semantically rich information in the shallow feature maps. In contrast, SE attention modules are incorporated between the convolutional layers of the deeper parts of the backbone and in the intermediate layers of the regression counting part. The SE attention module can assign higher weights to more important channels. The feature maps generated by the deeper convolutional layers have smaller sizes but more channels. At this stage, enabling the model to identify more important channels from the multitude of channels will be more beneficial for the model's performance.

Before feeding the feature maps extracted by the backbone into the regression counting head, the output of the 16th convolutional layer in the backbone is up-sampled. The width and height of the original feature map are doubled, and it is then fused with the output of the 12th convolutional layer to serve as the final output of the backbone.

3.4 Loss Function

The loss function comprises two primary components: the counting loss and the contrastive loss. Overall, the loss function of the model is:

$$Loss = L_{Count} + \alpha L_{Contra} \tag{1}$$

where α is the weight coefficient of the contrast loss, which in the experiment has a value of 0.1.

For the counting loss, this paper uses the combination of L1 loss and RMSE loss to calculate. For counting tasks, L1 loss is usually used to measure the difference between the predicted value and the target value, which directly affects the accuracy of the model for crowd counting. The formula is as follows:

$$\mathcal{L}_1 = \frac{1}{M} \sum_{i=1}^{M} |P_i - G_i| \tag{2}$$

where P_i and G_i are the predicted and GT number of people in image i, respectively, and M is the size of batch-size.

However, experimental results showed that using only the L1 loss for weakly supervised training led to significant variations in crowd counting results across different images. In most fully supervised models, density maps with location information are utilized for supervision. During the calculation of L1 loss with these density maps, pixel-level location supervision can be achieved. However, in weakly supervised models, computing the L1 loss merely boils down to comparing two numbers, which fails to provide effective guidance for deeper learning and consequently undermines the model's stability. To address this issue, the RMSE loss is introduced in this paper to measure the model's stability. The formula for calculating the RMSE loss is as follows:

$$\mathcal{L}_{RMSE} = \sqrt{\frac{1}{M} \sum_{i=1}^{M} (P_i - G_i)^2} \tag{3}$$

In summary, the final counting loss formula is as follows:

$$L_{Count} = \beta \mathcal{L}_1 + \mathcal{L}_{RMSE} \tag{4}$$

The presence of β is to make the model more biased towards the counting task, and it is set to 2 in the experiment.

In the model, the contrastive deep supervision component applies two distinct data augmentations to each image, and the two augmented images are fed into the model within the same batch. Let x_i and x_{i+M} denote the two augmented versions of image i, and $z = c(x)$ represent the outputs of the normalized projection branches in the contrastive deep supervision component. The contrastive loss function proposed in SimCLR [19] is adopted in this paper, and its calculation formula is as follows:

$$L_{\text{Contra}} = -\sum_{i=1}^{M} \log \frac{\exp(z_i \cdot z_{i+M})/\tau}{\sum_{k=1}^{2M} 1_{[k \neq i]} \exp(z_i \cdot z_k)/\tau} \tag{5}$$

In the formula, $1 \in \{0,1\}$ is an indicator function, whose value is 1 if $k \neq i$, and 0 otherwise. τ is a hyperparameter, which is set to 0.07 in the experiments of this paper.

4 Experimental Setup

4.1 Datasets

We evaluate our proposed method on five challenging datasets, including UCF-CC-50 [20], ShanghaiTech part A and part B [4], UCF-QNRF [21], and JHU-Crowd++ [22]. The details of these datasets are shown in Table 1.

The ShanghaiTech-A dataset, a widely recognized benchmark for crowd counting, contrasts with the ShanghaiTech-B dataset, which aligns more closely with real-world applications due to its composition of images captured by surveillance cameras on the streets of Shanghai. The UCF-QNRF dataset is notable for its higher crowd density and broader range of crowd counts, in addition to its inclusion of a diverse array of scenes.

The JHU-Crowd++ dataset can be categorized into three levels based on the number of individuals within each image: low density (0–50 people), medium density (51–500 people), and high density (above 500 people). The number of images in the three categories are 1228, 2512, and 632, respectively.

The UCF-CC-50 dataset, released earlier, consists of 50 images. Given the limited sample size of this dataset, we adopt a five-fold cross-validation approach for experimentation. The dataset is split evenly into five folds, with each fold serving as the validation set in turn, while the remaining four folds serve as the training set. Five experiments are conducted, and the average result is ultimately obtained.

4.2 Evaluation Metrics

Two metrics are employed for the experimental evaluation in this paper: mean absolute error (MAE) and mean squared error (MSE), which are defined as follows:

$$MAE = \frac{1}{M} \sum_{i=1}^{M} |P_i - G_i|, \tag{6}$$

$$MSE = \frac{1}{M} \sum_{i=1}^{M} |P_i - G_i|^2. \tag{7}$$

MAE and MSE are both commonly used evaluation criteria for regression models. MAE calculates the average difference between predicted and ground truth values,

Table 1. Details of the datasets used in this paper

Dataset	Scene	Image number				Image Resolution	Count statistics		
		Total	Train	Val	Test		Average	Min	Max
ShanghaiTech-A	Cross-scene	482	300	182	-	Average: 589 × 868	501	33	3139
ShanghaiTech-B	Single scene	716	400	316	-	Fixed: 768 × 1024	123	9	578
UCF-QNRF	Cross-scene	1535	1201	334	-	Average: 2013 × 2902	815	49	12865
JHU-Crowd++	Cross-scene	4372	2272	500	1600	Average: 910 × 1430	346	-	25791
UCF-CC-50	Cross-scene	50	-	-	-	Average: 2888 × 2101	1280	94	4543

directly reflecting the model's accuracy. However, the MAE metric does not directly reflect the model's stability. Even with similar MAE values, the stability of two models may still exhibit significant discrepancies under different scenarios. In contrast, MSE amplifies the discrepancy between predicted and ground truth values, making it more sensitive to outliers and better equipped to reflect the model's robustness in diverse situations. When conducting quantitative comparisons on the same dataset, lower values of these two metrics indicate superior performance of the model on that dataset.

4.3 Data Augmentation

To improve the model's generalization capacity and prevent premature overfitting during training due to multiple inputs of identical images, this paper incorporates the online data augmentation approach depicted in Fig. 3. For each image, we first randomly apply horizontal flipping with a 50% probability, followed by random proportional scaling with the same probability, while ensuring that the scaled image width remains at least 350 pixels. Additionally, three supplementary data augmentation techniques are employed for the image utilized in contrastive deep supervision: random horizontal flipping, random color jittering, and random grayscale adjustment. After these transformations, the original augmented images and the additionally augmented images are concatenated to form a batch, which is then fed into the model for training.

4.4 Implementation Details

The experimental platform used in this paper has an Intel(R) Core(TM) i5-11400 2.60 GHz CPU, an NVIDIA GeForce RTX 4070Ti GPU with 12GB of memory, and a Windows 11 23H2 operating system. The model is implemented based on Python 3.10

and Pytorch 1.11, and the CUDA version is 12.3. During training, all original images in this method are scaled to a size of 768 × 1152. The Adam optimizer is used for parameter optimization during training, with an initial learning rate of 10^{-5} and a batch size of 2. The total number of training epochs is 400.

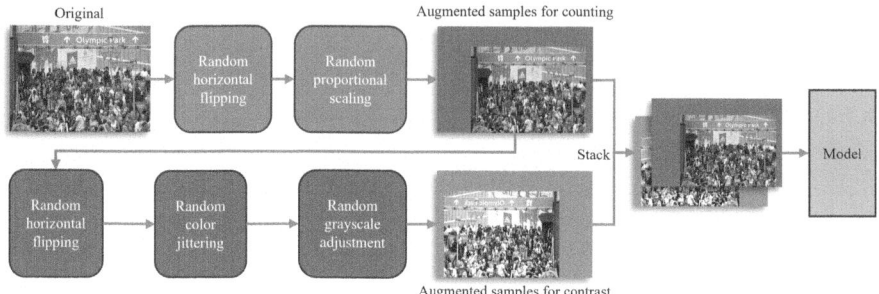

Fig. 3. Process of data augmentation

5 Experimental Result

For each dataset, the proposed method is quantitatively compared against prevalent crowd counting approaches. To validate the efficacy of the proposed method, this paper compares it with both mainstream weakly supervised and fully supervised crowd counting methods. The quantitative comparison results on UCF-CC-50, ShanghaiTech-A, ShanghaiTech-B and UCF-QNRF datasets are presented in Table 2.

Compared to weakly supervised models, the proposed method attains the best performance on ShanghaiTech-B and UCF-CC-50 datasets. In terms of MSE performance alone, the proposed method exhibits superior stability on UCF-CC-50, ShanghaiTech-A and ShanghaiTech-B compared to both TransCrowd methods. The MAE metrics also demonstrate that the proposed method achieves notable performance improvements on these three datasets. For the UCF-QNRF dataset, the proposed method only holds a slight advantage over TransCrowd-Token in terms of the MSE metric, which could be attributed to the challenges posed by the large crowd density variation within the images of this dataset.

While it may be considered unfair to directly compare the performance of weakly supervised models with fully supervised models, the proposed weakly supervised model still achieves commendable results, even surpassing several prevalent fully supervised crowd counting models in terms of MAE and MSE on certain datasets. For instance, on UCF-CC-50, ShanghaiTech-A, and ShanghaiTech-B datasets, the proposed method yields lower MAE and MSE values than the fully supervised model CSRNet. Additionally, on the UCF-QNRF dataset, the proposed method outperforms CAN in both metrics.

On the Val and Test subsets of JHU-Crowd++ dataset, the proposed method is quantitatively compared against other methods not only in terms of the overall performance

Table 2. Quantitative comparisons with different methods under different annotation levels on four datasets

Method	Label		UCF_CC_50		ShanghaiTech-A		ShanghaiTech-B		UCF_QNRF	
	Location	Number	MAE	MSE	MAE	MSE	MAE	MSE	MAE	MSE
Zhang [3]	✓	✓	467	498.5	181.8	277.7	32	49.8	-	-
MCNN [4]	✓	✓	377.6	509.1	110.2	173.2	26.4	41.3	-	-
CSRNet [5]	✓	✓	266.1	397.5	68.2	115	10.6	16	-	-
CAN [6]	✓	✓	212.2	243.7	62.3	100	7.8	12.2	107	183
DM-Count [7]	✓	✓	211	291.5	59.7	95.7	7.4	11.8	85.6	148.3
BL [27]	✓	✓	229.3	308.2	62.8	101.8	7.7	12.7	88.7	154.8
P2PNet [8]	✓	✓	172.72	256.18	**52.74**	85.06	6.25	9.9	85.32	154.5
CrowdFormer [10]	✓	✓	-	-	56.9	97.4	**5.7**	**9.6**	**78.8**	**136.1**
STNet [9]	✓	✓	**161.96**	**230.39**	52.85	**83.64**	6.25	10.3	87.88	166.44
YANG [12]	✗	✓	-	-	104.6	145.2	12.3	21.2	-	-
MATT [11]	Few	✓	355	550.2	80.1	129.4	11.7	17.5	-	-
TransCrowd-Token [13]	✗	✓	288.9	407.6	69	116.5	10.6	19.7	98.9	176.1
TransCrowd-GAP [13]	✗	✓	272.2	395.3	66.1	105.1	9.3	16.1	97.2	168.5
DSFormer [14]	✗	✓	-	-	**64.0**	**100.5**	9.2	17.1	**94.2**	**167.9**
Ours	✗	✓	**249.60**	**352.57**	65.12	102.58	**8.8**	**13.77**	106.47	174.09

on the entire data of each subset, but also on three categories of images classified based on the number of individuals within each image. The results are presented in Table 3 and Table 4, respectively.

On the Val subset of JHU-Crowd++, when trained solely with counting-level labels, the proposed method outperforms TransCrowd-GAP on the entire dataset. Furthermore, in comparison to common fully supervised methods, the proposed method even surpasses all fully supervised methods presented in Table 3 in terms of the overall performance on the entire Val subset. Notably, the exceptional performance in terms of the MSE metric demonstrates that the robustness of the proposed method on the Val subset is also competitive with fully supervised models. When considering different crowd densities, the proposed method still requires improvement in terms of low and medium density scenarios. However, it performs remarkably well on high-density crowd images, achieving reductions of 16.8% and 26.9% in MAE and MSE respectively compared to TransCrowd-GAP.

In comparison to fully supervised models, the proposed method exhibits significantly superior performance on the high-density subset of the Val set, but still shows a performance gap on medium and low-density images. This may be attributed to the fact that the objective function adopted in this paper does not incorporate crowd density as a weighting factor. Consequently, low and medium density images have smaller target values, and the corresponding counting loss obtained by feeding them into the model is also smaller compared to high-density images. This leads the model to be more inclined to optimize the prediction results for high-density crowd images.

Table 3. Quantitative comparison of the Val sets in the JHU-Crowd + dataset

Method	Label		JHU-Low		JHU-Medium		JHU-High		JHU-Total	
	Location	Number	MAE	MSE	MAE	MSE	MAE	MSE	MAE	MSE
MCNN[4]	✓	✓	90.6	202.9	125.3	259.5	494.9	856	160.6	377.7
CSRNet[5]	✓	✓	22.2	40	49	99.5	302.5	669.5	72.2	249.9
SA-Net[23]	✓	✓	13.6	26.8	50.4	78	397.8	749.2	82.1	272.6
CAN[6]	✓	✓	34.2	69.5	65.6	115.3	336.4	**619.7**	89.5	239.3
MBTTBF[24]	✓	✓	23.3	48.5	53.2	119.9	294.5	674.5	73.8	256.8
LSC-CNN[25]	✓	✓	**6.8**	**10.1**	**39.2**	**64.1**	504.7	860	87.3	309
SFCN[26]	✓	✓	11.8	19.8	39.3	73.4	297.3	679.4	62.9	247.5
BL[27]	✓	✓	6.9	10.3	39.7	85.2	**279.8**	620.4	59.3	229.2
TransCrowd-Token[13]	✗	✓	7.1	10.7	**33.3**	**54.6**	302.5	557.4	58.4	201.1
TransCrowd-GAP[13]	✗	✓	6.7	9.5	34.5	55.8	285.9	532.8	56.8	193.6
Ours	✗	✓	9.74	16.97	40.54	76.08	**237.9**	**389.52**	**55.37**	**149.61**

On the Test subset of JHU-Crowd++, the proposed method attains the best MAE and MSE performance on the entire dataset in comparison to the other methods listed in Table 4. Specifically, concerning the performance on the three density classifications, the proposed method still demonstrates optimal performance on high-density crowd images, yielding significant reductions in both MAE and MSE. In terms of medium-density image data, the proposed method also achieves the best results, with a 30.3% reduction in MSE compared to TransCrowd-Token. On the low-density crowd images in the Test subset of JHU-Crowd++, the proposed method exhibits certain shortcomings, but it still outperforms some fully supervised methods.

Figure 4 presents several test results of the proposed method on the JHU-Crowd++ dataset. These images are from the Val subset and were not involved in the model

Table 4. Quantitative comparison of the Test sets in the JHU-Crowd++ dataset

Method	Label		JHU-Low		JHU-Medium		JHU-High		JHU-Total	
	Location	Number	MAE	MSE	MAE	MSE	MAE	MSE	MAE	MSE
MCNN[4]	✓	✓	97.1	192.3	121.4	191.3	618.6	1166.7	188.9	483.4
CSRNet[5]	✓	✓	27.1	64.9	43.9	71.2	356.2	784.4	85.9	309.2
SA-Net[23]	✓	✓	17.3	37.9	46.8	69.1	397.9	817.7	91.1	320.4
CAN[6]	✓	✓	37.6	78.8	56.4	86.2	384.2	789	100.1	314
MBTTBF[24]	✓	✓	19.2	58.8	41.6	66	352.2	760.4	81.8	299.1
LSC-CNN[25]	✓	✓	10.6	**31.8**	34.9	55.6	601.9	1172.2	112.7	454.4
SFCN[26]	✓	✓	16.5	55.7	38.1	59.8	**341.8**	**758.8**	77.5	**297.6**
BL[27]	✓	✓	**10.1**	32.7	**34.2**	**54.5**	352	768.7	**75**	299.9
TransCrowd-Token[13]	✗	✓	8.5	23.2	33.3	71.5	368.3	816.4	76.4	319.8
TransCrowd-GAP[13]	✗	✓	7.6	16.7	34.8	73.6	354.8	752.8	74.9	295.6
Ours	✗	✓	12.26	33.89	**32.12**	**49.82**	320.99	718.16	**69.77**	**280.13**

training process. They encompass diverse weather conditions, indoor and outdoor scenarios, varying lighting conditions, and different crowd densities. The proposed method achieves promising prediction results in all these cases. Furthermore, by extracting the feature map of the last layer and applying color transformation, crowd density maps can be generated. Observations from these density maps reveal that despite the absence of location information during training, the model still learns near-precise crowd features and predicts the crowd distribution with an impressive level of accuracy, which is typically challenging for weakly supervised crowd counting methods.

Fig. 4. Crowd prediction results of some crowd images in the JHU-Crowd++ dataset

6 Ablation Experiment

To validate the effectiveness of each module incorporated in the proposed method, ablation experiments were conducted on the ShanghaiTech-A dataset to investigate their contributions. The results are presented in Table 5. The baseline model for comparison consists of the backbone combined with the regression counting head. For a fair comparison, all relevant parameter settings were kept consistent.

Adding contrastive deep supervision to the baseline model improved both MAE and MSE. Feature fusion further reduced the MSE compared to contrastive deep supervision alone. When both contrastive deep supervision and feature fusion were applied, the MAE was further reduced, and the MSE was also better than that of feature fusion alone.

With the addition of the multi-attention mechanism to contrastive deep supervision and feature fusion, the MAE and MSE of the model were reduced by 7.85% and 10.39% respectively compared to the baseline model, indicating that all three settings contribute to the prediction accuracy and stability of the model.

To further investigate the role of contrastive deep supervision, an ablation experiment was conducted where only feature fusion and the multi-attention mechanism were retained in the baseline model. The average error of this setting was larger than that of the final proposed model, indicating that contrastive deep supervision helps to improve the accuracy of crowd counting.

Table 5. Ablation experiments of different modules on the ShanghaiTech-A dataset

Model	ShanghaiTech-A	
	MAE	MSE
baseline	72.97	112.97
baseline + CDS	69.77	102.68
baseline + feature fusion	69.33	106.04
baseline + CDS + feature fusion	67.37	102.77
baseline + feature fusion + multi-attention	68.12	102.91
baseline + CDS + feature fusion + multi-attention(proposed method)	**65.12**	**102.58**

7 Conclusion

Employing weakly supervised learning methods to train crowd counting models can significantly reduce the labor costs associated with manual annotation, lower the deployment costs of crowd counting models in real-world applications, and expedite the deployment of crowd counting models across various domains. This paper proposes a weakly supervised crowd counting method that combines contrastive deep supervision and feature fusion. The proposed method only requires counting-level labels during training, which can avoid the large number of location-level labels required by fully supervised models.

The proposed method was validated on several popular crowd counting datasets, and the results demonstrated its effectiveness. The proposed method outperforms several weakly supervised methods in terms of MAE and MSE on multiple datasets, and even shows advantages over some fully supervised methods. The performance on the MSE metric in particular indicates that the proposed method is more stable. Additionally, the proposed model can still output relatively accurate crowd density maps without crowd location information involved in the training process.

However, it is also noted that the proposed method still has certain limitations on datasets with a large span of crowd density, since it does not consider balancing the loss for different crowd densities. Further improvements can be made in this direction in the future.

Acknowledgements. This paper is supported by the National Natural Science Foundation of China (NSFC) under grant No. 61976226 and No.72104254, and the Hubei Provincial Natural Science Foundation of China under grant No. 2022CFB469.

References

1. Chan, A.B., Liang, Z.-S.J., Vasconcelos, N.: Privacy preserving crowd monitoring: counting people without people models or tracking. In: 2008 IEEE Conference on Computer Vision and Pattern Recognition, pp. 1–7 (2008)
2. Zhang, L., Chen, X., Zhang, J., Dong, R., Ma, K.: Contrastive deep supervision. In: European Conference on Computer Vision, 1–19 (2022)
3. Zhang, C., Li, H., Wang, X., Yang, X.: Cross-scene crowd counting via deep convolutional neural networks. In: Proceedings of the IEEE Conference on Computer Vision and Pattern Recognition, pp. 833–841 (2015)
4. Zhang, Y., Zhou, D., Chen, S., Gao, S., Ma, Y.: Single-image crowd counting via multi-column convolutional neural network. In: Proceedings of the IEEE Conference on Computer Vision and Pattern Recognition, pp. 589–597 (2016)
5. Li, Y., Zhang, X., Chen, D.: CSRNET: dilated convolutional neural networks for understanding the highly congested scenes. In: Proceedings of the IEEE Conference on Computer Vision and Pattern Recognition, pp. 1091–1100 (2018)
6. Liu, W., Salzmann, M., Fua, P.: Context-aware crowd counting. In: Proceedings of the IEEE/CVF Conference on Computer Vision and Pattern Recognition, pp. 5099–5108 (2019)
7. Wang, B., Liu, H., Samaras, D., Nguyen, M.H.: Distribution matching for crowd counting. Adv. Neural. Inf. Process. Syst. **33**, 1595–1607 (2020)
8. Song, Q., et al.: Rethinking counting and localization in crowds: a purely point-based framework. In: Proceedings of the IEEE/CVF International Conference on Computer Vision, pp. 3365–3374 (2021)
9. Wang, M., Cai, H., Han, X.-F., Zhou, J., Gong, M.: STNet: scale tree network with multi-level auxiliator for crowd counting. IEEE Trans. Multimedia **25**, 2074–2084 (2023)
10. Yang, S., Guo, W., Ren, Y.: CrowdFormer: an overlap patching vision transformer for top-down crowd counting. In: Proceedings of the Thirty-First International Joint Conference on Artificial Intelligence, Vienna, Austria, pp. 23–29 (2022)
11. Lei, Y., Liu, Y., Zhang, P., Liu, L.: Towards using count-level weak supervision for crowd counting. Pattern Recogn. **109**, 107616 (2021)
12. Yang, Y., Li, G., Wu, Z., Su, L., Huang, Q., Sebe, N.: Weakly-supervised crowd counting learns from sorting rather than locations. In: Computer Vision–ECCV 2020: 16th European Conference, Glasgow, UK, 23–28 August 2020, Proceedings, Part VIII 16, 1–17 (2020)
13. Liang, D., Chen, X., Xu, W., Zhou, Y., Bai, X.: Transcrowd: weakly-supervised crowd counting with transformers. Sci. China Inf. Sci. **65**(6), 160104 (2022)
14. Hu, Z., Wang, B., Li, X.: Densitytoken: weakly-supervised crowd counting with density classification. In: IEEE International Conference on Acoustics, Speech and Signal Processing (ICASSP), Rhodes Island, Greece, 1–5 (2023)
15. Simonyan, K., Zisserman, A.: Very deep convolutional networks for large-scale image recognition. In: 3rd International Conference on Learning Representations (ICLR 2015), pp. 1–14 (2015)

16. Hou, Q., Zhou, D., Feng, J.: Coordinate attention for efficient mobile network design. In: Proceedings of the IEEE/CVF Conference on Computer Vision and Pattern Recognition, pp. 13713–13722 (2021)
17. Hu, J., Shen, L., Sun, G.: Squeeze-and-excitation networks. In: Proceedings of the IEEE Conference on Computer Vision and Pattern Recognition, pp. 7132–7141 (2018)
18. Chollet, F.: Xception: deep learning with depthwise separable convolutions. In: Proceedings of the IEEE Conference on Computer Vision and Pattern Recognition, pp. 1251–1258 (2017)
19. Chen, T., Kornblith, S., Norouzi, M., Hinton, G.: A simple framework for contrastive learning of visual representations. In: International Conference on Machine Learning, pp. 1597–1607 (2020)
20. Idrees, H., Saleemi, I., Seibert, C., Shah, M.: Multi-source multi-scale counting in extremely dense crowd images. In: Proceedings of the IEEE Conference on Computer Vision and Pattern Recognition, pp. 2547–2554 (2013)
21. Idrees, H., et al.: Composition loss for counting, density map estimation and localization in dense crowds. In: Proceedings of the European Conference on Computer Vision (ECCV), pp. 532–546 (2018)
22. Sindagi, V.A., Yasarla, R., Patel, V.M.: JHU-crowd++: large-scale crowd counting dataset and a benchmark method. IEEE Trans. Pattern Anal. Mach. Intell. **44**(5), 2594–2609 (2020)
23. Cao, X., Wang, Z., Zhao, Y., Su, F.: Scale aggregation network for accurate and efficient crowd counting. In: Proceedings of the European Conference on Computer Vision (ECCV), pp. 734–750 (2018)
24. Sindagi, V.A., Patel, V.M.: Multi-level bottom-top and top-bottom feature fusion for crowd counting. In: Proceedings of the IEEE/CVF International Conference on Computer Vision, pp. 1002–1012 (2019)
25. Sam, D.B., Peri, S.V., Sundararaman, M.N., Kamath, A., Babu, R.V.: Locate, size, and count: accurately resolving people in dense crowds via detection. IEEE Trans. Pattern Anal. Mach. Intell. **43**(8), 2739–2751 (2020)
26. Wang, Q., Gao, J., Lin, W., Yuan, Y.: Learning from synthetic data for crowd counting in the wild. In: Proceedings of the IEEE/CVF Conference on Computer Vision and Pattern Recognition, pp. 8198–8207 (2019)
27. Ma, Z., Wei, X., Hong, X., Gong, Y.: Bayesian loss for crowd count estimation with point supervision. In: Proceedings of the IEEE/CVF International Conference on Computer Vision, pp. 6142–6151 (2019)

The Detection and Rectification for Identity-Switch Based on the Unfalsified Control

Junchao Huang[1], Xiaoqi He[2(✉)], Yebo Wu[3], and Sheng Zhao[1]

[1] Shanghai Jiao Tong University, Shanghai, China
{j584356932549,shengzhao}@sjtu.edu.cn
[2] SJTU Ningbo Institute, Ningbo, China
hexiaoqi@niii.com
[3] Universidade de Macau, Zhuhai, China
yc37926@um.edu.mo

Abstract. The goal of multi-object tracking (MOT) is to continuously track and identify objects detected in videos. Currently, most methods for multi-object tracking model the motion information and combine it with appearance information to determine and track objects. However, overlapping between different targets can still lead to identity switch issues. To meet this challenge, we propose unfctrack, which employs unfalsified control to address the identity-switch problem in multi-object tracking. Specifically, we establish sequences of appearance information variations for the trajectories during the tracking process and a detection and rectification module is designed for identity-switch detection and recovery. Additionally, a simple and effective strategy is proposed to address the issue of ambiguous matching of appearance information during the data association process. Extensive experiments are conducted to evaluate the effectiveness of the unfctrack on the public MOT datasets. The results demonstrate that the unfctrack exhibits excellent effectiveness and robustness in handling tracking errors caused by occlusions and rapid movements.

Keywords: Multi-Object Tracking · Identity-Switch · Unfalsified Control

1 Introduction

Multi-object tracking [1] (MOT) aims to track and identify the trajectories of multiple objects in a video scene. With the rapid development of object detection methods, the current mainstream and effective approaches [2–4] still rely on detection-based tracking paradigms. Detection-based tracking methods transform the multi-object tracking problem into a data association problem, where the current frame detection boxes are associated with the detection boxes from the previous frame to establish object trajectories. However, errors in information acquisition, processing, and prediction during the tracking process can lead to matching errors in data association, resulting in ID-switch in multi-object tracking. Current research efforts have been focused on reducing the occurrence of ID-switch by addressing data sources and data association processes [5,6], but the approaches are always to find ways to reduce the occurrence of id-switch, rather than making rectification after it occurs.

In this work, we take a different perspective on the ID-switch problem. Specifically, instead of solely reducing the occurrence of ID-switch, we also focus on identifying whether ID-switch occur and attempt to correct it. We establish a multi-object tracking model based on unfalsified control [7], which enables the tracker to monitor the state of objects and includes the ID-switch detection module(IDSD). The tracker incorporates historical data that is often overlooked. Additionally, we introduce the ID-switch rectification module(IDSR) based on historical information to attempt the recovery of objects that have experienced ID-switch, making our tracker the first in the MOT field to address ID-switch and attempt rectification. The Ambiguous match improvement module(AMI) in our tracker effectively reduces the problems caused by small differences in appearance information during the data association process. Moreover, the IDSD, IDSR, and AMI modules of our tracker can be easily integrated into other tracking approaches. We conduct experiments on MOT datasets and achieve promising results. We believe that our approach provides a new possibility for addressing the ID-switch problem in multi-object tracking. Finally, we discuss the limitations and applicability of our approach.

2 Related Works

Different approaches in data processing lead to variations in multi-object tracking (MOT) methods, which can be broadly categorized into the following types: motion-based tracking, appearance-based tracking, and other types of learning-based tracking.

2.1 Motion-Based Tracking

Motion information is primarily used in the data association process. Motion-based trackers typically employ methods such as Kalman filtering [8] and particle filtering [9] to predict the motion of objects and then match their predicted positions with the detection boxes in the next frame to establish data association. SORT [2] utilizes Kalman filtering for box prediction and performs data association using IOU and the Hungarian algorithm [10]. Bytetrack [4] focuses on leveraging low-confidence detection boxes, while OCR-SORT [11] emphasizes modeling motion based on observed results, improving tracking robustness in nonlinear motion scenarios. These motion models employ Bayesian estimation to predict the next state and establish tracking trajectories through data association, but they ignore the utilization of other information such as appearance information.

2.2 Appearance-Based Tracking

With the advancements in the field of re-identification(ReID), effective methods for extracting appearance features have been proposed [12,13], leading to the integration of appearance information in multi-object tracking research. Deep-SORT [3] is one of the early trackers that incorporates appearance information by combining it with motion information in the data association process, improving the robustness of tracking systems under occlusion. ATOM [14] replaces Kalman filtering with deep learning for box estimation, while BOT-SORT [5] incorporates ReID features into high-resolution detection boxes. Finetrack [15] introduces a feature pyramid network that learns semantic flows between feature maps of different resolutions to correct spatial misalignments, enabling more accurate learning of appearance features. Approaches such as FairMOT [16,17] perform object detection and appearance feature extraction within a single network, allowing end-to-end training and reducing inference time. More recently, Deep OCR-SORT [18] adaptively integrates appearance matching into existing high-performance motion-based methods using object appearance, further enhancing tracking performance. The utilization of appearance information increases the robustness of the tracker in occlusion situations, but sometimes leads to fuzzy matching problems.

2.3 Other Types of Learning-Based Tracking

Motiontrack [6] employs trained interaction and patrol modules to handle complex motion in dense crowds and reidentify lost trajectories. CBIOU [19] extends the detection and tracking matching space by adding a buffer, mitigating the impact of irregular motion. MAAtrack [20] proposes a novel tracking association method that models fuzzy matching by searching for potential track detections with similar distances. In recent years, the successful application of transformer [21] in the visual domain, particularly the work by [22], has sparked a wave of combining transformer with multi-object tracking. Approaches such as [23–25] treat multi-object tracking as a sequence prediction problem, where each sequence corresponds to a trajectory of an object. MOTR [23], in particular, achieves end-to-end multi-object tracking by tracking queries and objects. Additionally, utilizing federated learning [26] can address data privacy issues in multi-object tracking processes.

In conclusion, existing methods are insufficient to rectify the occurrence of identity-switch. Therefore, we propose unfctrack, which efficiently addresses the identity-switch problem in multi-object tracking using unfalsified control.

3 Methods

In this section, we discuss the detailed design of our approach. Figure 1 represents the architecture and workflow of our approach. Specifically, we aim to clearly illustrate the following three modules: 1) ID-switch detection (IDSD) module, 2) ID-switch rectification (IDSR) module, and 3) ambiguous match improvement (AMI) module.

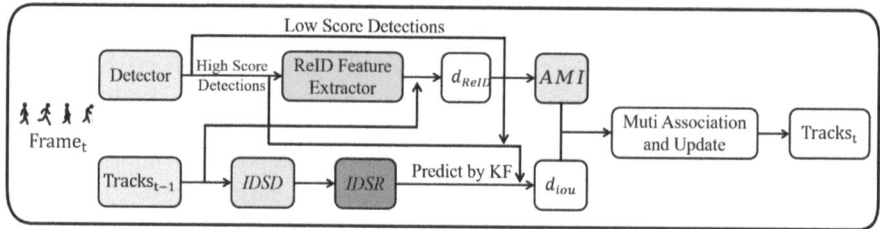

Fig. 1. Overview of the Unfctrack tracker's simplified channel diagram.

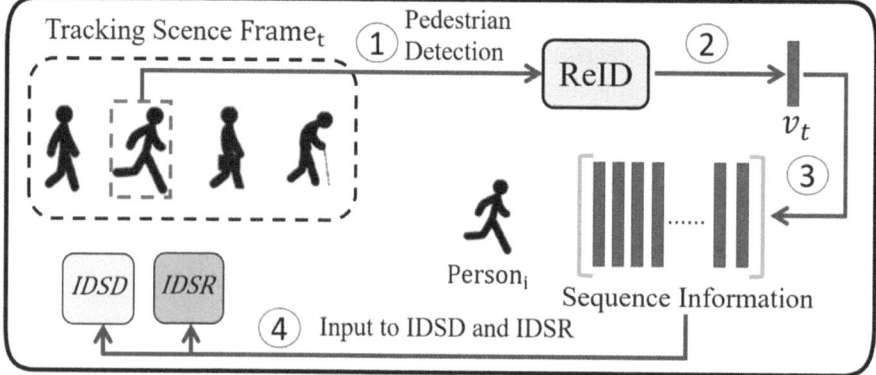

Fig. 2. The key to identifying identity switch lies in establishing a time series of appearance information, which is used for subsequent IDSD and IDSR modules.

3.1 ID-Switch Detection (IDSD)

Consider the state of the tracked object trajectory O_i at time t=i-1 as x_{i-1}, and the state of the object within the detection box K_i measured at time t=i as $\hat{x}_i$. We define the cost error as:

$$e_{K_i}^{O_i} = ||\hat{x}_i - x_{i-1}|| \tag{1}$$

In the data association process between the current frame's tracked object trajectories and detection boxes, data association is only considered when $e_{K_i}^{O_i}$ is less than a given threshold ϵ. Due to the existence of errors, multiple detection boxes may match with the same object trajectory. We include these multiple detection boxes in the candidate set K for trajectory matching. Suppose at time t=i, due to occlusion, there are two detection boxes in the candidate set K that match with the trajectory, $K=[k_1, k_2]$, and the correct tracked target in the current frame is k_2. However, we select k_1 with a smaller error for data association, leading to an ID-switch. When the occlusion ends, the appearance information extracted based on the detection box becomes more accurate. As the ID-switch occurs, the difference between the historical appearance information stored in the trajectory and the appearance information in the current frame will gradually increase as is shown in Fig. 2, and with time, it will exceed a threshold. Thus, we can determine that the trajectory has experienced an ID-switch. Therefore, the establishment of our unfalsified control model is as follows:

- Measurement information P_{data}: Appearance information extracted from objects during the tracking process.
- Candidate set K: Detection boxes used for data association with trajectories.
- Performance metric T_{spec}: The degree of change in appearance information of trajectories in a period of time.

To obtain measurement information P_{data}, we employ the BoT (SBS) [27] feature extraction method from the FastReID [28] library. We save appearance features every 5 frames, resulting in a sequence of appearance information with a length of 30. This sequence allows us to observe changes in appearance information. Even in the presence of occlusion-induced variations, the appearance information remains highly similar to the pre-occlusion state, providing data support for ID-switch detection. For the saved queue of appearance features, we establish another queue for post-processing to store the similarity costs between the current appearance feature and the previous appearance feature sequence. We calculate the cosine distance to measure the similarity between different appearance information. Then, we compute the variance of the similarity costs, which serves as the performance metric T_{spec} for judging ID-switch cases.

We select the appearance feature f of the current frame and calculate the cosine cost C between f and the previous 2/3 appearance features f_i in the trajectory queue. We establish a cosine cost queue with a length of 30, and the calculation formula for C is as follows:

$$C = (\sum_{i=1}^{n}(1 - \frac{f * f_i}{||f|| * ||f_i||}))/n \qquad (2)$$

Based on the values of C in the queue, we calculate T_{spec}, where $\overline{C}$ represents the average of C_i:

$$T_{spec} = \frac{\sum_i^n (C_i - \overline{C})^2}{n} \qquad (3)$$

When there are short-term variations in appearance features due to occlusion, the variance will remain at a low level. However, when an ID-switch occurs and the appearance information undergoes long-term changes, the performance metric T_{spec} will continue to rise. Once it exceeds a threshold T_θ, reaching the falsification criterion, we consider the trajectory to have undergone an ID-switch and remove the matched trajectory from the candidate set K.

3.2 ID-Switch Rectification (IDSR)

After falsifying the trajectories that have undergone an ID-switch using unfalsified control, we attempt to restore the true detection boxes corresponding to these trajectories. We establish a queue for each trajectory to store its appearance information. Therefore, we can select the appearance information extracted before the occurrence of the ID-switch, which represents the appearance information when the trajectory was not subjected to an ID-switch, as data support for ID correction.

To ensure the accuracy of the rectification process, we consider a trajectory to be associated with a detection box and update the trajectory only when the cosine cost is below a very small threshold, denoted as C_θ. In other words, the two appearance feature vectors are nearly identical. Furthermore, if we cannot find a suitable detection box to match the trajectory undergoing an ID-switch, we assign a new ID to the trajectory. This prevents it from continuing to be tracked using the incorrect ID.

3.3 Ambiguous Match Improvement (AMI)

The fusion of motion information and appearance information is performed in a similar manner to [3], using a weighted fusion approach. The motion information, represented by d_{iou}, and the appearance information, represented by d_{ReID}, are fused to obtain the fused information d_{dist}, using the following fusion method:

$$d_{dist} = \alpha * d_{iou} + (1 - \alpha) * d_{ReID} (0 < \alpha < 1) \tag{4}$$

The appearance information d_{ReID}, is obtained by extracting features from the detection boxes. However, many detection boxes suffer from overlap issues, resulting in significant ambiguity in some d_{ReID} values. This ambiguity can lead to severe fuzzy matching problems, potentially causing ID-switch and even discarding tracked trajectories for further processing in the next frame. To address this issue, we have designed a simple yet effective module called AMI to handle the problem of fuzzy matching. Specifically, we discard matches with confidence scores higher than a threshold d_θ, for low-confidence matches. For each row and column, we calculate the weights for high-confidence matches and low-confidence matches, respectively, and discard the low-confidence matches with lower weights (Fig. 3).

4 Experiments

4.1 Experimental Settings

Datasets. The experiments are conducted on the MOT17 [29] and MOT20 [30] datasets under the "private detection" protocol. The MOT17 and MOT20 datasets are widely used benchmarks in the field of multi-object tracking. Since both MOT17 and MOT20 do not provide a separate validation set, we follow the common practice [4,31] of splitting the training set into halves for training and validation (Fig. 4).

	Det1	Det2	Det3	Det4	Det5
Track1	1	0.7	1	0.1	1
Track2	0.03	1	1	1	0.8
Track3	0.18	0.03	1	1	1
Track4	1	1	0.07	0.6	1
Track5	1	1	1	1	0.15

	Det1	Det2	Det3	Det4	Det5
Track1	1	1	1	0.1	1
Track2	0.03	1	1	1	1
Track3	1	0.03	1	1	1
Track4	1	1	0.07	1	1
Track5	1	1	1	1	0.15

Fig. 3. AMI module addressing the ambiguous match issue between trajectories and detection boxes. Firstly, the module discards low-confidence matches with a threshold greater than $d_\theta = 0.2$, setting them to 1. For each row and column, the module also discards low-weight ambiguous matches. For example, Track3-Det1 and Track2-Det1 are compared, and since 0.18 is significantly greater than 0.03, the module discards the match with a weight of 0.18 and sets it to 1.

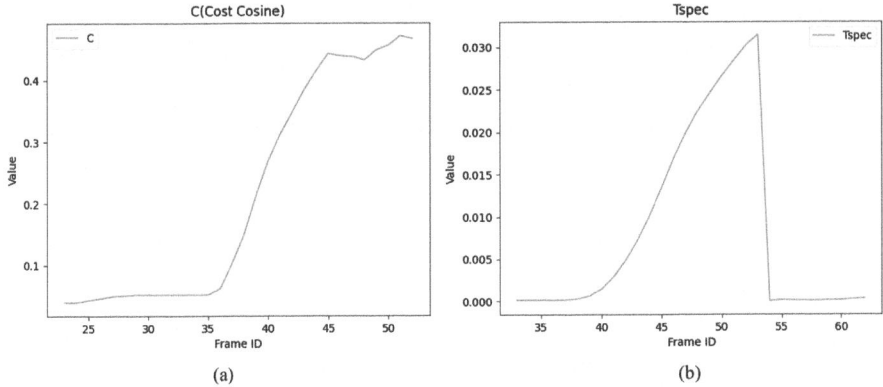

Fig. 4. Experimental results of IDSD and IDSR on the MOT17-01 dataset. The two subfigures illustrate the increasing cosine cost and T_{spec} after an ID-switch occurrence, as well as the variation of T_{spec} after ID rectification. (a)The change of cosine cost.(b)The change of T_{spec}.

Metrics. Existing methods in the field have not considered the possibility of recovering IDs after an ID-switch occurs. Therefore, widely accepted metrics in multi-object tracking, such as MOTA, HOTA, and IDSW [32], are not suitable for evaluating the performance of our tracker. We observe in our experiments that if the ID of a detected object changes once, IDSW increases by 1. However, if we correct the IDs of objects that have undergone an ID-switch, IDSW increases by 1 instead of decreasing by 1. This results in an increase in IDSW and a decrease in MOTA when we judge and correct ID-switch situations. Therefore, metrics like MOTA and IDSW cannot effectively evaluate our tracker, and we emphasize the potential of addressing the ID-switch problem from different perspectives. We demonstrate the effectiveness of our IDSD and IDSR modules through four metrics: RC (Recall, the proportion of IDSW correctly detected by the IDSD

Fig. 5. The three subfigures show the experimental image results at frames 24, 52, and 54. The IDSD model determines the ID-switch at frame 53, and the IDSD model rectify the ID at frame 54.

module), FPR (False Positive Rate, the proportion of IDSW incorrectly detected by the IDSD module), RA (Rectification Accuracy, the proportion of IDSW correctly rectified by the IDSR module), and RR (Renumber Ratio, the proportion of IDSW renumbered by the IDSR module).

Implementation Details. Our multi-object tracking method follows the detection-to-tracking paradigm. We use the publicly available YOLOX [33] as the detector, and the detection results are then used as input for our tracker. For ReID feature extraction, we utilize the SBS-50 model from the open-source FastReID [28], which is pre-trained on MOT17 and MOT20 [5]. Throughout the experiments, we set the default detection score threshold τ to 0.6 and remove a trajectory if it is lost for more than 30 frames. The threshold value for T_θ in IDSD is set to 0.01 by default, and the threshold value for the cosine cost C_θ in IDSR is set to 0.1 by default.

4.2 Testing and Experiments Results

In order to demonstrate the tracker's ability in detecting and correcting ID-switches, the AMI module is not used during the experimentation with the IDSD and IDSR modules.

ID-Switch Detection(IDSD). In the MOT17-01 dataset, we set the threshold T_θ for T_{spec} in IDSD to 0.01 to evaluate the tracker's ability to detect ID-switch situations. To exclude temporary variations in trajectory appearance features due to occlusion rather than ID-switch, we consider a trajectory to have undergone an ID-switch only when its performance metric T_{spec} exceeds T_θ for more than 10 consecutive frames. In the experiment, at frame 40, a new object enters from the right side of the field of view, resulting in an ID-switch for trajectory 6. We observe that the performance metric T_{spec} for trajectory 6 exceeds T_θ at frame 43, and the tracker determines the occurrence of an ID-switch for trajectory 6 at frame 53 which is shown in Fig. 5.

ID-Switch Rectification (IDSR). In the MOT17-01 dataset, after falsifying trajectory 6 for an ID-switch at frame 53 using unfalsified control, we retrieve the first appearance feature f_1 from the trajectory 6 queue. This feature f_1 was extracted before the ID-switch occurred. We match this feature with the appearance information of the current frame's detection box, calculate the cosine cost, and if the cosine cost is below the threshold C_θ, we perform ID rectification. Simultaneously, we remove the erroneous trajectory 23 and assign a new ID, 24, to the newly entered object on the right side. We observe that after correctly recovering the ID, the performance metric T_{spec} decreases below the threshold T_θ and stabilizes.

In the experiments conducted on other datasets in MOT17 and MOT20, our tracker demonstrates excellent ability in falsifying trajectories that have undergone ID-switch. It is worth noting that due to differences in camera angles and tracking environments across different datasets, there may be variations in setting the threshold T_θ for T_{spec} in IDSD. In the MOT17 test set, we validated the effectiveness of the IDSD and IDSR modules and presented the results in Table 1. In the experiment, the IDSD module was able to detect nearly half of the IDSW conditions (51.62 percent) with a relatively low false positive rate. The IDSR module was able to correct 23.1 percent of the IDSW and renumber the uncorrectable targets to prevent affecting the tracking results.

Ambiguous Match Improvement (AMI). We conduct ablation experiments on the AMI module using the training sets of MOT17 and MOT20. We evaluate the tracker using the official evaluation tool, Trackeval, from the MOT challenge. We find that applying the AMI algorithm to process the appearance information d_{ReID}, resulted in significant performance improvement in tracking.

Table 1. Metrics of IDSD and IDSR modules in the MOT17 test set.

MOT17-test	IDSW	RC	FPR	RA	RR
IDSD	554	51.62	5.3	/	/
IDSR	554	/	/	23.1	76.9

The experiments primarily emphasize the results of ID-switch detection and rectification. Although the metrics from [32] are not suitable for effectively evaluating our tracker, we still provide experimental results for the unfctrack tracker(without IDSD and IDSR modules) on the MOT17 dataset in Table 3.

4.3 Limitations

Unfctrack heavily relies on appearance feature information for the detection and recovery of ID-switch situations. However, excessive ReID feature extraction in dense scenes can be time-consuming, potentially compromising real-time performance. Additionally, the effectiveness of ReID feature extraction significantly affects the performance of IDSD and IDSR. Factors such as camera movement and significant environmental background variations may cause certain parameters of the unfctrack tracker to change. For example, the threshold value T_θ for the performance metric T_{spec} in IDSD may differ across different environments. For instance, $T_\theta = 0.01$ may be suitable for MOT17-01, while $T_\theta = 0.02$ may be more appropriate for MOT17-03. Adjustments may be necessary for T_θ in different environments. Finally, although Unfctrack demonstrates strong capabilities in detecting ID-switch situations, the correction and recovery of IDs still present significant challenges, which will be a focus of future research efforts (Table 2).

Table 2. Validation of the AMI module results on the train datasets of MOT17 and MOT20 using the official evaluation tool Trackeval from MOT-challenge.

Tracker	MOTA↑	FP↓	FN↓	IDSW↓
MOT17	87.492	3355	10162	529
MOT17(AMI)	90.042	2282	8540	361
MOT20	89.456	12703	37689	1093
MOT20(AMI)	92.762	6315	28430	594

Table 3. Performance metrics comparison of Unfctrack tracker and other trackers on the MOT17 dataset under the private detection protocol. Due to the metrics not being suitable for measuring our IDSD and IDSR processes, Unfctrack did not use these two modules in the results.

Tracker	MOTA↑	IDF1↑	HOTA↑	FP↓	FN↓	IDs↓	FPS↑
Tube-TK [34]	63	58.6	48	27060	177483	4137	3
GSDT [35]	66.2	68.7	55.5	43368	144261	3318	4.9
LMOT [36]	72	70.3	56.7	28113	126704	3071	28.6
MOTR [23]	73.4	68.6	57.8	/	/	2439	/
FairMOT [16]	73.7	72.3	59.3	27507	117477	3303	25.9
Transtrack [25]	75.2	63.5	54.1	50157	86442	3603	59.2
CrowdTrack [37]	75.6	73.6	60.3	25950	109101	2544	140.8
STC [38]	75.8	70.9	59.8	44952	87039	4533	9.5
FCG [39]	76.7	77.7	62.6	13284	116205	1737	4.9
OC-SORT [11]	78	77.5	63.2	15129	107055	1950	29
Bytetrack [4]	80.3	77.3	63.1	25491	83721	2196	29.6
Unfctrack(ours)	**79.8**	**77.9**	**63.5**	21960	90834	**1662**	8.3

5 Conclusions

In this paper, we propose unfctrack, which utilizes unfalsified control to identify and attempt to rectify ID-switch situations. By leveraging data-driven unfalsified control, our tracker can dynamically identify and rectify errors during the tracking process. To the best of our knowledge, this is the first tracker that focuses on detecting and attempting to correct ID-switch occurrences. The proposed method, which incorporates appearance information, can be easily integrated into other tracking frameworks. We hope that this work provides a new perspective for addressing ID-switch problems and contributes to the advancement of the field of multi-object tracking.

References

1. Luo, W., Xing, J., Milan, A., Zhang, X., Liu, W., Kim, T.-K.: Multiple object tracking: a literature review. Artif. Intell. **293**, 103448 (2021)
2. Bewley, A., Ge, Z., Ott, L., Ramos, F., Upcroft, B.: Simple online and realtime tracking. In: 2016 IEEE International Conference on Image Processing (ICIP), pp. 3464–3468. IEEE (2016)
3. Wojke, N., Bewley, A., Paulus, D.: Simple online and realtime tracking with a deep association metric. In: 2017 IEEE International Conference on Image Processing (ICIP), pp. 3645–3649. IEEE (2017)
4. Zhang, Y., et al.: Bytetrack: Multi-object tracking by associating every detection box. In: European Conference on Computer Vision, pp. 1–21. Springer (2022)
5. Aharon, N., Orfaig, R., Bobrovsky, B.Z.: Bot-sort: robust associations multi-pedestrian tracking. arXiv preprint arXiv:2206.14651 (2022)
6. Qin, Z., Zhou, S., Wang, L., Duan, J., Hua, G., Tang, W.: Motiontrack: learning robust short-term and long-term motions for multi-object tracking. In: Proceedings of the IEEE/CVF Conference on Computer Vision and Pattern Recognition, pp. 17939–17948 (2023)
7. Safonov, M.G., Tsao, T.-C.: The unfalsified control concept and learning. In: Proceedings of 1994 33rd IEEE Conference on Decision and Control, vol. 3, pp. 2819–2824. IEEE (1994)
8. Kalman, R.E.: Contributions to the theory of optimal control. Bol. Soc. Mat. Mexicana **5**(2), 102–119 (1960)
9. Djuric, P.M., et al.: Particle filtering. IEEE Signal Process. Mag **20**(5), 19–38 (2003)
10. Kuhn, H.W.: The Hungarian method for the assignment problem. Naval Res. Logistics Q. **2**(1–2), 83–97 (1955)
11. Cao, J., Pang, J., Weng, X., Khirodkar, R., Kitani, K.: Observation-centric sort: Rethinking sort for robust multi-object tracking. In: Proceedings of the IEEE/CVF Conference on Computer Vision and Pattern Recognition, pp. 9686–9696 (2023)
12. Li, W., Zhao, R., Xiao, T., Wang, X.: Deepreid: deep filter pairing neural network for person re-identification. In: Proceedings of the IEEE Conference on Computer Vision and Pattern Recognition, pp. 152–159 (2014)
13. Wang, G., Gong, S., Cheng, J., Hou, Z.: Faster person re-identification. In: European Conference on Computer Vision, pp. 275–292. Springer (2020)

14. Danelljan, M., Bhat, G., Khan, F.S., Felsberg, M.: Atom: accurate tracking by overlap maximization. In: Proceedings of the IEEE/CVF Conference on Computer Vision and Pattern Recognition, pp. 4660–4669 (2019)
15. Ren, H., Han, S., Ding, H., Zhang, Z., Wang, H., Wang, F.: Focus on details: online multi-object tracking with diverse fine-grained representation. In: Proceedings of the IEEE/CVF Conference on Computer Vision and Pattern Recognition, pp. 11289–11298 (2023)
16. Zhang, Y., Wang, C., Wang, X., Zeng, W., Liu, W.: Fairmot: on the fairness of detection and re-identification in multiple object tracking. Int. J. Comput. Vision **129**, 3069–3087 (2021)
17. Pang, J., et al.: Quasi-dense similarity learning for multiple object tracking. In: Proceedings of the IEEE/CVF Conference on Computer Vision and Pattern Recognition, pp. 164–173 (2021)
18. Maggiolino, G., Ahmad, A., Cao, J., Kitani, K.: Deep OC-sort: multi-pedestrian tracking by adaptive re-identification. arXiv preprint arXiv:2302.11813 (2023)
19. Yang, F., Odashima, S., Masui, S., Jiang, S.: Hard to track objects with irregular motions and similar appearances? make it easier by buffering the matching space. In: Proceedings of the IEEE/CVF Winter Conference on Applications of Computer Vision, pp. 4799–4808 (2023)
20. Stadler, D., Beyerer, J.: Modelling ambiguous assignments for multi-person tracking in crowds. In: Proceedings of the IEEE/CVF Winter Conference on Applications of Computer Vision, pp. 133–142 (2022)
21. Vaswani, A., et al.: Attention is all you need. In: Advances in Neural Information Processing Systems, vol. 30 (2017)
22. Carion, N., Massa, F., Synnaeve, G., Usunier, N., Kirillov, A., Zagoruyko, S.: End-to-end object detection with transformers. In: European Conference on Computer Vision, pp. 213–229. Springer (2020)
23. Zeng, F., Dong, B., Zhang, Y., Wang, T., Zhang, X., Wei, Y.: Motr: End-to-end multiple-object tracking with transformer. In: European Conference on Computer Vision, pp. 659–675. Springer (2022)
24. Meinhardt, T., Kirillov, A., Leal-Taixe, L., Feichtenhofer, C.: Trackformer: multi-object tracking with transformers. In: Proceedings of the IEEE/CVF Conference on Computer Vision and Pattern Recognition, pp. 8844–8854 (2022)
25. Sun, P., et al.: Transtrack: multiple object tracking with transformer. arXiv preprint arXiv:2012.15460 (2020)
26. Wu, Y., Li, L., Tian, C., Xu, C.: Breaking the memory wall for heterogeneous federated learning with progressive training. arXiv preprint arXiv:2404.13349 (2024)
27. Luo, H., Gu, Y., Liao, X., Lai, S., Jiang, W.: Bag of tricks and a strong baseline for deep person re-identification. In: Proceedings of the IEEE/CVF conference on Computer Vision and Pattern Recognition Workshops (2019)
28. He, L., Liao, X., Liu, W., Liu, X., Cheng, P., Mei, T.: Fastreid: a pytorch toolbox for real-world person re-identification. arXiv preprint arXiv:2006.02631 (2020)
29. Milan, A., Leal-Taixé, L., Reid, I., Roth, S., Schindler, K.: Mot16: a benchmark for multi-object tracking. arXiv preprint arXiv:1603.00831 (2016)
30. Dendorfer, P., et al.: Mot20: a benchmark for multi object tracking in crowded scenes. arXiv preprint arXiv:2003.09003 (2020)
31. Zhou, X., Koltun, V., Krähenbühl, P.: Tracking objects as points. In: European Conference on Computer Vision, pp. 474–490. Springer (2020)
32. Bernardin, K., Stiefelhagen, R.: Evaluating multiple object tracking performance: the clear mot metrics. EURASIP J. Image Video Process. **1–10**, 2008 (2008)

33. Ge, A., Liu, S., Wang, F., Li, Z., Sun, J.: Yolox: exceeding yolo series in 2021. arXiv preprint arXiv:2107.08430 (2021)
34. Pang, B., Li, Y., Zhang, Y., Li, M., Lu, C.: Tubetk: adopting tubes to track multi-object in a one-step training model. In: Proceedings of the IEEE/CVF Conference on Computer Vision and Pattern Recognition, pp. 6308–6318 (2020)
35. Wang, Y., Kitani, K., Weng, X.: Joint object detection and multi-object tracking with graph neural networks. In: 2021 IEEE International Conference on Robotics and Automation (ICRA), pp. 13708–13715. IEEE (2021)
36. Mostafa, R., Baraka, H., Bayoumi, A.E.M.: Lmot: efficient light-weight detection and tracking in crowds. IEEE Access **10**, 83085–83095 (2022)
37. Stadler, D., Beyerer, J.: On the performance of crowd-specific detectors in multi-pedestrian tracking. In: 2021 17th IEEE International Conference on Advanced Video and Signal Based Surveillance (AVSS), pp. 1–12. IEEE (2021)
38. Galor, A., Orfaig, R., Bobrovsky, B.-Z.: Strong-transcenter: improved multi-object tracking based on transformers with dense representations. arXiv preprint arXiv:2210.13570 (2022)
39. Girbau, A., Marqués, F., Satoh, S.: Multiple object tracking from appearance by hierarchically clustering tracklets. arXiv preprint arXiv:2210.03355 (2022)

LDSBC: Lightweight Detection Network for Student Behavior in Classroom Scenario

Minghua Jiang, Cheng Wang, Xingwei Zheng, Li Liu, and Feng Yu(✉)

Wuhan Textile University, Wuhan, China
{minghuajiang,l_liu,yufeng}@wtu.edu.cn, glkmnzd@yeah.net

Abstract. In modern smart education, accurate recognition of student classroom behavior is paramount. However, the inherent complexity of classroom environments, marked by a high concentration of students and limitations in computational resources of applicable devices, presents significant challenges for accurate behavior recognition. Existing methods often fall short regarding recognition accuracy in addressing these challenges. This paper proposes an innovative lightweight detection network for student behavior in classroom scenario (LDSBC) designed to detect student classroom behavior through object detection. We construct an efficient and lightweight feature extraction architecture that 1) replaces computationally intensive components in traditional structures with lighter convolution, substantially reduces the model parameters, and 2) incorporates an efficient multi-scale attention mechanism in the initial part of the deep feature extraction network, significantly enhancing the network's feature extraction capabilities. Furthermore, LDSBC introduces a more precise Intersection over Union (IoU) loss function strategy, enhancing the network's detection capabilities in dense scenarios. Experimental results demonstrate that our LDSBC, compared to the baseline model, sustains detection accuracy without compromise, achieves a 23.5% reduction in the number of parameters, and reduces algorithmic complexity by 19.8%.

Keywords: object detection · classroom behavior · model lightweight · muti-scale attention

1 Introduction

Behavior detection in analyzing student behavior in classroom surveillance videos provides an effective way to gain deeper insight into student engagement and learning performance [1,2]. Precise monitoring and analysis of student behavior through behavior detection technology can provide comprehensive and accurate feedback on educational and instructional goals, thus improving educational quality.

In the realm behavior analysis, researchers predominantly employ four types of algorithms: video action recognition [3,4], pose estimation [5,6], multi-sensor detection [7–9], and object detection [10,11]. These methods mentioned above may require substantial computational resources or hardware, which restricts their practical applicability in natural classroom settings. In contrast, object detection-based methods offer a more resource-efficient solution [12], allowing for real-time analysis without extensive hardware and making it more suitable for classroom scenarios. Consequently, this paper advocates using object detection-based methods for analyzing student behavior to achieve more precise and practical outcomes.

Despite significant advancements in Universal object detection, challenges persist in adapting these techniques to classroom settings. Primary include the diversity of student behaviors, encompassing variations in angles, individual differences, environmental factors, and classroom seating arrangements, often leading to obstructions in the line of sight, thereby increasing the complexity of classroom behavior detection. The effectiveness of object detection algorithms in practical applications depends significantly on the availability of high-quality datasets. Therefore, a comprehensive analysis of student behaviors in classroom scenarios was conducted, culminating in the creation of the Real-time Student Classroom Behavior Dataset (RSCB-Dataset). Subsequently, we propose a lightweight classroom scenario student behavior detection network called LDSBC.

Firstly, a lightweight feature extraction module is proposed to reduce the complexity of the overall network architecture. This module ingeniously utilizes partial convolution techniques to minimize unnecessary computational load effectively. Simultaneously, We integrate an efficient multi-scale attention mechanism to mitigate the potential adverse effects of lightweight, such as decreased detection accuracy. Additionally, integrating an enhanced IOU loss function [13] allows our approach to accurately pinpoint and address intricacies within dense scenarios, leading to optimized model performance.

The main contributions of this paper are summarized as follows:

- We design and implement a lightweight feature extraction module, significantly reducing the model's parameters and simplifying the network architecture's complexity.
- We integrate an effective multi-scale attention mechanism specifically tailored to mitigate the potential adverse effects of lightweighting, ensuring our model maintains high performance even with reduced resource requirements.
- We employ a precise IOU loss function, enabling our method to locate and address complexities within dense scenarios precisely.
- On our self-constructed dataset, the model has demonstrated exceptional performance improvements: an increase of 1.5% in the F1-Score, a reduction of 23.2% in the number of model parameters, a decrease of 19.8% in computational complexity, and a diminution of 21.5% in model size.

The rest of this paper is organized as follows: Sect. 2 provides a comprehensive review of general object detection algorithms and specific methods dedicated to classroom behavior detection. Section 3 details our proposed LDSBC. Section 4 is devoted to presenting and analyzing experimental results, while Sect. 5 summarizes the contributions of our proposed method.

2 Related Work

2.1 The Datasets of Student Classroom Behavior

As computer vision advances [14,15], neural networks can handle more tasks [16], making classroom student behavior monitoring increasingly feasible. Despite the abundance of datasets in the general computer vision domain [17–19], the field of education lacks large-scale, publicly available datasets. The paper [20] addresses this issue by providing a substantial dataset, comprising classroom videos from 128 different subjects and 11 distinct classrooms. This dataset is designed to automatically identify, detect, and describe student behavior, offering a rich resource for large-scale data-driven research. The ATL-BP [21] has created and released a labeled dataset, including 2,749 interaction samples from 54 students completing problems in an intelligent online math tutoring system. However, this dataset predominantly focuses on students' facial interaction expressions, with a relatively limited collection of other behavioral features. The SCBv3 [22] introduces a dataset named SCB-dataset3, containing 5686 images with 45578 labels, covering six primary student behaviors in the classroom, such as raising hands, reading, writing, etc. Notably, the samples in this dataset are extracted from frames of videos, resulting in some degree of repetition. The CBPH [23] has constructed a dataset named Student-Teacher Behavior Dataset (STBD-08), consisting of 4432 images covering eight typical classroom behaviors, totaling 151574 labeled anchor points. The introduction of these datasets provides robust support for in-depth research on student behavior while emphasizing the crucial importance of constructing diverse and comprehensive behavior datasets in education. However, due to concerns regarding student privacy, most of these datasets are not publicly available.

2.2 Students Classroom Behavior Detection

In recent years, computer vision has rapidly advanced and widely applied [24,25], with object detection technology particularly demonstrating exceptional performance and capturing increasing interest from researchers. However, the application of target detection technology in the classroom environment faces specific challenges, such as the diversity of student behaviors and issues related to the seating arrangement that leads to occlusions. The research [26] concentrates on the challenge of inconsistent action scales by creating a detection head designed explicitly for scale variations, successfully overcoming this issue. The research [11] propose a novel C2f-Res2block module by combining modules from Res2Net [27] and YOLOv8, enhancing detection accuracy, especially when dealing with challenges like target density and occlusion in classroom video images. The CBPH [23] introduces an advanced single-stage target detection named CBPH-Net, achieving higher performance through efficient feature extraction, multi-scale recognition, and techniques like elliptical boxes. The research [10] improve the YOLOv5 [27] for accurate detection of different student behaviors, demonstrating superior accuracy compared to YOLOv5.

However, behind these outstanding algorithms, we must also consider the practical application requirements in classroom environments, including limited computing power and the deployment demand for lightweight networks. The research [28] proposes a lightweight convolutional neural network model, addressing facial expression classification issues in small datasets for classroom behavior detection through techniques like depthwise separable convolution [29] and pre-activated residual units [30], making it suitable for real-time detection. The research [31] improves the SSH face detection algorithm by designing a new face loss function and applying a lightweight convolutional neural network on mobile terminals. This significantly reduces model complexity, decreases model size, enhances detection speed, and improves detection model performance through knowledge distillation, making it better suited for face detection devices on mobile terminals. In the BiTNet [32], outstanding accuracy and speed performance for real-time classroom behavior recognition tasks are achieved by introducing efficient Transformer blocks, Convolution Aggregation blocks, and a smaller detection head. In this context, our research aims to optimize the model's lightweight while maintaining high precision to meet the practical application requirements of classroom scenarios, ensuring the practicality and feasibility of the algorithm.

3 Method

This paper adopts YOLOv8n as the baseline model, with its network structure divided into two core parts. First is the feature extraction framework (C2f-F Block), which integrates faster and more lightweight convolutional modules. Second is the feature extraction framework (C2f-FEMA Block), which incorporates multi-scale attention mechanisms. Furthermore, we have introduced a more precise IoU loss function to enhance performance. The following sections will introduce our network structure and review our research findings.

3.1 LDSBC Network Architecture

The structure of our LDSBC network is shown in Fig. 1, which consists of a stack of complex network modules, including the CONV module, the C2f-F module, the C2f-FEMA module, the SPPF(Spatial Pyramid Pooling Fusion) module, the Upsample module, and the Head module. The CONV module consists of a 3X3 ordinary convolution, a bn layer, and a SiLU activation function, which helps the network extract features from images better and accelerates the network convergence during training. The C2f module of the original baseline network inspires the C2f-F module. It replaces the original structure with a Faster Block to process the feature data in a lighter-weight form. To reduce the loss caused by lightweight and to extract deeper information from the features, we added the

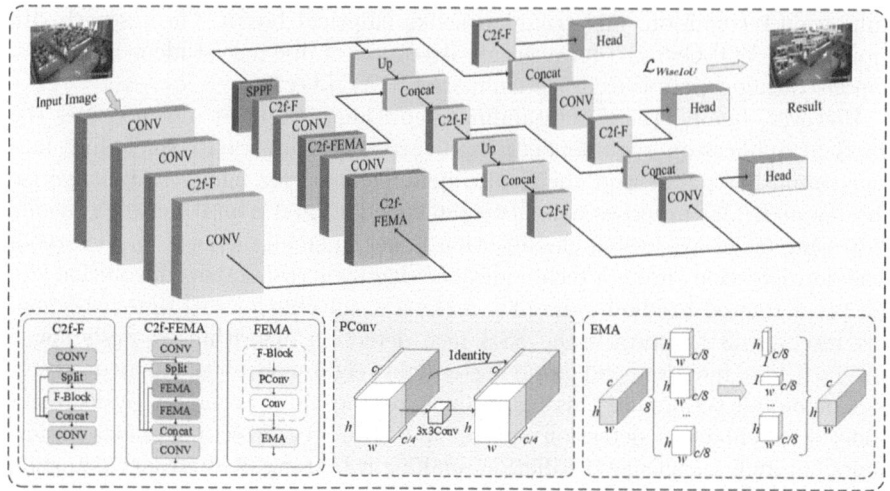

Fig. 1. The structure diagram of LDSBC.

EMA module to the Faster-Block to form the new C2f-FEMA module and add it in the first half of the network, which helps to extract more information from the network. The SPPF module handles variable-sized inputs and operates through spatial pyramid pooling to capture multi-scale features to generate fixed-length feature representations while preserving spatial information. Collectively, these components improve the overall performance of the LDSBC network.

To address the limitations of the original Yolov8n network architecture in the application of classroom behavior detection, this paper introduces the LDSBC network, incorporating Faster-Block and EMA modules to enhance the performance and efficiency of the original architecture. The improvements are as follows: 1) LDSBC introduces the Faster-Block module to replace the convolutional feature extractor in the original network's C2f construction module, forming the new C2f-F module. This modification aims to reduce the model's complexity while maintaining its effectiveness. 2) LDSBC integrates the EMA module within the C2f-F module, resulting in the new C2f-FEMA module designed to enhance the model's feature extraction capabilities without significantly increasing the model's parameters. 3) LDSBC adopts the Wise-IoU loss function to refine the network's efficacy in intricate and crowded classroom environments, improving detection precision and robustness.

3.2 C2f-F Module

The primary objective of this paper is to develop a lightweight network capable of accurately identifying student behaviors in classroom settings. By achieving this, the dependency on high-performance hardware will be reduced, facilitating easier deployment across classroom surveillance devices. We notice that the C2f module in the original yolov8 network architecture is used frequently and repeatedly.

Although the original authors consider a lightweight design for this core module, it still requires significant computational and memory resources. Therefore, we have improved the C2f module in the original network structure. The structure of the improved C2f-F module is depicted in the lower-left corner of Fig. 1.

In the original network architecture, the C2f module adjusts the channel number of the feature map by half through a 1×1 convolutional layer, followed by extracting further feature information through residual connections [30], and ultimately concatenating the extracted information to enhance the gradient flow of the model. The multi-branch and cross-layer connection structure theoretically enriches the information flow, but it decreases computational efficiency in practice.

Considering the original design of the feature extraction module, we realize that it includes two 3×3 convolution layers, where the first convolution layer is used to process the dimension-reduced feature map through residual connections and restore its dimension. In contrast, the second convolution layer reduces the parameter quantity and improves processing speed. Although this design performs well in reducing computational burden, there is still room for improvement in pursuing lightweight and optimized efficiency. To address this issue, we introduced the Faster-Block module in the LDSBC network to replace the original feature extraction module in the C2f module, thus forming the new C2f-F module.

The PConv (partial convolution strategy) [33] in the Faster-Block module uses a 3×3 convolution kernel to extract features from the front half (1/4) of the feature map, which are then fused with the feature map from the back half (3/4), and through BN layer and ReLU activation function to reduce gradient loss, ultimately adjusting the channel size through a 1×1 convolution. Compared to regular convolution, PConv utilizes the redundancy in the feature map and systematically applies standard convolution only to a portion of input channels without affecting the rest, fundamentally reducing FLOPs compared to standard convolution and better utilizing the computational capabilities of the device. Additionally, PConv is highly effective in extracting spatial features, contributing to improving network performance. By introducing the Faster-Block module, we aim to optimize network parameter quantity and computational efficiency further while maintaining or enhancing feature extraction capability to achieve a more efficient and precise deep learning model.

3.3 C2f-FEMA Module

After introducing the C2f-F module, there was a significant reduction in the network's parameter count and model complexity. However, this simplification somewhat compromised the network's recognition performance. Furthermore, while the LDSBC network's approach of channel dimensionality reduction for constructing cross-channel relationships is reasonable, it may inadvertently affect the extraction of deep visual representations. To address this issue, LDSBC introduces an efficient multi-scale attention mechanism (EMA) [34].

The design of the EMA module aims to retain channel-specific information while reducing computational load. The module reconstructs part of the channel information into batch dimensions, thereby preventing information loss typically associated with standard convolution, and further divides the channel dimension into eight sub-feature groups. This arrangement ensures a uniform distribution of spatial semantic features within each sub-feature group. Inspired by the Channel Attention [35] mechanism, we introduced a parallel network structure containing a 1×1 and a 3×3 convolutional kernel placed in two parallel sub-networks, respectively. This arrangement facilitates cross-dimensional interaction, effectively predicting channel or spatial attention. More precisely, the module not only encodes global information to recalibrate the channel weights in each parallel branch but also aggregates the output features of the two parallel branches through cross-dimensional interaction. This process captures pixel-level pairwise relationships, enhancing the model's representation capability.

The EMA module has been integrated into the previously proposed Faster-Block module and collaboratively functions with the original C2f module, forming a new C2f-FEMA module. The structure of this module is illustrated in the lower left corner of Fig. 1. Through innovative design, the C2f-FEMA module further optimized network parameters and complexity and enhanced the model's ability to capture detailed features and recognition accuracy. Introducing the EMA mechanism in the C2f-FEMA module compensated for potential information loss due to dimensionality reduction. By meticulously analyzing and allocating weights to features of different scales, the module substantially improved the model's understanding of spatial and channel relationships. Additionally, applying the multi-scale attention mechanism ensured the economical utilization of computational resources while maintaining the model's depth and width, thereby enhancing the feasibility and efficiency of the model in practical applications. In summary, by integrating the Faster-Block structure and EMA mechanism, the C2f-FEMA module not only achieved significant improvements in parameter efficiency and computational performance but, more importantly, enhanced the network's ability to recognize subtle features in complex visual tasks, making it more suitable for our scenario.

3.4 Loss Function

In optimizing the architecture of the LDSBC network, it was recognized that more than merely adjustments in the architectural framework were needed to surmount all the challenges inherent in object detection tasks. This realization was particularly pronounced in the context of complex and diverse classroom behavior scenarios, where the precision of the model's localization emerged as a pivotal factor in augmenting detection performance. Consequently, building upon the foundation of architectural optimization, an exploration into the design of loss functions was undertaken to enhance the model's localization precision. As evidenced by the widespread adoption and recognition of the YOLO series in real-time detection since its inception, a comprehensive and meticulously crafted loss function is paramount to the model's performance. Specifically, the design of the Bounding Box Regression (BBR) loss plays a decisive role in determining the model's performance in terms of localization accuracy.

Although the current designs of BBR loss functions are highly efficient, they are predominantly predicated on the assumption that the sample quality of the training data is uniform and of high caliber. However, this assumption often needs to be revised in practical educational scenarios, especially in the application of classroom behavior detection. In such contexts, where the quality of samples is highly variable, merely enhancing the fitting capability of the BBR loss may only sometimes lead to improved model performance. We introduced the Wise-IoU [13] loss function to address this challenge, offering a more flexible and robust solution. It is defined as follows:

$$\mathcal{L}_{Wise-IoU} = r\mathcal{R}_{WIoU}\mathcal{L}_{IoU} \qquad (1)$$

$$r = \frac{\beta}{\delta\alpha^{\beta-\delta}} \qquad (2)$$

$$\mathcal{R}_{WIoU} = \exp\left(\frac{(x-x_{gt})^2 + (y-y_{gt})^2}{(W_g^2 + H_g^2)^*}\right) \qquad (3)$$

where α, δ are hyperparameters, W_g and H_g are the dimensions of the minimum bounding box, and $W_g^2 + H_g^2$ is the diagonal length of the minimum bounding box. The superscript $*$ denotes the stripping operation, which is used to prevent the $\mathcal{R}_{WIoU}$ from generating gradients that prevent convergence, and $\mathcal{L}_{IoU}$ is the standard IoU formula.

The Wise-IoU loss function is predicated on the IoU. It incorporates the concept of dynamic, non-monotonic Frequency Modulation, enabling the model to handle anchor boxes of varying quality intelligently. By utilizing eccentricity rather than conventional IoU scoring, Wise-IoU can more precisely gauge the quality of anchor boxes. Moreover, it employs a sophisticated strategy of gradient gain allocation, which mitigates the competition among high-quality anchor boxes while concurrently diminishing the adverse gradient effects caused by low-quality samples. In this process, Wise-IoU predominantly enhances the performance of medium-quality anchor boxes, thereby elevating the overall detection efficacy and accuracy of the model.

Incorporating Wise-IoU enriches the array of loss function designs within the LDSBC network and furnishes a more nuanced approach to managing the intricate and variable scenarios encountered in classroom behavior detection. Through concerted efforts in architecture optimization and loss function design, the LDSBC network has further improved the precision and robustness of classroom behavior recognition while maintaining computational efficiency, which exemplifies its formidable application potential.

4 Experiments

In this section, we perform comprehensive experiments on our RSCB-Dataset to deliver an in-depth analysis of the LDSBC. All experiments are conducted on an

Ubuntu server with an Intel(R) Xeon(R) Gold 5118 CPU running at 2.30GHz and an NVIDIA Tesla V100 PCIe with 16GB of GPU memory.

4.1 Environmental Settings

4.1.1 Datasets

Positive classroom behaviors (such as raising hands, reading, and writing) and negative behaviors (like sleeping and using mobile phones) are critical indicators for assessing classroom quality. We particularly note that reading and writing behaviors have a high visual similarity in some scenarios, further complicating the detection process. In addition, variations in classroom environments and seating arrangements add complexity to the detection task. Changes in lighting conditions causing blurred images are another significant factor affecting detection. Moreover, students' classroom behaviors show substantial differences, presenting additional challenges for detection tasks.

To tackle these challenges, we continuously collect various classroom surveillance videos to create comprehensive datasets that include raising hands, reading, writing, sleeping, and using mobile phones. Our dataset consists of video frames captured by real surveillance cameras installed in various educational institutions, including primary, middle, and high schools and universities. To ensure a thorough behavioral analysis, we gather data from multiple perspectives, encompassing front, side, and rear views. We enhance the quality of our collected materials through rigorous data cleaning and improvement techniques. Following a meticulous process of annotation and review, we develop the RSCB-Dataset, which contains 5,221 images and 19,000 instances of specific behaviors.

4.1.2 Evaluation Metrics

The experiment uses precision (P), recall (R), F1 score (F1), average precision (AP), mean average precision (mAP), model parameters (Params), and model complexity (GFLOPs) as the main evaluation metrics. The definitions of these metrics are presented in Eqs. 1, 2, 3, 4, and 5.

$$P = \frac{TP}{(TP + FP)} \tag{4}$$

$$R = \frac{TP}{(TP + FN)} \tag{5}$$

$$F1 = \frac{2 \times (P \times R)}{(P + R)} \tag{6}$$

where TP represents the number of accurately predicted bounding boxes that match ground truth boxes. FP represents the number of falsely identified positive samples. FN represents the number of missed objects, where the ground truth boxes are not detected by the model.

$$AP = \sum_{i=1}^{n-1}(R_{i+1} - R_i)P_{interp}(R_{i+1}) \tag{7}$$

$$mAP = \frac{\sum_{i=1}^{K} AP_i}{K} \tag{8}$$

where AP can be defined as the area under the interpolated Precision-Recall (P-R) curve enveloped by the X-axis, where $R_1, R_2, ..., R_n$ are the recall values corresponding to the first interpolated precision P_{interp} at each segment, arranged in ascending order.

P and R are standard metrics for classifier performance, yet they individually gauge only accuracy or coverage without offering a balanced view. In contrast, the F1 and mAP present a more holistic evaluation of classifier efficacy. The F1 synthesizes precision and recall to provide a harmonized measure of classifier performance across varying thresholds.

Table 1. The results of comparative experiments

Model	Percision	Recall	F1	mAP	Parameters(m)	GFLOPs	ModelSize(MB)
FasterRCNN	73.6%	52.7%	0.614	78.9%	137.10	185	110
SSD	85.0%	49.9%	0.628	70.1%	24	62.7	95
SparseRCNN	71.2%	83.3%	0.768	90.1%	41	86	72
DAB-DERT	67.1%	84.9%	0.74	91.1%	44	94	246
YoloX-tiny	85.1%	86.2%	0.856	89.8%	54.1	77.9	19.4
Yolov7-tiny	80.2%	82.1%	0.811	84.8%	6.23	13.9	23.4
Yolov8n	84.8%	**87.4%**	0.861	92.0%	3.01	8.1	5.99
Ours	**87.1%**	85.3%	**0.862**	**92.2%**	**2.31**	**6.5**	**4.70**

Table 2. The results of ablation experiments

Faster-Block	EMA	Wise-IoU	Percision	Recall	F1	mAP	Parameters(m)	GFLOPs	ModelSize(MB)
			84.8%	87.4%	0.861	92.0%	3.007	8.1	5.99
✓			84.9%	86.0%	0.854	91.3%	**2.301**	**6.3**	**4.65**
✓	✓		85.1%	85.1%	0.851	91.6%	2.310	6.5	4.70
		✓	**87.6%**	**87.6%**	**0.876**	**92.6%**	3.007	8.1	6.03
✓	✓	✓	87.1%	85.3%	0.862	92.2%	2.310	6.5	4.70

4.2 Comparative Experiments

To validate the effectiveness of our work, we select several prominent networks for comparative experiments, including FasterRCNN [36], SSD [37], SparseR-CNN [38] anchor-free DAB-DETR [39], and the relatively lightweight YOLO series networks [40,41]. We select the RSCB-Dataset as the primary dataset for experiments. These experiments are designed to evaluate the accuracy of the algorithms by utilizing precision, recall, F1 score, and mAP while also considering parameters, model complexity, and model size to assess their lightweight nature. These metrics are essential for evaluating the performance of each algorithm in detecting student classroom behavior. The experimental results are shown in Table 1.

FatserRCNN and SSD are foundational in object detection and are known for their robustness and accuracy. However, their relatively lower performance in this experiment, especially in terms of mAP, underscores their limitations in dealing with the dynamic and diverse environments of classrooms. In contrast, our approach demonstrates superior performance in the experiments. Our model not only excels in key metrics such as accuracy, F1 score, and mAP, but also significantly surpasses FasterRCNN and SSD in terms of the number of Parameters, GFLOPs, and ModelSize.

DAB-DETR, as an anchor-free model, presents a significant leap in detection accuracy with a 91.1% mAP, merely one percentage point below than our approach, highlighting its effectiveness in handling varied classroom behaviors without the need for predefined anchor boxes. Nevertheless, its substantial parameter count, computational complexity, and model size also result in a heightened demand for computational resources. In comparison, our approach demonstrates significantly smaller requirements in these respects, thus embodying greater efficiency.

Our approach outperforms the established YOLO series, achieving 92.2% mAP and accurately identifying classroom behaviors. It also delivers well-balanced precision (87.1%) and recall (85.3%), with an F1 score of 0.862, indicating reliable performance in educational settings. Moreover, our model is efficient and compact, with only 2.31 billion parameters and a 4.70 MB size, suitable for environments with limited computing capabilities. It operates on just 6.5 GFLOPs, enabling real-time applications without high-end infrastructure.

In summary, our model provides high accuracy and efficiency in detecting student behaviors, offering an ideal solution for real-time use in education and balancing computational demands with performance.

4.3 Ablation Experiments

To comprehensively assess the LDSBC network introduced in this study and deepen our understanding of each module's performance, we conducted a series of ablation experiments. These experiments systematically integrated each module, enabling us to gauge their contributions to the overall effectiveness of the model precisely. The outcomes of these ablation experiments are detailed in Table 2.

When examining the performance of each module in isolation, the Faster-Block module stands out for its efficient extraction of spatial features through PconV's partial convolution while concurrently minimizing computational and memory redundancies. This markedly diminishes the model's complexity, parameter count, and size and underscores the module's role in bolstering network efficiency and performance without adversely affecting the model's mAP. Moreover, the Wise-IoU module introduces an optimized gradient gain allocation strategy, effectively reducing the rivalry among high-quality anchor frames and curtailing the negative gradients from lower-quality examples. This focus on mid-tier anchor frames by WIoU contributes to the detector's enhanced overall efficacy, with experiments indicating a 0.2% increase in mAP, achieved without an escalation in parameter count.

However, modeling cross-channel relationships through reducing channel dimensionality could potentially influence the extraction of in-depth visual representations. We integrated the EMA module into the Faster-Block module to address this in later experiments. This integration aims to preserve channel information and curtail computational demands. By reconfiguring some channels into batch dimensions and segmenting channel dimensions into various sub-features, this method ensures an even distribution of spatial semantic features across each feature group. Crucially, as the EMA module is independent of input size, it has a negligible impact on the model's total parameter count.

Overall, these experimental findings validate the efficacy of our proposed approach. The synergistic incorporation of these three modules enables our model to achieve a 20% reduction in weight while maintaining consistent accuracy.

5 Conclusion

This paper introduces a novel, lightweight, and efficient network for detecting student behavior in classroom surveillance footage. The Faster-Block module is incorporated to streamline feature extraction, thereby reducing the network's complexity and parameter count and facilitating easier deployment. Moreover, the EMA module enhances feature map utilization and behavior discrimination by grouping, concatenating, and reshaping while maintaining the model's lightweight design. To address the challenges presented by dense classroom settings, the Wise-IoU loss function is implemented, which improves the precision of bounding boxes and the accuracy of behavior detection. This paper also presents the RSCB-Dataset, which features five distinct behaviors validated through conventional detection methods. The proposed approach significantly reduces the model's parameters and complexity yet maintains high accuracy and improves precision, offering substantial benefits for educational environments by improving teaching efficiency and quality.

Acknowledgements. This work was supported by national natural science foundation of China (No.62202346), Hubei key research and development program (No.2021BAA042), China scholarship council (No.202208420109), Wuhan applied basic frontier research project (No.2022013988065212), MIIT's AI Industry Innovation Task unveils flagship projects (Key technologies, equipment, and systems for flexible customized and intelligent manufacturing in the clothing industry), and Hubei science and technology project of safe production special fund (No. SJZX20220908).

References

1. Yang, B., Yao, Z., Lu, H., Zhou, Y., Xu, J.: In-classroom learning analytics based on student behavior, topic and teaching characteristic mining. Pattern Recogn. Lett. **129**, 224–231 (2020)
2. Chen, W., Shen, Z., Pan, Y., Tan, K., Wang, C.: Applying machine learning algorithm to optimize personalized education recommendation system. J. Theory Pract. Eng. Sci. **4**(01), 101–108 (2024)
3. Wang, L., et al.: Videomae v2: scaling video masked autoencoders with dual masking. In: Proceedings of the IEEE/CVF Conference on Computer Vision and Pattern Recognition, pp. 14549–14560 (2023)
4. Liu, Z., et al.: Video swin transformer. In: Proceedings of the IEEE/CVF Conference on Computer Vision and Pattern Recognition, pp. 3202–3211 (2022)
5. Liu, Z., et al.: Disentangling and unifying graph convolutions for skeleton-based action recognition. In: CVPR, pp. 143–152 (2020)
6. Duan, H., Zhao, Y., Chen, K., Lin, D., Dai, B.: Revisiting skeleton-based action recognition. In: Proceedings of the IEEE/CVF Conference on Computer Vision and Pattern Recognition, pp. 2969–2978 (2022)
7. Yu, F., et al.: Intelligent wearable system with motion and emotion recognition based on digital twin technology. IEEE Internet Things J. **11**(15), 26314–26328 (2024)
8. Zaletelj, J., Košir, A.: Predicting students' attention in the classroom from kinect facial and body features. EURASIP J. Image Video Process. **2017**(1), 1–12 (2017)
9. Feng, Yu., Chen, Z., Jiang, M., Tian, Z., Peng, T., Xinrong, H.: Smart clothing system with multiple sensors based on digital twin technology. IEEE Internet Things J. **10**(7), 6377–6387 (2022)
10. Tang, L., Xie, T., Yang, Y., Wang, H.: Classroom behavior detection based on improved yolov5 algorithm combining multi-scale feature fusion and attention mechanism. Appl. Sci. **12**(13), 6790 (2022)
11. Chen, H., Zhou, G., Jiang, H.: Student behavior detection in the classroom based on improved yolov8. Sensors **23**(20), 8385 (2023)
12. Liao, W., Zhu, R., Ishizaki, T., Li, Y., Jia, Y., Yang, Z.: Can gas consumption data improve the performance of electricity theft detection? IEEE Trans. Ind. Inform. **20**(6), 8453–8465 (2024)
13. Tong, Z., et al.: Wise-IoU: bounding box regression loss with dynamic focusing mechanism. arXiv preprint arXiv:2301.10051 (2023)
14. Zhou, Y., Li, X., Wang, Q., Shen, J.: Visual in-context learning for large vision-language models. arXiv preprint arXiv:2402.11574 (2024)
15. Pan, B., et al.: Low-rank tensor regularized graph fuzzy learning for multi-view data processing. IEEE Trans. Consum. Electron. **70**(1), 2925–2938 (2023)
16. Wu, J., Vorobeychik, Y.: Robust deep reinforcement learning through bootstrapped opportunistic curriculum. In: International Conference on Machine Learning, pp. 24177–24211. PMLR (2022)

17. Everingham, M., Van Gool, L., Williams, C.K., Winn, J., Zisserman, A.: The pascal visual object classes (VOC) challenge. Int. J. Comput. Vis. **88**, 303–338 (2010)
18. Everingham, M., et al.: The pascal visual object classes challenge: a retrospective. Int. J. Comput. Vis. **111**, 98–136 (2015)
19. Lin, T.-Y., et al.: Microsoft COCO: common objects in context. In: Fleet, D., Pajdla, T., Schiele, B., Tuytelaars, T. (eds.) ECCV 2014. LNCS, vol. 8693, pp. 740–755. Springer, Cham (2014). https://doi.org/10.1007/978-3-319-10602-1_48
20. Sun, B., et al.: Student class behavior dataset: a video dataset for recognizing, detecting, and captioning students' behaviors in classroom scenes. Neural Comput. Appl. **33**, 8335–8354 (2021)
21. Ruiz, N., et al.: ATL-BP: a student engagement dataset and model for affect transfer learning for behavior prediction. IEEE Trans. Biometrics Behav. Identity Sci. **5**(3), 411–424 (2022)
22. Yang, F., Wang, t.: SCB-dataset3: a benchmark for detecting student classroom behavior. arXiv preprint arXiv:2310.02522 (2023)
23. Zhao, J., Zhu, H.: CBPH-net: a small object detector for behavior recognition in classroom scenarios. IEEE Trans. Instrum. Meas. **72**, 1–12 (2023)
24. Chenghu, D., et al.: VTON-SCFA: a virtual try-on network based on the semantic constraints and flow alignment. IEEE Trans. Multimedia **25**, 777–791 (2022)
25. Yu, F., Zhang, Y., Li, H., Du, C., Liu, L., Jiang, M.: Phase contour enhancement network for clothing parsing. IEEE Trans. Consum. Electron. **70**(1), 2784–2793 (2024)
26. Zheng, R., Jiang, F., Shen, R.: Intelligent student behavior analysis system for real classrooms. In: ICASSP 2020-2020 IEEE International Conference on Acoustics, Speech and Signal Processing (ICASSP), pp. 9244–9248. IEEE (2020)
27. Gao, S.H., Cheng, M.M., Zhao, K., Zhang, X.Y., Yang, M.H., Torr, P.: Res2net: a new multi-scale backbone architecture. IEEE Trans. Pattern Anal. Mach. Intell. **43**(2), 652–662 (2019)
28. Fang, J., et al.: A lightweight convolutional neural network student learning behavior analysis based on facial expression recognition. In: 2021 International Conference on Electronic Information Engineering and Computer Science (EIECS), pp. 593–596. IEEE (2021)
29. Chollet, F.: Xception: deep learning with depthwise separable convolutions. In: Proceedings of the IEEE Conference on Computer Vision and Pattern Recognition, pp. 1251–1258 (2017)
30. He, K., Zhang, X., Ren, S., Sun, J.: Deep residual learning for image recognition. In: Proceedings of the IEEE Conference on Computer Vision and Pattern Recognition, pp. 770–778 (2016)
31. Lingling, Z., Fucai, C., Chao, G.: Improvement of face detection algorithm based on lightweight convolutional neural network. In: 2020 IEEE 6th International Conference on Computer and Communications (ICCC), pp. 1191–1197. IEEE (2020)
32. Zhao, J., Zhu, H., Niu, L.: Bitnet: a lightweight object detection network for real-time classroom behavior recognition with transformer and bi-directional pyramid network. J. King Saud Univ. Comput. Inf. Sci. **35**(8), 101670 (2023)
33. Chen, J., et al.: Run, don't walk: chasing higher flops for faster neural networks. In: Proceedings of the IEEE/CVF Conference on Computer Vision and Pattern Recognition, pp. 12021–12031 (2023)
34. Ouyang, D., et al.: Efficient multi-scale attention module with cross-spatial learning. In: ICASSP 2023-2023 IEEE International Conference on Acoustics, Speech and Signal Processing (ICASSP), pp. 1–5. IEEE (2023)

35. Wang, Q., Wu, B., Zhu, P., Li, P., Zuo, W., Hu, Q.: ECA-net: efficient channel attention for deep convolutional neural networks. In: Proceedings of the IEEE/CVF Conference on Computer Vision and Pattern Recognition, pp. 11534–11542 (2020)
36. Ren, S., He, K., Girshick, R., Sun, J.: Faster R-CNN: towards real-time object detection with region proposal networks. In: Advances in Neural Information Processing Systems, vol. 28 (2015)
37. Liu, W., et al.: SSD: single shot multibox detector. In: Leibe, B., Matas, J., Sebe, N., Welling, M. (eds.) ECCV 2016. LNCS, vol. 9905, pp. 21–37. Springer, Cham (2016). https://doi.org/10.1007/978-3-319-46448-0_2
38. Sun, P., et al.: Sparse R-CNN: end-to-end object detection with learnable proposals. In: Proceedings of the IEEE/CVF Conference on Computer Vision and Pattern Recognition, pp. 14454–14463 (2021)
39. Liu, S., et al.: Dab-detr: dynamic anchor boxes are better queries for detr. arXiv preprint arXiv:2201.12329 (2022)
40. Ge, Z., Liu, S., Wang, F., Li, Z., Sun, J.: Yolox: exceeding yolo series in 2021. arXiv preprint arXiv:2107.08430 (2021)
41. Wang, C.Y., Bochkovskiy, A., Liao, H.Y.: Yolov7: trainable bag-of-freebies sets new state-of-the-art for real-time object detectors. In: Proceedings of the IEEE/CVF Conference on Computer Vision and Pattern Recognition, pp. 7464–7475 (2023)

YOLO-DPW: An Efficient Real-Time Fabric Defect Detection Model

Wentao Hu[1,2], Xinrong Hu[1,4(✉)], Rui Yang[3], Li Li[1], and Xiaoyun Yan[1]

[1] School of Computer Science and Artificial Intelligence, Wuhan Textile University, Wuhan 430200, China
hxr@wtu.edu.cn
[2] State Key Laboratory of New Textile Material and Advanced Processing Technologies, Wuhan 430200, China
[3] Electronic Information School, Wuhan University, Wuhan 430072, China
[4] Engineering Research Center of Hubei Province for Clothing Information, Wuhan Textile University, Wuhan 430200, China

Abstract. Fabric defects are characterized by a wide variety of types, varied scales, and similarity to the background. To address these challenges in detection, our research introduces a fabric defect detection algorithm named Yolo-DPW, which is an adaptation of the YOLOv8 model. This algorithm is designed to strike an optimal balance between detection accuracy and speed. The improved model in this research utilizes the PConv-C2 module to replace the C2f module in the original Backbone, which greatly reduces the number of parameters. The CIoU loss function used in the original YOLOv8 model is improved to WIoU loss function with dynamic non-monotonic focusing mechanism. At the same time, we use the D-Att module to improve the detection rate of defects with large differences in aspect ratio in the model. The experimental results show that the improved model improves the mean average precision (mAP) by 4.78% over the original model for the fabric defect detection task, while the detection speed reaches 203.17 FPS, which meets the detection requirements in industrial scenarios.

Keywords: attention mechanism · partial convolution · fabric detection · YOLOv8

1 Introduction

In the industrial production of fabric is very easy to produce a large number of defective fabric, and many textile companies still use the traditional manual methods to detect the defects of fabric, there are many problems with the traditional method of using manual fabric defect detection, including high labor costs, low efficiency and high leakage rate [1]. The use of computerized image detection technology can be a good solution to these problems. In the field of

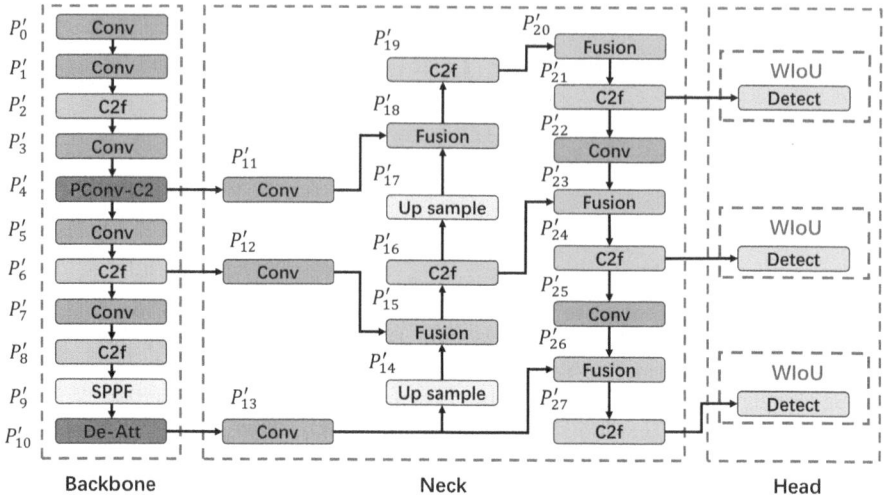

Fig. 1. Main Structure of YOLO-DPW

image detection, the current mainstream deep learning-based algorithms include single-stage algorithms represented by SSD [2]and YOLO [3] series and two-stage algorithms represented by R-CNN [4] and its improved algorithms. Among them, the single-stage lightweight algorithm model represented by YOLOv8 can have a high detection speed to achieve the real-time detection requirement with low arithmetic power of industrial scene detection equipment. Despite the deep learning has been applied and researched in the field of fabric defect detection, there are still more problems waiting to be solved. For instance, determining how to achieve an equilibrium between detection precision and speed, as well as enhancing the detection rates for defects with large differences in aspect ratio. To solve these problems, this research proposes an improved model named YOLO-DPW based on the YOLOv8n model.

2 Related Works

Fabric defects are highly variable in scale, with a large number of small target defects and large differences in aspect ratio defects, and it is difficult to obtain satisfactory performance by directly applying existing deep learning models. There are many researches on optimized models for fabric defect detection, Li et al. [5] proposed an improved fabric defect detection algorithm based on Faster R-CNN, which has high computational overhead and slow detection speed, and is not suitable for real-time detection tasks. Jing et al. [6] proposed an improved model based on the YOLOv3 model, which combines low-level features with the high-level information. Liu et al. [7] builds a new optimization model with YOLOv4 as the base model. For the scaling problem, it uses variability convolution to replace the original convolution module. Shi et al. [8] improves on the

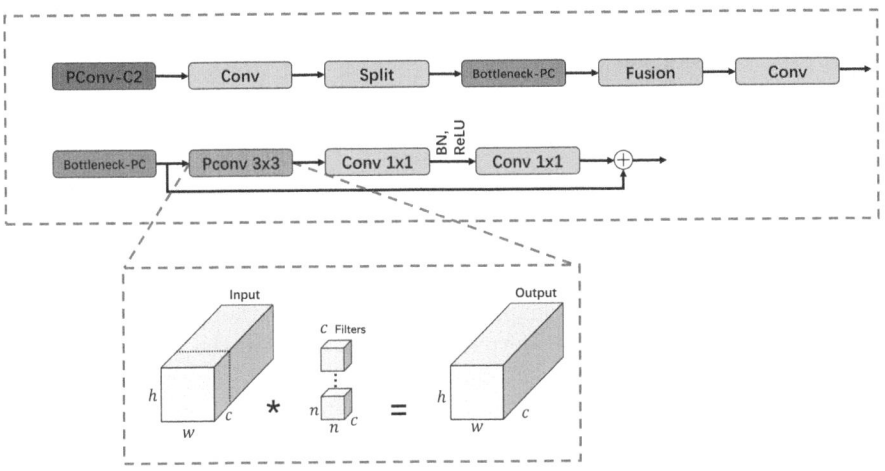

Fig. 2. Main structure of PConv-C2

YOLOv5 model. It introduces a multi-scale feature fusion module to produce more features, and also uses the Ghost module, which uses convolution for only some of the features and produces the others using linear operations, improving the detection speed.

3 Methods

3.1 Overall Framework

Our improved fabric defect detection model is shown in Fig. 1. By refining the modules within the Backbone architecture, we have achieved a substantial reduction in the model's parameters, which has concurrently enhanced the speed of detection. This lightweight architecture enables the model to run on resource limited edge devices. To enhance the model's capability to accurately detect targets of small scale and those with large differences in aspect ratio, we integrated a feature augmentation module into the Backbone architecture. Additionally, we employed a superior loss function to refine the detection performance further. Through this series of improvements, the model has significantly improved the detection ability and efficiency of the defects, which has great potential in practical applications.

3.2 PConv-C2 Block

Since the traditional convolutional operator produces high Floating-Point Operations (FLOPs) and has low Floating-Point Operations per Second (FLOPS), it is not favorable for real-time detection tasks in industrial scenarios. In this research, we introduce the idea of FasterNet [9] and use partial convolution (PConv) to reconstruct the original Bottleneck by replacing the original two convolution modules with one PConv module. PConv uses regular convolution for feature extraction only for some input channels, which reduces computational redundancy and significantly improves computational efficiency while maintaining certain performance levels. The feature maps exhibit high similarities among different channels. To address this, we employ a simple PConv-C2 module to simultaneously reduce computational redundancy and memory access. This module applies a regular convolution on only a subset of the input channels for spatial feature extraction, leaving the remaining channels untouched. For contiguous or regular memory access, we consider the first or last consecutive channels as representatives of the entire feature maps for computation. Without loss of generality, we assume that the input and output feature maps have the same number of channels.

$$h \times w \times n^2 \times c \tag{1}$$

Besides, PConv-C2 has a smaller amount of memory access.

$$h \times w \times 2c + n^2 \times c^2 \approx n \times w \times 2c \tag{2}$$

Equation 1 represents the memory access of convolution, while Eq. 2 represents the memory access of PConv-C2 which h, w, and c respectively represent the size of the input image, and n represents the size of the filter.

Figure 2 illustrates the specific structure, and the empirical data indicate a substantial reduction in both the model's parameters and FLOPs upon integrating the PConv-C2 module. Additionally, this modification yields a slight enhancement in performance compared to the baseline model.

3.3 Wise-IoU

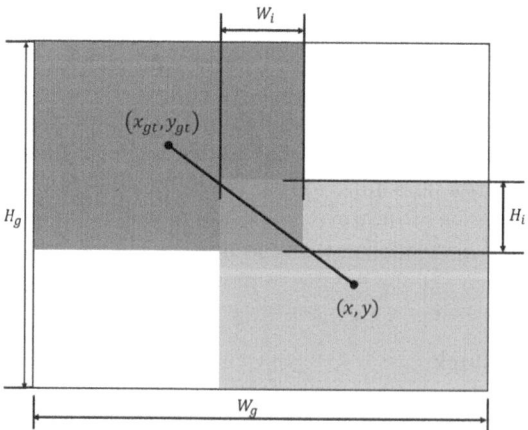

Fig. 3. The diagram of IoU

The Wise-IoU (WIoU) [10] loss function employs a dynamic non-monotonic focusing mechanism, which reduces the weight of high-quality anchor frames while reducing the harm caused by low-quality examples to the model. And because WIoU does not compare the computation of the horizontal to vertical ratio, it can achieve faster computation speed, which is favorable to meet the requirements of real-time detection (Fig. 3).

Jiahui Yu et al.'s Intersection over Union (IoU) [11] is used to measure the overlap between anchor boxes and target boxes in object detection tasks, with the formula for LIoU shown as Eqs. 3 and 4.

$$\mathcal{L}_{IoU} = 1 - \frac{W_i H_i}{S_u} \tag{3}$$

$$S_u = wh + w_{gt} h_{gt} - W_i H_i \tag{4}$$

However, it may suffer from the issue of vanishing gradients during back propagation, leading to the inability to update the width of the overlapping region. WIoU v1, which features a two-layer distance attention mechanism based on distance metrics, addresses this issue and it's shown as Eqs. 5 and 6.

$$\mathcal{L}_{WIoUv1} = \mathcal{R}_{WIoU} \cdot \mathcal{L}_{IoU} \tag{5}$$

$$R_{WIoU} = \exp\left(\frac{(x - x_{gt})^2 + (y - y_{gt})^2}{(W_g^2 + H_g^2)}\right) \tag{6}$$

WIoU v3 introduces the concept of outlier degree β (Eq. 7).

$$\beta = \frac{\mathcal{L}_{IoU}^*}{\mathcal{L}_{IoU}} \in [0, +\infty) \tag{7}$$

$$\mathcal{L}_{W\ IoUv\ 3} = r\mathcal{L}_{W\ IoUv\ 1}, r = \frac{\beta}{\delta \alpha^{\beta - \delta}} \tag{8}$$

When the outlier degree is low, denoted as $\mathcal{L}_{IoU}^*$ being small, indicates high anchor box quality, allowing for a small gradient boost to be allocated, facilitating the regression of bounding boxes towards anchor boxes of normal quality. For anchor boxes with larger outlier degree, indicating lower quality where the $\mathcal{L}_{IoU}^*$ loss is significant, a smaller gradient boost is assigned to effectively prevent low-quality examples from generating substantial harmful gradients. The formula is shown as Eq. 8. δ and α are two hyper-parameters that control r and β.

Our improved model in the research uses WIoUv3 and the hyper-parameter α is set to '1.9', and hyper-parameter δ is set to '3'.

3.4 D-Att Feature Enhance Block

Because the Backbone of the original model is stacked by simple convolutional modules, it is difficult to distinguish the target and background well, and there are a large number of textile blemishes with high horizontal to vertical ratios,

Table 1. Results of ablation experiments for the revised model

Model	With WIoU	With PConv-C2	With D-Att	mAP@0.5(%)	Parameters (M)	GFLOPs(G)
Baseline				48.1	3.0	8.1
YOLO-W	✔			48.9(+1.7)	3.0	8.1
YOLO-WP	✔	✔		49.6(+3.1)	3.0	7.8
YOLO-DW	✔		✔	50.1(+4.16)	3.2	8.3
YOLO-DPW	✔	✔	✔	50.4(+4.78)	3.2	8.0

Table 2. Results of PConv-C2 block. The prefixes "B" and "N" represent the replacement of modules in Backbone and Neck. The speed results are reported on 3070 GPU with FP16.

Model	mAP@0.5(%)	Parameters(M)	GFLOPs(G)	FPS
Baseline	48.9	3.0	8.1	246.1
B+N-P1-4	42.6	**2.3**	**6.3**	**257.7**
B-P1-4	46.3	2.6	7.0	253.6
N-P1-4	45.7	2.7	7.4	251.2
B-P1	48.3	3.0	7.9	249.0
B-P2	**49.6**	3.0	7.8	250.8
B-P3	47.8	2.9	7.8	249.4
B-P4	47.4	2.9	7.9	247.6

so the model needs more global information, but it is difficult for traditional convolutional neural networks to accept global feature information. Therefore, we invoke the idea of Deformable Attention [12] and use the D-Att module for feature enhancement in the model to obtain more low-frequency global information. With multiple sets of deformable sampling points, a more accurate focus region can be determined in the global information, so as to detect defects with large differences in aspect ratios.

$$\text{D-Att}\left(z_q, p_q, x\right) = \sum_{m=1}^{M} W_m \left[\sum_{k=1}^{K} A_{mqk} \cdot W'_m x \left(p_q + \Delta p_{mqk}\right)\right] \quad (9)$$

The D-Att module can be represented as Eq. 9, where x is the input feature for Key and Value, z is the input feature for query, M represents the number of heads in multi-head attention, K is the total number of sampled keys, Δp_{mqk} represents the position shift of the k-th sampling point relative to the reference point in the m-th attention head, A_{mqk} is the attention weight, p represents the position coordinate of z, and W_m and W'_m represent the offset matrices under

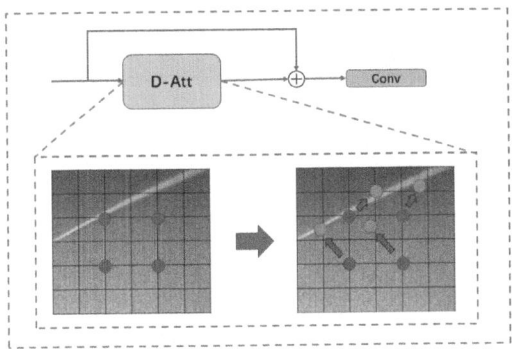

Fig. 4. D-Att Block

different inputs, respectively. The structure of the D-Att module is shown in Fig. 4.

Experiments show that the detection rate of the model for large differences in aspect ratio defects is improved by adding the D-Att module.

4 Experimental Results and Analysis

4.1 Experimental Datasets

The fabric images in the datasets of this research are all derived from Ali "Tianchi" [13] database, containing 5993 defective images, 9520 defective labels, and the resolution of the images are all 2446×1000. The datasets images are divided into training set, validation set, and test set in the ratio of 7:2:1. The training set contains 4802 images, the validation set contains 794 images, and the test set contains 397 images. Each defect image in the datasets contains at least one defect, covering 34 important defects in the textile industry. Given the restricted occurrences of certain defect categories, we employed procedures such as rotation, flipping, and splicing to enrich the dataset.

4.2 Experimental Environment and Parameter Settings

The same experimental environment was used for all experiments. The software environment was Ubuntu20.04, Cuda11.8, PyTorch2.0.0, and the hardware environment consists of a AMD EPYC 7543 and an NVIDIA Tesla A40 (48G) was used for training and computation. We augmented the data during model training and resized the data images to $1280 \times 1280 \times 3$. The model is trained with a stochastic gradient descent optimizer (SGD) to optimize the weights. The initial learning rate is set to 0.012, weight decay is set to 0.0005, batchsize is set to 16, and mixed precision (AMP) is turned on to train 300 epochs.

Table 3. Results of comparison experiment

Model	mAP@0.5(%)	mAP@0.95(%)	Parameters(M)	GFLOPs(G)	FPS
Faster R-CNN [14]	46.9	20.1	–	–	77.6
YOLOv3-tiny [15]	38.1	14.7	12.0	18.9	189.9
YOLOv5s [16]	47.5	21.3	2.7	7.4	241.2
YOLOv6n [17]	38.4	17.5	**2.5**	**7.1**	**257.5**
YOLOv8n [18]	48.1	22.9	3.0	8.1	246.1
YOLO-DPW	**50.4**	**24.3**	3.2	8.0	203.1

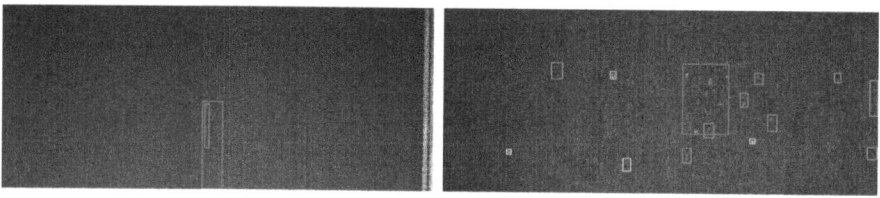

Fig. 5. Predictions of YOLO-DPW

4.3 Ablation Experiment

Ablation Study of the Improved Model. To confirm the efficacy of the enhancements made to the model, this research carried out a series of ablation tests. Based on the model improvements in this research, four ablation models were designed for this experiment: 'YOLO-W', where only WIoU was introduced; 'YOLO-WP', where the D-Att module was removed; 'YOLO-DW', where the PConv-C2 block removed; "YOLO-DPW", which introduces all improvements. The baseline model is YOLOv8n. The results of all the experiments are shown in Table 1, and the results show that the D-Att module and WIoU loss improve the detection performance of the model, and the PConv-C2 module substantially decreases the parameter count while enhancing the speed of detection. Ablation experiment results corroborate the effectiveness of the improvements introduced in this research.

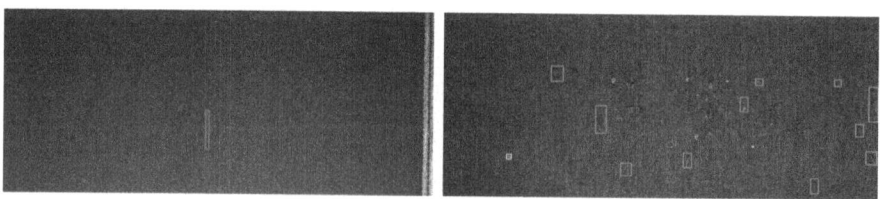

Fig. 6. Predictions of YOLOv8n

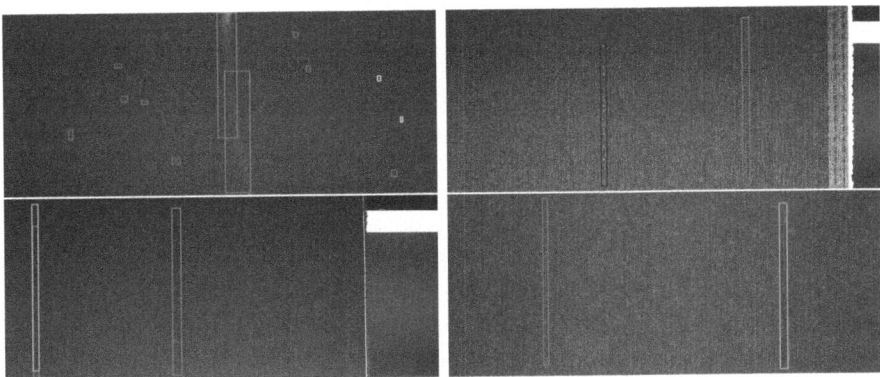

Fig. 7. Predictions with large differences in aspect ratio defects by YOLO-DPW

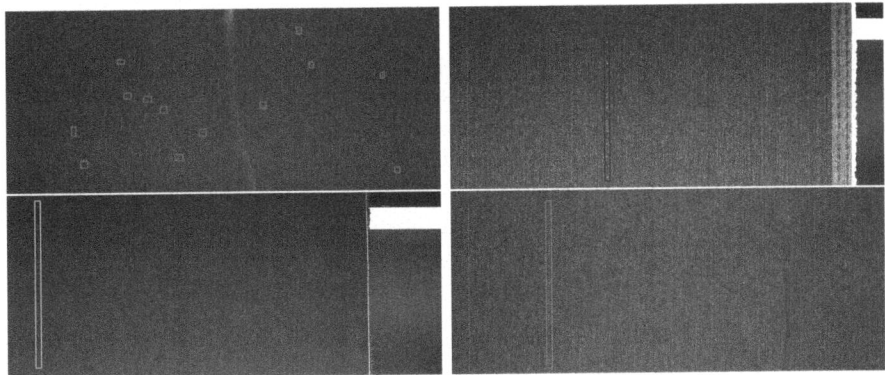

Fig. 8. Predictions with large differences in aspect ratio defects by YOLOv8n

The Effectiveness of Numbers and Placements of PConv-C2 Modules.
We attempted to integrate PConv-C2 modules into various positions within the Backbone layer of the model in order to determine the most effective location and the ideal number of insertion points. The outcomes of these experiments are presented in Table 2, using YOLOv8n as the reference baseline model. The experimental results show that although replacing all the C2 modules with Pconv-C2 modules results in a considerably higher detection speed, the detection accuracy is greatly reduced. Compared to Neck, using the Pconv-C2 module at Backbone resulted in higher detection speed and detection accuracy for the model. According to the experimental data, we only use the PConv-C2 module to replace the C2f module in the P2 layer of the backbone, which achieves the speed that meets the actual detection requirements while maintaining high detection accuracy, and the detection accuracy and detection speed are both higher than that of the baseline.

4.4 Comparison Experiment

Comparison with Other Models. To validate the enhanced model's superiority, this research conducts a comparative analysis against prevailing mainstream algorithms using an identical platform and dataset. The results of these comparative experiments are detailed in Table 3. The experimental results show that although the YOLOv6n model has a high detection speed, it exceeds the practical requirements and has a lower detection accuracy. While our model's detection speed is not as fast as that of contemporary leading detection models like YOLOv5n and YOLOv6n, it still satisfies the practical requirements for detection tasks. The detection accuracy of our model is higher than other mainstream models, with a maximum lead of 32.2%. In summary, the our model in this research achieves a mapping rate of 50.4% and a detection speed of 203.1 FPS, which can meet the demand for real-time detection of fabric imperfections in real-time scenarios.

Effectiveness of WIoU. To evaluate the performance of WIoU, we compared WIoU with CIoU [19] (used in YOLOv8) and other commonly used IoUs such as GIoU [20] and EIoU [21]. Based on the YOLOv8n as the base model, the comparison results of running the test set in the same experimental environment are shown in Table 4. WIoU v1 and WIoU v3 outperform almost all other IoUs in terms of precision (P), recall (R), and mean Average Precision (mAP), with WIoU v3 achieving the best scores across all evaluation metrics.

Table 4. Effectiveness of different IoUs

IoU	P(%)	R(%)	mAP@0.5(%)
CIoU	47.2	50.3	48.1
GIoU	46.7	47.6	47.5
EIoU	47.3	49.9	47.7
WIoU v1	47.7	50.2	48.1
WIoU v3	**48.5**	**51.1**	**48.9**

5 Conclusion

To meet the demand for real-time recognition of fabric defects, this study introduces an enhanced detection model called YOLO-DPW. This model is an improved version of YOLOv8, incorporating architectural innovations "PConv-C2" and "D-Att," along with WIoU, a superior loss function, to enhance detection performance. As shown in Figs. 5 and 6, the improved model in this study outperforms the baseline model in defect detection capabilities. As depicted in Figs. 7 and 8, the improved model demonstrates enhanced detection capabilities, particularly for challenging defects such as those with large differences in aspect ratio. The experimental results show that the YOLO-DPW model outperforms other leading models in terms of detection accuracy and speed, with an average precision mean (mAP) improvement of 4.78% and a detection speed increased to 257.5 FPS, meeting the requirements for real-time detection. Overall, our model has superior detection capabilities, and our goal is to further enhance the model's performance in detecting more subtle defects or in higher noise environments to address the latest challenges in the future.

References

1. Li, C., Li, J., Li, Y., He, L., Xiaokang, F., Chen, J.: Fabric defect detection in textile manufacturing: a survey of the state of the art. Secur. Commun. Networks **1–13**, 2021 (2021)
2. Liu, W., et al.: SSD: single shot multibox detector. In: Leibe, B., Matas, J., Sebe, N., Welling, M. (eds.) ECCV 2016. LNCS, vol. 9905, pp. 21–37. Springer, Cham (2016). https://doi.org/10.1007/978-3-319-46448-0_2
3. Redmon, J., Divvala, S., Girshick, R., Farhadi, A.: You only look once: unified, real-time object detection. In: Proceedings of the IEEE Conference on Computer Vision and Pattern Recognition, pp. 779–788 (2016)
4. Girshick, R., Donahue, J., Darrell, T., Malik, J.: Rich feature hierarchies for accurate object detection and semantic segmentation. In: Proceedings of the IEEE Conference on Computer Vision and Pattern Recognition, pp. 580–587 (2014)
5. Zhou, H., Jang, B., Chen, Y., Troendle, D.: Exploring faster RCNN for fabric defect detection. In: 2020 Third International Conference on Artificial Intelligence for Industries (AI4I), pp. 52–55. IEEE (2020)
6. Jing, J., Zhuo, D., Zhang, H., Liang, Y., Zheng, M.: Fabric defect detection using the improved yolov3 model. J. Eng. Fibers Fabr. **15**, 1558925020908268 (2020)
7. Liu, T., Chen, S.: Yolov4-DCN-based fabric defect detection algorithm. In: 2022 37th Youth Academic Annual Conference of Chinese Association of Automation (YAC), pp. 710–715. IEEE (2022)
8. Shi, L., Song, J., Gao, Y., Cheng, G., Hao, B.: Yolo-GFD: a fast and accurate fabric defect detection model. In: 2023 4th International Conference on Big Data, Artificial Intelligence and Internet of Things Engineering (ICBAIE), pp. 229–233. IEEE (2023)
9. Chen, J., et al.: Run, don't walk: chasing higher flops for faster neural networks. In: Proceedings of the IEEE/CVF Conference on Computer Vision and Pattern Recognition, pp. 12021–12031 (2023)
10. Tong, Z., Chen, Y., Xu, Z., Yu, R.: Wise-iou: bounding box regression loss with dynamic focusing mechanism (2023)
11. Jiahui, Yu., Jiang, Y., Wang, Z., Cao, Z., Huang, T.: An advanced object detection network, Unitbox (2016)
12. Xia, Z., Pan, X., Song, S., Li, L.E., Huang, G.: Vision transformer with deformable attention. In: Proceedings of the IEEE/CVF Conference on Computer Vision and Pattern Recognition, pp. 4794–4803 (2022)
13. Tianchi: Smart diagnosis of cloth flaw dataset (2020). https:// tianchi. aliyun. com/ dataset/ 79336

14. Ren, S., He, K., Girshick, R., Sun, J.: Faster R-CNN: towards real-time object detection with region proposal networks. IEEE Trans. Pattern Anal. Mach. Intell. **39**(6), 1137–1149 (2016)
15. Redmon, J., Farhadi, A.: Yolov3: an incremental improvement (2018)
16. Glenn, J.: Yolov5 release v7.0 (2022). https://github.com/ultralytics/yolov5/tree/v7.0
17. Li, C., Chu, X.: Yolov6 v3. 0: a full-scale reloading (2023)
18. Glenn, J.: Yolov8 (2023). https://github.com/ultralytics/ultralytics/tree/main
19. Zheng, Z., Wang, P., Liu, W., Li, J., Ye, R., Ren, D.: Distance-IoU loss: faster and better learning for bounding box regression. In: Proceedings of the AAAI Conference on Artificial Intelligence, vol. 34, pp. 12993–13000 (2020)
20. Rezatofighi, H., Tsoi, N., Gwak, J., Sadeghian, A., Reid, I., Savarese, S.: Generalized intersection over union: a metric and a loss for bounding box regression. In: Proceedings of the IEEE/CVF Conference on Computer Vision and Pattern Recognition, pp. 658–666 (2019)
21. Zhang, Y.F., Ren, W., Zhang, Z., Jia, Z., Wang, L., Tan, T.: Focal and efficient IoU loss for accurate bounding box regression. arXiv preprint arXiv:2101.08158 (2021)

Quadrotor Unmanned Aerial Vehicle Trajectory Tracking Under Event-Triggered Sliding Mode Control

Han Jiang, Ruhui Yin, Zilin Shu , Ziang Ren, Hongyu Zhu, and Zixin Huang(✉)

School of Electrical and, Information Engineering, Wuhan Institute of Technology, Wuhan, China
huangzx@wit.edu.cn

Abstract. This paper considers an event-triggered sliding mode control approach for quadrotor unmanned aerial vehicle (UAV) to solve the trajectory tracking control problem under communication resource constraints. Firstly, the rigid-body dynamics model of the quadrotor is analyzed and briefly described event-triggering mechanisms (ETM) for general non-linear systems. Separate controllers were designed for the position and attitude of the quadrotor, and analysed the stability of the closed-loop system using Liapunov theory. Then, it is proved that Zeno phenomenon does not exist When closed loop controlling. The simulations verify that the proposed method can effectively reduce the number of controller updates while maintaining good trajectory tracking efficiency of the quadrotor UAV under different tracking commands. Meanwhile, it reduces the amount of controller computation and improves the system resource utilization.

Keywords: Event-triggered · Quadrotor UAV · Trajectory tracking · Sliding mode control · Lyapunov theory

1 Introduction

Quadrotor unmanneda aerial vehicle (UAV) is a typical rotor UAV with good stability and manoeuvrability, as well as superb carrying capacity. It is widely used in aerial photography, logistics, agriculture, surveying and other fields [1]. It consists of four control inputs of propeller lift and three-axis torque, and six degree of freedom outputs of position and attitude, and is characterised by nonlinearity, underactuated and strong coupling [2].

Scholars from various locations have researched and discussed the flight control of quadrotors. Liu et al. proposed a fully actuated system approaches (FASA)-based quadrotor trajectory tracking control method inspired by ADRC [3]. Huang et al. used adaptive control to estimate the upper limit of external perturbations online [4]. Najm et al. proposed the use of a nonlinear PID controller to stabilise the translation and rotation of quadrotor [5]. Peng et al.

Presented a comprehensive review of the progress in research on event-triggered communication and control [6]. Zhang et al. designed a dynamic event-triggered communication mechanism for coherent quadrotor velocity and attitude tracking [7]. Bisheban proposed geometric adaptive controller with artificial neural network for quadrotor. [8].

The literature above proposes effective control methods for the trajectory tracking of quadrotor. However, it does not consider the problem of stable trajectory tracking control for quadrotor under limited communication resources and external interference. Traditional time-triggered schemes usually require the collection of the vehicle's state information at a fixed high sampling frequency.

2 Preliminaries

2.1 System Model of QuadRotor

Assuming the quadrotor deformation is ignored, Fig. 1 shows the rigid body model of the quadrotor. We can derive the dynamic equations of the quadrotor based on the Newton-Euler equations. The rotational speeds of the four rotor motors are defined as ω_1, ω_2, ω_3 and ω_4. The total lift of the vehicle is represented by f, and the rotational moments around the fuselage X, Y and Z, are represented by τ_x, τ_y, and τ_z, respectively. From this, it can be concluded that

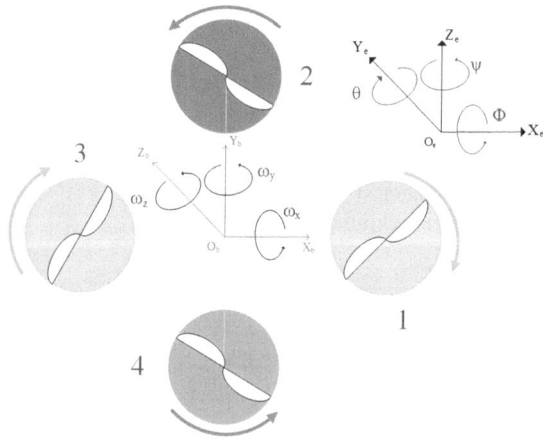

Fig. 1. Quadrotor rigid body model

$$\begin{bmatrix} f \\ \tau_x \\ \tau_y \\ \tau_z \end{bmatrix} = \begin{bmatrix} k_L(\omega_1^2 + \omega_2^2 + \omega_3^2 + \omega_4^2) \\ dk_L(\omega_2^2 - \omega_4^2) \\ dk_L(-\omega_1^2 + \omega_3^2) \\ b(\omega_1^2 - \omega_2^2 + \omega_3^2 - \omega_4^2) \end{bmatrix} \quad (1)$$

The lift coefficient is represented by k_L, b is counter torque coefficient, the distance between the rotor centre and the centre of UAV is d. The dynamics of the rigid body quadrotor is modelled as

$$\begin{bmatrix} \ddot{x} \\ \ddot{y} \\ \ddot{z} \\ \ddot{\phi} \\ \ddot{\theta} \\ \ddot{\psi} \end{bmatrix} = \begin{bmatrix} -\frac{f}{m}(c\phi s\theta c\psi + s\phi s\psi) - \frac{k_t \dot{x}}{m} + \frac{f_{dx}}{m} \\ -\frac{f}{m}(c\phi s\theta s\psi - s\phi c\psi) - \frac{k_t \dot{y}}{m} + \frac{f_{dy}}{m} \\ -\frac{f}{m}\cos\phi\cos\theta - g - \frac{k_t \dot{z}}{m} + \frac{f_{dz}}{m} \\ \frac{1}{I_x}[(I_z - I_y)\omega_y\omega_z + \tau_x] + \tau_{dx} \\ \frac{1}{I_y}[(I_x - I_z)\omega_x\omega_z + \tau_y] + \tau_{dy} \\ \frac{1}{I_z}[(I_y - I_x)\omega_y\omega_x + \tau_z] + \tau_{dz} \end{bmatrix} \quad (2)$$

The centre of mass of the UAV is represented by x, y, and z in the inertial coordinate system. The roll angle, pitch angle, and yaw angle are represented by ϕ, θ, and ψ respectively. $s = sin, c = cos$. The inertia of the three axes is represented by I_x, I_y, and I_z. m is the mass of the UAV, while g is the gravitational acceleration. k_t is drag coefficient. The variables f_{dx}, f_{dy}, f_{dz} represent external disturbance forces, while τ_{dx}, τ_{dy}, and τ_{dz} represent external disturbance moments.

2.2 Common Paradigm for Event Triggering

We analysis focuses on nonlinear systems whose control forms are as follows

$$\dot{x} = f(x, u), x \in \mathbb{R}^n, u \in \mathbb{R}^m \quad (3)$$

Setting up a closed-loop system with a feedback control gain of $k : \mathbb{R}^n \to \mathbb{R}^m$.

$$\dot{x} = f(x, k(x + e)) \quad (4)$$

Input to state stabilisation (ISS) for measurement error e. Assuming an ISS stabilising Liapunov smooth function V. α, $\underline{\alpha}$, $\overline{\alpha}$ and γ are $\mathcal{K}_\infty$ functions. Simultaneously satisfying all $x, e \in \mathbb{R}^n$.

$$\underline{\alpha}(\|x\|) \leq V(x) \leq \overline{\alpha}(\|x\|) \quad (5)$$

$$\nabla V(x) \cdot f(x, u) \leq -\alpha\|x\| + \gamma\|e\| \quad (6)$$

The actual control input of the controller on the digital platform is

$$u(t_i) = k(x(t_i)), \forall t \in [t_i, t_{i+1}), i \in \mathbb{N} \quad (7)$$

The control inputs are calculated and updated using the time series parameter t_i. Defining

$$e(t) = x(t_i) - x(t), \forall t \in [t_i, t_{i+1}), i \in \mathbb{N} \quad (8)$$

The system is shaped as a closed-loop system Eq. (4). In an event-triggered control system, the execution is triggered based on an event generated by a system state rule. This mechanism is known as the event-triggered mechanism (ETM). An important consideration in event triggering control is the presence of a minimum interaction time, which must exceed a certain threshold $\varepsilon > 0$. Failure to do so would result in an infinite number of event triggers. General event triggering means two things:

(1) Design an appropriate event trigger law that determines when and how the control action is performed.
(2) Create a suitable control law that considers the stability properties of the system convergence, tracking performance, and other relevant aspects to ensure that the controller can quickly and accurately respond to changes in the system state, achieving optimal control results.

3 Controller Design

3.1 Position Controller

The control law for the position system in Eq. (2) needs to be designed virtually:

$$\begin{cases} u_x = u_1(c\phi s\theta c\psi + s\phi s\psi) \\ u_y = u_1(s\phi s\theta c\psi - c\phi s\psi) \\ u_z = u_1 c\phi c\psi \\ u_1 = -\dfrac{f}{m} \end{cases} \quad (9)$$

The description of the positional state model can be rephrased as

$$\begin{cases} \ddot{x} = u_x - \dfrac{k_t \dot{x}}{m} + \dfrac{f_{dx}}{m} \\ \ddot{y} = u_y - \dfrac{k_t \dot{y}}{m} + \dfrac{f_{dy}}{m} \\ \ddot{z} = u_z - g - \dfrac{k_t \dot{z}}{m} + \dfrac{f_{dz}}{m} \end{cases} \quad (10)$$

The position tracking error is defined as

$$\begin{cases} e_x = x - x_d \\ e_y = y - y_d \\ e_z = z - z_d \end{cases} \quad (11)$$

where the command for tracking quadrotor's position is $x_r = \dot{x}_d - c_x e_x$, $y_r = \dot{y}_d - c_y e_y$, $z_r = \dot{z}_d - c_z e_z$. $c_i > 0$ $(i = x, y, z)$ is constant gain. Based on Lyapunov stability theory and backstepping method, the sliding mode controller is designed as

$$\begin{cases} u_x = \frac{k_t \dot{x}}{m} + \ddot{x}_d - c_x \dot{e}_x - e_x \\ -K_1 s_x - \eta_1 \text{sgn} s_x \\ u_y = \frac{k_t \dot{y}}{m} + \ddot{y}_d - c_y \dot{e}_y - e_y \\ -K_2 s_y - \eta_2 \text{sgn} s_y \\ u_z = \frac{k_t \dot{z}}{m} + \ddot{z}_d - c_z \dot{e}_z - e_z \\ +g - K_3 s_z - \eta_3 \text{sgn} s_z \end{cases} \quad (12)$$

The sliding mode surface of the position system is given by $s_x = \dot{x} - x_r$, $s_y = \dot{y} - y_r$, $s_z = \dot{z} - z_r$. K_i is the non-negative gain. η_i is larger than the corresponding perturbation of each subsystem. Set the Lyapunov function of the system as

$$V = \frac{1}{2}(e_x^2 + e_y^2 + e_z^2 + s_x^2 + s_y^2 + s_z^2) \quad (13)$$

The derivation of (13) and the introduction of virtual control inputs result in:

$$\dot{V} = s_x(\ddot{x} + c_x \dot{e}_x - \ddot{x}_d) - c_x e_x^2 + e_x s_x \\ + s_y(\ddot{y} + c_y \dot{e}_y - \ddot{y}_d) - c_y e_y^2 + e_y s_y \\ + s_z(\ddot{z} + c_z \dot{e}_z - \ddot{z}_d) - c_z e_z^2 + e_z s_z \quad (14)$$

By substituting the position system Eq. (10) and the control law Eq. (12) into equation Eq. (14), the following is obtained:

$$\dot{V} = s_x \frac{f_{dx}}{m} - c_x e_x^2 - K_1 s_x^2 - \eta_1 |s_x| \\ -c_y e_y^2 + s_y \frac{f_{dy}}{m} - K_2 s_y^2 - \eta_2 |s_y| - \\ c_z e_z^2 + s_z \frac{f_{dz}}{m} - K_3 s_z^2 - \eta_3 |s_z| \leqslant \\ |s_x||\frac{f_{dx}}{m}| - c_x e_x^2 - K_1 s_x^2 - \eta_1 |s_x| \\ -c_y e_y^2 + |s_y||\frac{f_{dy}}{m}| - K_2 s_y^2 - \eta_2 |s_y| - \\ c_z e_z^2 + |s_z||\frac{f_{dz}}{m}| - K_3 s_z^2 - \eta_3 |s_z| \leqslant 0 \quad (15)$$

For the system to be asymptotically stable, by Liapunov stability theorem, a positive definite scalar function must exist that satisfies the negative determination of its first-order derivative function. The system is asymptotically stable when $c_i, k_i > 0$ and $\dot{V} < 0$.

3.2 Attitude Controller

The quadrotor's dynamical model is characterized by underactuated, with coupling between the attitude and position control systems. The expected Euler angles for the attitude subsystem tracking are extracted from the position subsystem.

$$\psi_d = \arctan(\frac{s\phi_d c\phi_d u_x - c^2\phi_d u_y}{u_z}) \tag{16}$$

Assuming that the angle θ varies within the range of $\left(-\frac{\pi}{2}, \frac{\pi}{2}\right)$.

$$\theta_d = \frac{c\phi_d(c\phi_d u_x + s\phi_d u_y)}{u_z} \tag{17}$$

The vector $\Phi_d = [\phi\ \theta\ \psi]^T$ as the desired attitude angle. The attitude tracking error is $\Phi e = \Phi - \Phi_d$. The design attitude sliding mode surface function is

$$s(t) = J\Phi_e(t) + \dot{\Phi}_e(t) = [s_\phi\ s_\theta\ s_\psi]^T \tag{18}$$

J is the positive diagonal matrix. Defining the attitude angle tracking error as

$$e_\Phi(t) = \Phi_e(t_i) - \Phi_e(t), \forall t \in [t_i, t_{i+1}) \tag{19}$$

Assume that $\Phi_d, \dot{\Phi}_d, \ddot{\Phi}_d$ is all bounded. Thus, consider the control law for the attitude subsystem as

$$\begin{aligned}u(t) &= (AC\Phi_E(t_i) + k\mathrm{sgn}(s(t_i))) \\ &-(AB)^{-1}, \Phi_E(t_i) = \left[\Phi_e(t_i), \dot{\Phi}_e(t_i)\right]^T\end{aligned} \tag{20}$$

The event-triggere d condition is

$$\|A\|\,\|C\|\,\|E_\Phi(t)\| < \alpha \tag{21}$$

where:

$$A = [J\ I_{3\times 3}],\ B = [0\ I_{3\times 3}]^T,\ C = [0\ C_1],$$
$$C_1 = [I_{3\times 3}\ -lKI\ ]^T, E_\Phi(t) = [e_\Phi(t)\ \dot{e}_\Phi(t)]^T.$$

K is the controller gain matrix, I is the rotational inertia matrix, and l is the radius length of the quadrotor.

The control law Eq. (20) enables the attitude tracking error to be stabilised to a range around $s(t) = 0$. To prove the existence of the slip mode surface, take the Lyapunov function as

$$V(t) = \frac{1}{2} s^T(t)s(t) \tag{22}$$

Derivation of V to introduce an event triggered sliding mode control law

$$\begin{aligned}\dot{V} &= k\mathrm{sgn}(s(t_i)) - s^T(t)(ACE_\Phi(t)- \\ &D_\Phi + lKI\dot{\Phi}_d + \ddot{\Phi}_d)\end{aligned} \tag{23}$$

If $t = t_i$, we get $\dot{V} < 0$ and the attitude subsystem is asymptotically stable. It can be obtained based on the event triggering conditions, attitude tracking error and controller gain.

$$\dot{V} < s^{\mathrm{T}}(t_i))\mathrm{sgn}(s(t_i)) - \eta(s^{\mathrm{T}}(t) - \\ s^{\mathrm{T}}(t_i) = -\eta s(t_i) + \eta\alpha \parallel C \parallel^{-1} \tag{24}$$

When $\|s(t_i)\| > \alpha\|C\|^{-1}$, the controller is updated when the event trigger condition is met, and the trigger time minimum interval must be a non-negative constant to prevent the Zeno phenomenon. $T = \min\{t_{i+1} - t_i\} > 0$. The conditions that trigger the event and the ranges within which the parameters are bound.

$$T_i \geqslant \frac{1}{\|C\|}\ln(1+ \parallel A \parallel^{-1} \parallel C \parallel^{-1} \\ \frac{\alpha\|C\|}{\rho(\|\Phi_{\mathrm{E}}(t_i)\|) + \beta}) \geqslant 0 \tag{25}$$

Therefore, the existence of a normal number lower bound on the time interval between neighbouring event triggers avoids the Zeno phenomenon of infinite triggers in a finite period of time.

4 Simulation Results and Analysis

In this paper, we validate the proposed control algorithm through a MATLAB/Simulink model, employing parameters detailed in Table 1 to represent the quadrotor dynamics.

Table 1. Quadrotor Model Parameters

Variant	Value
m(kg)	2
l(m)	0.315
g(m·s^{-2})	9.81
I_x, I_y(Nm·s^2/rad)	0.0820
I_z(Nm·s^2/rad)	0.1377
k_t(N(m/s)$^{-2}$)	0.01

The quadrotor's initial position coordinates and attitude angles are all set to 0. The desired position is $p_{\mathrm{d}} = [1.44\cos t, 1.44\sin t, 1.5t - 1]^{\mathrm{T}}$ and $p'_{\mathrm{d}} = [-2\sin t, 3\cos t, 3sin^2 t + 1]^{\mathrm{T}}$. The desired yaw angle is $\psi_{\mathrm{d}} = 0.1\pi sint - 1$,

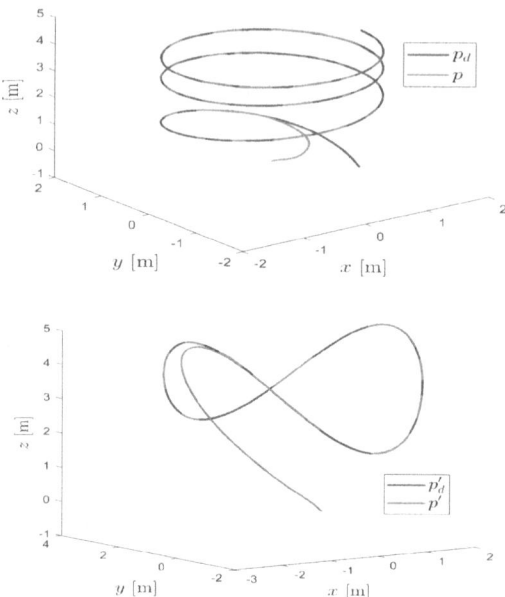

Fig. 2. 3D trajectory tracking effect

$\psi'_d = \sin t$. Expect roll and pitch to be 0. Positional sliding mode surface coefficient $c_i = 5$ ($i = 1, 2, 3$), controller Gains $K_i = 5$, $\eta_i = 0.1$. Sliding mode surface factor of attitude ring is 0.5, controller gain $K = \text{diag}\{0.5, 0.5, 2\}$, event trigger limit $\alpha = 0.85$.

The simulation time is set to 30 s and the sampling period is 0.0015 s. Figures 2 and 3 display the simulation results of two sets of quadrotor tracking 3D spatial trajectories to verify the tracking effect of the designed controller. The results indicate that during take-off, the quadrotor's position and attitude change significantly compared to the initial position. However, during the tracking process, the parameters change gradually and smoothly along the trajectory, resulting in effective tracking after approximately 3 s.

Figure 4 displays the attitude angle tracking of both groups. The reference signal is accurately tracked, and the pitch and roll angles remain relatively stable with slight fluctuations around 0 after approximately 3 s. The p'_d group exhibits a slight periodic fluctuation, but the magnitude is small. The yaw angle varies smoothly with the desired command. During the 30-second simulation, a total of 30,000 samples were taken. The event triggering condition was triggered 4586 times, and the event interval scatter is shown in Fig. 5. To reduce the number

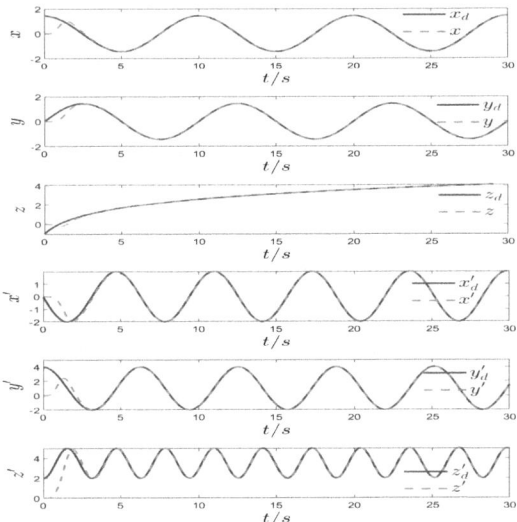

Fig. 3. Trajectory tracking in x, y, z

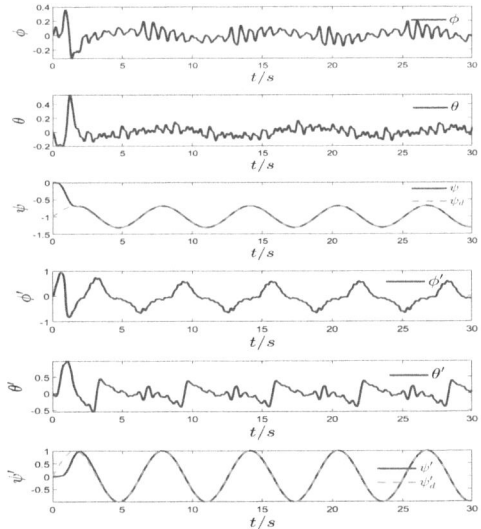

Fig. 4. Attitude angle tracking curve

of samples by 84.71% without affecting the control performance of the trajectory tracking system. This dramatically reduces the amount of controller data transmission and saves communication resources.

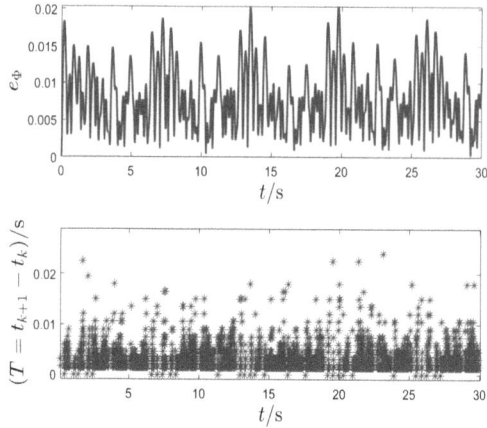

Fig. 5. Event-triggered scatterplot

5 Conclusions

The study introduces an event-triggered sliding mode control approach to address trajectory tracking for a quadrotor UAV subject to limited resources. The control law is updated solely when the error exceeds a predefined limit. System stability and tracking error bounds are established via Lyapunov analysis, eliminating the occurrence of Zeno behavior.

The simulations confirm that the suggested control scheme effectively reduces the number of controller updates while ensuring the quadrotor's tracking performance. This reduces the controller computation and improves system resource utilization. In the future, we will consider event-triggered control methods that can maintain the stability of quadrotor trajectory tracking in the presence of nonlinear complex perturbation systems and external disturbances.

References

1. Yao, H., Qin, R., Chen, X.: Unmanned aerial vehicle for remote sensing applications-a review. Remote Sens. **11**(12), 1443 (2019)
2. Huang, X., Ralescu, A.L., Gao, H., Huang, H.: A survey on the application of fuzzy systems for underactuated systems. Proc. Inst. Mech. Eng. **233**(3), 217–244 (2019)
3. Liu, G., Li, B., Duan, G.: An optimal FASA approach for UAV trajectory tracking control. Guidance Navig. Control **3**(03), 2350015 (2023)
4. Huang, J., Wang, W., Wen, C., Li, G.: Adaptive event-triggered control of nonlinear systems with controller and parameter estimator triggering. IEEE Trans. Autom. Control **65**(1), 318–324 (2020)
5. Najm, A.A., Azar, A.T., Ibraheem, I.K., Humaidi, A.J.: A nonlinear PID controller design for 6-DOF unmanned aerial vehicles. In: Unmanned Aerial Systems, pp. 315–343 (2021)
6. Peng, C., Li, F.: A survey on recent advances in event-triggered communication and control. Inf. Sci. **457**, 113–125 (2018)

7. Zhang, B., Sun, X., Lv, M., Liu, S.: Distributed coordinated control for fixed-wing UAVs with dynamic event-triggered communication. IEEE Trans. Veh. Technol. **71**(5), 4665–4676 (2022)
8. Bisheban, M., Lee, T., et al.: Geometric adaptive control with neural networks for a quadrotor in wind fields. IEEE Trans. Control Syst. Technol. **29**(4), 1533–1548 (2021)

Emotion Loss Attacking: Adversarial Attack Perception for Skeleton Based on Multi-dimensional Features

Feng Liu[1(✉)], Qing Xu[2], and Qijian Zheng[1]

[1] East China Normal University, Shanghai, China
lsttoy@163.com
[2] Beijing University of Posts and Telecommunications, Beijing, China

Abstract. Adversarial attack on skeletal motion is a hot topic. However, existing researches only consider part of dynamic features when measuring distance between skeleton graph sequences, which results in poor imperceptibility. To this end, we propose a novel adversarial attack method to attack action recognizers for skeletal motions. Firstly, our method systematically proposes a dynamic distance function to measure the difference between skeletal motions. Meanwhile, we innovatively introduce emotional features for complementary information. In addition, we use Alternating Direction Method of Multipliers(ADMM) to solve the constrained optimization problem, which generates adversarial samples with better imperceptibility to deceive the classifiers. Experiments show that our method is effective on multiple action classifiers and datasets. When the perturbation magnitude measured by l norms is the same, the dynamic perturbations generated by our method are much lower than that of other methods. What's more, we are the first to prove the effectiveness of emotional features, and provide a new idea for measuring the distance between skeletal motions.

Keywords: adversarial attack · skeleton · optimization · emotion loss attacking · computational perception

1 Introduction

Affective computing [1] is one of the hotspots in today's AI research, which includes and is not limited to the research of facial emotion recognition [2], speech emotion recognition [3,4], gesture emotion recognition [5], multimodal emotion recognition [6,7] and some personality recognition [8] based on dynamic expression recognition [9] and other related technologies [10]. As the research of skeleton-based action recognition is becoming more and more popular, its robustness in practical application scenarios has attracted extensive attention and exploration [11–13]. Researches in adversarial attack has revealed that deep learning methods are vulnerable to carefully devised data perturbations. Adversarial attacks on static data such as images and text have been widely studied

[14], but the research on time-series data especially skeleton data is relatively lack and immature [15–17]. The adversarial attack on skeleton sequences mainly faces two challenges: low redundancy and perceptual sensitivity, which is unique from static data and other time-series data. A skeletal motion is composed of joints and physical relationships among joints. That means the action domain of skeletal motions is limited, and the requirements of imperceptibility for adversarial samples become more stringent. A skeletal motion usually has less than 100 Degrees of freedom (Dofs), much lower than images/meshes. What's more, any sparsity based perturbation (on a single joint or a single frame) will greatly affect the dynamics (leading to jitter or bone-length violation) and is very obvious to the observer.

There are many typical attack methods for classified networks which can be divided into gradient based and optimization based. These methods are mostly based on images [18]that are also called European structure. However, skeletal motion is with non European structure. That means the distance measurement of skeletal motion can not be simply measured by l0, l2 and others. However, the existing researches [19,20] don't consider it and only use perturbations magnitude as the metric to judge the imperceptibility [20], which is unreasonable for skeletal motions. Therefore, we take the unique dynamics into consideration comprehensively when generating adversarial samples.

Research on emotion recognition is becoming more and more popular, such as speech-based emotion recognition [21], text-based emotion recognition [22], multimodal emotion recognition [23,24] and action-based emotion recognition [25]. Previous studies have revealed that emotion can be reflected from action. Moreover, the dynamic features mentioned earlier can measure the visual difference between the two samples, and the emotional features can reveal the logical relationship between skeleton joints. Therefore, we try to introduce emotional feature as one of the indicators to measure the difference between samples, and explore the impact of emotional features.

To this end, in this paper we propose an adversarial attack method for skeletal motions. Firstly, we define a novel distance function based on multi-dimensional features that considers dynamics and introduce emotional features for the first time. The distance considers spatial dynamic such as bone length and bone angle and temporal dynamic like speed. In addition, we use Alternating Direction Method of Multipliers(ADMM) to ensure the imperceptibility. Our proposed attack method is evaluated on three kinds of state-of-the-art models. Extensive evaluations show that our attack method can achieve 100% success rate with almost no violation of the constraints mentioned above. To summarize, the contributions of this paper are as follows:

(1) We define a novel distance method based on multi-dimensional features to measure skeletal motions, which includes dynamic distance and innovatively incorporate emotional features as complementary information.
(2) We propose an effective optimization algorithm based on Alternating Direction Method of Multipliers(ADMM) to solve the primal constrained problem,

which generates adversarial skeletal motion samples with perturbations as few as possible.
(3) We fully evaluate multiple state-of-the-art models and multiple datasets and verify that the adversarial samples generated by ours can successfully deceive models with fewer perturbations and lower imperceptibility.

2 Methodology

Given a skeleton sample x, l is the predicted label of x of a trained classifier. We denote $\Theta(x)$ as the result of the probability of each class before softmax layer and F as softmax function. We aim to find minimum perturbation added

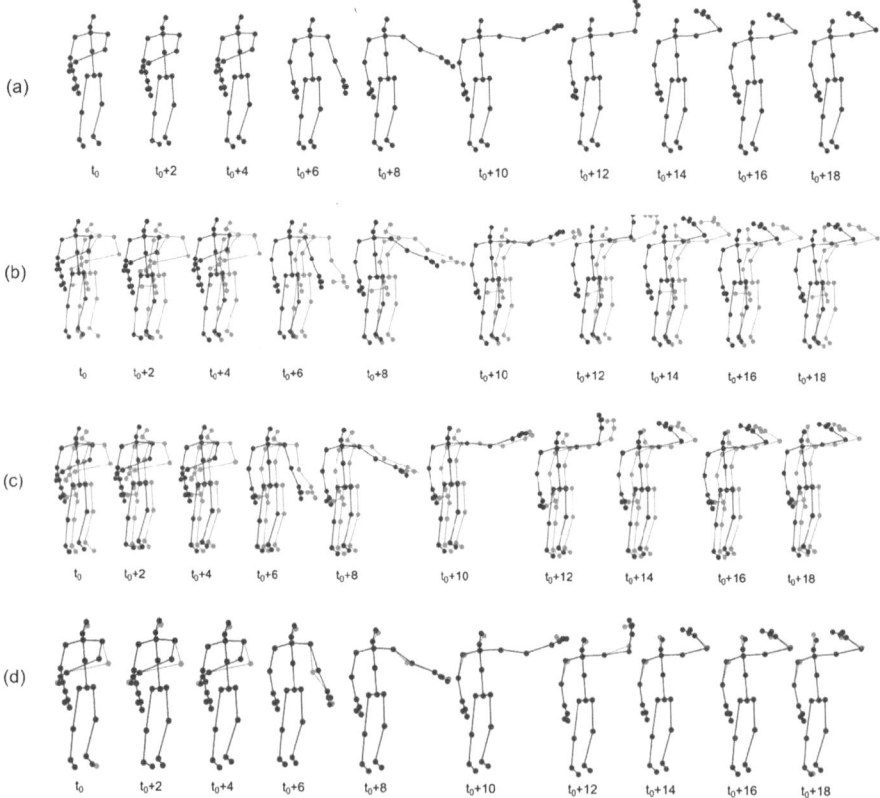

Fig. 1. Visual comparison. The green joints represent the original sample and the red ones represent the adversarial sample. (a) shows the original sample, (b) shows attack results of C&W, (c) shows attack results of SMART, (d) shows attack results of our method. (Color figure online)

to original sample to get adversarial sample x' and $F(\Theta(x)) \neq F(\Theta(x'))$. The problem can be formulated as:

$$\begin{aligned} min \quad & D(x, x') \\ subject\ to \quad & F(\Theta(x')) = l', x' \in [0,1]^n \end{aligned} \qquad (1)$$

where D is the distance function to measure original sample and adversarial sample, l' is the predicted label of adversarial sample x' and $l' \neq l$ is a hard constraint. The hard constraint of classification is defined according to different attack modes. In addition, we use emotion feature as supplementary expression of skeletal motion.

2.1 Skeleton-Based Dynamic Distance

For the motion $m = \{m_0, m_1, \cdots, m_t\}$, m_t at time t consists of not only 3D coordinates of joints but the connected topological structure. A skeleton has its dynamic information and we can represent dynamics of a skeleton from spatial and temporal aspects.

From spatial perspective, we need static and dynamic information. To ensure imperceptibility bone lengths should remain the same in adversarial samples. So we use bone length as static spatial dynamic constraint. A bone corresponds to two joints so a bone can be represented as a vector $B = (x_s - x_t, y_s - y_t, z_s - z_t)$ where (x_s, y_s, z_s) is coordinate of source joint and (x_t, y_t, z_t) is target joint. In this regard, length of the i_{th} bone at the t_{th} frame is defined as $B_i^t = \sqrt{(x_s - x_t)^2 + (y_s - y_t)^2 + (z_s - z_t)^2}$. Normally, the length of the bone should be the same between original sample and adversarial sample. It can be represented as $b(x, x') = |B_i^t - B_i'^t|/B_i^t$ where B_i^t and $B_i'^t$ represent the original sample and the adversarial sample respectively.

We use angle between bones as measurement of change of skeletons. Every two connected bones form an angle, and the change of angles means the extent of bone rotation. So we introduce angle constraint into skeleton dynamic distance. To avoid gradient explosion, we compute change of the i_{th} angle at t frame A_i^t by [12]. Similar to bone length, we use function $a(x, x')$ to measure changes of angles.

From temporal perspective, it is necessary to ensure temporal smooth of adversarial samples. So we introduce joint's speed as an index of temporal measurement. We can estimate speed of the i_{th} joint at frame t by the Euclidean distance between two consecutive temporal frames. The speed of the i_{th} joint at frame t is computed as $S_i^t = \sqrt{(x_i^{t+1} - x_i^t)^2 + (y_i^{t+1} - y_i^t)^2 + (z_i^{t+1} - z_i^t)^2}$. The measure is represented as $s(x, x') = |S_i^t - S_i'^t|/S_i^t$ where S_i^t and $S_i'^t$ represent the joint of original sample and adversarial sample respectively. Similar to spatial constraints, ε_s is maximum change value.

Algorithm 1. Generating adversarial samples

1: **Input:** original sample x, maximum numbers of iterations I, Classification Loss Function C, Dynamic Distance Function D_d, Emotion Distance Function D_e
2: **Initialization:** $x'_0 = x$, Lagrangian Variable: λ
3: **while** $i \leq I - 1$ **do**
4: $\quad x'(i+1) = argmin_x L(x'(i), \lambda(i))$;
5: $\quad l_d, l_e, l_c = D_d(x'(i+1)), D_e(x'(i+1)), C(x'(i+1))$;
6: $\quad l_c = \lambda \times l_c + \frac{\gamma}{2}(||l_c||_2^2)$;
7: $\quad loss = l_d + l_e + l_c$;
8: $\quad$ Backward(loss);
9: $\quad \lambda(i+1) = \lambda(i) + \gamma C(x'(i+1))$;
10: **end while**

2.2 Classification Loss

Untargeted Setting. In mode of untargeted attack, $F(\Theta(x')) \neq l$ means that predicted label of the classifier can be any label other than the ground truth l. That means maximum value of possibility must not be l, which can be represented as $max(\Theta(x')) > \Theta_l(x')$. Based on this, We can denote classification loss as $max(\Theta(x')) - \Theta_l(x') > conf$ where $conf$ is expected value of wrong prediction of classifiers. Note that the inequality constraints in the original problem impose inequality constraints on the corresponding Lagrangian variables in the dual problem. So we convert inequality constraint to equality constraint as:

$$max(\Theta_l(x') - max(\Theta(x')) + conf) = 0 \qquad (2)$$

Targeted Setting. Under the setting of targeted attack, we aim to get $F(\Theta(x')) = l_t$. That is to say, $max(\Theta(x')) = \Theta_{l_t}(x')$. So we can use $\Theta_{l_t}(x') - max_{l \neq l_t}(\Theta(x')) > conf$ as classification loss. The equation form is expressed as follows:

$$max(\Theta(x')) - \Theta_{l_t}(x') = 0 \qquad (3)$$

2.3 Emotion Loss

In addition to dynamics, skeletal motions may also contain emotional features. Therefore, we innovatively introduce emotions as non-dynamic features to measure the distance. Specifically, we use the emotion classifier in literature [26] to extract the emotional features of skeletal motions. The model embeds the skeletal motion sequence into images for training, and obtains the predicted emotional features through four group convolution. Group convolution allows the network to learn independently from different parts of the input, so as to determine the joint interval that has the greatest impact on the final category. We put gait-based skeletal motions and the generated adversarial samples into the pre-training model to obtain the distance loss of emotion in non-dynamic features. We use E as emotional features. The specific formula is $e(x, x') = ||E(x) - E(x')||$.

2.4 Optimal Dual Method

The objective function of the constrained optimization problem formulated as Eq. 1. $D(x, x^{'})$ is distance function and $D(x, x^{'}) = b(x, x^{'}) + a(x, x^{'}) + s(x, x^{'}) + e(x, x^{'})$. The hard constraint is loss of classification as denoted in Eqs. 2 and 3. In optimization theory, the optimization problem of objective function under constraints can be transformed into a corresponding dual problem. Due to its strong duality, the solution of the original problem can be obtained by solving the dual problem. We introduce the Alternating Direction Method of Multiplier to solve the dual problem. We denote Lagrange expression as $L(x, \lambda) = b(x, x^{'}) + a(x, x^{'}) + s(x, x^{'}) + e(x, x^{'}) + \lambda C(l, l^{'}) + \frac{\gamma}{2}||C(l, l^{'})||_2^2$ where λ is Lagrange multiplier and C is classification loss. In order to effectively find the local optimal solution, we use Adam optimization algorithm for Adam optimization algorithm always converges faster than vanilla SGD. The process of generating adversarial samples is described as Algorithm 1.

3 Experiments

3.1 Models and Datasets

NTU RGB+D consists of 25 joint points in each skeleton. The original paper recommends two benchmarks: (1) Cross-subject: the subject in training set and validation set are different. (2) Cross-view: training set captured by camera 2 and 3 and validation set captured by camera 1. **Kinetics-400** [27] contains 18 joints in each skeleton. The adversarial samples of following experiments are generated on the validation set on two datasets.

We select HCN [28], 2 s AGCN [29], SGN [30] and investigate their vulnerability under different scenarios. HCN [28] has achieved state-of-the-art performance before GCN related work and 2 s AGCN [29] is an effective GCN-based model. SGN [30] introduces semantics for the first time and achieves great performance.

3.2 Evaluation Metrics

For the adversarial attack method, the effectiveness refers to the extent to which the method can provide "successful" adversarial samples. On this premise, we evaluates the quality of adversarial samples from two aspects: misclassification and imperceptibility.

(1) *Misclassification* refers to the degree of deception of adversarial samples, reflected in the following indicators.
   Attack Success Rate(SR), that is, the proportion of adversarial samples wrongly classified (in untarget mode) or wrongly classified to the specified class (in target mode). $SR_{UA} = \frac{1}{N}\sum_{j=0}^{N} sum(F(x) \neq l_t)$ is under untarget mode and $SR_{TA} = \frac{1}{N}\sum_{j=0}^{N} sum(F(x) = l_t)$ is under target mode.

(2) *Imperceptibility*. We defined four evaluation metrics for the original sample x and adversarial sample x': the average deviation percentage of bone length $\triangle \mathbf{B}/\mathbf{B} = \frac{\sum_{i=0}^{N}(\sum_{j=0}^{M}(B_j^i - B_j'^i)/B_j^i)}{N \times M}$, the average deviation percentage of bone angle $\triangle \mathbf{A}/\mathbf{A}$, the deviation percentage of joint speed $\triangle \mathbf{S}/\mathbf{S} = \frac{\sum_{j=0}^{N}||x_s - x_s'||_2}{F \times N \times O}$ and the l2 distance between the original sample and adversarial sample $\mathbf{l2} = \frac{\sum_{j=0}^{N}||x-x'||_2}{F \times N}$ where N is the total number of adversarial samples, F is the total number of frames in a motion and O and M are the total number of joints and frames in a skeleton.

3.3 Attack Results

Misclassification. The quantitative results of untargeted attack mode are shown in Table 1. Our method achieves high success rates across different datasets and target models. For targeted attack mode, results are shown in Table 2. It is not surprising to turn 'reading' into 'writing'. Therefore we choose 'drinking water' as targeted skeletal motion class for obvious differences are existed. For classifier model 2 s AGCN and SGN, we can see that the adversarial samples successfully deceives the two models but more perturbations are added to the adversarial samples to deceive SGN compared with 2 s AGCN. This shows that even though the network of SGN is relatively simple, its defense capability exceeds that of 2 s AGCN. What's more, it is also proved that semantics can greatly enhance the ability of network to learn logical and dynamic features of skeletal motions.

Table 1. The results of our method with untargeted attack mode on NTU RGB+D.

Models	γ	NTU RGB+D CV					NTU RGB+D CS				
		$\triangle$B/B	$\triangle$A/A	$\triangle$S/S	SR	l2	$\triangle$B/B	$\triangle$A/A	$\triangle$S/S	SR	l2
HCN	0.1	0.9%	4.2%	3.2%	100%	0.26	0.8%	4.1%	3.3%	100%	0.24
	1.0	1.3%	6.7%	4.2%	100%	0.21	1.3%	6.7%	4.2%	100%	0.21
	10.0	2.4%	15.1%	7.5%	100%	0.22	2.3%	13.7%	7.1%	100%	0.20
2 s AGCN	0.1	0.4%	2.5%	1.8%	100%	0.07	0.6%	2.8%	1.6%	100%	0.06
	1.0	0.6%	2.7%	2.2%	100%	0.08	0.5%	2.1%	1.9%	100%	0.07
	10.0	2.3%	12.0%	6.9%	100%	0.15	1.4%	7.8%	4.1%	100%	0.12
SGN	0.1	0.6%	3.1%	2.1%	100%	0.15	0.8%	3.0%	1.8%	100%	0.14
	1.0	0.9%	4.8%	2.4%	100%	0.12	0.9%	4.9%	1.7%	100%	0.12
	10.0	2.6%	12.6%	7.5%	100%	0.18	1.8%	10.6%	4.5%	100%	0.13

Imperceptibility. Our method obtains adversarial samples with much lower perturbation as shown in Table 4. Therefore, it is also proved that the dynamic

Table 2. The results of our method on targeted attack mode on NTU RGB+D with cross view setting.

	△B/B	△A/A	△S/S	SR	l2
HCN	3.1%	15.4%	7.5%	100%	0.62
2s AGCN	1.1%	4.8%	3.1%	100%	0.21
SGN	2.9%	15%	4.2%	100%	0.44
AeS-GCN [5]	**10.5%**	**41.2%**	**21.9%**	**73.9%**	**5.92**

distance proposed is more effective than l2 distance for skeletal motions. Compared with the existing methods, strict perceptual control is used as the optimization target problem to improve the imperceptibility. Taking the adversarial sample generated based on SGN as an example in Fig. 1, we sample 10 frames from sequence for visual display. Since the previous results show that SGN produces greater perturbations when it is successfully attacked. The label of original sample is 'throwing' and after attack the predicted label is 'brushing teeth' under targeted attack mode. When comparing two samples carefully, we can find that differences are existed in some joints. However, when two samples are played as video sequences, differences are hard to find. In addition, we also find that the perturbations added to adversarial samples are concentrated on arms and hands, which contain obvious dynamics. This may remind us that we should consider to reduce sensitivity to special data when designing classifiers.

Table 3. The effectiveness of emotional features on HCN on NTU RGB+D with cross view setting.

	△B/B	△A/A	△S/S	SR	l2
Ours w emotion	1.3%	6.7%	4.2%	100%	0.21
Ours w/o emotion	1.2%	7.1%	4.8%	100%	0.24

We also verify the role of emotional features. Table 3 shows the effectiveness of emotional features. Emotional features can control the perception of adversarial samples from overall perspective. However, the improvement is not obvious, which may be due to the accuracy of the emotion recognizer used. Therefore, it can be expected that with in-depth study of emotion recognition, emotional features will be better integrated.

Table 4. The results of C&W on HCN on NTU RGB+D.

		$\Delta B/B$	$\Delta A/A$	SR	l2
Untargeted	NTU CV	4.67%	24.1%	100%	0.28
	NTU CS	4.09%	21.1%	100%	0.24
Targeted	NTU CV	8.8%	46.8%	100%	0.51
	NTU CS	9.5%	50.7%	100%	0.52

4 Conclusion

To summarize, in order to explore the vulnerability of skeleton-based action recognizers, we propose a novel attack method for based on multi-dimensional features. We fuse dynamics and emotional features of skeletal motions and generate successful adversarial samples based on ADMM. A large number of experiments show that our method has fewer perturbations and better imperceptibility than other methods. Our method is effective on multiple datasets and the state-of-the-art models. In the future, we will systematically study how to improve the defense ability of models to resist attacks.

Acknowledgements. This work supported by Beijing Key Laboratory of Behavior and Mental Health in School of Psychological and Cognitive Sciences, Peking University. We would also like to thank the colleagues in the CiL lab at East China Normal University for their efforts on this project, and the reviewers for their time and hard work.

References

1. Picard, R.W.: Affective Computing. MIT Press (2000)
2. Zhang, J., Liu, F., Zhou, A.: Off-tanet: a lightweight neural micro-expression recognizer with optical flow features and integrated attention mechanism. In: Pacific Rim International Conference on Artificial Intelligence, pp. 266–279. Springer (2021)
3. Liu, F., Shen, S.-Y., Zi-Wang, F., Wang, H.-Y., Zhou, A.-M., Qi, J.-Y.: LGCCT: a light gated and crossed complementation transformer for multimodal speech emotion recognition. Entropy **24**(7), 1010 (2022)
4. Shen, S., Liu, F., Zhou, A.: Mingling or misalignment? temporal shift for speech emotion recognition with pre-trained representations. In: ICASSP 2023 - 2023 IEEE International Conference on Acoustics, Speech and Signal Processing (ICASSP), pp. 1–5 (2023)
5. Qing, X., LiU, F., Ziwang, F., Zhou, A., Qi, J.: AES-GCN: attention-enhanced semantic-guided graph convolutional networks for skeleton-based action recognition. Comput. Animation Virtual Worlds **33**(3–4), e2070 (2022)
6. Ziwang, F., Liu, F., Qing, X., Xiangling, F., Qi, J.: LMR-CBT: learning modality-fused representations with CB-transformer for multimodal emotion recognition from unaligned multimodal sequences. Front. Comp. Sci. **18**(4), 184314 (2024)

7. Liu, F., Fu, Z., Wang, Y., Zheng, Q.: TACFN: transformer-based adaptive cross-modal fusion network for multimodal emotion recognition. CAAI Artif. Intell. Res. **2** (2023)
8. Liu, F., et al.: OPO-FCM: a computational affection based OCC-pad-ocean federation cognitive modeling approach. IEEE Trans. Comput. Soc. Syst. (2022)
9. Wang, H., et al.: Rethinking the learning paradigm for dynamic facial expression recognition. In: Proceedings of the IEEE/CVF Conference on Computer Vision and Pattern Recognition (CVPR), pp. 17958–17968 (2023)
10. Liu, F., et al.: EvoGAN: an evolutionary computation assisted GAN. Neurocomputing **469**, 81–90 (2022)
11. Liu, J., Akhtar, N., Mian, A.: Adversarial attack on skeleton-based human action recognition. IEEE Trans. Neural Netw. Learn. Syst. (2020)
12. Zheng, T., Liu, S., Chen, C., Yuan, J., Li, B., Ren, K.: Towards understanding the adversarial vulnerability of skeleton-based action recognition. arXiv preprint arXiv:2005.07151 (2020)
13. Bai, X., Yang, M., Liu, Z.: On the robustness of skeleton detection against adversarial attacks. Neural Netw. **132**, 416–427 (2020)
14. Xiao, C., Yang, D., Li, B., Deng, J., Liu, M.: Meshadv: adversarial meshes for visual recognition. In: Proceedings of the IEEE/CVF Conference on Computer Vision and Pattern Recognition, pp. 6898–6907 (2019)
15. Karim, F., Majumdar, S., Darabi, H.: Adversarial attacks on time series. IEEE Trans. Pattern Anal. Mach. Intell. (2020)
16. Fawaz, H.I., Forestier, G., Weber, J., Idoumghar, L., Muller, P.A.: Adversarial attacks on deep neural networks for time series classification. In: 2019 International Joint Conference on Neural Networks (IJCNN), pp. 1–8. IEEE (2019)
17. Jia, S., Ma, C., Song, Y., Yang, X.: Robust tracking against adversarial attacks. In: European Conference on Computer Vision, pp. 69–84. Springer (2020)
18. Xiao, C., Li, B., Zhu, J.Y., He, W., Liu, M., Song, D.: Generating adversarial examples with adversarial networks. arXiv preprint arXiv:1801.02610 (2018)
19. Diao, Y., Shao, T., Yang, Y.L., Zhou, K., Wang, H.: Basar: black-box attack on skeletal action recognition. In: Proceedings of the IEEE/CVF Conference on Computer Vision and Pattern Recognition, pp. 7597–7607 (2021)
20. Wang, H., et al.: Understanding the robustness of skeleton-based action recognition under adversarial attack. In: Proceedings of the IEEE/CVF Conference on Computer Vision and Pattern Recognition, pp. 14656–14665 (2021)
21. Morais, E., Hoory, R., Zhu, W., Gat, I., Damasceno, M., Aronowitz, H.: Speech emotion recognition using self-supervised features. In: ICASSP 2022-2022 IEEE International Conference on Acoustics, Speech and Signal Processing (ICASSP) (2021)
22. Li, Y., Bell, P., Lai, C.: Fusing ASR outputs in joint training for speech emotion recognition. arXiv preprint arXiv:2110.15684 (2021)
23. Liu, P., Li, K., Meng, H.: Group gated fusion on attention-based bidirectional alignment for multimodal emotion recognition. arXiv preprint arXiv:2201.06309 (2022)
24. Fu, Z., Liu, F., Xu, Q., Fu, X., Qi, J.: LMR-CBT: learning modality-fused representations with CB-transformer for multimodal emotion recognition from unaligned multimodal sequences. arXiv preprintarXiv:2112.01697 (2021)
25. Hu, C., Sheng, W., Dong, B., Li, X.: Tntc: two-stream network with transformer-based complementarity for gait-based emotion recognition. arXiv preprint arXiv:2110.13708 (2021)

26. Narayanan, V., Manoghar, B.M., Dorbala, V.S., Manocha, D., Bera, A.: Proxemo: Gait-based emotion learning and multi-view proxemic fusion for socially-aware robot navigation. In: 2020 IEEE/RSJ International Conference on Intelligent Robots and Systems (IROS), pp. 8200–8207. IEEE (2020)
27. Kay, W., et al.: The kinetics human action video dataset. arXiv preprint arXiv:1705.06950 (2017)
28. Li, C., Zhong, Q., Xie, D., Pu, S.: Co-occurrence feature learning from skeleton data for action recognition and detection with hierarchical aggregation. arXiv preprint arXiv:1804.06055 (2018)
29. Shi, L., Zhang, Y., Cheng, J., Lu, H.: Two-stream adaptive graph convolutional networks for skeleton-based action recognition. In: Proceedings of the IEEE/CVF conference on Computer Vision and Pattern Recognition, pp. 12026–12035 (2019)
30. Zhang, P., Lan, C., Zeng, W., Xing, J., Xue, J., Zheng, N.: Semantics-guided neural networks for efficient skeleton-based human action recognition. In: Proceedings of the IEEE/CVF Conference on Computer Vision and Pattern Recognition, pp. 1112–1121 (2020)

Method of Ionospheric Delay Positioning Error Correction Based on Transformer Model Prediction

Hongteng Ma[1], Mengying Lin[1(✉)], Die Zou[1], Ziang Wei[1], Zhengke Wen[2], and Zixin Huang[1]

[1] School of Electrical and Information Engineering, Wuhan Institute of Technology, Wuhan, China
{linmengying,huangzx}@wit.edu.cn
[2] School of Mechanical and Electrical Engineering, Wuhan Institute of Technology, Wuhan, China

Abstract. Aiming at the problem of limited ionospheric delay correction accuracy of current single-frequency receiving equipment, this paper proposes an ionospheric delayed positioning error correction method based on Transformer. Firstly, according to the spatiotemporal characteristics of total electron content (TEC) relevant parameters of solar/geomagnetic activities in China surrounding regions, features such as periodicity at various time scales and local spatial correction are designed and conducted, and TEC prediction model is built on the basis of Transformer self-attention mechanism. Next, the TEC grid data are predicted by the Transformer model, following with TEC estimation on arbitrary geographical location by space-time bilinear inverse interpolation. Finally, the ionospheric delay correction is used for pseudorange positioning error compensation and comparing with current ionospheric delay correction method of Klobuchar model, verifying the excellent performance of the proposed method for predicting and correcting positioning errors in advance.

Keywords: Ionospheric delay · TEC prediction · Positioning error · Transformer model

1 Introduction

The ionospheric space is about 60–1000 km from the ground and is a necessary route for transmitting signals from the Global Navigation Satellite System (GNSS). The ionospheric refraction effect produces a delay effect by accelerating the phase velocity of the signal carrier and reducing the velocity of the pseudo-code group, resulting in the distance delay of the pseudo-code and the carrier and resulting in navigation and positioning errors. The ionospheric delay error introduced by the carrier range is small, but it is limited by the cycle jump generated by the ionospheric disturbance and the difficulty in estimating the unknown whole cycle ambiguity [1,2]. The distance above errors caused by the ionosphere are usually in the range of several meters or even a hundred meters and have now become a significant source of error that cannot be ignored in the demand for high-precision navigation and positioning [3]. Weakening the ionospheric delay error as much as possible remains one of the critical concerns in improving the accuracy and precision of navigation and positioning at present.

Some scholars have used various neural network methods to obtain more dimensional TEC temporal and spatial information in this context. Using higher accuracy TEC prediction results provides new and improved optimization ideas for ionospheric delay modeling. It allows single-frequency receivers to enhance higher positioning accuracy than the traditional model [4,5]. For example, literature [6] used the TEC prediction results output from the segmented long and short-term memory model to estimate the ionospheric delay error value, which had more robust convergence and stability in terms of single-point localization accuracy compared with the traditional Klobuchar empirical model and the regional ionospheric grid model. Additionally, literature [7] utilized the TEC predicted by the multilayer perceptual modeling to carry out Brazilian region single-frequency receiver ionospheric delay correction, and the proposed model localized with 27% and 33% reduction in error compared with the effect of the traditional NeQuick G empirical model and grid ionosphere TEC map (GIM) based ionospheric delay correction, respectively.

In summary, Neural network models excel at extracting TEC feature data and enhancing ionospheric delay error correction. However, further research is needed to optimize specific correction techniques for efficient and accurate results.

2 Ionospheric Delay Estimates Based on Transformer Model Predictions

2.1 VTEC Prediction Based on the Transformer Model

In order to reduce the TEC prediction error to improve the accuracy of receiver ionospheric delay estimation, this paper proposes to use the vertical TEC(VTEC) value predicted by the Transformer model, then obtain the VTEC value at any receiver position by inverse distance bilinear interpolation, and finally obtain the ionospheric delay error estimation to correct the receiver pseudorange error. By fully extracting and maximizing the use of TEC temporal periodicity and spatial correlation, embedding the spatial information into the model, and combining the model self-attention mechanism, the method predicts the TEC values for the next 24 h by taking the previous five days' TEC historical data, spatial feature elements and solar/geomagnetic activity-related feature parameters as inputs. Based on the relevant feature information, the feature vector constructed in this paper is shown in the following equation

$$x = \left\{ \begin{array}{l} TEC, SSN, F10.7, Kp, ap, \\ AE, Dst, Lat, Lon \end{array} \right\} \tag{1}$$

where x denotes the feature vector for a particular hour, and Lat and Lon are latitude and longitude, respectively. In the model training, a total of 120 sets of feature vector values for each hour of the first five days are used as feature inputs, that is $\mathbf{X} = \{x_1, x_2, ..., x_{120}\}$, and the corresponding feature label $\mathbf{Y} = \{TEC_1, TEC_2, ..., TEC_{24}\}$ is the TEC prediction for day 6. The model training and test sets are derived from historical data related to the two most recent solar activity cycles, including 1998–2015 and 2016–2018 data, respectively, and each sample contains five days of feature data and the corresponding 6th day of labeled data, with a sliding window step of 1 day between samples, which ultimately yields 6,418 training and 1,096 test samples.

The structure of the TEC prediction model is shown in Fig. 1, and the whole consists of an input layer, N identical Transformer encoding blocks, a linear decoding layer, and an output layer. The right side of the figure shows the detailed structure of each encoding block stacked together, and each block includes two sub-layers. The first sub-layer is the self-attention layer that computes the self-attention information of the model inputs, and the second sub-layer is the Fully Connected Feed-Forward Neural Network (FFN) consisting of the two Fully Connected Linear Layers ReLU activation functions, which is $FFN(x) = \max(0, xW_1 + b_1)W_2 + b_2$, where W and b are the weights and biases of the linear layers, respectively. Each sublayer uses residual network structure and layer normalization operation, and its output is $LayerNorm\,(x + Sublayer\,(x))$, where $Sublayer\,(x)$ is the x-mapping result of the sublayer pair. In the self-attention mechanism of the model, attention is paid to all positions of the entire input sequence by treating each input position as a query. In the self-attention mechanism, each position of the input sequence has a corresponding key and value, and the dot product of the query and all keys for that position is computed to compute the attention score, which is the weight value between that position and all other positions. The values of each position are weighted and summed according to the corresponding attention weights to obtain the output representation of that position. For the first input vector $\mathbf{x}_1$, the output matrix expression obtained by the single-head self-attention mechanism for the input vector is

$$\begin{aligned} x_{1, Attention} &= \text{Attention}(q_1, K, V) \\ &= \sum_{i=1}^{120} \text{softmax}(\frac{q_1 k_i^T}{\sqrt{d_k}}) \nu_i \\ &= \sum_{i=1}^{120} \hat{\alpha}_{1,i} \nu_i \end{aligned} \qquad (2)$$

where $q_1 = x_1 W^Q$, $k_i = x_i W^K$, and $v_i = x_i W^V$, are query vectors, key vectors, and value vectors obtained by linear transformation matrices W^Q, W^K, and W^V, respectively.

Similarly, the corresponding self-attention score vectors can be computed for the other input vectors $x_2, x_3..., x_{120}$, resulting in a self-attention matrix of dimension 120×11, and the self-attention score matrix $X_{Attention} = \{x_{1,Attention}, x_{2,Attention}, ..., x_{120,Attention}\}$. The application of the self-attention mechanism allows the model to be useful for capturing long-range dependencies in the input sequences, and its parallel mode allows the model to achieve efficient computation without losing the feature information of the data before and after. In addition, the multi-head self-attention mechanism can enhance the model's

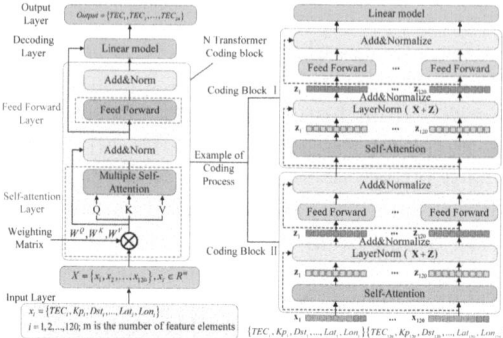

Fig. 1. Self-attention structure of model.

ability to model sequence data by introducing multiple single-head self-attention mechanisms to form multiple subspaces to focus on encoded information in different dimensional spaces. Since the feature vector of the TEC prediction model contains 9, better feature extraction can be achieved by using a single-head self-attention mechanism, for which a single-head self-attention mechanism is set up in each stacked block.

In the encoding process of the TEC prediction model, the model is trained on each set of inputs by batch $batch\_size$ and outputs a matrix of dimension $batch\_size \times 120 \times 9$ after stacked block feature information extraction, and combines and transforms the latter two-dimensional data into a two-dimensional matrix of $batch\_size \times (120 \times 9)$ as input information for the decoding part. According to the TEC prediction task, which is to predict the 24-hour TEC prediction on day 6, a linear transformation is applied to transform each sample input data of each batch into a vector with 24 elements, which is

$$\mathbf{Output} = \mathbf{Z_{in}} \cdot \mathbf{W}_L + \mathbf{b_L} = \begin{bmatrix} TEC_1 \\ TEC_2 \\ \vdots \\ TEC_{24} \end{bmatrix}^T \quad (3)$$

where $\mathbf{Z_{in}}$ is the coded output vector for each sample of dimension $1 \times (120 \times 9)$, $\mathbf{W}_L$ is the linear transformation matrix of dimension $(120 \times 9) \times 24$, and $\mathbf{b_L}$ is the 1×24-bias vector of dimension.

2.2 Ionospheric Delay Estimation Based on VTEC Predictions

After the VTEC value of the grid predicted by the Transformer model, the VTEC prediction value of any geographic location can be obtained by using the spatiotemporal inverse distance bilinear interpolation, based on which the ionospheric delay error at the location of the receiver can be estimated, and the specific steps are as follows:

(1) Calculation of the geocentric angle in the geographic coordinate system of the earth's core.

$$\alpha = \frac{\pi}{2} - Ele - \arcsin\left(\frac{R_e}{R_e + H}\cos(Ele)\right) \quad (4)$$

(2) Calculation of latitude and longitude at the ionospheric pierce point of the satellite signal.

$$\begin{cases} \phi_{IPP} = \arcsin\left(\begin{array}{c}\sin\alpha\cos\varphi_r\cos Az \\ + \cos\alpha\sin\varphi_r\end{array}\right) \\ \lambda_{IPP} = \lambda_r + \arcsin\frac{\sin\alpha\sin Az}{\cos\phi_{IPP}} \end{cases} \quad (5)$$

where λ_r is the geographic longitude of the receiver and φ_{IPP} and λ_{IPP} are calculated from the satellite altitude and azimuth angles observed at the receiver location, respectively.

(3) Interpolated to obtain $VTEC(t, \phi_{IPP}, \lambda_{IPP})$ at the ionospheric pierce point, the ionospheric delay (unit: m) is calculated as

$$d_{iono}^s = \frac{1}{\cos(z')}\frac{40.3\times 10^{16}}{f_i} \times VTEC(t, \phi_{IPP}, \lambda_{IPP}) \quad (6)$$

where $VTEC(t, \phi_{IPP}, \lambda_{IPP})$ can be obtained by interpolating the temporal and spatial latitude based on the VTEC values of the grid around the pierce point in the GIM, and $z' = \arcsin\left(\frac{R_e}{R_e+H}\cos(Ele)\right)$. As shown in Fig. 2 for the relationship between the puncture point and the neighboring TEC map and grid point, the VTEC of the signal received at the time of the receiver at the pierce point $(\phi_{IPP}, \lambda_{IPP})$ is calculated as follows:

(1) By time linear interpolation, the VTEC of the moment is calculated based on the two TEC maps that are near the receiver's moment t. Assuming that $T_i < t < T_{i+1}(i = 0, 1, ..., 24)$, T_i denote the moments corresponding to the ith TEC map, the value of VTEC at moment t is

$$\begin{aligned}VTEC(\phi_{\text{IPP}}, \lambda_{\text{IPP}}, t) \\ = \frac{T_{i+1}-t}{T_{i+1}-T_i}VTEC\begin{pmatrix}\phi_{IPP}, \lambda_{IPP} \\ +\Delta\lambda_i, T_i\end{pmatrix} \\ + \frac{t-T_i}{T_{i+1}-T_i}VTEC\begin{pmatrix}\phi_{IPP}, \lambda_{IPP} \\ +\Delta\lambda_{i+1}, T_{i+1}\end{pmatrix}\end{aligned} \quad (7)$$

where the difference in longitude needs to be adjusted for the time difference, taking into account the rotation of the Earth and the close correlation between the TEC and the position of the Sun; thus, $\Delta\lambda_i = \omega(t - T_i)$, $\Delta\lambda_{i+1} = \omega(t - T_{i+1})$, and $\omega = 2\pi/86400$ is the rotational angular velocity of the Sun relative to the Earth.

(2) After determining the TEC maps of two neighboring moments, spatial inverse distance bilinear interpolation is used to find $(\phi_{IPP}, \lambda_{IPP} + \Delta\lambda_{i+1})$ and $(\phi_{IPP}, \lambda_{IPP} + \Delta\lambda_i)$ in the maps respectively. Taking the ith map as an example, the four surrounding grid points $P_{11}(\phi_1, \lambda_1)$, $P_{12}(\phi_1, \lambda_2)$, $P_{21}(\phi_2, \lambda_1)$ and $P_{22}(\phi_2, \lambda_2)$ latitude and longitude are all subjected to inverse distance linear interpolation, and the VTEC expression at the point $IPP_i(\phi_{IPP}, \lambda_{IPP} + \Delta\lambda_i)$ to be sought is obtained as follows

$$VTEC(\phi, \lambda) \approx \frac{\lambda_2 - \lambda}{\lambda_2 - \lambda_1} \frac{\phi_2 - \phi}{\phi_2 - \phi_1} VTEC(\phi_1, \lambda_1) \\ + \frac{\lambda - \lambda_1}{\lambda_2 - \lambda_1} \frac{\phi_2 - \phi}{\phi_2 - \phi_1} VTEC(\phi_1, \lambda_2) \\ + \frac{\lambda_2 - \lambda}{\lambda_2 - \lambda_1} \frac{\phi - \phi_1}{\phi_2 - \phi_1} VTEC(\phi_2, \lambda_1) \\ + \frac{\lambda - \lambda_1}{\lambda_2 - \lambda_1} \frac{\phi - \phi_1}{\phi_2 - \phi_1} VTEC(\phi_2, \lambda_2) \tag{8}$$

where the grid point VTEC data is obtained from the Transformer model prediction, and $\lambda_1 < \lambda = \lambda_{IPP} + \Delta\lambda_i < \lambda_2$, $\phi_1 < \phi = \phi_{IPP} < \phi_2$. Similarly, the VTEC value at $IPP_{i+1}(\phi_{IPP}, \lambda_{IPP} + \Delta\lambda_{i+1})$ is obtained by making $\phi_1 < \phi = \phi_{IPP} < \phi_2$, $\lambda_1 < \lambda = \lambda_{IPP} + \Delta\lambda_{i+1} < \lambda_2$, on the basis of the $(i+1)$th TEC map.

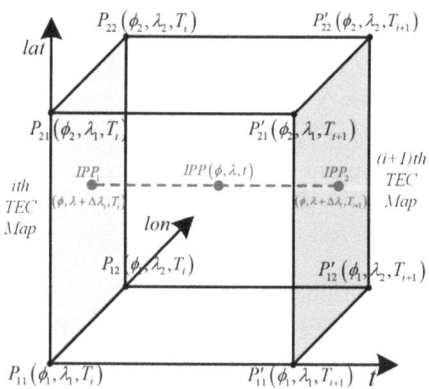

Fig. 2. Space-time inverse distance interpolation diagram.

The ionospheric delay estimate can be obtained by substituting the VTEC obtained from Eq. (7) into Eq. (6). In order to verify the effectiveness of this method in positioning error correction, this paper compares the above ionospheric delay estimates predicted based on the Transformer model with the GIM hindcast products, takes the GIM hindcast TEC grid data as input, and obtains the ionospheric delay estimates according to Eqs. (4)–(8) to evaluate its effectiveness in positioning error correction.

3 Positioning Error Experimental Study

In order to compare the effect of the model proposed in this paper on the ionospheric delayed positioning error correction, this experiment compares the positioning error correction effect of GNSS observatories with/without ionospheric delayed correction modes for the entire period of 2018. Considering that the Transformer model's TEC prediction region is China and its surrounding area, in order to maximize the comparison of the model's positioning improvement effect under each calendar element, this experiment takes the GNSS station BJFS (39.606°N, 115.892°E) in China as an example for experimental validation to ensure that, as far as possible, the satellite signals received by the station are at the ionosphere pierce point is located within the prediction range of the Transformer model TEC.

3.1 Positioning Error Correction Strategies

In this paper, we use three ionospheric delay correction strategies plus a localization error benchmark, where the localization error benchmark (without ionospheric delay correction) is used to compare the localization effects under the three correction strategies; The bilinear interpolation method based on the post VTEC grid data corresponding to strategy II uses the GIM post product provided by CODE network; the bilinear interpolation method corresponding to the predicted VTEC grid data of strategy III and predicts the resulting VTEC data by using the Transformer model proposed in this paper. The VTEC grid data in Strategy II has a high accuracy of ionospheric delay estimation. However, the official website has a certain time delay, which makes it difficult to achieve real-time positioning error compensation. At the same time, Strategy III can predict the VTEC grid data in advance. If it has the same positioning error correction effect as strategy II, it proves the feasibility of the method proposed in this paper.

In order to ensure the accuracy of the experiment, the other error factors besides the ionospheric delay were corrected using the strategy presented in Table 1. Based on this, the root-mean-square (RMS) errors of the positioning errors were separately analyzed in the four modes mentioned above, using the coordinates of the measurement stations included in the observation files as the reference frame. In addition, considering the accuracy of the reference coordinates of the stations, this experiment further compares and analyses the rms positioning errors under the ionospheric delay correction strategy of each model using the average positioning result of each calendar element in a single day as the reference benchmark, reflecting the fluctuation of the model in the northeasterly direction and its positional stability under each calendar element after the correction of the ionospheric delay error.

Table 1. Error correction models and parameter configurations on standard single positioning

Relevant parameters and sources of error	Setup and correction strategies
Station coordinates	IGS station coordinates
Epoch interval	30 s
Satellite cut-off altitude angle	15°
Stellite ephemeris	Broadcast ephemeris
Satellite clock bias	Corrected by broadcast ephemeris calculation
Receiver clock offsets	Least-squares estimation
Tropospheric delay	Saastamoinen mode
Earth's rotation effect	Sagnac effect correction
Relativistic effect	Corrected by broadcast ephemeris calculation
Antenna phase center change	/

3.2 Positioning Performance Evaluation

This experiment aims to evaluate the positioning errors of different ionospheric delay correction models in the E, N, and U directions during various ionospheric active periods. For this purpose, we have used daily observation files from the BJFS observatory for the entire year of 2018, broadcast ephemeris files, a post IONEX files from the CODE network, and TEC prediction data based on the Transformer model. To ensure data consistency, we have calculated the latitude and longitude of the ionospheric pierce point of the satellite signals received at the station for each calendar element according to Eq. (5). We have excluded the calendar elements outside of China and the surrounding regions where the latitude and longitude are located. Additionally, we have excluded all the calendar elements in the four sets of positioning experiments under the ionospheric delayed correction mode. The positioning results corresponding to the remaining calendar elements have been taken as the objects for the comparative analysis. The frequency of the calendar element provided by the IGS observational data is 30 s. To simplify the comparison data, the experiment proposes to use the monthly average of the root-mean-square (RMS) errors of the localization errors in each direction as the evaluation criterion.

$$RMSE_d = \sqrt{\frac{1}{M_d} \sum_{i=1}^{M_d} \left(POS_i^d - POS_{baseline}\right)^2} \quad (9)$$

$$\overline{RMSE}_m = \frac{1}{N_m} \sum_{d=1}^{N_m} RMSE_d \quad (10)$$

Where M_d denotes the number of valid calendar elements for the ith day of the month, POS_i^d is the positioning result corresponding to the ith valid calendar element, and N_m is the number of valid days corresponding to the mth month.

Due to the strong influence of the ionosphere on the satellite signals in the U direction, the monthly averages of the root-mean-square (RMS) errors of the station for each month of 2018 were compared under the four ionospheric delay correction strategies using the coordinates provided in the observation files of the BJFS station as a baseline, as shown in Fig. 3.

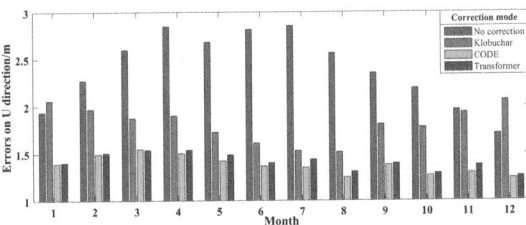

Fig. 3. Monthly mean values of U-direction RMSE on BJFS station in 2018 (based on station coordinates).

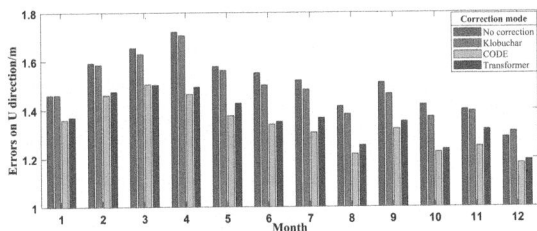

Fig. 4. Monthly mean values of U-direction RMSE on BJFS station in 2018 (based on daily mean values).

The experimental results show that the Klobuchar model corresponding to strategy I reduces the positioning error of the BJFS observatory by 1.39% to 46.42% from February to October, and the ionospheric delay correction effect is very significant, especially in July. However, the positioning accuracy appears to be reduced by 6.4% and 20.86% in January and December, respectively, which is presumed to be due to the abnormally high frequency of ionospheric activity in the region during this period. The current ionospheric delay error is assumed to be difficult to estimate from the empirical model due to the widespread ionospheric activities in the region during this period. The ionospheric delay correction models based on the CODE network hindcast TEC grid data and the Transformer model predicted TEC grid data in Strategy II and Strategy III, respectively, improve the station positioning error accuracy by 27.66%–52.69% and 26.38%–50.18% respectively, and reduce the positioning error to 1.5 m or even lower in each month, which is more stable and correctable than Strategy I. The correction of Strategy I is more stable and correctable than Strategy II. Strategy I has more stable correction accuracy. At the same time, Strategy I and Strategy II have consistency in ionospheric delay correction, which further illustrates the effectiveness of the ionospheric delay positioning error correction method based on the Transformer model prediction proposed in this paper, which can provide a higher precision ionospheric delay correction for single-frequency receivers, and then provide the feasibility of high-precision ionospheric delay error correction for real-time positioning.

Taking the daily averages of observation station positioning results under each ionospheric delay model correction as a benchmark, the monthly averages of the root mean square error in the U-direction are compared for each month of 2018 at the BJFS observation station, as shown in Fig. 4. As can be seen from the figure, the Klobuchar model corresponding to strategy I has little correction effect in the U-direction, and the positioning accuracy is improved by −1.82% to 3.55%, while the positioning accuracy of strategy II and strategy III is improved by 6.91% to 14.09% and 5.82% to 12.91%, respectively. The statistical results show that the correction model corresponding to strategy III is slightly lower than that of strategy II in terms of positioning accuracy by 1.85%, indicating that the two correction performances have a high degree of consistency, which can achieve the correction of ionospheric delay positioning errors in different ionospheric active periods.

The above grid point VTEC data are provided by the GIM with the post product, which is better than the traditional Klobuchar model in terms of correction accuracy, but the product has a certain time lag. For this reason, this paper proposes a VTEC prediction method based on the Transformer model instead of the GIM product to provide ionospheric delay correction predictions for receivers at any location in the region, and the temporal and space-time interpolation process of this method is the same as above.

4 Conclusions

Aiming at the problems of limited accuracy of existing models for ionospheric delay error correction of single-frequency receivers and the difficulty of implementing high-precision real-time correction, this paper proposes a method of ionospheric delayed positioning error correction based on the prediction of the Transformer model, which transforms the problem of real-time improvement of receiver positioning accuracy into the problem of ionospheric VTEC prediction. Firstly, based on the CODE network post VTEC historical data and solar/geomagnetic activity-related feature parameters, a spatial information embedded Transformer model is established for predicting the VTEC grid data in China and the neighboring regions. Secondly, the VTEC value at the ionospheric pierce point of the satellite signal received by the receiver is estimated by spatio-temporal inverse distance bilinear interpolation to calculate the ionospheric delay error, which is ultimately used for pseudorange error compensation to achieve the improvement of positioning accuracy.

References

1. Noble, B.G., Sneddon, I.N.: On certain integrals of Lipschitz-Hankel type involving products of Bessel functions. Philos. Trans. R. Soc. London Ser. A, Math. Phys. Sci. **247**(935), 529–551 (1955)
2. Maxwell, J.C.: A Treatise on Electricity and Magnetism. Clarendon Press, Oxford (1873)
3. Yang, H.: Research on GNSS Ionospheric Delay Modeling in China. Guilin University of Technology, Guilin (2020)
4. Gao, X., Yao, Y.: A storm-time ionospheric TEC model with multichannel features by the spatiotemporal ConvLSTM network. J. Geodesy **97**(1), 9 (2023)
5. Liu, H., Lei, D., Yuan, J., et al.: Ionospheric TEC prediction in China based on the multiple-attention LSTM model. Atmosphere **13**(11), 1939 (2022)
6. Xie, T., Dai, Z., Zhu, X., et al.: LSTM-based short-term ionospheric TEC forecast model and positioning accuracy analysis. GPS Solutions **27**(2), 66 (2023)
7. Silva, A., Moraes, A., Sousasantos, J., et al.: Using deep learning to map ionospheric total electron content over Brazil. Remote Sens. **15**(2), 412 (2023)

RFBR-IR: Regularized Frequency BRDF Reconstruction Inverse Rendering

Xiuyuan zheng[1], Weibing Wan[1(✉)], Zhijun Fang[2], and Dezhi Liu[1]

[1] Shanghai University of Engineering Science, Shanghai, China
{xyzheng,wbwan}@sues.edu.cn
[2] Donghua University, Shanghai, China

Abstract. The advancements in implicit neural rendering representations and differentiable rendering have facilitated the capture of multi-view RGB images from unknown illumination while simultaneously recovering the estimated object's geometry, lighting, and materials. However, a key challenge in inverse rendering is appropriately incorporating priors and regularization during the optimization process to mitigate ill-posed situations. Currently, most methods rely on modeling lighting from different materials based on multi-view cameras using spherical Gaussians (SG), often resulting in the blurring of high-frequency details. In this study, we propose a novel inverse rendering representation called RFBR-IR. This method reduces overfitting by regularizing frequency stability during the learning process. Simultaneously, it introduces a gradient-based edge-aware factor and regularization to alleviate edge smoothness constraints in edge regions, preserving more details. Through joint optimization of radiance field, materials, and lighting, we significantly improve performance and achieve a physically-based and easily optimized inverse rendering approach. Extensive experiments demonstrate that our method outperforms state-of-the-art methods on multiple synthetic datasets, achieving superior rendering quality.

Keywords: inverse rendering · regularization frequency · neural radiation field · view reconstruction · edge perception factor

1 Introduction

Decomposing the appearance of an image into latent intrinsic properties, such as geometry, materials, and lighting conditions, has long been a persistent challenge in computer vision and graphics. The key issue in inverse rendering is appropriately introducing priors and regularization during the optimization process to mitigate ill-posed situations. The high-quality geometry and radiance field modeled by Neural Radiance Fields (NeRF) have proven particularly useful for inverse rendering. However, addressing the severe ill-posedness in inverse rendering remains a significant challenge. Some methods [1–3] use this hybrid rendering approach, where neural radiance fields and physically-based rendering mutually influence each other to implement high-quality rendering. Although effective, these methods struggle to seamlessly integrate high-frequency detail information. Due to the superiority of this hybrid representation approach, we propose an efficient, simple, and compact method to reconstruct scenes.Specifically, we use voxel grids to separately store the initial state information of density and appearance points. Density features and appearance features are stored in different grids, and appearance features are decomposed into radiance networks, shadow normal networks, and material networks.

Physically-based rendering of scenes [4,5] faces two main challenges: (1) accurate geometric reconstruction and (2) modeling secondary shading effects. In this paper, our goal is to estimate the Bidirectional Reflectance Distribution Function (BRDF) of objects based on multi-view RGB images captured under unknown static lighting. Our main technical innovation lies in a spectrum refinement process during the inverse rendering, progressing from coarse to fine. This approach avoids overfitting to 2D images in the early stages, unlike NeRF. Simultaneously, we employ joint modeling with radiance fields and physics-based methods to reconstruct the scene. Radiance fields [6,7] rendering can be directly used to provide more accurate indirect illumination for physics-based rendering. We model indirect illumination using Multi-Layer Perceptrons (MLP), which map 3D surface points to their indirect incoming lighting.

To robustly optimize the scene, we initially employ existing methods [7]to learn the geometric shape of objects and the outgoing radiance field from input images. Both are represented using Multi-Layer Perceptrons (MLP). For the entire model, a dynamic strategy is adopted to control the contribution of frequency in the position encoding. This is achieved by deforming frequencies to adjust the input position encoding components of the network. By zeroing out high-frequency components at the beginning, the network avoids instability in the early training stages, mitigating the susceptibility to high-frequency signal effects. Subsequently, with the gradual introduction of higher frequencies during optimization, the entire scene undergoes continuous refinement. Simultaneously, to preserve more details while reducing smoothness constraints in edge regions, we encourage smoothness in non-edge areas. This is accomplished by introducing a gradient-based edge-aware factor to optimize spatial consistency. To enhance the model's predictions of normal directions, we design a direction loss function that includes additional regularization terms. This regularization term penalizes predictions of normals with significant differences from the expected normal direction.

Our method achieves advanced quality in scene reconstruction (geometry and material properties) and rendering (novel view synthesis). In summary:

- We introduce a novel model for representing inverse rendering, achieving high-quality reconstruction on synthetic datasets.
- We apply a progressively refined frequency regularization and utilize a new occlusion regularizer to enhance optimization performance for high-frequency details, enabling generalization across datasets.

- We mitigate noise and optimize noisy normal fields by introducing a smoothness loss.
- We propose an edge-aware factor that encourages smoothness in non-edge areas while reducing smoothness constraints in edge regions to preserve more details.

2 Related Work

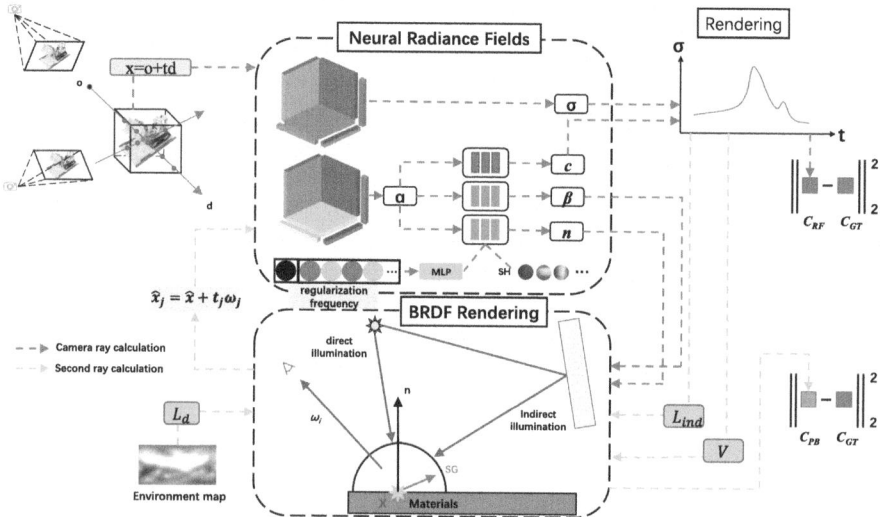

Fig. 1. The method proposes an approach to optimize the continuous 5D neural radiance field representation of a scene (volume density and viewpoint-dependent color at any continuous location). The scene is represented using neural radiance fields and physically-based rendering by parameterizing components. It utilizes tensor factorization and multiple MLPs to regress volume density σ, viewpoint-dependent color c, normals n, and material properties (i.e., BRDF parameters) β for radiance field rendering and physically-based rendering. Additionally, it incorporates regularization frequencies to dynamically control the contribution of frequencies in the encoding.

Single/Multi-view Inverse Rendering. Traditional methods for inverse rendering are applicable to a single RGB image or multi-view, multi-modal inputs. Recovering shape, albedo, and lighting from a single RGB view is highly constrained and often yields poor results in scene-level reconstruction and partial material reconstruction in the real world. More practical approaches involve reconstructing shape from multi-view RGB images [6–12] and simplifying the corresponding assumptions. Most previous research combines prior knowledge such as lighting, shape, and shadows, as well as additional observations like scanned geometry [13,14] and known lighting conditions [15], to ensure appropriate regularization during the rendering component optimization process. This includes neural radiance field algorithms constructed based on photo collections captured in unconstrained environments as well as algorithms that factorize latent variables for shape and reflectance (like NeRFactor [3] and NeRD [16]) for view and lighting re-synthesis. To more efficiently achieve the decomposition of the NeRF radiance field implicit function space and latent space variables (such as lighting, normals, diffuse reflection, spatial surface representation), subsequent research introduced radiance synthesis computational models, such as NeRFactor and NeRV algorithms, drawing inspiration from the computational principles of highly realistic rendering in computer graphics. In comparison, our work builds upon the latest advancements in implicit neural representation [17], achieving stronger inverse rendering capabilities, and enhancing the model's generalization by effectively modeling indirect illumination.

Regularization Frequency. Position encoding are core components of the neural radiance field. Previous research [18,19] has shown that using position encoding enables neural networks to better learn high-frequency functions from low-dimensional networks. The use of sine functions with different frequencies effectively addresses this issue, encoding different inputs to alleviate the problem. Recent works [11,20] demonstrate the benefits of introducing input frequencies in various applications, such as surface reconstruction and fitting functions with broader frequency ranges. In essence, we propose a coarse-to-fine regularization to prevent the model from getting stuck in local minima.

Physically-Based Rendering. Since the flourishing development of Neural Radiance Fields (NeRF), numerous works have proposed methods based on neural radiance fields to address inverse rendering problems.However, many works make use of simplified assumptions, such as known lighting conditions [2], neglecting shadow effects [16,21,22], or assuming constant reflectance [22]. NeRFactor [3] is the first to comprehensively estimate the fundamental physical properties of a scene (geometry, albedo, BRDF, and lighting) under a single unknown natural illumination while considering shadow effects. Following the overall framework of NeRFactor, InvRender [23] is based on state-of-the-art methods for shape and radiance field reconstruction [7,24], proposing to model indirect illumination by refining a pre-trained NeRF as an auxiliary MLP. However, it does not model indirect illumination, and known surface-based inverse rendering processes are prone to local minima. Recently, TensoIR [25] utilizes a fast radiance field data structure [8] and precise visibility and indirect illumination estimation through ray marching.

3 Method

In the given set of scene RGB images with camera poses, our goal is to use the model to fit the scene, construct an implicit volume representation of the scene, and model appearance and density. We aim to recover material properties, including their textures and lighting. We utilize parameterized components for forward rendering and employ a comprehensive analytical approach to address the inverse rendering problem. Similar to previous works, we model and represent the scene through neural radiance fields and physics-based rendering. An overview of the model is illustrated in Fig. 1.

3.1 Regularization Frequency

Positional Encoding. Based on previous research [6], it has been demonstrated that MLP networks struggle to learn high-frequency information. Directly using MLP for learning can result in generated images being too blurry when viewed up close and producing aliasing artifacts when viewed from a distance. Therefore, positional encoding is introduced to enable NeRF to synthesize views with high fidelity. This involves mapping 3D coordinates (x) to a higher-dimensional deterministic space using different sine functions as bases. This allows MLP to simultaneously learn both high and low-frequency information, enhancing clarity. Directly optimizing NeRF on the original input (x, d) often leads to issues with high-frequency details in the synthesized output. To address this problem, recent works use sine functions of different frequencies to map the input to a higher-dimensional space [6]:

$$x' = [x, \gamma_L(x)] \tag{1}$$

This will be used to concatenate applied to coordinate input and view direction input.

Frequency Encoding. Position encoding allows coordinate-based neural networks (typically bandwidth-limited) to represent higher-frequency signals with faster convergence behavior [18]. High-frequency inputs may lead to overfitting issues in neural rendering. [18] suggests that mapping higher frequencies may cause the rapid convergence of high-frequency information, potentially resulting in neural radiance field artifacts biased towards sky blurring (even in shallow networks). Therefore, we propose a method of frequency regularization aimed at addressing the position encoding issue, particularly in parts that are more sensitive to noise. During the training process, we aim to gradually introduce high-frequency details so that the model first captures the rough structure of the scene and then learns more detailed features. We investigated the impact of encoding different numbers of frequency bands on the overall reconstruction results, as shown in Fig. 3. We observed a decrease in performance as higher-frequency inputs were provided to the model. For example, at an embedding rate of 10%, we achieved a PSNR of 35.29, while at 100% visible position encoding rate, the PSNR was only 33.38. Based on this observation, we propose a method of frequency regularization (Eq. 1). To achieve this goal, we use masked encoding to train our radiance field. Specifically, during training with only radiance field rendering, we mask the frequency band-encoded positions. Although the generated alphaMask significantly reduces GPU memory costs, it also reduces the subsequent reconstruction quality. Given the length $L + 1$ of the position encoding, we use linearly increasing frequencies ν masks to adjust the visible spectrum based on training time steps. Here, we briefly present our research results, and experimental details will be deferred to Sect. 4.3.

$$\gamma_L(t,T;x) = \gamma_L(x) \odot \nu(t,T,L), \tag{2}$$

$$\text{with } \nu_i(t,T,L) = \begin{cases} 1 \\ (\frac{t*2}{\zeta \cdot T} \cdot L) - \lfloor (\frac{t*2}{\zeta \cdot T} \cdot L) \rfloor \\ 0 \end{cases} \tag{3}$$

In this context, ν_i (t;T;L) represents the i-th value of ν (t;T;L), where t and T are the current training iteration and the total number of iterations, respectively, and ζ is a hyperparameter used to assess the impact of frequency regularization over time. For components less than or equal to $(\frac{t*2}{\zeta \cdot T} \cdot L) + 1$, the mask is 1, meaning that these low-frequency components are always visible throughout the entire training process. For components between these values, the mask's value linearly increases from 0 to 1, and the specific increase depends on the ratio between the current iteration count and the total iteration count. Specifically, we start with the original input without position encoding and progressively increase the length of the entire encoding during training, linearly increasing the visible frequency by 1 bit. Our frequency regularization avoids the model being sensitive to high-frequency signals at the beginning of training, mitigating instability at the start of training. By gradually providing high-frequency information while avoiding excessive smoothing, it effectively addresses the ill-posed nature of the inverse rendering process. With this approach, we found that in the early stages of training, the model might tend to fit noise or details in the training data that are not important. By restricting access to high-frequency information, we can reduce the risk of overfitting. As the model gradually encounters higher-frequency information, it can better learn the details of the data while maintaining the generalized features learned at low frequencies.

3.2 Rendering

Scene Representation. For volume rendering, we employ differentiable volume rendering. For each pixel, we trace the ray $r = o + td$ by sampling a set of points and computing the pixel's color, as shown in Eq. 4:

$$\begin{cases} \hat{C} = \sum_{i=1}^{N} \tau_i(1 - \exp(-\sigma_i \Delta_i))c_i \\ \tau_i = \exp\left(-\sum_{j=1}^{i-1} \sigma_j \Delta_j\right) \end{cases} \tag{4}$$

where c_i and σ_i represent the color and density values computed at the sampling point position x_i; Δ_i is the ray step size, and τ_i represents the transmittance. Similar to previous methods [3,6], the surface point is naturally determined by the volume rendering weights and the sampling points defined by Eq. 4:

$$w_j = \tau_i(1 - \exp(-\sigma_i \Delta_i)) \qquad (5)$$

The surface rendering equation proposed by [26] is a fundamental equation in computer graphics that describes the physical process of light transport in a scene. It can be used to simulate complex lighting effects such as reflection, refraction, global illumination, etc. Similarly, we apply a physically based rendering BRDF model [27] f_r and use it with the camera rays at the surface points to predict geometric and material properties for performing physically based rendering.

$$L_o(\mathbf{x}, \omega_o) = L_e(\mathbf{x}, \omega_o) + \int_\Omega L_{in}(\mathbf{x}, \omega_i) f_r(\mathbf{x}, \omega_i, \omega_o)(\omega_i \cdot \mathbf{n}) d\omega_i \qquad (6)$$

where: $L_o(\mathbf{x}, \omega_o)$ is the radiance emitted from point $\mathbf{x}$ along the direction ω_o. $L_e(\mathbf{x}, \omega_o)$ is the radiance emitted from point $\mathbf{x}$ in the direction ω_o. For non-emissive surfaces, this term is zero. $\int_\Omega$ represents the integral over all incoming directions ω_i in the hemisphere Ω, capturing the cumulative effect of light rays from all possible incoming directions.

To effectively improve the computational efficiency, we adopt a scene representation based on tensor decomposition, modeling volume density σ, view-dependent color c, shading normal n, and material properties β (including diffuse reflectance and roughness). In this work, we utilize the vector-matrix factorization technique proposed by TensoRF, employing two separate VM decompositions to model volume density and appearance, where the appearance tensor is followed by multiple lightweight multi-layer perceptrons (MLPs) to regress various appearance attributes.

3.3 Normal Optimization

Previous NeRF-based methods compute the shadow using the negative direction of the volume density gradient as the normal: $n_\sigma = \frac{\nabla_x \sigma}{\|\nabla_x \sigma\|}$. However, we found that normals derived this way have noise and lack fine details, impacting the quality of reconstruction. To further reduce noise and alleviate the occurrence of artifacts, we attempted to add smoothness losses for reflectance and roughness:

$$\mathcal{L}_n = \sum_j w_j (\|n_j - n_{\sigma,j}\|_2^2 + \|n_j - \tilde{n}'\|_2^2) \qquad (7)$$

where w_j is the volume rendering weight (as described in Eq. 5) allocating larger weights to points around the object's surface, n_j is the predicted normal vector, $n_{\sigma,j}$ is the normal vector computed based on density, and $\tilde{n}'$ represents a smoothing term with added 0.002 times Gaussian noise on n. This regularization term propagates gradients back to the appearance tensor (via the normal network) and the density tensor, further relating the geometry and appearance of the entire scene for more accurate normal reconstruction.

3.4 Joint Reconstruction and Training Loss

To reconstruct the scene, we optimize the radiance field for each scene by minimizing the breadth loss using a set of multi-view input images with known camera poses:

Rendering Loss: We use the ground truth color C_{gt} to supervise the radiance field rendering color C_{RF} and the BRDF-based rendering color C_{PB}:

$$\mathcal{L}_{RF} = \|C_{RF} - C_{gt}\|_2^2, \quad \mathcal{L}_{PB} = \|C_{PB} - C_{gt}\|_2^2 \tag{8}$$

Smoothness Loss. We aim to encourage smoothness in non-edge regions while reducing smoothness constraints at edges to preserve more details. To achieve this, we introduce a gradient-based edge-aware factor E_x. This factor attenuates the smoothness loss in edge regions by assigning smaller weights, while assigning larger weights in non-edge (smooth) regions when computing the smoothness loss. We detect edges by computing gradients of material properties and reduce the loss weights in these regions. This approach helps optimize spatial consistency of material properties without sacrificing important visual features.

$$E_x = exp(-\lambda \|\nabla \beta_x\|_2) \tag{9}$$

Here, $\nabla \beta_x$ represents the spatial gradient of material properties at point x, and λ is a hyperparameter. The new smoothness loss is given by:

$$\mathcal{L}_\beta = \sum_{j, x=r(t_j)} w_j E_x \left(\frac{\|\beta_x - \beta_{x+\xi}\|_2}{\max(\|\beta_x\|_2, \|\beta_{x+\xi}\|_2)} \right)^2 \tag{10}$$

Direction Loss. We aim to introduce an additional regularization term to encourage reasonable orientations for normals. If there isn't enough information to determine the exact normal direction at a point, we can use normal information from neighboring points to guide the prediction or bias towards some default direction. Specifically, we aim to enhance the model's prediction of normal directions, making them tend towards natural, smooth, and physically plausible directions in uncertain situations. To achieve this, we consider two improvements:1. Encouraging normals to point outward and be smooth, i.e., penalizing normals that point inward or deviate from smooth surfaces. 2. Guiding normals towards a default or expected direction in regions lacking exact information. This direction can be based on neighboring normal information or some prior knowledge.Based on this idea, we design a direction loss function that includes an additional regularization term. This regularization term penalizes predicted normals that deviate significantly from the expected normal direction. Assuming we have an expected direction $\hat{n}$, we can define a regularization term $R(n_j, \hat{n})$:

$$R(n_j, \hat{n}) = (1 - (n_j \cdot \hat{n})^2) \tag{11}$$

Here, $n_j \cdot \hat{n}$ represents the dot product between the predicted normal n_j and the expected normal $\hat{n}$. Thus, the new directional loss is formulated as:

$$\mathcal{L}_d = \sum_j w_j \left(\max(0, n_j \cdot d) + \mu R(n_j, \hat{n}) \right) \tag{12}$$

where μ is a hyperparameter used to balance the weight between the directional error and the regularization term for normal direction. In both cases, we control the sensitivity of edge detection and the strength of normal direction regularization through two regularization losses. The purpose is to ensure that when the material properties of two points are very close (i.e., in non-edge regions), the loss function encourages smoothness. However, when encountering edges or texture regions, the loss function allows for larger differences due to significant disparities, preserving detailed information.

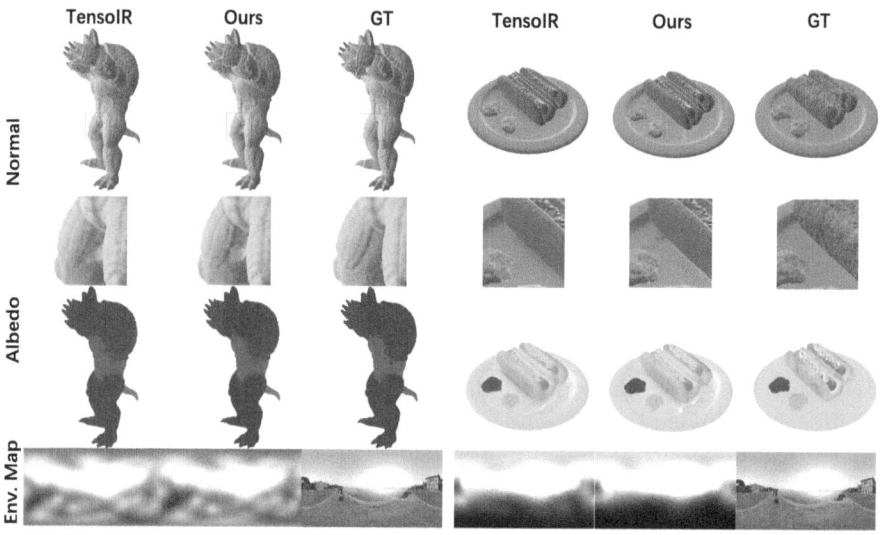

Fig. 2. Visual comparison with baseline methods. Our approach produces higher-quality inverse rendering results with more detailed normals and accurate reflectance, resulting in more realistic relighting results.

4 Experiments

In this section, we first provide our specific implementation details in Sect. 4.1. Next, in Sect. 4.2, we present and demonstrate the comparison of our method with other NeRF-related methods. Finally, in Sect. 4.3, we conduct ablation experiments to study the impact of different parameters and components on the model.

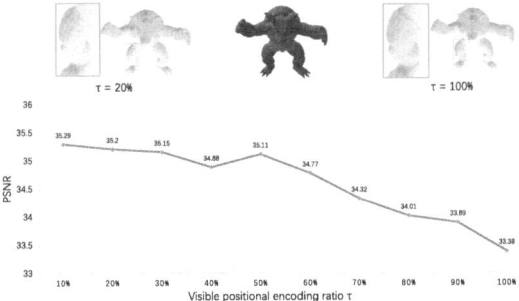

Fig. 3. The figure displays the peak signal-to-noise ratio (PSNR) variation with the ratio of visibility encoding frequencies on the Armadillo dataset.

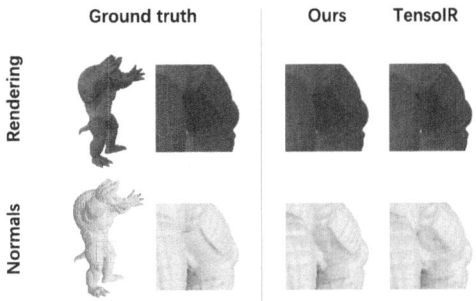

Fig. 4. Our model exhibits accurate glossy appearance and recovers finer geometric details. TensoIR [25] is capable of estimating accurate specular reflection and normal vectors but fails to capture details at finer scales.

4.1 Implementation Details

Training Details. We ran the model on a single RTX 3080 Ti GPU (16GB memory) to obtain all our results. For fair comparison, baseline methods (InvRender [23] and TensoIR [25]) were also re-run and tested with the same GPU. The model is implemented in PyTorch and trained with the Adam optimizer at a learning rate of $5e^{-4}$ for the entire model; for TensoRF, we used initial learning rates of 0.03 and 0.0005 for the tensor factor and MLP, respectively. We assume the material of the object is dielectric (non-conductive), so we fixed the Fresnel coefficient to 0.05. For fairness, the total number of training iterations is set to 80k. Rapid convergence on high frequencies can lead to the radiance field not exploring low-frequency information well and exhibiting a trend toward undesired offset artifacts. Here, we restrict this by setting $pos = pos * 0$ during the initial 5k iterations, effectively masking out positions in the frequency band. We also performed multiple upsampling of our spatial tensor factors during training. Except for the lego dataset, where we started with an initial resolution of $N_0^3 = 128^3$, we used linear and bilinear sampling of vectors and matrices at 5000, 15000, 25000, and 35000 steps until reaching the final spatial resolution

Table 1. Quantitative comparison on synthetic datasets. Our (single-light) results outperform baseline results by generating more accurate reflectance and normals, leading to improved results in more realistic novel multi-view synthesis and relighting. Render quality comparisons are reported on various datasets, including PSNR, SSIM, and LPIPS, compared with methods from different categories in reflectance, multi-view synthesis, and remapping.

Scene	Method	Normal	Albedo			Novel View Synthesis			Relighting		
		MAE↓	PSNR↑	SSIM↑	LPIPS↓	PSNR↑	SSIM↑	LPIPS↓	PSNR↑	SSIM↑	LPIPS↓
Lego	NeRFactor [3]	9.976	25.444	0.937	0.112	26.076	0.881	0.151	23.246	0.865	0.156
	InvRender [23]	9.980	21.435	0.882	0.160	24.391	0.883	0.151	20.117	0.832	0.171
	InvRender [23]	5.980	25.240	0.900	0.145	34.700	0.968	0.037	28.581	0.944	0.081
	RFBR-IR	5.971	25.886	0.916	0.144	35.124	0.966	0.036	28.601	0.945	0.079
Hotdog	NeRFactor [3]	5.579	24.654	0.950	0.142	24.498	0.940	0.141	22.713	0.914	0.159
	InvRender [23]	3.708	27.028	0.950	0.094	31.832	0.952	0.089	27.630	0.928	0.089
	TensoIR [25]	4.050	30.370	0.947	0.093	36.820	0.976	0.045	27.927	0.933	0.115
	RFBR-IR	3.825	29.896	0.943	0.095	36.929	0.976	0.043	27.988	0.935	0.113
Armadillo	NeRFactor [3]	3.346	28.001	0.946	0.096	26.479	0.947	0.095	26.887	0.944	0.102
	InvRender [23]	1.723	35.573	0.959	0.076	31.446	0.968	0.057	27.814	0.949	0.069
	TensoIR [25]	1.950	34.360	0.989	0.059	39.050	0.986	0.039	34.504	0.975	0.045
	RFBR-IR	1.884	35.293	0.988	0.055	39.924	0.988	0.033	35.102	0.978	0.043
Ficus	NeRFactor [3]	6.442	22.402	0.928	0.085	21.664	0.919	0.095	20.684	0.907	0.107
	InvRender [23]	4.884	25.335	0.942	0.072	22.131	0.934	0.057	20.330	0.895	0.073
	TensoIR [25]	4.420	27.130	0.964	0.044	29.780	0.973	0.041	24.296	0.947	0.068
	RFBR-IR	4.453	27.582	0.967	0.042	30.424	0.970	0.040	24.737	0.951	0.061

Table 2. The contrastive impact of frequency regularization on the model. We conducted ablation experiments in a fair environment, where RF stands for Regularized Frequency.

	PSNR↑	SSIM↑	LPIPS↓
w/o RF	34.98	0.990	0.058
w/ $RF_{10\%}$	35.29	0.987	0.055
w/ $RF_{20\%}$	35.20	0.988	0.057
w/ $RF_{30\%}$	35.15	0.988	0.058

of $N^3 = 300^3$. Additionally, we performed linear interpolation of voxel counts in logarithmic space between the initial and final spatial resolutions. We report the inverse rendering details in Fig. 2, where our method yields higher-quality inverse rendering results.

Ray Details. During training, when computing indirect illumination and visibility, we sampled 1024 secondary rays at each surface point, with each ray having 96 sampling points. Half of the rays were filtered in the direction of the surface normal, i.e., those with normal vectors in the upper hemisphere. The directions of sampled rays were obtained through hierarchical sampling.

By using spherical coordinates formulas to convert latitude and longitude into vectors in three-dimensional space, we obtained the light area weights for each pixel in the environment map, ultimately determining the direction of incident rays. The incident ray directions were then reshaped and extended to match the number of surface points, and the calculated ray directions were L2 normalized. We obtained the visibility map from the visibility network and created a mask to occlude half of the incident rays behind the surface, computing the secondary shadow shading effect.

Table 3. The impact of normal smoothness on the model. Here, NN represents the normal smoothness term with added Gaussian noise, NE represents the introduction of a gradient-aware factor, and RD represents the introduction of the direction loss regularization term.

	Normal MAE↓	PSNR ↑	SSIM ↑	LPIPS ↓
w/ NN	1.99	39.96	0.987	0.033
w/ NE	1.93	39.76	0.987	0.035
w/ RD	1.95	39.75	0.986	0.034
RFBR-IR	1.88	39.97	0.988	0.033

4.2 Evaluation

In comparison to previous methods, we conducted a comparison of our method and previous inverse rendering-based methods (NeRFactor [3], InvRender [23], and TensoIR [25]) using images captured under a single unknown illumination in different scenes. Table 1 shows the evaluation of the accuracy of reflectance, normals, and relighting results using metrics such as PSNR, SSIM, and LPIPS [28]. It can be observed from the table that, using the same metrics for evaluation, our single-light results outperform other baseline methods. Compared to the baseline methods, our results are closer to the ground truth, demonstrating the superiority of our method. Our method produces smoother results without losing details compared to other methods, which can be attributed to our efficient encoding strategy and additional regularization terms, ensuring satisfactory performance in both reconstruction and decomposition quality. At the same time, we report in Fig. 4 that compared to baseline methods, RFBR-IR is better at capturing fine-scale details.

4.3 Ablation Study

In this section, we validate our experiments on synthetic datasets to investigate the impact of a series of key components designed in our method on experimental factors, focusing mainly on high-frequency details to demonstrate the effectiveness of our approach. For fairness, similar to TensoRF, we apply the

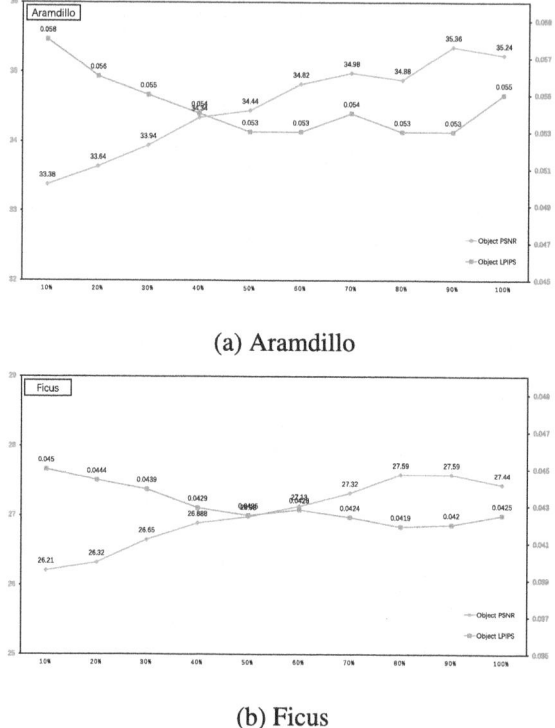

(a) Aramdillo

(b) Ficus

Fig. 5. The impact of regularization frequency duration was investigated by setting the regularization frequency end to $\mathcal{T} = \lfloor total_{iteration} \times x\% \rfloor$. Our RFBR-IR achieved quite satisfactory results across a wide range of choices.

Table 4. The influence of different weights (μ) on the model.

	ratio	Albedo PSNR ↑	NVS PSNR ↑	SSIM ↑
	0.1	35.27	39.864	0.988
μ	0.5	35.13	39.627	0.986
	0.9	35.05	39.513	0.986

$\mathcal{L}_1$ regularization on all tensor factors in the tensor decomposition as the former. We showcase the differences between our method and TensoIR [25] on two synthetic datasets in Fig. 2, illustrating that our method exhibits significantly better reconstruction results in terms of smoothness handling.

Variable Spectrum. We investigated the impact of different spectra on the model, as shown in Table 2. It can be observed that the smaller the frequency regularization mask, the more pronounced the effect on the model. This is because we found that in the early stages of training, the model may tend to fit noise or unimportant details in the training data. By limiting access to high-frequency information, we can reduce the risk of overfitting. Additionally, we studied the influence of the regularization frequency duration T in Fig. 5. Regarding the PSNR scores for the Aramdillo and Ficus datasets, we found that the best performance was achieved around 80%-90% of the time. Furthermore, we noticed that there should be a trade-off between peak signal-to-noise ratio (PSNR) scores and image similarity metric (LPIPS) scores. While longer regularization frequency durations tend to increase PSNR scores, they also slightly decrease LPIPS scores. Therefore, we believe 85% strikes the best balance. Consequently, we adopt it as our default regularization frequency.

Smoothness Loss. In Table 3, we display the influence of normal smoothness on the model, evaluating the differences between our RFBR-IR and normal smoothness with only Gaussian noise added, gradient-aware smoothing factor, and only direction loss regularization introduced. It can be observed that the effect is worst when only the direction loss regularization term is introduced, as there is insufficient information guiding the areas lacking exact information, particularly in the absence of sufficient information in the edge areas. However, after introducing the edge-aware factor, we are able to optimize the spatial consistency of the material properties, resulting in improved effects. Furthermore, we quantitatively compare the rendering effects of the Armadillo synthetic dataset using different λ values in Fig. 6. Smaller weights lead to poorer PSNR reconstruction quality, while larger weights lead to better PSNR reconstruction quality. It can be observed that the overall reconstruction effect is best when $\lambda = 0.7$. Therefore, in practical applications, we comprehensively consider rendering quality to choose an appropriate λ value.

Direction Loss. In Table 4, we evaluate the influence of different direction weights on the model. It can be seen that the model performs best when the weight is 0.1. We find that smaller weights can better balance the direction error and the regularization strength of normal direction. This is because the regularization term penalizes predicted normals that differ greatly from the expected normal direction, thereby enhancing the model's prediction of normal direction.

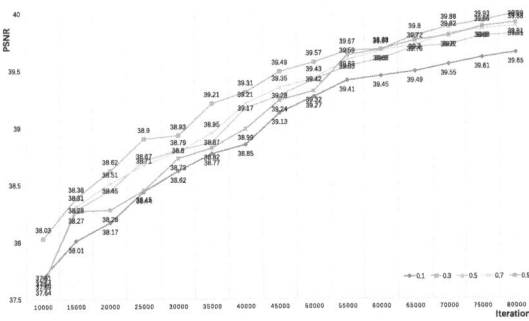

Fig. 6. Quantitative comparison of rendering results on the Armadillo synthetic dataset using different λ values.

5 Conclusion

In this paper, we propose RFBR-IR, a physically-based and easily optimized inverse rendering method that combines physics-based rendering to achieve higher-quality decomposition of lighting and materials in multi-view images. The regularization frequency we propose reveals the impact of input frequency on model reconstruction, refining the visible frequency band through a coarse-to-fine process, dynamically controlling the contribution of encoding frequency, and thus more precisely controlling the introduction of high-frequency information. We also introduce a gradient-based edge-aware factor to optimize spatial consistency and encourage smoothness in adjacent regions when material properties are similar, preserving more detailed information. RFBR-IR outperforms existing state-of-the-art methods on multiple datasets with minimal overhead. Our method achieves a reasonable balance between speed and quality, but there are still opportunities for further research in the future.

References

1. Boss, M., Jampani, V., Braun, R., Liu, C., Barron, J., Lensch, H.: Neural-PIL: neural pre-integrated lighting for reflectance decomposition. Adv. Neural. Inf. Process. Syst. **34**, 10691–10704 (2021)
2. Srinivasan, P.P., Deng, B., Zhang, X., Tancik, M., Mildenhall, B., Barron, J.T.: Nerv: Neural reflectance and visibility fields for relighting and view synthesis. In: Proceedings of the IEEE/CVF Conference on Computer Vision and Pattern Recognition, pp. 7495–7504 (2021)
3. Zhang, X., Srinivasan, P.P., Deng, B., Debevec, P., Freeman, W.T., Barron, J.T.: NeRFactor: neural factorization of shape and reflectance under an unknown illumination. ACM Trans. Graph. (ToG) **40**(6), 1–18 (2021)
4. Sai Bi, et al.: Neural reflectance fields for appearance acquisition. arXiv preprint arXiv:2008.03824 (2020)
5. Li, Z., Zexiang, X., Ramamoorthi, R., Sunkavalli, K., Chandraker, M.: Learning to reconstruct shape and spatially-varying reflectance from a single image. ACM Trans. Graph. (TOG) **37**(6), 1–11 (2018)
6. Mildenhall, B., Srinivasan, P.P., Tancik, M., Barron, J.T., Ramamoorthi, R., Ng, R.: NeRF: representing scenes as neural radiance fields for view synthesis. Commun. ACM **65**(1), 99–106 (2021)
7. Yariv, L., et al.: Multiview neural surface reconstruction by disentangling geometry and appearance. Adv. Neural. Inf. Process. Syst. **33**, 2492–2502 (2020)
8. Chen, A., Xu, Z., Geiger, A., Yu, J., Su, H.: TensoRF: tensorial radiance fields. In: Avidan, S., Brostow, G., Cissé, M., Farinella, G.M., Hassner, T. (eds.) European Conference on Computer Vision, pp. 333–350. Springer (2022). https://doi.org/10.1007/978-3-031-19824-3_20
9. Li, Z., Niklaus, S., Snavely, N., Wang, O.: Neural scene flow fields for space-time view synthesis of dynamic scenes. In: Proceedings of the IEEE/CVF Conference on Computer Vision and Pattern Recognition, pp. 6498–6508 (2021)
10. Müller, T., Evans, A., Schied, C., Keller, A.: Instant neural graphics primitives with a multiresolution hash encoding. ACM Trans. Graph. (ToG) **41**(4), 1–15 (2022)

11. Park, K., et al.: Nerfies: deformable neural radiance fields. In: Proceedings of the IEEE/CVF International Conference on Computer Vision, pp. 5865–5874 (2021)
12. Zhang, K., et al.: ARF: artistic radiance fields. In: Avidan, S., Brostow, G., Cissé, M., Farinella, G.M., Hassner, T. (eds.) European Conference on Computer Vision, pp. 717–733. Springer (2022). https://doi.org/10.1007/978-3-031-19821-2_41
13. Lensch, H.P., Kautz, J., Goesele, M., Heidrich, W., Seidel, H.P.: Image-based reconstruction of spatial appearance and geometric detail. ACM Trans. Graph. (TOG), **22**(2), 234–257 (2003)
14. Schmitt, C., Donne, S., Riegler, G., Koltun, V., Geiger, A.: On joint estimation of pose, geometry and svBRDF from a handheld scanner. In: Proceedings of the IEEE/CVF Conference on Computer Vision and Pattern Recognition, pp. 3493–3503 (2020)
15. Cheng, Z., Li, H., Asano, Y., Zheng, Y., Sato, I.: Multi-view 3D reconstruction of a texture-less smooth surface of unknown generic reflectance. In: Proceedings of the IEEE/CVF Conference on Computer Vision and Pattern Recognition, pp. 16226–16235 (2021)
16. Boss, M., Braun, R., Jampani, V., Barron, J.T., Liu, C., Lensch, H.: NeRD: neural reflectance decomposition from image collections. In: Proceedings of the IEEE/CVF International Conference on Computer Vision, pp. 12684–12694 (2021)
17. Liu, D., Wan, W., Fang, Z., Zheng, X.: GsNeRF: fast novel view synthesis of dynamic radiance fields. Comput. Graph. **116**, 491–499 (2023)
18. Tancik, M., et al.: Fourier features let networks learn high frequency functions in low dimensional domains. Adv. Neural. Inf. Process. Syst. **33**, 7537–7547 (2020)
19. Sitzmann, V., Martel, J., Bergman, A., Lindell, D., Wetzstein, G.: Implicit neural representations with periodic activation functions. Adv. Neural. Inf. Process. Syst. **33**, 7462–7473 (2020)
20. Wang, Y., Skorokhodov, I., Wonka, P.: HF-NeuS: improved surface reconstruction using high-frequency details. Adv. Neural. Inf. Process. Syst. **35**, 1966–1978 (2022)
21. Munkberg, J., et al.: Extracting triangular 3D models, materials, and lighting from images. In: Proceedings of the IEEE/CVF Conference on Computer Vision and Pattern Recognition, pp. 8280–8290 (2022)
22. Zhang, K., Luan, F., Wang, Q., Bala, K., Snavely, N.: PHYSG: inverse rendering with spherical gaussians for physics-based material editing and relighting. In: Proceedings of the IEEE/CVF Conference on Computer Vision and Pattern Recognition, pp. 5453–5462 (2021)
23. Zhang, Y., Sun, J., He, X., Fu, H., Jia, R., Zhou, X.: Modeling indirect illumination for inverse rendering. In: Proceedings of the IEEE/CVF Conference on Computer Vision and Pattern Recognition, pp. 18643–18652 (2022)
24. Wang, P., Liu, L., Liu, Y., Theobalt, C., Komura, T., Wang, W.: NEUS: learning neural implicit surfaces by volume rendering for multi-view reconstruction. arXiv preprint arXiv:2106.10689 (2021)
25. Jin, H., et al.: TensoIR: tensorial inverse rendering. In: Proceedings of the IEEE/CVF Conference on Computer Vision and Pattern Recognition, pp. 165–174 (2023)
26. Kajiya, J.T.: The rendering equation. In: Proceedings of the 13th Annual Conference on Computer Graphics and Interactive Techniques, pp. 143–150 (1986)
27. Burley, B., Studios, W.D.A.: Physically-based shading at disney. In: ACM Siggraph, vol. 2012, pp. 1–7 (2012)
28. Zhang, R., Isola, P., Efros, A.A., Shechtman, E., Wang, O.: The unreasonable effectiveness of deep features as a perceptual metric. In: Proceedings of the IEEE Conference on Computer Vision and Pattern Recognition, pp. 586–595 (2018)

A Lightweight Camouflaged Object Detection Model Based on Improved Attention Mechanism

Jinyu Song[1], Xianzhi Luo[1], Li Jiang[2(✉)], Yan Zhang[2], and Chun Liu[2]

[1] School of Artificial Intelligence, Hubei University, Wuhan, China
[2] School of Computer Science and Information Engineering, Hubei University, Wuhan, China
121695221@qq.com

Abstract. In computer vision tasks, camouflaged object detection aims to detect highly covert objects, which has important practical significance in military reconnaissance, medical monitoring and other fields. In recent years, camouflaged object detection models based on Transformer have become a new research hotspot. However, the training cost of classic Transformer models is high, and the dot-product attention mechanism has a quadratic computational complexity, which will cause excessive memory usage and limit their application on embedded edge devices with limited memory and computing resources. In view of the above issues, a lightweight camouflaged target detection model E-UGTR with improved attention mechanism is proposed. By introducing a linear complexity attention mechanism to reduce the computational complexity of the model, a flexible attention mechanism control strategy is adopted to enhance the performance compatibility of the model under different computing resource requirements. Then, based on the UGTR model, a universal linear attention module E-Attention is introduced to design and implement a lightweight adaptive camouflaged object detection model E-UGTR. The experimental results show that on the common public data set, the training speed of the E-UGTR model is about 1.8 times that of the UGTR model, and the inference speed is about 1.5 times that of the UGTR model. When compared with other classic SOTA models, the E-UGTR model has strong compatibility and can maintain good detection performance while being lightweight.

Keywords: computer vision · camouflaged object detection · attention mechanism · lightweight · transformer

1 Introduction

Camouflage is a crucial mechanism employed by organisms in the natural world for self-protection. It enables a target to possess features such as color and shape that closely resemble the environment, making it challenging to be detected [1]. For instance, as depicted in Fig. 1, fish, spiders, artificial camouflage, and polyps all exhibit a high degree of similarity to their backgrounds. In computer vision tasks, Camouflaged Object Detection (COD) aims to identify highly hidden and similar camouflage targets, which is of great practical significance in military reconnaissance, medical monitoring and other fields.

Camouflaged object detection is an extremely challenging task, mainly because camouflaged objects, unlike general or salient objects, are more difficult to discern as they blend into the background environment. This characteristic makes traditional detection methods less effective in complex scenarios. With the rapid development of deep learning techniques, camouflaged object detection models based on Transformers have become a current research focus. The Transformer model [2] is a deep learning model based on self-attention mechanisms, completely abandoning recurrent and convolutional operations. The traditional Transformer model consists of encoders and decoders, and includes self-attention, cross-attention, and multi-head attention mechanism. Self-attention is the core part of the Transformer model which effectively captures long-range dependencies in processing long sequence data and focuses on critical information. Cross-attention is used to handle and fuse relationships between two different sequences which enhances the model's ability to interact with information from various data. Multi-head attention allows the model to run multiple self-attention mechanisms on the same input sequence, with each mechanism focusing on different parts of the sequence, capturing richer information. Compared to traditional Convolutional Neural Networks (CNN), the Transformer model has stronger parallelism, better ability to acquire global information, and better modeling ability for long sequences. Therefore, the Transformer has been introduced into computer vision tasks, leading to various variant models such as ViT [3], DETR [4], PVT [5], and others. The ViT model, proposed by the Google team in 2020, adopted a pure Transformer structure, divided the input image into patches and inputted them into the model, which achieved good results in image classification tasks. DETR is an end-to-end object detection model proposed by Facebook, it combined CNN and Transformer, simplified the process of object detection and improved detection accuracy and efficiency. Compared with the ViT model, the PVT model only had a single-scale feature. It adopted a pyramid structure and was divided into four stages, so that the model can process images with different resolutions and multi-scale features. In recent years, Transformer models have also been introduced into the camouflaged target detection task. Compared with CNN, Transformer-based camouflaged object detection models can rapidly expand the receptive field, characterize more diverse feature space, and do not lose fine-grained information. They are more suitable for tasks that require rich contextual information, such as camouflaged object detection. However, current Transformer-style camouflaged object detection models are facing challenges such as large model parameter sizes, high computational costs, long training times, and the need for substantial computing power and time. These issues make it difficult to meet the requirements of edge computing and real-time systems. Therefore, researches on the lightweighting of Transformer-style camouflaged target detection models have significant practical implications. Model acceleration is one of the important techniques for the lightweighting of the model. It can effectively reduce the computational burden of the model and make the model run more efficiently in the environments with limited resources.

(a)Camouflaged Fish (b)Camouflaged Spider (c)Artificial Camouflage (d)polyp

Fig. 1. Examples of camouflaged objects

To address these challenges and reduce the demand of memory occupation and computing resources of the Transformer-style camouflaged target detection model, a lightweight camouflaged object detection method with an improved attention mechanism is proposed. This approach introduces a linear complexity attention mechanism to reduce the model's computational complexity. It replaces the traditional self-attention and cross-attention in Transformer with a linear attention module, reducing model training time, enhancing model inference speed, and adopting a flexible attention control strategy to improve the model's performance compatibility with different computational resource demands.

2 Related Work

In recent years, there has been a growing interest in camouflaged object detection models based on Transformer [6–10]. Yang et al. introduced Bayesian learning into camouflaged object detection and proposed the UGTR [6] (Uncertainty-guided Transformer Reasoning) which used probability to model uncertain regions. Liu et al. presented a camouflaged object detection model named DTINet [7], which can precisely locate camouflage objects and capture their detailed boundaries simultaneously. Zhang et al. introduced a progressive network called TPRNet [8] which consists of a Progressive Refinement Module (TPRM) and a Semantic-Spatial Interaction Enhancement Module (SIEM). In the TPRM module, high-level semantics are guided and refined, while in the SIEM module, refined semantic features interact with low-level features to enhance boundary features. Different from the above methods, Yin et al.'s Camo-Former [9] focuses on the effective use of self-attention mechanisms. It uses the Masked Separable Attention (MSA) method to separates multi-head self-attention into three parts, This method can treat camouflage objects and backgrounds separately. Through a top-down approach, it captures high-resolution semantics progressively, gradually improving the segmentation accuracy of camouflage targets. Although these methods have achieved good detection results, they do not emphasize lightweight design. The models have large computational requirements. They require significant computing power and time and can not meet the application needs on the equipments with limited resources. This is mainly due to the quadratic temporal and spatial complexity of the attention mechanism in the Transformer model. Especially when the input sequence is longer, the calculation amount of the model and occupation of memory will show a square-level increase. In response to this problem, this paper studies a lightweight camouflaged object detection model based on an improved attention mechanism to reduce computational complexity and achieve model acceleration. Reference [11] employs linear attention to address the quadratic computational complexity issue in the Transformer model, mapping the self-attention's Softmax function as the linear dot product of kernel features, and utilizing the associativity of matrix multiplication to reduce the computational complexity from $O(N^2)$ to $O(N)$. Specifically, linear attention uses a separate kernel function to replace the Softmax function in self-attention, reducing the need for pairwise computations. Based on the associativity property of matrix multiplication, linear attention changes the computation order by first calculatin QK^T to decrease the computational complexity from $O(N^2d)$ to $O(Nd^2)$. The core challenge in the linear attention module's design is to make it equivalent to Softmax attention. Performer [12] uses a new fast attention orthogonal random feature method to approximate the Softmax attention kernel. Performer operates with linear space and time complexity and does not rely on prior conditions such as sparsity or low-rankness. Hydra attention [13] replaces Softmax with cosine similarity and employs an extremely multi-head attention mechanism, where each feature has an independent attention head. Each feature does not attend to all features but focuses only on other features related to it, making the attention computation complexity linear with the number of features and tokens. SOFT [14] replaces the dot-product similarity with a Gaussian kernel function, which can make an approximation of the complete self-attention matrix through low-rank matrix decomposition. Efficient Attention [15] normalizes rows and columns separately for Q and K using Softmax, so that the sum of QK^T each row equals 1.

Inspired by this, this paper introduces a linear attention module into the Transformer-based camouflaged object detection model, exploring how to lightweight the Transformer-style camouflaged object detection model to achieve model acceleration.

3 Research Methodology

This paper proposes a lightweight camouflaged target detection method which will reduce model computational complexity through replacing the traditional dot-product attention mechanism with an improved attention mechanism. At the same time, an Attention Control Module (ACM) is designed to enhance the performance compatibility of the model under different computational resource requirements by setting control strategies for the attention mechanism. Additionally, based on the UGTR model, an linear attention module, E-Attention, is introduced, which will realize a camouflaged target detection model E-UGTR compatible with lightweight scenarios.

3.1 The Overall Architecture of the E-UGTR Model

The overall structure of the E-UGTR model is illustrated in Fig. 2. The E-UGTR model consists of four main components: the Uncertainty Quantization Network (UQN), the E-uncertainty-guided transformer (E-UGT), the E-prototyping transformer (E-PT), and the Attention Control Module (ACM). On the original UGTR model architecture, the E-UGTR model primarily replaces the multi-head attention in the UGTR model, including self-attention and cross-attention, with the E-Attention module based on Efficient Attention. This replacement aims to achieve model lightweighting. Furthermore, an Attention Control Module (ACM) is introduced to enhance the performance compatibility of the model in different resource environments.

The UQN network comes from the UGTR model and consists of two parts: the feature extraction network and the probability module. ResNet50 is selected as the feature extraction network to extract features. Through the ResNet50 network, an RGB image $I \in R^{H \times W \times 3}$ is mapped to a c-dimensional feature embedding $F \in R^{h \times w \times c}$. To obtain the uncertainty map, Gaussian distribution modeling is applied to the pixel-level feature embedding, resulting in mean map $\mu \in R^{h \times w \times 1}$ and variance map $\sigma \in R^{h \times w \times 1}$. For the variance map, a standard Gaussian distribution is added to ensure end-to-end differentiation. Subsequently, K camouflaged samples are drawn from the distribution to generate uncertainty maps.

The E-PT serves as an auxiliary module designed for learning and reasoning about higher-level semantics. E-PT transforms the feature embedding $F \in R^{h \times w \times c}$ into t learnable semantic prototype $X = x_1, ...x_t \in R^{tc}$. These prototypes X are employed to assist the final inference. E-PT initially acquires initial prototype features Xinit using an iterative strategy and subsequently processes Xinit through a Transformer block to obtain the final prototype features $X \in R^{c \times t}$. $X \in R^{c \times t}$ carries essential global semantics.

E-UGT takes feature embedding $F \in R^{c \times hw}$, semantic prototypes $X \in R^{c \times t}$, and uncertainty mapas $U \in R^{1 \times hw}$ as inputs, and then generates refined features $F_o \in R^{(h \times w) \times c}$ for camouflaged target detection in a sequence-to-sequence manner. To enhance contextual reasoning ability, especially in challenging (uncertain) regions, the Uncertainty-Guided Random Masking algorithm (UGRM) from the UGTR model is incorporated into E-UGT. The UGRM algorithm is embedded in E-UGT and guided by the uncertainty map U, ensuring that challenging detection areas are more likely to be masked during the training process.

The Attention Control Module (ACM) is a module capable of dynamically switching attention mechanisms based on different computational resource environments.

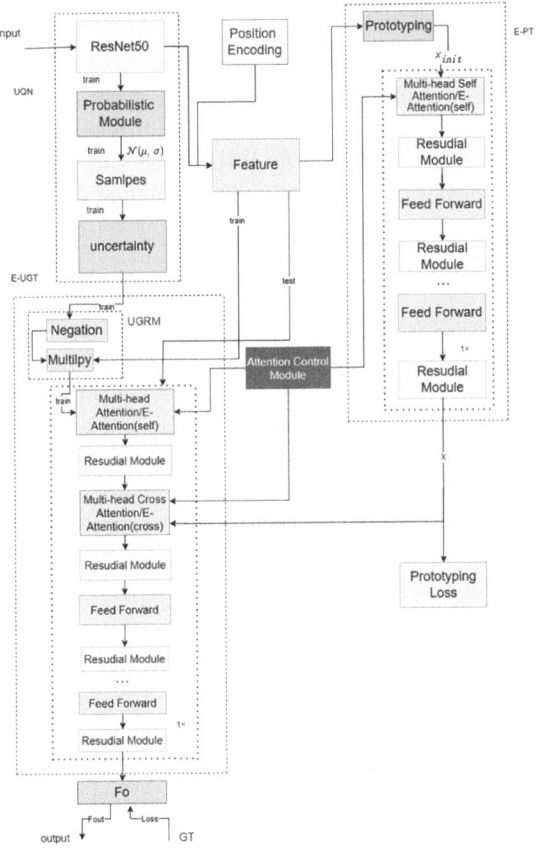

Fig. 2. E-UGTR Model

The four modules work together to infer the context and produce the decamouflaged result F_o. Finally, F_o is mapped into the ultimate prediction result output through an output function F_{out}, which comprises a reshaping layer, a 1×1 convolutional layer, and an up-sampling layer.

3.2 Attention Control Module (ACE)

Performance compatibility of the model on devices with different computational resources, the E-UGTR model incorporates an Attention Control Module (ACE). On devices with sufficient computational resources, the E-UGTR model can utilize the traditional scaled dot-product attention of the Transformer model to achieve better detection accuracy. On devices with limited computational resources, the E-UGTR model can switch to a lightweight mode, employing the linear attention module (E-Attention) to reduce model computational complexity, lower computational requirements, decrease training time, and enhance inference speed.

3.3 The Scaled Dot-Product Attention Mechanism

On devices with sufficient computational resources, the E-UGTR model can utilize the traditional scaled dot-product attention of the Transformer model to achieve better detection accuracy. In the specific implementation of the traditional Transformer model, both the multi-head self-attention mechanism and the cross-attention mechanism are achieved through scaled dot-product attention. The calculation formula for dot-product attention is as follows:

$$D(Q, K, V) = \rho(QK^T)V \qquad (1)$$

Among them, $Q, K, V \in R^{N \times d}$. The main drawback of the dot-product attention mechanism lies in its high computational resource requirements, with a memory complexity of $O(N^2)$ and a computational complexity of $O(dN^2)$. Therefore, the resource demands of dot-product attention become prohibitively high for large inputs, posing a significant obstacle to its application on devices with limited resources. The scaled dot-product attention introduces a scaling factor on top of the dot-product attention to maintain numerical stability and prevent gradient explosions. The mathematical expression for the scaled dot-product attention mechanism is shown in Eq. (2):

$$D(Q, K, V) = Softmax(\frac{QK^T}{\sqrt{d_k}})V \qquad (2)$$

d_k denotes the dimension of the Key.

3.4 The Linear Attention Module E-Attention, Based on the Efficient Attention

Motivated by the effective reduction in computational complexity brought about by the linear attention mechanism, this paper introduces the Efficient Attention into the camouflaged object detection model. It designs a linear attention module named E-Attention based on the Efficient Attention, which can replace the traditional Transformer model's attention mechanism with the specific implementation of scaled dot-product attention as needed. The E-Attention module is embedded and operates within both E-PT and E-UGT. The structure of the E-Attention module is illustrated in Fig. 3.

In the E-Attention module, instead of interpreting K as N feature vectors in R^d, the query matrix $Q \in R^{N \times d}$, key matrix $K \in R^{N \times d}$ and value matrix $V \in R^{N \times d}$ are treated as d single-channel feature maps. The E-Attention module considers each map as a weighting over all positions, aggregating features through weighted summation to form a global context vector. This vector does not correspond to a specific position but serves as a global description of the input features.

The linear attention computation formula in the E-Attention module is defined as follows (Eq. 3):

$$E(Q, K, V) = Softmax_{row}(\frac{Q}{\sqrt{d_k}})(Softmax_{col}(K^T)V) \qquad (3)$$

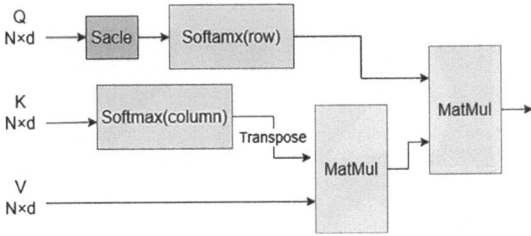

Fig. 3. Structure of the E-Attention Module

In the context of the E-Attention module, $Softmax_{row}(\bullet)$ and $Softmax_{col}(\bullet)$ represent the application of the Softmax function along each row or each column of the matrix, respectively. The Softmax operation in Eq. (2) is essentially equivalent to $Softmax_{row}(\bullet)$. Although the two Softmax operations on Q and K are not exactly equivalent to a single Softmax operation on QK^T, they closely approximate the original Softmax operation. The key property of $\sigma_{row}(\frac{QK^T}{\sqrt{d_k}})$ is that each of its rows sums up to be very close to 1, indicating a normalized attention distribution across all positions. The Softmax variant on the matrix $\sigma_{row}(\frac{Q}{\sqrt{d_k}})\sigma_{col}(K)^T$ is similar to a variant of the scaled dot-product attention mechanism.

Table 1. Performance Comparison of Various Models

Networks	CHAMELEON				CAMO				COD10K			
	$S_\alpha \uparrow$	$E_\phi \uparrow$	$F_\beta^\omega \uparrow$	MAE↓	$S_\alpha \uparrow$	$E_\phi \uparrow$	$F_\beta^\omega \uparrow$	MAE↓	$S_\alpha \uparrow$	$E_\phi \uparrow$	$F_\beta^\omega \uparrow$	MAE↓
FPN [16]	0.794	0.783	0.590	0.075	0.684	0.677	0.483	0.131	0.697	0.691	0.411	0.075
MaskRCNN [17]	0.643	0.778	0.518	0.099	0.574	0.715	0.430	0.151	0.613	0.748	0.402	0.080
PSPNet [18]	0.773	0.758	0.555	0.085	0.663	0.659	0.455	0.139	0.678	0.680	0.377	0.080
UNet++ [19]	0.695	0.762	0.501	0.094	0.599	0.653	0.392	0.149	0.623	0.672	0.350	0.086
PiCANet [20]	0.769	0.749	0.536	0.085	0.609	0.584	0.356	0.156	0.649	0.643	0.322	0.090
MSRCNN [21]	0.637	0.686	0.443	0.091	0.617	0.669	0.454	0.133	0.641	0.706	0.419	0.073
PoolNet [22]	0.776	0.779	0.555	0.081	0.702	0.698	0.494	0.129	0.705	0.713	0.416	0.074
BASNet [23]	0.687	0.721	0.474	0.118	0.618	0.661	0.413	0.159	0.634	0.678	0.365	0.105
PFANet [24]	0.679	0.648	0.378	0.144	0.659	0.622	0.391	0.172	0.636	0.618	0.286	0.128
HTC [25]	0.517	0.489	0.204	0.129	0.476	0.442	0.174	0.172	0.548	0.520	0.021	0.088
A-Net [26]	–	–	–	–	0.682	0.685	0.484	0.126	–	–	–	–
SINet [1]	0.869	0.891	0.740	0.044	0.751	0.771	0.606	0.100	0.771	0.806	0.551	0.051
E-UGTR	0.823	0.885	0.685	0.054	0.734	0.817	0.599	0.109	0.764	0.845	0.550	0.052

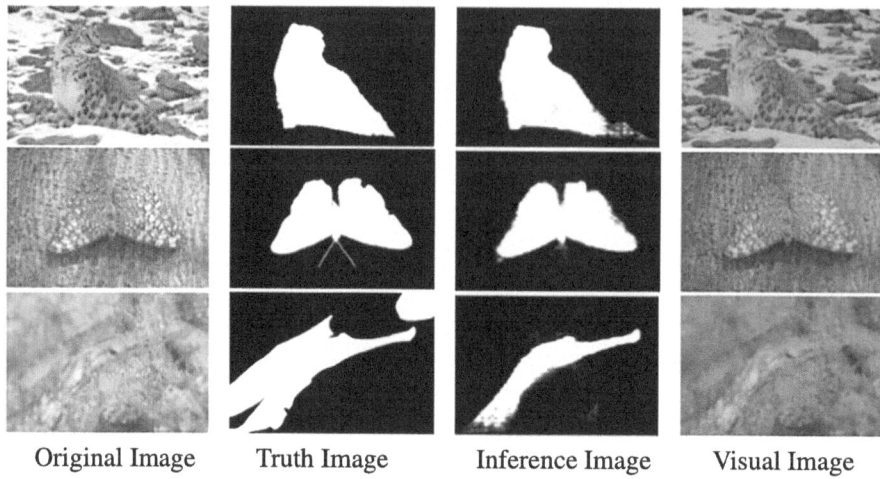

Original Image Truth Image Inference Image Visual Image

Fig. 4. Visualization of E-UGTR Inference Results

Table 2. Training Time Comparison between E-UGTR and UGTR

Model Name	epoch	Training Time per Epoch	Total Training Time for 50 Epochs
UGTR	50	900 s	13.25h
E-UGTR	50	496 s	7.31h

Table 3. Comparative Inference Speeds of E-UGTR and UGTR on Various COD Datasets

Dataset Name	UGTR	E-UGTR
CAMO	17 s	12 s
NC4K	238 s	163 s
COD10K	121 s	81 s

Table 4. Comparison of E-UGTR and UGTR on CAMO Dataset Indicators

Evaluating Indicator	UGTR	E-UGTR
S_α	0.785	0.734
E_ϕ	0.859	0.817
F_β^ω	0.686	0.599
MAE	0.086	0.109

Table 5. Performance Comparison of E-UGTR and UGTR on CHAMELEON Dataset

Evaluating Indicator	UGTR	E-UGTR
S_α	0.888	0.823
E_ϕ	0.918	0.885
F_β^ω	0.796	0.685
MAE	0.031	0.054

Table 6. Performance Comparison of E-UGTR and UGTR on COD10K Dataset Indicators

Evaluating Indicator	UGTR	E-UGTR
S_α	0.818	0.764
E_ϕ	0.850	0.845
F_β^ω	0.667	0.550
MAE	0.035	0.052

4 Experimental Evaluation

4.1 Experiment Setup

The experiments are conducted in the environment configured with CUDA 11.3, PyTorch 1.12.1, Python 3.8.5, and a GPU of NVIDIA GeForce RTX 4060 Ti 16G. For the feature extraction network ResNet50 in the model, we use its pre-trained weight parameters on the ImageNet dataset. During the network training phase, this chapter transforms the size of the training images to 473×473 through preprocessing, and set the batch size (batch size) to 1, the base learning rate (base lr) to 10^{-7}, the exponent (power) of learning rate decay to 0.9, the auxiliary loss weight to 0.4 and the weight decay to 10^{-5}.

4.2 Dataset

To evaluate the performance of the E-UGTR model with the E-Attention module(referred to as E-UGTR), assessments are conducted on four publicly available camouflaged detection datasets. In the CAMO dataset [26], 1,000 camouflaged images belong to the training set, and 250 camouflaged images are part of the test set. The CHAMELEON dataset [27] consists of 76 camouflaged images, which are all in the test set. The COD10K dataset [1] contains a total of 5,066 camouflaged images, with 3,040 images in the training set comprising and 2,026 images in the test set. The NC4K dataset [28] has a test set with 4,121 images for the camouflaged object detection task. For a fair comparison, this paper uses the same training dataset as Yang et al. [6], combining the COD10K and CAMO datasets to form the training set, which includes a total of 4,040 camouflaged images. Although the datasets provide both image-level and pixel-level annotations, only per-pixel labels are required for model training.

4.3 Evaluation Metrics

The effectiveness of the E-UGTR model with the E-Attention module is evaluated on three widely adopted datasets for camouflaged object detection: CAMO, CHAMELEON, and COD10K. The evaluation utilizes four commonly used performance metrics, namely Mean Absolute Error (MAE) [29], E-measure (E_ϕ) [30], S-measure (S_α) [31], and F-measure (F_ω^β) [32]. A smaller MAE indicates better model performance, while higher values for the other three metrics signify improved model performance.

(1) Structural Measure (S-measure, S_α): This metric is used to evaluate the structural similarity between the predicted camouflage image and the ground truth image. Unlike pixel-level error metrics, S_α assesses region-level errors. It involves two parameters, namely S_o and S_r, where S_o calculates the target perception, and S_r is used to acquire region observation features. The expression for the S-measure is as follows:

$$S_\alpha = \alpha \times S_o + (1 - \alpha) \times S_r \tag{4}$$

S_o represents the target-based structural metric and S_r represents the region-based structural metric; α is the weight parameter, $\alpha \in [0, 1]$ with the default value of 0.5, which is used to balance S_o and S_r.

(2) The Enhanced-alignment measure (E-measure, E_ϕ) is a method based on visual perception mechanisms. It evaluates the overall and local accuracy of the camouflaged target detection results by comparing the differences between the predicted and ground truth images with both image-level and pixel-level statistics. Its formula is defined as follows:

$$E_\phi = \frac{1}{W \times H} \sum_{x=1}^{W} \sum_{y=1}^{H} \phi(C(x,y) - G(x,y)) \tag{5}$$

ϕ represents the enhanced consistency matrix, W and H denote the width and height of the input, while C and G represent the predicted and ground truth images, respectively.

(3) The Weighted F-measure (F_ω^β), primarily based on region similarity, calculates the relationship between precision P and recall R. It can compute the average harmonic measure between P and R and display its numerical value. The formula is defined as follows:

$$F_\beta^\omega = \frac{(1 + \beta^2) P \times R}{\beta^2 \times P + R} \tag{6}$$

P and R represent the weighted precision and recall, and β is a balancing hyperparameter for P and R. β^2 is set to 0.3 by default.

(4) MAE (Mean Absolute Error): It is used to calculate the average absolute error between the prediction map and the true image, serving as a metric to

measure the quality of the model's predicted image. The formula is defined as follows:

$$MAE = \frac{1}{W \times H} \sum_{x=1}^{H} \sum_{y=1}^{W} |C(x,y) - G(x,y)| \tag{7}$$

W and H represent the width and height of the image; $C(x,y) \in [0,1]$ denotes the pixel value at location (x,y) in the prediction map, while $G(x,y) \in [0,1]$ represents the pixel value at location (x,y) in the ground truth image.

4.4 Experimental Results and Analysis

The E-UGTR model, equipped with the E-Attention module (referred to as E-UGTR), is quantitatively compared with some state-of-the-art (SOTA) methods on the CAMO, CHAMELEON, and COD10K datasets, as shown in Table 1. In comparison with these SOTA methods, the E-UGTR model outperforms them on all metrics. On the CAMO dataset, compared to the ANet model, the MAE metric decreases by 1.2% points, S-measure increases by 3.5% points, E-measure increases by 11.6% points, and F-measure increases by 9.7% points. On the COD10K dataset, compared to the SINet model, the lightweight mode of the E-UGTR model sees a slight drop in the S-measure evaluation index by 0.7% points, but the MAE evaluation index only increases by 0.1% points, with the F-measure evaluation index showing virtually no difference, being only 0.1% points lower, whereas the E-measure evaluation index improves by 3.9% points. The visualization of the inference results of E-UGTR is shown in Fig. 4.

4.5 Ruling Out Experiment

On a well-resourced device with the same experimental setup, a comparison was made between the E-UGTR model (equipped with the E-Attention module) and the UGTR model in terms of training time and inference time. Since the E-Attention module reduces the complexity of model computations, the training duration is effectively shortened. Detailed data is presented in Table 2. Under the experimental condition with 4040 images in the training dataset, E-UGTR achieved a training time of 7.31 h, while UGTR had a training duration of 13.25 h, resulting in a 44 reduction in training time. It can be observed that the use of the linear attention mechanism significantly reduces the model's training time, making the training speed of the E-UGTR model 1.81 times faster than the UGTR model.

In terms of inference speed, we conducted a comparison of inference times on classic datasets such as CAMO, NC4K, and COD10K, as shown in Table 3. For the CAMO dataset with 250 images, the UGTR model requires 17 s for inference, while the E-UGTR model only takes 12 s, which is a 1.42-fold speedup compared to the original model. In the case of the NC4K dataset with 4121 images, the UGTR model requires 238 s for inference, whereas the E-UGTR model only takes 163 s, achieving a 1.46-fold speedup. Similarly, for the COD10K dataset with 2026 images, the UGTR model takes 121 s for inference, while the

E-UGTR model only requires 81 s, resulting in a 1.49-fold increase in inference speed. This indicates that on GPU platforms, the E-UGTR model, based on efficient attention mechanisms, achieves approximately 1.46 times acceleration compared to the UGTR model.

E-UGTR model has significant advantages over the UGTR model in terms of training time, inference speed, and consumption of memory and computational resources. This is due to the introduction of the Efficient Attention replaces the scaled dot-product attention mechanism in the UGTR model, which reduces the model's memory complexity fromto, and computational complexity fromto. However, the E-UGTR model still exhibits a certain degree of loss in accuracy compared to the UGTR model. The performance comparison on the CAMO dataset is shown in Table 4, with the S-measure evaluation index decreasing by 5.1% points, the E-measure evaluation index decreasing by 4.2% points, the F-measure evaluation index decreasing by 8.7% points, and the MAE increasing by 2.3% points; the comparison on the CHAMELEON dataset is shown in Table 5, with the S-measure evaluation index decreasing by 6.5% points, the E-measure evaluation index decreasing by 3.3% points, the F-measure evaluation index decreasing by 11.1% points, and the MAE increasing by 2.2% points; the comparison on the most challenging COD10K dataset is shown in Table 6, with the S-measure evaluation index decreasing by 5.4% points, the E-measure evaluation index decreasing by 0.5% points, the F-measure evaluation index decreasing by 11.7% points, and the MAE increasing by 1.7% points. Overall, the E-UGTR model with the enabled E-Attention module effectively alleviates the quadratic computational complexity issue of traditional Transformer models' attention mechanisms. While ensuring acceptable accuracy losses, it achieves significant advantages in terms of model training time, inference speed, as well as memory and computational resource consumption compared to traditional Transformer models.

5 Conclusions

This paragraph discusses the challenges posed by mainstream Transformer-based camouflaged object detection models and highlights some issues, such as lengthy training times, data consumption, large parameter counts, and high demands on memory and computational resources which limited their applicability on resource-constrained devices. To address these challenges, the paper introduces a lightweight camouflaged object detection method based on an improved attention mechanism. This approach leverages a linear complexity attention mechanism to enhance the traditional Transformer's attention mechanism which will accelerate the model. Additionally, we design an Attention Control Module (ACM) to achieve flexible attention mechanism strategy for the model. Finally, we build a lightweight adaptive camouflaged target detection model E-UGTR, which use an universal linear attention module (E-Attention) based on the UGTR. The E-UGTR model significantly reduces computational resource requirements compared to the UGTR model. It demonstrates approximately 1.8

times faster training speed and 1.5 times faster inference speed. By comparing the E-UGTR model with other classic SOTA methods, the E-UGTR model achieves a better balance between detection performance and efficiency.

Acknowledgements. This work is supported by the National Natural Science Foundation of China (No. 62377009, 62102136), the Key R & D projects in Hubei Province (No. 2021BAA184, 2021BAA188), the Science and Technology Innovation Program of Hubei Province (No. 2020AEA008), The Major Program (JD) of Hubei Province (2023BAA018), and in part by the Hubei Province Project of Key Research Institute of Humanities and Social Sciences at Universities (Research Center of Information Management for Performance Evaluation).

References

1. Fan, D.-P., Ji, G.-P., Sun, G.-L., Cheng, M.-M., Shen, J.-B., Lin, S.: Camouflaged object detection. In: CVPR, pp. 2774–2784, Seattle, WA, USA. IEEE (2019)
2. Vaswani, A., et al.: Attention is all you need. In: NeurIPS, pp. 6000–6010, Long Beach, California, USA. Curran Associates Inc. (2017)
3. Dosovitskiy, A., et al.: An image is worth 16 × 16 words: transformers for image recognition at scale. In: ICLR (2021)
4. Carion, N., Massa, F., Synnaeve, G., Usunier, N., Kirillov, A., Zagoruyko, S.: End-to-end object detection with transformers. In: Vedaldi, A., Bischof, H., Brox, T., Frahm, J.-M. (eds.) ECCV 2020. LNCS, vol. 12346, pp. 213–229. Springer, Cham (2020). https://doi.org/10.1007/978-3-030-58452-8_13
5. Wang, W., et al.: Pyramid vision transformer: a versatile backbone for dense prediction without convolutions. In: ICCV, pp. 548–558, Montreal, QC, Canada. IEEE (2021)
6. Yang, F., et al.: Uncertainty-guided transformer reasoning for camouflaged object detection. In: ICCV, pp. 4126–4135, Montreal, QC, Canada. IEEE (2021)
7. Liu, Z., Zhang, Z., Wu, W.: Boosting camouflaged object detection with dual-task interactive transformer. In: ICPR, pp. 140–146, Montreal, QC, Canada. IEEE (2022)
8. Zhang, Q., Ge, Y., Zhang, C., Bi, H.: TPRNet: camouflaged object detection via transformer-induced progressive refinement network. Vis. Comput. **39**, 4593–4607 (2023)
9. Yin, B., Zhang, X., Hou, Q., Sun, B.-Y., Fan, D.-P., Gool, L.V.: CamoFormer: masked separable attention for camouflaged object detection (2022). https://arxiv.org/abs/2212.06570
10. Mao, Y., et al.: Transformer transforms salient object detection and camouflaged object detection (2021). https://arxiv.org/abs/2104.10127
11. Katharopoulos, A., Vyas, A., Pappas, N., Fleuret, F.: Transformers are RNNs: fast autoregressive transformers with linear attention. In: ICML, pp. 5156—5165. JMLR.org (2020)
12. Choromanski, K., et al.: Rethinking attention with performers. In: ICLR (2021)
13. Bolya, D., Fu, C.-Y., Dai, X., Zhang, P., Hoffman, J.: Hydra attention: efficient attention with many heads. In: Karlinsky, L., Michaeli, T., Nishino, K. (eds.) Computer Vision - ECCV 2022 Workshops, pp. 35–49, Tel Aviv, Israel (2023)

14. Jiachen, L., et al.: SOFT: softmax-free transformer with linear complexity. Adv. Neural. Inf. Process. Syst. **34**, 21297–21309 (2021)
15. Shen, Z., Zhang, M., Zhao, H., Yi, S., Li, H.: Efficient attention: attention with linear complexities. In: CVPR, pp. 3530–3538, Waikoloa, HI, USA. IEEE (2021)
16. Lin, T.-Y., Dollár, P., Girshick, R., He, K., Hariharan, B., Belongie, S.: Feature pyramid networks for object detection. In: CVPR, pp. 936–944, Honolulu, HI, USA. IEEE (2017)
17. He, K., Gkioxari, G., Dollár, P., Girshicke, R.: Mask R-CNN. In: ICCV, pp. 2980–2988, Venice, Italy. IEEE (2017)
18. Zhao, H., Shi, J., Qi, X., Wang, X., Jia, J.: Pyramid scene parsing network. In: CVPR, pp. 6230–6239, Honolulu, HI, USA. IEEE (2017)
19. Zhou, Z., Siddiquee, Md.M.R., Tajbakhsh, N., Liang, J.: UNet++: a nested U-Net architecture for medical image segmentation. In: Stoyanov, D., et al. (eds.) DLMIA, pp. 3–11, Granada, Spain. Springer, Cham (2018). https://doi.org/10.1007/978-3-030-00889-5_1
20. Liu, N., Han, J., Yang, M.-H.: PiCANet: learning pixel-wise contextual attention for saliency detection. IEEE Trans. Image Process. **28**, 6438–6451 (2020)
21. Huang, Z., Huang, L., Gong, Y., Huang, C., Wang, X.: Mask scoring R-CNN. In: CVPR, pp. 6402–6411, Long Beach, CA, USA. IEEE (2019)
22. Liu, J.-J., Hou, Q., Cheng, M.-M., Feng, J., Jiang, J.: A simple pooling-based design for real-time salient object detection. In: CVPR, pp. 3912–3921, Long Beach, CA, USA. IEEE (2019)
23. Qin, J., Zhang, Z., Huang, C., Gao, C., Dehghan, M., Jagersand, M.: BASNet: boundary-aware salient object detection. In: CVPR, pp. 7471–7481, Long Beach, CA, USA. IEEE (2019)
24. Zhao, T., Wu, X.: Pyramid feature attention network for saliency detection. In: CVPR, pp. 3080–3089, Long Beach, CA, USA. IEEE (2019)
25. Chen, K., et al.: Hybrid task cascade for instance segmentation. In: CVPR, pp. 4969–4978, Long Beach, CA, USA. IEEE (2019)
26. Le, T.-N., Nguyen, T.V., Nie, Z., Tran, M.T., Sugimoto, A.: Anabranch network for camouflaged object segmentation. Comput. Vis. Image Underst. **184**, 45–56 (2019)
27. Wu, Z., Su, L., Huang, Q.: Cascaded partial decoder for fast and accurate salient object detection. In: CVPR, pp. 3902–3911, Long Beach, CA, USA. IEEE (2019)
28. Lv, Y., et al.: Simultaneously localize, segment and rank the camouflaged objects. In: CVPR, pp. 11589–11596, Nashville, TN, USA. IEEE (2021)
29. Perazzi, F., Krähenbühl, P., Pritch, Y., Hornung, A.: Saliency filters: contrast based filtering for salient region detection. In: CVPR, pp. 733–740, Providence, RI, USA. IEEE (2012)
30. Fan, D.-P., Ji, G.-P., Qin, X., Cheng, M.-M.: Cognitive vision inspired object segmentation metric and loss function. Comput. Vis. Image Underst. **184**, 1 (2021)
31. Fan, D.-P., Cheng, M.-M., Liu, Y., Li, T., Borji, A.: Structure-measure: a new way to evaluate foreground maps. In: ICCV, pp. 4558–4567, Venice, Italy. IEEE (2017)
32. Margolin, R., Zelnik-Manor, L., Tal, A.: How to evaluate foreground maps. In: CVPR, pp. 248–255, Columbus, OH, USA. IEEE (2017)

A Fabric Defect Detection Method Based on Improved YOLOv5

Chi Zhang[1,2], Cancan Rao[1,2], Hongjun Li[1,3(✉)], Chengjun Chang[1,2], Jun Wang[1,2], Aijie Yin[1,2], and Zixuan Wang[1,2]

[1] School of Mechanical Engineering and Automation, Wuhan Textile University, Wuhan, China
lhj@wtu.edu.cn
[2] Hubei Key Laboratory of Digital Textile Equipment, Wuhan, China
[3] Hubei Engineering Research Center for Intelligent Assembly of Industrial Detonators, Wuhan, China

Abstract. Fabric defect detection algorithms currently suffer from low detection accuracy, slow processing speeds, and high rates of missing subtle defects, severely limiting the application of this technology. To address this challenge, this paper proposes a fabric defect detection algorithm called GDC-YOLO, which contributes as follows: (1) To reduce network parameters and computational costs, we utilize the Ghost module to enhance the detection capability of tiny defects while lowering model complexity. (2) We introduce a novel DWAM attention mechanism, leveraging depthwise separable convolution, to resolve the issue of spatial and channel attention interfering with each other. (3) To better understand contextual information in feature maps and spatial relationships, we incorporate coordinate information into the feature maps, thereby enhancing the model's generalization ability. (4) Addressing the issue of long-tailed data, we effectively mitigate the impact of imbalanced positive and negative samples on detection results using Focal Loss, thereby improving the accuracy and stability of fabric defect detection. On the SDCF dataset, compared to YOLOv5, GDC-YOLO significantly reduces network parameters by 20.4%, while simultaneously improving , accuracy, and recall by 5.5%, 6%, and 5.2%, respectively. Additionally, the proposed DWAM attention mechanism serves as a superior alternative to CBAM, significantly increasing by 1.7% in experiments.

Keywords: fabric defect detection · YOLOv5 · Ghost · DWAM · CoordConv

1 Introduction

Currently, the vast majority of textile enterprises rely on manual visual inspection for fabric defect detection. Manual visual inspection is influenced by subjective factors, such as limited worker experience, unstable lighting conditions on-site, and worker fatigue, as well as objective factors. Often, this method fails to guarantee the accuracy and precision of detection. Fabric images are characterized by dense warp and weft threads and complex textures. To achieve higher detection rates manually, more time is required for inspection, which is insufficient to meet the demands of large-scale industrial inspection. With the development of computer and deep learning technologies, utilizing image processing techniques for intelligent and automated detection has become a research hotspot in fabric defect detection [1].

There are numerous target detection algorithms based on deep learning [2–5], which can be categorized into two-stage target detection algorithms and single-stage target detection algorithms in terms of the structure of the detection network. The representative network of the two-stage target detection algorithm is Faster R-CNN [6]. Faster R-CNN obtains the input image features through a feature extraction network, generates the candidate region of the target based on the features using RPN [7] (Region proposal network), and finally filters out the most accurate box as the output through NMS [8]. Single-stage target detection algorithm utilizes the whole image as the input of the network and directly outputs the coordinate position of the Bounding box and the labeled category in the output layer, the representative networks are SSD [9] and YOLO series network [10–12], this kind of algorithm completely abandons the step of generating candidate regions, greatly improves the detection speed, and can satisfy the speed requirements of real-time detection However, the detection accuracy is relatively low.

Some scholars use target detection algorithms applied to fabric defect detection. Chen [13] et al. combine the Gabor filter with Faster R-CNN, which dramatically improves the recognition rate of fabric defects with Faster R-CNN, but reduces the detection speed. Xie [14] combines YOLOv1 with their image acquisition system and completes a complete fabric defect detection system. Jing et al. [15] used the improved YOLOV3 for fabric defect detection, and the addition of feature layers can better detect small defects. Guo [16] et al. proposed to add a convolution to the SE network to combine the two outputs to improve the detection ability and added the ASPP module to obtain a larger sensory field, which improved the accuracy of fabric defect detection, but the correspondingly increases the computational complexity of the network. The detection speed of both schemes has decreased significantly, and it is difficult to meet the requirements of real-time detection.

Xie [17] et al. to solve the problem of the poor generalization ability of the target detection model, added the FCCA attention mechanism and the connecting block for enhanced feature transfer (BA-TCB) to RefineDet, which greatly improved the generalization ability of the model, and was able to detect fabric defects with no pattern, regular pattern, and irregular patterned backgrounds. Liu et al. [18] proposed to integrate the layer features and the source model information to improve the robustness and recognition rate of the model, which solves the needs of limited samples and automatically obtains accurate quantification, but it cannot be integrated with real-time monitoring systems at present.

Existing scholars have proposed a variety of fabric defect detection techniques based on image processing, such as Zhang [19] and Kang [20], etc., respectively, proposed the use of the Gabor filter to achieve feature selection and parameter optimization, the method can achieve the defect-recognition in complex texture background, but for the complex background are required to set different parameters. To detect fabrics with complex textures and small defects, Tong [21] et al. proposed to utilize non-local similarity in the image for defect detection by adopting a non-locally concentrated sparse representation model, which is effective in detecting small defects but less effective in detecting defects in large areas.

Defect detection algorithms have been widely used in industry. However, due to the complexity of the fabric background texture interlacing, and the existence of part of the texture and defect similarity, different types of defects of different shapes, the same type of defects of different sizes, making the current defect detection algorithms on the fabric of the detection of the effect is not good. Therefore, this paper focuses on researching target detection algorithms with less number of parameters, faster detection speed, and more accurate localization of fabric defect detection. The main contributions of this paper are as follows:

1). Use the lightweight network module C3_Ghost to replace the C3 module in the Neck network to speed up the feature extraction, and reduce the number of network parameters while the model performance degradation is not obvious.
2). Propose a customized attention mechanism DWAM (Depthwise Attention Model), add in the lightweight YOLOv5 neck network, through the experimental comparison of the model detection with CBAM, SE, ECA, and other attention mechanisms, it proves that the depth separable convolution in DWAM can effectively alleviate the channel attention and spatial attention interfere with each other, and can effectively improve the detection of fabric defects.
3). Use CoordConv to replace the ordinary convolution in the neck network of YOLOv5, and improve the generalization ability of the network by adding coordinate channels to obtain the position information of the input data.
4). for the problem of long-tailed data, this paper uses the Focal Loss loss function to replace the original cross-entropy loss function. This loss function can reduce the focus on easy-to-categorize samples, which makes the model pay more attention to samples that are difficult to classify.

2 Methodology

2.1 C3_Ghost

The structure diagrams of C3 and BottleNeck are illustrated in Fig. 1, where Conv_BN_SiLU consists of Conv, BatchNormal, and SiLU.

In the C3 module, BottleNeck can effectively extract the features in the image, and the one-time 1x1 conv2D and one-time 3×3 conv2D are used in BottleNcek, and the final output is the convolved feature layer added with the input feature layer, as shown in BottleNeck in Fig. 1. However, using conventional convolution makes the network's parameter amount larger, which brings the problem of slower detection.

To address the above problems, this paper uses Ghost_module to reduce the amount of computation and improve the detection speed, the operation of Ghost_module is shown in Fig. 2. The specific practice is: the first step is to use less convolution kernel to generate a part of the feature maps; the second step is to use cheap operations on the feature maps generated in the first step to obtain another part of the feature maps, the cheap operations are to use 3x3 or 5x5 for the depth separable convolution so that the feature maps can be convolved one by one, and the first part of the similar feature maps

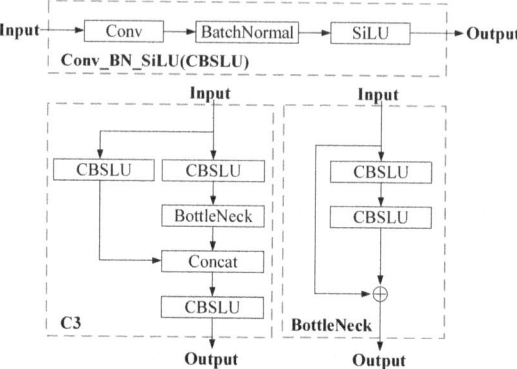

Fig. 1. Structural Diagram of C3, Conv_BN_SiLU, and Similar Module

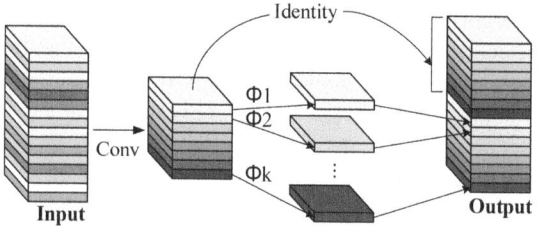

Fig. 2. The Ghost module

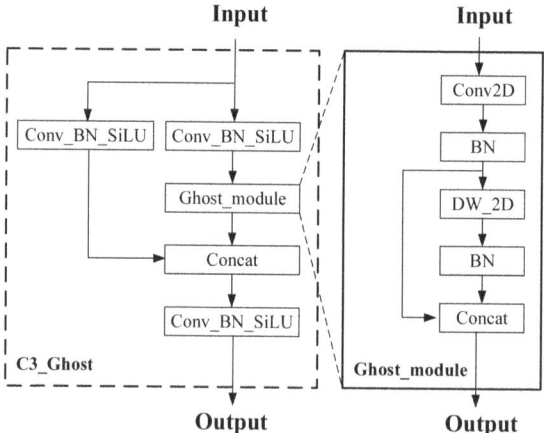

Fig. 3. C3_Ghost and Ghost_module detailed structure diagram

are generated by simple operations., compared with BottleNeck, the overall network computation can be greatly reduced.

Therefore, this article proposes using the Ghost Module to replace the BottleNeck module in C3. The detailed structures of C3_Ghost and the Ghost Module are shown in

Fig. 3. In YOLOv5, we replace all C3 modules in the Neck with C3_Ghost, as shown in Fig. 6. We did not use C3_Ghost to replace the C3 in the Backbone because we believe that in the main feature extraction network, the emphasis is more on obtaining features from the image. If replace the BottleNeck with the Ghost Module, it alters the randomness of convolutional feature extraction, potentially weakening the feature extraction capability. However, in the feature fusion network of the Neck, the algorithm focuses more on feature fusion, The key in this section is how to fuse existing feature maps faster and better. Therefore, using Ghost_module will not have much impact on the feature extraction of the overall network.

Analyzing Ghost module gains in memory usage and theoretical speedups: assuming input shape = c × h × w, output shape = n × h' × w', the convolution kernel size is k × k, then when using traditional convolution:

$$FLOPs_1 = n \times h' \times w' \times c \times k \times k \tag{1}$$

When using Ghost_module, we define the number of channels for the partial feature maps generated in the first step as: m = n/s, and the depthwise separable convolution kernel size as $d \times d$. Can calculate:

$$FLOPs_2 = m \times h' \times w' \times c \times k \times k \\ +(n-m) \times h' \times w' \times 1 \times d \times d \tag{2}$$

The theoretical speedup ratio for upgrading a normal convolution with the Ghost module is:

$$r_s = \frac{FLOPs_1}{FLOPs_2} \\ = \frac{c \times k \times k}{\frac{1}{s} \times c \times k \times k + \left(1-\frac{1}{s}\right) \times d \times d} \\ \approx \frac{s \times c}{c+s-1} \approx s \tag{3}$$

FLOPs can be reduced to 1/s of the original, so the acceleration of Ghost module quite significant.

2.2 Depthwise Attention Model

The improved attention mechanism DWAM based on CBAM is shown in Fig. 4, which mainly consists of (a) Channel Attention Mechanism and (b) Depthwise Spatial Attention Module. The attention mechanism can adaptively adjust weights, allowing the network to focus on areas that require more attention. In the spatial attention mechanism part of CBAM, the algorithm first performs average pooling and maximum pooling for all channels and concatenates, and then uses standard convolution to obtain the feature layer for a single channel. However, the standard convolution designs the interaction of spatial and channel dimensions, which leads to confusing spatial weights with channel weights [22], affecting the algorithm's ability to extract features in fabric-complex texture backgrounds. This problem is solved using depth separable convolution and the proposed attention mechanism in DWAM is shown in Fig. 4.

The channel attention mechanism part of DWAM is the same as CBAM's. The Channel attention module first uses average pooling and max pooling operations to

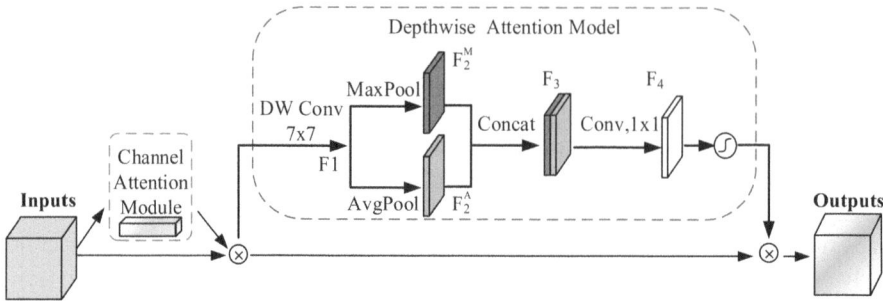

Fig. 4. DWAM Network Structure

aggregate the spatial information of feature maps. The input shape $= c \times h \times w$, the output shapes of max pooling feature F_M^c and average pooling feature F_A^c are $c \times 1 \times 1$. Then, F_M^c and F_A^c are fed into two fully connected neural networks with shared parameters, and the two resulting new feature maps are added. Finally, the output weight coefficients are processed by the sigmoid function. As shown in Fig. 4, the input feature map first goes through the Channel attention module to adaptively adjust the channel weights of the feature map, then goes through the Depthwise Spatial Attention Module to adjust the spatial weights of the feature map, and outputs the final feature map.

Assuming input shape $= c \times h \times w$, after depthwise separable convolution, the output feature layer F_1's shape is also $c \times h \times w$. The operation of MaxPool in space is to find the maximum value of feature points at the same position on the c channels of F_1. We use $P_{k,i,j}$ to represent the feature point in the k-th channel, with coordinate position (i, j), $k \in [1, c], i \in [0, h), j \in [0, w)$. Then the output feature point $P_{i,j}^{Max}$ calculation formula of MaxPool is shown in Eq. 4:

$$P_{i,j}^{Max} = max\left(P_{1,i,j}, P_{2,i,j} \ldots \ldots P_{k,i,j}\right) \quad (4)$$

The operation of AvgPool is to average the feature points at the same position on the c channels of F_1, and the output feature point $P_{i,j}^{Avg}$ calculation formula is shown in Eq. 5:

$$P_{i,j}^{Avg} = \frac{\sum_{k=1}^{c} P_{k,i,j}}{c} \quad (5)$$

After the above calculations, the output feature layers F_2^M, F_2^A of F_1 after MaxPool and AvgPool have a shape of $1 \times h \times w$. We then concatenate F_2^M and F_2^A into F_3 with a shape of $2 \times h \times w$ and use 1×1 convolution to reduce F_3's channel number to 1. Finally, F_3 is processed by the sigmoid function, limiting each feature point on the feature map between 0 and 1, outputting F_4. F_4 is then multiplied by the input feature map, completing the spatial attention mechanism calculation.

2.3 Coordinate Convolution

The ordinary convolution mainly focuses on the content information of the input data while ignoring the spatial position information of pixels. CoordConv [23] introduces

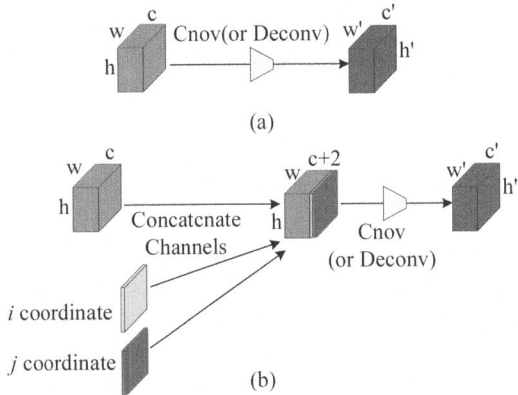

Fig. 5. CoordConv Structure. (a) Calculation process of regular convolution; (b) Calculation process of CoordConv

coordinate information by adding coordinate channels in the input feature map, enabling the neural network to perceive the position information of the input data. Each pixel contains its coordinate information in the input image, which enables the neural network to better understand the contextual information and spatial relationships of the feature map, thereby improving the network's generalization ability. The structure diagram is shown in Fig. 5.

Compared to traditional convolution, CoordConv adds two additional channels to the input feature map: one for the x-coordinate and one for the y-coordinate. Then, a standard convolution operation is performed. When the coordinate channels of Coord-Conv do not learn any information, it behaves like a regular convolution, exhibiting the translational invariance of standard convolution. However, when the coordinate channels contain learned information, CoordConv exhibits some degree of translational dependence. Furthermore, it only increases the number of channels by two, resulting in a relatively modest increase in computational complexity.

In the context of fabric defect detection, where backgrounds are complex and target sizes vary, incorporating CoordConv in YOLOv5 allows the network to acquire spatial information about the target's coordinates, and enhances the network's detection performance.

2.4 Focal Loss

Due to the presence of intricately textured backgrounds in the fabric dataset and the relatively small spatial occupation of fabric defects in the images, there are a large number of unmatched negative samples during model training. This imbalance between positive and negative samples can significantly affect the detection results. To address this issue, we adopted the Focal Loss [24] function to replace the original cross-entropy loss function. This loss function reduces the focus on easily classified samples, thereby directing the model's attention toward harder-to-classify samples. This approach effectively mitigates the impact of the imbalance between positive and negative samples on detection results, thereby enhancing the accuracy and stability of fabric defect detection. The cross-entropy loss function L is given by:

$$L(p, y) = -y\ln p - (1-y)\ln(1-p) = \begin{cases} -\ln(p) & if\ y = 1 \\ -\ln(1-p) & otherwise \end{cases} \quad (6)$$

In Eq. (6), y represents the true value of the sample, and p represents the probability predicted by the model that a certain sample is a positive sample. For positive samples with true labels as defects, a larger p indicates a more accurate prediction by the model. Similarly, for negative samples with true labels as back ground, a smaller p indicates a more accurate prediction by the model. Therefore, if there are too many background negative samples, it can lead to slow iteration of the loss function and may not optimize to the optimum.

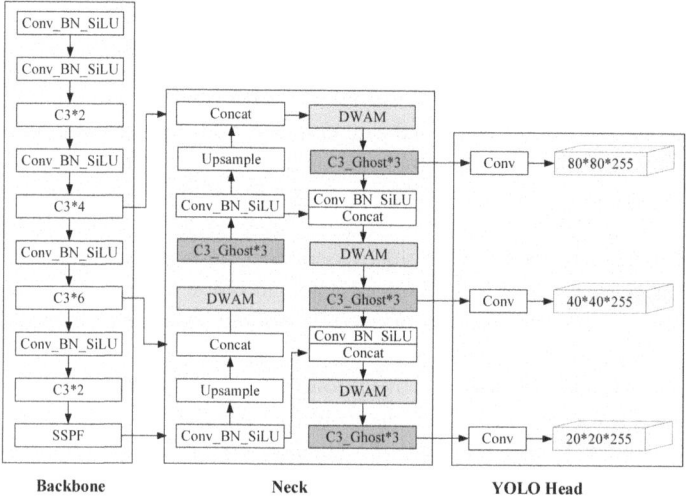

Fig. 6. The network framework diagram of GDC-YOLO

To distinguish between hard and easy samples, Focal Loss introduces a coefficient γ > 0, as shown in Eq. (8). This coefficient reduces the loss contribution of easy samples, making the training focus more on difficult samples. Focal Loss adds a coefficient α to mitigate the impact of positive-negative sample imbalance, where α_t is defined as shown in Eq. (7):

$$\alpha_t = \begin{cases} \alpha & if\ y = 1 \\ 1-\alpha & otherwise \end{cases} \quad (7)$$

After summarization, the Focal Loss function is represented as Eq. (8):

$$FL = \begin{cases} -\alpha(1-p)^\gamma \ln p & if\ y = 1 \\ -(1-\alpha)p^\gamma \ln(1-p) & otherwise \end{cases} \quad (8)$$

2.5 Overview of GDC-YOLO

The architectural diagram of the GDC-YOLO network is shown in Fig. 6. We first replace the C3 module in the Neck with the C3_Ghost module, aiming to reduce the computational parameters and enhance the running speed while maintaining the existing feature extraction accuracy. To improve the algorithm's capability to detect defects against complex fabric textures, we have integrated a custom attention mechanism (DWAM), which consists of channel and spatial attention based on depthwise separable convolutions. This allows the network to adaptively focus on the defects we aim to detect through training, thereby increasing the recognition accuracy. Subsequently, we employ CoordConv in place of standard convolutions, adding coordinate channels to perceive the positional information of the input data, which enhances the network's detection performance.

3 Experiment Details

3.1 Dataset

The Smart Diagnosis of Cloth Flaw Dataset (referred to as SDCF datasets in the following) used in our paper was released by Tianchi in 2020 as part of a competition dataset. This dataset comprises 5913 images of defective fabric and 3663 images of normal fabric. It encompasses 20 different types of fabric defects, such as water stains, knots, lint, broken threads, and more. By the classification approach outlined in [1], this paper categorizes defects into four classes: (I) dot_defects, (II) stain_defects, (III) warp_defects, and (IV) weft_defects. Additionally, a portion of normal fabric images was included as challenging samples. To address the low sample count in warp_defect and weft_defect classes, we employed data augmentation techniques including mirroring, flipping, translation, and Mosaic to expand the dataset. Finally, the dataset curated in this paper is presented in Table 1.

3.2 Parameter Details

The training and inference environment for GDC-YOLO is TensorFlow 2.4.0, with the host utilizing an NVIDIA RTX3060 GPU with 12GB of memory. During training, the Adam optimizer is employed with a momentum setting of 0.937. Parameters are initialized using a warm-up strategy. The learning rate is updated using one-dimensional linear interpolation for each iteration. Mosaic data augmentation is applied, with the initial learning rate set to 0.001. The input image size is 608 pixels × 608 pixels.

3.3 Evaluation Metrics

In the experimental section, we utilize mAP@0.5, mAP@0.5:0.95, P, R, and F1-score as evaluation metrics to assess the accuracy of the detection models. In the object detection task, the algorithm outputs an A(bounding box) to denote the position of the target, and a B(ground truth) in the test set exists to mark the real target. We use Intersection over Union (IOU) to measure the degree of overlap between the two regions. If the IOU of the algorithm's output A and the actual ground truth B exceeds a predefined threshold, then A is considered as an effective detection. The calculation of IOU is represented by the following formula:

$$IoU = \frac{A \cap B}{A \cup B} \quad (9)$$

mAP@0.5 refers to the mean Average Precision when the IOU threshold is set to 0.5, while mAP@0.5:0.95 represents the average of 10 mAP values calculated at IOU thresholds ranging from 0.5 to 0.95 (with a step size of 0.05). P(Precision) indicates the proportion of correctly predicted defects out of all predicted defects by the model. R(Recall) represents the proportion of correctly predicted defects out of all true labeled defects. F1(F1 Score) combines both precision and recall metrics to provide a comprehensive evaluation of the model's performance. Their calculation methods are as follows:

Table 1. Defect Count Statistics of the Fabric Defect Dataset Used in This Paper

Datasets	Dot	Stain	Warp	Weft	Normal	Total
SDCF	2021	1663	1571	1763	1488	8466

Table 2. Comparison of GDC-YOLO with Other Object Detection Algorithms

Model	Size	P (%)	R (%)	F1 (%)	mAP@0.5	mAP@0.5:0.95	Speed (ms)	Weight (MB)	GFLOPs
YOLOv5s	608	78.5	37.2	50	52.6	26.4	12.5	13.7	15.8
SSD	608	53.1	32.1	40	39.2	15.2	42.7	92.1	61.1
YOLOv4	608	61.4	18.8	29	37.6	13.4	52.1	245.4	127.8
YOLOv7	608	82.3	39.7	54	54.9	25.0	35.2	142	105.2
Faster R-CNN	608	46.1	36.3	42	36.2	9.0	71.3	108.7	233.2
GDC-YOLO	608	**84.5**	**42.4**	**56**	**58.7**	**32.1**	**11.2**	**10.9**	**11.3**

In Table 2, the best results are shown in bold.

Table 3. Comparison of mAP@0.5 for Different Defect Categories across Various Algorithms

Class	YOLOv4	YOLOV7	FasterR-CNN	SSD	YOLOv5s	GDC-YOLO
Dot	60.4	**65.5**	31.5	28.1	62.4	**65.6**
Stain	33.3	60.3	42.2	57.3	59.1	**65.9**
Warp	20.3	40.1	39.8	36.4	52.4	**55.2**
Weft	36.3	37.8	31.3	34.9	36.4	**47.9**

In Table 3, the best results are shown in bold

$$P = \frac{X_{TP}}{X_{TP}+X_{FP}} \times 100\% \quad (10)$$

$$R = \frac{X_{TP}}{X_{TP}+X_{FN}} \times 100\% \quad (11)$$

$$F1 = \frac{2\times(P\times R)}{P+R} \times 100\% \quad (12)$$

In Eqs. (10) and (11): X_{TP} represents the number of defects detected correctly by the model; X_{FP} represents the number of false detections where the model detects defects but there are actually none present; X_{FN} represents the number of missed detections where there are defects present but the model fails to detect them; X_{FC} represents the number of misclassifications where the model detects defects but assigns them to the wrong class.

4 Results

4.1 Quantitative Experimental Results

In the task of target detection, the accuracy of algorithmic detection is important, as is the speed of detection of the model and the complexity of the algorithm. Table 2 shows the evaluation results of the model proposed in this paper on SDCF datasets, Obtained by training according to the parameter scheme in Subsect. 5.1, GDC-YOLO is evaluated by eight metrics: P, R, F1, mAP@0.5, mAP@0.5: 0.9, single detection time (Speed), size of the model (Weight), and algorithmic complexity GFLOPs. We conduct comparison experiments with YOLOv5, SSD, YOLOv4, YOLOv7, Faster R-CNN, and thus determine the good performance of the proposed improvements in GDC-YOLO. Table 3 presents the comparison of mAP@0.5 for different defect categories. Figure 7 displays the detection performance comparison between GDC-YOLO and other detection algorithms on the validation set. As indicated by the data in Table 2, it can be concluded that the proposed GDC-YOLO outperforms YOLOv5 and YOLOv7 in terms of smaller GFLOPs, while achieving higher mAP@0.5 and precision. This suggests that GDC-YOLO achieves superior detection results with fewer parameters in fabric defect detection. Our algorithm achieves the highest values in mAP@0.5, mAP@0.5:0.95, Precision, and Recall, demonstrating superior detection performance even in complex fabric texture backgrounds. Compared to other object detection models like YOLOv4, SSD, and Faster R-CNN, GDC-YOLO exhibits significant advantages, with a 21.2% higher mAP@0.5 than YOLOv4, 19.5% higher than SSD, and 22.5% higher than Faster R-CNN. Moreover, GDC-YOLO outperforms YOLOv5s and YOLOv7 by 6.1% and 3.8%, respectively. Through comparative analysis, our approach achieves high detection rates and low parameter counts in fabric defect detection, especially in complex texture backgrounds.

Analyzing Table 3, we observe that GDC-YOLO demonstrates the best detection performance for dot defects, stain defects, warp defects, and weft defects. Compared to YOLOv5s, it achieves improvements of 3.2%, 6.8%, 2.8%, and 11.5%, respectively.

4.2 Qualitative Experimental Analysis

In Fig. 7, we can visually compare the improved detection performance of GDC-YOLO. It exhibits excellent detection results for weft defects, accurately identifying defects comprehensively. Additionally, by comparing with the utilization of DWAM attention, the algorithm demonstrates enhanced attention to defects on complex texture backgrounds. For instance, in the case of stain defects depicted in the figure, GDC-YOLO shows superior detection capability, able to detect subtle defects effectively. Combining detection speed and GFLOPs, our method achieves higher detection rates and faster detection speeds while utilizing fewer parameters.

4.3 Ablation Experiment of DWAM

As described in Sect. 4.5, we replaced the C3 module in the neck network of YOLOv5 with C3_Ghost, and incorporated the DWAM attention mechanism to address the issue of defect detection in complex texture backgrounds. This section, we will conduct comparative experiments to validate the superiority of DWAM over other algorithms.

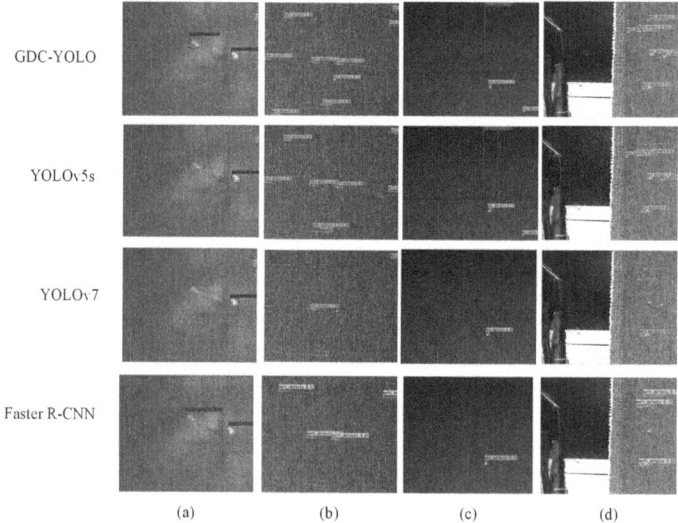

Fig. 7. Comparison of Detection Results between GDC-YOLO and Other Algorithms

In Table 4, the best results are shown in bold.

We used the network after replacing C3 with C3_Ghost as the base network and conducted comparative experiments using SE, ECA, CBAM, and DWAM attention mechanisms. The results are shown in Table 4. By comparing the mAP@0.5 for each fabric defect with different attention mechanisms, we found that DWAM performs the best in stain_defects and weft_defects, with detection rates of 62.8% and 42.3%, respectively. It is evident that overall defect detection, the DWAM attention mechanism slightly outperforms other attention mechanisms. Using DWAM can effectively improve the

Table 4. Comparative Analysis of Different Attention Mechanisms in Optimizing Our Algorithm

Model	Dot	Stain	Warp	Weft	mAP@0.5	mAP@0.5:0.95
C3_Ghost	65.2%	61.4%	40.4%	40.9%	52.0%	26.2%
C3_Ghost + SE	**65.7%**	59.0%	48.1%	38.0%	52.7%	26.8%
C3_Ghost + ECA	63.6%	59.6%	45.3%	42.0%	52.6%	26.7%
C3_Ghost + CBAM	64.4%	60.9%	50.5%	36.3%	53.0%	27.0%
C3_Ghost + DWAM	64.9%	62.8%	48.9%	42.3%	54.7%	27.2%
C3_Ghost + DWAM + CoordConv	65.3%	65.1%	54.6%	47.5%	58.1%	29.8%
C3_Ghost + DWAM + CoordConv + Focal loss	65.6%	**65.9%**	**55.2%**	**47.9%**	**58.7%**	**32.1%**

algorithm's detection rate for defects. This demonstrates that using depth-wise separable convolutions in spatial attention mechanisms provides greater performance benefits than traditional convolutions, confirming that depth-wise separable convolutions can effectively address the problem of interference between channel attention and spatial attention.

Building upon C3_Ghost and DWAM, we further added CoordConv to the network. It can be observed that the mAP@0.5 for Stain, Warp, and Weft defects all achieved maximum values, demonstrating a significant improvement in detection performance by incorporating this module to obtain target coordinate information in the network.

To further analyze the impact of attention mechanisms on object detection algorithms, we conducted comparative experiments using Grad-CAM (Gradient Class Activation Mapping). By generating visualizations of class activation maps, we can observe which regions of the target the network emphasizes. As shown in Fig. 8, we employed YOLOv5, C3_Ghost + CBAM, and C3_Ghost + DWAM to detect fabric defects in input images, where (a), (b), (c), (d) represent a lateral comparison of Grad-CAM for the same fabric defect image using different algorithms.

It can be observed that in figures (b) and (c), YOLOv5 with CBAM has fewer Grad CAM masks covering the target areas compared to DWAM. Some targets awaiting detection do not have masks covering them, resulting in a decrease in detection performance. By contrast, in figures (a) and (d), it is evident that the masks generated by DWAM are more concentrated in the defect areas, with correspondingly higher scores for the target class. Therefore, based on observations, we infer that after using the DWAM attention mechanism, the high-response masks indeed concentrate on the regions we consider most conducive to detection. In summary, employing the DWAM attention mechanism effectively enhances the algorithm's ability to detect defects in complex fabric texture backgrounds.

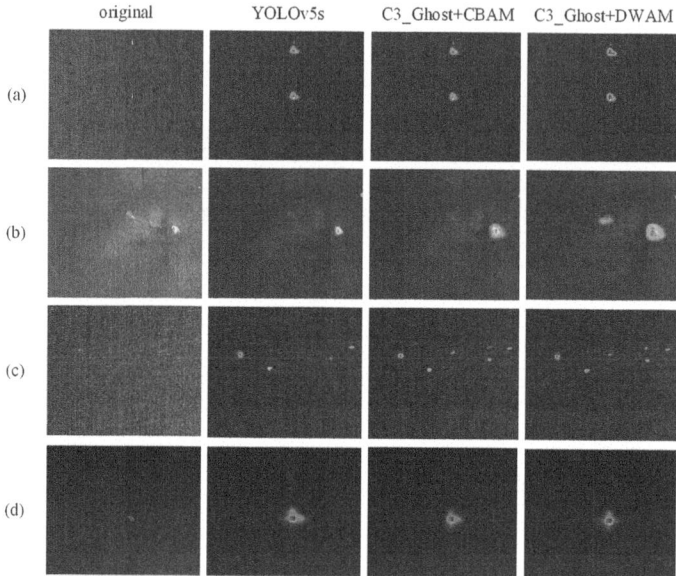

Fig. 8. Visualization of Class Activation Maps for Fabric Defect Detection Using Different Algorithms

4.4 Ablation Experiment of Focal Loss

As shown in Fig. 9, the left plot displays the loss curve obtained after training with the initial cross-entropy loss function using YOLOv5, while the right plot displays the loss curve obtained after training with Focal Loss. It is evident from the graphs that employing Focal Loss significantly enhances the rate of decrease in loss during training, thereby accelerating the model's Fitting speed.

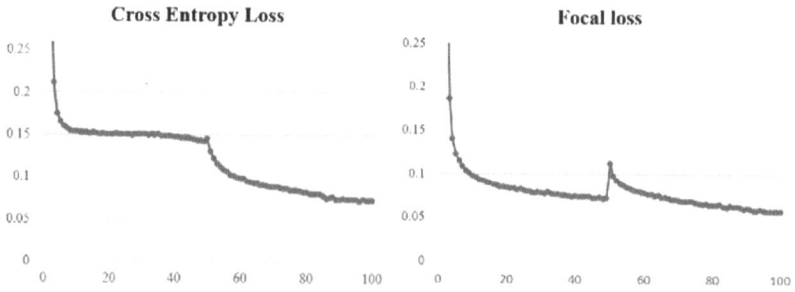

Fig. 9. Loss value comparison chart after using different loss functions

5 Conclusions

To reduce the detection complexity of fabric defects in object detection algorithms, improve detection efficiency, and mitigate the impact of complex texture backgrounds, we propose a detection algorithm called GDC-YOLO based on the improved YOLOv5. GDC-YOLO integrates several state-of-the-art techniques in computer vision, including Ghostnet, attention mechanisms, depth-wise separable convolutions, the addition of coordinate channels to input images, data augmentation, and various training techniques.

The contributions of this paper include: Use of C3_Ghost to replace the C3 module in the YOLOv5 neck network, which can maintain the original feature extraction effect, reduce the number of parameters, and speed up feature extraction; To address the challenge of extracting features in the complex texture backgrounds of fabrics, we optimized the ordinary convolutions in CBAM with depth-wise separable convolutions. This optimization resolves the issue of confusion between spatial weights and channel weights in attention mechanisms; At the same time, in the neck network, we replaced ordinary convolutions with CoordConv to enable the network to focus more on the positional information of targets. This enhancement effectively improves the detection performance and generalization capability of the network.

To validate the effectiveness of the improvements, we conducted tests using the SDCF datasets. Compared to YOLOv5, GAW-YOLO achieves a 6.1% increase in mAP@0.5 while reducing parameters by 20.4%. With other conditions remaining unchanged, the use of the DWAM attention mechanism, compared to CBAM, results in a 1.7% increase in mAP@0.5. These results indicate that the algorithm indeed exhibits a superior detection effect in fabric defect detection in complex texture backgrounds.

In future work, we will focus on how to utilize small-sample fabric defect data for transfer learning. We aim to maintain the existing detection speed and model size while achieving good detection performance on other fabric defect datasets, thereby enhancing the universality and generalization capabilities of our algorithm.

Acknowledgements. This research was supported by the National Natural Science Foundation of China (51875414) and the mission statement of the Hubei Provincial Key Research and Development Program (2023BAB195).

References

1. Wen-qing, H., Qiang, W.: Image retrieval algorithm based on convolutional neural network. Curr. Trends Comput. Sci. Mech. Autom. **1**, 304–314 (2017)
2. Bochkovskiy, A., Wang, C.-Y., Liao, H.-Y.M.: YOLOv4: optimal speed and accuracy of object detection. CoRR (2020)
3. Wang, C.-Y., Bochkovskiy, A., Liao, H.-Y.M.: Scaled-YOLOv4: scaling cross stage partial network. In: Proceedings of the IEEE Computer Society Conference on Computer Vision and Pattern Recognition, pp. 13024–13033 (2021)
4. Cai, Z., Vasconcelos, N.: Cascade R-CNN: delving into high quality object detection. In: Proceedings of the IEEE Computer Society Conference on Computer Vision and Pattern Recognition, pp. 6154–6162 (2018)

5. Jiang, Z., Zhao, L., Li, S., Jia, Y.: Real-time object detection method based on improved YOLOv4-tiny. CoRR (2020)
6. Shaoqing, R., Kaiming, H., Ross, G., Jian, S.: Faster R-CNN: towards real-time object detection with region proposal networks. IEEE Trans. Pattern Anal. Mach. Intell. **39**(6), 1137–1149 (2017)
7. Fan, Q., Zhuo, W., Tang, C.K., et al.: Few-shot object detection with attention-RPN and multi-relation detector. In: Proceedings of the IEEE/CVF Conference on Computer Vision and Pattern Recognition, pp. 4013–4022 (2020)
8. Neubeck, A., Van Gool, L.: Efficient non-maximum suppression. In: Proceedings - International Conference on Pattern Recognition, vol. 3, p. 850 (2006)
9. Liu, W., et al.: SSD: single shot multibox detector. LNCS, vol. 9905, pp. 21–37 (2016)
10. Jiang, P., Ergu, D., Liu, F., et al.: A review of YOLO algorithm developments. Procedia Comput. Sci. **199**, 1066–1073 (2022)
11. Ge, Z., Liu, S., Wang, F., et al.: YOLOx: exceeding YOLO series in 2021. arXiv preprint arXiv:2107.08430 (2021)
12. Wang, Y., Wang, H., Xin, Z.: Efficient detection model of steel strip surface defects based on YOLO-V7. IEEE Access **10**, 133936–133944 (2022)
13. Chen Mengqi, Y., Lingjie, Z.C., Runjun, S., Shuangwu, Z., Zhongyuan, G., Yuming, Z.: Improved faster R-CNN for fabric defect detection based on Gabor filter with Genetic Algorithm optimization. Comput. Ind. **134**, 103551 (2022)
14. Xie Guosheng, X., Zhiqi, Y.Y., Yize, S.: An intelligent defect detection system for warp-knitted fabric. Text. Res. J. **92**(9–10), 1394–1404 (2022)
15. Jing, J., Zhuo, D., Zhang, H., Liang, Y., Zheng, M.: Fabric defect detection using the improved YOLOv3 model. J. Eng. Fibers Fabrics **15** (2020)
16. Guo, Y., Kang, X., Li, J., et al.: Automatic fabric defect detection method using AC-YOLOv5. Electronics **12**(13), 2950 (2023)
17. Huosheng, X., Zesen, W.: A robust fabric defect detection method based on improved RefineDet. Sensors **20**(15), 4260 (2020)
18. Qiang, L., Chuan, W., Yusheng, L., Mingwang, G., Jingao, L.: A fabric defect detection method based on deep learning. IEEE Access **10**, 4284–4296 (2022)
19. Zhang, J., Li, Y., Luo, H.: Defect detection in textile fabrics with optimal Gabor filter and BRDPSO algorithm. J. Phy. Conf. Ser. **1651**(1) (2020)
20. Kang, X., Yang, P., Jing, J.: Defect detection on printed fabrics via Gabor filter and regular band. J. Fiber Bioeng. Inform. **8**(1), 195–206 (2015)
21. Le, T., Wong, W.K., Kwong, C.K.: Fabric defect detection for apparel industry: a nonlocal sparse representation approach. IEEE Access **5**, 5947–5964 (2017)
22. Han, K., Wang, Y., Tian, Q., Guo, J., Xu, C., Xu, C.: GhostNet: more features from cheap operations. In: Proceedings of the IEEE Computer Society Conference on Computer Vision and Pattern Recognition, pp. 1577–1586 (2020)
23. Liu, R., Lehman, J., Molino, P., et al.: An intriguing failing of convolutional neural networks and the coordconv solution. In: Advances in Neural Information Processing Systems, vol. 31 (2018)
24. Lin, T.Y., Goyal, P., Girshick, R., et al.: Focal loss for dense object detection. In: Proceedings of the IEEE International Conference on Computer Vision, 2980–2988 (2017)

UBAViz: User Behavior Analyzing in Literature Resources by Modeling User Behavior Sequences

Junxiang Cao[1], Xiaoju Dong[1,2(✉)], Zhiyuan Wu[1], and Xuefei Tian[1]

[1] Department of Computer Science, Shanghai Jiao Tong University, Shanghai, China
{cjxqaq,wzy605399,13487426939}@sjtu.edu.cn
[2] Shanghai Key Laboratory of Trusted Data Circulation and Governance in Web3, Shanghai, China
xjdong@sjtu.edu.cn

Abstract. Recently, network technology and internationalization of scientific research have pushed researchers to turn to electronic literature resources. In the face of changes in user behavior, e-documentation platforms need to efficiently manage and deeply understand the sequence of user behavior in order to improve the accuracy and satisfaction of their services. Our study introduces an innovative methodology for analyzing user behavior within literature resource platforms through modeling sequential patterns of user actions. By leveraging the word2vec technique from natural language processing, we transform user behavior sequences comprising both the nature of the actions and the characteristics of the accessed documents into meaningful vector representations. This transformation enables the detection of anomalies in the behavioral patterns by examining clusters in the vector space. Based on this approach, we design and implement a visual analysis system of abnormal access: UBAViz. The system allows analysts to check and analyze the results of modeling user behavioral sequences and to improve the understanding of anomalous access users. Through two user cases, we demonstrate how our approach and system help to detect and analyze abnormal users, showing that the system allows managers to fully and carefully mine the behavioral patterns of different users.

Keywords: literature access · visualization · rare category · anomaly detection

1 Introduction

In the 21st century, with the development of network information technology and the internationalization of scientific research, the way researchers read papers has gradually changed from paper resources in libraries to electronic resources on the Internet. Electronic literature resources have the advantages of simple preparation, low storage cost, easy to use and fast retrieval. The number of people accessing electronic literature resources through online channels is increasing, and the management of users by the electronic literature resource platforms that provide the service is particularly important. Through an in-depth understanding of user behavior, electronic literature resource platforms can better meet the needs of users and provide more accurate services. This requires us to be able to mine the user behavioral patterns from their behavioral sequences and interpret them. For managers, understanding users' behavioral patterns can help them develop a more intelligent and personalized literature access system. However, most current studies only focus on a single type of user behavior such as downloading behavior, or only analyze the content of the literature accessed by the user, ignoring the correlation between different types of consecutive user behaviors and the pattern information they have. In addition, since user behavior data are usually unstructured and high-dimensional, suitable algorithms are needed to extract useful information.

At present, various literature resource platforms do not have a clear categorization of abnormal users, and simply regard users who download literature in excess of a certain threshold as violating the law. The method proposed in this paper takes into account the user's other behaviors besides downloading such as searching and browsing, as well as the sequence order between the user's downloading behavior and other behaviors and the semantic information of the literature associated with each behavior, and based on these rich multidimensional features, an advanced neural network model is applied to map the user's access behavior into a high-dimensional embedding space to generate the corresponding embedding vectors. Subsequently, through the method of rare category analysis, we can identify different user behavior patterns from the user group, which may include those users who unintentionally misuse the literature resources or access behaviors with malicious intent. By combining the visual analytics system with algorithms to dig deeper into the categorized user behaviors, we can not only identify abnormal access patterns, but also deeply understand the meaning behind these patterns. For example, certain users may frequently download large amounts of literature due to research needs, and although this behavior may trigger security mechanisms, it is inherently harmless. In this case, the organization can adapt its policies to meet the specific needs of this group of users while preventing the system from misjudging them. On the other hand, using the data mining capabilities of a visual analytics system, we can mine rare categories and find users whose access patterns are more unusual and who may be harmful. For example, some users may take advantage of platform vulnerabilities to maliciously download and distribute unauthorized literature, or misuse resources to cause excessive server load. Through visualization methods, we can intuitively see the difference between the activities of these users and those of other users, and take appropriate measures, such as restricting their access privileges, warning or prohibiting them from using the service, to protect the normal operation of the platform and the rights and interests of the majority of users.

We propose a method to mine and categorize user behavior patterns from the behavior sequences generated when users access electronic literature resources which consist of three actions: downloading, browsing, and searching. The method is divided into three parts:

1. Generating a content feature for each behavior corresponding to the title or search term of the document, and comparing it with the content feature of the previous behavior to generate a "context similarity".

2. Sampling from temporal behavior sequences to get "words" and "sentences" for training, randomly 2–4 consecutive behaviors as a "word". The embedding vectors of the sentences are obtained by skip-gram training.

3. After obtaining the vector representation of the behavior sequences, we perform clustering analysis according to its euclidean distance in the vector space to automatically find different behavioral patterns.

To enhance the understanding of infrequent categories, we have developed a visual analysis system. This system exhibits the outcomes of user clustering generated through the pattern classification algorithm. Moreover, it facilitates a more profound and intuitive exploration of user behavior by empowering analysts with the ability to visualize the precise behavioral data of specific user categories via charts and graphs. Such an implementation promotes a deeper comprehension of user patterns and tendencies. In addition, we also conducted experiments on a real literature resource platform user access dataset, and discussed the effectiveness of our system through two user cases.

2 Relative Work

This chapter introduces two types of existing abnormal access behavior detection methods for electronic literature resources, and briefly introduces the existing methods of rare category analysis.

2.1 Detection of Abnormal Electronic Resources Access

There are mainly two ways to detect the abnormal access of electronic literature resources.

One is to analyze user download traffic and data packets. Wang et al. [1] introduced bypass monitoring technology to explore the design idea of library restricting excessive download of digital resources. Lei et al. [2] proposed the method of log analysis to determine anomalies by information in one session, i.e., the behaviors of users between logging in and leaving the website, and proposes various characteristics of anomalous behavior such as abnormal traffic, abnormal number of IPs, abnormal number of logins, and abnormal log size. The drawback of this method is that the threshold value needs to be set artificially in advance, and too high a threshold value will lead to missed detection and too low a threshold value will lead to false detection, which needs to be adjusted and determined according to the actual situation. The statistical method of data messages requires additional traffic interception and mirroring devices at the exit of university campus network, while for the electronic resource platform serving all users on the Internet, it is difficult to conduct similar data message statistics due to the complexity of the network topology, and can only be analyzed based on log files.

Another method is to judge by the topic relevance of the user's downloaded literature content. Guo [3] proposes an idea of using topic relevance to determine user downloading behavior by performing topic clustering on literature downloaded by users within a sliding event window to analyze whether they are topic related, and then perform malicious download detection judgments.

Both methods use only the user's downloading behavior for judgment, and do not correlate with other behaviors such as browsing and retrieval. Hence we propose a method to detect abnormal access to documents based on user behavior sequences and cross-validate it with these two existing methods.

2.2 Rare Category Analysis

Rare category analysis, as one of the important research directions in the field of data mining, is particularly important when dealing with highly unbalanced datasets, especially unlabeled datasets. This problem has practical application needs in several fields, such as network intrusion detection, medical diagnosis, and research on social and political issues. The key role of rare category analysis in the field of data mining is that it can reveal new phenomena or behaviors that are hidden in huge amounts of data, which are limited in number but crucial.

Rare category analysis is mainly divided into two steps: rare category detection and rare category exploration. The goal of the former is to discover at least one data sample from each rare class, which requires first selecting candidate data samples of rare classes from unlabeled datasets, and then handing over to human experts to give the true class labels of the samples, so effective rare class detection algorithms should minimize the number of queries required to discover all rare classes.

Interleave [4], a pioneering work in the field of rare class detection, is a probabilistic model-based methodology that assumes that the data follows a Gaussian mixture model and employs a Gaussian Bayesian classifier to select those instances of the data that are assigned the lowest generative probability by the mixture model until a sample of the data is found for each class. The NNDM algorithm [5] and the GRADE algorithm [6] assumes that the probability distribution function of the main classes is locally smooth and each rare class is concentrated in a small local region, i.e., the local density changes drastically when the rare class appears. The method selects the data samples in the region with large changes in local density as the candidate samples of rare classes. CLOVER algorithm [7] uses the characteristics of rare classes to innovatively introduce the criterion of local variability (LVD), which utilizes the difference in the number of Mutual k-Nearest Neighbors (MkNN) to differentiate between the rare classes and outliers, and uses each data sample with its k-nearest neighbor to distinguish rare classes and outliers. Hierarchical clustering-based algorithms study the rare class characteristics of clusters at different levels, of which HMS [8] is a typical algorithm. The algorithm uses mean drift with different bandwidths to construct a hierarchical structure of clusters, and then selects from all clusters those that meet the criteria of compactness and segregation, and from these, the data samples that are closest to the cluster center are selected as candidate rare category samples. The Farpoint algorithm [9] employs an iterative, split-type hierarchical clustering mechanism to recursively refine large clusters in an interactive query process, splitting them into purer, smaller-scale subclusters. In order to enhance the clustering effect and adapt to various heterogeneous dataset structures, the researchers combined Farpoint algorithm with other clustering methods and introduced two fusion versions: Farpoint-COPK and Farpoint-HA [10]. These two improved algorithms not only enhance the clustering accuracy, but also solve the parameterization problem.

The core goal of rare category exploration is to reveal all undiscovered members of a rare category or to construct a compact representation of the category with the help of one to more known rare category data samples, thus serving as a key step after rare category detection. Mainstream approaches transform this problem into a local clustering problem, i.e., treating labeled rare category samples as starting seeds and focusing on forming compact clusters around these seeds instead of globally traversing the entire dataset. The LERI [11] algorithm employs a targeted approach that relies on only single-labeled rare category samples (i.e., seeds) and efficiently identifies all data instances in arbitrary morphological rare all data instances in the category. In each local search iteration, the algorithm looks up the k nearest neighbors of newly visited data points to extend the clustering boundaries. In addition, Spielman and Teng [12] devised a local clustering algorithm optimized for large-scale graph structures, which is able to efficiently locate and extract a compact subset of local clusters around the seed nodes of a rare category with an approximately linear relationship between size and runtime.

3 Anomaly Detection Method

The pattern classification methods of literature access behavior we proposed is divided into three main parts, as shown in the Fig. 1.

The first part is the data processing part, which focuses on adding the characteristics of the visited or retrieved literature to each user behavior, and processing the raw data into sequences of user behaviors and more expressive sets of ngrams of events required by anomaly detection algorithms.

The second part transforms the sequences into high dimensional embedding vectors using the mixed-ngram2vec method, which incorporates the event-group slicing parameters from the data processing part above and a simple skip-gram neural network to learn the embedding vectors of the sequences.

In the third part, the embedding vectors from the previous section are clustered in a high dimensional vector space using the DBSCAN clustering algorithm to obtain clustering results, which are examined for rare categories and anomalies to find anomalous behavior sequences, and the clustering results of the embedding vectors are visualized by t-SNE downscaling to a two-dimensional plane to help find and explain the rare categories.

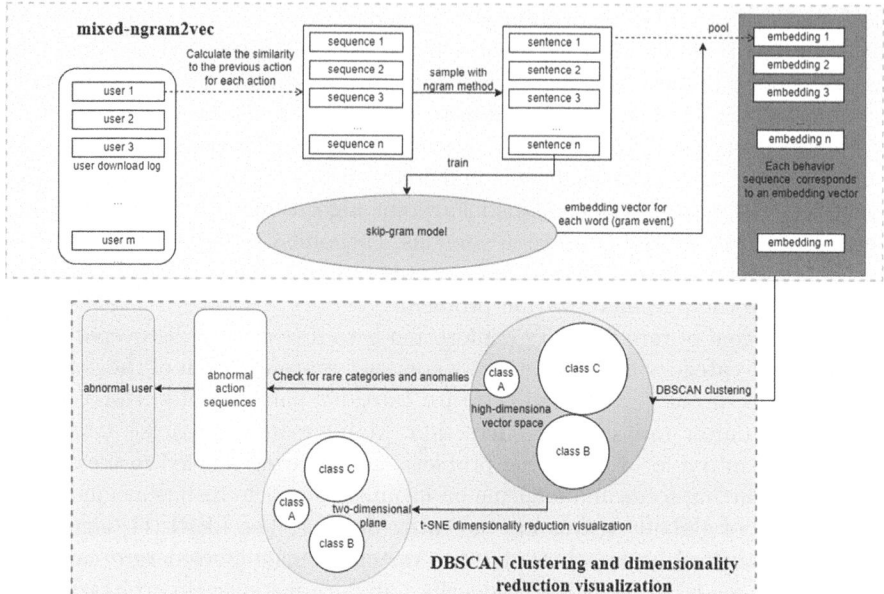

Fig. 1. User behavior sequence analysis process

3.1 Data Preprocess

The data we use are the user action log data of an electronic literature resource platform in 2020, including searching logs, browsing logs and downloading logs. The total number of users and total number of documents involved after the user identification ID and literature de-duplication are counted and shown in Table 1.

Table 1. Statistics for three types of logs

	search	browse	download
Number of entries	11051649	13417978	13417978
Number of users	1440726	952240	387609
Number of Literature	-	10513669	1300453

The search data fields contain user ID, search terms, date-time, the download and browse data fields contain user ID, document ID, document title, date-time, keywords, class code, author, and other unused fields such as administration area are not listed. One of the data fields is shown in the Fig. 2.

In the data processing process, first, the embedding vectors are computed for the document features attached to each behavior, which are document titles

USER_ID	SEARCH_WORD	DATETIME
bcbbcce0	"Ureter Matching"	2020-01-29 01:51:05

USER_ID	ARTICLE_ID	ARTICLE_TITLE	DATETIME	KEYWORDS	CLASSCODE	AUTHOR
1b3178784	zgsyzd012	Correlation of high-sensitivity troponin T with chronic heart failure and its differential value for acute myocardial infarction	2020-01-14 00:14:40	Chronic heart failure;acute myocardial infarction;high-sensitivity troponin T;differential value	R541	Ren MeiYing; Liu ying; GuoXiaojie

Fig. 2. One of the data fields: above is the search log data, below is the download and browse log data

in the download and browse behaviors and search terms in the retrieval behavior. The corresponding word vectors for each keyword are obtained from the pre-trained Chinese word vectors [13] after splitting the document title and the retrieval word, and the average pooling yields the document feature vector for that behavior. After getting the literature feature vector for each behavior, the cosine similarity between 0–1 is calculated with the feature vector of the previous behavior. Based on this similarity, a behavior can be expanded into two categories: high relevance and low relevance, and thus the three types of behaviors are expanded into six types of behaviors.

Secondly, each user in the user behavior log is divided into individual sequences every 24 h to take into account its relevance in a short period of time while avoiding long sequences and the list of user behavior sequences $T_S = \{S_1, S_2, ..., S_m\}$ is obtained. Second, in order to obtain a uniform embedding vector representation for the variable-length user behavior sequences, each sequence needs to be split into multiple subsequences of length n to represent an operational event of the user in the behavior sequence (called an n-gram, e.g., retrieval-browse-download, which is also a word in sentence for nlp model), each sequence in the set of user behavior sequences is split into a list consisting of several n-gram subsequences $S_i = \{s_1, s_2, ..., s_k\}$. Since the length of the combination of successive operations representing events (i.e., n in the n-gram) is difficult to determine and is likely to have a variable length, we use a hybrid n-element subsequence embedding method to obtain a representation of the user behavior sequence in a high dimensional vector space. This is a method that applies a sliding window. Specifically, the values of n are sampled uniformly in 2, 3, and 4, and each time the current n-gram is obtained, the new start position is shifted two places back from the current position in the sequence. Since there are only six types of behavior-relevance in the sequence of behavioral events, there are 6^n possible cases for an n-element subsequence, so the size of the pattern set of this mixed-n-element subsequence is up to $6^2 + 6^3 + 6^4 = 1548$.

The next section consists of transforming these n-element subsequences obtained in this section into embedding vectors, and thus obtaining a vector representation of this user's action sequence.

This method can be applied to sequence data of arbitrary length containing any kind of behavior, so that the action sequence can be transformed into an embedding vector focusing on both local and overall information of the sequence for deeper analysis.

3.2 Sequence Vectorization

In natural language processing, machines cannot understand the semantics of natural language, so an algorithm is needed to generate a word vector that can express the semantics for all words in the corpus given an unlabeled corpus, by which the semantic similarity between two words can be calculated. Word2vec is a set of correlation models used to generate word vectors. Skip-gram is one of the models in word2vec, which was proposed by Guthrie et al. in 2006 [14].

We use skip-gram to embed each n-gram to a high dimensional vector, and the dimension of the embedding vector for natural language words is generally chosen to be 50–200, considering that the size of the vocabulary set in this experiment is only 1548, which is much smaller than that of natural language, the dimension of the embedding vector is chosen to be 30. We set the window size to 2, each word will only be trained with words that are within two distance of the training sample.

After obtaining the embedding vectors of all mixed-ngram, the representation of the original sequence in the vector space is obtained using global averaging.

3.3 Clustering To Find Rare Categories

On the basis of obtaining a vector representation of the sequences, we apply a clustering method based on Euclidean distance to cluster the samples and group the similar sequences together for analysis. In this paper, we choose to use the Density-Based Spatial Clustering of Applications with Noise (DBSCAN), which was proposed by Ester et al. in 1996 [15].

Since the clustering results of DBSCAN are sensitive to hyperparameters such as minpts, eps, etc., and the hyperparameters that achieve the best results may be varied for different datasets. In order to achieve the best differentiation effect, it may be necessary to adjust the parameters several times in this process. In this paper, after several experiments, the recommended settings are minpts = 100, eps = 0.115 under the current data set. We will leave the specific experimentation of the parameters for future work, while also reserving the possibility of implementing this step of the parameter tuning process through visual interaction.

4 Visual Analysis System

The difficulty of anomalous access detection is that it is impossible to know that rare category belongs to meaningful anomalies without a priori knowledge, and the relevant managers may need a visual analytics system to centrally analyze and interpret all the possible results to determine whether they are meaningful anomalies or not. Based on this consideration, this paper designs and implements a visual analysis system for literature access to support the interpretation of anomaly detection algorithms and to understand the characteristics of anomalous users. The main design requirements are summarized below.

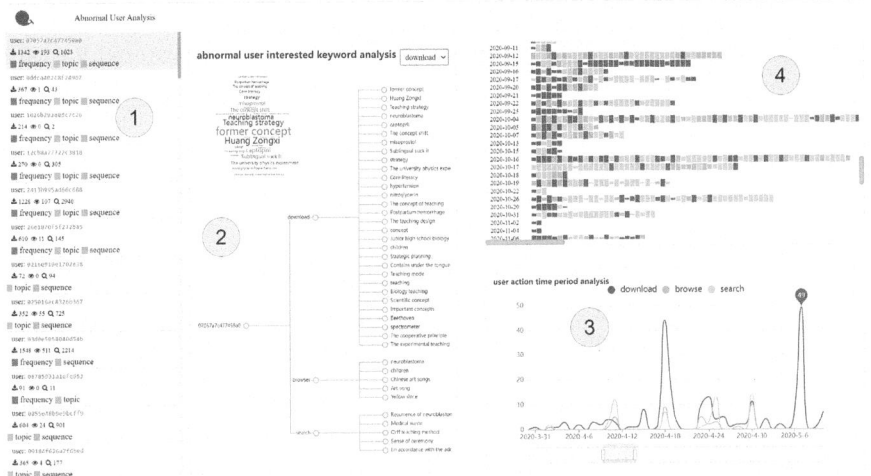

Fig. 3. UBAViz supports viewing and analyzing the behavior details of abnormal users. (1) Abnormal User List. (2) Abnormal user Interested keyword analysis view. (3) User action time period analysis view. (4) User action sequence analysis view

R1: Support inspection and visualization of large amounts of historical log data. The log data of a literature resource platform is usually large and complicated, and the system should be able to quickly filter the data needed for analysis from the historical log data and build efficient visual charts for large amounts of data.

R2: Automated rare analysis. The system should be able to automate the rare category detection and analysis process, provide a variety of common literature access anomaly detection algorithms, and annotate and sort the results.

R3: Provide interpretations about abnormal data. The system should be able to visualize the key data patterns on which each anomaly detection algorithm makes its judgments in an easily understandable form.

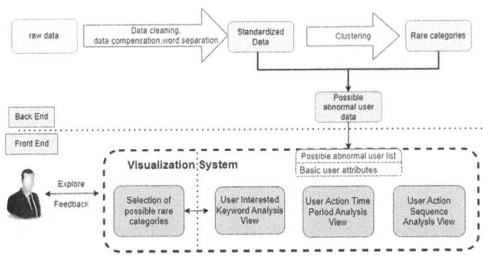

Fig. 4. Visualization System Framework

As shown in Fig. 4, in the backend, the raw data is preprocessed as described above to obtain normalized data, and the normalized data is clustered for rare category analysis, and the obtained clustering results are sent to the front-end for the user to select the cluster of users that can be interested in the category of users, i.e., the possible abnormal users. The data and information to be used in the front-end visualization and interaction system are extracted from the normalized data based on the list of possible abnormal users and then sent to the front-end through the designed interface.

The system only needs to perform a full traversal when processing new data for the first time to obtain normalized data for input and visualization of the anomaly detection algorithm, and automatically saves the results of the anomaly detection algorithm, after which an efficient and fast visualization chart can be built on the already obtained result data (R1). After the initial processing of the data, the system can perform automatic anomaly analysis using the pre-set anomaly detection algorithm and rank the anomalous users according to the annotation results of the anomaly detection algorithm (R2). The obtained list of anomalous users and their action log data will be transferred to the front-end to visualize the features on which anomaly detection relies and present them to users in an easy-to-understand manner (R3).

The system interface is structured into two primary sections. The first part, focused on rare category selection, is illustrated in Fig. 5. The main part in the upper left corner to show the user's behavioral sequence embedded vector clustering after downscaling to the two-dimensional plane, and through the interactive way to support the user to select one of the rare categories for in-depth analysis. The remaining part of the display of the data of some basic statistical information, such as: the distribution of the distribution of download time line graphs, the ratio of the number of downloads of literature to the number of browsing of different categories, as well as the keyword word cloud of the downloaded literature.

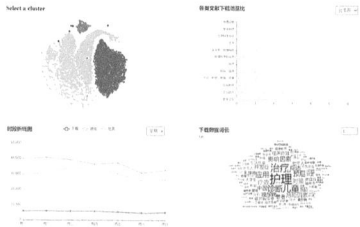

Fig. 5. Analysts view and select the rare categories to be explored in the upper left corner, and other charts present some statistical information about the full current literature access dataset.

The second part of the abnormal user analysis section is shown in Fig. 3, which mainly includes (1) user list, (2) user interested keyword analysis view,

(3) user action time period analysis view and (4) user action sequence analysis view.

When a category in the clustering view is selected, the system will jump to the abnormal user analysis view, analyze the current cluster category as an abnormal cluster category, and import the literature access data generated by the users of the section into the section of abnormal user analysis, in which the list of users shows the unique ids of all the users of the category currently selected by the analyst and some of their basic attributes, such as number of downloads, number of browsing, number of searches. The other three are analysis views for displaying individual abnormal user access log information.

4.1 User List

The user list view is shown in Fig. 3(1), displaying the number of downloads, browsing, and searching of the current user, and showing which types of anomaly detection algorithms have determined the user to be anomalous.

4.2 User Interested Keyword Analysis View

The user interest keyword analysis section is organized into two distinct parts, as depicted in Fig. 3(2). A key element of this section is the display of a word cloud representing the keywords related to the actions performed by the currently selected user. System analysts can utilize options in the top right corner of the interface to specify the source of the word cloud data, which can be either the keywords from documents downloaded by the user, the set of keywords from browsed documents, or a subset derived from search actions. This design of the word cloud presentation area aims to swiftly and intuitively convey the user's areas of interest to the observer, summarizing the data graphically to avoid the need for exhaustive data scrutiny, thereby accelerating the comprehension process.

The other part is a word tree diagram, in which all three types of user keywords are listed down in a tree diagram according to their frequency of use from highest to lowest. The analyst can carefully observe on this tree diagram that the current user is more interested in the keywords and that the keywords of lesser interest to the user are also accessible, and at the same time, in the word tree diagram, it is convenient for the analyst to directly compare the difference between the keywords of interest to the user in his three behaviors without switching the type of user behavior, and the analyst can also click on a node to collapse a behavior type to compare the other two types in a more focused manner.

4.3 User Action Time Period Analysis View

As shown in Fig. 3(3), the user action time period analysis view provides the download, browse, and search data of the currently selected user for each day under the whole year range. The line graph allows the analyst to easily discover the total number of documents downloaded, documents browsed, and search operations performed by the user on a given day, and to compare the number of the three behaviors to find anomalies among them. It is also able to observe the changes in the number of the three actions of users over a period of time, and to understand whether the downloading, browsing, and searching performed by users are sudden actions or habitual actions that last for a period of time.

To facilitate the analyst's use of the view, the view provides a timeline based zoom feature that allows the analyst to focus on user action data over a period of days or to observe changes in user action data over a time scale of months. Also, analysts can filter by specific behavior types using the legend above the view.

4.4 User Action Sequence Analysis View

The user action sequence analysis view is to enable the analyst to understand the number as well as the sequence of download, browsing, and searching actions of the user per day, and to be able to further explore the user's action trajectory on that day, and to provide an explanation for the anomaly detection method based on user action sequence in this paper. Each row in the view corresponds to a sequence of behaviors of that user in a given day, with the three behaviors of downloading, browsing, and retrieving represented by three colors, and the corresponding contextual relevance of the behaviors is encoded by the size of the rectangles.

With this view, the analyst can clearly see the sequence of user actions, and can get a good explanation of the user's anomalous behavior sequence detection algorithm's flagging, for example, an anomalous user only performed downloading actions on a certain day, but no searching or browsing actions, and only sporadic searching or browsing actions on a few days. And there is no searching operation before they perform downloading or the relevance between a sequence of downloads is low.

5 Case Study

We conducted experiments on the user action log dataset of this literature resource service platform for empirical analysis. The anomaly detection method based on download frequency statistics and the anomaly detection method based on topic relevance detected 28 and 36 anomalous users, which were labeled with *frequence* and *topic*, respectively, in the user list. The VENN plots of the users detected by these two methods and the users detected by our proposed method are shown in Fig. 6. Their specific comparisons will be shown in the following two specific cases.

The analyst selected the top green cluster category in Fig. 5, then the system imported the users contained in the corresponding cluster and jumped to the abnormal user sharing view, in which the analyst detected in detail the

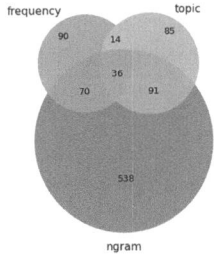

Fig. 6. VENN plots of anomalous users detected by the three methods

behavioral characteristics of the users in that rare category. In the following, we explain the anomalous action detection algorithm and introduce the visual analysis system on abnormal access detection by taking two of the anomalous users as examples.

Case 1: user "07057a7c477459a0": As shown in Fig. 7 upper left, after selecting this user, the system will change the background color of this user in the abnormal user list, and we can see that the total number of downloads for this user is 1342, the total number of browsing is 193, and the total number of searches is 1023. This user is marked as abnormal download frequency, abnormal topic relevance, and abnormal action sequence at the same time.

Fig. 7. Upper left: user list, Lower left: action time period analysis view Right: keyword analysis view

The user's interested keyword analysis view is shown in Fig. 7 lower left, which shows that the two largest words in the keyword cloud downloaded by the user are "former concept" and "Huang Zongxi", of which the term "former concept" is a psychological term that refers to everyday concepts, as opposed to scientific concepts, while Huang Zongxi" is one of the "Four Enlightenment thinkers of the late Ming and early Qing dynasties", which is a historical term. The keyword tree (browsing and searching keywords are collapsed interactively to focus on the downloading keywords) shows that the user also has the educational term "teaching strategy" and the biomedical term "neuroblastoma". Each of these terms belongs to a vastly different research area, reflecting the user's low topic relevance when downloading literature, so this user is marked as an anomalous user by the topic relevance anomaly detection algorithm.

The visualization of the temporal analysis of this user's behavior is depicted in Fig. 7 on the right-hand side. Evidently, it reveals that on January 6, 2020, the user executed 340 downloads, a figure that significantly surpasses the established threshold for malicious activity of 90 downloads within a 24-hour period. Consequently, the user was flagged as anomalous by the download frequency anomaly detection algorithm.

This user's action sequence analysis view is shown in Fig. 8. Due to its high number of active dates, this case study only shows its action sequence records for two periods of time, which are the abnormal action sequence between January and March and the normal action sequence between September and October.

Fig. 8. Left: Abnormal action sequence Right: Normal action sequence

This user did not browse or search between January and March, but performed a large number of downloads, and a large number of consecutive downloads with low similarity occurred among them. After vectorization, this kind of action sequence belongs to abnormal cluster type in high dimensional space, so this action sequence is also judged as an abnormal behavior sequence. And between September and October, the user's actions were more diverse, with a more balanced distribution of downloading, browsing, and searching actions, and all focusing on the same topics in phases, which is consistent with the general user's behavior of accessing electronic documents. However, since his action sequence had been anomalous before, the action sequence anomaly detection algorithm marked him as an anomalous user.

Case 2: user "7c9ab01e0c68e6b6": The user is not marked as anomalous by the topic relevance anomaly detection algorithm and does not reach the download frequency threshold, but it is determined to be an anomalous user by the action sequence anomaly detection algorithm. Several main views of the user is shown in Fig. 9.

In the visual analysis system, it can be found that the literature keywords downloaded by this user are more thematically focused, while it can be seen from the action time period analysis view that its peak download frequency is only 45, which is less than the download frequency threshold in this experiment. This user was identified as an abnormal user because he or she had performed only download operations and no other normal operations on a particular day. As shown in the Fig. 9, the user's action sequence on April 4th, 2020 contains

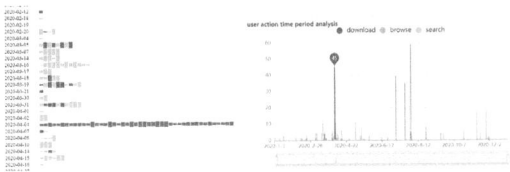

Fig. 9. Case 2 user's analysis panel

only download and has low document similarity between downloads, which is clearly anomalous, and thus is also detected and marked as anomalous by the action sequence anomaly detection algorithm.

6 Conclusion

Based on the user behavior log data of the literature resource platform, we propose a method for analyzing access to electronic literature resources based on the vectorization of user behavioral sequence, which integrally considers three kinds of user behaviors and the literature keyword features corresponding to the behaviors. Then a visual analysis system was designed, which functions to display the results of the algorithm's classification and supports in-depth examination of rare categories of interest to the analyst, as well as support for examination of the reasoning behind anomaly detection algorithms. Finally, we conduct experiments on real datasets and analyze two anomalous cases with the system to demonstrate the utility of the visual analytics system and the reasonableness of the electronic literature resource access analysis method based on user behavioral sequences.

References

1. Wang, Z., Yu, X., Jin, Y.: Using sniffer technology to constraint electronic resource excessive downloading. New Technol. Libr. Inf. Serv. **12**, 95–100 (2015)
2. Lei, D., Guo, Z.: Research on abnormal access to electronic resources based on EZproxy logs. J. Mod. Inf. **36**(7), 101–106 (2016)
3. Guo, S.: Research and implementation of sliding event window based malicious download detection system for library resource. Master's thesis, Beijing University of Posts and Telecommunications (2019)
4. Pelleg, D., Moore, A.: Active learning for anomaly and rare-category detection. In: Advances in Neural Information Processing Systems, vol. 17 (2004)
5. He, J., Carbonell, J.: Nearest-neighbor-based active learning for rare category detection. In: Platt, J., Koller, D., Singer, Y., Roweis, S. (eds.) Advances in Neural Information Processing Systems, vol. 20. Curran Associates, Inc. (2007)
6. He, J., Liu, Y., Lawrence, R.: Graph-based rare category detection. In: 2008 Eighth IEEE International Conference on Data Mining. IEEE (2008)
7. Huang, H., He, Q., Chiew, K., Qian, F., Ma, L.: CLOVER: a faster prior-free approach to rare-category detection. Knowl. Inf. Syst. **35**(3), 713–736 (2013)

8. Vatturi, P., Wong, W.-K.: Category detection using hierarchical mean shift. In: Proceedings of the 15th ACM SIGKDD International Conference on Knowledge Discovery and Data Mining, New York, NY, USA. ACM (2009)
9. Loveland, R., Amdahl, J.: Far point algorithm: active semi-supervised clustering for rare category detection. In: Proceedings of the 3rd International Conference on Vision, Image and Signal Processing, pp. 1–5 (2019)
10. Loveland, R., Kaplan, N.: Combining active semi-supervised learning and rare category detection. In: Troiano, L., et al. (eds.) Advances in Deep Learning, Artificial Intelligence and Robotics. LNNS, vol. 249, pp. 217–229. Springer, Cham (2022). https://doi.org/10.1007/978-3-030-85365-5_21
11. Huang, H., Yan, Q., Wei, L., Lin, H., Gao, Y., Chen, L.: LERI: local exploration for rare-category identification. IEEE Trans. Knowl. Data Eng. **32**(9), 1761–1772 (2019)
12. Spielman, D.A., Teng, S.-H.: A local clustering algorithm for massive graphs and its application to nearly linear time graph partitioning. SIAM J. Comput. **42**(1), 1–26 (2013)
13. Qiu, Y., Li, H., Li, S., Jiang, Y., Hu, R., Yang, L.: Revisiting correlations between intrinsic and extrinsic evaluations of word embeddings. In: Sun, M., Liu, T., Wang, X., Liu, Z., Liu, Y. (eds.) CCL/NLP-NABD -2018. LNCS (LNAI), vol. 11221, pp. 209–221. Springer, Cham (2018). https://doi.org/10.1007/978-3-030-01716-3_18
14. Guthrie, D., Allison, B., Liu, W., Guthrie, L., Wilks, Y.: A closer look at skip-gram modelling. In: LREC, vol. 6, pp. 1222–1225. Citeseer (2006)
15. Ester, M., Kriegel, H.-P., Sander, J., Xu, X.: Density-based spatial clustering of applications with noise. In: International Conference on Knowledge Discovery and Data Mining, vol. 240 (1996)

ACDiff: Angle Craft Diffusion Model for Novel View Synthesis

Huangqianyu Luo(✉)

Wuhan Textile University, Wuhan, China
lllhqy03@163.com

Abstract. Single-view novel view synthesis, the process of generating images from new perspectives using only a single reference image, is a vital yet formidable task. Traditional methods often employ conventional computer graphics techniques or deep learning approaches, but these frequently grapple with issues such as limited adaptability to intricate scenes, inability to maintain fine-grained details, and challenges in handling occlusions and texture inconsistencies. To tackle these challenges, we present the Angle Craft Diffusion Model (ACDiff), a groundbreaking network framework specifically tailored to merge CLIP's multimodal understanding with the unique demands of our task. This innovative approach effectively bridges the gap between angle-specific textual descriptions and visual data in novel view synthesis. Moreover, within the ACDiff framework, we integrate a refining module that uses the image generated in the previous phase as a conditioning factor. This module is instrumental in restoring texture and enhancing the consistency of fine details in the synthesized images. Our method's superior fidelity and realism are evidenced through both qualitative and quantitative results, underscoring its ability to produce visually compelling images that closely resemble the ground truth across various evaluation metrics.

1 Introduction

Novel view synthesis is a crucial task in computer vision with profound significance across various applications. This task involves generating images or views of a scene from perspectives not present in the original data, enabling the creation of unseen viewpoints. The significance of novel view synthesis lies in its potential to enhance visual perception and understanding. Creating new views of a scene allows us to gain a more comprehensive understanding of complex environments, which enhances our ability to interpret and analyze them. This capability is particularly valuable in fields such as content creation [1,2], robotic manipulation and navigation [3], object re-identification [4–7] and Virtual Reality [8], where a diverse set of viewpoints is essential for accurate decision-making and interaction with the environment.

In the field of novel view synthesis, there are several challenges. These include scene understanding, viewpoint consistency, occlusion handling, generalization across scenes, data sparsity, learning from limited data, and meeting user expectations for perceptual quality. Previous methods can be broadly categorized into geometric-based and learning-based approaches. Geometric-based methodologies involve explicit modeling of scene geometry and camera parameters, often requiring time-consuming iterative optimization for obtaining novel view images. Exemplary works within this category include RealFusion [9], NeuralLift [10], and SSDNerf [11]. However, challenges inherent in these methods revolve around the intricate nature of handling complex scenes, where sensitivity to the accuracy of geometric modeling during iterative optimization poses a significant hurdle.

Another category of past methods primarily embraces learning-based approaches. These techniques leverage neural networks to implicitly capture the complex mapping relationships between input images and desired novel views. Noteworthy for their efficiency, they can accomplish the synthesis task with a single forward process. Representative works encompass MCC [12], Graf [13], and Zero123 [14]. Despite their speed and efficacy, challenges in this category include potential overfitting, a demand for extensive training data, and difficulties in achieving robust generalization, particularly when dealing with complex scenes.

To address this, we propose an innovative approach integrating CLIP's [15] multimodal understanding with task-specific requirements. Leveraging CLIP and SD [16] layers while adapting representations through adaptable layers like Linear, LayNorm [17], and cross-attention, our method enhances model interpretability and integration of textual and visual details. This enables generation of contextually accurate and visually compelling images. Additionally, a refining module is introduced to enhance texture detail and image quality by leveraging coarse-grained target images and employing DINOv2 image encoder. Texture features are incorporated using an across-attention mechanism, steering the model towards texture restoration and fine detail coherence. The main contributions of this paper are summarized as follows:

- We introduce the Angle Craft Diffusion Model (ACDiff) to boost the fidelity of single-view synthesis by employing a controllable multimodal conditional generation model.
- we propose a refining model that repairs the generated image in the previous stage through the texture details of the source image.
- We conduct extensive experiments on two datasets to demonstrate that the proposed method is superior to the state-of-the-art approaches.

2 Related Work

2.1 Novel View Synthesis

Geometric-based Methods for novel view synthesis rely on explicit modeling of the underlying geometric structures in a scene. One notable approach is the seminal work of [18], which introduced a depth-based method for novel view synthesis. By capturing the geometric relationships between pixels and depths, the model could synthesize new views by extrapolating the scene geometry. This geometric paradigm extends further with the work of [19], which employs a neural network to predict 3D geometry from images, allowing for more accurate geometric representations in the novel view synthesis process. Geometric-based methods excel in preserving fine-grained structural details, making them valuable in scenarios where accurate geometric understanding is crucial.

Learning-based Approaches for novel view synthesis leverage neural networks to directly learn the mapping between input views and desired output views. A notable example is the work by [20], which introduced the concept of multiplane images (MPI) for synthesizing novel views. By formulating the scene as a set of image planes with associated depths, the model learned to generate new views through a learned mapping, effectively combining depth and appearance information. Learning-based methods, such as this, are advantageous for their ability to capture complex, non-linear relationships between input and output views, allowing for more flexible and adaptive novel view synthesis. Recently, [12] integrates extensive cross-domain training using diverse RGB-D video datasets. It is designed to compress input appearance and geometry collectively, enabling the prediction of 3D structure through interactions with a specialized 3D-aware decoder.

Currently, Neural Radiance Fields (NeRF) [21] proposes to achieve the result of synthesizing novel views of complex scenes by optimizing the underlying continuous volume scene function using a sparse set of input views. DreamFields [22] demonstrates the versatility of NeRF, showcasing its capability to serve as a primary component within a 3D generative system. Recently, researchers leverage various 3D representations for this task, including 3D point clouds [23–25], as well as layered formats such as layered depth images [8,26], and multiplane images [27]. However, the above method has the following limitations:(1) Difficulties may be encountered when dealing with scenes with complex textures and dealing with inaccuracies in depth estimation or occlusion. (2) When the model encounters scenes that are significantly different from its training data, it leads to potential artifacts and synthetic inaccuracies. Therefore, our work explores addressing these challenges through the integration of advanced neural network architectures and leveraging multimodal understanding from CLIP to enhance the fidelity and adaptability of single-view novel view synthesis.

2.2 Diffusion Model

Denoising diffusion probabilistic models (DDPMs) [28,29], commonly referred to as diffusion models, are a class of generative models characterized by a two-stage framework. The first stage, known as the forward process or "diffuse" phase, involves diffusing input data into a random distribution through multiple steps, achieved by introducing Gaussian noise. Subsequently, in the reverse process, the model undergoes training to reverse the diffusion, effectively denoising the perturbed data. This dual-stage approach allows DDPMs to learn and characterize the underlying data distribution through the iterative interplay of diffusion and denoising processes. Diffusion models achieve impressive results in various fields, with notable applications including image generation [30–32], image-to-image translation [33,34], audio synthesis [35], image super-resolution [36], and image editing [37,38].

The pioneering work of 3DiM [39] introduced a diffusion model tailored for the task of novel view synthesis. This model, when provided with a source view and corresponding pose as input, proficiently produces a novel view aligned with the target pose as its output. SparseFusion [40] presents an approach aimed at deducing 3D neural representations from sparsely observed views, marking a significant stride in extracting intricate 3D details from casually captured images. However, a notable constraint lies in the dependence on pre-determined camera poses during the observation process. [41] introduces an innovative view synthesis technique employing geometry-based priors and diffusion models to generate views from a single image. Nevertheless, there is the potential for slight inconsistencies and drift when confronted with challenging real-world datasets. Zero1-to-3 [14] solves zero-shot, single-image novel view synthesis and 3D reconstruction problems. Leveraging stable diffusion models [16,42] pre-trained on Internet-scale data, capturing rich semantic and geometric priors, and demonstrating state-of-the-art performance on a variety of benchmarks by expertly leveraging robust object shape priors. Nevertheless, ensuring the coherence of both geometry and color in the produced images proves to be an ongoing challenge. Utilizing a geometry-aware deep model, Consistent 1-to-3 [43] initiates the process with a transformer, generating an intentionally blurry yet geometrically correct image. Subsequently, the model employs a diffusion model to refine the details, achieving the production of high-quality and 3D-consistent novel view synthesis from either a single image or a few short images. Our research, alongside recent investigations [44–47], is dedicated to overcoming previous constraints and pushing the boundaries in this domain.

3 Proposed Method

3.1 Preliminaries

Generative diffusion techniques offer a complex framework for data synthesis and evolution. These models involve a two-stage process. In the first stage, known as the diffusion stage, data is continuously modified by adding Gaussian noise over a sequence of T steps using a Markov chain mechanism. In the second stage, the process is reversed, and a trained model is used to predict the original data from its noisy state. Notably, diffusion models can be customized to include additional inputs, such as augmenting text descriptions in text-to-image conversions. These models are trained to minimize an objective function, which is a refined version of the variational bound. The objective function focuses on predicting the noise component and can be represented by the following expression:

$$L_{simple} = \mathbb{E}_{Z_0, \epsilon \sim \mathcal{N}(0,1), c, t} \|\epsilon - \epsilon_\theta(Z_t, c, t)\|^2. \tag{1}$$

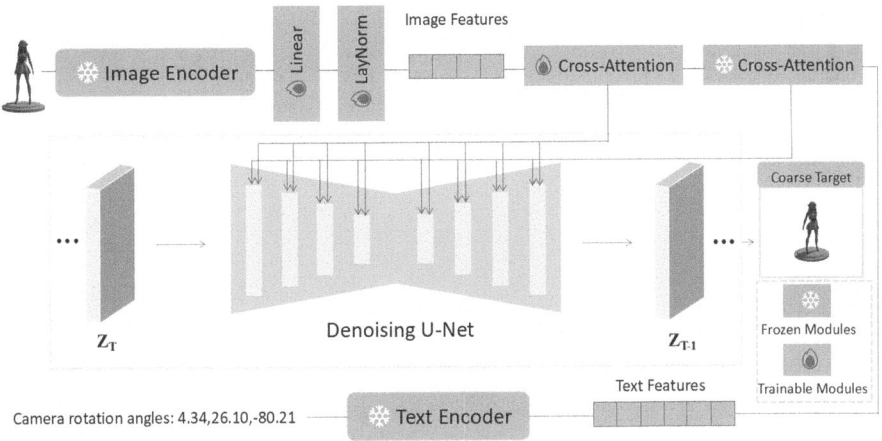

Fig. 1. Overview of the ACDiff. ACDiff exclusively trains the Linear, LayNorm, and an additional cross-attention layer, while maintaining the parameters of the remaining modules in a frozen state

Here, the term Z_t denotes the interplay between the original signal Z_0 and the introduced noise ϵ, adjusted over the course $[0, T]$ to reflect the balance struck at each interval t:

$$Z_t = \sqrt{\alpha_t} Z_0 + \sqrt{1-\alpha_t}\epsilon.$$

This mathematical relationship underscores the model's ability to traverse from an initial data point through a noise-induced trajectory, and back to a state of clarity, all while being modulated by a set of scaling factors α_t.

In the realm of enhancing fidelity and pattern coherence within generative diffusion models, one often harnesses a classifier as a directive guide [48]. This necessitates a distinct training process for an image classification module, operating independently from the diffusion model. Nevertheless, under the classifier-free guidance [49] approach, the training procedure encompasses both conditional and unconditional diffusion models, with control conditions c being subject to random exclusion. The sampling phase's noise estimation is governed by this equation:

$$\hat{\epsilon}_\theta(Z_t, c, t) = \omega \epsilon_\theta(Z_t, c, t) + (1-\omega)\epsilon_\theta(Z_t). \qquad (2)$$

Here, ω denotes the weighting factor that calibrates the adherence to the specified conditions c within the output. The generative model foundational to this work is SD, which maps visual data into a more tractable latent space instead of operating directly within the high-dimensional pixel space. This adaptation, which utilizes the SD framework, considerably diminishes the complexity of the diffusion process. Within this modified SD architecture, a U-Net [50] model, trained to serve as the core of the noise prediction mechanism, incorporates a cross-attention layer. This layer is strategically positioned within the U-Net's

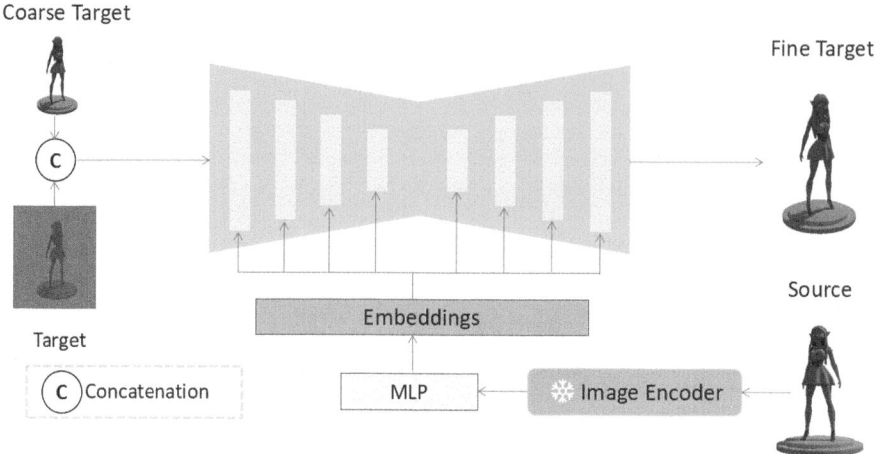

Fig. 2. The overall framework of refining module. The refining module utilizes the preliminary coarse-grained image produced in the preceding stage to rectify textures and maintain coherence

intermediate stages to infuse the control information c directly into the image synthesis pipeline. The operation of the cross-attention layer is encapsulated as:

$$\text{Attention}(Q, K, V) = \text{softmax}\left(\frac{QK^T}{\sqrt{d}}\right) \cdot V, \qquad (3)$$

where $Q = W_Q \cdot \phi(Z_t), K = W_K \cdot \tau(c)$, and $V = W_V \cdot \tau(c)$. Here, W_Q, W_K, and W_V represent matrices of learnable weights, $\phi(Z_t)$ is a function that transforms the latent representation into a sequence amenable to attention mechanisms, and $\tau(c)$ is a domain-specific encoder transforming the conditions c into an appropriate format for the model.

3.2 Dual Cross-Attention

In the training process, the precise integration of reference images and angles into the diffusion model is imperative. Ensuring that the synthesized images are not only visually compelling but also maintain a sense of authenticity and credibility is crucial. To successfully inject these conditions into the diffusion model, we employ a frozen CLIP image encoder, derived from the SD model, augmented with a trainable linear layer (Linear) and Layer Normalization (LayNorm). The primary objective of this configuration is to process the dispersed image features x and map them to an optimized feature c' that aligns seamlessly with the desired effect and is compatible with the text embedding dimension. The linear layer computes $y = W'x + b$, while the LayNorm transforms the input into a control condition imbued with corresponding angle characteristics, resulting in the feature c':

$$\begin{cases} c' = g \odot \dfrac{y - \mu}{\sqrt{\sigma^2 + \epsilon}} + b', \\ \mu = \dfrac{1}{H} \sum_{i=1}^{H} y_i, \\ \sigma = \sqrt{\dfrac{1}{H} \sum_{i=1}^{H} (y_i - \mu)^2}. \end{cases} \quad (4)$$

In the above equation, the terms W', b, g, and b' represent tunable parameters, H stands for the total number of hidden units, and $\odot$ indicates element-wise multiplication. Subsequently, we can incorporate the derived feature c' into the ensuing cross-attention layer:

$$\text{Attention}(Q, K', V') = \text{softmax}\left(\frac{QK^T}{\sqrt{d}}\right) \cdot V, \quad (5)$$

where $Q = W_Q \cdot \phi(Z_t)$, $K' = W'_K \cdot \tau(c')$, and $V' = W'_V \cdot \tau(c')$. Here, W_K and W_V are learnable parameters for the new cross-attention layer. Consequently, this structure facilitates the merging of cross-attention layers that are informed by text encoding angular characteristics, as well as by reference image features, into a singular dual cross-attention scheme:

$$\begin{aligned} \text{Attention}_{\text{new}} = {} & (1 - \alpha) \cdot \text{Attention}(Q, K, V) \\ & + \alpha \cdot \text{Attention}(Q, K', V'). \end{aligned} \quad (6)$$

Our dual cross-attention mechanism integrates the features of reference images with angle information, delivering rich and targeted visual information. Adopting the idea of unguided classifiers, we introduce an α parameter (default set at 0.5) to modulate the trade-off between the accuracy and diversity of the generated images via weight adjustments.

3.3 Combined with Stable Diffusion

To resolve the disconnect between angle-specific textual descriptions and the corresponding visual data in novel view synthesis, we propose an innovative approach that harmonizes the strengths of CLIP's multimodal understanding with our task-specific requirements. Our method builds upon the proven methodology of training an Adapter with CLIP and SD layers held constant, enabling a focus on fine-tuning a more compact set of parameters. By freezing the foundational architecture of CLIP and SD, we harness their powerful pre-trained representations and contrastive learning benefits, while our network learns to adapt these representations to the demands of synthesizing new viewpoints through a minimal set of adaptable layers-Linear, LayNorm, and cross-attention. This strategy not only streamlines the training process but also imbues our model with the ability to interpret and integrate angle information provided in textual form with the intricate visual details captured by the image encoder. Consequently, our method is tailored to effectively bridge the gap between text-based angle descriptions and high-fidelity visual outputs, thus enabling the generation of images that are both contextually accurate and visually compelling.

In the training stage, we concurrently map the features of reference images and the corresponding descriptive angle information into a unified dimensional framework, injecting these dual inputs into the U-Net's intermediate layers through dual cross-attention mechanism. This technique not only harmonizes the visual and textual modalities but also empowers the model to generate views that are intricately aligned with the specified angles and visual cues. To bolster the model's resilience and adaptability, we strategically introduce a probabilistic conditioning element by setting image and text conditions to empty according to the probability of $p_\emptyset=0.05$ and set both conditions as empty at the same time under the same probability. This practice trains the model to perform reliably even when confronted with incomplete data, promoting an internal capacity for inferring missing information and achieving robust synthesis outcomes. The integration of this probabilistic approach into our training objectives ensures that the model remains versatile across various degrees of input completeness, thereby enhancing its utility in real-world applications where data sparsity is commonplace. We established the following goals for the model's training regimen:

$$L_{\text{new}} = \mathbb{E}_{Z_o, \epsilon \sim \mathcal{N}(0,I), c, c', t} \|\epsilon - \epsilon_\theta(Z_t, c, c', t)\|^2. \tag{7}$$

Thus, the aim of predicting noise is established as:

$$\tilde{\epsilon}_\theta(Z_t, c, c', t) = w\epsilon_\theta(Z_t, c, c', t) + (1-w)\epsilon_\theta(Z_t, t). \tag{8}$$

3.4 Refining Module

Following the preceding phase, we acquire an initial coarse-grained target image generated through preliminary processes. To augment image quality and enhance texture detail, we introduce a refining module. Leveraging the coarse-grained image produced in the prior stage as a reference, this module aims to enhance the quality and fidelity of the synthesized image. We initiate the process by integrating the coarse-grained target image with the noisy image across the channels. This can be accomplished by making adjustments to the first convolutional layer within the diffusion model, which is designed based on the UNet architecture. Subsequently, we employ the DINOv2 image encoder, along with a trainable MLP layer, to capture distinctive features from the source image. Ultimately, we introduce texture features into the network through across-attention mechanism to steer the model towards texture restoration and to enhance the coherence of fine details.

Given that the features of the coarse target i_{ct} and those from the source image Z_s are known, the loss function for the refinement procedure is articulated as:

$$L_{prior} = \mathbb{E}_{Z_0, \epsilon, i_{ct}, Z_s, t} \|\epsilon - \epsilon_\theta(Z_t, i_{ct}, Z_s, t)\|^2. \tag{9}$$

For the inference phase, the model applies the subsequent formulation:

$$\epsilon_\theta(Z_t, i_{ct}, f_s, t) = w\epsilon_\theta(Z_t, i_{ct}, f_s, t) + (1-w)\epsilon_\theta(Z_t, t), \tag{10}$$

where f_s represent the feature embeddings derived from the source features.

The architectural overview of ACDiff is presented in Fig. 1. We input the reference image into the image encoder to obtain its feature representation, while simultaneously feeding the relevant angle information into the text encoder to acquire the corresponding textual feature representation. These two feature representations are then passed into the model. The model learns to transform the feature representation of the reference image into an image corresponding to the target viewpoint. By combining image and angle information, our approach effectively captures semantic details and spatial variations crucial for novel view synthesis tasks. The merit of this method lies in its exploitation of multimodal information, thereby enhancing the synthesis of images from novel viewpoints. To expedite the process of generating novel view synthesis, we utilized DDIM [51],a rapid sampling technique that employs a non-Markov diffusion process to emulate the reverse progression of Markov diffusion. To achieve texture restoration and enhance fine-detail consistency, we introduce a refining module, shown as Fig. 2. This module utilizes the coarsely generated image from the previous stage as a condition.

4 Experiment and Analysis

To validate the proposed ACDiff's superiority, it is compared with multiple state-of-the-art novel view synthesis approaches on two large-scale datasets, namely, Objaverse [52], Google Scanned Objects [53].

Table 1. Results for novel view synthesis on Objaverse.

	↑ PSNR	↑ SSIM	↓ LPIPS	↓ FID
ImageVariation [54]	6.53	0.526	0.571	13.956
Zero-1-to-3 [14]	19.56	0.798	0.215	0.302
SJC-I [55]	7.89	0.546	0.527	14.857
Consistent-1-to-3 [43]	20.78	0.878	0.108	1.623
Ours	**21.13**	**0.883**	**0.106**	**0.224**

4.1 Datasets

Objaverse. Our diffusion model undergoes fine-tuning utilizing the released Objaverse dataset, which encompasses a broad array of high-quality 3D models characterized by intricate geometry, many exhibiting fine-grained details and unique material properties. Leveraging the processed rendering data sourced from Zero123, we capitalize on the availability of 12 diverse views per object. The evaluation of our model takes place using the Objaverse's designated test partition facilitated by Zero123.

Google Scanned Objects. To gauge the robustness of our model, we conduct assessments on data beyond its training distribution, opting to evaluate it on the Google Scanned Objects dataset. This dataset encompasses meticulously scanned household items of exceptional quality, furnishing a rich assortment of objects for rigorous testing and validation purposes. To ensure consistency and comparability in our experiments, we standardize all images in the dataset to a resolution of 256 × 256, with a uniform white background applied.

4.2 Evaluation Metrics

We gauge the fidelity of rendered images against ground truth images by employing four metrics: Peak Signal-to-Noise Ratio (PSNR), Structural Similarity Index (SSIM) [56], Learned Perceptual Image Patch Similarity (LPIPS) [57], and Fréchet Inception Distance (FID) [58].

4.3 Implementation Details

We utilize CLIP ViT-H/14 [59] as the image encoder and SD v1.5 as the backbone network. ACDiff's parameters were lightweight and enabled training on a 24 GB RTX 3090 graphics card with 80 GB RAM. Employing AdamW [60] as the optimizer, we train for 160k global steps on Objaverse with a learning rate set at 1×10^{-4} and a weight decay of 0.01. DDIM served as the sampling acceleration algorithm, executing 50 sampling steps during inference. The coefficient α in dual cross-attention defaulted to 0.5.

4.4 Comparison with State-of-the-Art Methods

Table 2. Results for novel view synthesis on Google Scanned Objects.

	↑ PSNR	↑ SSIM	↓ LPIPS	↓ FID
ImageVariation [54]	5.92	0.527	0.531	18.562
Zero-1-to-3 [14]	17.96	0.893	0.218	0.429
SJC-I [55]	8.014	0.594	0.541	8.122
Consistent-1-to-3 [43]	19.48	0.863	0.143	0.395
Ours	**20.56**	**0.927**	**0.117**	**0.215**

4.4.1 Comparisons Using the Objaverse Dataset

In Table 1, we showcase quantitative findings for NVS across datasets within the distribution. Our method not only surpasses the state-of-the-art approach in terms of PSNR, achieving higher scores compared to Zero 1-to-3 on the Objaverse

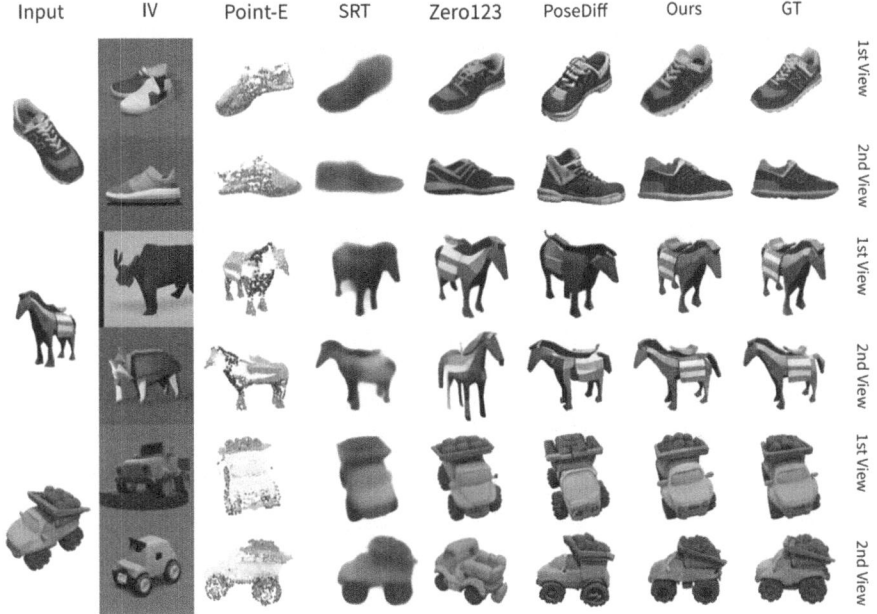

Fig. 3. NVS visualization. We present a comprehensive visualization of NVS outcomes across various methodologies using the Objaverse dataset. Our method surpasses competitive benchmarks by generating highly realistic images

dataset, but also excels in SSIM, consistently outperforming Consistent-1-to-3. This improvement underscores our method's dual focus: prioritizing image fidelity for PSNR and preserving structural similarity for SSIM. As a result, we achieve a more effective integration of conditions, reflecting our method's comprehensive approach to image quality enhancement.

4.4.2 Comparisons Using Google Scanned Objects Dataset

Quantitative outcomes for NVS on datasets beyond the distribution are displayed in Table 2. In terms of LPIPS, our method surpasses the state-of-the-art approach, achieving higher scores compared to ImageVariation on the Google Scanned Objects dataset. Additionally, our method excels in FID, consistently outperforming SJC-I. This improvement underscores our method's dual focus: emphasizing the perceptual differences between images for LPIPS and prioritizing the similarity of feature distributions between images for FID. As a result, our method combines various conditions smoothly, showing how effectively it improves image quality.

4.5 Ablation Studies and Analysis

The comparison results presented in Table 1 and Table 2, demonstrate that our method is superior to many state-of-the-art methods. In what follows, our

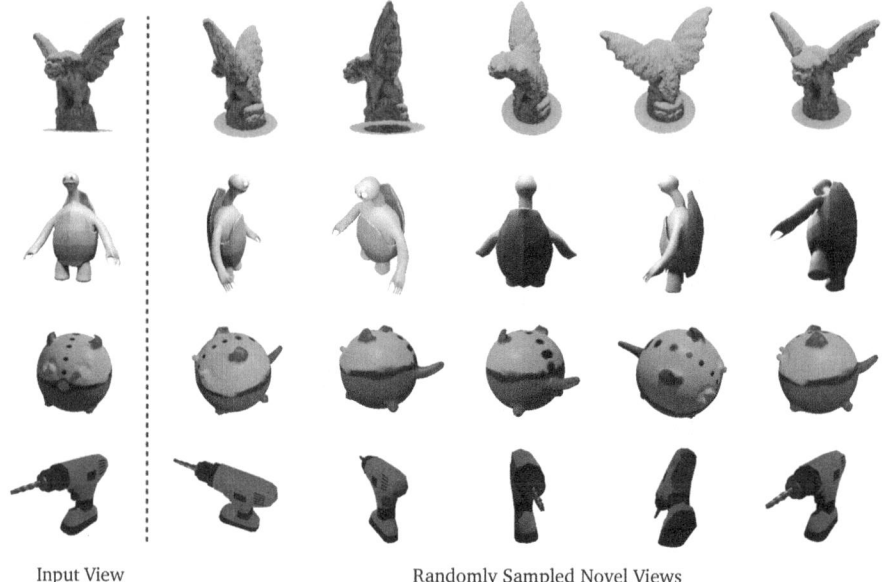

Fig. 4. Novel view synthesis on the Objaverse.

method is comprehensively analyzed from five aspects to investigate the logic behind its superiority.

Table 3. Ablation study on Objaverse.

	↑ PSNR	↑ SSIM	↓ LPIPS	↓ FID
w.o. dual cross-attention	18.83	0.845	0.145	0.436
w.o. probabilistic conditioning	20.67	0.863	0.131	0.316
w.o. refining module	20.81	0.872	0.115	0.247
full model	**21.13**	**0.883**	**0.106**	**0.224**

(1) Role of Dual Cross-Attention. The experimental results in Table 3 demonstrate the crucial role of the dual cross-attention mechanism in novel view synthesis. Removal of this mechanism had mixed effects on performance metrics: while PSNR and SSIM decreased, LPIPS and FID increased. This suggests that without dual cross-attention, the model's ability to align textual angle descriptions with visual features may be compromised, impacting its capacity to generate high-fidelity and contextually accurate visual outputs. Despite varying impacts on individual metrics, these findings collectively emphasize the significance of dual cross-attention in enhancing the overall performance and robustness of novel view synthesis frameworks.

(2) Impact of Probabilistic Conditioning. Based on the experimental results in Table 3, the impact of probabilistic conditioning on novel view synthesis model performance is evident. Using probabilistic conditioning significantly enhances performance metrics over scenarios that do not include it. Specifically, the model achieves higher PSNR and SSIM, and lower LPIPS and FID values with probabilistic conditioning. This trend indicates the significant contribution of probabilistic conditioning to model resilience and adaptability, enabling reliable performance with incomplete data. By strategically setting image and text conditions to empty with a certain probability, the model effectively infers missing information, enhancing synthesis outcomes. These findings highlight the importance of integrating probabilistic conditioning into novel view synthesis frameworks, improving model versatility across varying input completeness levels and enhancing utility in real-world applications with common data sparsity issues.

(3) Influence of Refining Module. From the results in Table 3, the refining module significantly impacts the model's performance in novel view synthesis. Its inclusion led to better performance in certain metrics compared to scenarios without it, including higher PSNR and SSIM values, indicating improved image fidelity and structural similarity. Additionally, lower LPIPS and FID values were observed, suggesting reduced perceptual differences and feature distributional differences. These results emphasize the refining module's crucial role in enhancing various aspects of image synthesis, yielding more visually appealing and contextually accurate outcomes.

(4) Complexity Analysis. In our complexity analysis, we meticulously examine the computational implications and model intricacies of each component in our proposed framework. Firstly, we delve into the computational overhead introduced by key components like the dual cross-attention mechanism, probabilistic conditioning, and refining module. We quantify the additional computational operations required during both training and inference phases, providing insights into their impact on overall runtime performance. Secondly, we scrutinize the model's parameter count and memory footprint with and without each component, shedding light on its scalability and resource efficiency. Furthermore, we rigorously evaluate the model's inference time and memory consumption across diverse hardware platforms, including CPUs and GPUs, to assess its practical feasibility for deployment. Through this detailed analysis, we aim to offer a comprehensive understanding of the computational demands and intricacies of our framework, aiding informed decision-making regarding its applicability in real-world scenarios.

(5) Sensitivity Analysis. In our sensitivity analysis, we rigorously explore our framework's robustness and sensitivity to parameter and configuration variations. We systematically vary parameters like learning rates, batch sizes, and architectural hyperparameters to optimize model performance while ensuring stability and convergence in training. Additionally, extensive experiments assess the framework's sensitivity to changes in input data characteristics, such as image resolution, noise levels, and textual descriptions' specificity. By varying these factors, we gain insights into the framework's adaptability and generalization across diverse input conditions. Furthermore, we investigate its sensitivity to hardware configurations and computational resources, such as CPU and GPU specifications, to assess its robustness in real-world deployment scenarios. Through this analysis, we provide valuable insights into the resilience and adaptability of our framework, aiding informed decisions for practical applications.

4.6 Visualization

Figure 3 illustrates a comparative analysis of NVS outcomes on the Objaverse dataset, featuring our method alongside all baseline approaches. The SRT [61] outcomes depicted in the figure are derived from training the SRT component within Consistent-1-to-3 solely utilizing the reconstruction loss. While Point-E, SRT and ImageVariation exhibit consistency with inputs but struggle to generate realistic images, diffusion-based baselines such as Zero123 and PoseDiff can produce realistic images but often fail to align with the ground truth. In contrast, our approach stands out as the only method achieving both fidelity and consistency. Figure 4 showcases our model's robustness in handling objects with intricate geometry and diverse textures. Moreover, it illustrates the model's proficiency in synthesizing high-fidelity viewpoints while preserving the object's characteristics, identity, and low-level details. This demonstrates the versatility and effectiveness of our approach in handling challenging scenarios and producing visually compelling results across a variety of object types and environmental conditions.

5 Conclusion

In conclusion, we introduced ACDiff, a novel network framework designed to seamlessly integrate CLIP's multimodal understanding with our specific task requirements in single-view novel view synthesis. While our method demonstrated significant advancements in generating visually compelling images from fresh perspectives using only one reference image, there were inherent limitations that warranted consideration. ACDiff's performance might have suffered when applied to extremely complex scenes with intricate structures or extreme lighting conditions, and further research was needed to address these challenges. Additionally, while our method aimed to preserve fine-grained details and handle occlusions and texture inconsistencies, there was room for improvement in these aspects. Moreover, the computational complexity of ACDiff might have limited its practical applicability in real-time or resource-constrained environments, necessitating future efforts in improving efficiency without compromising performance. **Future Work.** Although ACDiff produces high-fidelity images, its use in real-time or resource-constrained environments presents limitations. Future work will focus on optimizing the algorithm to reduce computational demands, thereby expanding its applicability across various practical scenarios.

References

1. Yen-Chen, L., Florence, P., Barron, J.T., Lin, T.-Y., Rodriguez, A., Isola, P.: NeRF-supervision: learning dense object descriptors from neural radiance fields. In: 2022 International Conference on Robotics and Automation (ICRA), pp. 6496–6503. IEEE (2022)
2. Poole, B., Jain, A., Barron, J.T., Mildenhall, B.: DreamFusion: text-to-3D using 2D diffusion. arXiv preprint arXiv:2209.14988 (2022)
3. Moreau, A., Piasco, N., Tsishkou, D., Stanciulescu, B., de La Fortelle, A.: LENS: localization enhanced by NeRF synthesis. In: Conference on Robot Learning, pp. 1347–1356. PMLR (2022)
4. Shen, F., et al.: An efficient multiresolution network for vehicle reidentification. IEEE Internet Things J. **9**(11), 9049–9059 (2021)
5. Shen, F., Peng, X., Wang, L., Zhang, X., Shu, M., Wang, Y.: HSGM: a hierarchical similarity graph module for object re-identification. In: 2022 IEEE International Conference on Multimedia and Expo (ICME), pp. 1–6. IEEE (2022)
6. Shen, F., Xie, Y., Zhu, J., Zhu, X., Zeng, H.: GiT: graph interactive transformer for vehicle re-identification. IEEE Trans. Image Process. (2023)
7. Shen, F., Shu, X., Du, X., Tang, J.: Pedestrian-specific bipartite-aware similarity learning for text-based person retrieval. In: Proceedings of the 31th ACM International Conference on Multimedia (2023)
8. Kopf, J., et al.: One shot 3D photography. ACM Trans. Graph. (TOG) **39**(4), 76:1–76:13 (2020)
9. Melas-Kyriazi, L., Laina, I., Rupprecht, C., Vedaldi, A.: RealFusion: 360° reconstruction of any object from a single image. In: Proceedings of the IEEE/CVF Conference on Computer Vision and Pattern Recognition, pp. 8446–8455 (2023)
10. Xu, D., Jiang, Y., Wang, P., Fan, Z., Wang, Y., Wang, Z.: NeuralLift-360: lifting an in-the-wild 2D photo to a 3D object with 360° views. In: Proceedings of the IEEE/CVF Conference on Computer Vision and Pattern Recognition, pp. 4479–4489 (2023)
11. Ranade, S., et al.: SSDNeRF: semantic soft decomposition of neural radiance fields. arXiv preprint arXiv:2212.03406 (2022)
12. Wu, C.-Y., Johnson, J., Malik, J., Feichtenhofer, C., Gkioxari, G.: Multiview compressive coding for 3D reconstruction. In: Proceedings of the IEEE/CVF Conference on Computer Vision and Pattern Recognition, pp. 9065–9075 (2023)
13. Schwarz, K., Liao, Y., Niemeyer, M., Geiger, A.: GRAF: generative radiance fields for 3D-aware image synthesis. Adv. Neural. Inf. Process. Syst. **33**, 20154–20166 (2020)
14. Liu, R., Wu, R., Van Hoorick, B., Tokmakov, P., Zakharov, S., Vondrick, C.: Zero-1-to-3: zero-shot one image to 3D object. In: Proceedings of the IEEE/CVF International Conference on Computer Vision, pp. 9298–9309 (2023)
15. Radford, A.,, et al.: Learning transferable visual models from natural language supervision. In: International Conference on Machine Learning, pp. 8748–8763. PMLR (2021)
16. Yao, J., et al.: NDC-scene: boost monocular 3D semantic scene completion in normalized device coordinates space. In: 2023 IEEE/CVF International Conference on Computer Vision (ICCV), pp. 9421–9431. IEEE Computer Society (2023)

17. Ba, J.L., Kiros, J.R., Hinton, G.E.: Layer normalization. arXiv preprint arXiv:1607.06450 (2016)
18. Eigen, D., Fergus, R.: Predicting depth, surface normals and semantic labels with a common multi-scale convolutional architecture. In: Proceedings of the IEEE International Conference on Computer Vision, pp. 2650–2658 (2015)
19. Tatarchenko, M., Dosovitskiy, A., Brox, T.: Multi-view 3D models from single images with a convolutional network. In: Leibe, B., Matas, J., Sebe, N., Welling, M. (eds.) ECCV 2016. LNCS, vol. 9911, pp. 322–337. Springer, Cham (2016). https://doi.org/10.1007/978-3-319-46478-7_20
20. Flynn, J., Broxton, M., Debevec, P., DuVall, M., Fyffe, G., Overbeck, R., Snavely, N., Tucker, R.: DeepView: view synthesis with learned gradient descent. In: Proceedings of the IEEE/CVF Conference on Computer Vision and Pattern Recognition, pp. 2367–2376 (2019)
21. Mildenhall, B., Srinivasan, P.P., Tancik, M., Barron, J.T., Ramamoorthi, R., Ng, R.: NeRF: representing scenes as neural radiance fields for view synthesis. Commun. ACM **65**(1), 99–106 (2021)
22. Jain, A., Mildenhall, B., Barron, J.T., Abbeel, P., Poole, B.: Zero-shot text-guided object generation with dream fields. In: Proceedings of the IEEE/CVF Conference on Computer Vision and Pattern Recognition, pp. 867–876 (2022)
23. Aliev, K.-A., Sevastopolsky, A., Kolos, M., Ulyanov, D., Lempitsky, V.: Neural point-based graphics. In: Vedaldi, A., Bischof, H., Brox, T., Frahm, J.-M. (eds.) ECCV 2020. LNCS, vol. 12367, pp. 696–712. Springer, Cham (2020). https://doi.org/10.1007/978-3-030-58542-6_42
24. Koh, J.Y., et al.: Simple and effective synthesis of indoor 3D scenes. In: Proceedings of the AAAI Conference on Artificial Intelligence, vol. 37, pp. 1169–1178 (2023)
25. Meshry, M., et al.: Neural rerendering in the wild. In: Proceedings of the IEEE/CVF Conference on Computer Vision and Pattern Recognition, pp. 6878–6887 (2019)
26. Shih, M.-L., Su, S.-Y., Kopf, J., Huang, J.-B.: 3D photography using context-aware layered depth inpainting. In: Proceedings of the IEEE/CVF Conference on Computer Vision and Pattern Recognition, pp. 8028–8038 (2020)
27. Zhou, T., Tucker, R., Flynn, J., Fyffe, G., Snavely, N.: Stereo magnification: learning view synthesis using multiplane images. arXiv preprint arXiv:1805.09817 (2018)
28. Ho, J., Jain, A., Abbeel, P.: Denoising diffusion probabilistic models. Adv. Neural. Inf. Process. Syst. **33**, 6840–6851 (2020)
29. Song, Y., Ermon, S.: Generative modeling by estimating gradients of the data distribution. Adv. Neural Inf. Process. Syst. **32** (2019)
30. Ho, J., Saharia, C., Chan, W., Fleet, D.J., Norouzi, M., Salimans, T.: Cascaded diffusion models for high fidelity image generation. J. Mach. Learn. Res. **23**(1), 2249–2281 (2022)
31. Nichol, A., et al. GLIDE: towards photorealistic image generation and editing with text-guided diffusion models. arXiv preprint arXiv:2112.10741 (2021)
32. Zheng, G., et al.: Entropy-driven sampling and training scheme for conditional diffusion generation. In: Avidan, S., Brostow, G., Cissé, M., Farinella, G.M., Hassner, T. (eds.) Computer Vision – ECCV 2022: 17th European Conference, Tel Aviv, Israel, October 23–27, 2022, Proceedings, Part XXII, pp. 754–769. Springer, Cham (2022). https://doi.org/10.1007/978-3-031-20047-2_43
33. Sasaki, H., Willcocks, C.G., Breckon, T.P.: UNIT-DDPM: unpaired image translation with denoising diffusion probabilistic models. arXiv preprint arXiv:2104.05358 (2021)

34. Tumanyan, N., Geyer, M., Bagon, S., Dekel, T.: Plug-and-play diffusion features for text-driven image-to-image translation. In: Proceedings of the IEEE/CVF Conference on Computer Vision and Pattern Recognition, pp. 1921–1930 (2023)
35. Kong, Z., Ping, W., Huang, J., Zhao, K., Catanzaro, B.: DiffWave: a versatile diffusion model for audio synthesis. arXiv preprint arXiv:2009.09761 (2020)
36. Saharia, C., Ho, J., Chan, W., Salimans, T., Fleet, D.J., Norouzi, M.: Image super-resolution via iterative refinement. IEEE Trans. Pattern Anal. Mach. Intell. **45**(4), 4713–4726 (2022)
37. Kawar, B., et al.: Imagic: text-based real image editing with diffusion models. In: Proceedings of the IEEE/CVF Conference on Computer Vision and Pattern Recognition, pp. 6007–6017 (2023)
38. Couairon, G., Verbeek, J., Schwenk, H., Cord, M.: DiffEdit: diffusion-based semantic image editing with mask guidance. arXiv preprint arXiv:2210.11427 (2022)
39. Watson, D., Chan, W., Martin-Brualla, R., Ho, J., Tagliasacchi, A., Norouzi, M.: Novel view synthesis with diffusion models. arXiv preprint arXiv:2210.04628 (2022)
40. Zhou, Z., Tulsiani, S.: SparseFusion: distilling view-conditioned diffusion for 3D reconstruction. In: Proceedings of the IEEE/CVF Conference on Computer Vision and Pattern Recognition, pp. 12588–12597 (2023)
41. Chan, E.R., et al.: Generative novel view synthesis with 3D-aware diffusion models. arXiv preprint arXiv:2304.02602 (2023)
42. Shen, F., Ye, H., Zhang, J., Wang, C., Han, X., Yang, W.: Advancing pose-guided image synthesis with progressive conditional diffusion models. arXiv preprint arXiv:2310.06313 (2023)
43. Ye, J., Wang, P., Li, K., Shi, Y., Wang, H.: Consistent-1-to-3: consistent image to 3D view synthesis via geometry-aware diffusion models. arXiv preprint arXiv:2310.03020 (2023)
44. Lin, Y., Han, H., Gong, C., Xu, Z., Zhang, Y., Li, X.: Consistent123: one image to highly consistent 3D asset using case-aware diffusion priors. arXiv preprint arXiv:2309.17261 (2023)
45. Liu, Y., et al.: SyncDreamer: generating multiview-consistent images from a single-view image. arXiv preprint arXiv:2309.03453 (2023)
46. Weng, H., et al.: Consistent123: improve consistency for one image to 3D object synthesis. arXiv preprint arXiv:2310.08092 (2023)
47. Liu, M., et al.: One-2-3-45++: fast single image to 3D objects with consistent multi-view generation and 3D diffusion. arXiv preprint arXiv:2311.07885 (2023)
48. Dhariwal, P., Nichol, A.: Diffusion models beat GANs on image synthesis. Adv. Neural. Inf. Process. Syst. **34**, 8780–8794 (2021)
49. Ho, J., Salimans, T.: Classifier-free diffusion guidance. arXiv preprint arXiv:2207.12598 (2022)
50. Ronneberger, O., Fischer, P., Brox, T.: U-Net: convolutional networks for biomedical image segmentation. In: Navab, N., Hornegger, J., Wells, W.M., Frangi, A.F. (eds.) MICCAI 2015. LNCS, vol. 9351, pp. 234–241. Springer, Cham (2015). https://doi.org/10.1007/978-3-319-24574-4_28
51. Song, J., Meng, C., Ermon, S.: Denoising diffusion implicit models. arXiv preprint arXiv:2010.02502 (2020)
52. Deitke, M., A universe of annotated 3D objects. In: Proceedings of the IEEE/CVF Conference on Computer Vision and Pattern Recognition, pp. 13142–13153 (2023)
53. Downs, L., et al.: Google scanned objects: a high-quality dataset of 3D scanned household items. In: 2022 International Conference on Robotics and Automation (ICRA), pp. 2553–2560. IEEE (2022)

54. Stable diffusion image variations - a hugging face space by lambdalabs
55. Wang, H., Du, X., Li, J., Yeh, R.A., Shakhnarovich, G.: Score Jacobian chaining: lifting pretrained 2D diffusion models for 3D generation. In: Proceedings of the IEEE/CVF Conference on Computer Vision and Pattern Recognition, pp. 12619–12629 (2023)
56. Wang, Z.: Image quality assessment: form error visibility to structural similarity. IEEE Trans. Image Process. **13**(4), 604–606 (2004)
57. Zhang, R., Isola, P., Efros, A.A., Shechtman, E., Wang, O.: The unreasonable effectiveness of deep features as a perceptual metric. In: Proceedings of the IEEE Conference on Computer Vision and Pattern Recognition, pp. 586–595 (2018)
58. Heusel, M., Ramsauer, H., Unterthiner, T., Nessler, B., Hochreiter, S.: GANs trained by a two time-scale update rule converge to a local NASH equilibrium. Adv. Neural Inf. Process. Syst. **30** (2017)
59. Ilharco, G., et al.: OpenCLIP, July 2021
60. Loshchilov, I., Hutter, F.: Decoupled weight decay regularization. arXiv preprint arXiv:1711.05101 (2017)
61. Yao, J., Pan, X., Wu, T., Zhang, X.: Building lane-level maps from aerial images. In: ICASSP 2024-2024 IEEE International Conference on Acoustics, Speech and Signal Processing (ICASSP), pp. 3890–3894. IEEE (2024)

A Training and Evaluation System for Magnetic-Actuated Virtual Vessel Interventional Surgery

Bosi Cai[1], Jianhui Zhao[1(✉)], Zhiyong Yuan[1], Tingbao Zhang[2], and Yu Feng[2]

[1] School of Computer Science, Wuhan University, Wuhan, China
{jianhuizhao,zhiyongyuan}@whu.edu.cn
[2] Zhongnan Hospital of Wuhan University, Wuhan University, Wuhan, China

Abstract. Interventional surgery is an efficient and safe surgical method with the advantages of less trauma and quick recovery. However, the current interventional surgery training is mainly based on teachers' hands-on guidance of the students, which has problems such as low efficiency and high risks. Therefore, to help doctors who want to conduct interventional surgery training, we have designed a virtual interventional surgery training system based on bone model guide wires. By designing the bone model and movement of the guidewire, linking it with the haptic device of Geomagic TOUCH, and reconstructing the real vascular surgery scene, we can simulate the manipulation of doctors on the guidewire during interventional surgery, and evaluate and score the training process to make the training more practical and evaluable. Users can check their operating level and accumulate experience. We then design a simulation of vascular interventional surgery based on magnetic-actuation in this system. The experimental results show that, compared with the traditional interventional surgery simulation mode, simulation based on magnetic-actuation can effectively improve the performance of the trainer. This system is designed to enhance the reality of the surgical simulation process, help trainers become familiar with interventional surgery scenarios, and provide a real practical experience for practicing both traditional and magnetic-actuation interventional surgeries.

Keywords: Interventional Surgery · Surgical Simulation System · Training and Evaluation · Magnetic-actuation · Virtual Reality

1 Introduction

Interventional surgery is a minimally invasive treatment technology that, under the guidance of medical imaging, introduces special guide wires, catheters, and other precision instruments into the human body to diagnose and treat diseased areas in the body. Its advantages include less trauma, faster recovery, and better results.

However, training process of interventional surgery is still mainly based on teachers' personal guidance of students. Not only is the efficiency relatively low, but there may also be safety risks and other issues. To allow doctors to conduct surgical training in a lower-cost and safer manner and to simulate various surgical scenarios for the pre-operative planning, researchers combined interventional surgery and virtual reality technology into virtual interventional surgery [1]. This technology used simulated precision instruments such as guide wires and catheters to diagnose and treat simulated internal disease areas of the human body, such as simulating intestinal anastomosis in virtual reality [2] or virtual training systems for vascular interventional surgery [3].

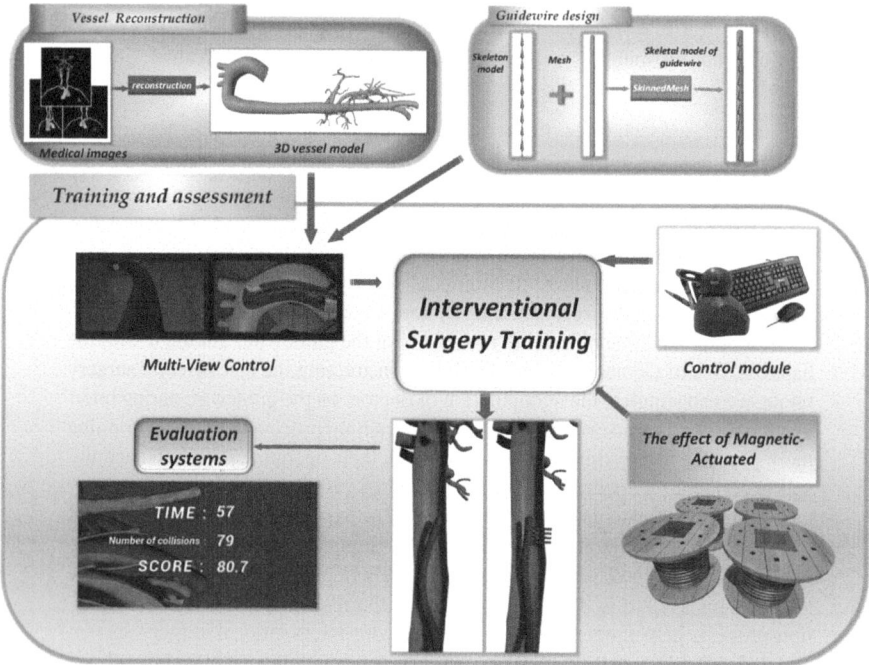

Fig. 1. The system structure

Although the virtual interventional surgery research has been widely used, there are few studies on its training and evaluation. It is undoubtedly of great significance to help doctors train in the operating level and proficiency of interventional surgery. Therefore, in this paper we design a virtual interventional surgery training system (shown in Fig. 1), the guidewire model is innovatively designed based on bones and integrated with the simulation hardware platform to achieve real-time tactile and visual feedback and also magnetic drive simulation, completing complex interventional surgery training within the reconstructed three-dimensional vascular scene. At the same time, a novel evaluation and scoring model has been designed in this system to evaluate and derive the trainer's operating level in real time, providing a realistic training environment and efficient training means for doctors to conduct simulated surgery training.

2 Related Work

The virtual surgical intervention simulation has made rapid progress in recent years, giving rise to numerous innovative technologies revolving around the construction of surgical scenarios, design of surgical procedures, and automation of interventional surgery.

The construction of virtual surgical scenes can be mainly categorized into two types: image-driven and physics-driven. Image-driven methods rely on medical imaging data such as CT and MRI images to reconstruct the patient's anatomical structures, thereby achieving the personalized surgical simulation [4, 5]. However, these methods may struggle to capture the physical properties of the tissues, and their performance may be unsatisfactory in surgical scenarios that require force feedback.

In contrast, physics-driven methods utilize biomechanical modelling algorithms to better simulate both tissue deformation and cutting processes [6, 7]. A method proposed by [8] leverages deep learning to predict the tissue deformation, achieving more accurate results through extensive training data. [9] employs machine learning to automatically adjust the parameters of biomechanical models, thereby achieving the goal of personalized simulation. To improve real-time performance and stability of organ simulation, some researchers have adopted the techniques such as precomputation [10] or model reduction [11].

The use of robots in interventional surgery can also enhance the efficiency and precision of surgeries [12], as demonstrated by studies on learning-based vascular interventional surgical robots [13] and the magnetically guided and propelled guidewire robots in surgery [14].

Regarding the design and simulation of interventional guidewires, [15] provided a novel method for designing interventional guidewires and conducting physical simulations, allowing doctors to perform the simulated experiments before actual surgery. [16] used finite element methods to model the bending behavior of guidewires and studied the effects of different design parameters on guidewire performance.

In terms of the integration of hardware and software and the human-computer interaction, innovative methods such as GPU-based parallel computing [17] have effectively accelerated the solution process of finite element models. Customized FPGA hardware has been used to achieve real-time physical simulation [18], and haptic devices have been employed to simulate force feedback during surgical procedures [19]. Additionally, a magnetic drive network physical system for interventional surgery [20] has been developed to enhance the accuracy and efficiency of simulation by designing and optimizing hardware devices, allowing doctors to experience the sensation of operating the guidewires more realistically.

Regarding the virtual vascular surgery [21], research has developed virtual heart surgery planning software for specific vascular grafts [22]. Studies have also achieved autonomous vascular guidewire navigation based on machine learning in the porcine hepatic venous system [23]. Similarly, some research has focused on the interactive experience and training of virtual surgical simulation, such as virtual simulation training based on metrics or sensors [24, 25], including deformation of vascular models in virtual training systems [26] or preoperative simulation [27], and the current status and improvement needs of plastic surgery simulation education [28]. The development of cloud computing and VR technology has also brought new possibilities to the virtual interventional surgical simulation. For example, cloud-based surgical training systems have been implemented to facilitate the multi-user online collaborative training [29], and the potential application of VR technology in liver surgery training [30].

To establish a virtual vascular interventional surgery training and evaluation system, it is necessary to achieve high real-time tactile feedback. The system must be able to capture the user's operations in a timely manner and convey the tactile information to the user in an appropriate manner. Secondly, to achieve high-fidelity surgical instruments and blood vessel scenes, it is necessary to accurately simulate the shape, material and movement of surgical tools, as well as the structure, elasticity and physiological characteristics of blood vessels. Finally, proper evaluation and scoring of simulation level requires the design of effective evaluation indicators and algorithms to ensure that the evaluation results can objectively and accurately reflect the user's operating skills and decision-making ability, which is undoubtedly very challenging.

3 Design of Interventional Surgery Training System

3.1 Systems Architecture

The structural diagram of this surgical training system (Fig. 1) mainly includes three modules: reconstruction of the interventional surgical environment, design of the guidewire skeleton model, and surgical training and evaluation. We obtain medical images such as CT images from the hospital and use Mimics software to reconstruct the CT images into a three-dimensional blood vessel model as a surgical scene for the vascular interventional surgery. The design of the guide wire is to first create the skeletal part of the guide wire and connect it to the overall skeleton of the guide wire, then complete the skinning and motion design of the skeleton to achieve a realistic guidewire appearance and also a guidewire deformation that fit the real situation well, and finally obtain the guidewire bone model. During the surgical training process, the trainer controls the movement of the guidewire through tactile devices and keyboards. At the same time, this system provides two viewing angles: a bird's-eye view and a third-person perspective, and the trainer can switch in real-time according to his or her needs.

The training evaluation and scoring system can output the operation records and training results on the screen after the training is completed, and export them in the form of a CSV file to help trainers view results in real-time and summarize shortcomings. This system also helps discuss whether the influence of the magnetic field on the deflection of the guidewire head can improve the training performance in the case of magnetic drive. Experiments have proved that in the case of magnetic-actuation, the performance of trainers will generally be better than the traditional interventional surgery mode.

3.1.1 Design of Guidewire Skeletal Model

The mass-spring model is a physical modelling method widely used in computer graphics. It simulates the deformation and movement of objects by discretely representing objects as a series of mass points and using spring models to connect these mass points. However, in the simulations, the mass point spring model cannot well represent the actual properties of the guide wire. For a guide wire that is driven by the links one by one, the mass-spring model cannot accurately simulate the movement of the front end from the tail end. And because the particle spring model requires interaction calculations for each particle, it may be inefficient in large-scale simulations or real-time applications, and thus it cannot achieve good results in real-time medical simulations.

Therefore, in this paper we propose a bone-based guidewire continuous model (Fig. 2), which adjusts the posture of the object based on the rotation constraints and transformation information of the joint, and can simulate the deformation of the object more accurately.

Compared to the skeletal body model, which can better handle collisions between objects because of its precise collision response based on joint constraints and collision detection algorithms, the mass point spring model may require more calculations and logic processing in terms of collision handling. And because the skeletal body guide wire only needs to perform transformation calculations on the skeletal joints during movement, and does not need to perform complex interaction calculations for each particle, the skeletal body model is more efficient in real-time applications and large-scale simulations.

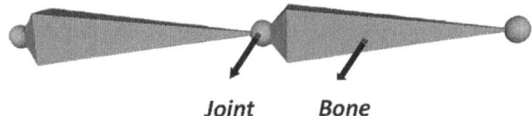

Fig. 2. Skeleton model components

In a skeletal model, parent and child nodes are the concepts used to describe the skeletal hierarchy. A skeletal model can consist of multiple bones, where each bone has a parent node. A parent node is the upper-level bone of the current bone, which is the direct superior of the current bone. A child node is the next level of bone of the current bone, which is a direct descendant of the current bone. Each bone can have zero or more child nodes, but only one parent node.

When the parent node is transformed, all the child nodes will be affected, forming a bone hierarchy with a linkage effect. This structure is usually used to describe the relationship between bones in character animation and to realize a hierarchical control of the position and rotation of the bones. Skeletal models are extremely flexible and accurate, reflecting the movements and deformations of the guidewire in subtle and complex ways, thus accurately simulating the actual surgical situation in a virtual environment. The guidewire movement based on the skeletal model can be finely controlled and adjusted, making it ideal for surgical simulations that require the precise guidewire movement paths.

3.1.2 Skinning Design of the Guidewire

To further enhance the realism and to make the model look more similar to the actual guidewire, we cover the outer layer of the skeletal model with a mesh body as the skin for skinning. This not only fits the skeletal model well but also provides the possibility to simulate the physical properties of the guidewire (e.g., elasticity and resistance). Skinning is the process of binding the mesh's vertices to the bones. Each vertex is affected by the motion of the nearby bones, although each bone has a different weight on the vertex, and the number of bones that can affect the vertex is generally less than four. When the skeleton undergoes a translation or rotation transformation, the vertices correspondingly drive the mesh body to transform together. In this system, since the guidewire consists of a whole bone with no extra branches, a linear hybrid skinning algorithm is used, the basic principle of which can be expressed by the following equation:

$$V' = \sum_{i=1}^{n-1} w_i M_i V, \sum_{i=1}^{n} w_i = 1 \tag{1}$$

In formula (1), V represents the position in the world coordinate system before the vertex transformation, V' represents the position after the vertex transformation, and i represents the number of bones that affect the vertex at the same time, generally taking a value between 2–4. w_i represents the influence weight exerted by the i-th bone on the vertex, taking a value between 0 and 1, and the sum of all w_i is 1. M_i indicates that in the initial reference pose of the model, the i-th bone related to the vertex is converted from the local coordinates to the world coordinates (the absolute matrix of bone transformation). Through the matrix M_i, bone i can be converted from the initial position to the new position when the animation data arrives. $M_i \times V$ represents the position of V under the separate influence of bone i.

By adding mesh skinning to a skeletal model (Fig. 3), we create a model that can accurately simulate the movement of the guidewire while also realistically represent its appearance. The advantages of this design method are obvious. First, the bone-based model makes the movement of the guide wire more accurate; second, the outer mesh skin makes the guide wire look more realistic, further enhancing the fidelity of the surgical simulation.

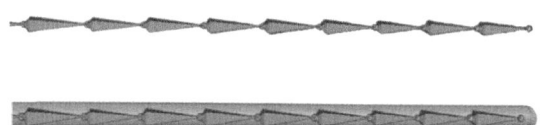

Fig. 3. Guidewire skeleton (top) and skinned guidewire model (bottom)

3.1.3 Guidewire Motion System

In this paper, the guidewire motion is based on a skeletal model where child nodes' movements are linked and driven by parent nodes. This closely mirrors the actual intervention process during surgery, where pushing forces from posterior nodes are transmitted to each node, facilitating movement and directional changes.

(1) Node coordinate conversion in the skeleton's resting state (reference posture)

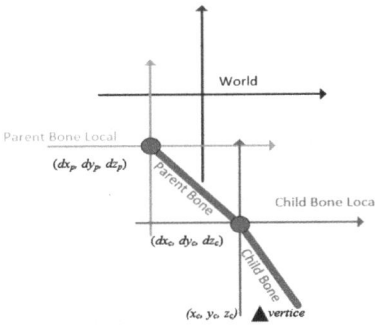

Fig. 4. Bone coordinate system

Take Fig. 4 as an example, there are three coordinate systems nested in each other: the child bone coordinate system, the parent bone coordinate system, and the world coordinate system. First, we do not consider the movement of the bones. Let V_c be the position of the vertex V in the local coordinate system of the child bone. When each bone is stationary, to obtain the world coordinates of the child bone, we need to first convert from the child bone coordinates to the parent bone coordinates:

$$V_p = V_c * M_{L \to P} \tag{2}$$

Then convert from parent bone coordinates to world coordinates:

$$V_w = V_p * M_{P \to W} \tag{3}$$

Therefore, the process of direct conversion from child bone coordinates to world coordinates is:

$$V_w = V_c * M_{L \to P} * M_{P \to W} \tag{4}$$

Among them, V_c can be expressed as a row vector represented by $V_c = (x_c, y_c, z_c, 1)$, $M_{C \to P}$ and $M_{P \to W}$ are two matrices of the translation, (d_{xp}, d_{yp}, d_{zp}) and (d_{xc}, d_{yc}, d_{zc}) are the positions of the coordinate system origins of the parent and child bones in the world coordinate system:

$$M_{C \to P} = \begin{bmatrix} 1 & 0 & 0 & 0 \\ 0 & 1 & 0 & 0 \\ 0 & 0 & 1 & 0 \\ d_{xc} - d_{xp} & d_{yc} - d_{yp} & d_{zc} - d_{zp} & 1 \end{bmatrix} \tag{5}$$

$$M_{P \to W} = \begin{bmatrix} 1 & 0 & 0 & 0 \\ 0 & 1 & 0 & 0 \\ 0 & 0 & 1 & 0 \\ d_{xp} & d_{yp} & d_{zp} & 1 \end{bmatrix} \tag{6}$$

(2) Calculation of skeletal motion accumulation transformation

Let's further consider the situation of bone movement. The method of describing the movement of a bone in this article is to decompose its movement into rotation and translation relative to its local coordinate system (usually rotation first, then translation). Its rotation and translation can be simply used as the rotation quadrature *Quarternion* and the translation vector *Translation*. For simplicity, both of them are unified into a single form of transformation matrix.

Assume that the transformation of the child bone relative to its local coordinate system is M_{tc}, and the transformation of the parent bone relative to its local coordinate system is M_{tp}, the transformation from the local child bone to the parent bone coordinates is:

$$V'_p = V_c * M_{tc} * M_{C \to P} \tag{7}$$

Then we transform V'_p to the world coordinate system, and finally get the new position of V_c in the world system after the bone movement:

$$V'_w = V'_p * M_{tp} * M_{P \to W} \tag{8}$$

and we have:

$$V'_w = V_c * \left[M_{tc} * M_{C \to P} * \left(M_{tp} * M_{P \to W} \right) \right] \tag{9}$$

For any bone, we can find its new position in the world coordinate system after the bone moves based on the position of the vertex in the local coordinate system of the bone.

The process is a (transformation in the local coordinate system) * (transformation to the parent coordinate system) * (transformation within the parent coordinate system) * (transformation to the ancestor coordinate system) *… Way until the transformation to the world coordinate system.

(3) Calculation of mesh node coordinates associated with bones

When the world coordinates of each node on the mesh, the accumulated transformation matrix of each bone, and the position of the origin of the local coordinate system of each bone in the world system are available, we need the world coordinates of each mesh node after the bone movement. To apply the bone accumulation transformation to obtain new world coordinates of a node, we need to convert the node's world coordinates into local coordinates in the bone coordinate system associated with it.

In other words, for a node V that is connected to a sub-skeleton, we know the world coordinate V_w of V and the accumulated transformation matrix of the sub-skeleton, and we need to calculate the new world coordinate of V after movement. We consider the situation where the bones are at rest, that is, the initial state of all bones (*Reference Pose*). For each bone, there is an initial matrix associated with it, and this transformation is called the initial inverse transformation of the bone in the reference posture. Its function is to convert the world coordinates of the node associated with the bone in the reference posture into the local coordinates of the bone, which are used to transform V_w to V_c.

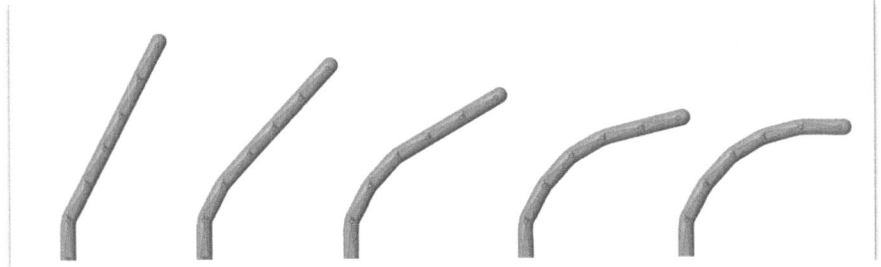

Fig. 5. Parent bone transformation passed to child bone's frame animation

For example, assuming that the initial inverse transformation of the sub-skeleton in the reference posture is $M_{W \to C}$, there is:

$$M_{W \to C} = M_{C \to W}^{-1} = \begin{bmatrix} 1 & 0 & 0 & 0 \\ 0 & 1 & 0 & 0 \\ 0 & 0 & 1 & 0 \\ -d_{xc} & -d_{yc} & -d_{zc} & 1 \end{bmatrix} \quad (10)$$

Then we get the result after translation.

As shown in Fig. 5, after the parent bone is transformed, the child bones and mesh nodes will also transform following its movement.

3.2 Reconstruction and Modelling of Blood Vessels

The modelling of blood vessels is based on CT files. The blood vessel CT slice files provided by doctors are segmented and reconstructed using Mimics software. This process can completely reveal the structure and details of blood vessels. After processing, we export the results to FBX file format.

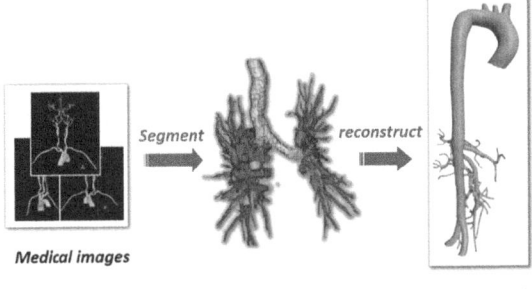

Fig. 6. Vascular reconstruction process

In the reconstruction modelling of CT images in this article (Fig. 6), the main reconstruction uses the Marching cubes algorithm based on surface rendering and the Raycasting algorithm based on volume rendering. The former focuses on outlining the 3D model by constructing the surface mesh of the 3D model, while the latter directly draws each pixel of the 3D data, and then constructs a 3D model containing internal spatial information.

The principle of three-dimensional organ reconstruction using Mimics software is based on the following steps:

(1) Import CT files locally and perform the image pre-processing, including adjusting the brightness and contrast of the image, and applying techniques such as smoothing filtering and edge enhancement to optimize the image quality.
(2) Segmenting the organ, first select a suitable slice as the reference, and draw the outline of the vascular region on the slice. The contours are then automatically traced and extended on other slices via an interpolation algorithm for the organ.
(3) Based on the traced contour information of the ROI, use the segmentation function of the Mimics software to help segment each blood vessel accurately.
(4) Clean and edit the segmentation results. The preliminary segmentation results may contain noise and incomplete or inaccurate parts, and they need to be adjusted.
(5) Connect the boundaries and contours in the segmentation results to obtain a complete three-dimensional model representing the external shape of the organ.

In this system, the human thoracic aorta and descending aorta are mainly reconstructed, and the situation of the guide wire traveling in these two blood vessels is simulated, which is used as the demonstration for the virtual interventional surgery and evaluation.

3.3 Connection of Surgical Training System with Haptic Device

To provide the trainers with a more realistic surgical simulation experience, we use 3D Systems' Geomagic Touch® device to control the guidewire in the virtual interventional surgery training system. Geomagic Touch® device is a tactile device that provides universal movement. It can provide real-feel physical touch and 3D navigation, allowing users to truly perceive the virtual world.

Its precise, powerful, and flexible control experience is particularly suitable for doctors to simulate the surgical operations. The core advantage of this device is its ability to convey very precise three-dimensional scene perception and tactile feedback to users through a handheld tactile pen. As illustrated in Fig. 7, the advancement of the handheld tactile pen is mapped to the advancement of the guidewire in the system. In addition, to simulate the doctor's rotation of the guide wire to change the bending angle of the guide wire head during actual surgery, in this system we also design the circumferential rotation of the guide wire head. That is, during the simulated interventional surgery, the trainer rotates the tactile pen by rotating the guide wire. The end is used to control the circumferential rotation transmitted from the end of the guidewire to the front end, to facilitate the guidewire to be pushed into the correct branch in the complex vascular pathway. This design allows doctors to simulate surgical operations more directly and is consistent with the movement of the guidewire in the real interventional surgery scenarios to the greatest extent.

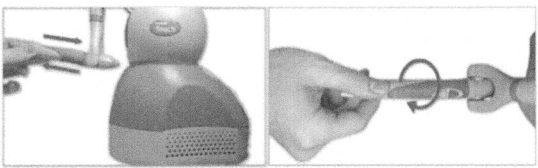

control and rotation control

Fig. 7. Guidewire advance and retreat control and rotation control

In addition, inspired by the work of SHAN [20] and others, in this system we design a set of magnetic coils to create an external magnetic field to control the deflection of the guidewire head. To simulate the impact of magnetic-actuation on the guidewire head, the AD key on the keyboard will control the direction of the magnetic field, forcing the head of the guidewire to shift to the left or right. This allows the trainer to control the guidewire to enter different forks and find the correct path in a complex interventional surgical environment the way (as shown in Fig. 8). Since this type of new device has emerged for interventional surgery based on the magnetic-actuation, it is important to simulate it in our system and also evaluate its performance.

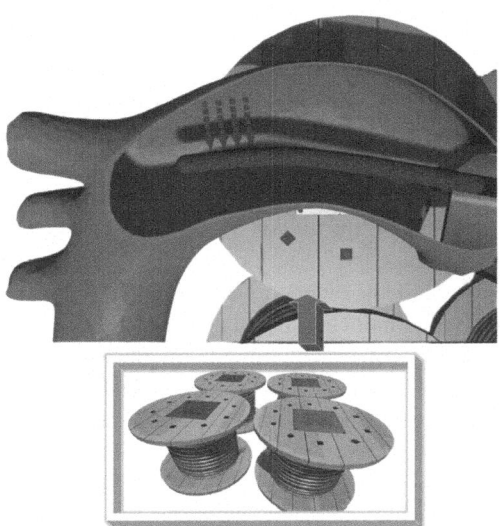

Fig. 8. Magnetic-actuation affects the guide wire head

With the combination of both software and hardware, the trainer's operations can be efficiently transmitted to the guidewire in the virtual surgery system in real-time, helping the guidewire to move and find paths in complex surgical scenes, and to minimize collisions with the blood vessel wall. This creates an easy-to-use, powerful surgical training system for the interventional surgery.

4 Evaluation of the Interventional Surgery Training System

4.1 Evaluation Criteria for Interventional Surgery Simulation

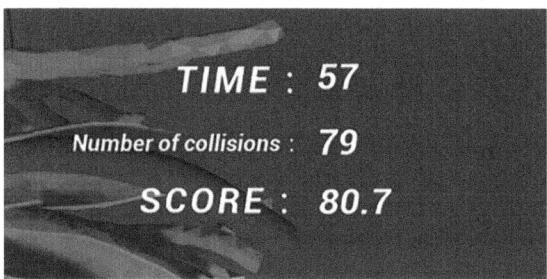

Fig. 9. Training results on the monitor

The scoring criteria for virtual surgery are mainly based on two criteria: the number of collisions between the guide wire and the blood vessel wall and the time it takes for the guide wire to pass through the entire vascular branch.

First, we focus on the number of collisions between the guide wire and the blood vessel wall. In interventional surgery, the goal of the guidewire is to collide with the vessel wall as little as possible. Collisions can cause damage or discomfort to the vessel wall, so reducing the number of collisions can improve the safety and success of the procedure.

Second, we consider the speed at which the guidewire passes through the blood vessel. In interventional surgery, the guidewire needs to pass through the blood vessel quickly and smoothly to reduce the surgery time and risk to the patient. Therefore, the fewer times the guidewire hits the blood vessel wall and the shorter the time it takes to pass through the blood vessel branches, the higher the score.

The final judging criteria are based on the normalized values of time and number of collisions, and a linear combination is used to calculate the final score. Because our vascular environment mainly extends from the human thoracic aorta to the descending aorta, taking into account its internal structure, the average passing time, and the number of collisions during multiple trainings, we set the passing time as t, the maximum time value t_{max}=300s, the number of collisions as n, the maximum number of collisions n_{max}=400, and perform normalization processing to obtain:

$$t' = \frac{t}{t_{max}}, n' = \frac{n}{n_{max}} \qquad (11)$$

During the training process, we believe that the impact of passing time on the training level is greater than the number of collisions. We set the weight of time to 0.8 and the weight of the number of collisions to 0.2. After balancing the weights of these two factors, the calculation formula for the score is:

$$Score = 100 \times \left(1 - 0.8t' - 0.2n'\right) \tag{12}$$

After the simulation is completed, the system displays the score on the screen (Fig. 9), and the corresponding evaluation data is exported through a CSV file, so that trainers can check their proficiency in the simulated surgical process. This can help trainers become better familiar with the interventional simulation process and lay a good foundation for actual interventional surgery.

4.2 Training Simulation of Interventional Surgery

The system contains a blood vessel model with a complex structure and numerous forks. The trainer simulates the surgical process by controlling the guide wire to travel in this model. This system aims to reproduce the various situations that may be encountered in the real surgery, thereby providing the comprehensive interventional surgery training.

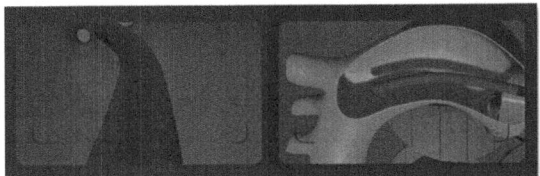

Fig. 10. 3D view (left) and cross-sectional bird's-eye view (right)

In the experiment, we complete ten trainings in environments with and without magnetic fields and record the data and results of each training session. To better observe the operation process, the system supports switching between a three-dimensional perspective and a cross-sectional bird's-eye view (Fig. 10), and the trainer can choose according to their needs.

Through the haptic device, the trainer can intuitively and accurately control the progress of the guidewire. Using the universal movement and force arm advancement of the Touch® device, the trainer can continuously push the guidewire to travel in the blood vessel, and then rotate the touch pen end to control the circumferential rotation of the guidewire, or apply a magnetic field to change the deflection direction of the guidewire head, thereby turn to the right road at the fork and complete the training process.

During the surgical training, we record the changes in the training level of Trainer 1 during ten training sessions under magnetic-actuation conditions. It can be seen in Fig. 11 that as the number of training increases, the trainer's passing time and number of collisions in the two training modes are constantly decreasing, which shows that the trainer can complete the simulation process faster and with fewer collisions, and the training results are also steadily increasing, proving that this system can effectively help trainers practice the virtual interventional surgery.

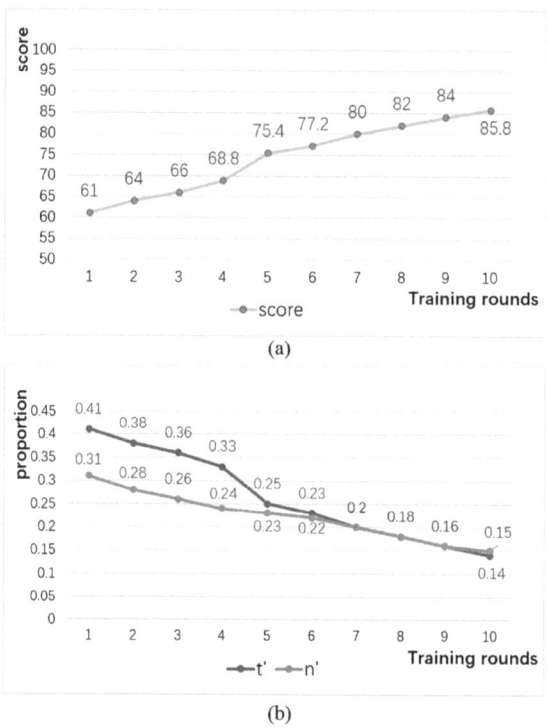

Fig. 11. The score change chart (a) and t', n' proportion change chart (b)

Table 1. Comparison of average training performance between the two modes

Training rounds	Without magnetic-actuation			With magnetic-actuation		
	Time	Number of collisions	Score	Time	Number of collisions	Score
1	158	148	50.5	118	121	62.5
2	152	140	53.0	109	114	65.3
3	143	132	55.3	100	106	68.1
4	128	127	59.6	90	102	70.9
5	120	121	62.0	86	92	72.5
6	111	114	64.7	74	87	76.0
7	97	103	69.0	66	85	78.2
8	85	98	72.5	59	79	80.4
9	79	91	74.4	50	71	84.2
10	69	83	77.4	42	63	85.7

4.3 Comparative Experiment Between the Magnetic-Actuated and Traditional Modes

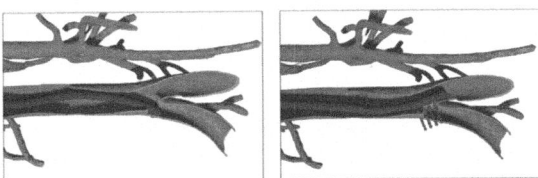

Fig. 12. Effects of magnetic-actuation at forks of vessels

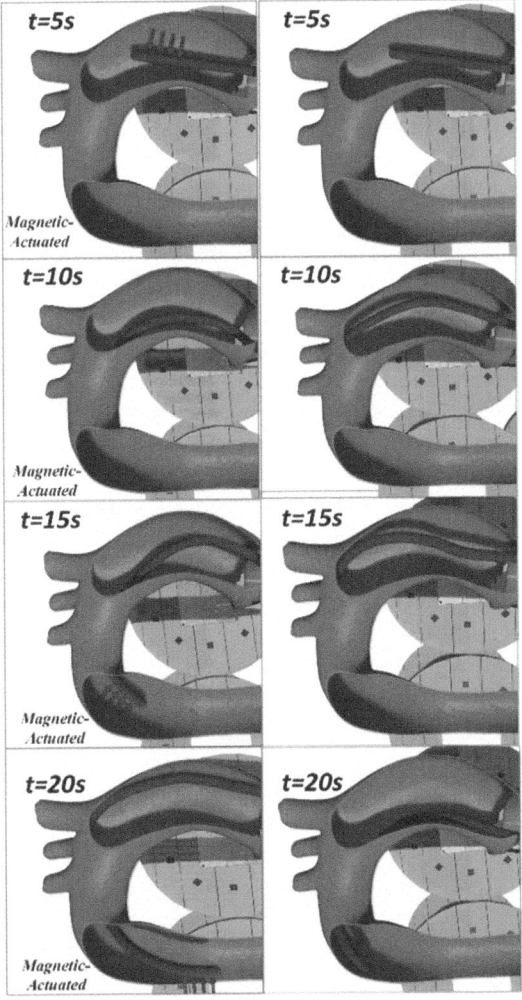

Fig. 13. Comparison of two modes passing through the same blood vessel

In the training of vascular interventional surgery, if there is magnetic-actuation to affect the deflection of the guide wire head, the direction of guide wire advancement can be effectively controlled, and the posture of the guide wire can be adjusted to reduce collision with the blood vessel wall (Fig. 12).

To intuitively compare the experimental performance of the magnetic-actuated and traditional modes, we complete a training process under these two conditions. It can be seen in Fig. 13 that under the magnetic-actuated condition, the distance traveled by the guidewire at the same time is longer and there is less contact with the vessel wall.

To quantitatively explore whether magnetic-actuated control of guidewire head deflection can effectively improve the level of simulated interventional surgery training, we record the average results of ten training sessions (Table 1). By comparing the average scores with and without magnetic-actuation, it can be found that with the magnetic-actuation, trainers can more flexibly control the direction of the guidewire, reduce the number of collisions with blood vessel walls at corners and forks, and complete the training more quickly, thus the training performance is generally higher than that under no magnetic-actuated conditions.

5 Conclusion and Outlook

Traditional interventional surgery needs to be practiced on real patients, but this approach involves certain risks and high costs. Through software simulation, doctors can perform the surgical operations in a virtual environment, improve their skill level and experience, and reduce their reliance on real patients. We implement a virtual training system for vessel interventional surgery, which includes multiple elements such as the guidewire design and movement, interaction with a haptic device, three-dimensional blood vessel reconstruction, and interventional surgery scoring.

Looking to the future, we can further improve the system and add more surgical scenarios and functional modules. For example, different types of vascular lesions and surgical operations can be simulated to provide a more diverse training experience. At the same time, artificial intelligence technology can be introduced to enable the system to automatically learn and optimize surgical plans or add pathfinding functions to improve the safety and success rate of surgery. In addition, we are also considering introducing magnetic drive technology into real interventional surgeries to help doctors more flexibly control guidewires and improve the accuracy and stability of operations. In general, interventional surgery training systems have great potential in field of medical applications, such as education and research.

Acknowledgements. This work was supported by National Natural Science Foundation of China (No. 62372338, No. 62073248) and Key R&D projects in Hubei Province (No. 2023BCB133).

References

1. Cameron, B.M., MS, Robb, R.A.: Virtual-reality-assisted Interventional Procedures. Clinical Orthopaedics Related Res. **442**, 63–73. https://doi.org/10.1097/01.blo.0000194684.40624.a8
2. Qi, D., De, S.: Split and join: an efficient approach for simulating stapled intestinal anastomosis in virtual reality. Comput. Anim. Virtual Worlds **34**(6), e2151 (2023). https://doi.org/10.1002/cav.2151
3. Li, P., et al.: Virtual training system for vascular interventional surgery. In: 2023 9th International Conference on Virtual Reality (ICVR), 413–418 (2023). https://doi.org/10.1109/ICVR57957.2023.10169546
4. Kerckhoffs, R.C.: Patient-specific modeling of cardiac electrophysiology in heart-failure patients. Comput. Math. Appl. **64**(12), 3723–3734 (2012)
5. Venugopal, A., Moccia, S., Foti, S., et al.: Real-time vessel segmentation and reconstruction for virtual fixtures for an active handheld microneurosurgical instrument. Int. J. CARS **17**, 1069–1077 (2022). https://doi.org/10.1007/s11548-022-02584-5
6. Wang, Y., Jiang, C., Schroeder, C., Teran, J.: An adaptive virtual node algorithm with robust mesh cutting. In: Proceedings of the ACM SIGGRAPH/Eurographics Symposium on Computer Animation, pp. 77–85 (2014)
7. Yang, X., Chen, L., Zhang, Y.: A novel material point method for simulating deformable objects. Visual Comput. **34**(9), 1225–1235 (2018)
8. Huang, M., Li, Y., Hu, J., et al.: Deformation prediction of soft tissue via deep learning for interactive simulation of virtual surgery. Int. J. Comput. Assist. Radiol. Surg. **14**(7), 1167–1175 (2019)
9. Qin, C., Bao, P., Liu, Y., et al.: Automatic parameter adjustment of soft tissue physical properties for surgical simulation based on machine learning. IEEE Trans. Biomed. Eng. **66**(4), 1155–1163 (2019)
10. Liu, T., Bargteil, A.W., O'Brien, J.F., Kavan, L.: Fast simulation of mass-spring systems. ACM Trans. Graph. **32**(6), 214:1–214:7 (2013)
11. Barbic, J., James, D.L.: Real-time subspace integration for St. Venant-Kirchhoff deformable models. ACM Trans. Graph. **24**(3), 982–990 (2005)
12. Zhao, Y., Mei, Z., Luo, X., et al. (2022). Remote vascular interventional surgery robotics: a literature review. Quant Imaging Med Surg, 12(4), 2552–2574. https://doi.org/10.21037/qims-21-792
13. Chen, X., Chen, Y., Duan, W., et al.: Design and evaluation of a learning-based vascular interventional surgery robot. Fibers **10**(12), 106 (2022). https://doi.org/10.3390/fib10120106
14. Fu, S., Chen, B., Li, D., et al.: A magnetically controlled guidewire robot system with steering and propulsion capabilities for vascular interventional surgery. Adv. Intell. Syst. **5**, 2300267 (2023). https://doi.org/10.1002/aisy.202300267
15. Suh, Y.S., Kang, S., Baybach, T., et al.: Preoperative virtual simulation and three-dimensional printing techniques for the surgical management of horseshoe kidney with a giant aneurysm of renal isthmus artery. Korean J. Urol. **57**(2), 148–152 (2016)
16. Zhao, X., Wang, G., Liu, Q., et al.: Modeling and Simulation of the Bending Behavior of Vascular Guidewires. Bio-Med. Mater. Eng. **27**(2–3), 235–246 (2016)
17. Courtecuisse, H., Allard, J., Kerfriden, P., et al.: Parallel dense GPU solver for real-time surgical simulation. Graph. Models **73**(5), 89–102 (2011)
18. Dequidt, J., Marchal, D., Duriez, C., et al.: Interactive simulation of embolization coils: modeling and experimental validation. In: MICCAI '08 Proceedings of the 11th International Conference on Medical Image Computing and Computer-Assisted Intervention - Volume Part I, pp. 695–702 (2008)

19. Kuching, M., Legner, A., Lorenz, T., et al.: Tactile perception: a comparison of three surgical simulation scenarios. Int. J. Med. Robot. Comput. Assisted Surg. **15**(1), e1955 (2019)
20. Shan, C., Zhao, J., Zhao, W., et al.: Magnetic-actuated cyber-physical system for interventional surgery. Human-centric Comput. Inf. Sci. **12**(37) (2022)
21. Haiser, A., Aydin, A., Kunduzi, B., et al.: A systematic review of simulation-based training in vascular surgery. J. Surg. Res. **279**, 409–419 (2022). https://doi.org/10.1016/j.jss.2022.05.009
22. Kim, B., Nguyen, P., Loke, Y., et al.: Virtual reality cardiac surgical planning software (CorFix) for designing patient-specific vascular grafts: development and pilot usability study. JMIR Cardio **6**(1), e35488 (2022). https://doi.org/10.2196/35488
23. Karstensen, L., Ritter, J., Hatzl, J., et al.: Learning-based autonomous vascular guidewire navigation without human demonstration in the venous system of a porcine liver. Int. J. CARS **17**, 2033–2040 (2022). https://doi.org/10.1007/s11548-022-02646-8
24. Schneider, M.S., Sandve, K.O., Kurz, K.D., et al.: Metric based virtual simulation training for endovascular thrombectomy improves interventional neuroradiologists' simulator performance. Interventional Neuroradiol. **29**(5), 577–582 (2023). https://doi.org/10.1177/15910199221113902
25. Fischer, N., Marzi, C., Meisenbacher, K., et al.: A sensorized modular training platform to reduce vascular damage in endovascular surgery. Int. J. CARS **18**, 1687–1695 (2023). https://doi.org/10.1007/s11548-023-02935-w
26. Fan, Z., Guo, J., Guo, S., Song, Y.: Study on deformation of vascular model in virtual training system. In: 2022 IEEE International Conference on Mechatronics and Automation (ICMA), pp. 1165–1170 (2022). https://doi.org/10.1109/ICMA54519.2022.9856209
27. Seong, H., Yun, D., Yoon, K.S., Kwak, J.S., Koh, J.C.: Development of pre-procedure virtual simulation for challenging interventional procedures: an experimental study with clinical application. Korean J. Pain **35**(4), 403–412 (2022). https://doi.org/10.3344/kjp.2022.35.4.403
28. Noel, O.F., Lopez, J., Alperovich, M., Prsic, A., Lin, A., Hsia, H.C.: Surgical simulation education in plastic surgery: current state of the art and need for improvement (2023)
29. Yao, Y., Zhang, L., Pan, Z., et al.: Cloud-based surgical planning and navigation system for online collaborative medical education. ACM Trans. Multimed. Comput. Commun. Appl. (in press)
30. Peters, J., Meng, Z., Suter, D.: Mixed reality serious games for surgical training. Virtual Reality **23**(2), 101–112 (2019). 10.1002/c

Self-Adapting NeRF: Non-ideal Video Based NeRF for High-Quality Novel View Synthesis

Tao Huang[1], Dengming Zhu[2(✉)], Min Shi[3], and Zhaoqi Wang[1]

[1] Institute of Computing Technology, Chinese Academy of Sciences, Beijing, China
[2] Institute of Computing Technology, Chinese Academy of Sciences, Taicang-ZK Institute of Information and Technology, Beijing, China
mdzhu@ict.ac.cn
[3] North China Electric Power University, Beijing, China

Abstract. We propose Self-Adapting NeRF for high-quality novel view synthesis based on non-ideal video input. We first using Lie algebra to encode camera poses, which were dynamically controlled by parameters from the precomputed Fourier transform encoding in the NeRF network input, achieving joint optimization of poses and the model. Subsequently, by monitoring intermediate training results, we supplement areas with poor performance, implementing a training strategy based on keyframe supplementation and gradient prioritization. This addresses the challenge of achieving high-quality novel view synthesis with NeRF-series in non-ideal input scenarios. Finally, we employ a strategy of geometry and material information separation, along with a reflection lighting model, to address issues in scenes with specular reflections.

Keywords: Novel View Synthesis · Neural Rendering · Non-ideal input · Illumination model

1 Introduction

NeRF [1] require a certain level of ideal data input to achieve satisfactory results. Compared to sparse view 3D reconstruction, NeRF utilizes end-to-end supervision through the color values of 2D image pixels, primarily focusing on the quality of synthesized 2D viewpoint images rather than the accuracy of obtaining a precise 3D model output. In other words, NeRF may not capture precise 3D model information of the scene, yet it can still generate high-quality 2D images. Conversely, sparse view 3D reconstruction places more emphasis on the correctness of 3D information and typically requires a 3D model as supervision. For input data, it requires at least hundreds of 2D images with known and precise pose information. In this work, we have investigated methods for extracting video keyframes in the context of novel view synthesis. And we optimized the pose information and neural network parameters, establishing a neural rendering

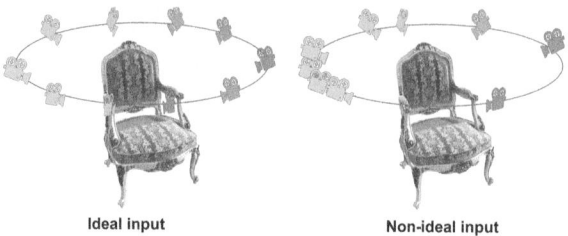

Fig. 1. Ideal and Non-ideal input

model under non-ideal conditions. Utilizing video input, we achieved keyframe selection and pose estimation for video keyframes.

As in Fig. 1, for non-ideal input, when selecting keyframes, we ensure a uniform spatial distribution based on the poses of images in space. Subsequently, we encode the poses into high-dimensional vectors using Lie algebra, serving as the pose network. This allows us to perform joint optimization of camera poses and scene representation networks, transforming the optimization objective from pose estimation to image quality. This approach addresses the issue of local optima in pose optimization. Due to the non-existence of overfitting issues in NeRF's neural rendering, we address rendering deficiencies by monitoring the training process. This involves supplementing keyframes with suboptimal rendering and prioritizing batch pixels based on the absolute gradient values. These strategies aim to enhance rendering performance under non-ideal inputs. NeRF integrates object geometry and material information (color, reflectance, etc.) into a single network, limiting its fitting capability, especially for smooth and specular surfaces in complex scenes. We employ a method that separates geometry and material networks, disentangling object geometry information from surface material information. This enhances the network's ability to encode complex scenes. NeRF is a neural rendering method based on ray-casting, hard to handle complex lighting environments [2,3]. We incorporate a rendering model with added reflection components to address the issue of poor rendering performance under complex lighting conditions.

In summary, our contributions are as follows: As shown in Fig. 2, a framework based on NeRF to achieve high-quality view synthesis under non-ideal inputs. Additionally, a neural rendering strategy for specular lighting based on a reflection model is implemented.

1. Adapting Net for Enhanced Self-Adapting Rendering: Separating scene geometry and material information, and provides accurate pose estimation results, reducing the likelihood of falling into local optima.

2. Training Strategy based on Keyframe Supplementary and Gradient Priority: Targeted optimization is performed for poorly-performing segments during training, enabling adaptive modifications to the training set.

3. **Rendering Model based on Physical Reflection:** The adoption of a reflection-based rendering model allows rendering under complex lighting conditions.

2 Related Work

Neural Rendering. Data-driven methods integrate traditional computer graphics algorithms with machine learning, replace certain steps in traditional rendering methods with learnable components. Besides static scenes, neural scene representations can be employed for various high-level semantic tasks [4,5], leading to functional extensions such as dynamic scenes [6]. Currently, research in neural rendering can be broadly categorized into two main types: those based on Neural Volumes [7–9] and those based on MLP [10–12]. One line of work, exemplified by Sitzmann et al.'s DeepVoxels [8], replaces the physical information in traditional voxel grids with high-dimensional features encoded by neural networks. Neural Sparse Voxel Field (NSVF) [13] learns sparser voxel representations of the scene, and Neural Volumes [9] focuses on learning dynamic representations for scenes, enabling the representation of dynamic scene content. Neural Volumes occupy more memory space, but their decoding computational cost is lower, resulting in faster rendering speeds. The compactness of storing feature information is inversely proportional to the complexity of decoding, leading to a trade-off between storage space and computational efficiency.

Coordinate-MLP, encoding the scene with MLP parameters involves using coordinate-based MLPs to fit the mapping between spatial coordinates and corresponding physical properties. This is based on the assumption of lower semantics in coordinate mapping tasks, eliminating the need for introducing advanced semantic fitting network structures like convolutional neural networks. Many works still drew inspiration from traditional methods, using neural networks to simplify the reconstruction process, such as the combination of neural networks and Signed Distance Functions (SDFs) [14]. These methods, although exhibiting a degree of generalization [15], tended to compromise the quality of synthesized images and were often limited to the representation of specific object classes. These approaches required a substantial number of labeled 3D models for supervision during the network training process, raising the algorithmic barrier.

NeRF Improvements. NeRF has achieved state-of-the-art results in terms of image synthesis quality. However, it has notable limitations. Improved works based on NeRF [16–18] have addressed these issues to varying extents. Currently, these methods commonly require a sufficient number of viewpoint images and corresponding pose information, which often needs to be estimated through additional steps (SFM). This estimation process is prone to subtle errors, leading to a decrease in the quality of synthesized images.

Expanding the input format of neural radiance fields to videos [19–22] addresses the issue of the number of viewpoint images. For instance, NeRFlow [23] focuses on rendering dynamic scenes, but its treatment of videos is relatively coarse. Typically, it directly extracts a sufficient number of viewpoint images from fixed frames, using established pose estimation algorithms like colmap [24] to obtain relatively accurate pose estimates. However, due to non- uniform camera motion in videos, methods based on fixed frame extraction may result in viewpoint repetitions, failing to ensure coverage of a broader range of perspectives. Additionally, mature pose estimation algorithms like colmap can only provide relatively accurate pose estimates, which may not meet the requirements of neural radiance fields. Video-formatted input for neural radiance fields is commonly used for rendering dynamic scenes, with current mainstream methods incorporating temporal information into neural radiance fields to achieve dynamic object rendering [6,25].

In works combining camera poses with NeRF [26–29], such as NeRF- [29], pose estimation is integrated into NeRF by introducing an optimization module for camera poses. These methods optimize both the NeRF network and pose information simultaneously. Deep learning-based depth estimation modules can also be incorporated to introduce depth information into the input data [30]. This guides NeRF's rendering and sampling strategies, improving rendering quality. NeRF-, for instance, directly uses the orthogonal vectors of the original poses as training parameters. it may not perform optimally on larger datasets with 360° views.

3 Self-adapting

3.1 Pose Estimation Based on Joint Optimization

We employ a preliminary screening of video frames based on the Structural Similarity Index (SSIM) of image structures. This helps eliminate redundant frames with minimal camera motion or even stationary frames. Then we employ colmap to obtain the rough poses of the frames after the initial screening.

Subsequently, based on the calculated rotation angle θ and displacement threshold t_0 of the camera's external parameters, we further filter the images that will be ultimately fed into the network, ensuring that selected keyframes are evenly distributed in spatial perspectives.

We address the issue of local optima by jointly optimizing the camera pose information and the scene representation network, transforming the optimization objective of pose estimation into image quality. When performing joint optimization of the pose $[R, t]$ and the neural radiance field, we first convert it into the Lie algebra encoding form.

$$\phi = \arccos\left(\frac{trace(R)-1}{2}\right),$$
$$u = \ln\left[\frac{trace(R-R^T)}{2\sin\phi}\right] \tag{1}$$

From optimization perspective, a rotation matrix, as a Lie group element, needs to maintain the constraint of being an orthogonal matrix, which introduces certain limitations in the constrained optimization process. Conversely, the three-dimensional vector in its corresponding Lie algebra releases the inherent

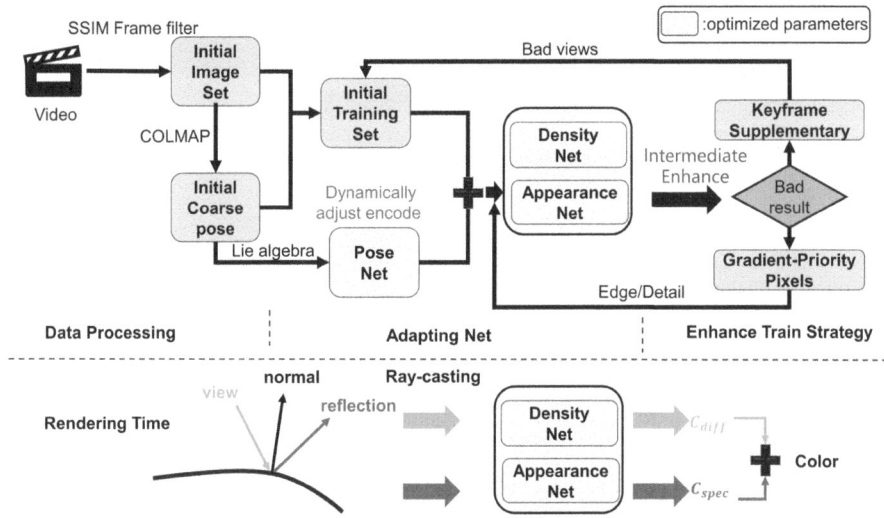

Fig. 2. Self-Adapting NeRF pipeline overview. We design a "Self-Adapting NeRF" rendering framework for enabling high-quality new view synthesis in non-ideal situations. First, filter out trainable images based on SSIM, and use colmap to obtain the initial rough pose as the initial training set. For network structure, we use Lie algebra to encode poses and dynamic encoding adjustments of coordinate inputs to implement pose net training; meanwhile, we decouple geometry and material information and use density net and appearance net to characterize scene features respectively. During training, we use regular intermediate supervision to supplement training set based on bad views and gradients with poor results. In the rendering part, based on the reflection lighting model, we use ray-casting to render the diffuse reflection color C_{diff} and the specular reflection component C_{spec} respectively to improve the effect of the network in specular reflection scenes.

constraints, making its solution more convenient. Similarly, in dealing with pose representation, operations such as transformation combination, inverse transformation, integration, differentiation, uncertainty, and more, have been simplified and enhanced in terms of properties through mathematical tools like Lie groups and Lie algebras. Therefore, we adopted Lie algebra as a more sophisticated encoding scheme.

As the pose estimation process is prone to getting stuck in local optima, we implemented a strategy for dynamically adjusting the complexity of the network encoding. This strategy is based on the fact that low-frequency signals are less likely to fall into local optima during the pose alignment process. It ensures that, during the early stages of network training, the weighting of the encoding is higher in the low-frequency components, reducing the probability of the pose alignment getting trapped in local optima.

We achieve this by dynamically adjusting the encoding weights of the neural radiance field, ensuring that, during the early stages of network training, the

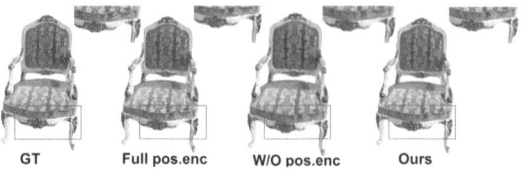

Fig. 3. Dynamically Pose Encoding strategy

encoding weights are higher in the low-frequency components. This helps reduce the probability of the pose alignment getting trapped in local optima, as shown in Fig. 3, we use full weights and zero weights for high-frequency compare with our strategy.

$$w_k(\alpha) = \begin{cases} 0 & if \alpha < k \\ \frac{1-\cos((\alpha-k)\pi)}{2} & if 0 \leq \alpha - k < 1 \\ 1 & if \alpha - k > 1 \end{cases} \quad (2)$$

where $\alpha \in [0, maxSteps]$ is a measure of the training progress. As the training progresses, the weights of the high-frequency components gradually increase until reaching 1.

3.2 Geometry and Texture Net

The original NeRF network structure integrates object geometry and texture information (color, reflectance etc.) into a single set of network parameters. Due to the simplicity of the native network structure, it's fitting capability is limited, making it hard to model more complex objects and scenes, especially in rendering scenarios involving smooth and specular surfaces. In Fig. 4, we separate geometric and texture networks, decoupling object geometry information from surface texture information, thereby enhancing the capability to encode complex scenes.

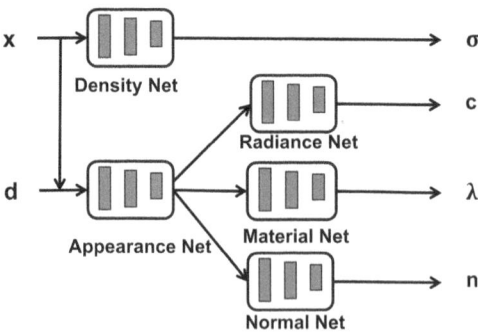

Fig. 4. Separate network structure

The Density Net serves as the network for encoding geometric information, specifically designed to learn the geometry information present in the original network, such as volume density σ. Appearance Net utilizes networks to learn interpretable surface texture parameters, primarily consisting of three components: ① color information C of the object; ② material properties (texture roughness, specular reflectance); ③ surface normals n of the object. These parameters are used to enhance rendering effects for complex object textures and lighting scenarios. Due to the lack of explicit normal supervision in the native training process, but considering NeRF's relatively accurate fitting of geometric density information, we approximated the normals (GT) by computing the gradient of density values. This approximation was employed as supervisory information for the normal part.

$$\widehat{n}(x) = -\frac{\nabla \tau(x)}{\|\nabla \tau(x)\|} \quad (3)$$

Relying solely on the aforementioned strategy as normal supervisory information still resulted in insufficient precision. The estimated normals often exhibited poor continuity and occasional abrupt changes. This issue arises because the volume rendering method used for density estimation can be deceptive; the learned scene density often encompasses both the surface and interior of the scene. Furthermore, the density distribution may not necessarily match the actual distribution, yet correct colors can still be obtained through the integration equation of ray-marching. We introduced a regularization penalty strategy for normal fitting.

$$loss_n = w * \max(0, n \cdot d) \quad (4)$$

where the $loss_n$ penalizes the part where the normals align with the viewing direction. Specifically, on the object surface, when the normal vector n is opposite to the viewing direction d ($¿$ 90°), it conforms to common observational experience and realistic density distribution. In such cases, the penalty term is set to 0. The parameter W serves as the penalty coefficient, and in this context, the volume density is used. This ensures that in regions where the object is closer to the surface and the volume is denser, the penalty for normal estimation has a more significant impact, thereby yielding more accurate normal estimation results in those areas.

4 Optimizing Strategy

NeRF has a relatively fixed training method: ① The training set is fixed, and once the set of perspective images for training is determined, there will be no addition or reduction of images during the training process; ② Pixel selection strategy is fixed, generally involving random selection or sequential traversal of image pixels, without distinguishing between foreground and background or handling high-frequency edge details in the images.

A fixed training strategy can achieve decent rendering results under ideal inputs. However, for non-ideal input scenarios, especially in the context of video information, the fixed strategy may not fully utilize the input information, resulting in suboptimal performance. Therefore, we have adopted a set of training strategies that dynamically adjust the keyframe training set during the training process and prioritize image pixels based on gradients.

4.1 Keyframe Supplementary Strategy

Due to variations in the geometric shapes, colors, and materials of the scene from different viewpoints, the difficulty of fitting the network also varies across different view ranges. The theoretically optimal training set needs to distinguish the differences in various view ranges, composing a training dataset with an adaptive distribution of images based on the rendering effects from different perspectives.

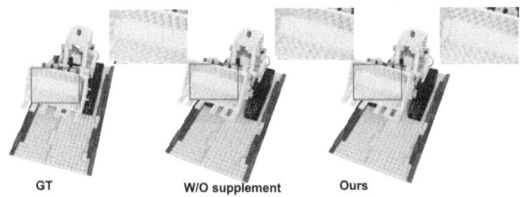

Fig. 5. Keyframe supplement contrast

After a certain number of training steps, rendering tests on the test set reveal suboptimal performance (PSNRs) within a specific range of viewpoints. To address this, we identify the corresponding range in the original video frames, select new keyframes, and incorporate them into the training set for further training, as shown in Fig. 5.

In Fig. 6, based on the initial screening strategy, we obtain a source set I. We periodically evaluate the rendering performance as intermediate supervision. And based on the result, we identify portions where there is a significant drop in rendering quality (or set a specific threshold). We detect viewpoints V_{bad} with subpar results. Subsequently, we supplement the training set by selecting additional frames from the source set I within the range of V_{bad}.

4.2 Gradient-Priority Training Strategy

Due to the limitation of GPU memory, the batch size for training is restricted (typically around 4096). This means that in each training batch, only a randomly selected batch size of pixels is used for fitting. The extensive background consumes a significant portion of the training cycles. The strategy of randomly selecting pixels for training results in insufficient training cycles allocated to the detailed parts of the image, ultimately leading to poor rendering details. In a

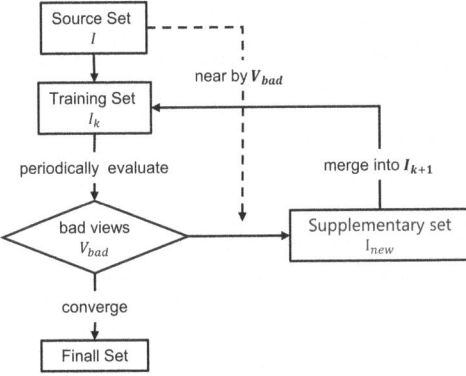

Fig. 6. Training set change process

single batch, parts of the tensor with larger absolute gradient values often indicate regions where the network's fitting capability is weaker. In the context of NVS tasks, these regions are usually associated with the areas with complex geometric information, such as object edges. Therefore, during training, these parts with larger absolute gradient values can be included in the batch to improve the network's performance in fitting such challenging regions.

$$P_{k+1} = P_{random} + W_{edge} * P_{edge} + W_{new} * P_{new} \tag{5}$$

Specifically, in the k-th batch training, a pixel list P_k is chosen. Based on the results of the network's forward pass, the gradient $_k$ for each pixel is obtained. Sorting the pixels based on the absolute gradient values, a subset of pixels P_{edge} with significantly larger gradients compared to others is selected. This subset is then treated as a new pixel list and added to the training in the next batch. Additionally, as mentioned earlier, there is periodic training set supplementation for poorly rendered viewpoints during the training process. This involves another set of randomly selected pixels P_{new} from the newly supplemented dataset, which is also added to the training in the next batch.

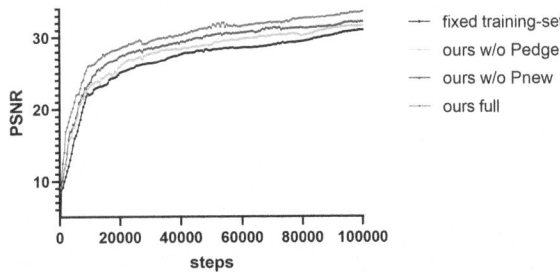

Fig. 7. Gradient-Priority statistics comparison

In each batch, pixels is not exclusively from the current training set I_k; instead, it is distributed according to a certain ratio. A portion of the pixels, obtained through the original random selection scheme, forms the pixel list P_{random}. Simultaneously, during the training process, a subset with larger gradient descent values (likely representing image edges or detailed regions) P_{edge} is maintained, and more significant weights are assigned to it. Additionally, for newly introduced training images, a subset of pixels P_{new} is randomly chosen, and again, larger weights are assigned for training. Through this strategy, it helps address issues of suboptimal performance in certain viewpoints or image edge and detail regions. In Fig. 7, we use different batch pixels to verify our analysis.

5 Reflection-Enhanced Rendering Model

Due to the native NeRF method considering only a single ray integral when rendering a pixel, it fails to account for the fact that the color of an object in a real scene is the result of the blending of multiple rays. In traditional computer graphics, various models exist for approximating physical lighting. For instance, the Phong lighting model separates the observed color into diffuse and specular reflection components as perceived by the human eye. Based on the principle of reversible light paths and leveraging more accurate normal estimates obtained in the previous section, we calculate the reflection direction of the viewing angle on the object surface. We then use this reflection direction to render the color component of the reflected light, which is added to the final rendering result.

$$C = C_{diff} + C_{Spec} \quad (6)$$

where C_{diff} is diffuse reflection from the original viewing direction and C_{spec} is specular reflection highlight (Fig. 8).

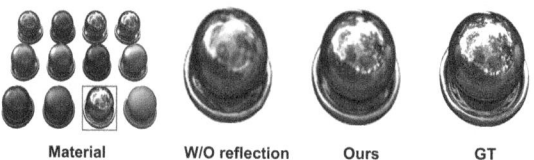

Fig. 8. Lighting model comparison

6 Experiment

We evaluate our model in some challenging scenes. We first modified commonly used data sets according to the characteristics of the research problem, and then designed some ablation studies to verify the effectiveness of our model improvements and strategies, and compare them with the current state-of-the-art methods.

6.1 Implement Details

We still adopted the most commonly used Synthetic 360° Blender dataset in the NeRF series, primarily because it belongs to the 360° scene type, facilitating comparisons of 3D consistency and pose alignment results. On the other hand, the pose information in the Blender dataset is nearly perfectly accurate, while other datasets use colmap's pose estimation results as pose information. In this work, we consider that colmap's estimated pose information cannot serve as the ground truth for poses, thus it cannot fully demonstrate the advantages of our work in terms of pose optimization. Additionally, to further highlight the advantages of our method, we intentionally introduced random perturbations to the accurate poses in Blender, using them as input with inaccurate pose information for comparison with the ground truth.

6.2 Ablation Model Components and Strategies

We conducted ablation experiments separately for the pose estimation, training strategy, and rendering strategy of the Self-Adapting NeRF rendering framework.

Table 1. Comparison of Pose Estimation Strategy

Method	Rotation	Translation	PSNR	SSIM	LPIPS
colmap	-	-	26.80	0.919	0.091
W/O pos.enc	0.616	1.303	22.12	0.821	0.205
Full pos.enc	0.202	0.768	26.78	0.917	0.087
Ours	0.193	0.756	27.50	0.930	0.065

In the comparison section of the effects of pose joint optimization, as shown in Table 1, Rotation and Translation illustrate the comparison between the joint optimization of pose and the accurate pose. It can be observed that when using NeRF with high-frequency encoding on colmap's relatively accurate poses, the rendering performance deteriorates as the pose step size increases. On the other hand, the rendering effect based on dynamic encoding outperforms the original rough pose, demonstrating the effectiveness of our pose joint optimization and dynamic encoding.

In the comparison section of the effects of keyframe supplementation and gradient-priority training strategy, as shown in Table 2, compared to the NeRF training strategy with a fixed training set, our training strategy shows improvement in various indicators of rendering quality. Additionally, our training strategy can also serve as an acceleration strategy for network convergence to some extent. This is because in the early stages of training, with fewer iterations, the network has not fully converged, and there are significant differences in gradient values calculated for different parts of the image. Therefore, prioritizing the

Table 2. Comparison of Training Strategies

Method	PSNR30+(h)	Converge(h)	PSNR	SSIM	LPIPS
Fixed set	1.0-1.5	3	33.40	0.871	0.024
W/O P_{edge}	1.0-1.2	4-5	34.48	0.821	0.015
W/O P_{new}	0.8-1.0	5-6	34.89	0.964	0.017
Ours	0.5-0.6	7-8	35.21	0.981	0.009

parts with more noticeable improvement results in an earlier arrival of PSNR values reaching 30. As the number of network training iterations increases and the network converges, the fitting effects for various parts become ideal, and gradient values reach lower levels. Therefore, in the later stages of training with further iterations, the improvement in the effectiveness of our training strategy becomes less significant.

Table 3. Comparison of Rendering Strategies

Method	PSNR ↑	SSIM↑	LPIPS↓
W/O Reflection	29.47	0.944	0.084
W/O transmittance	32.65	0.964	0.057
Ours	34.23	0.973	0.045

In the comparison section of the reflection lighting model, as shown in Table 3, it can be observed that reducing the reflection component has a greater impact on the overall rendering effect, while canceling the visibility part has a smaller impact on the final result. A more complex lighting model can achieve specular reflection effects, making full use of obtained material information (normals).

6.3 Comparisons with Related Methods

We compare Self-Adapting NeRF with the state-of-the-art neural rendering and pose estimation methods, NeRF– [29] and Self-Calibrating [31], as shown in Table 4. Additionally, we compare it with the rendering results under rough poses obtained from colmap. Beyond rendering performance, we also showcase the accuracy of pose estimation based on camera extrinsics RT. It can be observed that our pose optimization method (using noisy poses as a baseline) outperforms the previous two methods in most metrics, demonstrating the superiority of our approach (Fig. 9).

We also conducted tests on some real-world scenes, as shown in Fig. 10. It can be observed that our method is equally effective in addressing the issue of image blurriness in partial viewpoints of real scenes (Table 4).

Table 4. Comparison of Pose Optimization-Related Methods

Method	Rotation	Translation	PSNR	SSIM	LPIPS
colmap	-	-	26.80	0.919	0.091
NeRF- -	0.257	0.805	27.37	0.921	0.079
Self-Calibrating	0.224	0.787	27.42	0.916	0.069
Ours	0.193	0.756	27.50	0.930	0.065

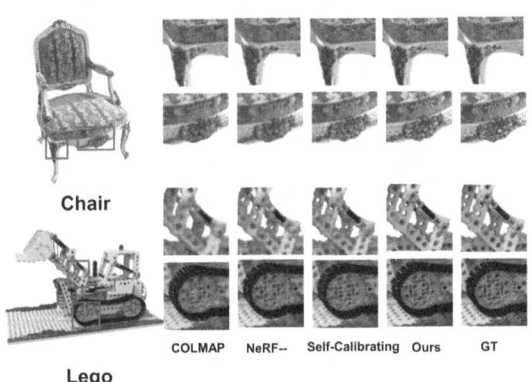

Fig. 9. Comparison of Pose Optimization-Related Methods

Table 5. Validation of Method Universality

Method	PSNR ↑	SSIM ↑	LPIPS ↓
NeRF	26.80	0.919	0.091
Ours+NeRF	27.50	0.930	0.065
Plenoxels	32.49	0.927	0.073
Ours+Plenoxel	33.14	0.934	0.058
Instant-NGP	31.27	0.922	0.081
Ours+NGP	31.86	0.930	0.062
Plenoctree	31.87	0.925	0.077
Ours+octree	32.40	0.933	0.059

In the end, we integrate the Self-Adapting NeRF rendering framework as a general module into the current state-of-the-art methods for optimizing NeRF rendering effects, including Plenoxels [32], Plenoctree [2], and Instant-NGP [7], using rough pose inputs obtained from colmap as a baseline. As shown in Table 5, our method not only works for the original NeRF but also for other improved NeRF methods, as long as they still adopt the native NeRF rendering framework. This demonstrates the versatility of our approach.

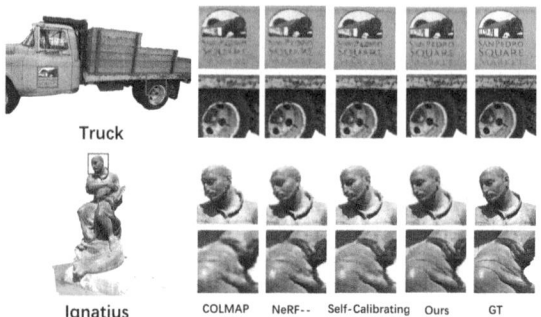

Fig. 10. Results on real-world scene

7 Limitations

Although Self-Adapting NeRF has improved to some extent the handling of non-ideal scene datasets and information extraction compared to previous methods, it increased computational complexity for network training and rendering, leading to a decrease in both scene fitting and view synthesis speeds. And while the lighting fitting based on the reflection model is superior to the native method, it cannot handle more complex real-world lighting scenarios.

8 Conclusion

Our contributions include demonstrating the limitations of prior NeRF-based methods in accurately handling view synthesis in non-ideal input scenarios, especially those with highlights and reflections. Our model introduces a novel framework for handling keyframes and poses under non-ideal inputs, along with improvements to the training strategy. These contributions result in enhancement of accuracy in view synthesis under non-ideal inputs for Self-Adapting NeRF in synthetic scenes. Additionally, we employ a texture-separation-based approach for more accurate normal estimation and a reflection-based lighting model, addressing challenges related to specular reflections. We believe that this work represents progress in lowering the barriers to the practical application of NeRF technology.

Acknowledgements. We extend our appreciation to the Institute of Computing Technology, Chinese Academy of Sciences, and the Virtual Reality Laboratory for their indispensable support. The collaborative efforts of colleagues have significantly contributed to this work. We also acknowledge the participants for their cooperation. Gratitude is expressed to family and friends for their unwavering support throughout this endeavor.

References

1. Mildenhall, B., Srinivasan, P.P., Tancik, M., Barron, J.T., Ramamoorthi, R., Ng, R.: Nerf: representing scenes as neural radiance fields for view synthesis. Commun. ACM **65**(1), 99–106 (2021)
2. Yu, A., Li, R., Tancik, M., Li, H., Ng, R., Kanazawa, A.: Plenoctrees for real-time rendering of neural radiance fields. In: Proceedings of the IEEE/CVF International Conference on Computer Vision, pp. 5752–5761 (2021)
3. Aliev, K.-A., Sevastopolsky, A., Kolos, M., Ulyanov, D., Lempitsky, V.: Neural Point-Based Graphics. In: Vedaldi, A., Bischof, H., Brox, T., Frahm, J.-M. (eds.) ECCV 2020. LNCS, vol. 12367, pp. 696–712. Springer, Cham (2020)
4. Sitzmann, V., Rezchikov, S., Freeman, B., Tenenbaum, J., Durand, F.: Light field networks: neural scene representations with single-evaluation rendering. Adv. Neural. Inf. Process. Syst. **34**, 19313–19325 (2021)
5. Reiser, C., Peng, S., Liao, Y., Geiger, A.: Kilonerf: speeding up neural radiance fields with thousands of tiny mlps. In: Proceedings of the IEEE/CVF International Conference on Computer Vision, pp. 14335–14345 (2021)
6. Li, T., et al.: Neural 3d video synthesis from multi-view video. In: Proceedings of the IEEE/CVF Conference on Computer Vision and Pattern Recognition, pp. 5521–5531 (2022)
7. Müller, T., Evans, A., Schied, C., Keller, A.: Instant neural graphics primitives with a multiresolution hash encoding. ACM Trans. Graph. (TOG) **41**(4), 1–15 (2022)
8. Sitzmann, V., Thies, J., Heide, F., Nießner, M., Wetzstein, G., Zollhofer, M.: Deepvoxels: learning persistent 3d feature embeddings. In: Proceedings of the IEEE/CVF Conference on Computer Vision and Pattern Recognition, pp. 2437–2446 (2019)
9. Lombardi, S., Simon, T., Saragih, J., Schwartz, G., Lehrmann, A., Sheikh, Y.: Neural volumes: learning dynamic renderable volumes from images. arXiv preprint arXiv:1906.07751 (2019)
10. Tewari, A., et al.: Advances in neural rendering. In: Computer Graphics Forum, vol. 41, pp. 703–735. Wiley Online Library (2022)
11. Barron, J.T., Mildenhall, B., Tancik, M., Hedman, P., Martin-Brualla, R., Srinivasan, P.P.: Mip-nerf: a multiscale representation for anti-aliasing neural radiance fields. In: Proceedings of the IEEE/CVF International Conference on Computer Vision, pp. 5855–5864 (2021)
12. Garbin, S.J., Kowalski, M., Johnson, M., Shotton, J., Valentin, J.: Fastnerf: high-fidelity neural rendering at 200fps. In: Proceedings of the IEEE/CVF International Conference on Computer Vision, pp. 14346–14355 (2021)
13. Liu, L., Gu, J., Lin, K.Z., Chua, T.-S., Theobalt, C.: Neural sparse voxel fields. Adv. Neural. Inf. Process. Syst. **33**, 15651–15663 (2020)
14. Park, J.J., Florence, P., Straub, J., Newcombe, R., Lovegrove, S.: Deepsdf: learning continuous signed distance functions for shape representation. In: Proceedings of the IEEE/CVF Conference on Computer Vision and Pattern Recognition, pp. 165–174 (2019)
15. Izadi, S., et al.: Kinectfusion: real-time 3d reconstruction and interaction using a moving depth camera. In: Proceedings of the 24th Annual ACM Symposium on User Interface Software and Technology, pp. 559–568 (2011)
16. Zhang, K., Riegler, G., Snavely, N., Koltun, V.: Nerf++: analyzing and improving neural radiance fields. arXiv preprint arXiv:2010.07492 (2020)

17. Sun, C., Sun, M., Chen, H.-T.: Direct voxel grid optimization: super-fast convergence for radiance fields reconstruction. In: Proceedings of the IEEE/CVF Conference on Computer Vision and Pattern Recognition, pp. 5459–5469 (2022)
18. Hedman, P., Srinivasan, P.P., Mildenhall, B., Barron, J.T., Debevec, P.: Baking neural radiance fields for real-time view synthesis. In: Proceedings of the IEEE/CVF International Conference on Computer Vision, pp. 5875–5884 (2021)
19. Lombardi, S., Simon, T., Schwartz, G., Zollhoefer, M., Sheikh, Y., Saragih, J.: Mixture of volumetric primitives for efficient neural rendering. ACM Trans. Graph. (ToG) **40**(4), 1–13 (2021)
20. Xian, W., Huang, J.-B., Kopf, J., Kim, C.: Space-time neural irradiance fields for free-viewpoint video. In: Proceedings of the IEEE/CVF Conference on Computer Vision and Pattern Recognition, pp. 9421–9431 (2021)
21. Du, Y., Zhang, Y., Yu, H.-X., Tenenbaum, J.B., Wu, J.: Neural radiance flow for 4d view synthesis and video processing. In: 2021 IEEE/CVF International Conference on Computer Vision (ICCV), pp. 14304–14314. IEEE Computer Society (2021)
22. Nießner, M., Zollhöfer, M., Izadi, S., Stamminger, M.: Real-time 3d reconstruction at scale using voxel hashing. ACM Trans. Graph. (ToG) **32**(6), 1–11 (2013)
23. Li, Z., Niklaus, S., Snavely, N., Wang, O.: Neural scene flow fields for space-time view synthesis of dynamic scenes. In: Proceedings of the IEEE/CVF Conference on Computer Vision and Pattern Recognition, pp. 6498–6508 (2021)
24. Fisher, A., Cannizzaro, R., Cochrane, M., Nagahawatte, C., Palmer, J.L.: Colmap: a memory-efficient occupancy grid mapping framework. Robot. Autonomous Syst. **142**, 103755 (2021)
25. Saito, S., Huang, Z., Natsume, R., Morishima, S., Kanazawa, A., Li, H.: Pifu: pixel-aligned implicit function for high-resolution clothed human digitization. In: Proceedings of the IEEE/CVF International Conference on Computer Vision, pp. 2304–2314 (2019)
26. Meng, Q., et al.: Gnerf: gan-based neural radiance field without posed camera. In: Proceedings of the IEEE/CVF International Conference on Computer Vision, pp. 6351–6361 (2021)
27. Schwarz, K., Liao, Y., Niemeyer, M., Geiger, A.: Graf: Generative radiance fields for 3d-aware image synthesis. Adv. Neural. Inf. Process. Syst. **33**, 20154–20166 (2020)
28. Yen-Chen, L., Florence, P., Barron, J.T., Rodriguez, A., Isola, P., Lin, T.-Y.: inerf: inverting neural radiance fields for pose estimation. In: 2021 IEEE/RSJ International Conference on Intelligent Robots and Systems (IROS), pp. 1323–1330. IEEE (2021)
29. Wang, Z., Wu, S., Xie, W., Chen, M., Prisacariu, V.A.: Nerf–: Neural radiance fields without known camera parameters. arXiv preprint arXiv:2102.07064 (2021)
30. Deng, K., Liu, A., Zhu, J.-Y., Ramanan, D.: Depth-supervised nerf: Fewer views and faster training for free. In: Proceedings of the IEEE/CVF Conference on Computer Vision and Pattern Recognition, pp. 12882–12891 (2022)
31. Jeong, Y., Ahn, S., Choy, C., Anandkumar, A., Cho, M., Park, J.: Self-calibrating neural radiance fields. In: Proceedings of the IEEE/CVF International Conference on Computer Vision, pp. 5846–5854 (2021)
32. Fridovich-Keil, S., Yu, A., Tancik, M., Chen, Q., Recht, B., Kanazawa, A.: Plenoxels: radiance fields without neural networks. In: Proceedings of the IEEE/CVF Conference on Computer Vision and Pattern Recognition, pp. 5501–5510 (2022)

AnisoVector: Separable Anisotropic Set Abstraction and Group Vector Attention for Efficient Point Cloud Analysis

Zhicheng Wen and Lei Wang(✉)

East China University of Technology, Fuzhou, China
wlei598@163.com

Abstract. The rapid evolution of laser radar technology has enabled the widespread acquisition of three-dimensional point cloud data, posing challenges in real-time analysis and efficient information extraction. The focus of this research is to solve a key problem in 3D point cloud data processing: to achieve rapid and efficient analysis of point cloud classification and semantic segmentation tasks. We propose the AnisoVector network, which divides local point cloud processing into two distinct stages: point position processing and point feature processing, thereby significantly enhancing the model's inference speed. By introducing anisotropic functions, our approach enables Multilayer Perceptrons (MLPs) to differentially process each local point cloud, thus augmenting the model's capacity for fine-grained point cloud analysis (Separable Anisotropic - SAM). Furthermore, vectors with size and directional properties enhance the flexibility of point cloud representation, enabling the network to handle diverse point cloud shapes more effectively and enhance the ability to extract local point cloud features (Point Vector - PVM). By employing a group vector attention mechanism, efficient capture of feature information within local point clouds has been achieved, thereby enhancing the efficiency and generalization performance of the model (Group-Former - GFM). Experimental results across ModelNet40, ShapeNetPart, and S3DIS datasets demonstrate superior performance in tasks like classification and segmentation.

Keywords: point cloud · classification · semantic segmentation · rapid and efficient extraction

1 Introduction

The understanding of point clouds serves as the foundation for analyzing three-dimensional scenes [1–3], such as autonomous driving and augmented reality. In comparison to 2D images, 3D point cloud data encapsulates richer geometric information about objects. However, due to the irregular and unordered nature of 3D point clouds, the direct processing of such data by deep learning networks is constrained.

In recent years, as the demand for analyzing point cloud data continues to grow, many deep learning methods based on 3D point clouds have been evolving. These methods can broadly be categorized into three classes: projection-based methods [4, 5], voxel-based methods [6–8], and point-based methods [9–23, 25]. Projection-based methods involve transforming point clouds into a set of images, processing them using two-dimensional convolutions, and then converting the results back into point clouds. Voxel-based methods convert point clouds into a regularized voxel representation, employ sparse convolutions for processing, and subsequently transform the results into point clouds. However, both of these approaches may lead to the loss of geometric details during the transformation process. Point-based methods can directly operate on 3D point clouds without the need for intermediate data representations. Some methods dedicated to point cloud analysis have achieved satisfactory performance, such as RandLA-Net [16] and PointTransformer [20]. However, the majority of existing point cloud analysis methods [16, 18, 20, 22] have yet to address a critical issue: how to achieve real-time analysis of point clouds while ensuring accuracy? There is a need to devise a method that can effectively learn meaningful features from point clouds and rapidly perform tasks such as point cloud classification and semantic segmentation under real-time constraints.

Taking inspiration from several point cloud methods [18–20, 22] that have demonstrated promising performance in point cloud analysis, this study investigates how to efficiently extract meaningful feature information from point clouds for rapid analysis. The above-mentioned issues are decomposed into three specific yet crucial questions to provide clearer guidance for the research direction of this paper:

1) How can the most representative and discriminative feature information be rapidly extracted within local regions of point clouds?
2) How can effective point cloud representation methods be designed to comprehensively capture the structural information of 3D point clouds and achieve better performance in point cloud tasks?
3) How can the model be empowered to comprehensively understand the local point cloud features by enlarging the receptive field, thereby enhancing its ability to analyze and recognize point clouds?

Addressing these three issues, we propose the AnisoVector network, which primarily consists of three modules: Separable Anisotropic (SAM), Point Vector (PVM), and GroupFormer (GFM). Initially, SAM employs Multilayer Perceptrons (MLPs) to process global three-dimensional points, subsequently utilizing a grouping algorithm to acquire local point clouds, and ultimately leveraging anisotropic functions to differentially consider each local point cloud, thereby rapidly and efficiently learning complex feature information within the locality. Subsequently, PVM integrates vectors with size and directional properties with the coordinate attributes of three-dimensional points to enhance the flexibility of point cloud representation. Finally, GFM facilitates information exchange among local point cloud features through grouped vector attention, enabling the learning of more intricate point cloud features. We propose a three-dimensional point cloud analysis network based on the U-Net architecture, termed AnisoVector. In summary, this paper contributes as follows:

- We employ Separable Anisotropic (SAM), which enables rapid learning of fine-grained feature information within local point clouds.

- Point Vector (PVM) is utilized to merge vectors with size and directional properties with the coordinate attributes of three-dimensional points, enhancing the flexibility of point cloud representation.
- GroupFormer (GFM) is adopted to facilitate information exchange among local point cloud features through grouped vector attention, thereby enhancing the efficiency and generalization performance of the model.
- Our approach is evaluated on three datasets, namely ModelNet40, ShapeNetPart, and S3DIS, for point cloud classification, point cloud part segmentation, and point cloud semantic segmentation tasks, surpassing many methods and achieving good performance (Fig. 1).

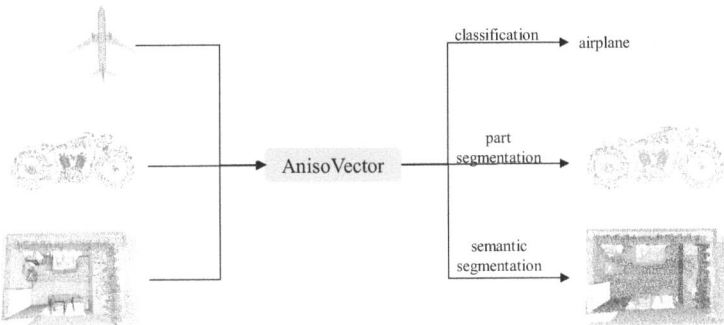

Fig. 1. AnisoVector for point cloud classification, point cloud part segmentation, and point cloud semantic segmentation tasks.

2 Related Work

In this chapter, we comprehensively review previous research methods, namely projection-based methods, voxel-based methods, and point-based methods.

Projection-Based Methods: Due to the mature application of 2D convolutions on images and their outstanding performance, many works [4, 5] transform point clouds into images and process them with 2D convolutions. However, this approach leads to geometric information loss during the transformation process and generates a large number of images, resulting in significant computational overhead.

Voxel-Based Methods: This approach converts three-dimensional points into voxel representations and processes them using 3D convolutions. Many methods [6, 7] unavoidably compute empty voxels during processing, leading to unnecessary resource consumption. To address this issue, sparse convolution methods [8] have been proposed to mitigate the additional resource consumption caused by empty voxels. However, geometric information loss in point clouds still occurs during the data transformation process.

Point-Based Methods: Due to the unstructured nature of point clouds, traditional convolutions are challenging to apply directly. PointNet [9] utilizes per-point Multilayer Perceptrons (MLPs) to process global point clouds and resolves the unorderedness issue through max-pooling aggregation. To capture finer features, PointNet++ [10] processes global point clouds in groups. RandLA-Net [16] extends the receptive field by connecting LocSe and Attentive Pooling by using Dilated Residual Blocks, achieving rapid point cloud processing through random sampling. PCT [17] and PointTransformer [20] introduce attention mechanisms to effectively model global and local features, thereby improving point cloud task performance. However, they are time-consuming and cannot meet real-time requirements. To address this challenge, our proposed AnisoVector network offers at least three advantages: 1) Local point cloud processing is divided into two independent stages, and each local point cloud is differentially considered using anisotropic functions, enabling rapid learning of effective feature information within local point clouds; 2) Fusion of vector data with scalar data of three-dimensional point coordinates enhances the flexibility of point cloud representation; 3) Grouped vector attention is employed to learn complex point cloud features, improving model efficiency and generalization performance.

3 Methodology

Firstly, Sect. 3.1 will review operations for processing local point clouds. Subsequently, Sect. 3.2 will provide a detailed introduction to Separable Anisotropic (SAM) for efficient handling of local point clouds. Following this, Sect. 3.3 will introduce Point Vector (PVM) to further enhance the network architecture. Additionally, Sect. 3.4 will present GroupFormer (GFM) to further improve performance. Finally, Sect. 3.5 will provide a detailed description of the overall architecture of the AnisoVector network.

3.1 Preliminary

According to the operations performed on local point clouds, they can be categorized into the following two types:
- Group-MLP-Aggregate
- MLP-Group-Aggregate

In the first approach, the global point cloud is initially partitioned into groups, followed by processing the point cloud data within each group using multilayer perceptrons (MLPs), and finally integrating the information of each local point cloud using aggregation functions. The FLOPs of this method are denoted as $C \times C \times N \times k \times L$. In contrast, the second approach adopts a different strategy. It preprocesses the global point cloud data using MLPs first, then divides the processed data into multiple groups. The FLOPs of this method are denoted as $C \times C \times N \times L$. The ratio of FLOPs between the two methods is represented as k, indicating that the FLOPs of the first method are k times those of the second method. Here, N represents the number of points, k denotes the number of neighboring points, C signifies the number of feature channels, and L represents the number of MLP layers. The comparison between the two approaches is illustrated in Fig. 2 (Table 1).

Table 1. Performance of different methods on PointNet++.

	FLOPs(G)
(1)PointNet++	1.0
(2)PointNet++ (MLP-Group)	0.53

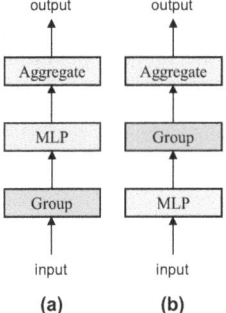

Fig. 2. (a) represents the Group-MLP-Aggregate approach, while (b) represents the MLP-Group-Aggregate approach.

Although utilizing the MLP-Group-Aggregate approach significantly reduces the time complexity of processing point clouds, this method fails to encode the geometric information of the point clouds effectively, resulting in a decrease in model performance. Specifically, geometric information can be represented by any relative information (e.g., edge information) between neighboring points and the central point, such as relative positions in PointNet++ $(p_i - p_i^k)$.

3.2 Separable Anisotropic

As previously mentioned, this paper adopts the MLP-Group-Aggregate approach to process point cloud data, aiming to avoid introducing excessive FLOPs. However, this method may lead to information loss, especially when dealing with complex local structures within point clouds. Traditional MLP operations may not always effectively capture the nonlinear relationships within point clouds, potentially blurring or overlooking key features, thus diminishing the model's performance in point cloud segmentation.

To address this issue, the Separable Anisotropic (SAM) approach is employed. SAM focuses on addressing the challenge of information loss while swiftly processing point clouds. By introducing anisotropic functions, SAM selectively considers the differences among each local point cloud, facilitating a more effective learning of complex structural information within the local context. Compared to traditional MLPs, SAM better captures the nonlinear relationships within point clouds during information propagation, preventing key features from being blurred or overlooked.

$$f_{i'} = \text{MLP}(f_i) \tag{1}$$

$$f_{i'}^k = \text{Group}(f_{i'}) \tag{2}$$

$$f_i^{\text{ani}} = \text{Agg}\left(\Delta x_i^k f_{i'}^k \oplus \Delta y_i^k f_{i'}^k \oplus \Delta z_i^k f_{i'}^k\right) \tag{3}$$

$$p_i^{\text{encode}} = \text{Agg}\left(\text{MLP}\left(p_i - p_i^k\right)\right) \tag{4}$$

$$f_i^{\text{result}} = p_i^{\text{encode}} \oplus f_i^{\text{ani}} \tag{5}$$

Here, Δx_i^k, Δy_i^k and Δz_i^k denote the relative positions of the central point p_i and the neighboring point p_i^k in the x, y and z dimensions, with $\oplus$ representing concatenation (Fig. 3).

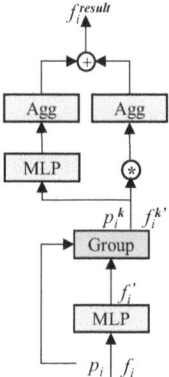

Fig. 3. Separable Anisotropic (SAM).

Firstly, this module processes global point cloud features f_i using MLP. Subsequently, based on the Cartesian coordinate system, the K-nearest neighbors (KNN) algorithm is employed to obtain the neighboring points p_i^k for each point along with their corresponding features $f_i^{k'}$. Thirdly, the features of neighboring points are scaled using three relative positional information. Then, these scaled features of neighboring points are concatenated and fed into the aggregation layer. Fourthly, the relative positional information of local points is encoded and aggregated. Finally, the results of the two aggregations are concatenated to obtain the output of this module.

3.3 Point Vector

In previous research efforts [10, 16, 20, 22], encoding of the coordinate information of point clouds has been conducted. However, the coordinate information of point clouds consists of scalar data on three dimensions, x, y, and z, which imposes limitations on the representation flexibility of point clouds. To address this issue, Point Vector is utilized in this study, as depicted in Fig. 4. In contrast to utilizing scalar coordinate information, this study enhances the representation flexibility of point clouds by introducing vectors with size and directional attributes, thereby augmenting their expressiveness. The specific steps are as follows:

Compute Distances and Angles. Apply the coordinates of points in the Cartesian coordinate system to Eqs. (6) to (8) to calculate distances (dis_i^k) and angles(θ_i^k, φ_i^k). Here, dis_i^k denotes the distance between p_i and p_i^k, while θ_i^k, φ_i^k represents the angle between p_i and p_i^k.

$$dis_i^k = \sqrt{x_i^{k^2} + y_i^{k^2} + z_i^{k^2}} \tag{6}$$

$$\theta_i^k = \arctan\left(\frac{z_i^k}{\sqrt{x_i^{k^2} + y_i^{k^2}}}\right) \tag{7}$$

$$\varphi_i^k = \arctan\left(\frac{y_i^k}{x_i^k}\right) \tag{8}$$

Here, (x_i^k, y_i^k, z_i^k) represents the coordinates of p_i in the Cartesian coordinate system.

Calculation of Centroid Angles. The centroid p_i^c is computed based on the coordinates of points within the local region. In this study, the direction from point p_i to point p_i^c is defined as the local direction. This definition offers two advantages: 1) the centroid can reflect the overall characteristics of the local region; 2) utilizing the centroid helps reduce the randomness introduced by downsampling. The centroid angles θ_i^c, φ_i^c are calculated according to Eqs. (7) and (8).

Calculation of Relative Angles. Subtracting the angle of each point within the region from the angle of the centroid yields the relative angles $\theta_i^{k\prime}$, $\varphi_i^{k\prime}$.

$$\theta_i^{k\prime} = \theta_i^k - \theta_i^c \tag{9}$$

$$\varphi_i^{k\prime} = \varphi_i^k - \varphi_i^c \tag{10}$$

3.4 GroupFormer

In order to expand the receptive field of each point to acquire more feature information, attention mechanisms are introduced, categorized into scalar attention and vector attention. Scalar attention processes query and key using matrix multiplication, followed by scaling the result to obtain attention weights w_i^k. The specific formula is as follows:

$$w_i^k = query_i^k \otimes key_i^k / \sqrt{C} \tag{11}$$

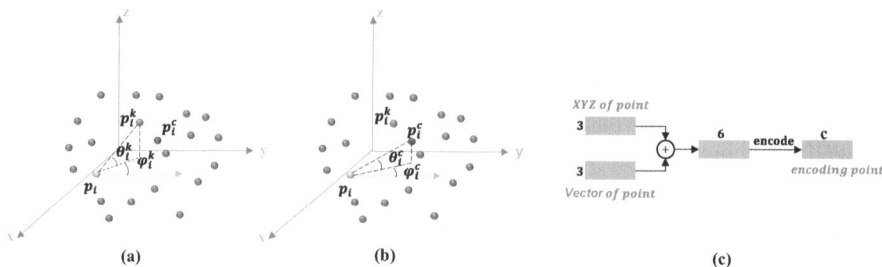

Fig. 4. Point Vector (PVM).

$$f_i^{\text{attn}} = \sum_k \text{Softmax}(w_i)^k \odot v_i^k \qquad (12)$$

Here, C represents the number of feature channels for the query. In vector attention, the relationship between the query and key is mapped to a vector through a weight encoding function, as illustrated in Fig. 5(a). The specific representation of vector attention is as follows:

$$w_i^k = \omega\left(\gamma\left(query_i^k, key_i^k\right)\right) \qquad (13)$$

$$f_i^{\text{attn}} = \sum_k \text{Softmax}(w_i)^k \odot v_i^k \qquad (14)$$

where γ represents the relational function, and $\omega \in R^c \rightarrow R^c$ denotes the learnable weight encoding. Scalar attention treats each feature element equally, while vector attention processes them differently based on their distinct characteristics. Therefore, vector attention is more adept at capturing meaningful feature information in complex scenarios.

However, in vector attention, as the network deepens and the number of feature channels increases, the parameter count in the weight encoding layer sharply rises, restricting the efficiency and generalization capability of the model. To overcome this limitation, a grouping mechanism is introduced, as illustrated in Fig. 5(b). The feature channels of the value $v \in R^c$ are evenly divided into g groups($1 \leq g \leq c$). The weight encoding layer outputs grouped attention vectors with g feature channels. Within the same attention group, the feature channels of the value share the same attention weights from the grouped attention vectors. The formula is as follows:

$$f_i^{\text{attn}} = \sum_k \sum_{l=1}^{g} \sum_{m=1}^{c/g} \text{Softmax}(w_i)_l^k \odot v_i^{klc/g+m} \qquad (15)$$

At the core of GroupFormer lies vector attention, as depicted in Fig. 5(c). This module consists of vector attention and a residual connection. The input data comprises the global point cloud coordinates and the corresponding point features. The GroupFormer facilitates information exchange among the feature vectors of local points, generating new feature vectors as its output. These new feature vectors not only integrate the intrinsic characteristics of point feature vectors but also consider the overall spatial arrangement of these point feature vectors in three-dimensional space.

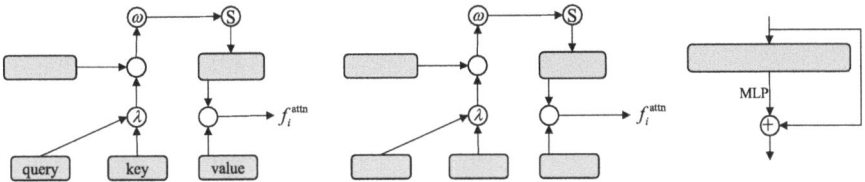

Fig. 5. The components composition of GroupFormer (GFM).

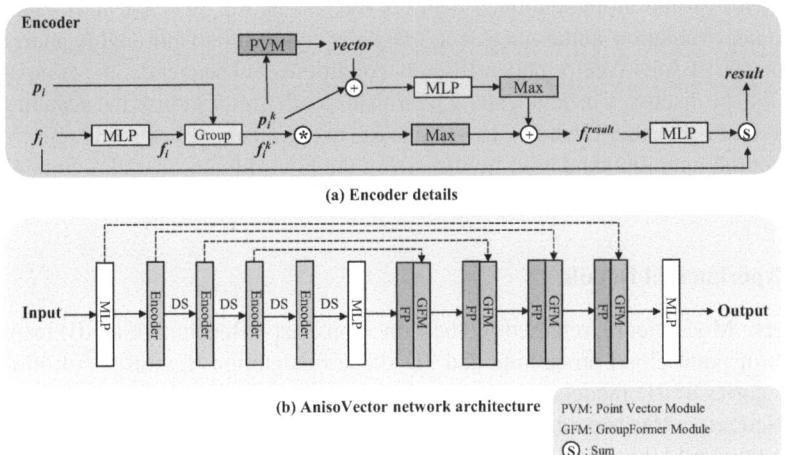

Fig. 6. Overview of AnisoVector.

3.5 Network Architecture

The three-dimensional point cloud analysis network AnisoVector is constructed based on SAM, PVM, and GFM, as illustrated in Fig. 6.

Backbone Structure. The classic U-Net architecture is employed. This architecture consists of 4 encoder and decoder stages, with skip connections between each encoder and its corresponding decoder. Each encoder stage extracts contextual information from the point cloud and performs downsampling. Each decoder stage restores the original number of points.

Output Head. For point cloud classification task, the feature vectors generated by the 4 decoder stages are globally max-pooled. Subsequently, the results are concatenated along the feature channel dimension, and an MLP is applied to the concatenated result to obtain the final classification result. For point cloud part and semantic segmentation tasks, an MLP is utilized to map the feature vector generated by the last decoder stage to produce the final prediction vector.

4 Experiments

To validate the effectiveness of the proposed method, the AnisoVector introduced in this paper will be employed for point cloud classification, part segmentation, and semantic segmentation tasks on three datasets: ModelNet40, ShapeNetPart, and S3DIS, respectively.

This chapter will provide a detailed description of the AnisoVector method implementation (see Sect. 4.1) and compare its performance with advanced methods through experiments on the aforementioned datasets (see Sects. 4.2, 4.3, and 4.4). Additionally, extensive ablation studies (see Sect. 4.3) were conducted to thoroughly analyze the performance of AnisoVector under different conditions. Subsequently, the comparative results will be discussed in detail, along with an in-depth exploration of the advantages of AnisoVector over other methods. In the ablation experiments of Sect. 4.3, AnisoVector underwent systematic validation by dissecting the contribution of each component to ensure the robustness and interpretability of this method.

4.1 Experimental Details

Datasets. ModelNet40, released by the Princeton Shape Benchmark (PSB) team, is a dataset for point cloud processing and 3D shape recognition. It consists of 40 different categories of 3D models, with each category containing 1000 point cloud models. ShapeNetPart, a 3D shape dataset for part segmentation, was created by the ShapeNet team at Stanford University. It comprises 16 object categories, 50 semantic categories, totaling 16846 3D objects. S3DIS is a large-scale 3D point cloud dataset for indoor scene understanding, composed of 271 rooms within 6 regions, encompassing 13 semantic categories. To adhere to the common protocol, Area 5 serves as the test set, while the remaining areas serve as the training set.

Evaluation Metric. For classification task, Overall Accuracy (OA) is employed as the evaluation metric. The formula for calculating OA is as follows:

$$OA = \frac{TP}{TP + FP} \tag{16}$$

where TP denotes the number of correctly classified instances, and FP represents the number of misclassifications.

For part segmentation and semantic segmentation tasks, mIoU (mean Intersection over Union) is used as the evaluation metric. It is described as follows:

$$mIoU = \frac{1}{C} \sum_{i=0}^{C} \frac{P_i \cap G_i}{P_i \cup G_i} \tag{17}$$

where P_i and G_i represent the correct predictions and true labels for the i-th category respectively, and C represents the number of categories.

Network Configuration. As depicted in Fig. 6, the architecture employs four Encoder-Decoder stages as the backbone to extract feature information from point clouds. The downsampling ratios and output channels for the Encoder stages are set as [N/4, N/16, N/64, N/128] and [64, 128, 256, 512], respectively. For the Decoder stages, the upsampling ratios and output channels are [N/64, N/16, N/4, N] and [256, 128, 64, 32], respectively, where N represents the number of input point.

Training Details. The AnisoVector network is trained from scratch using the AdamW optimizer and employs Cross-Entropy loss with label smoothing. For the ModelNet40 dataset, the batch size and learning rate are set to 16 and 0.1 respectively, and the training is conducted for 200 epochs. For the ShapeNetPart dataset, the batch size and learning rate are set to 8 and 0.01 respectively, and training is conducted for 250 epochs. Regarding the S3DIS dataset, the batch size and learning rate are set to 4 and 0.01 respectively, and training is performed for 100 epochs. All experiments are conducted on a single NVIDIA 3080 GPU.

4.2 3D Shape Classification and Segmentation

ModelNet40. We conduct classification experiments on the ModelNet40 dataset using our proposed method, AnisoVector, and compare the results with previous approaches. As shown in Table 2, our method exhibits superior performance compared to other methods, demonstrating its effectiveness.

Table 2. Shape classification on ModelNet40.

Method	mAcc (%)	OA (%)	Speed (ins./sec.)
PointNet [9]	86.0	89.2	39.4
PointNet++ [10]	-	91.9	24.7
PointCNN [11]	88.1	92.5	26.7
KPConv [14]	-	92.9	5.2
DGCNN [12]	90.2	92.9	30.9
PointASNL [15]	-	92.9	17.8
PCT [17]	-	93.2	20.1
PointStack [21]	89.6	93.3	-
AnisoVector (Ours)	89.8	93.4	44.8

ShapeNetPart. We conduct part segmentation experiments on the ShapeNetPart dataset using our proposed method. Table 3 presents a quantitative comparison of the performance of our method, AnisoVector, with other advanced approaches on the ShapeNetPart dataset. Our method outperforms most previous methods in part segmentation performance. The part segmentation results are visualized in Fig. 7, the segmented output closely resembles the ground truth.

Table 3. Part segmentation on ShapeNetPart.

Method	mIoU (%)	Speed (ins./sec.)
PointNet [9]	83.7	39.2
PointNet++ [10]	85.1	24.3
DGCNN [12]	85.2	31.1
PointCNN [11]	86.1	26.8
KPConv [14]	86.1	5.3
PCT [17]	86.4	20.1
PointStack [21]	87.2	-
AnisoVector (Ours)	87.2	44.7

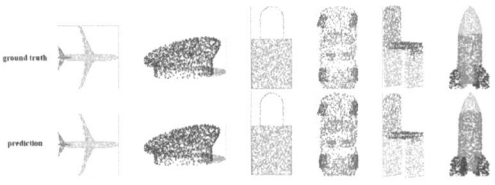

Fig. 7. Partial point cloud visualization results in ShapeNetPart.

4.3 3D Scene Segmentation

Semantic segmentation experiments are conducted on the S3DIS dataset using our proposed method, AnisoVector. The quantitative results of semantic segmentation are shown in Table 4. KPConv achieves leading performance with 67.1% mIoU and 72.8% mAcc. However, in terms of speed, AnisoVector (our method) surpasses all other methods with a processing speed of 36.6 instances per second while maintaining high performance, with 66.6% mIoU, 73.2% mAcc, and the highest overall accuracy (OA) of 89.2%. This indicates that our method significantly improves segmentation speed while ensuring high accuracy.

To visually observe the effectiveness of semantic segmentation, Fig. 8 illustrates the visualization results of Area5. Due to the complexity of large-scale 3D point cloud scenes, some misclassifications of categories are inevitable, such as incorrectly predicting windows as doors.

4.4 Ablation Study

We conducted detailed ablation experiments to assess the effectiveness of each module within the proposed methodology. The ablation experiments were performed on S3DIS Area5.

Number of Neighbors. To investigate the impact of the number of neighboring points on segmentation performance, we conducted ablation experiments on AnisoVector, and

Table 4. Semantic segmentation on S3DIS Area5.

Method	mIoU (%)	mAcc (%)	OA (%)	Speed (ins./sec.)
PointNet [9]	41.1	49.0	-	32.4
DGCNN [12]	49.9	58.7	82.3	25.4
LAP-DGCNN [31]	53.6	62.3	-	-
PointNet++ [10]	54.5	67.1	81.0	20.4
PointCNN [11]	57.3	63.9	85.9	21.7
PCT [17]	61.3	67.6	-	16.4
RandLA-Net [16]	62.4	71.4	87.2	19.1
PointASNL [15]	62,6	68,5	87.7	14.6
SCF-Net [18]	63.4	-	-	19.3
DeepViewAgg [32]	64.7	-	-	-
IFE [33]	65.2	73.6	88.3	-
ASSANet [19]	66.8	-	-	11.4
KPConv [14]	67.1	72.8	-	4.2
AnisoVector (Ours)	66.6	73.2	89.2	36.6

Fig. 8. Partial room visualization results in S3DIS Area5.

the results are presented in Table 5. The best performance was observed when the number of neighbors was set to 16. However, for values of 4 or 8, the model might lack a sufficient number of points for predicting contextual semantics effectively. In the case of a setting with a value of 32, PVM provided abundant directional vector data for each point within the local region, and GFM supplied data information for neighboring points. Nevertheless, due to the likelihood of many points being more distant, resulting in lower correlation, an excessive amount of noise was introduced, leading to a reduction in the model's performance.

Table 5. Ablation study of number of neighbour point.

K	mIoU (%)
4	61.4
8	64.7
16	66.6
32	65.4

SAM. Specifically, we investigated the differences in semantic segmentation accuracy and speed between the Separable Anisotropic module (SAM) and other Set Abstraction modules. The results are presented in Table 6.

Table 6. Ablation study of SAM. The structure of SA is the same as SA of PointNet++.

Module	mIoU (%)	Speed (ins./sec.)
SA	53.3	36.1
SA + LSE [16]	54.9	30.6
Separable SA (SSA)	50.7	46.8
SSA + Relative Position	56.2	46.0
Separable Anisotropic SA	59.9	51.6

These findings suggest that Separable Anisotropic Module outperforms the 'SA + LSE' and other Set Abstraction modules in both segmentation accuracy and speed. Anisotropic kernels are crucial for capturing the fine-grained structures and varying shapes of objects in point clouds. Combining SA with additional feature-aware modules can be beneficial. Both the LSE and relative position infomation, when incorporated alongside SA, lead to improvements in segmentation accuracy. This indicates that explicitly incorporating features like local environment cues and spatial relationships between points can further enhance the model's understanding of the scene. The Separate Anisotropic module achieve both the highest accuracy and the fastest processing speed (59.9% mIoU and 51.6 ins./s.).

PVM. To validate the efficacy of vectors endowed with both distance and directional attributes in representing features compared to scalars, pertinent experimental results are presented in Table 7.

In our model, 'xyz' denotes the processing of scalar data exclusively along the x, y, and z dimensions. Introducing 'xyz + distance' involves inputting coordinate data with magnitude attributes into the model. Similarly, 'xyz + direction' entails providing coordinate data with directional attributes to the model. The expression 'xyz + PVM' signifies the input of coordinate data with both magnitude and directional attributes into the model. This observation implies that vectors endowed with both distance and

Table 7. Ablation study of PVM.

Module	mIoU (%)
xyz	59.9
xyz + distance	60.5
xyz + direction	60.8
xyz + PVM	61.6

direction exhibit greater expressiveness in capturing point cloud features compared to scalar data.

GFM. We conducted a study on different types of attention, and the experimental results are presented in Table 8.

Table 8. Ablation study of GFM.

Module	mIoU (%)	Speed (ins./sec.)	Param (M)
replace with MLP + max	61.9	35.1	2.10
replace with scalar attention	62.4	24.8	2.21
replace with vector attention	65.5	31.1	2.45
group vector attention	66.6	36.6	2.54

The ablation study which replaces GFM (GroupFormer) with different methods reveals insightful findings. From Table 8, it can be observed that scalar attention is able to capture more feature information compared to 'MLP + max', resulting in a 0.5% increase in mIoU; however, it comes at the cost of slower processing speed. There is a significant performance gap between vector attention and scalar attention, with the mIoU and processing speed of former outperforming the latter by 3.1% and 6.3 instances per second, indicating the effectiveness of the learnable weight encoding layer ω. In comparison with vector attention, the proposed group vector attention surpasses all other mechanisms, achieving the highest mIoU of 66.6% and the fastest processing speed of 36.6 instances per second, albeit with a slightly increased parameter count. These results underscore the superiority of group vector attention in capturing features within local point clouds, thus enhancing both efficiency and performance in point cloud analysis tasks.

5 Conclusion

In this study, we propose a novel network architecture named AnisoVector aimed at efficiently extracting valuable information from point cloud data to address challenges in real-time analysis and efficient information extraction. The AnisoVector network consists of three key modules: Separable Anisotropic (SAM), Point Vector (PVM), and GroupFormer (GFM). These modules collectively enhance not only the inference speed of the model but also the analysis capability of fine-grained features in point clouds. The SAM module significantly improves the learning efficiency of the model for local feature information by dividing local point cloud processing into two independent stages and introducing an anisotropic function. The PVM module increases the degree of freedom in point cloud representation by introducing vectors with size and direction attributes, thereby better capturing the geometric features of point clouds. The GFM module efficiently exchanges feature information of local point clouds and improves the efficiency and generalization performance of the model. Experimental results on the ModelNet40, ShapeNetPart, and S3DIS datasets demonstrate the outstanding performance of AnisoVector in point cloud classification, point cloud part segmentation, and point cloud semantic segmentation tasks. Compared with existing methods, AnisoVector exhibits significant improvements in accuracy, speed, and generalization ability. Particularly, in the semantic segmentation task on the S3DIS dataset, AnisoVector achieves high real-time performance with 36.6 inferences per second while maintaining high accuracy, demonstrating its potential in practical applications. Furthermore, we conduct ablation experiments to validate the contributions of each component of AnisoVector, ensuring the robustness and interpretability of the method. These experimental results further confirm the effectiveness and practicality of AnisoVector in the field of point cloud analysis. Overall, the AnisoVector network provides a new perspective for point cloud understanding, potentially advancing the development of fields such as autonomous driving and augmented reality.

Acknowledgements. This work was supported by Jiangxi Nuclear Geoscience Data Science and System Engineering Technology Research Center Foundation JELRGBDT202202 and Jiangxi Province Radiogeoscience Big data technology Engineering Laboratory open fund JELRGBDT202103.

References

1. Xiao, A., Huang, J., Guan, D., et al.: Unsupervised point cloud representation learning with deep neural networks: a survey. IEEE Trans. Pattern Anal. Mach. Intell. (2023)
2. Zhang, H., Wang, C., Tian, S., et al.: Deep learning-based 3D point cloud classification: a systematic survey and outlook. Displays, 102456 (2023)
3. Stilla, U., Xu, Y.: Change detection of urban objects using 3D point clouds: a review. ISPRS J. Photogramm. Remote. Sens. **197**, 228–255 (2023)
4. Boulch, A., Le Saux, B., Audebert, N.: Unstructured point cloud semantic labeling using deep segmentation networks. 3dor@ eurographics **3**, 17–24 (2017)
5. Lawin, F.J., Danelljan, M., Tosteberg, P., et al.: Deep projective 3D semantic segmentation. In: Computer Analysis of Images and Patterns: 17th International Conference, CAIP 2017, Ystad, Sweden, 22–24 August 2017, Proceedings, Part I 17, pp. 95–107. Springer, Cham (2017)
6. Huang, J., You, S.: Point cloud labeling using 3D convolutional neural network. In: 2016 23rd International Conference on Pattern Recognition (ICPR), pp. 2670–2675. IEEE (2016)
7. Tchapmi, L., Choy, C., Armeni, I., et al.: Segcloud: semantic segmentation of 3D point clouds. In: 2017 International Conference on 3D Vision (3DV), pp. 537–547. IEEE (2017)

8. Graham, B., Engelcke, M., Van Der Maaten, L.: 3D semantic segmentation with submanifold sparse convolutional networks. In: Proceedings of the IEEE Conference on Computer Vision and Pattern Recognition, pp. 9224–9232 (2018)
9. Qi, C.R., Su, H., Mo, K., et al.: Pointnet: deep learning on point sets for 3D classification and segmentation. In: Proceedings of the IEEE Conference on Computer Vision and Pattern Recognition, pp. 652–660 (2017)
10. Qi, C.R., Yi, L., Su, H., et al.: Pointnet++: deep hierarchical feature learning on point sets in a metric space. In: Advances in Neural Information Processing Systems, vol. 30 (2017)
11. Li, Y., Bu, R., Sun, M., et al.: PointCNN: convolution on x-transformed points. In: Advances in Neural Information Processing Systems, vol. 31 (2018)
12. Wang, Y., Sun, Y., Liu, Z., et al.: Dynamic graph CNN for learning on point clouds. ACM Trans. Graph. (ToG) **38**(5), 1–12 (2019)
13. Wu, W., Qi, Z., Fuxi, L.: PointConv: deep convolutional networks on 3D point clouds. In: Proceedings of the IEEE/CVF Conference on Computer Vision and Pattern Recognition, pp. 9621–9630 (2019)
14. Thomas, H., Qi, C.R., Deschaud, J.E., et al.: KPConv: flexible and deformable convolution for point clouds. In: Proceedings of the IEEE/CVF International Conference on Computer Vision, pp. 6411–6420 (2019)
15. Yan, X., Zheng, C., Li, Z., et al.: PointASNL: robust point clouds processing using nonlocal neural networks with adaptive sampling. In: Proceedings of the IEEE/CVF Conference on Computer Vision and Pattern Recognition, pp. 5589–5598 (2020)
16. Hu, Q., Yang, B., Xie, L., et al.: RandLa-net: efficient semantic segmentation of large-scale point clouds. In: Proceedings of the IEEE/CVF Conference on Computer Vision and Pattern Recognition, pp. 11108–11117 (2020)
17. Guo, M.H., Cai, J.X., Liu, Z.N., et al.: PCT: point cloud transformer. Comput. Vis. Media **7**, 187–199 (2021)
18. Fan, S., Dong, Q., Zhu, F., et al.: SCF-Net: learning spatial contextual features for large-scale point cloud segmentation. In: Proceedings of the IEEE/CVF Conference on Computer Vision and Pattern Recognition, pp. 14504–14513 (2021)
19. Qian, G., Hammoud, H., Li, G., et al:. Assanet: an anisotropic separable set abstraction for efficient point cloud representation learning. In: Advances in Neural Information Processing Systems, vol. 34, pp. 28119–28130 (2021)
20. Zhao, H., Jiang, L., Jia, J., et al:. Point transformer. In: Proceedings of the IEEE/CVF International Conference on Computer Vision, pp. 16259–16268 (2021)
21. Wijaya, K.T., Paek, D.H., Kong, S.H.: Advanced feature learning on point clouds using multi-resolution features and learnable pooling. arXiv preprint arXiv:2205.09962 (2022)
22. Qian, G., Li, Y., Peng, H., et al.: Pointnext: revisiting pointnet++ with improved training and scaling strategies. In: Advances in Neural Information Processing Systems, vol. 35, pp. 23192–23204 (2022)
23. Ma, X., Qin, C., You, H., et al.: Rethinking network design and local geometry in point cloud: a simple residual MLP framework. arXiv preprint arXiv:2202.07123 (2022)
24. Park, C., Jeong, Y., Cho, M., et al.: Fast point transformer. In: Proceedings of the IEEE/CVF Conference on Computer Vision and Pattern Recognition, pp. 16949–16958 (2022)
25. Deng, X., Zhang, W.Y., Ding, Q., et al.: PointVector: a vector representation in point cloud analysis. In: Proceedings of the IEEE/CVF Conference on Computer Vision and Pattern Recognition, pp. 9455–9465 (2023)
26. Thomas, H., Goulette, F., Deschaud, J.E., et al.: Semantic classification of 3D point clouds with multiscale spherical neighborhoods. In: 2018 International Conference on 3D Vision (3DV), pp. 390–398. IEEE (2018)

27. Ye, X., Li, J., Huang, H., et al.: 3D recurrent neural networks with context fusion for point cloud semantic segmentation. In: Proceedings of the European Conference on Computer Vision (ECCV), pp. 403–417 (2018)
28. Zhang, Z., Hua, B.S., Yeung, S.K.: Shellnet: efficient point cloud convolutional neural networks using concentric shells statistics. In: Proceedings of the IEEE/CVF International Conference on Computer Vision, pp. 1607–1616 (2019)
29. Zhao, C., Zhou, W., Lu, L., et al.: Pooling scores of neighboring points for improved 3D point cloud segmentation. In: 2019 IEEE International Conference on Image Processing (ICIP), pp. 1475–1479. IEEE (2019)
30. Zhao, H., Jiang, L., Fu, C.W., et al.: Pointweb: enhancing local neighborhood features for point cloud processing. In: Proceedings of the IEEE/CVF Conference on Computer Vision and Pattern Recognition, pp. 5565–5573 (2019)
31. Lin, L., Huang, P., Fu, C.W., et al.: On learning the right attention point for feature enhancement. Sci. China Inf. Sci. **66**, 112107 (2023)
32. Robert, D., Vallet, B., Landrieu, L.: Learning multi-view aggregation in the wild for large-scale 3D semantic segmentation. In: Proceedings of the IEEE/CVF Conference on Computer Vision and Pattern Recognition, pp. 5575–5584 (2022)
33. Yang, Z., Ye, Q., Stoter, J., et al.: Enriching point clouds with implicit representations for 3D classification and segmentation. Remote Sens. **15**(1), 61 (2022)

Automatic Code Generation from GUI Screenshots with Vision-Language Models

Jingbin Liang, Jing Liang[✉], and Shuang Li

School of Computer Science and Artificial Intelligence, Wuhan Textile University, Wuhan, China
{2115363083,2215363064}@mail.wtu.edu.cn, shinelight@wtu.edu.cn

Abstract. There are two challenges in the GUI code generation tasks: insufficient image feature extraction capability and low accuracy of code generation. Existing methods can handle simple GUI datasets well but have difficulty with complex GUI datasets. We propose a method for automatic code generation from GUI screenshots with vision-language models. Our method uses a multimodal information fusion module to fuse feature information from images and code efficiently. To improve the accuracy and feature extraction capability of GUI code generation, we use a combination of automated metrics to evaluate the performance of our method. The multiple experimental results demonstrate that our method achieves better performance among existing methods on both existing public and newly constructed datasets in the GUI code generation field. In particular, the BLUE4 score has been improved by 27% on the newly constructed dataset. The vision-language model architecture in our method can meet the diversity of code generation tasks and provide a helpful solution for GUI development in various domains.

Keywords: GUI · code generation · vision-language models · attention mechanism · multimodal fusion

1 Introduction

In recent years, the GUI code generation task [1] has become an increasingly popular research topic. Beltramelli et al. [2] pioneered this field and introduced the pix2code model, which uses Convolutional Neural Networks(CNN) and Long Short-Term Memory(LSTM) to translate UI screenshots into Domain-Specific Language(DSL). Subsequently, other researchers have proposed many optimization methods based on the pix2code model. Liu et al. [3] replaced LSTM with Bidirectional LSTM(Bi-LSTM) to obtain richer contextual information. Zhu et al. [4] proposed a method that combines an attention mechanism with a hierarchical LSTM. Chen et al. [5] used GRU instead of LSTM and added an attention mechanism. These models mentioned above have shown advancements in code generation accuracy compared to the pix2code model. However, the models based on CNN-RNN still present suboptimal performance, particularly when dealing with complex GUI datasets. Further enhancements are needed to improve the accuracy of the GUI code generation.

Transformer [6] is renowned for its powerful attention mechanism, which performs well when dealing with sequential textual data. Li et al. [7] designed two versions of Transformer-based tree decoders, which can predict layout structures and semantic properties well. He et al. [8] employed a convolutional network to enhance image feature extraction capabilities and a text encoder based on Transformer for text feature extraction. These studies show that the Transformer architecture has a significant advantage in capturing global features and improving end-to-end code generation accuracy by handling global dependencies.

Large language models [9] based on the Transformer architecture perform well in the Natural Language Processing (NLP) area. Vision Transformer(ViT) [10] has successfully applied the Transformer architecture to computer vision. Many studies have utilized vision-language models [11] based on the Transformer architecture in image captioning tasks [12]. Vision-language models integrate a large vision model [13] and a large language model to generate corresponding textual descriptions from images. In the field of image captioning, Luo et al. [14] introduced an end-to-end framework for generating image captions, which can learn the alignment between vision and language to create accurate image descriptions. Li et al. [15] proposed a Querying Transformer (Q-Former) pre-trained with a new two-stage pretraining strategy to achieve effective vision-language alignment. Due to advantages in visual and textual information processing, vision-language models are widely used in image captioning tasks.

The GUI code generation task can be regarded as a specialized form of image captioning task, which can achieve end-to-end GUI code generation. The GUI code generation task is different from the image description task in that it needs to accurately reflect the layout information of the user interface, which requires the generated code to have higher quality and more precise. This paper proposes a GUI code generation model based on vision-language models. It is a multimodal information fusion module that can handle the problem of aligning cross-modal information and improves the generalization capabilities when dealing with complex GUI datasets.

The contributions of this paper are as follows:

- We propose img2code, an end-to-end generative model based on vision-language models for GUI code generation that outperformed the baseline model.
- We design a simple and efficient multimodal information fusion module that can integrate image and code information effectively.
- We use a method of randomly generating training datasets that constructs a complex dataset, establishing a new baseline for future research.
- We extensively evaluate the effectiveness and limitations of img2code using both public and newly constructed datasets and compare it to traditional approaches in GUI code generation. Additionally, we conduct ablation experiments to assess the impact and improvement of the multimodal information

fusion module. The experimental results demonstrate that img2code achieves excellent results across multiple evaluation metrics.

2 Related Work

The motivation of GUI code generation research is to realize automatically converting GUI images into code. Beltramelli et al. [2] proposed pix2code, a model based on CNN and LSTM, capable of converting GUI screenshots into Domain-Specific Languages (DSL) with an accuracy of 77%. Some researchers have optimized the pix2code model. Liu et al. [3] introduced Bidirectional LSTM(Bi-LSTM) to replace the original LSTM in the pix2code model, which captures contextual information better and improves the accuracy to 85% on the pix2code dataset. Zhu et al. [4] introduced a hierarchical LSTM with an attention mechanism, which can generate hierarchically structured code in consistency with the hierarchical layout of the graphic elements in the GUI. Pang et al. [16] proposed HGui2Code, a model that utilizes a hybrid attention mechanism to combine GUI features with semantic features of DSL code, which achieves a 5.5% improvement in accuracy compared to the pix2code model. Xu et al. [17] improved the CNN architecture of the pix2code model and incorporated object detection techniques.

Li et al. [7] proposed a tree-structured generation model based on Transformer, which encodes layout information from GUI images to predict the tree structure of the code. He et al. [8] replaced the text encoder of the pix2code model with a Transformer encoder, followed by a bidirectional LSTM decoder. This approach increased the BLEU score from 0.81 to 0.85 on publicly available datasets and from 0.547 to 0.575 on newly created datasets. Zhang et al. [18] utilized a Transformer decoder, where the multi-head attention mechanism within the decoder can focus on feature information from both images and code. Ge et al. [19] proposed a model with an encoder-decoder architecture that uses a Swin Transformer instead of CNN for image feature extractors. Soselia et al. [20] introduced ViCT based on reinforcement learning. This model utilizes ViT and Distilled Transformer(DiT) [21] as encoders and GPT-2 as a decoder, achieving notable performance across multiple evaluation metrics. Wang et al. [22] achieved impressive performance across benchmark tests by utilizing large-scale pretraining on visual-textual data and fine-tuning for the target task.

Although research on GUI code generation has been conducted extensively, no approach has been based on vision-language models. In addition, there is still a lot of room for exploration in the task of GUI code generation, especially in improving the quality of the dataset, enhancing the accuracy of code generation, and improving the performance of the model.

3 Methodology

In this paper, we introduce an approach based on vision-language models. Our model uses ViT as an image encoder and GPT2 as a text decoder. ViT is trained by rich information from the large-scale dataset ImageNet [23], which has strong migration capability across various visual tasks. It can extract semantic and structural features from the GUI screenshots very well. At the same time, GPT-2 is utilized as a textual decoder in language models, which is trained from a large amount of textual data and has good text generation capabilities.

3.1 Common Vision-Language Models Architecture

GPT-2 cannot process visual information directly. A common practice is to insert a randomly initialized cross-attention module between the multi-head self-attention(MHSA) and Feedforward Network(FFN) layers in GPT-2 to handle the image features extracted by the image encoder, as is exemplified in Fig. 1. This approach may render the pretraining weights of GPT-2 ineffective, necessitating retraining the model on large-scale datasets. However, directly injecting visual knowledge into the GPT-2 destroys the integrity of its structure, causing it to continuously learn visual information, known as Continual Lifelong Learning [24]. This learning process may pose some challenges and is highly possible to cause the catastrophic forgetting problem [25] because a modal gap exists between language and vision, harming the original language generation knowledge and severely affecting the model's overall performance.

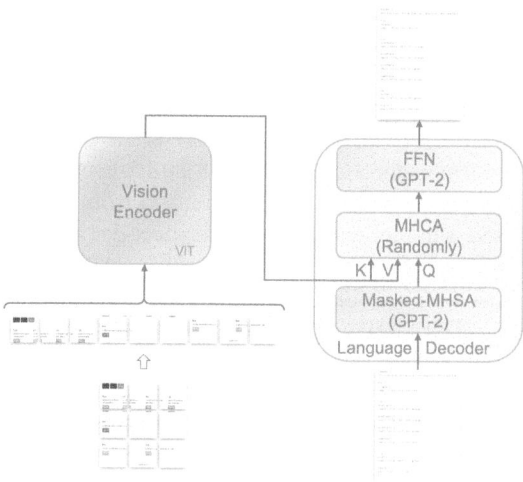

Fig. 1. The model architecture integrates multimodal information using a randomly initialized cross-attention module.

3.2 Vanilla Model Architecture

Figure 2 illustrates the architecture of the vanilla model, which connects vision-language models using a pre-fusion method. This method involves repeated stacking of the CLS Tokens from the output hidden layer of the ViT, ensuring that the sequence length of CLS Tokens representing image features matches the size of the text sequence. Subsequently, the concatenated vectors of the image sequence and text sequence are used as inputs to the language model. This approach enables each word vector to incorporate image features, allowing the language model to handle visual features effectively. Specifically, the calculation formula for adding the output of ViT with a text vector is as follows:

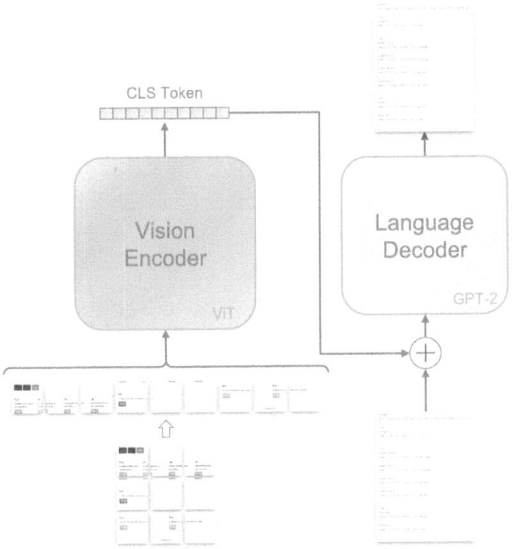

Fig. 2. The architecture of the vanilla model.

$$I = \left(v^{cls}, v_1, \ldots, v_m\right) \tag{1}$$

$$X = (x_1, \ldots, x_n) \tag{2}$$

$$C = \left(v_1^{cls}, \ldots, v_n^{cls}\right) \tag{3}$$

$$Z = X + C \tag{4}$$

where I represents the output of ViT hidden layers, v^{cls} denotes the CLS Token, $(v_1, \ldots, v_m)$ represents the remaining Patch Tokens, where m is the length of Patch Tokens. X is the text vector, and n is the length of the text sequence. C is a vector obtained by stacking the v^{cls} vector n times to match the length of the text sequence, and Z is the vector obtained by concatenating X and C.

The CLS Token can effectively provide an overall feature representation of the image. Still, its granularity is coarse and cannot fully capture the local detailed information in the GUI screenshots. Despite its limitations, utilizing the CLS token in the ViT remains an effective approach in practical scenarios.

3.3 Img2code Model Architecture

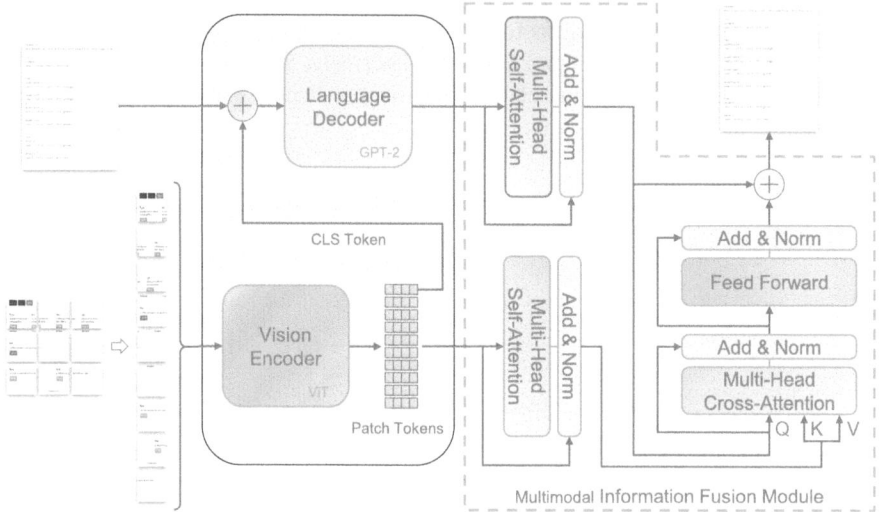

Fig. 3. The architecture of the img2code model.

The general architecture of the img2code model is shown in Fig. 3. This model constructs a visual encoder and a language decoder based on ViT and GPT-2, respectively. We have designed a simple and efficient multimodal information fusion module to effectively capture the relationship between local image features and the generated code. Specifically, the details of this module are as follows:

(a) The introduction of a multi-head self-attention mechanism. This mechanism enables each feature vector to focus on other feature vectors dynamically and improves the capability to handle intrinsic relationships between local features. The formula for the multi-head self-attention mechanism is as follows:

$$MultiHead(Q, K, V) = Concat(head_1, head_2, \ldots, head_h) \cdot W^O \quad (5)$$

where $head_i$

$$= Attention\left(Q \cdot W_i^Q, K \cdot W_i^K, V \cdot W_i^V\right) \quad (6)$$

$$Attention(Q,K,V) = softmax\left(\frac{Q \cdot K^T}{\sqrt{d_k}}\right) \cdot V \quad (7)$$

$$Q = X \cdot W^Q \quad (8)$$
$$K = X \cdot W^K \quad (9)$$
$$V = X \cdot W^V \quad (10)$$

where the projections are parameter matrices $W^Q \in \mathbb{R}^{d_{model} \times d_k}$, $W^K \in \mathbb{R}^{d_{model} \times d_k}$, $W^V \in \mathbb{R}^{d_{model} \times d_v}$, and $W^O \in \mathbb{R}^{d_{model} \times hd_v}$, $i \in h$. In this work, we employ $h = 8$ self-attention heads. For each of these, we use $d_k = d_v = d_{model}/h = 64$.

(b) Residual connections and Layer Normalization are applied to the output of the multi-head self-attention layer. This step can stabilize the learning process of the model and alleviate the problem of gradient vanishing and gradient explosion during the training process, consequently improving the model's performance.

(c) The outputs of the language decoder and the vision encoder are processed through multi-head self-attention layers, followed by a multi-head cross-attention mechanism. This step effectively integrates the image's feature information and the generated code's semantics. The formula for the multi-head cross-attention attention mechanism is as follows:

$$MultiHead(Q_T, K_I, V_I) \\ = Concat\,(head_1, head_2, \ldots, head_h) \cdot W^{O_T} \tag{11}$$

where $head_i$
$$= Attention\left(Q_T \cdot W_i^{Q_T}, K_I \cdot W_i^{K_I}, V_I \cdot W_i^{V_I}\right) \tag{12}$$

$$Attention(Q, K, V) = softmax\left(\frac{Q \cdot K^T}{\sqrt{d_k}}\right) \cdot V \tag{13}$$

$$Q = Q_T \cdot W^{Q_T} \tag{14}$$
$$K = K_I \cdot W^{K_I} \tag{15}$$
$$V = V_I \cdot W^{V_I} \tag{16}$$

where the projections are parameter matrices $W_i^{Q_T} \in \mathbb{R}^{d_{model} \times d_k}$, $W_i^{K_I} \in \mathbb{R}^{d_{model} \times d_k}$, $W_i^{V_I} \in \mathbb{R}^{d_{model} \times d_v}$, and $W^{O_T} \in \mathbb{R}^{d_{model} \times hd_v}$, $i \in h$. Q_T comes from the language decoder, while K_I and V_I come from the vision encoder. In this work, we employ $h = 8$ self-attention heads. For each of these, we use $d_k = d_v = d_{model}/h = 64$.

(d) The output from the previous step is further processed through an FFN to extract and abstract feature information. Additionally, we introduce the Gelu activation function and set $d_{model} = 512, d_{ff} = 2048$, and $dropout = 20\%$. The calculation formula for the feedforward network is as follows:

$$FFN(x) = Gelu\,(W_2 \cdot Gelu\,(W_1 \cdot x + b_1) + b_2) \tag{17}$$

(e) Finally, we combine the output of the FFN layer and the production of GPT-2 through the multi-head self-attention layer with a residual connection.

The multimodal information fusion module can efficiently handle the complex relationship between images and generated codes by introducing an attention mechanism to assign weights dynamically. This mechanism improves the ability of our model to learn features while maintaining the respective characteristics of ViT and GPT-2. It is particularly effective in handling multimodal information, producing more accurate output results.

Fig. 4. The Web UI screenshot of the pix2code dataset(a) and the img2code dataset(b).

4 Experiments and Results

4.1 Dataset

The synthetic dataset constructed by Beltramelli et al. [2] has been widely used for GUI code generation. This dataset comprises three types of data: Web, Android, and iOS. There are 1742 web screenshots with their corresponding code in the Web-type dataset. The Web-type dataset mainly covers buttons, titles, and text, as shown in Fig. 4(a). This dataset is too small in scale and does not include complex interface elements, thus limiting its utility in Transformer models. To solve this problem, we propose a method for generating training datasets randomly, as shown in Fig. 5. This method randomly generates the Domain Specific Language(DSL) labels based on the requirements. Then, DSL tags are compiled into markup languages, like HTML or XML. Finally, the rendering engine renders the interface graphics corroding to the markup language, and the screenshot is saved.

We synthesize 36000 UI images with their corresponding DSL using the above mentioned method. The image screenshot in the synthetic dataset is shown in Fig. 4(b). We named it the img2code dataset, which is utilized for subsequent research on GUI code generation. We add new components such as "input", "toggle", "img" and "checkbox" and expand the number of colors for buttons to 5. The average length of characters has increased by about two times over the pix2code dataset. Table 1 shows the data comparison between the img2code dataset and the pix2code dataset.

Table 1. Comparison of datasets.

Dataset	Quantities	Elements	Btn-colors	Characters
pix2code	1742	6	3	336
img2code	36000	10	5	641

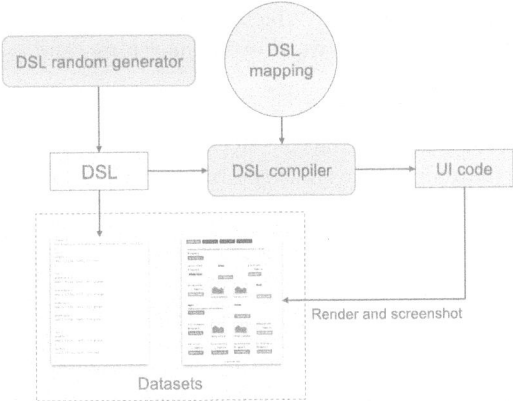

Fig. 5. Methodology for dataset Generation.

4.2 Evaluation Metrics

In terms of experimentation, we employ a set of evaluation metrics commonly used in text-generation tasks to facilitate comparative experiments with baseline papers. We evaluate the model's performance by measuring the similarity between the generated code and the reference DSL text of the image.

Accuracy is a metric that measures how well the generated code matches the reference text, providing an intuitive reflection of the model's performance. The formula for calculating the accuracy score is as follows:

$$Accuracy = \frac{N}{M} \quad (18)$$

where N is the number of texts correctly predicted by the model, and M is the total number of texts.

BLEU [26](Bilingual Evaluation Understudy) is a widely used metric in machine translation to evaluate the quality of the generated text by comparing n-gram matches. The formula for calculating the BLEU score is as follows:

$$BLEU = BP \cdot \exp\left(\sum_{n=1}^{N} w_n \log P_n\right) \quad (19)$$

where BP is the brevity penalty for length difference, N is the maximum n-gram order, w_n is the weight assigned to n-grams for weighting, and P_n is the precision of n-grams.

METEOR [27] improves BLEU by considering additional factors such as word order and synonyms. The formula for calculating the METEOR score is as follows:

$$METEOR = (1 - penalty) \cdot \frac{P \cdot R}{\alpha P + (1 - \alpha) R} \quad (20)$$

where *penalty* represents the penalty factor for repetitions, P is the precision of word matching, R is the recall of word order matching, and α is the parameter balancing precision and recall.

These metrics collectively provide a comprehensive assessment of the quality of the generated code, considering the accuracy of n-gram matching, content overlap, and word matching, as well as the balance between precision and recall.

4.3 Experimental Environment and Parameters

We implemented the img2code model in PyTorch and optimized it using the AdamW optimization algorithm with a batch size 48 and an initial learning rate set to 0.00005. Additionally, adaptive learning rate adjustment was performed with a learning rate scheduler. The training can be stopped when the model training loss gradually converges after 50 epochs.

Table 2. Scoring results of different models on the pix2code dataset.

Model	Accuracy	BLEU-1	BLEU-2	BLEU-3	BLEU-4	METEOR
pix2code	0.8285	0.8985	0.9218	0.8950	0.8620	0.8246
vanilla model	0.9105	0.9597	0.9761	0.9694	0.9558	0.9412
img2code	0.9560	0.9796	0.9857	0.9797	0.9687	0.9577

Table 3. Scoring results of different models on the img2code dataset.

model	Accuracy	BLEU-1	BLEU-2	BLEU-3	BLEU-4	METEOR
pix2code	0.2471	0.5496	0.5029	0.4485	0.3953	0.3798
vanilla model	0.3686	0.9170	0.8772	0.8227	0.7656	0.7161
img2code	0.4244	0.9254	0.8871	0.8341	0.7780	0.7260

4.4 Comparative Experiments

We compared our img2code model with the pix2code model [2] and additionally conducted ablation experiments on the vanilla model of the img2code model by removing the multimodal information fusion module. Table 2 and Table 3 show the results on the pix2code and img2code datasets respectively.

The experiments show that the img2code model significantly outperforms the pix2code model across multiple evaluation metrics. It demonstrates that employing vision-language models is more effective than traditional methods. At the same time, it is noteworthy that the performance of the img2code model with the addition of the multimodal information fusion module is significantly better than that of the vanilla model. The img2code model is more effective in handling component recognition and their corresponding relationships in GUI screenshots.

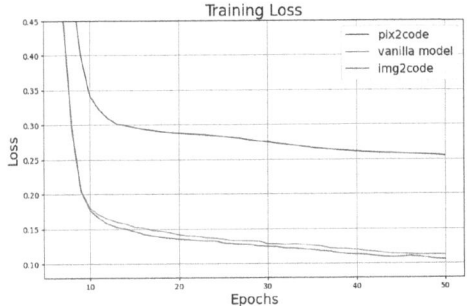

Fig. 6. Training loss of the models.

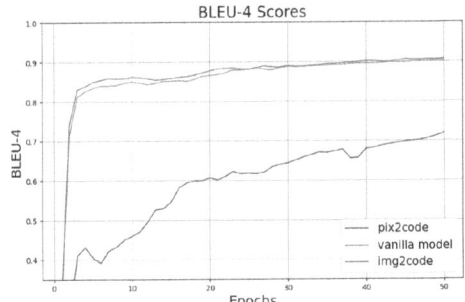

Fig. 7. Validation accuracy of the models.

Figures 6 and 7 show the variations of the training loss and the validation BLEU-4 scores across epochs for each model on the img2code dataset. The img2code converges well on the training loss on the training set and achieves the same verification accuracy faster than the pix2code. When dealing with large-scale datasets, pix2code's training loss convergence value is significantly higher than that of the img2code. It indicates that traditional models have difficulty learning the detailed feature information effectively on complex and large-scale datasets, leading to a significant decrease in the accuracy of the models. The img2code model improves 38% over the pix2code model on the BLUE4 metric. It can effectively learn feature information on complex datasets. The experiments demonstrate that the img2code model with the multimodal information fusion module has good generalization capability and robustness.

5 Conclusion and Prospect

In this paper, we propose img2code, a model based on vision-language models for the end-to-end GUI code generation task. We introduce a multimodal information fusion module with the vision encoder and the language decoder, which successfully fuses the image and code information efficiently, and improves the model's performance and generalization capability. The experimental results demonstrate that the img2code model outperforms traditional models across multiple evaluation metrics.

In future work, we will explore more effective multimodal fusion techniques to handle the alignment of images and code information. Additionally, we plan to utilize more powerful code generation models like CodeGeeX or Code Llama to improve the code generation quality.

References

1. de Souza Baulé, D., von Wangenheim, C.G., von Wangenheim, A., Hauck, J.C.R.: Recent progress in automated code generation from GUI images using machine learning techniques. J. Univers. Comput. Sci. **26**(9), 1095–1127 (2020)
2. Beltramelli, T.: pix2code: generating code from a graphical user interface screenshot. In: Proceedings of the ACM SIGCHI Symposium on Engineering Interactive Computing Systems, pp. 1–6 (2018)
3. Liu, Y., Hu, Q., Shu, K.: Improving pix2code based bi-directional LSTM. In: 2018 IEEE International Conference on Automation, Electronics and Electrical Engineering (AUTEEE), pp. 220–223. IEEE (2018)
4. Zhu, Z., Xue, Z., Yuan, Z.: Automatic graphics program generation using attention-based hierarchical decoder. In: Jawahar, C.V., Li, H., Mori, G., Schindler, K. (eds.) ACCV 2018. LNCS, vol. 11366, pp. 181–196. Springer, Cham (2019). https://doi.org/10.1007/978-3-030-20876-9_12
5. Chen, W.-Y., Podstreleny, P., Cheng, W.-H., Chen, Y.-Y., Hua, K.-L.: Code generation from a graphical user interface via attention-based encoder-decoder model. Multimed. Syst. **28**(1), 121–130 (2022)
6. Vaswani, A., et al.: Attention is all you need. In: Advances in Neural Information Processing Systems, vol. 30 (2017)
7. Li, Y., Amelot, J., Zhou, X., Bengio, S., Si, S.: Auto completion of user interface layout design using transformer-based tree decoders. arXiv preprint arXiv:2001.05308 (2020)
8. He, X., Wang, J., Liu, Z., Xie, L., Wang, H., et al. Automatic generation of frontend code from design interface. In: 2023 13th International Conference on Information Science and Technology (ICIST), pp. 94–99. IEEE (2023)
9. Zhao, W.X., et al. A survey of large language models. arXiv preprint arXiv:2303.18223 (2023)
10. Dosovitskiy, A., et al.: An image is worth 16×16 words: transformers for image recognition at scale. arXiv preprint arXiv:2010.11929 (2020)
11. Zhou, K., Yang, J., Loy, C.C., Liu, Z.: Learning to prompt for vision-language models. Int. J. Comput. Vision **130**(9), 2337–2348 (2022)
12. Xu, K., et al.: Show, attend and tell: neural image caption generation with visual attention. In: International Conference on Machine Learning, pp. 2048–2057. PMLR (2015)

13. Wang, J., et al.: Review of large vision models and visual prompt engineering. Meta-Radiology **1**, 100047 (2023)
14. Luo, Z., Xi, Y., Zhang, R., Ma, J.: A frustratingly simple approach for end-to-end image captioning. arXiv preprint arXiv:2201.12723 (2022)
15. Li, J., Li, D., Savarese, S., Hoi, S.: Blip-2: Bootstrapping language-image pre-training with frozen image encoders and large language models. arXiv preprint arXiv:2301.12597 (2023)
16. Pang, X., Zhou, Y., Li, P., Lin, W., Wu, W., Wang, J.Z.: A novel syntax-aware automatic graphics code generation with attention-based deep neural network. J. Netwo. Comput. Appl. **161**, 102636 (2020)
17. Yong, X., Bo, L., Sun, X., Li, B., Jiang, J., Zhou, W.: image2emmet: automatic code generation from web user interface image. J. Softw. Evol. Process **33**(8), e2369 (2021)
18. Zhang, Z., Ding, Y., Huang, C.: Automatic front-end code generation from image via multi-head attention. In: 2023 4th International Conference on Computer Engineering and Application (ICCEA), pp. 869–872. IEEE (2023)
19. Jin, G.E., Xuesong, L.U.: Automatic generation of web front-end code based on UI images. J. East China Norm. Univ. Nat. Sci. **2023**(5), 100 (2023)
20. Soselia, D., Saifullah, K., Zhou, T.: Reinforcement learning finetuned vision-code transformer for UI-to-code generation. arXiv preprint arXiv:2305.14637 (2023)
21. Li, J., Xu, Y., Lv, T., Cui, L., Zhang, C., Wei, F.: DIT: self-supervised pre-training for document image transformer. In: Proceedings of the 30th ACM International Conference on Multimedia, pp. 3530–3539 (2022)
22. Wang, J., et al.: GIT: a generative image-to-text transformer for vision and language. arXiv preprint arXiv:2205.14100 (2022)
23. Deng, J., Dong, W., Socher, R., Li, L.-J., Li, K., Fei-Fei, L.: Imagenet: a large-scale hierarchical image database. In: 2009 IEEE Conference on Computer Vision and Pattern Recognition, pp. 248–255. IEEE (2009)
24. Parisi, G.I., Kemker, R., Part, J.L., Kanan, C., Wermter, S.: Continual lifelong learning with neural networks: a review. Neural Netw. **113**, 54–71 (2019)
25. Kaushik, P., Gain, A., Kortylewski, A., Yuille, A.: Understanding catastrophic forgetting and remembering in continual learning with optimal relevance mapping. arXiv preprint arXiv:2102.11343 (2021)
26. Papineni, K., Roukos, S., Ward, T., Zhu, W.-J.: BLEU: a method for automatic evaluation of machine translation. In: Proceedings of the 40th Annual Meeting of the Association for Computational Linguistics, pp. 311–318 (2002)
27. Banerjee, S., Lavie, A.: Meteor: an automatic metric for MT evaluation with improved correlation with human judgments. In: Proceedings of the ACL Workshop on Intrinsic and Extrinsic Evaluation Measures for Machine Translation and/or Summarization, pp. 65–72 (2005)

SymMoment: A Symbol Recognition System Using Multiple Moments and Multicore Computing

Zili Zhang[1], Tao Peng[2], Xinrong Hu[3], and Jun Zhang[4(✉)]

[1] School of Computer and Artificial Intelligence, Wuhan Textile University, Wuhan, China
[2] Hubei Provincial Engineering Research Center for Intelligent Textile and Fashion, Wuhan, China
[3] Engineering Research Center of Hubei Province for Clothing Information, Wuhan, China
[4] School of Computer Science and Engineering, Wuhan Institute of Technology, Wuhan, China
zjun@wit.edu.cn

Abstract. Conventional symbol recognition approaches overlook the critical issues of multiple moments and multicore programming. In this study, we develop a symbol recognition system - *SymMoment* - running multiple moments on a multicore processor. *SymMoment* integrates multiple moments to speed up the process of symbol recognition.*SymMoment* optimizes a moment's order through multiple threads in parallel, thereby tremendously boosting system performance. *SymMoment* adopts an open-ended design and; therefore, other moments are readily incorporated as plugins. We make use of 6710 symbol samples to evaluate *SymMoment*. Compared against the popular moments including the *Zernike* and *Tchebichef* moments, *SymMoment* improves the recognition accuracy of the existing moment-based schemes by up to **89.1%** with an average of **52.5%**. *SymMoment*'s multicore computing speeds up the performance by up to **21.1%** with an average of **8.5%**. Furthermore, *SymMoment* reduces the optimization time of the Zernike and Tchebichef moments by averages of **10.1%** and **6.6%**.

Keywords: Symbol Recognition System · Multiple Moments · Multicore Computing · Robustness · Zernike Moments · Tchebichef Moments

1 Introduction

1.1 Motivations

Conventional feature extraction methods for symbol recognition [1,2] include Fourier descriptors, shape signatures, curvature scale space, chain code representations. The existing symbol recognition approaches overlook the critical issues of multiple moments and multicore programming. In this study, we apply multiple-moment-based representations to optimize accuracy and robustness in symbol recognition. We show that in the process of symbol recognition, the *Zernike* [3] and *Tchebichef* [4] moments exhibit compact representation, invariance properties, and robustness to noise. We develop a symbol recognition system called *SymMoment*, at the heart of which are two feature extraction algorithms offering high accuracy and robustness. We optimize *SymMoment*'s system performance by configuring the order of a moment.

Symbol recognition plays an important role in the area of pattern recognition [5–7]. Symbol recognition becomes indispensable for a wide range of applications, including architectural drawings, engineering drawings, maps, circuit diagrams, musical notations, mathematical expressions, to name a few.

In general, symbol recognition methods are classified into three camps, namely, statistical, structural, and hybrid methods. All the three types of methods promise satisfactory overall performance; importantly, descriptors for representing symbols are crucial. Moments, a family of powerful descriptors, are employed in statistical and hybrid methods.

We pay particular attention to the *Zernike* and *Tchebichef* moments, because these two moments have the following three promising characteristics to facilitate the development of our *SymMoment* system. First, compared with other moments, the *Zernike* and *Tchebichef* moments tend to exhibit smaller information redundancy in extracted features. Second, the *Tchebichef* moment is free of approximation errors generated by converting a continuous coordinate space to a discrete image space.

Little attention has been paid toward optimizing the performance of moments-based symbol recognition methods. We are motivated to propose *SymMoment* - an approach to optimizing *Zernike*-based and *Tchebichef*-based symbol recognition systems. Our optimization methods can be extended to any moment-based scheme (e.g., *Krawtchouk* moment [8]).

Profiling the performance of multiple moments (see Sects. 6.1 and 6.2), we discover that the execution time and recognition accuracy largely depend on image sizes and shapes. Regardless of moments, increasing image size enlarges the recognition processing time.

A straightforward way of optimizing accuracy is to profile the moment performance by varying the order in a certain range. This optimization process is time consuming. We are motivated to design a multicore-based algorithm, which assigns multiple profiling tasks to multiple cores to tremendously speed up the optimization procedure,

1.2 Contributions

Our overarching goal is to develop the *SymMoment* system, which executes multiple moments on a multicore system to recognize symbols for a wide range of applications in the architectural and electrical fields. We develop a multi-moment algorithm to significantly improve symbol-recognition performance. We also implement a multicore algorithm to optimize the recognition accuracy of *SymMoment* by tuning a moment's order on a multicore processor.

We evaluate the performance of our *SymMoment* system processing a total of 6710 symbol samples. The experimental results indicate that *SymMoment* improves the symbol-recognition accuracy of the other moment-based schemes by up to **89.12%** with an average of **52.52%**. The multicore-based algorithm speeds up the recognition performance by up to **21.1%** with an average of **8.5%**. *SymMoment* reduces the optimization time of Zernike and Tchebichef by averages of **10.1%** and **6.6%**.

We summarize the six main contributions as follows:

- We develop a symbol recognition system - *SymMoment* - using multiple moments on a multicore processor.
- We implement the multi-moment algorithm to improve symbol-recognition performance.
- We design the multicore algorithm to boost recognition accuracy by adjusting the order of a moment.
- We investigate the feasibility of combining the *Zernike* and *Tchebichef* moments to recognize symbols.
- We conduct an empirical study to assess the impacts of symbol shape and size on system performance.
- We evaluate the performance of *SymMoment* driven by a database comprised of 6710 symbol samples.

The remainder of this paper is organized as follows. In the next section, past research on symbol recognition is reviewed from the viewpoints of statistical, structural, and hybrid methods. Section 3 presents nine moments and their corresponding invariant moments. Multi-moment and multi-core Computing can be found in Sect. 4. Section 5 introduces the evaluation methodology. Section 6 evaluates the performance of *SymMoment* with respect to performance and accuracy. Finally, Sect. 7 concludes this paper with future research directions.

2 Related Work

2.1 Structural-Based Schemes

An increasing number of structural-based methods have been developed to address key issues in symbol recognition. For example, Horne *et al.* [9] proposed an algorithm that segments symbol regions to recognize the symbols in prosthetic vision. Santosh *et al.* [10] employed spatio-structural description of a "vocabulary" of extracted visual elementary parts to recognize symbols.

A handful of prior studies were focused on structural-based approaches to classifying symbols. For example, Coustaty *et al.* [11] proposed using structural signatures and a Galois lattice as a classifier to recognize symbols. The structural signatures consist of three parts: segment extraction, computation of topological graphs, and computation of the structural signature. Deufemia *et al.* [12] proposed a two-stage algorithm to extract features followed by classifying symbol parts. Tirkaz et al. [13] presented a method in which semi-supervised clusters are used to learn the visual appearances of drawings and a supervised step is used to classify objects.

Mathematical symbol recognition [14] introduces challenging issues due to various mathematical symbols and complex background content. To deal with the challenges, Li et al. [15] proposed a descriptor for geometric relationships of line-segment pairs. Because structural approaches are vector-based, some musical score recognition methods [16] have adopted the graph-structure-based strategy.

The drawbacks of the aforementioned structural-based schemes are two-fold. First, the efficiency of the graph matching algorithms (see, for example, [17]) suffers due to a performance bottleneck. Second, these methods are sensitive to error decomposition of symbols. We address the two challenging issues by adopting moments to automatically recognize symbols.

2.2 Statistical-Based Schemes

Let us now analyze the prior research on statistical-based symbol recognition approaches.

Intriguing research on classifying symbols can be found in the literature. For example, Zhang et al. [18] investigated a strategy for similarity measurement of two symbols based on the statistical trait of similar symbols to meet various conditions in symbol recognition. Fornés et al. [19] proposed to apply the dynamic time warping (DTW) algorithm to compute matching distances of symbols, which are classified by the k-nearest neighbor algorithm.

Recently, a handful of studies were focused on handwritten music symbol recognition [20]. For example, Su et al. [21] proposed a neural-network-based approach, which recognizes handwritten digits and music. Miyao and Maruyama [22] developed an online handwritten music symbol recognition system. Subsequently, Hse and Newton's [23] scheme recognizes hand-sketched symbols by means of Zernike moment descriptors.

The disadvantage of the above statistical methods are two-folds. First, some existing statistical schemes are impractical due to their low efficiency. Second, most of the existing solutions become inadequate for symbols with rotation and scale-invariance. Unlike these approaches, our solution exhibits high robustness and low time complexity during the process of recognizing symbols.

2.3 Hybrid Approaches

Hybrid schemes offer the advantages by combining structural-based and statistical-based methods. For example, Visani et al. [24] developed an innovative protocol to improve symbol description from various angles. Santosh et al. [25] adopted attributed relational graphs to construct spatial relations between visual vocabulary elements. Unsupervised clustering approach was applied to capture shape variations within a vocabulary class, thereby advancing the discriminative power.

In general, one descriptor cannot provide perfect discrimination; therefore, several approaches are typically combined to classify symbols. Barrat and Tabbone [26] combined three descriptors and shape measures to classify architectural symbols, thereby obtaining satisfactory results. Delaye and Anquetil [27] investigated a generic representation mechanism that combines dynamic features, visual features, Hu moments, and convex hull features to recognize symbols.

Some of the aforementioned hybrid solutions suffer from high computation overload, whereas the other algorithms lack either extensibility and parallel computing. Compared with the exiting hybrid schemes, our multicore-based and multi-moment-based *SymMoment* system is efficient, domain-independent, and extensible.

3 Moments

3.1 Overview

Descriptors facilitate feature extraction in pattern recognition applications. Evidence indicates that image moments - being able to describe image contents - perform as ideal descriptors [3]. A handful of novel moments have been investigated in recent years. *Non-orthogonal* (see Sect. 3.2) and *orthogonal* moments (see Sect. 3.3) are two image representation mechanisms, which have distinctive properties of moment kernel functions.

Non-orthogonal standard moments include *Hu* moments [28], *complex* moments [29], and *geometric* moments [30]. Orthogonal standard moments are classified into continuous and discrete orthogonal moments. Representative continuous orthogonal moments include *Zernike*, *Pseudo-Zernike* [3], *Legendre* [3], and *Fouire-Mellin* moments [31]. Representative discrete orthogonal moments are *Krawtchouk* and *Tchebichef* moments.

In this study, we apply the *Zernike* (see Sect. 3.4) and *Tchebichef* (see Sect. 3.5) moments to build a symbol recognition system. We also exploit moment invariants of the standard orthogonal and non-orthogonal moments. We show how to optimize system performance by tuning the *Zernike* and *Tchebichef* moments. The notation and symbols used throughout this paper are summarized in Table 1.

3.2 Non-orthogonal Moments

In 1962, Hu [28] proposed the *Hu* moment using algebraic invariants. This moment has desired invariant properties, specifically, translation, scaling, and rotation. Thanks to Hu moment's computational advantages (i.e., only compute seven values), it is widely used for pattern recognition, object classification, template matching, edge detection, robot vision, and data compression. The *complex* moment [29] (see (1)) and *geometric* moment [30] (see (2)) are two fundamental tools constructing other moments.

$$C(p,q) = \int_0^\infty \int_0^{2\pi} r^{p+q+1} e^{i(p-q)\theta} f(r,\theta) dr d\theta. \tag{1}$$

Table 1. Notation, Symbols, and Default Values

Symbol	Meaning	Default Value
p	Order of a moment function	$p \in \mathbb{N}$
q	Order of a moment function	$q \in \mathbb{N}$
r	Polar axis in polar coordinates	$r \in [0,1]$
θ	Polar angle in polar coordinates	$\theta \in [0, 2\pi]$
x	X coordinate	$x \in [0..N]$
y	Y coordinate	$y \in [0..N]$
$f(x,y)$	Intensity functions in Cartesian coordinates	N/A
$f(r,\theta)$	Intensity functions in polar coordinates	N/A
e	Base of the natural logarithm	2.74
i	Imaginary unit	$\sqrt{-1}$
j	Imaginary unit	$\sqrt{-1}$
N	Width of an image	N/A
M	Height of an image	N/A

$$M_{pq} = \sum_{x=1}^{N} \sum_{y=1}^{N} x^p y^q f(x,y). \qquad (2)$$

3.3 Orthogonal Moments

In 1980, Teague [3] proposed orthogonal moments, namely, *Zernike* moment, *Pseudo-Zernike* moment, and *Legendre* moment. Orthogonal moments possess advantages such as robust and minimal redundancy information in moments set. To address these problems, Mukundan et al. [4] proposed discrete *Tchebichef* orthogonal moment (see also Sect. 3.5), which avoids any approximation of continuous integrals without requiring coordinate space transformations.

3.3.1 Legendre Moments

The *Legendre* moment, which has been widely adopted in pattern recognition, is defined in a unit square. The *Legendre* moment function is specified by (3).

$$L_{pq} = \frac{(2p+1)(2q+1)}{4} \int_{-1}^{1} \int_{-1}^{1} P_p(x) P_q(y) f(x,y) dx dy; \qquad (3)$$

where $x, y \in [-1, 1]$;

$$P_p(x) = \sum_{k=0}^{p} \{ (-1)^{\frac{p-k}{2}} \frac{1}{2^p} \frac{(p+k)! x^k}{(\frac{p-k}{2})!(\frac{p+k}{2})!k!} \}. \qquad (4)$$

where $p - k = even$. $P_p(x)$ and $P_q(y)$ are polynomials with respect to x and y, respectively. The key element of both polynomials is ratio of $(p+k)!x^k$ and $(\frac{p-k}{2})!(\frac{p+k}{2})!k!$. The other parameters are found in Table 1.

3.3.2 Orthogonal Fourier-Mellin Moments

The orthogonal *Fourier-Mellin* moment or *OFMM* [31], proposed by Sheng and Arsenault, can be envisioned as a generalized version of the *Zernike* moment and orthogonalized *complex* moment. The *OFMM* function is defined in (5). OFMM is defined in polar coordinates. $Q_p(r)$ is a polynomial with respect to r. The main part of $Q_p(r)$ is the ratio of $(p+k+1)!$ and $(p-k)!k!(k+1)!$. The other parameters are shown in Table 1.

$$FM_{pq} = \frac{p+1}{\pi} \int_0^{2\pi} \int_0^1 Q_p(r)e^{-jq\theta} f(r,\theta) r dr d\theta, \qquad (5)$$

where

$$Q_p(r) = \sum_{k=0}^{p} (-1)^{p+k} \frac{(p+k+1)!}{(p-k)!k!(k+1)!} r^k. \qquad (6)$$

where $p = 0, 1, 2, ..., \infty$; $|q| \geq 0$; $\theta = tan^{-1}(y/x)$.

In 2010, Zhang et al. [32] constructed a complete set of *OFMM* invariants with scale and rotation invariant properties.

3.3.3 Krawtchouk Moments

The *Krawtchouk* moment [8], proposed by Yap et al., is a well-known discrete orthogonal moment. The *Krawtchouk* moment obtains local information by tuning parameters p_1 and p_2. Its moment function is given as follows (see (7)).

$$Q_{nm} = \sum_{x=0}^{N-1} \sum_{y=0}^{M-1} \bar{K}_n(x; p_1, N-1) \bar{K}_m(y; p_2, M-1) f(x,y); \qquad (7)$$

$$\bar{K}_n(x; p, N) = K_n(x; p, N) \sqrt{\frac{\omega(x; p, N)}{\rho(n; p, N)}}; \qquad (8)$$

$$K_n(x; p, N) = \sum_{k=0}^{n} \frac{(-n)_k (-x)_k}{(-N)_k} \frac{(\frac{1}{p})^k}{k!}; \qquad (9)$$

$x, n = 0, 1, 2, ..., N$; $p \in (0, 1)$;

$$\omega(x; p, N) = \binom{N}{x} p^x (1-p)^{N-x}; \qquad (10)$$

$$\rho(n; p, N) = (-1)^n \left(\frac{1-p}{p}\right)^n \frac{n!}{(-N)_n}; \qquad (11)$$

$n, m = 1, 2, ..., N$; $(a)_k$ is the Pochhammer symbol, as defined in Eq. 12:

$$(a)_k = a(a+1)...(a+k-1); \qquad (12)$$

These formats consist of permutation factors. The other parameters are shown in Table 1.

3.4 Zernike Moments

The *Zernike* and *Pseudo-Zernike* moments are limited in a unit circle. The functions of the *Zernike* and *Pseudo-Zernike* moments are specified by (13) and (15), respectively.

$$A_{pq} = \frac{p+1}{\pi} \int\int_D f(x,y) V_{pq}^*(x,y) dx dy, \qquad (13)$$

In (13), $V_{pq}^*(x,y)$ are complex conjugates of *Zernike* functions. In (14), the key part of $V_{pq}(x,y)$ is the ratio of $(-1)^s(p-s)! r^{p-2s}$ and $s!(\frac{p+|q|}{2} - s)!(\frac{(p-|q|)}{2} - s)!$.

$$V_{pq}(x,y) = \sum_{s=0}^{(p-|q|)/2} \frac{(-1)^s (p-s)! r^{p-2s}}{s!(\frac{p+|q|}{2} - s)!(\frac{(p-|q|)}{2} - s)!} e^{jq\theta}, \qquad (14)$$

where $0 \leq |q| \leq p$; $p - |q| = even$; $\theta = tan^{-1}(y/x)$; $r = \sqrt{x^2 + y^2}$.

$$Z_{pq} = \frac{p+1}{\pi} \int_0^{2\pi} \int_0^1 V_{pq}^*(r,\theta) f(r,\theta) r dr d\theta, \qquad (15)$$

where $0 \leq |q| \leq p$; $*$ denotes complex conjugate; $V_{pq}(r,\theta)$ is defined in (16).

$$V_{pq}(r,\theta) = \sum_{s=0}^{p-|q|} \frac{(-1)^k (2p+1-s)! r^{p-s}}{s!(p-|q|-s)!(p+|q|+1-s)!} e^{jq\theta}. \qquad (16)$$

The other parameters are shown in Table 1.

3.5 Tchebichef Moments

Similar to the *Krawtchouk* moment, the *Tchebichef* moment proposed by Mukundan et al. is a discrete orthogonal moment [4]. The *Tchebichef* moment function is defined in (17).

$$T_{pq} = \frac{1}{\tilde{\rho}(p,N)\tilde{\rho}(q,N)} \sum_{x=0}^{N-1} \sum_{y=0}^{N-1} \tilde{t}_p(x)\tilde{t}_q(y) f(x,y); \qquad (17)$$

In (18), $\tilde{\rho}(n,N)$ is a ratio of $\beta(n,N)$ and $\rho(n,N)$. In (19), $\rho(n,N)$ is the product of $(2n)!$ and $\binom{N+n}{2n+1}$.

$$\tilde{\rho}(n,N) = \frac{\rho(n,N)}{\beta(n,N)^2}; \qquad (18)$$

$$\rho(n,N) = (2n)! \binom{N+n}{2n+1}; \qquad (19)$$

where $n = 0, 1, ..., N-1$.

In (20), $\beta(n,N)$ is derived as N to the power of n (i.e., $\beta(n,N) = N^n$).

$$\beta(n,N) = N^n; \qquad (20)$$

$$\tilde{t}_n(x) = \frac{t_n(x)}{\beta(n,N)}; \qquad (21)$$

$$t_n(x) = n! \sum_{k=0}^n (-1)^{n-k} \binom{N-1-k}{n-k} \binom{n+k}{n} \binom{x}{k}; \qquad (22)$$

The other parameters are shown in Table 1.

4 Multi-moment and Multicore Computing

4.1 System Design

Figure 1 outlines the system framework of *SymMoment*, which takes images as input files to recognition symbols. At the heart of *SymMoment*, there are three key modules - the feature extraction module, the classification module, and the performance evaluation module.

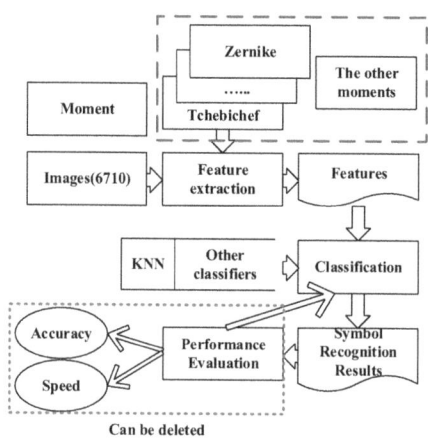

Fig. 1. The framework of the *SymMoment* system.

The Feature Extraction Module: The implementation of feature extraction relies on moments (see Sect. 3), which capture features from input symbols.

The Classification Module: The input data of the classification module is a feature file generated by the above feature extraction module.

The Performance Evaluation Module: The purpose of the performance evaluation module is to assess the symbol-recognition speed and accuracy of the *SymMoment* system (see Sect. 6 for evaluation results).

4.2 Integrating Multiple Moments

SymMoment seamlessly integrates multiple moments and moment invariants running on a multicore system. *SymMoment* is comprised of the standard-moment-based schemes as well as the invariant-moment-based schemes. The nine standard moments implemented in *SymMoment* include *Complex* moment (CM), *Geometric* moment (GM), *Tchebichef* moment (TM), *Zernike* moment (ZM), *Orthogonal Fourier Mellin* moment (*OFMM*), *Legendre* moment (LM), *Radial Tchebichef* moment (RTM) [33], and *Pseudo-Zernike* moment (PZM), and *Krawtchouk* moment (KM).

Apart from standard moments, *SymMoment* also embraces seven moment invariants, including *Hu* moment (HM), *Legendre* Translation Invariants moment(LTI) [34], *Radial Tchebichef* moment invariant (RTMI) [35], *Pseudo-Zernike* scale moment invariant (PZSMI) [36], *Orthogonal Fourier Mellin* moment invariant (OFMMI) [32], and *Zernike* Translation moment invariant (ZTMI) [37].

SymMoment is extensible in the way that the other moments can be readily integrated into the system as plug-in modules.

4.3 Improving Performance with Multiple Moments

4.3.1 Basic Idea of Multi-moment Computing

Recall that some moments are more sensitive to image sizes and shapes than their counterparts. For example, the *Tchebichef* moments are more sensitive to image size and shape than the *Zernike* moments (see Sect. 6.3).

Table 2. Notation for Algorithms 1 (see Sect. 4.3.2) and 2 (see Sect. 4.4.2).

Symbol	Meaning	Symbol	Meaning
s	Symbol	SD	Symbol database
m	Moment	M	Moment set
t_m	Thread for moment m	p	59 Symbol template
f_m	Features by the fastest thread	tf	A template feature file
sc	Symbol class	SS	Standard symbol set
mr	Maximal rate	oo	Optimal order

We design a multi-moment-based algorithm running on a multicore processor to speed up the recognition process for symbols with uncertain size and shape. Each core may focus on a single moment to independently recognize symbols; thus, a multi-core system (e.g., four cores) is able to handle multiple moments in parallel. When one moment is finished by a core, a notification is delivered to all the other cores to terminate their computing. Such terminations allow *SymMoment* to improve system utilization by allocating computing resources to process other symbols. Table 2 summarizes the notation used in Algorithm 1 (see Sect. 4.3.2) and Algorithm 2 (see Sect. 4.4.2).

4.3.2 The Multi-moment Algorithm

Algorithm 1 illustrates the pseudo-code of multi-moment computing, where multiple moments are concurrently running. The algorithm starts by loading template features p from a file tf (see Line 3). The template features facilitate symbol recognition (see Line 12). Multiple threads are created during the initialization phase (see Lines 5–7).

Algorithm 1. Improving Performance with Multiple Moments.

1: **Input:** tf-template features, SD-symbol database, M-moment set
2: **Output:** sc-symbol class
3: $p \leftarrow features\_read(tf)$; /* load template features from a file */
4: **for all** $s \in SD$ **do**
5:    **for all** $m \in M$ **do**
6:       $t_m \leftarrow thread\_create()$; /* create/run moment thread t_m */
7:    **end for**
8:    **for all** threads except the current thread **do**
9:       $thread\_cancel(t_m), m \in M$; /* terminate other slow thread */
10:    **end for**
11:    Synchronize all threads;
12:    $sc \leftarrow symbol\_recognize(f_m, p)$; /*$p$ is template, f_m is in Table 2*/
13: **end for**

Once all the threads are constructed, the threads concurrently handles multiple moments. After the fastest thread completes its moment calculation, all the other slow and unfinished threads are immediately terminated (see Lines 8–10). The synchronization phase occurs in Line 11, followed by symbol recognition (Line 12) using the template features (Line 3) and those extracted by the multiple cores (Lines 4–10).

4.4 Improving Accuracy with Multi-core Computing

4.4.1 Basic Idea of Optimizing Accuracy

The orders of moments impose vital impacts on recognition rates. The terms recognition rate and accuracy are used interchangeably throughout this paper. Given a moment, *SymMoment* aims to determine an optimal order that leads to a high accuracy.

4.4.2 The Multicore Computing Algorithm

The pseudo-code of optimizing recognition accuracy on a multicore process can be found in Algorithm 2. This algorithm takes a list of candidate orders as an input; the algorithm outputs the maximal recognition rate and an optimal order.

In the initialization phase, the algorithm loads the standard symbols as well as a symbol database (see Lines 3–4), followed by the creation of the multiple threads (see Line 6). Each thread is in charge of evaluating the accuracy of a moment configured with a candidate order (see Lines 7–12). Line 13 is a synchronization point, where the parent thread waits for all the child threads to produce recognition rates. Next, the parent thread choose the maximal rate among all the rates offered by the child thread (see Lines 15-20). Finally, Line 21 returns the maximal rate and optimal order kept in mr and oo (see Lines 15 and 18).

Algorithm 2. Improving Accuracy on Multi-core Processors.

1: **Input:** CO-candidate orders;
2: **Output:** mr-maximal recognition rate, oo-optimal order
3: $SS \leftarrow standard\_symbol\_load()$
4: $SD \leftarrow symbol\_database\_load()$
5: **for all** candidate order $o \in CO$ **do**
6:    $t\_o \leftarrow thread\_create()$; /* create and run thread t_o */
7:    $P\_o \leftarrow standard\_symbol\_feature\_extract(o, SS)$
8:    **for all** $s \in SD$ **do**
9:       $s\_o \leftarrow symbol\_feature\_extract(o, s)$;
10:      $sc\_o \leftarrow symbol\_recognize(s\_o, P\_o)$;
11:    **end for**
12:    $r\_o \leftarrow recognition\_rate\_compute(sc)$; /*$sc$-symbol class*/
13:    $thread\_wait(t\_o)$, $o \in CO$; /* wait for all the threads */
14: **end for**
15: $mr \leftarrow 0$; $oo \leftarrow 1$;
16: **for all** $o \in CO$ **do**
17:    **if** $r\_o > mr$ **then**
18:       $mr \leftarrow r\_o$; $oo \leftarrow o$;
19:    **end if**
20: **end for**
21: $return(mr, oo)$;

5 Evaluation Methodology

5.1 Experimental Environment

We design experiments (see Sect. 6) to demonstrate that the *SymMoment* system shortens symbol-recognition time while optimizing recognition accuracy.

We run *SymMoment* on a multicore server with two Xeon(R) X5650 @2.80GHz (4 cores) CPUs, 12 GB DDR3 memory, the Intel X58 Chipset Mainboard, and West Digital's Enterprise WD1002FBYS SATA2 disks. The operating system is CentOS 7.0 X86 64 (Kernel 2.6.32).

5.2 Datasets and Experiment Groups

To conduct an overall performance evaluation, we make use of the data obtained from the GREC'03 symbol recognition contest[1] to drive our tests. Figure 2 shows the tested dataset that contains a total of 59 ideal models, where linear symbols are made of lines, arcs, and simple geometric primitives. These symbols cover two application domains, namely, architectural and electronics.

We conduct extensive experiments, where we process the five image groups (see Table 3).

---

[1] http://www.cvc.uab.es/grec2003/SymRecContest/index.htm.

Table 3. The five image groups evaluated in our experiments.

Group	Image Type	Notation
Group 1	Sample Scanned Images	SSI
Group 2	Binary Degradations	BD
Group 3	Binary Degradations and Vectorial Distortions	$BDVD$
Group 4	Vectorial Distortions	VD
Group 5	Standard	N/A

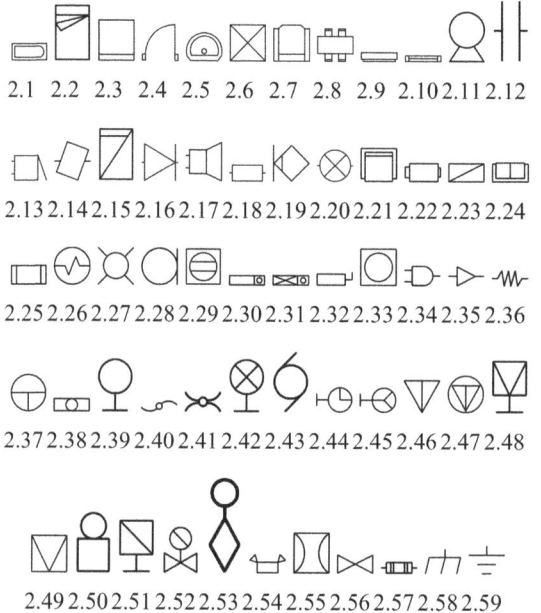

Fig. 2. Ideal Models

5.3 Evaluation Metrics

We consider two performance metrics. The first metric is symbol-recognition accuracy RA. The second one is recognition speed RS measured in the unit of millisecond. Recognition speed is the summation of the feature extraction and classification times; which approximately equal to feature extraction namely.

6 Experimental Results

6.1 Standard Moments

We compared the results obtained for nine standard moments in the five groups of images.

SSI: Table 4 shows that for the degraded images in Level 0, ZM has the highest accuracy; for the degraded images in Level 1, TM, ZM and RTM share the same accuracy. The accuracy of CM is the lowest among its peers.

Table 4. Recognition rates of standard moments (%)

Moments		CM	GM	TM	ZM	OFMM	RTM	PZM	KM	LM
SSI	Level 0	43.3	53.3	95.0	**98.3**	73.3	93.3	86.7	65.0	86.7
	Level 1	41.7	45.0	**95.0**	**95.0**	60.0	**95.0**	85.0	45.0	68.3
BD	Set 1	24.2	22.2	77.2	**77.8**	23.9	45.6	51.0	47.2	33.3
	Set 2	21.7	22.1	88.9	**90.2**	22.7	47.7	52.7	61.9	29.6
BDVD	Level 1	9.3	7.7	**89.4**	72.6	4.1	27.7	35.3	47.9	14.6
	Level 2	9.3	7.0	**86.9**	76.8	2.7	25.4	49.0	56.2	12.1
	Level 3	8.3	9.3	**83.0**	77.0	4.2	19.9	35.2	42.2	12.5
VD	Set 1	7.3	9.6	**77.6**	77.3	2.7	36.7	51.8	57.6	16.4
	Set 2	3.7	3.7	39.3	**46.4**	11.4	35.9	31.6	37.9	17.4
Standard		100	100	100	100	100	100	100	100	100
Mean Rate		16.3	16.3	**84.5**	81.6	15.4	39.1	47.8	55.4	23.7

BD: The noise in this group is simulated and generated by scanning, printing, and photocopying. ZM has the highest accuracy rate, whereas TM is a runner up. GM and OFMM have the lowest recognition rates, meaning that these moments are sensitive to noise.

BDVD: There are 2430 degraded and distorted images. Table 4 reveals that TM is the best moment across all the three levels. ZM is in the second place, whereas OFMM and GM are the worst two on the list.

VD: In this test, images simulate the chirography of people's handwriting.

Table 4 shows that the rotation and scale-rotation images have the lowest recognition rate. In Set 1, KM exhibits the highest rate among the rotation images; RTM - a radial moment function - has the highest rate among scale-rotation images. The runner ups in sets 1 and 2 are ZM and TM, respectively. Again, OFMM and GM are at the bottom of the ranking list.

Standard: Table 4 shows that the accuracies of all the moments are 100% when there is no degradation.

6.2 Invariant Moments

Now we compare the performance of moment invariants (see also Sect. 4.2).

SSI: As shown in Table 5, *ZTMI* outperforms all the other competitors at Levels 0 and 1. *LTI*'s performance is the worst among its peers.

Table 5. Recognition rates of the invariant moments (%)

Moments		HM	LTI	RTMI	PZSMI	KMI	OFMMI	ZTMI
SSI	L0	70.0	20.0	35.0	95.0	85.0	65.0	**100**
	L1	50.0	25.0	30.0	91.7	91.7	60.0	**95.0**
BD	S1	18.3	32.8	21.7	34.4	48.3	**72.2**	61.1
	S2	12.8	21.9	25.4	33.0	41.3	58.1	**60.8**
BDVD	L1	0.6	18.3	13.6	16.3	19.9	29.9	**48.6**
	L2	0.9	5.7	6.5	22.0	12.6	38.2	**64.3**
	L3	1	8.0	7.3	11.7	19.0	27.5	**50.4**
VD	S1	3.8	11.8	16.0	16.9	16.2	35.1	**57.6**
	S2	10.8	8.6	12.0	15.4	4.3	**22.8**	5.1
Standard		100	100	100	100	100	100	100
Mean Rate		9.5	17.4	18.9	26.8	30.5	46.0	**56.4**

BD: Table 5 shows that when it comes to the BD images, *OFMMI* and *ZTMI* are the winners in *set 1* and *set 2*, respectively. In both sets, *HM* is the worst moment. The standard moment ZM - the best one for the BD images - is noticeably superior to the winning invariant moments (i.e., *OFMMI* and *ZTMI*).

BDVD: Like the SSI case, in the BDVD case the best invariant moment at all the three levels is *ZTMI* (see Table 5). HM is the worst invariant moment (i.e., rate < 1%).

VD: Table 5 reveals that *ZTMI* delivers the highest rates for the three distortion images (i.e., 57.6% in set 1); however, *ZTMI* is inappropriate for recognizing the VD images (i.e., 5.1% in set 2). Interestingly, all the invariant moments obtain fairly poor results for set 2.

No Degradation: Like the standard moments, the invariant moments exhibit expected symbol recognition behaviors for the images without degradations. The results for this group of experiments can be found in Table 5.

Stand Moments vs. Invariant Moments: The total average rates of all the invariant moments are listed in Table 5. With the highest rate at the level of 56.4%, we conclude that invariant moments have extremely poor performance. Among all the standard moments, *TM* and *ZM* achieve a recognition rate as high as 84.5% and 81.6%, respectively.

6.3 Performance Improvements with Multiple Moments

Overall Improvements: Table 6 shows the execution times of *SymMoment* coupled with the TM- and ZM-based approaches (i.e., *TM* and *ZM*). Here, we refer to symbols 9, 10, 21, and 29 in Fig. 2 as $s1$, $s2$, $s3$, and $s4$, respectively, recognized to test the performance of multi-moment computing. *TM* processes

$s1$ and $s2$ fast, whereas the ZM-based scheme or *ZM* efficiently handles $s3$ and $s4$. Importantly, when these two group symbols are exchanged or all the four symbols are jointly tested, *SymMoment*'s multi-moment computing starts earning its superiority over *TM* and *ZM*.

Table 6. Performance improvements of *SymMoment* over the ZM- and TM-based approaches.

Symbols	s1+s2	s3+s4	s1+s3	s2+s4	s1+s4	s2+s3	s1-s4
ZM	449.9	445.6	450.0	445.5	448.6	446.8	447.7
TM	388.3	617.1	483.7	521.6	519.3	486.1	502.7
MM	386.7	445.6	416.4	415.9	415.1	417.2	416.1
Impr._ZM	14.0%	0%	6.9%	6.6%	7.5%	6.6%	7.1%
Impr._TM	0.4%	27.8%	13.9%	20.3%	20.1%	14.2%	17.2%

The results listed in Table 6 show that *SymMoment*'s capacity of multi-moment computing noticeably speeds up the performance of *ZM* and *TM* in 12 out of all the 14 test cases. For example, *SymMoment* improves ZM and TM by up to 14.0% and 27.8% with averages of 7.0% and 16.2%, respectively.

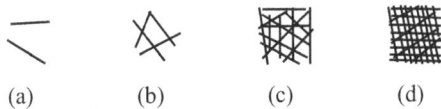

Fig. 3. Four synthetic symbols to evaluate the impacts of shapes on *SymMoment*, the ZM- and TM-based schemes.

Impacts of Symbol Shape on Performance: To evaluate the impacts of symbol shapes on *SymMoment*, the ZM- and TM-based schemes, we test the execution times of the three approaches processing four synthetic symbols ranging from simple to complicated ones (see Fig. 3). The size of each symbol is 512 by 512 pixels.

Figure 4 shows that *SymMoment* outperforms of ZM and TM in most cases; *SymMoment* and ZM share similar performance when it comes to symbols c and d. Table 7 clearly indicates that on average *SymMoment* shortens the execution times of ZM and TM by 9.0% and 35.0%.

Figure 4 also illustrates that the execution times of *SymMoment* and TM go up when we increase the complexity of symbol shape; the opposite is true for ZM. We observe that TM is a whole lot more sensitive to symbol shape than SymMoment and ZM.

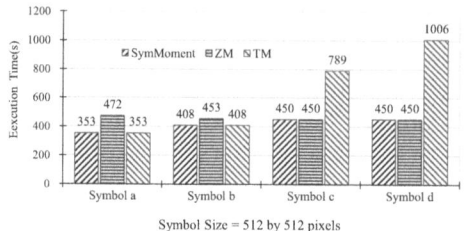

Fig. 4. Performance improvements of *SymMoment* over the Zernike (ZM) and Tchebichef (TM) moments in the cases of four synthetic symbols ranging from simple (symbol a in Fig. 3(a)) to complicated ones (symbol d in Fig. 3(d)).

Table 7. Average performance improvements of *SymMoment* over the Zernike (ZM) and Tchebichef (TM) moments under various symbol complexities. Std Dev: Standard Deviation. Mean EXE_T: execution time.

Moments	ZM	TM	SymMoment
Mean EXE_T	456.1(ms)	638.8(ms)	415.1(ms)
Std Dev.	10.5	312.2	46.2
Improvement	9.0%	35.0%	–

Impacts of Symbol Size on Performance: Now we process symbols in Fig. 3(a) and 3(c) to test the impacts of symbol size on the performance of *SymMoment*. We set the size of each symbol as 256 by 256, 512 by 512, and 896 by 896 pixels, respectively. Figure 5 reveals that in 10 out of 12 cases, *SymMoment* is superior to ZM and TM. We observe from Table 8 that SymMoment speeds up the performance of ZM and TM by averages of 14.1% and 28.7%, respectively.

Figure 5 indicates that symbol size has noticeable impacts on all the three schemes. In particular, regardless of the shape complexity, the improvement of *SymMoment* over TM becomes pronounced when symbol size grows.

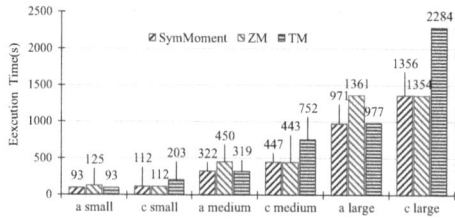

Fig. 5. Performance improvements of *SymMoment* over the Zernike (ZM) and Tchebichef (TM) moments in the cases of two synthetic symbols with varied size. a: symbol a, b: symbol b, c: symbol c. Small size:256 by 256 pixels, medium size: 512 by 512 pixels, large size 896 by 896 pixels.

Table 8. Average performance improvements of *SymMoment* over the Zernike (ZM) and Tchebichef (TM) moments under various symbol size. Std Dev: Standard Deviation. Mean EXE_T: execution time.

Moments	ZM	TM	Multi-moment
Means EXE_T	640.8(ms)	771.7(ms)	550.2(ms)
Std Dev.	574.1	814.7	508.0
Improvement	14.1%	28.7%	–

Table 9. Improvement of total time

Symbols	SSI		BD		BDVD			VD		Standard
	Level 0	Level 1	Set 1	Set 2	Level 1	Level 2	Level 3	Set 1	Set 2	
Number	60	60	180	3120	810	810	810	450	351	59
Totaltime_ZM(ms)	26592	26580	79543	1385509	358649	236598	237989	358925	358883	26215
Totaltime_TM(ms)	24359	24251	70202	1355107	350537	238763	217832	354776	402826	24797
Totaltime_multicore(ms)	23902	23829	66450	1247735	322133	222163	208621	325428	333751	23732
STD EV_ZM	8.1	8.1	10.8	12.4	11.4	226.5	322.6	12.2	9.8	11.3
STD EV_TM	51.6	49.9	104.7	98.2	97.3	224.2	326.6	95.9	178.2	70.9
STD EV_multicore	40.3	39.6	77.7	51.8	54.7	208.8	300.9	54.5	46.7	46.1
Improvement_ZM	10.1%	10.4%	16.5%	9.9%	10.2%	6.1%	12.3%	9.3%	7.0%	9.5%
Improvement_TM	1.9%	1.7%	5.3%	7.9%	8.1%	7.0%	4.2%	8.3%	17.2%	4.3%

Table 9 highlights the performance improvements of SymMoment over ZM and TM. We set the order of ZM and TM to 32 and 20, because the accuracy of ZM and TM are maximized under these two orders. The results confirm that SymMoment boosts the processing speeds of ZM and TM in all the image groups.

Table 10. Features fusion of TM and ZM (%).

Symbols	SSI	BD		BDVD			VD		Standard	Mean Rate
		Set 1	Set 2	Level 1	Level 2	Level 3	Set 1	Set 2		
TM+ZM	100	79.4	83.6	88.5	91.1	87.0	**80.9**	41.9	100	88.4
TM		95.0	**80.0**	**94.6**	**90.7**	**91.2**	**91.1**	80.7	40.2	100	**89.1**
ZM		97.5	78.9	89.3	76.7	83.6	83.8	77.6	**43.6**	100	83.2

6.4 Optimizing Performance and Accuracy

Combining TM and ZM: We evaluate the idea of combining two moments to improve accuracy. We consider TM and ZM in this experiment, because these two moments are outstanding among their peers. Table 10 shows combining TM and ZM achieves SSI recognition rate of 100%, which is better than the two individual moments. However, in the other subgroups, the combination of the two moments exhibit no superiority (Table 11).

Table 11. Comparison of original and fast methods

Orders	2	4	6	8	10
Original Method	10015	23095	40670	61402	91058
Fast Method	1529	3276	6302	8970	13541
Orders	12	14	16	18	20
Original Method	122491	161351	208635	250661	303795
Fast Method	18315	23509	31690	37066	45519

7 Conclusion

In this study, we developed the *SymMoment* system running multiple moments on a multicore processor to recognize symbols. We designed a multi-moment algorithm to significantly speed up the process of symbol recognition. To optimize recognition accuracy, we implemented a multicore algorithm in *SymMoment* to evaluate a moment's order through multiple threads in parallel. *SymMoment* is an open-ended platform, because other moments are readily incorporated in our system as plugins.

Testing a total of 6710 symbol samples, we evaluated *SymMoment* by comparing it with the popular moments including the *Zernike* and *Tchebichef* moments. The extensive experiments confirm that *SymMoment* improves the accuracy of the existing moment-based schemes by up to **89.12%** with an average of **52.52%**. The multicore-based algorithm in *SymMoment* speeds up the performance by up to **21.1%** with an average of **8.5%**. Importantly, *SymMoment* shortens the optimization time of *Zernike* and *Tchebichef* by averages of **10.1%** and **6.6%**.

References

1. Keysers, D., Deselaers, T., Rowley, H.A., Wang, L.L., Carbune, V.: Multi-language online handwriting recognition. IEEE Trans. Pattern Anal. Mach. Intell. **39**(6), 1180–1194 (2017)
2. Sakshi, Vinay, K.: A retrospective study on handwritten mathematical symbols and expressions: classification and recognition. Eng. Appl. Artif. Intell. **103**(104292), 1–32 (2021)
3. Kaur, P., Pannu, H.S., Malhi, A.K.: Comprehensive study of continuous orthogonal moments-a systematic review. ACM Comput. Surv. **2**(4), 67:1–67:30 (2019)

4. Mukundan, R., Ong, S.H., Lee, P.A.: Image analysis by Tchebichef moments. IEEE Trans. Image Process. **10**(9), 1357–1364 (2001)
5. Kherallah, M., Bouri, F., Alimi, A.M.: On-line Arabic handwriting recognition system based on visual encoding and genetic algorithm. Eng. Appl. Artif. Intell. **22**(1), 153–170 (2009)
6. Surinta, O., Karaaba, M.F., Schomaker, L.R.B., Wiering, M.A.: Recognition of handwritten characters using local gradient feature descriptors. Eng. Appl. Artif. Intell. **45**, 405–414 (2015)
7. Zaiz, F., Babahenini, M.C., Djeffal, A.: Puzzle based system for improving Arabic handwriting recognition. Eng. Appl. Artif. Intell. **56**, 222–229 (2016)
8. Yap, P.-T., Paramesran, R., Ong, S.-H.: Image analysis by krawtchouk moments. IEEE Trans. Image Process. **12**(11), 1367–1377 (2003)
9. Lachlan, H., Nick, B., Chris, M., He, X.: Image segmentation for enhancing symbol recognition in prosthetic vision. Conf. Proc. IEEE Eng. Med. Biol. Soc. **2012**, 2792–2795 (2012)
10. Santosh, K.C., Lamiroy, B., Wendling, L.: Symbol recognition using spatial relations. Pattern Recogn. Lett. **33**(3), 331–341 (2012)
11. Coustaty, M., Bertet, K., Visani, M., Ogier, J.-M.: A new adaptive structural signature for symbol recognition by using a Galois lattice as a classifier. IEEE Trans. Syst. Man Cybern. Part B **41**(4), 1136–1148 (2011)
12. Deufemia, V., Risi, M., Tortora, G.: Sketched symbol recognition using latent-dynamic conditional random fields and distance-based clustering. Pattern Recogn. **47**(3), 1159–1171 (2014)
13. Tirkaz, C., Yanikoglu, B.A., Metin Sezgin, T.: Sketched symbol recognition with auto-completion. Pattern Recogn. **45**(11), 3926–3937 (2012)
14. Jin-Wen, W., Yin, F., Zhang, Y.-M., Zhang, X.-Y., Liu, C.-L.: Handwritten mathematical expression recognition via paired adversarial learning. Int. J. Comput. Vision **128**(6), 2386–2401 (2020)
15. Li, T., Shu, B., Qiu, X., Wang, Z.: A complete descriptor of line-segment-pair for symbol recognition. In: Proceedings of the 2009 Computer Graphics International Conference, CGI 2009, p. 89C95, New York, NY, USA, 2009. Association for Computing Machinery (2009)
16. Na In Seop and Kim Soo Hyung: Music symbol recognition by a lag-based combination model. Multimed. Tools Appl. **76**(24), 25563–25579 (2017)
17. Lladós, J., Martí, E., Villanueva, J.J.: Symbol recognition by error-tolerant subgraph matching between region adjacency graphs. IEEE Trans. Pattern Anal. Mach. Intell. **23**(10), 1137–1143 (2001)
18. Zhang, W., Wenyin, L., Zhang, K.: Symbol recognition with kernel density matching. IEEE Trans. Pattern Anal. Mach. Intell. **28**(12), 2020–2024 (2006)
19. Fornés, A., Lladós, J., Sánchez, G., Karatzas, D.: Rotation invariant hand-drawn symbol recognition based on a dynamic time warping model. Int. J. Doc. Anal. Recogn. (IJDAR) **13**(3), 229–241 (2010)
20. Alfaro-Contreras, M., Valero-Mas, J.J.: Exploiting the two-dimensional nature of agnostic music notation for neural optical music recognition. Appl. Sci. **11**(3621), 1–16 (2021)
21. Chun, S.M., Hua, C.H., Chi, C.W.: A neural network based approach to optical symbol recognition. Neural Process. Lett. **15**(2), 117–135 (2002)
22. Hidetoshi, M., Minoru, M.: An online handwritten music symbol recognition system. Int. J. Doc. Anal. Recogn. (IJDAR) **9**(1), 49–58 (2007)
23. Hse, H.H., Newton, A.R.: Sketched symbol recognition using Zernike moments. In: ICPR (1), pp. 367–370 (2004)

24. Visani, M., Terrades, O.R., Tabbone, S.: A protocol to characterize the descriptive power and the complementarity of shape descriptors. Int. J. Doc. Anal. Recogn. (IJDAR) **14**(1), 87–100 (2011)
25. Santosh, K.C., Lamiroy, B., Wendling, L.: Integrating vocabulary clustering with spatial relations for symbol recognition. Int. J. Doc. Anal. Recogn. (IJDAR) **17**(1), 61–78 (2014)
26. Barrat, S., Tabbone, S.: A Bayesian network for combining descriptors: application to symbol recognition. Int. J. Doc. Anal. Recogn (IJDAR) **13**(1), 65–75 (2010)
27. Delaye, A., Anquetil, É.: Hbf49 feature set: a first unified baseline for online symbol recognition. Pattern Recogn. **46**(1), 117–130 (2013)
28. Ming-Kuei, H.: Visual pattern recognition by moment invariants. IRE Trans. Inf. Theory **8**(2), 179–187 (1962)
29. Davis, P.J.: Plane regions determined by complex moments. J. Approx. Theory **19**(2), 148–153 (1977)
30. Papakostas, G.A., Karakasis, E.G., Koulouriotis, D.E.: Efficient and accurate computation of geometric moments on gray-scale images. Pattern Recogn. **41**(6), 1895–1904 (2008)
31. Sheng, Y., Arsenault, H.H.: Experiments on pattern recognition using invariant Fourier-Mellin descriptors. J. Opt. Soc. Am. A. **3**(6), 771–776 (1986)
32. Zhang, H., Shu, H.Z., Haigron, P., Li, B.-S., Luo, L.M.: Construction of a complete set of orthogonal Fourier-Mellin moment invariants for pattern recognition applications. Image Vision Comput. **28**(1), 38–44 (2010)
33. Mukundan, R.: Radial Tchebichef invariants for pattern recognition. In: TENCON 2005 2005 IEEE Region 10, pp. 1–6. IEEE (2005)
34. Chong, C.-W., Raveendran, P., Mukundan, R.: Translation and scale invariants of Legendre moments. Pattern Recogn. **37**(1), 119–129 (2004)
35. Xiao, B., Ma, J.-F., Tao Cui, J. Invariant pattern recognition using radial Tchebichef moments. In: 2010 Chinese Conference on Pattern Recognition, pp. 1–5. IEEE (2003)
36. Chong, C.-W., Raveendran, P., Mukundan, R.: The scale invariants of pseudo-Zernike moments. Pattern Anal. Appl. **6**(3), 176–184 (2003)
37. Chong, C.-W., Raveendran, P., Mukundan, R.: Translation invariants of Zernike moments. Pattern Recogn. **36**(8), 1765–1773 (2003)

DBFF-PCGC: Dual-Branch Feature Fusion for Point Cloud Geometry Compression

Shiyu Lu[1], Cheng Han[1(✉)], Huamin Yang[1(✉)], and Fudong Yu[2]

[1] Changchun University of Science and Technology, Changchun, Jilin, China
{hancheng,yanghuamin}@cust.edu.cn
[2] Jilin Zhongnong Sunshine Data Co., Ltd., Changchun, Jilin, China

Abstract. Point cloud is an important three-dimensional data representation applied in fields such as driverless driving and virtual reality. Due to the high resolution of point clouds, data transmission requires a large amount of network bandwidth and storage resources, which seriously hinders further promotion. This aims at the problem that most current point cloud geometric compression algorithms based on deep learning only consider the local feature information or global feature information of the point cloud separately. To this end, a point cloud geometric compression network based on dual-branch feature fusion is proposed. First, to capture local features with rotation invariance, the point cloud resnet module is introduced to extract local features with low computational complexity. Second, To capture the high-dimensional information in the compression process, a Transformer for point clouds is designed. At the same time, to further effectively utilize features, a point cloud attentional feature fusion block is designed, which contains the point cloud channel attention blocks for local and global features effective fusion extraction. Finally, To compensate for the feature loss in the sampling process and reduce the dynamic memory footprint of model training, the autoencoder adopts a multi-scale progressive structure. Experimental results demonstrate that on the 8iVFB, Owlii, and MVUB datasets, which average Bjontegaard Delta Rate (BD-Rate) gains of 89.11% and 88.17% compared to Geometry-based Point Cloud Compression (G-PCC).

Keywords: Point Clouds · Geometry Compression · Feature Fusion

1 Introduction

Point clouds are widely used to depict geometric information in Augmented Reality (AR), Virtual Reality (VR) and Mixed Reality (MR) [1]. Due to its large amount of data and irregular structure, it poses a challenge to store and transmit point clouds. Our work is dedicated the compression of one fundamental aspect of point cloud compression (PCC), the geometry. Moreover, deep learning has been introduced to address the challenges in PCC, including lossless coding [2–5] and lossy coding [6–10]. The point cloud lossy compression method employs a neural network to learn associated features between points and reconstructs the point cloud through these features, compensating for the information loss caused by quantization. Quach et al. [6] introduced a learning approximation model, GeoCNNv2, based on neural networks. This model utilizes octree partitioning to divide the point cloud into blocks of the same size, encodes it through the scale super-prior entropy model, and then employs multi-layer convolutional transformations to learn features of partitioned point clouds. The Learned-PCGC method [7] first voxelizes the point cloud, obtains non-overlapping squares of the same size after scaling and partitioning, and uses a CNN-based Variational Autoencoder (VAE) to learn potential features to complete Smooth surface reconstruction. André et al. [8] and Wang et al. [9] improved the compression effect by adding modules to the multi-scale point cloud geometry compression network. Lu et al. [10] introduced a lightweight Transformer into the point cloud geometry compression network, improving coding efficiency while maintaining computational efficiency. The existing methods either extract only the local geometric information of the point cloud or only the global information. This fails to fully utilize all the features of the point cloud. Therefore, we are proposing a point cloud geometric compression network based on dual-branch feature fusion.

Main contributions of this paper are fourfold: (i) We have designed a new dual-branch feature fusion network. Among all the compared methods, our method exhibits the best performance. (ii) The 3D convolutional operations in neural networks with fixed sense fields and weights face limitations in aggregating sufficient information from sparse and disordered point clouds. To address this, we have developed a Transformer capable of handling point clouds, allowing

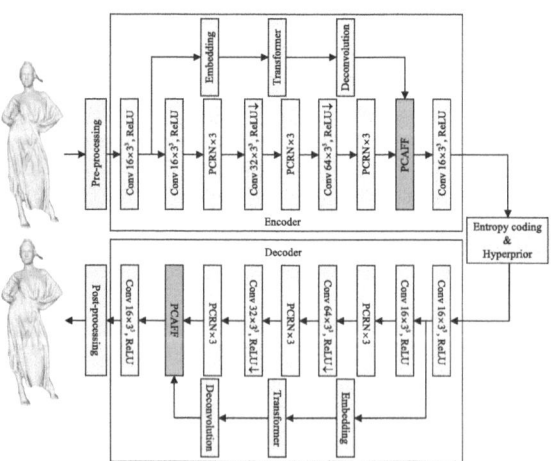

Fig. 1. DBFF-PCGC. "Conv" denotes the number of output channels, and the kernel size, "×3" indicates the cascading of three PCRNs, and "↑" and "↓" signify the operations of zoom-in and zoom-out. "ReLU" refers to the rectified linear unit.

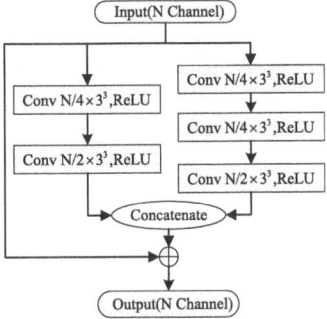

Fig. 2. PCRN Blocks.

us to extract rich global features. (iii) To avoid the problem of underutilizing the extracted feature information, a solution that better integrates global and local features is needed. Therefore, we designed point cloud attention feature fusion blocks(PCAFF), which solves the problems that arise when fusing global and local features. (iv)We also propose a point cloud channel attention blocks (PCCA), which solves the problems that occur when fusing features of different scales.

2 Deep Feature Coding for PCC

The encoder-decoder of DBFF-PCGC is mainly composed of Transformer, point cloud resnet (PCRN), point cloud attention feature fusion (PCAFF) and point cloud channel attention(PCCA) blocks, as shown in Fig. 1. These four blocks are used to respectively extract global and local features of the point cloud. Since the decoder shares the same modules as the encoder, they will be introduced together in the following subsection.

2.1 Point Cloud Resnet

In the point cloud compression algorithm based on double branch feature fusion, PCRN architecture is used for local feature extraction, as shown in Fig. 2. From the name and structure of the PCRN, it can be seen that it is a simple variant of Inception-ResNet [11]. By fusing shallow features with high-level features, feature reuse can be achieved and the problem of gradient disappearance in deep networks can be avoided. At the same time, the shallow features are added to the high-level features through another branch, achieving improved network performance and stability. To reduce computational complexity in the 3D convolution layer, $3 \times 3 \times 3$ and $1 \times 1 \times 1$ convolution kernels are used. In order to obtain compact local feature information from voxel, 18 PCRN are used in both the encoder and decoder stages.

2.2 Transformer

Transformer's ability to capture long-range dependencies between elements has led to great success in many artificial intelligence fields, such as natural language processing, computer vision, and speech processing [12]. The Transformer consists of two main parts: a multi-head self-attention(MHSA) mechanism and a multi-layer perceptron blocks, as shown in Fig. 3. The MHSA mechanism is a feature enhancement technique that can fully extract the global feature features in the point cloud, as shown in Eq. 1. Among them, the output value $head_i$ of all single-head self-attention (SHSA) mechanisms is connected and multiplied by the total weight W^O to obtain the MHSA mechanism output value. $head_i$ is calculated by Eq. 2, expressed as the output value of a SHSA mechanism, and the SHSA mechanism learns four weight matrices: W_i^Q is the query weight, W_i^K is the key weight, W_i^V is the value weight, and W_O is the total weight. The main process is to divide the input 64×64×64 point cloud into non-overlapping patches through patch partitioning, and the size of each patch is fixed at 8×8×8. These patches are flattened into one-dimensional vectors and Sent to the Transformer. These vectors are projected to the desired vector dimension C using a linear embedding, and the number of vectors is kept $[H/4, W/4, D/4]$ by the encoder's Transformer. The vectors are restored from $[H/4, W/4, D/4]$ to $[H, W, D]$ using two 3D deconvolution operations in the decoder. By utilizing the global feature information extracted by the Transformer, the encoder can retain more information, leading to more accurate probabilistic predictions in the decoder. In addition, it can remove low-probability point clouds for accurate point cloud refinement in the decoder, ultimately leading to better decoding performance.

$$MH(Q, K, V) = concat(head_1, \cdots, head_h)W^O \quad (1)$$

$$head_i = soft(\frac{Q_i K_i^T}{\sqrt{d_K}})V_i \quad (2)$$

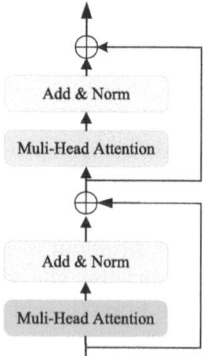

Fig. 3. Transformer Blocks.

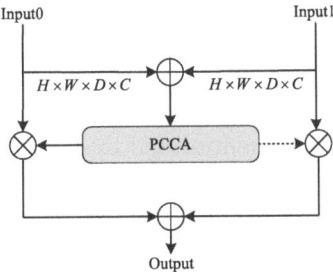

Fig. 4. PCAFF Blocks.

2.3 Point Cloud Attentional Feature Fusion

Inspired by Attentional Feature Fusion [13], we designed PCAFF, as shown in Fig. 4. Feature fusion is an important method in the field of pattern recognition. As a special pattern classification problem, the point cloud geometric compression problem still has many challenges. The feature fusion method can neutralize multiple features, realize the complementary advantages of multiple features, and obtain more robust and accurate classification results. Currently, the features of different layers or branches are usually implemented using simple linear operations (such as summation or concatenation).This method assigns features fixed weights irrespective of content differences, which may not always be the optimal choice.To address this limitation, PCAFF is introduced to address issues that arise when mixing different point cloud feature information. Given local features X, global features Y are used for feature fusion. PCAFF can be expressed as:

$$Z = V(X \uplus Y) \otimes X + (1 - V(X \uplus Y)) \otimes Y \tag{3}$$

where V is PCCA blocks, $V(X) \in R^{C \times H \times W \times D}$ is the fused feature, and $\uplus$ denotes the initial feature integration. Where $1 - V(X \uplus Y)$ represents the dashed portion in Fig. 4. It should be noted that the fusion weights $V(X \uplus Y)$ consist of real numbers between 0 and 1, as do the values of $1 - V(X \uplus Y)$. These values enable the network to perform a soft selection or weighted averaging between X and Y.

2.4 Point Cloud Channel Attention

To better fuse features of different scales, we propose the PCCA, which solves the problems that arise when fusing features of different scales, as shown in Fig. 5. PCCA combines local and global features on 3DCNN and uses an attention mechanism to fuse features in space. To make PCCA as lightweight as possible, PCCA uses 3D point-by-point convolution to focus on the scale of the channel instead of convolution kernels of different sizes. Among them, the channel attention of local features is shown:

$$L(X) = \delta \left(PWConv_2 \left(\delta \left(PWConv_1(X) \right) \right) \right) \tag{4}$$

Among them, $PWConv_1(X)$ represents the use of $1 \times 1 \times 1$ point convolution to reduce the number of input feature X channels to the original $1/r$, δ represents the ReLU activation function, and $PWConv_2$ represents the use of $1 \times 1 \times 1$. The point convolution of 1 restore the number of channels to the same number as the original input channels. r is represented by the channel scaling ratio, which is set to 4 in this paper.

The channel attention of global features $G(X)$, as shown in Eq. 5. The difference from $L(X)$ is that the input X needs to be processed by a global average pooling first. The calculated weight value is used to perform attention operations on the input feature X to obtain the output X', as shown in Eq. 6, where $\otimes$ represents the multiplication of corresponding elements of the two feature maps, σ represents the Sigmoid operate and $\oplus$ represents the add of corresponding elements of the two feature maps.

$$G(X) = \delta\left(PWCon_2\left(\delta\left(PWCon_1(GVA(X))\right)\right)\right) \tag{5}$$

$$X' = X \otimes V(X) = X \otimes \sigma(L(X) \oplus G(X)) \tag{6}$$

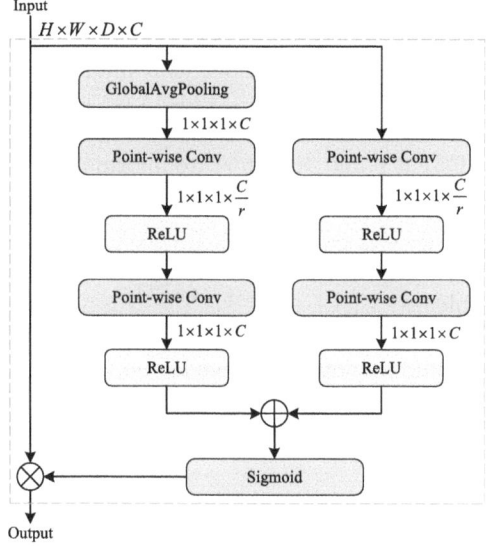

Fig. 5. PCCA Blocks.

2.5 Entropy Coding

The arithmetic coding in entropy coding is widely used for its superior compression performance [7]. To obtain more accurate probability estimates in neural networks, Eq. 7 is used to approximate the actual bitstream of quantized features, where E is the quantization operation and $p_{\hat{y}}(\hat{y})$ is the probability density function of $\hat{y}$. In existing learned image compression algorithms [14,15], a VAE structure is enforced to have both main and hyper codecs, as shown in Fig. 6. Since hyperpriors are mainly used for modeling the entropy of latent features [16], we apply three successive lightweight 3D convolutions used to extract hyperprior information z in the hyper-encoder. The hyper-decoder is then used to estimate the bitstream of $\hat{y}$. The quantization strategy is applied to hidden feature y and hyperprior z. The entropy model is a fully factorized probability model of z, as shown in Eq. 8, where U is a uniform distribution and $\psi^{(i)}$ is the parameter of each univariate distribution $p_{\hat{z}_i|\psi^{(i)}}$. As for $\hat{y}$, assuming it follows a Laplace distribution $\mathcal{L}$, the probability density function is estimated based on hyperprior $\hat{z}$, as shown in Eq. 9, where σ_i, μ_i, and the parameters of each element of $\hat{y}_i$ are obtained through hyperprior $\hat{z}_i$.

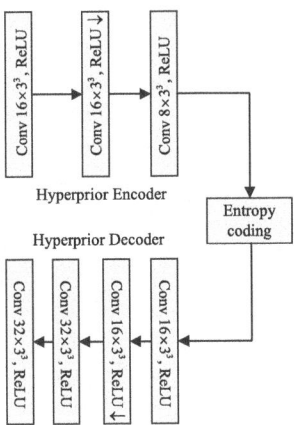

Fig. 6. Hyperprior Blocks.

$$R_{\hat{y}} = E\left[-log_2 p_{\hat{y}}(\hat{y})\right] \tag{7}$$

$$p_{\hat{z}|\psi}(\hat{z}|\psi) = \prod_i (p_{\hat{z}_i|\psi^{(i)}}(\psi^{(i)}) \times U(-\frac{1}{2},+\frac{1}{2}))(\hat{z}_i) \tag{8}$$

$$p_{\hat{y}|\hat{z}}(\hat{y}|\hat{z}) = \prod_i (\mathcal{L}(\mu_i,\sigma_i) \times U(-\frac{1}{2},+\frac{1}{2}))(\hat{y}_i) \tag{9}$$

2.6 Loss Function

To optimize the compression of point cloud data, it is common to consider both bitstream and distortion simultaneously. Therefore, a joint loss function utilizing Lagrangian loss and weighted binary cross-entropy is employed. This optimization approach allows for a balance between bitstream and distortion, achieving a compression and distortion equilibrium as expressed in Eq. 10, where λ controls the weight of BD-Rate, R represents bitstream, and D represents distortion.

$$J_{loss} = R + \lambda D \tag{10}$$

3 Experiments and Analysis

3.1 Experimental Environment and Dataset

The experimental platform used was Ubuntu 22.04, with the deep learning framework being TensorFlow 2.4. The CPU was an Intel Xeon(R) Gold 6134, with a memory of 256GB and GPU was an NVIDIA GeForce RTX 3090. All the algorithms involved were trained or tested on this experimental platform. During the training phase, the original point cloud data from the ShapeNet [18] dataset was voxelized into 256×256×256 voxelized, and the voxel was randomly cropped into non-repeating voxel blocks of 64×64×64 for training. A total of 3×10^5 voxel blocks were used in the training process. The loss function was specified in Eq. 10, with the initial BD-Rate set to 10, learning rate set to 10^{-4}, batch size set to 8, Adam optimizer used, and the model began to converge after 2×10^5 iterations.

3.2 Experimental Results

The proposed DBFF-PCGC was compared and analyzed against other point cloud geometry compression algorithms, including G-PCC [17], ADL-PCC [8], GeoCNNv2 [6], Learned-PCGC [7] and TransPCGC [10]. ADL-PCC, GeoCNNv2, and TransPCGC all utilize the provided model experimental data for comparative analysis. Objective comparisons were made using BD-Rate analysis for lossy compression, measuring point-to-point error (D1), point-to-plane error (D2), and PSNR derived from both metrics. Additionally, the bits per input point (bpp) were used to assess the compression rate.

We first conduct a comparative analysis on the 8i Voxelized FullBodies(8iVFB) [19] dataset, and the results are presented in Tables 1 and 2. Our method achieves averaged -92.74% and -93.50% gains against G-PCC [17], −42.07% and −43.84% gains against ADL-PCC [8], −42.75% and −38.32% gains against GeoCNNv2 [6], −23.48% and −23.91% gains against Learned-PCGC [7], −17.79% and −16.73% gains against TransPCGC [10], as measured by respective D1 and D2 based BD-Rate. Secondly, we plotted the rate-distortion curves for the different point clouds on the Owlii [20] dataset using the provided experimental results, as illustrated in Fig. 7. Observing the results, it is evident that the D1 and D2 metrics of DBFF-PCGC outperform significantly when compared to all other algorithms across various bit rates.

For a thorough comparison, we evaluate all point clouds from the 8iVFB, Owlii, and Microsoft Voxelized Upper Bodies(MVUB) [21] datasets, as summarized in Table 3. ADL-PCC and GeoCNNv2 were omitted from the comparison due to incomplete experimental results. Table 3 illustrates that DBFF-PCGC achieves averaged −89.11% and −88.17% gains against G-PCC, −20.44% and −23.22% gains against Learned-PCGC, −15.89% and −14.28% gains against TransPCGC. These results showcase the superior performance of our method in comparison to other methods across multiple datasets.

In Table 4, we compare the running time of different methods. The table displays the encoding and decoding time of each method. The traditional method G-PCC [17] has the fastest encoding and decoding time, which is slightly increased compared to Learned-PCGC [7]. However, compared to ADL-PCC [8] and TransPCGC our method still has a significant advantage. The slightly slower encoding time of our method is mainly because more point cloud feature information is utilized in the encoding process.

Table 1. BD-Rate reducest G-PCC [17], ADL-PCC [8] , GeoCNNv2 [6], Learned-PCGC [7] and TransPCGC [10] in D1 based BD-Rate measurement (percentage/%).

Point Clouds	D1(p2point)				
	G-PCC [17]	ADL-PCC [8]	GeoCNNv2 [6]	Learned-PCGC [7]	TransPCGC [10]
Longdress_vox10	−94.33	−46.61	−43.47	−24.93	−18.26
Red&black_vox10	−91.93	−37.95	−45.50	−23.78	−17.23
Loot_vox10	−92.38	−42.21	−39.23	−23.36	−18.55
Soldier_vox10	−92.31	−41.51	−42.80	−21.84	−17.10
Average	−92.74	−42.07	−42.75	−23.48	−17.79

Table 2. BD-Rate reducest G-PCC [17], ADL-PCC [8] , GeoCNNv2 [6], Learned-PCGC [7] and TransPCGC [10] in D2 based BD-Rate measurement (percentage/%).

Point Clouds	D2(p2plane)				
	G-PCC [17]	ADL-PCC [8]	GeoCNNv2 [6]	Learned-PCGC [7]	TransPCGC [10]
Longdress_vox10	−94.97	−47.12	−39.23	−23.89	−16.78
Red&black_vox10	−91.53	−39.08	−36.94	−22.72	−15.86
Loot_vox10	−94.37	−45.79	−37.45	−25.18	−17.40
Soldier_vox10	−93.12	−43.36	−39.65	−23.83	−16.89
Average	−93.50	−43.84	−38.32	−23.91	−16.73

In Fig. 8, we provide a visual comparison between the original point cloud and the decompressed point clouds. To visualize the geometric details of the point

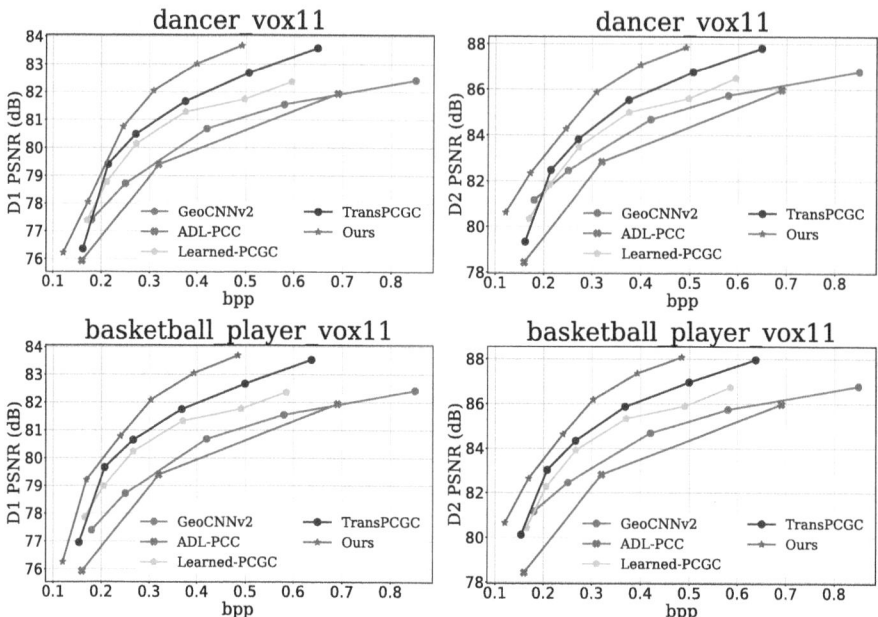

Fig. 7. R-D curves of Owlii examples: (left) D1 based PSNR, (right) D2 based PSNR.

Table 3. BD-Rate reducest G-PCC [17], Learned-PCGC [7] and TransPCGC [10] in D1 and D2 based BD-Rate measurement(percentage/%).

Point Clouds	G-PCC [17]		Learned-PCGC [7]		TransPCGC [10]	
	D1	D2	D1	D2	D1	D2
8iVFB	−92.74	−93.50	−23.48	−23.91	−17.79	−16.73
Owlii	−83.50	−80.92	−22.08	−24.80	−20.96	−17.79
MVUB	−91.10	−90.10	−15.76	−20.94	−8.01	−8.33
Average	−89.11	−88.17	−20.44	−23.22	−15.89	−14.28

cloud, we initially compute the normal vectors for each point using the surrounding 20 neighboring points and render the point cloud. This approach provides a superior visual effect. Additionally, we generate error maps based on the D1 error between the decompressed and original point cloud, allowing us to visualize the error distribution. Comparing the resulting point clouds from different compression methods, our method stands out in preserving intricate details and generating visually superior point clouds, as indicated by the red and blue boxes in Fig. 8. It is noteworthy that G-PCC [17] exhibit sparser reconstructed point clouds with significant quantization loss compared to other methods. This phenomenon occurs because octree-based encoding methods often lose details in leaf nodes at low bit rates. On the contrary, ADL-PCC [8], GeoCNNv2 [6], Learned-

Table 4. Compare the average Enc and Dec time of different methods (unit: second/s)

	G-PCC [17]	Learned-PCGC [7]	ADL-PCC [8]	TransPCGC [10]	Ours
Enc time	0.7	2.9	19.1	2.1	6.2
Dec time	5.2	2.9	6.5	12.85	5.8

Table 5. Ablation for Transformer and PCAFF Blocks on the "longdress" point cloud.

Ablation	Variant	bpp	D1	D2
Baseline	Learned-PCGC	0.63	75.09	79.43
Transformer	Transformer×1	**0.54**	76.21	80.43
	Transformer×2	0.56	**76.27**	**80.49**
	Transformer×3	0.55	76.19	80.41
Fusion Module	Add	0.55	76.10	80.28
	Mulit	0.54	76.11	80.28
	PCAFF	**0.54**	**76.29**	**80.51**

PCGC [7] and TransPCGC [10] demonstrate better preservation of details and fill a significant number of holes. With less bitrate consumption, DBFF-PCGC not only provides a lower reconstruction error but also presents a more visually pleasant point cloud with more realistic textures when compared with the ground truth.

3.3 Ablation Experiment

This section conducts a series of ablation studies to understand the contribution of each module in DBFF-PCGC. We train all models using ShapeNet by default. The comparison anchor is the Learned-PCGC. We study the modular contribution of the DBFF-PCGC used for Transformer and PCAFF derivation and results are reported in Table 5. We conducted a superposition operation on the Transformer module within the dense point cloud geometry compression algorithm to examine whether the Transformer module would perform better when utilized in a triple-layered structure similar to the PCRN. It can be seen that when we superimpose the Transformer, its bpp, and PSNR are not effectively

Table 6. Ablation for PCCA Blocks on the "longdress" point cloud.

Ablation	bpp	D1	D2
Add	0.56	76.20	80.40
Resnet	0.55	76.25	80.45
PCCA	**0.54**	**76.29**	**80.51**

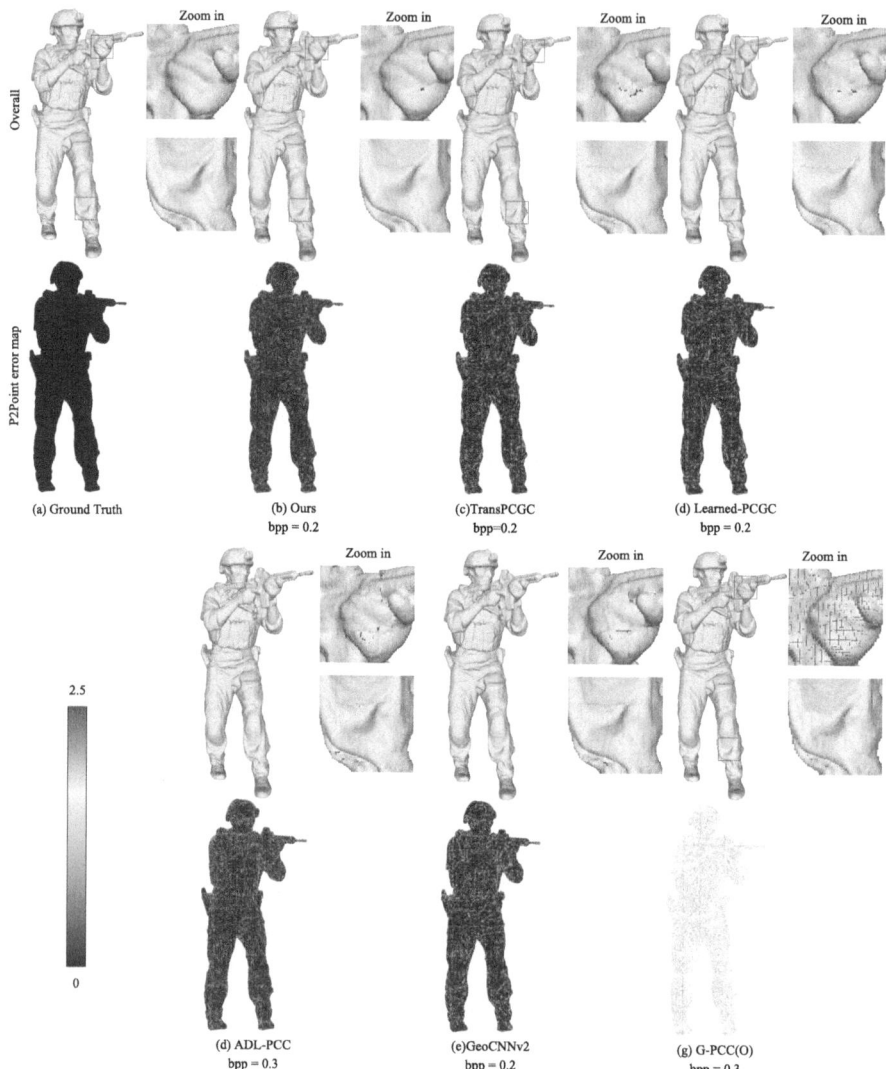

Fig. 8. Visual comparison of "soldier" for ground truth, Ours, TransPCGC, Learned-PCGC, ADL-PCC, GeoCNNv2 and G-PCC.

improved. Therefore, we only use one layer of Transformer for global feature extraction.

We also replace the fusion block and use addition and multiplication respectively to replace the PCAFF. However, it can be seen from Table 5 that when using the PCAFF, the best experimental results are obtained, which proves the effectiveness of our proposed fusion module. Similarly, we also conducted ablation experiments on the PCCA, and the experimental results are shown in Table 6.

When PCCA is replaced by Add or Resnet, experimental results are worse than PCCA, which also proves the effectiveness of our proposed PCCA.

4 Conclusion

Addressing the quandary wherein prevailing algorithms for point cloud geometric compression tend to focus solely on either a singular local feature or a global feature, we proffer a dual-branch feature fusion network tailored for the compression of point cloud geometry. Initially, rotational-invariant local features and globally extensive features are extracted utilizing the Point Cloud ResNet and Transformer, respectively. A sophisticated feature fusion ensues through the deployment of the Point Cloud Attention Feature Fusion and the Point Cloud Channel Attention Blocks to amalgamate the local and global features effectively. Leveraging multi-scale asymptotic outcomes mitigates the dynamic memory footprint during model training. Feature encoding employs entropy coding, while the joint loss function incorporates Lagrangian loss and weighted binary cross-entropy, thereby significantly enhancing the efficacy of point cloud compression. The proposed DBFF-PCGC fully demonstrates its effectiveness by conducting extensive evaluations and fair comparisons across three different datasets. Future work may include the extension of the proposed geometry compression solution to the attribute compression domain for point clouds.

Acknowledgements. This research was funded by the National Key RD Program of China, grant number: (No. 2020YFB1709200).

References

1. Chen, A., et al.: An introduction to point cloud compression standards. GetMobile Mobile Comp. Comm. **27**(1), 11–17 (2023)
2. Nguyen, D.T., Quach, M., Valenzise, G., Duhamel, P.: Learning-based lossless compression of 3d point cloud geometry. In: ICASSP 2021 - 2021 IEEE International Conference on Acoustics, Speech and Signal Processing (ICASSP), pp. 4220–4224 (2021)
3. Nguyen, D.T., Kaup, A.: Learning-based lossless point cloud geometry coding using sparse tensors. In: 2022 IEEE International Conference on Image Processing (ICIP), pp. 2341–2345 (2022)
4. Nguyen, D.T., Kaup, A.: Lossless point cloud geometry and attribute compression using a learned conditional probability model. IEEE Trans. Circuits Syst. Video Technol. **33**(8), 4337–4348 (2023)
5. Wang, J., Ding, D., Li, Z., Feng, X., Cao, C., Ma, Z.: Sparse tensor-based multiscale representation for point cloud geometry compression. IEEE Trans. Pattern Anal. Mach. Intell. **45**(7), 9055–9071 (2023)
6. Quach, M., Valenzise, G., Dufaux, F.: Improved deep point cloud geometry compression. In: 2020 IEEE 22nd International Workshop on Multimedia Signal Processing (MMSP), pp. 1–6 (2020)

7. Wang, J., Zhu, H., Liu, H., Ma, Z.: Lossy point cloud geometry compression via end-to-end learning. IEEE Trans. Circuits Syst. Video Technol. **31**(12), 4909–4923 (2021)
8. Guarda, A.F.R., Rodrigues, N.M.M., Pereira, F.: Adaptive deep learning-based point cloud geometry coding. IEEE J. Sel. Top. Signal Process. **15**(2), 415–430 (2021)
9. Wang, J., Ding, D., Li, Z., Ma, Z.: Multiscale point cloud geometry compression. In: 2021 Data Compression Conference (DCC), pp. 73–82 (2021)
10. Lu, S., Yang, H., Han, C.: TransPCGC: point cloud geometry compression based on transformers. Algorithms. **16**(10), 484 (2023)
11. Szegedy, C., Ioffe, S., Vanhoucke, V., A.A. Alemi. Inception-v4, inception-resnet and the impact of residual connections on learning. In: Proceedings of the Thirty-First AAAI Conference on Artificial Intelligence, pp. 4278–4284 (2017)
12. Han, K., et al.: A survey on vision transformer. IEEE Trans. Pattern Anal. Mach. Intell. **45**(1), 87–110 (2023)
13. Dai, Y., Gieseke, F., Oehmcke, S., Wu, Y., Barnard, K.: Attentional feature fusion. In 2021 IEEE Winter Conference on Applications of Computer Vision (WACV), pp. 3559-3560 (2021)
14. Haisheng, F.F., et al.: Learned image compression with gaussian-Laplacian-logistic mixture model and concatenated residual modules. IEEE Trans. Image Process. **32**, 2063–2076 (2023)
15. Bai, Y., Liu, X., Wang, K., Ji, X., Xiaolin, W., Gao, W.: Deep lossy plus residual coding for lossless and near-lossless image compression. IEEE Trans. Pattern Anal. Mach. Intell. **46**(5), 3577–3594 (2024)
16. Chen, T., Ma, Z.: Variable bitrate image compression with quality scaling factors. In: ICASSP 2020 - 2020 IEEE International Conference on Acoustics, Speech and Signal Processing (ICASSP), pp. 2163–2167 (2020)
17. Mpeg.information technology-coded representation of immersive media - part9:geometry-based point cloud compression (G-PCC). ISO/IEC, pp. 223090–5 (2021)
18. Chang, A.X., et al.: Shapenet: an information-rich 3d model repository. arXiv preprint arXiv:1512.03012 (2015)
19. d'Eon, E., Harrison, B., Myers, T., Chou, P.A.: 8i voxelized full bodies-a voxelized point cloud dataset. ISO/IEC JTC1/SC29 Joint WG11/WG1 (MPEG/JPEG) input document WG11M40059/WG1M74006. **7**(8), 11 (2017)
20. Xu, Y., Lu, Y., Wen, Z.: Owlii dynamic human mesh sequence dataset. In: ISO/IEC JTC1/SC29/WG11 m41658, 120th MPEG Meeting, vol. 1 (2017)
21. Loop, C., Cai, Q., Escolano, S.O., Chou, P.A.: Microsoft voxelized upper bodies-a voxelized point cloud dataset. ISO/IEC JTC1/SC29 Joint WG11/WG1 (MPEG/JPEG) input document m38673 M. **72012**, 2016 (2016)

Camouflaged Object Detection Based on Edge-Feature Interation

Aiqing Zhu, Xiaomei Kuang, Junbin Yuan, and Qingzhen Xu[✉]

School of Computer Science, South China Normal University, Guangzhou, China
zhuaiqing_913@163.com, xqz1997@163.com, 2022023183@m.scnu.edu.cn

Abstract. Camouflaged object detection (COD), segmenting hidden objects that are integrated with the surrounding environment, is a valuable challenging task. Existing deep learning methods often struggle to accurately identify disguised objects with complete and refined object structures. For this purpose, we proposes a new edge-feature interaction network (EFINet) for COD. Our method explores and fully utilizes rich edge semantics to force the model to generate prominent object structure features, and then fuses context information to promote precise localization of camouflage object, thereby improving the effectiveness of COD. Extensive experiments on three challenging benchmark datasets have shown that our EFINet outperforms the existing 14 state-of-the-art methods under four widely used evaluation metrics.

Keywords: camouflaged object detection · edge clue guidance · context fusion · interactive fusion

1 Introduction

Camouflage, also known as mimicry in biology, is a widespread phenomenon in the natural world, wherein animals attempt to alter their shapes to "perfectly" blend into the surrounding environment, thereby avoiding predators [1]. This mechanism also significantly influences human society, such as military, art, medicine, etc. In recent years, identifying camouflaged objects from the environment, namely camouflaged object detection (COD), has attracted increasing research interest in the field of computer vision [2]. It promotes various valuable downstream applications and has broad prospects, such as animal protection [3], medical image segmentation [4], and so on. However, due to the inherent characteristic of the camouflage mechanism, high intrinsic similarity between candidate objects and chaotic backgrounds, the recognition of camouflaged objects is very difficult [5].

To tackle these challenges, deep learning techniques have been adopted in COD task. Deep learning-based COD methods utilize robust feature extraction capabilities and autonomous learning to model disguised targets, greatly improving the performance of camouflage object detection models, such as C2F-Net [9], S-MGL [10] and SINet [11].

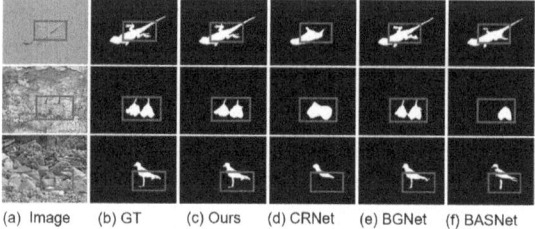

Fig. 1. Visual examples of camouflaged object detection in some challenging scenarios. Our method outperforms cutting-edge methods (e.g., CRNet [6], BGNet [7] and BASNet [8]), with accurate predictions of complete boundaries, as shown in the red box. (Color figure online)

Although the methods proposed recently have achieved outstanding results, there are still some issues and shortcomings. Externally, the inherent deceptive edge-blurring characteristics and texture similarity to the background of camouflaged objects make it challenging for existing methods to identify the structure and details of objects [12]. Internally, in model design perspective, there are two reasons leading to suboptimal prediction results. Firstly, the contours of segmentation object are blurred due to insufficient capability in capturing structural features [7,13]. Secondly, insufficient modeling of contextual features leads to segmentation anomalies, such as segmentation localization errors or segmentation object errors [14]. As shown in the 1st row of Fig. 1, state-of-the-art models lose many details about lizard legs in prediction results when the boundary of camouflaged object is indefinable. Based on the above experience, it is imperative to extend the study on effectively capturing structural features while enhancing the model's capability in context information modeling, which will promote precise localization and fine segmentation in COD.

To this end, we propose a novel network model named edge-feature interaction network (EFINet), which leverages multi-channel edge information to enhance the performance of camouflaged object detection. Initially, we introduce the edge exploration module (EEM) that explores multi-channel edge information with rich structural features related to the boundaries of camouflage objects. Subsequently, we carefully design the cross edge-feature module (CEFM) to fuse the edge information extracted by EEM with multi-layer backbone features, using edge clues to guide structural representation learning. Furthermore, to enhance semantic feature representation, we construct a context enhance module (CEM) that utilizes spatial attention mechanisms and cross-scale dilated convolutions interaction to aggregate multi-scale contextual semantics. Note that, compared to previous methods, we innovatively propose to fully exploit rich object boundary information by using cross-attention mechanism and further enhance contextual semantic information by aggregating spatial attention mechanism and cross-scale interactions. Benefiting from well-designed modules, the proposed EFINet achieves more accurate object localization and stronger preservation of object structures. In summary, our main contributions are as follows:

- To enhance structural feature representation, we innovatively propose the cross edge-feature module (CEFM) that sufficiently utilizes edge information.
- To enhance semantic feature representation, we build the context enhance module (CEM), modeling long and short-range dependencies and capturing contextual information.
- For the COD task, our proposed method EFINet, which integrates CEFM and CEM, has been verified effectiveness through comparative experiments and ablation experiments.

2 Related Work

2.1 Edge-Guided Camouflage Object Detection

Facing the challenges brought by inherent similarity and edge interruptions, as mentioned in previous research [15], edge information can play a crucial role in emphasizing contours and providing shape information. However, existing edge prior methods often employ simple concatenation methods to combine edge information with feature information, failing to maximize its guiding effect. To our best knowledge, MGL [10] is the first to explicitly utilize edge information to improve COD performance. Subsequently proposed methods is as followed. BASNet [8] learns the residual between coarse prediction maps and ground truth (GT) and utilizes a hybrid loss function. ERRNet [16] achieves refinement by fusing edge priors with other prior knowledge, but the excessive use of prior knowledge tends to overshadow valuable clues. BGNet [7] enhances features through edge perception. However, it only explores single-channel edge clues and aggregates them simply with backbone feature information, failing to fully explore and utilize edge information.

2.2 Attention

In deep neural networks, attention mechanism allow the model to assign different weights to different positions in the input sequence, enabling the model to focus on the most relevant parts when processing each sequence element, enhancing the importance of key information. In the field of computer vision, various attention mechanisms are widely used, including spatial attention mechanism, channel attention mechanism and cross-attention mechanism. The cross-attention mechanism, introduced in SPNet [17], enhances cross-modal feature learning by utilizing the correlation between two modes effectively. The spatial attention mechanism and channel attention mechanism proposed in CBAM [18] focus on specific information in the image. Channel attention emphasizes certain specific information in the image, informing the model which features in the given image are more important, enhancing structural features. Spatial attention focuses on specific positions in the image, informing the model where the information is rich, enhancing semantic features. In this paper, we aim to improve the model's ability to capture structural information about predicted objects by using interactive attention and channel attention. Additionally, enhance the model's ability to locate predicted objects by utilizing spatial attention.

3 Proposed Method

In this section, we first present the overall architecture of the proposed EFINet. Then, we detail three key modules in our EFINet. Finally, we describe the loss function for the proposed COD method.

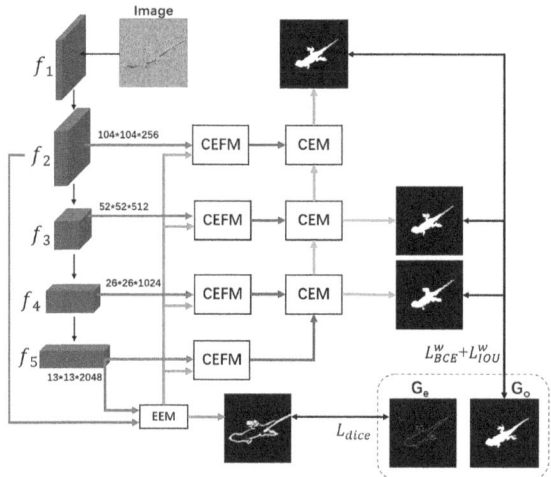

Fig. 2. The overall architecture of the proposed EFINet, which consists of three key modules, i.e., edge exploration module (EEM), cross edge-feature fusion module (CEFM) and context enhance module (CEM). See Sect. 3 for details.

3.1 Overview

The overall architecture of the proposed EFINet is depicted in Fig. 2, which integrates edge information and utilizes contextual features to improve the model's performance. Specifically, we adopt Res2Net-50 as the backbone network to extract multi-level features, denoted as f_i ($i \in \{2, 3, 4, 5\}$), from the input image. Then, under the supervision of GT graph of object boundary, EEM is used to mine rich multi channel edge semantics related to camouflaged objects. Secondly, multiple CEFMs are used to integrate the edge information of EEM with the backbone features (f_2-f_5) to enhance boundary representation. Finally, multiple CEMs are employed to gradually aggregate multilevel fusion features in a top-down manner to find camouflage objects. In testing, the prediction of the last CEM will be selected as the final result.

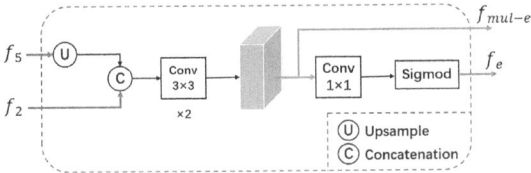

Fig. 3. Diagram of the edge exploration module (EEM), which is designed to explore rich edge clues related to camouflaged object.

3.2 Edge Exploration Module

Good edge clues can play a crucial role in correct object detection through emphasizing contours and providing shape information [15]. Inspired by BGNet [7], high-level semantic information can be used to weaken the noise associated with low-level features containing rich edge details, and the combination of the two promotes the exploration of edge features related to disguised objects. In EEM, we integrate low-level local edge information (f_2) and high-level global position information (f_5) from backbone to generate rich edge clues relevant to disguised objects, as shown in Fig. 3. Specifically, we integrate f_2 and upsampled f_5 through connection operations. Then we gain the rich edge information f_{mul-e} with 256 channels after fusing feature by two 3 × 3 convolutional layer, which provide rich edge information for next module CEFM. After that, use one 1×1 convolutional layer followed by the Sigmoid function to generate edge prediction map for edge GT graph supervision. This module dedicates to generating effective multi-channel edge information for CEFM, whose effectiveness is shown in Table 2.

3.3 Cross Edge-Feature Fusion Module

To enhance the structural features of objects, we design a cross edge-feature fusion module (CEFM) to sufficiently integrate edge cues and backbone fea-

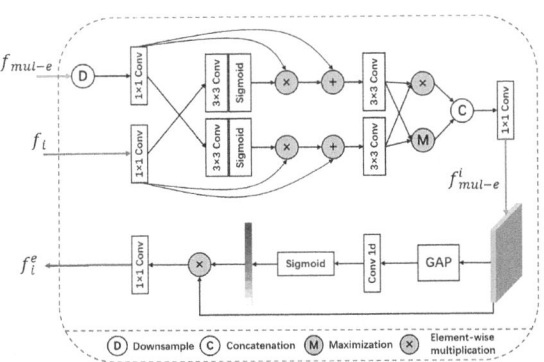

Fig. 4. Diagram of the cross edge-feature fusion module (CEFM) adopted to fully infuse edge clues into feature learning process.

ture. As known in SP-Net [17], interactive attention mechanism could effectively capture the correlation between two input sources. Additionally, local channel attention mechanism [7] excels at enhancing key structural features through interaction among channels with different structural information. In order to achieve optimal integration and generate powerful representation, our method utilizes the both mechanisms simultaneously.

Specifically, as shown in Fig. 4, given input features f_i ($i \in \{2, 3, 4, 5\}$) and edge information f_{mul-e}, we initially reduce the channel number by half respectively through a 1×1 convolution for acceleration, i.e., $f_i' = conv_1(f_i)$ and $f_m' = conv_1(D(f_{mul-e}))$, where D is down-sampling and $conv_1$ is 1×1 convolution.

Subsequently, we apply a 3×3 convolutional layer with a Sigmoid function to obtain feature attention maps of two inputs. To exploit the correlation between the two features, we perform cross attention weighting between them to adaptively enhance feature representation. Beside, we utilize a residual connection to combine the enhanced features with their original to preserve the original features. The above can be formulated as:

$$\begin{cases} f_{mul-e}^a = f_m' + f_m' \otimes \sigma(conv_3(f_i')), \\ f_i^a = f_i' + f_i' \otimes \sigma(conv_3(f_m')), \end{cases} \quad (1)$$

where $conv_3$ is 3×3 convolution. σ is the logistic Sigmoid activation function and $\otimes$ denotes element-wise multiplication. To leverage the advantages of different fusion strategies, we use element-wise multiplication and maximization simultaneously and then concatenate two results to effectively fuse f_{mul-e}^a and f_i^a. Subsequently, a 1×1 convolutional layer is used to compress the channel of the concatenated features to result in f_{mul-e}^i. It can be formulated as:

$$\begin{cases} p_{mul} = conv_3(f_{mul-e}^a) \otimes conv_3(f_i^a), \\ p_{max} = M(conv_3(f_{mul-e}^a), conv_3(f_i^a)), \\ f_{mul-e}^i = conv_1([p_{mul}, p_{max}]), \end{cases} \quad (2)$$

where [*] is concatenation operation and M denotes Maximization. Following is the stage of local channel attention, enhancing key channels. We utilize global average pooling (GAP) to aggregate the features f_{mul-e}^i. Then, we employ 1D convolution and a Sigmoid function to obtain the corresponding channel attention weights. Instead of using a computationally expensive fully-connected operation, we adopt a localized approach to learn channel attention weights, focusing on exploring the interactions between k neighboring channels. After that, we multiply channel attention weights with original f_{mul-e}^i to highlight key feature channels and suppressing redundant channels or noise. At last, we reduce channels by a 1×1 convolution to obtain the final output f_e^i. It can be formulated as:

$$\begin{cases} f_{att} = \sigma\left(F_{1D}^k(GAP(f_{mul-e}^i))\right), \\ f_i^e = conv_1(f_{att} \otimes f_{mul-e}^i), \end{cases} \quad (3)$$

where F_{1D}^k is 1D convolution with kernel size k. The kernel size k can be calculate as $k = |(1 + \log_2(C))/2|_{odd}$, where $|*|_{odd}$ denotes the nearest odd number and C is the channels of f^i_{mul-e}. It is worth noting that the proposed CEFM can fully leverage the guidance of edge cues in constructing target features, enhancing the structural representation.

3.4 Context Enhancement Module

We designed a context enhancement module (CEM) to enhance semantic feature representation by exploring long-range and short-range contextual semantics. Unlike existing ASPP [19], BGNet [7] and GR-module [20], we leverage the complementarity [21,22] of dilation convolutions at different scales to capture short-range contextual information while incorporate a spatial attention mechanism to capture long-range contextual information. By combining these two mechanisms, we effectively enhance feature representation with long and short-range information.

Specifically, as shown in Fig. 5, we first concatenate the two inputs followed by a 1×1 convolutional layer to obtain the initial aggregated feature f_m. Next, we input it into two processing pathways, short-range dependency mining and long-range dependency mining, respectively. In the short-range dependency mining, we divide the feature map f_m into four feature maps $(f^1_m, f^2_m, f^3_m, f^4_m)$ by averaging along the channel dimension. Then, we perform interactive learning between different dilated convolutions to integrate features of different scales. It can be defined as:

$$f^{j'}_m = F^j_{conv}\left(f^{j-1}_m \oplus f^j_m \oplus f^{j+1}_m\right), \quad (4)$$
$$j \in \{1, 2, 3, 4\},$$

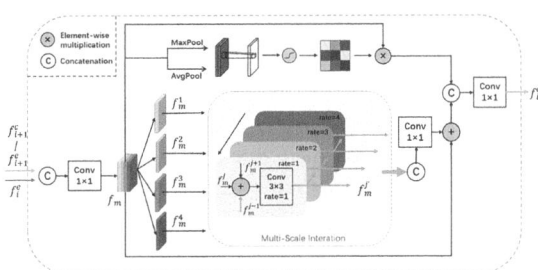

Fig. 5. Diagram of the context enhancement module (CEM) used to capture long-short distance context dependencies.

where F^j_{conv} indicates a 3 × 3 atrous convolution with a dilation rate of j. In our experiments, we set $j = \{1, 2, 3, 4\}$. Then, we concatenate these four multiscale features followed by a 1×1 convolution and a residual connection, which can be formulated as:

$$f^a_i = conv_1\left(\left[f^{j'}_m\right]\right) \oplus f_m, \quad (5)$$

Meanwhile, in long-range dependency mining, we employ average-pooling and max-pooling to aggregate spatial information from f_m. Then, we perform concatenation, convolution, and activation operations on the two pooling results to generate spatial attention map f_{s_a}. To leverage long-range dependency relationships to enhance the crucial features, we multiply this attention map f_{s_a} with the feature map f_m. It can be denoted as:

$$\begin{cases} f_{s\_a} = \sigma(conv_7([\mathrm{A}(f_m), \mathrm{M}(f_m)])), \\ f_i^s = f_{s\_a} \otimes f_m, \end{cases} \quad (6)$$

where $conv_7$ represents a convolution operation with the filter size of 7, A indicates average-pooling and M is max-pooling. After the two processes, we concatenate their results (f_i^s and f_i^a) followed by a 1×1 convolution to obtain the CEM's final output f_i^c, which can be denoted as: $f_i^c = conv_1([f_i^s, f_i^a])$. By another 1×1 convolution, we can gain the final prediction map P_i ($i \in \{2,3,4\}$) of camouflaged objects.

3.5 Loss Function

As shown in Fig. 2, our model contains two supervisions for camouflage object prediction (P_i, $i \in \{2,3,4\}$) and camouflage object edge prediction (P_e), respectively. In object supervision, we apply weighted binary cross-entropy loss (L_{BCE}^w) and weighted IOU loss (L_{IOU}^w) [23] to process each pixel differently by assigning different weights to each pixel. In edge supervision, we apply dice loss (L_{dice}) [24] to measure the difference between the predicted distribution and the target distribution. To treat each supervisions equally, we define our loss function as follows:

$$L_{total} = \sum_{i=2}^{4}(L_{BCE}^w(P_i, G_o) + L_{IOU}^w(P_i, G_o))/3 + L_{dice}(P_e, G_e), \quad (7)$$

where G_o represents the ground truth mask for camouflage objects, and G_e represents the ground truth mask for camouflage object edges.

4 Experiment

4.1 Implementation Details

We implement EFINet on PyTorch and employ Res2Net50 [25], pre-trained on the ImageNet, as the backbone architecture. We employ Adam optimizer [26] to train our model. To ensure consistency, all input images are resized to a resolution of 416×416 and augment them by random horizontal flipping. During training, the batch size is set to 16 and the maximum epoch is set to 40. The learning rate and gradient clipping margin are set to 1e-4 and 0.5, respectively. Accelerated by an NVIDIA V100-32GB GPU, the whole training takes approximately 4 h.

4.2 Datasets

To validate the effectiveness of the proposed mode, we evaluate our method on three public benchmark datasets: CHAMELEON [27], CAMO [28] and COD10K [11]. Following previous works, we use the training sets of CAMO and COD10K for training and employ their testing sets along with CHAMELEON for testing.

4.3 Evaluation Metrics

We employ four widely used metrics to evaluate the performance of our method: mean absolute Error (MAE, M) [29], weighted F-measure (F_β^w) [30], structure-measure (S_α) [31], and average E-measure (E_ϕ) [32].

4.4 Performance Comparison

The effectiveness of our method is demonstrated through a comparison with 14 state-of-the-art methods, including SINet [11], PFNet [33], S-MGL [10], R-MGL [10], LSR [34], UGTR [35], C2FNet [36], JCSOD [37], BASNet [8], BGNet [7], C2F-Net [9], BSA-Net [38], CRNet [6] and FLCNet [39]. For fair comparison, all result data of these methods are obtained based on the same evaluation code [11].

Quantitative Comparison. Table 1 presents the quantitative results of different COD methods on three benchmark datasets. Compared with existing SOTA methods, including existing edge prior methods [7,8,10], our EFINet performs better on most metrics. Especially, compared to the optimal edge prior method BGNet [7], our method reduces M by 6.9% on average, which is a rare achievement on a high-level benchmark.

Qualitative Comparison. Figure 6 illustrates the qualitative comparison with various COD methods on several typical samples from test dataset, covering diverse scenes such as forests, deserts, oceans, and various complex scenarios. As depicted in Fig. 6, existing methods perform poorly in predicting complex scenes (e.g. cluttered scenes and tiny camouflaged objects). However, our method, with its powerful ability to capture structural and semantic features, can still accurately locate and finely segment camouflaged objects in these complex scenes. These results intuitively demonstrate the superior performance of the proposed method.

Table 1. Quantitative comparison with state-of-the-art COD methods using four widely used evaluation metrics (S_α, E_ϕ, F_β^w and M) across three benchmarks." ↑" / "↓" means that larger/smaller is better. The best results are highlighted in bold for clarity.

Methods	Pub/Year	CHAMELEON				CAMO-TEST				COD10K-TEST			
		$S_\alpha\uparrow$	$E_\phi\uparrow$	$F_\beta^w\uparrow$	$M\downarrow$	$S_\alpha\uparrow$	$E_\phi\uparrow$	$F_\beta^w\uparrow$	$M\downarrow$	$S_\alpha\uparrow$	$E_\phi\uparrow$	$F_\beta^w\uparrow$	$M\downarrow$
SINet	CVPR'20	–	–	–	–	0.745	0.804	0.644	0.092	0.776	0.864	0.631	0.043
PFNet	CVPR'21	–	–	–	–	0.782	0.841	0.695	0.085	0.800	0.877	0.660	0.040
S-MGL	CVPR'21	–	–	–	–	0.772	0.806	0.664	0.089	0.811	0.844	0.654	0.037
R-MGL	CVPR'21	–	–	–	–	0.775	0.812	0.673	0.088	0.814	0.851	0.666	0.035
UGTR	ICCV'21	–	–	–	–	0.784	0.821	0.683	0.086	0.817	0.852	0.665	0.036
LSR	CVPR'21	–	–	–	–	0.787	0.838	0.696	0.080	0.804	0.880	0.673	0.037
JCSOD	CVPR'21	–	–	–	–	0.800	0.859	0.728	0.073	0.809	0.884	0.684	0.035
BASNet	CORR'21	–	–	–	–	0.749	0.808	0.646	0.096	0.802	0.870	0.677	0.038
C2FNet	IJCAI'21	0.888	0.935	0.828	0.032	0.796	0.854	0.719	0.080	0.813	0.890	0.686	0.036
BGNet	IJCAI'22	0.899	0.959	0.848	0.028	0.812	0.870	0.749	0.073	0.831	0.901	0.722	0.033
C2F-Net	TCSVT'22	0.893	0.947	0.845	0.028	0.800	0.869	0.730	0.077	0.811	0.891	0.691	0.036
BSA-Net	AAAI'22	0.895	0.946	0.841	0.027	0.796	0.851	0.717	0.079	0.818	0.891	0.699	0.034
CRNet	AAAI'23	0.818	0.897	0.744	0.046	0.735	0.815	0.641	0.092	0.733	0.832	0.576	0.049
FLCNet	EJ'23	0.891	0.948	0.837	0.028	0.808	0.873	0.741	0.071	0.818	0.893	0.700	0.034
EFINet (Ours)		**0.902**	**0.964**	**0.856**	**0.025**	**0.808**	**0.875**	0.741	**0.070**	**0.831**	**0.906**	**0.729**	**0.031**

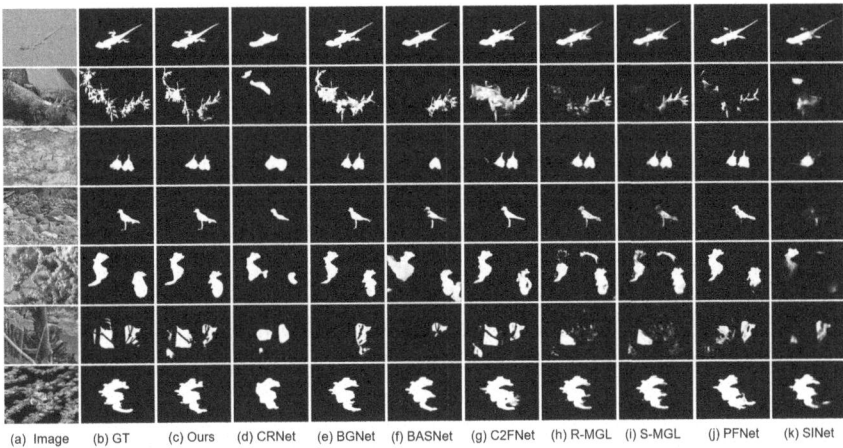

Fig. 6. Visual comparison of proposed model with eight state-of-the-art COD methods. It is obvious that our approach can accurately segment camouflaged objects with clearer boundaries.

Table 2. Quantitative evaluation of ablation study on three datasets. The best results are highlighted in bold. B means baseline. M means model.

M	Methods	CHAMELEON				CAMO-TEST				COD10K-TEST			
		$S_\alpha \uparrow$	$E_\phi \uparrow$	$F_\beta^w \uparrow$	$M \downarrow$	$S_\alpha \uparrow$	$E_\phi \uparrow$	$F_\beta^w \uparrow$	$M \downarrow$	$S_\alpha \uparrow$	$E_\phi \uparrow$	$F_\beta^w \uparrow$	$M \downarrow$
a	B	0.893	0.955	0.836	0.029	0.806	0.871	0.732	0.077	0.822	0.903	0.704	0.033
b	B+CEM	0.893	0.950	0.839	0.028	0.805	**0.875**	0.736	0.074	0.827	0.902	0.715	0.033
c	B+EEM	0.896	0.955	0.846	0.028	0.807	0.870	0.734	0.075	0.826	0.905	0.717	0.032
d	Ours-CEFM	0.899	0.952	0.850	0.028	0.805	0.873	0.738	0.074	0.827	0.900	0.718	0.032
e	Ours	**0.902**	**0.964**	**0.856**	**0.025**	**0.808**	**0.875**	**0.741**	**0.070**	**0.831**	**0.906**	**0.729**	**0.031**

4.5 Ablation Study

To validate the effectiveness of each key component, we conduct several ablation experiments, and the results are reported in Table 2. For the baseline model (B), we remove all additional modules (i.e., EEM, CEFM, and CEM), retaining only four 1×1 convolutions to reduce the channel of backbone features (f_i, $i \in \{2,3,4,5\}$), and employ the initial aggregation operation from CEM to fuse multi-level features in a top-down manner.

Effectiveness of CEM. Comparing with method B, it's evident that method B+CEM performs better. Particularly, B+CEM exhibits a greater advantage in the F_β^w metric on COD10K-TEST dataset, with a performance improvement of 1.50%.

Effectiveness of EEM. To validate the effectiveness of object-relevant edge clues, we exclude the interference of other modules. Method B+EEM, replacing CEFM and CEM with two 1×1 convolutions and concatenation, shows superior performance compared to the baseline model (method B). Especially in terms of F_β^w, the average performance across all datasets improves by 1.1%.

Effectiveness of CEFM. On the basis of whole model (model e), we remove CEFM to verify the effectiveness of interactive fusion for edge clues and backbone features. From Table 2, it is obvious that model e has a significant improvement in performance compared with model d. In terms of E_ϕ and F_β^w, the average performances increase by 0.71% and 0.87%, respectively. Furthermore, our entire model comprehensively utilizes the structural feature modeling ability of CEFM and the semantic feature modeling ability of CEM, ultimately achieving high performance, especially reducing M by a large margin of 6.1% and improving F_β^w by 2.4% on average compared with baseline (model a).

5 Conclusion

To address the issues of inaccurate and imprecise predictions in COD, the paper propose an effective edge-feature interaction network (EFINet), which contains edge exploration module, edge-feature interaction fusion module and context enhancement module. Ablation study verifys the necessity of three modules and the superiority of EFINet. Extensive comparative experiments shows that EFINet outperforms state-of-the-art methods on three benchmarks. In summary, with the structural feature modeling ability of CEFM and the semantic feature capture ability of CEM, EFINet predicts accurate results with fine object boundaries against existing state-of-the-art methods.

References

1. Price, N., Green, S.: Background matching and disruptive coloration as habitat-specific strategies for camouflage. Sci. Rep. **9**(1), 7840 (2019)
2. Liang, Y., Qin, G.: A systematic review of image-level camouflaged object detection with deep learning. Neurocomputing, p. 127050 (2023)
3. Pérez-de la Fuente, R., Delclòs, X.: Early evolution and ecology of camouflage in insects. Proc. Natl. Acad. Sci. **109**(52), 21414–21419 (2012)
4. Fan, D.-P., Zhou, T.: Inf-net: Automatic COVID-19 lung infection segmentation from CT images. IEEE Trans. Med. Imaging **39**(8), 2626–2637 (2020)
5. Bi, H., Zhang, C.: Rethinking camouflaged object detection: models and datasets. IEEE Trans. Circuits Syst. Video Technol. **32**(9), 5708–5724 (2021)
6. He, R., Dong, Q.: Weakly-supervised camouflaged object detection with scribble annotations. Proc. AAAI Conf. Artif. Intell. **37**, 781–789 (2023)
7. Sun, Y., Wang, S.: Boundary-guided camouflaged object detection. In: Proceedings of the Thirty-First International Joint Conference on Artificial Intelligence, pp. 1335–1341 (2022)
8. Qin, X., Fan, D.-P.: Boundary-aware segmentation network for mobile and web applications. CoRR, abs/2101.04704 (2021)
9. Chen, G., Liu, S.-J.: Camouflaged object detection via context-aware cross-level fusion. IEEE Trans. Circuits Syst. Video Technol. **32**(10), 6981–6993 (2022)

10. Zhai, Q., Li, X.: Mutual graph learning for camouflaged object detection. In: Proceedings of the IEEE/CVF Conference on Computer Vision and Pattern Recognition, pp. 12997–13007 (2021)
11. Fan, D.-P., Ji, G.-P.: Camouflaged object detection. In: Proceedings of the IEEE/CVF Conference on Computer Vision and Pattern Recognition, pp. 2777–2787 (2020)
12. Zhu, J., Zhang, X.: Inferring camouflaged objects by texture-aware interactive guidance network. Proc. AAAI Conf. Artif. Intell. **35**, 3599–3607 (2021)
13. Lv, Y., Zhang, J.: Towards deeper understanding of camouflaged object detection. IEEE Trans. Circuits Syst. Video Technol. **33**, 3462–3476 (2023)
14. Shi, C., Ren, B.: Camouflaged object detection based on context-aware and boundary refinement. Appl. Intell. **53**(19), 22429–22445 (2023)
15. Zhao, J.-X., Liu, J.-J.: Egnet: Edge guidance network for salient object detection. In: Proceedings of the IEEE/CVF International Conference on Computer Vision, pp. 8779–8788 (2019)
16. Ji, G.-P., Zhu, L.: Fast camouflaged object detection via edge-based reversible re-calibration network. Pattern Recogn. **123**, 108414 (2022)
17. Zhou, T., Fu, H.: Specificity-preserving RGB-D saliency detection. In: Proceedings of the IEEE/CVF International Conference on Computer Vision, pp. 4681–4691 (2021)
18. Woo, S., Park, J., Lee, J.-Y., Kweon, I.S.: CBAM: convolutional block attention module. In: Ferrari, V., Hebert, M., Sminchisescu, C., Weiss, Y. (eds.) ECCV 2018. LNCS, vol. 11211, pp. 3–19. Springer, Cham (2018). https://doi.org/10.1007/978-3-030-01234-2_1
19. Chen, L.-C., Zhu, Y.: Encoder-decoder with Atrous separable convolution for semantic image segmentation (2018)
20. Xu, X., Chen, S.: Guided multi-scale refinement network for camouflaged object detection. Multimed. Tools Appl. **82**(4), 5785–5801 (2023)
21. Wang, Z., Ji, S.: Smoothed dilated convolutions for improved dense prediction. In: Proceedings of the 24th ACM SIGKDD, July 2018
22. Yu, W., Yang, K.: Exploiting the complementary strengths of multi-layer CNN features for image retrieval. Neurocomputing **237**, 235–241 (2017)
23. Wei, J., Wang, S.: F^3net: fusion, feedback and focus for salient object detection. Proc. AAAI Conf. Artif. Intell. **34**, 12321–12328 (2020)
24. Milletari, F., Navab, N.: V-net: fully convolutional neural networks for volumetric medical image segmentation. In: 2016 Fourth International Conference on 3D Vision, pp. 565–571. IEEE (2016)
25. Gao, S.-H., Cheng, M.-M.: Res2net: a new multi-scale backbone architecture. IEEE Trans. Pattern Anal. Mach. Intell. **43**(2), 652–662 (2019)
26. Kingma, D.P., Ba, J.: Adam: a method for stochastic optimization. arXiv preprint arXiv:1412.6980 (2014)
27. Skurowski, P., Abdulameer, H.: Animal camouflage analysis Chameleon database. **2**(6), 7 (2018, Unpublished Manuscript)
28. Le, T.-N., Nguyen, T.V.: Anabranch network for camouflaged object segmentation. Comput. Vis. Image Underst. **184**, 45–56 (2019)
29. Perazzi, F., Krähenbühl, P.: Saliency filters: Contrast based filtering for salient region detection. In: 2012 IEEE Conference on Computer Vision and Pattern Recognition, pp. 733–740. IEEE (2012)
30. Margolin, R., Zelnik-Manor, L.: How to evaluate foreground maps? In: Proceedings of the IEEE Conference on Computer Vision and Pattern Recognition, pp. 248–255 (2014)

31. Fan, D.-P., Cheng, M.-M.: Structure-measure: a new way to evaluate foreground maps. In: Proceedings of the IEEE International Conference on Computer Vision, pp. 4548–4557 (2017)
32. Fan, D.-P., Ji, G.-P.: Cognitive vision inspired object segmentation metric and loss function. Sci. Sin. Inform. **6**(6), 1–7 (2021)
33. Mei, H., Ji, G.-P.: Camouflaged object segmentation with distraction mining. In: Proceedings of the IEEE/CVF Conference on Computer Vision and Pattern Recognition, pp. 8772–8781 (2021)
34. Lv, Y., Zhang, J.: Simultaneously localize, segment and rank the camouflaged objects. In: Proceedings of the IEEE/CVF Conference on Computer Vision and Pattern Recognition, pp. 11591–11601 (2021)
35. Yang, F., Zhai, Q.: Uncertainty-guided transformer reasoning for camouflaged object detection. In: Proceedings of the IEEE/CVF International Conference on Computer Vision, pp. 4146–4155 (2021)
36. Sun, Y., Chen, G.: Context-aware cross-level fusion network for camouflaged object detection. In: Proceedings of the Thirtieth International Joint Conference on Artificial Intelligence, pp. 1025–1031 (2021)
37. Li, A., Zhang, J.: Uncertainty-aware joint salient object and camouflaged object detection. In: Proceedings of the IEEE/CVF Conference on Computer Vision and Pattern Recognition, pp. 10071–10081 (2021)
38. Zhu, H., Li, P.: I can find you! boundary-guided separated attention network for camouflaged object detection. Proc. AAAI Conf. Artif. Intell. **36**, 3608–3616 (2022)
39. Wang, T., Wang, J.: Camouflaged object detection with a feature lateral connection network. Electronics **12**(12), 2570 (2023)

EyeGlove: Enhancing Smart Glove with Visual Information to Assist Students in Conducting Chemistry Experiments in Mixed Reality Laboratory

Hong Cui, Dehui Kong, and Zhiquan Feng(✉)

University of JiNan, Jinan, China
`ise.fengzq@ujn.edu.cn`

Abstract. Virtual intelligent experiments in education often struggle with limitations, such as the inability to manipulate real objects and accurately understand user intentions. This study introduces EyeGlove, a smart glove with enhanced visual capabilities, and its associated smart laboratory. The aim is to enable students to interact with real chemical laboratory equipment in a mixed-reality environment. To address challenges in prior virtual experiments, we propose the MUFD algorithm, based on fuzzy reasoning and Dempster-Shafer evidence theory, to enhance intention understanding. MUFD analyzes speech, visual, and gesture information to determine users' experimental intentions. Experimental results show EyeGlove, supported by MUFD, effectively addresses challenging experiment steps, demonstrating robustness in handling incomplete and uncertain information. Through hands-on experiences and surveys with 20 participants, our system proves advantageous in reducing task load and enhancing subjective emotional experiences.

Keywords: Smart gloves · Intelligent Experiments · Mixed Reality

1 Introduction

Envision the challenges of conducting experiments in a real chemistry laboratory, where the threats and dangers of chemical reactions are prevalent. However, with the continuous development of Augmented Reality (AR), Virtual Reality (VR), and Mixed Reality (MR) technologies, the teaching approach in intelligent laboratories is becoming increasingly mainstream.

The intelligent laboratory, as a carrier of smart systems, comprehensively assesses and precisely controls the laboratory by real-time perception of the laboratory's state and coordinating various functional modules [1]. It can provide users with a more immersive, interactive, and digitized experimental experience through technologies such as AR, VR, and MR [2]. Although students can simulate actual experiments in virtual laboratories, this may hinder learners from focusing on more experimental information [3], thus reducing the effectiveness of experimental teaching. In contrast, MR experiments integrate the real and virtual [4, 5], enhancing the physical and realistic tactile sensations during the experimental process. However, in real MR experiments, due to issues with Bluetooth communication or networks, there may be loss or incompleteness of sensor information from experimental devices and user behavior information, affecting the system's accurate perception of the operator's experimental intent. Overall, whether it's AR, VR, or MR, relying solely on visual or sensor information from head-worn devices may lead to biases in understanding due to device malfunctions or the user expressing vague or incomplete information. Additionally, mutual obstruction between devices during experiments may lead to misidentification of some instruments, increasing the complexity of operations (Fig. 1).

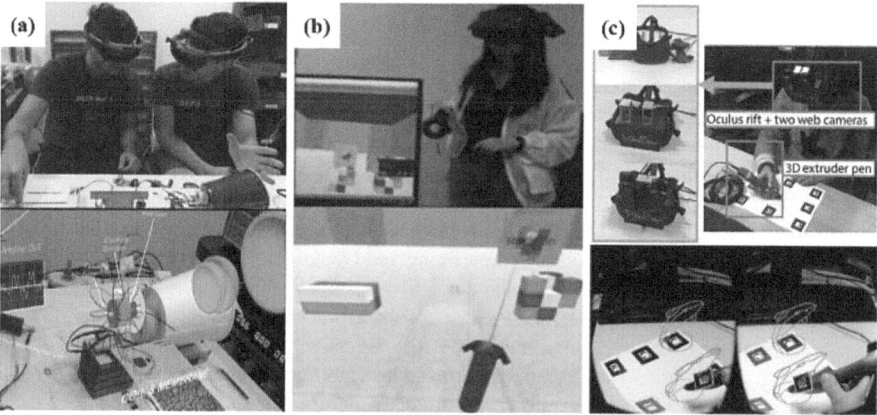

Fig. 1. (a) Augmented Reality system [3], (b) Virtual Reality system [6], (c) Mixed Reality system [7]

Therefore, to address the aforementioned issues, we make the following contributions:

(1) Designed an intelligent glove, EyeGlove, with an added visual channel, and based on this, developed a virtual-real hybrid intelligent laboratory for chemistry experiment teaching.
(2) Introducing a multimodal fusion algorithm based on fuzzy reasoning and Dempster-Shafer (DS) evidence theory. This algorithm integrates gesture motion channels, speech channels, and visual channels to determine user's fuzzy or incomplete intentions.

2 Related Work

With the transformation of information technology, educators are continuously developing new teaching methods [12]. Currently, intelligent experiments can be broadly categorized into AR, VR, and MR forms. AR experimental teaching can assist students in learning subjects that are challenging to practically operate [8, 13]. VR technology enables highly immersive interaction with virtual environments [9, 10], allowing users to conduct various experimental operations within these virtual settings [11, 12]. However, the virtual nature of AR or VR experiments makes it challenging for operators to obtain a sense of reality during operations [8], and the requirement to wear headsets may limit users' comfortable experience with the experimental process. In contrast, MR experiments offer higher interactivity and a sense of realism. MR experiments often incorporate additional modal information to more accurately identify the operator's operational intent [5, 15], but MR experiments often face challenges such as complex experimental equipment [14].

In the process of human-computer collaboration, flexible and wearable human-computer interaction is an inevitable trend for the future, providing better participant experiences and fascinating applications such as virtual scenes, compared to traditional rigid and bulky interaction devices [16]. Smart gloves can enhance immersion, expressiveness, and presence in virtual/mixed reality. Although traditional data gloves provide valuable information in perceiving motion and touch [17], relying solely on these sensing information may not meet users' needs for comprehensive perception in some application scenarios.

Visual information plays a crucial role in the reasoning process [18]. As one of the primary human senses, vision is essential for understanding and interacting in human-computer interfaces. Particularly in tasks that require a more comprehensive understanding and interaction, accurate understanding of the appearance, shape, and gestures of objects is crucial. However, traditional smart gloves primarily focus on tactile and motion perception, capturing hand movements through sensors [19], but lack detailed visual information about the user's environment. To address this limitation, the innovative solution of adding a visual channel to the smart glove, EyeGlove, allows it to capture the scenes the experimenter sees, providing richer and more comprehensive information about user behavior and intentions.

In response, we attempt to answer the following research question:

RQ1:How do we design EyeGlove to facilitate scene perception during the experiment?

RQ2:How can fuzzy reasoning and DS evidence theory be used to achieve understanding of fuzzy and uncertain user intentions?

3 Intelligent Glove System

3.1 Hardware Components of EyeGlove

This paper designs and implements the hardware structure of the smart glove, EyeGlove (Fig. 2(a)), consisting of bend sensors (aruino flex sensor 2.2–4.5), attitude sensors (JY61), pressure sensors (RP-C18.3-LT), and binocular cameras (MS4231). Particularly, a binocular camera is added to the wrist part of the glove. By integrating the camera in the relatively flat and stable viewing angle of the glove's wrist, the issue of other parts of the hand potentially blocking the camera is avoided. This enables EyeGlove to capture and transmit visual information, thus more accurately perceiving user actions. Additionally, a multimodal fusion intent perception smart glove system based on EyeGlove is proposed (Fig. 2(b) and Fig. 2(c)). When using the system, the operator wears EyeGlove to manipulate real experimental instruments, and the virtual experimental phenomena (such as gases) are displayed on the computer screen. This not only makes the experimental process safer, enhancing the operator's sense of reality and immersion but also makes some less observable experimental operations clearer and more visible (Fig. 2(d)).

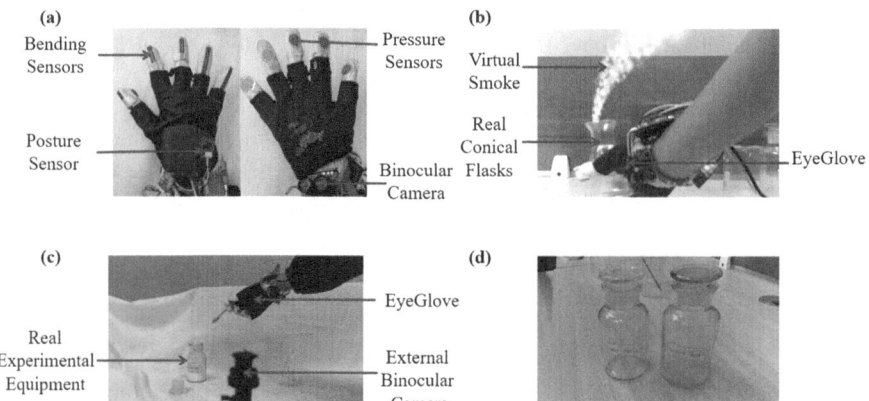

Fig. 2. (a): Hardware Structure of EyeGlove, (b): Smart Glove System,(c) System Experiment Scenario,(d) Similar experimental equipment, and subtle experimental phenomena

3.2 Intention Understanding

The process of intent understanding often encounters issues with incomplete and uncertain information. Fuzzy reasoning allows the use of fuzzy sets in handling ambiguous and uncertain information, while Dempster-Shafer (DS) evidence theory provides an effective framework for dealing with uncertainty and conflicts. Therefore, this paper proposes a multimodal intent understanding method based on fuzzy reasoning and DS evidence theory (MUFD). The general framework of the smart glove system is shown in Fig. 3.

Firstly, In the scene perception channel, we utilize the YOLOv5 algorithm to obtain the planar information of the scene and use the SGBM algorithm to obtain the depth visual information of the scene. The intention probability sets of visual channels obtained separately by the camera of EyeGlove and external binocular cameras (YSA algorithm), as well as the final user experimental intention probability set obtained by entropy weight method (MAG algorithm). Next, in the gesture motion channel, the user's gesture intention is judged by comprehensive analysis of the bending sensor and pressure sensor of EyeGlove. Then, the input intentions of users in each channel of visual channel, gesture motion channel, and voice channel are fuzzified to obtain the user experimental intention sets of each channel. After fuzzifying the user experimental intention sets of each channel, a fuzzy intention set is formed, and the membership degree of each channel fuzzy set is calculated using Gaussian membership function. The membership degrees of user fuzzy intentions in each channel are normalized to obtain the credibility distribution of each channel for a certain fuzzy intention. Based on expert knowledge

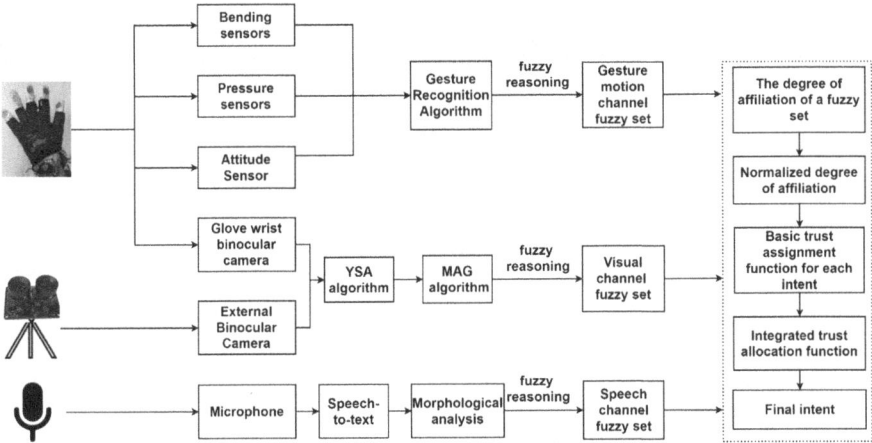

Fig. 3. Multimodal intention understanding method based on fuzzy reasoning and DS evidence theory.

and task requirements, we adjusted the importance of different channels in intention classification to obtain the weight of each channel. The fuzzy sets of user experimental intentions of each channel are taken as evidence sources, and basic belief assignment functions are constructed for each evidence source according to the weights of each channel to represent the support of the channel for each possible intention. Using the DS synthesis rule, the basic belief assignment functions for a certain fuzzy intention under different channels are combined to obtain the comprehensive belief assignment function of that intention. Based on the comprehensive belief assignment function, we calculate the confidence of each possible fuzzy intention, and the fuzzy intention with the highest confidence is the user's final fuzzy intention. The fuzzy sets of each channel are used as evidence for reasoning, and the user's current intention judgment is obtained through fusion, and the user's final intention is obtained after de-fuzzification.

4 Methodology

4.1 Participants

The experiment invited 20 volunteers to participate, including 8 males and 12 females, aged between 23 and 27, with an average age of 24.3 years and a total variance of 0.91. The volunteers participating in the experiment had no previous experience with intelligent experiments but had experience with real chemical experiments. The experiment adopted a within-subjects design. To eliminate the influence of individual differences on the experimental results, we adopted several methods: Firstly, we used random grouping to ensure that subjects were assigned to different experimental condition groups, reducing potential individual differences. Secondly, we employed a balanced design to ensure that each subject received an equal number of test conditions, and the occurrence of each condition was balanced. Additionally, we used a crossover design where each subject was tested in different condition orders to reduce errors caused by individual differences.

Finally, we controlled external variables in the experiment, such as environmental conditions, as much as possible to minimize their impact on the results. Through these methods, we aimed to minimize the effects of individual differences and other potential errors on the experimental results, making the results more reliable and trustworthy. All volunteers participating in the experiment signed informed consent forms, were mentally healthy, capable of independent learning, and actively participated in the questionnaires. The experiment lasted no more than 2 h and was divided into two stages: teaching and operation. Participants maintained a seated posture throughout the experiment, taking a 20-min break in the lounge after completing a section to ensure the experiment was not affected.

4.2 Assessment of the Necessity of the Camera at the Glove's Wrist

To investigate the impact of wrist cameras on the system's understanding of volunteers' experimental intentions, we designed a set of comparative experiments. Volunteers used smart glove systems with and without wrist cameras to perform 4 hard-to-identify experimental steps, each step conducted 3 times. To reduce interference from other factors on the experimental results, all volunteers received the same system usage instructions before the experiment. This research design aims to gain a deeper understanding of the impact of wrist cameras on experimental operations to ensure the reliability and repeatability of the experimental results.

Table 1. Key Steps in the Experimental Process That Are Difficult to Identify.

Step 1	Step 2	Step 3	Step 4
A narrow-necked bottle containing concentrated sulfuric acid	A narrow-necked bottle containing concentrated ammonia solution	Pick up the medicine spoon	Pick up the pipette

The reason for selecting the above steps is because we observed significant issues in real experiments. The experimental instruments in Steps 1 and 2 are difficult to distinguish in appearance, mainly due to their similarities in color and shape, except for the labels. Similarly, the instruments between Steps 3 and 4, being relatively small, also face difficulties in recognition. These key steps that are difficult to identify directly impact the accuracy and overall effectiveness of the experimental results.

4.3 Multi-modal Intention Understanding Method Based on Fuzzy Reasoning and Dempster-Shafer Evidence Theory (MUFD)

To delve into the performance of the MUFD algorithm in handling incomplete and uncertain information, we designed a comparative experiment. Volunteers used the smart glove system to express 22 experimental intentions for the reaction between 'solid sodium chloride and concentrated sulfuric acid,' including incomplete or uncertain expressions, such as expressing the voice intention of 'pick up the beaker' as 'beaker' or 'cup,' etc. We recorded the number of successful identifications of experimental intentions by these 20 volunteers in these situations to assess the robustness and adaptability of the MUFD algorithm. This experimental design allows us to gain a deep understanding of the performance of the MUFD algorithm in handling complex contexts that may be encountered in practical applications.

4.4 Intelligent Glove System

To delve into the impact of the smart glove system on user task load and subjective emotions, we designed a set of comparative experiments. The experiments included three perceptual channel environments: Experiment Environment 1 (unimodal visual channel), Experiment Environment 2 (bimodal visual and voice channels), and Experiment Environment 3 (trimodal, including visual, voice, and gesture motion channels). Volunteers completed tasks in each environment, including difficult-to-identify key steps and incomplete, uncertain expressions, simulating the complexity of user-system interactions in the real world. The specific descriptions and objectives of the tasks were detailed in the experimental design to ensure consistency and comparability of tasks. After the experiments, we distributed two questionnaires to 20 volunteers, assessing task load and subjective emotional experiences separately. These questionnaires used validated standard scales and a series of open-ended questions to ensure comprehensive and in-depth questionnaire design.

4.4.1 Task Load (STLX)

To assess the task load of users when operating the smart glove system, we employed an adapted version of the NASA Task Load Index (NASA TLX) [20]. At the end of each experimental session in every environment, volunteers rated their perceived load across three dimensions: Cognitive Task Load, Physiological Task Load, and Behavioral Task Load using a Likert scale ranging from 1 to 10. We set the significance level at 0.05 a priori.

4.4.2 Subjective Emotional Experience(SAM) [21]

This questionnaire serves as a reliable measure of users' subjective emotional experiences when operating the smart glove system. At the end of each experiment in each environmental setting, participants provided written ratings for the Valence, Arousal, and Dominance dimensions of their current experiment.

5 Results

5.1 Evaluation of the Glove Wrist Camera

The experimental results, as shown in the Fig. 4, indicate that the smart glove system with a wrist-mounted camera significantly outperforms the system without a wrist-mounted camera in handling challenging recognition steps, with the vertical axis representing the

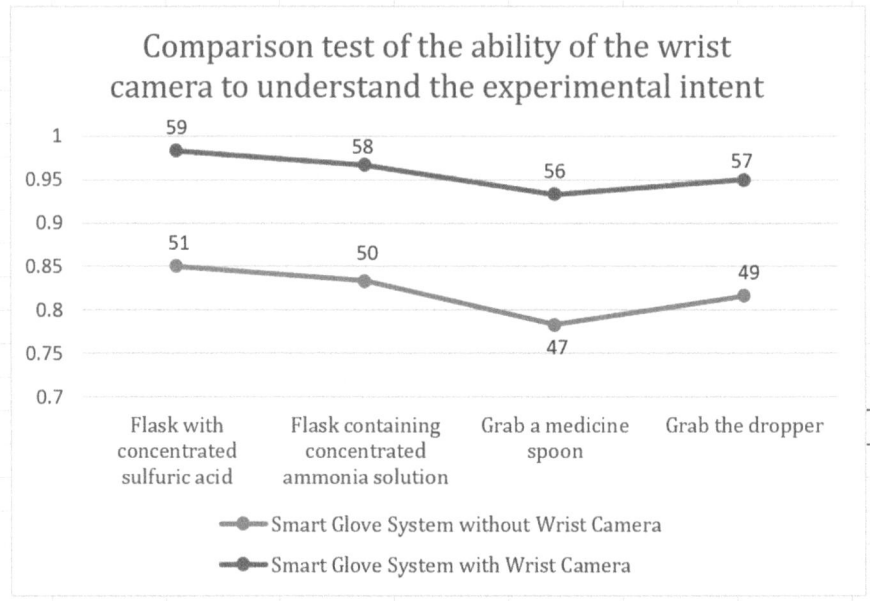

Fig. 4. Comparative experiment on the impact of the glove wrist camera on intention understanding ability.

recognition rate. The use of a wrist camera enhances the accuracy of volunteer experimental operations, demonstrating a positive impact on the system's understanding of participants' experimental intentions. These findings not only address issues in experimental design but also provide a reliable foundation for overall performance improvement. The wrist camera exhibits potential applications in addressing challenging key steps, offering valuable insights for future research and technological development.

5.2 Multi-modal Intent Understanding Method Based on Fuzzy Reasoning and DS Evidence Theory (MUFD)

During the testing process of 22 experimental intentions among 20 volunteers, each intention was expressed five times, including experimental intentions with incomplete or uncertain information. Among the 2200 expressions, the success rate of the MUFD algorithm exceeded 90%. This demonstrates the robustness of the MUFD algorithm to incomplete and uncertain information, highlighting its significant superiority in handling incomplete and uncertain information of user experimental intentions. This provides positive insights into the reliability and adaptability of the smart glove system in practical applications and offers valuable guidance for future improvements and optimizations of the MUFD algorithm to better meet user needs.

Table 2. STLX Experimental Results

Groups	N	Score
Experimental environment 1	60	7.47 ± 1.23^b
Experimental environment 2	60	6.98 ± 0.86^b
Experimental environment 3	60	3.38 ± 1.11^c
F		256.910
P		0.000

5.3 STLX

The experimental results are shown in Table 2. Among them, experimental environment 1 is (single-modal visual channel), experimental environment 2 is (dual-modal visual and voice channels), and the experimental environment 3 of this smart glove system (trimodal, including visual, voice, and gesture motion channels). To validate the significant differences in volunteer experiences under different experimental environments, the Friedman test was employed, yielding a p-value < 0.001, indicating highly significant differences in volunteer experience assessments across the three experimental environments. Further analysis using the Duncan test revealed significant differences in volunteer experience assessments. From the obtained experimental results, it is evident that there is a substantial difference in volunteer experience evaluations between experimental environments 1 and 2 compared to experimental environment 3. These results not only enhance the understanding of user experiences but also provide robust support for further in-depth analysis (Table 1).

5.4 SAM

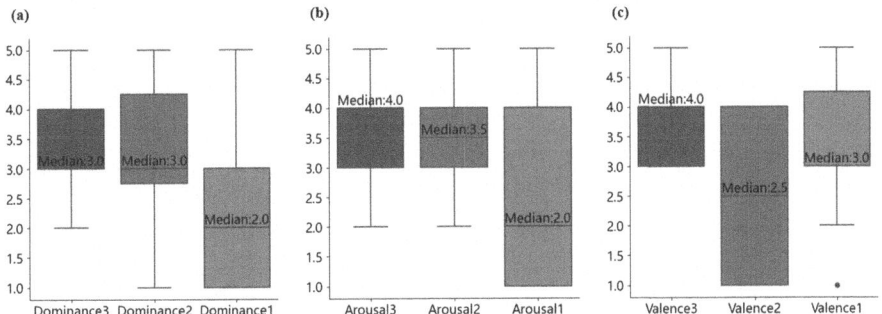

Fig. 5. SAM Ratings Under Different Experimental Conditions (a) Valence (b) Arousal (c) Dominance

Figure 5 presents SAM results under these three experimental conditions, with a significance level set at 0.05. The obtained results for Valence(F(2,57) = 3.79, p

= 0.028,η_p^2= 0.12), Arousal (F(2,57) = 5.85, p = 0.0048,η_p^2=0.17) and Dominance (F(2,57) = 4.37, p = 0.017,η_p^2=0.13). So indicate that, across different experimental environments, the combined use of three modalities on participants results in increased pleasure (Valence), decreased arousal (Arousal), and enhanced dominance (Dominance). Overall, SAM results reveal the multifaceted impact of multi-modal interaction on volunteers' emotional experiences. Significant differences in pleasure, arousal, and dominance offer an opportunity for a detailed understanding of the nuanced effects of multi-modal interaction on user experiences.

6 Discussion

In summary of the above experimental results, we conducted an in-depth discussion on the role and impact of the wrist camera, MUFD algorithm, and multimodal interaction in the intelligent glove system to better understand their functions in the system.

Firstly, through the comparative experiment shown in Fig. 4, we clearly observe that the intelligent glove system with a wrist camera is significantly superior in resolving challenging key steps compared to the system without a wrist camera. This implies that the introduction of the wrist camera has a positive impact on enhancing the system's understanding of participants' experimental intentions, providing a reliable foundation for the overall performance improvement of the intelligent glove system, and demonstrating potential application prospects in addressing challenging key steps in experiments. Secondly, the experimental results of the MUFD algorithm indicate that, in situations where experimental intentions contain incomplete or uncertain information, the algorithm has successfully achieved an average accuracy of over 90%. This provides positive insights into the reliability and adaptability of the intelligent glove system in practical applications, emphasizing the significant superiority of the MUFD algorithm in handling user experimental intentions with incomplete and uncertain information. These findings not only guide future improvements and optimizations of the MUFD algorithm but also offer reliable solutions to issues in experimental design. Finally, in terms of multimodal interaction, SAM results show significant differences in Valence, Arousal, and Dominance under different experimental conditions. This implies that acquiring participants' experimental operation intentions through three modalities can contribute to increased pleasure, decreased arousal, and enhanced dominance. This provides important reference and guidance for designing emotionally effective intelligent systems and deepens the understanding of the impact of multimodal interaction on user experience.

In summary, these experimental results not only provide substantial support for the technological development of the smart glove system but also offer important reference and inspiration for future research and technological improvements.

7 Limitation

This study has limitations that need to be considered. The diversity of volunteers in the experiment is relatively limited, not comprehensively covering various age groups, cultural backgrounds, and physical conditions, this study has limitations that need to be considered. The diversity of volunteers in the experiment is relatively limited, not comprehensively covering various age groups, cultural backgrounds, and physical conditions, in addition, the issue of user adaptability is a direction for future research.

Despite these limitations, the study's findings provide valuable insights for multiple domains. EyeGlove demonstrates significant advantages in laboratory work, offering feasible technological support to enhance experimental accuracy. The successful application of the MUFD algorithm in user intent recognition introduces a new perspective for human-computer interaction, holding the potential to improve intelligent devices' understanding of user commands. The intelligent glove system for multimodal interaction recognition shows broad potential applications in enhancing user experience and understanding intent. Additionally, the system presents intriguing possibilities in the field of education. These potential applications will be further explored in future research to ensure the feasibility and effectiveness of the technology in practical scenarios.

8 Conclusion

In this work, we proposed placing a camera on the wrist of a glove and introduced an intelligent experimental system with multimodal fusion based on this smart glove, along with a multimodal intent understanding method based on fuzzy reasoning and DS evidence theory. By comprehensively evaluating the performance of the smart glove system in experimental scenarios, we explored the wrist camera, MUFD algorithm, and the multimodal fusion smart glove system. Firstly, the experimental results clearly indicate that the smart glove with a wrist camera exhibits significant advantages in solving key steps that are not easily identifiable in experiments, providing strong support for enhancing the system's understanding of participants' experimental intentions. Secondly, the MUFD algorithm demonstrates robustness in handling incomplete and uncertain information in experimental intent, providing reliable algorithmic support for improving the accuracy of user experimental intent recognition. Finally, the experimental results of the multimodal fusion smart glove system reveal the multifaceted impact of the system on participants' emotional experiences, offering important reference and guidance for designing more emotionally effective intelligent systems. Overall, this study provides valuable insights for the improvement of smart glove systems in experimental operations and user interactions, offering crucial references for research and technological development in related fields.

Acknowledgements. I would like to thank those who helped me in the preparation of my thesis.

References

1. Liao, X.: Doctoral Thesis on Theoretical Research and Design of Intelligent Laboratory, University of Chinese Academy of Sciences (Shanghai Institute of Technical Physics, Chinese Academy of Sciences) (2017). (in Chinese)
2. Çankaya, S.: Use of VR headsets in education: a systematic review study. J. Educ. Technol. Online Learn. 2(1), 74–88 (2019)
3. Radu, I., Schneider, B.: What can we learn from augmented reality (AR)? Benefits and drawbacks of AR for inquiry-based learning of physics. In: Proceedings of the 2019 CHI Conference on Human Factors in Computing Systems, pp. 1–12 (2019)
4. Tang, Y.M., Au, K.M., Lau, H.C., Ho, G.T., Wu, C.H.: Evaluating the effectiveness of learning design with mixed reality (MR) in higher education. Virtual Reality 24(4), 797–807 (2020)
5. Yu, M., Liu, Y.J., Zhao, G., Wang, C.C.: Tangible interaction with 3D printed modular robots through multi-channel sensors. In: SIGGRAPH Asia 2018 Posters, pp. 1–2 (2018)
6. Li, N., et al.: vMirror: enhancing the interaction with occluded or distant objects in vr with virtual mirrors. In: Proceedings of the 2021 CHI Conference on Human Factors in Computing Systems, pp. 1–11 (2021)
7. Yue, Y.T., Zhang, X., Yang, Y., Ren, G., Choi, Y.K., Wang, W.: Wiredraw: 3D wire sculpturing guided with mixed reality. In Proceedings of the 2017 CHI Conference on Human Factors in Computing Systems, pp. 3693–3704 (2017)
8. Shelton, B.E., Hedley, N.R.: Using augmented reality for teaching earth-sun relationships to undergraduate geography students. In: The First IEEE International Workshop Agumented Reality Toolkit, p. 8. IEEE (2002)
9. Holly, M., Pirker, J., Resch, S., Brettschuh, S., Gütl, C.: Designing VR experiences–expectations for teaching and learning in VR. Educ. Technol. Soc. 24(2), 107–119 (2021)
10. Slavova, Y., Mu, M.: A comparative study of the learning outcomes and experience of VR in education. In: 2018 IEEE Conference on Virtual Reality and 3D User Interfaces (VR), pp. 685–686. IEEE (2018)
11. Horváth, I.: Evolution of teaching roles and tasks in VR/AR-based education. In: 2018 9th IEEE International Conference on Cognitive Infocommunications (CogInfoCom), pp. 000355–000360. IEEE (2018)
12. Dede, C.: Immersive interfaces for engagement and learning. Science 323(5910), 66–69 (2009)
13. Rasheed, F., Onkar, P., Narula, M.: Immersive virtual reality to enhance the spatial awareness of students. In: Proceedings of the 7th Indian Conference on Human-Computer Interaction, pp. 154–160 (2015)
14. Speicher, M., Hall, B.D., Nebeling, M.: What is mixed reality?. In: Proceedings of the 2019 CHI Conference on Human Factors in Computing Systems, pp. 1–15 (2019)
15. Matovu, H., et al.: Immersive virtual reality for science learning: Design, implementation, and evaluation. Stud. Sci. Educ., 1–40 (2023)
16. Chhabria, S.A., Dharaskar, R.V., Thakare, V.M.: Survey of fusion techniques for design of efficient multimodal systems. In: 2013 International Conference on Machine Intelligence and Research Advancement, pp. 486–492. IEEE (2013)
17. Sánchez-Margallo, F.M., Pérez-Duarte, F.J., Sánchez-Margallo, J.A., Lucas-Hernández, M., Matos-Azevedo, A.M., Díaz-Güemes, I.: Application of a motion capture data glove for hand and wrist ergonomic analysis during laparoscopy. Minim. Invasive Ther. Allied Technol. 23(6), 350–356 (2014)
18. Hammer, E.: Logic and visual information (1995)
19. Takada, R., Kadomoto, J., Shizuki, B.: A sensing technique for data glove using conductive fiber. In: Extended Abstracts of the 2019 CHI Conference on Human Factors in Computing Systems, pp. 1–4 (2019)

20. Hart, S.G., Staveland, L.E.: Development of NASA-TLX (Task Load Index): Results of empirical and theoretical research. In: Advances in Psychology, vol. 52, pp. 139–183. North-Holland (1988)
21. Bradley, M.M., Lang, P.J.: Measuring emotion: the self-assessment manikin and the semantic differential. J. Behav. Ther. Exp. Psych. **25**(1), 49–59 (1994)

Multilevel Topology Structure-Aware Network for 3D Hand Pose Estimation

Yanjun Liu[1], Wanshu Fan[1], Xiaopeng Wei[2], and Dongsheng Zhou[1(✉)]

[1] Dalian University, Dalian, China
liuyanjun@s.dlu.edu.cn, {fanwanshu,zhouds}@dlu.edu.cn
[2] Dalian University of Technology, Dalian, China
xpwei@dlut.edu.cn

Abstract. 3D hand pose estimation from monocular RGB images is an essential topic in computer vision and pattern recognition, which is widely used in various fields, especially for virtual reality, human-computer interaction, and gesture recognition, but often grapples with challenges such as pose complexity and self-occlusions. Most existing methods often fail to sufficiently capture the skeletal representation of the hand due to the complex topology relationships between hand joints. To mitigate these challenges, we introduce the Multilevel Topology Structure-aware Network (MTS-Net), a novel deep learning architecture designed for further exploring the hierarchy of hand topology to improve 3D hand pose estimation. Specifically, we propose a Multi-features Cross-Attention module (MCA) to enhance the interaction of multi-level information from different hierarchical topologies of joint, part, and hand. Finally, to validate the effectiveness of the proposed model, we conduct experimental verification on three commonly used public datasets: Rendered Hand Dataset (RHD), Stereo Hand Pose Benchmark (STB), and First-Person Hand Action Benchmark (FPHA). The experimental results surpassed those of the existing state-of-the-art models.

Keywords: 3D Hand Pose estimation · Transformer · GCN · Geometric Feature

1 Introduction

3D hand pose estimation serves as a fundamental research area with extensive applications in fields such as human-computer interaction [1], virtual reality [2,3], hand reconstruction [4–6], and gesture recognition [7–10] etc. Despite significant progress in the field of research over the past few years, the precise determination of 3D hand joint positions from monocular RGB images continues to pose a substantial difficulty. Factors contributing to this difficulty include complex hand topologies, self-occlusion, depth ambiguity, complex hand poses, and limited information in monocular images.

To address complex hand topologies, geometric modeling techniques provide a foundation for understanding and representing the hand's topology structure. These models define the hierarchical relationships between joints and parts, which can help improve the accuracy of pose estimation by reducing ambiguity. Existing methods [11–13] often employ the GCN layer or Transformer to represent the topological structure of hand joints. To extract sufficient usable information from monocular RGB images, many works focus on constructing various features to represent hand keypoints [11] utilize pose features, shape features, and camera features as the feature representation of 3D hand keypoints [14] believe that the pose of the hand is also related to the state of the arm, so they incorporate arm features into the model when estimating 3D hand poses. Guo et al. [15] obtain 2D heatmaps of keypoints and skeletons through the Hourglass, and complete the interaction of two types of features through the designed Feature Chat Block, thereby estimating the 3D hand pose. Chen et al. [16] capture the u-coordinate features and v-coordinate features of the keypoints through vertical single-column convolution and horizontal single-row convolution, respectively, and then estimate the z-coordinate features with the global features obtained by pooling. Although the aforementioned works achieve great achievements in estimating 3D hand poses using various types of features, most of them do not establish connections between different features.

Unlike the aforementioned works, to model keypoints from different hierarchies, we use joint features, part features, and hand features as the feature representation of keypoints. To construct the relationship between joints, it is also possible to construct the relationship between features at different levels, we adopt TNT [17] as the baseline to focus on the relationship between joints and between the different levels of hand. However, if the interaction of multiple features is simply established using the Multi-head Self-Attention of Transformer, it will face the problem of incomplete interaction. To work around this limitation, we design a Multi-feature Cross-Attention module (MCA) to ensure that the ternary input can construct comprehensive interactions.

The main contributions of this paper can be summarized as follows:

- We propose a Multilevel Topology Structure-aware Network (MTS-Net) for 3D hand pose estimation, which not only establishes dependencies among hand joints but also incorporates the features of multiple semantic levels.
- We propose a Multi-features Cross-Attention module (MCA) to better fuse multiple features, enabling effective interaction from different hierarchical topologies of joint, part, and hand.
- We quantitatively and qualitatively conduct experimental verification on three commonly used benchmarks. The experimental results show that our method is superior to the existing state-of-the-art methods.

We organize the structure of this paper within the following arrangement: We introduce the related work including Transformer for 3D hand pose estimation and Multiple features for joint expression in Sect. 2. We detailedly introduce our MTS-Net in Sect. 3. We present experiments both quantitatively and qualitatively in Sect. 4. We conclude our MTS-Net in Sect. 5.

2 Related Works

Significant progress has been made in 3D hand pose estimation in recent years, especially with the advent of the Transformer model. With its ability to construct global relationships, it propels the development of 3D hand pose estimation. In this part, we only briefly describe some recent 3D hand pose estimation methods that are relevant to our approach.

Transformer for 3D Hand Pose Estimation. Some works [12,13,18] consider using the Transformer to construct relationships between global keypoints. Huang et al. [12] adopt a non-autoregressive decoder to prevent Transformer from modeling the sequence of hand poses. Wang et al. [13] utilize Transformer to construct global similarity dependencies while using the GCN layer to establish keypoint relationships that are only applicable to hand structures. Yin et al. [18] infer the context between hand and object features through the Transformer, encoding hand features and object features in different ways to improve the accuracy of gesture recognition and pose estimation. Although the above works adopt Transformer for 3D hand pose estimation from different directions and achieve great success, they only establish relationships between keypoints. Therefore, we model hand information from different levels of the hand and design MTS-Net based on TNT [17], which not only constructs relationships between keypoints but also completes the interaction of different hierarchy features of keypoints.

Multi-feature for Joint Expression. To enrich the representation of keypoints, many methods [11,14–16] construct various keypoint features to ensure the robustness and accuracy of keypoint position estimation. He et al. [11] utilize pose features, shape features, and camera features to form keypoint representations for estimating 3D hand poses. Liu et al. [14] believe that the pose of the hand is also related to the state of the arm, hence they jointly estimate the 3D pose of the hand using arm and hand features. Chen et al. [16] capture the u-coordinate features and v-coordinate features of the keypoints through vertical single-column convolution and horizontal single-row convolution, respectively, and then estimate the z-coordinate features with the globally pooled features. Although this compensates for the instability of representing keypoints with a single feature, it does not interactively align different types of features, resulting in suboptimal keypoint representation. Recently, [15] achieve interaction between two types of features using a unique feature interaction mechanism. They first obtain the 2D heatmaps of keypoints and skeletons through an hourglass, and complete the interaction of two types of features through a uniquely designed feature interaction block (Feature chat block), and estimate the 3D hand pose. Although these methods construct joint features from different aspects, they still struggle to resolve the issues brought by the complex topology of the hand. To address this challenge, we model the joint topology from different levels of the hand and use a Multi-features Cross-Attention module (MCA) in TNT to interact with features at different levels, thereby achieving state-of-the-art performance on three commonly used public datasets: RHD, STB, and FPHA.

3 Proposed Approach

In this paper, we adopt a single monocular RGB image as input for 3D hand pose estimation. Our proposed MTS-Net is illustrated in Fig. 1. We first utilize Hourglass [19] as the feature extractor. Then, we construct part features and hand features in different ways from the obtained joint features. The new keypoint feature representation is jointly represented by joint features, part features, and hand features, and serves as the input to the baseline, TNT, to obtain uv coordinate features. Similarly, keypoints represented by multiple hierarchy features are input into another TNT to obtain d coordinate features. Then the uv coordinate features and d coordinate features are jointly estimated to obtain the d coordinate, thereby reducing the difficulty of the 2D-to-3D mapping.

3.1 TNT for Hand Pose

To establish global dependency relationships between joints, and to enable interaction between multi-feature representations of joints, we discover that TNT [17] can pay attention to the relationships between joints and the different features of joints at the same time. Therefore, we use TNT [17] as the baseline and modify TNT to be suitable for the task of 3D hand pose estimation, TNTPose. Next, we first provide a brief overview of TNT in Sect. 3.1.1, followed by a detailed introduction of our proposed TNTPose in Sect. 3.1.2.

3.1.1 Review for TNT

Due to the abundant details and color information in natural images, it is necessary to mine object features at different scales and positions with a finer granularity of patches. Therefore, TNT [17] propose dividing local patches (e.g., 16×16) into smaller patches (e.g., 4×4). TNT structure they proposed is capable of learning both global and local information in an image. First, a 2D image is divided into n patches $\chi = [X^1, X^2, \ldots, X^n] \in \mathbb{R}^{n \times p \times p \times 3}$, where (p,p) is the resolution of each patch. And then, each patch is further split into m sub-patches, $X^i \to [x^{i,1}, x^{i,2}, \ldots, x^{i,m}]$, where $x^{i,j} \in \mathbb{R}^{s \times s \times 3}$ is the j-th sub-patch of the i-th patch, (s,s) is the size of sub-patches.

In TNT, two data streams process the sub-patches and patches separately. For the sub-patches, they utilize an inner transformer block to build the relation between sub-patches:

$$Y^i = [y^{i,1}, y^{i,2}, \ldots, y^{i,m}], y^{i,j} = FC(Vec(x^{i,j})), \tag{3.1a}$$

$$Y_l^{'i} = Y_{l-1}^i + MSA(LN(Y_{l-1}^i)), \tag{3.1b}$$

$$Y_l^i = Y_l^{'i} + MLP(LN(Y_l^{'i})). \tag{3.1c}$$

Where $y^{i,j} \in \mathbb{R}^c$ is the j-th sub-patch, c is the dimension of sub-patch, $Vec(*)$ is the vectorization operation. $l = 1, 2, \ldots, L$ is the index of the l-th inner transformer block, and L is the total number of stacked inner transformer blocks.

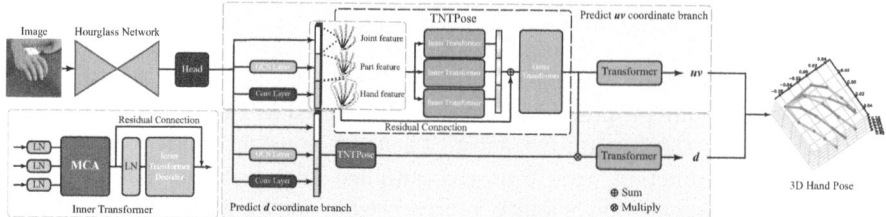

Fig. 1. Overview of the proposed MTS-Net. Our model first utilizes the Hourglass network as a feature extractor to obtain joint features. Subsequently, these joint features are used to construct part features through a GCN layer and hand features through a convolution operation with a kernel size of 1. These three types of features are concatenated to form joint features. The joint features are then processed through two branches of TNT to obtain uv coordinate features and d coordinate features respectively. The uv coordinate features are transformed into uv coordinates using a standard transformer. The d coordinate features are concatenated with the uv coordinate features and a standard transformer is used for joint estimation of the d coordinates. Ultimately, this results in the 3D hand pose.

$MSA(*)$ is the Multi-head Self-Attention module. $LN(*)$ is the Layer Normalization.

For the patches, they adopt an outer transformer block for transforming the patch embeddings:

$$Z_{l-1}^i = Z_{l-1}^i + FC(Vec(Y_l^i)), \qquad (3.2\text{a})$$

$$\mathcal{Z}_0 = [Z_{class}, Z_0^1, Z_0^2, \ldots, Z_0^n] \in \mathbb{R}^{(n+1)\times d} \qquad (3.2\text{b})$$

$$\mathcal{Z}_l' = \mathcal{Z}_{l-1} + MSA(LN(\mathcal{Z}_{l-1})), \qquad (3.2\text{c})$$

$$\mathcal{Z}_l = \mathcal{Z}_l' + MLP(LN(\mathcal{Z}_l')). \qquad (3.2\text{d})$$

Where $Z_{l-1}^i \in \mathbb{R}^d$, $FC(*)$ is the fully-connected layer. Z_{class} is the class token.

3.1.2 TNTPose

Inspired by TNT, we construct relationships at different levels between hand joint points and between different hierarchy features of the joints. For different hierarchy features of joints, we obtain the joint feature vector $V_j \in \mathbb{R}^{n\times d}$ by passing the feature map output from the hourglass through the *head* module. This joint feature vector is then used to construct the part feature vector $V_p \in \mathbb{R}^{n\times d}$ of the joints through the GCN layer, with its adjacency matrix set by prior knowledge of the hand. Simultaneously, the hand feature vector $V_h \in \mathbb{R}^{n\times d}$ is constructed from the joint feature vector through a convolution with a kernel size of 1. Therefore, a joint is jointly represented by the joint feature vector, part feature vector, and hand feature vector. Then, we use the inner transformer to facilitate interactions between different levels features. To enable effective interaction of the tripartite features, we design a Multiple features Cross-Attention module (MCA) for use within the inner transformer, as described in Sect. 3.2.

This process is formally represented as follows:

$$X = Concat(V_j, V_p, V_h), \quad (3.3a)$$
$$V_{j,l} = MLP(MCA(LN(V_{j,l-1}),$$
$$LN(V_{p,l-1}), LN(V_{h,l-1}))), \quad (3.3b)$$
$$V_{p,l} = MLP(MCA(LN(V_{p,l-1}),$$
$$LN(V_{j,l-1}), LN(V_{h,l-1}))), \quad (3.3c)$$
$$V_{h,l} = MLP(MCA(LN(V_{h,l-1}),$$
$$LN(V_{j,l-1}), LN(V_{p,l-1}))), \quad (3.3d)$$
$$X_l = X_{l-1} + Concat(V_{j,l}, V_{p,l}, V_{h,l}). \quad (3.3e)$$

Where $Concat(*)$ is the concatenate operation. $V_{*,l}$ is the output of the l-th inner transformer block. $MCA(*)$ is the Multiple features Cross-Attention module. $MLP(*)$ is the multilayer perceptrons.

For the joints, we adopt the standard transformer as our outer transformer to establish connections between joints:

$$\chi = [X_0, X_1, \ldots, X_n], \chi \in \mathbb{R}^{n \times 3d}, \quad (3.4a)$$
$$\chi'_l = \chi_{l-1} + MSA(LN(\chi_{l-1})), \quad (3.4b)$$
$$\chi_l = \chi'_l + MLP(LN(\chi'_l)). \quad (3.4c)$$

Where $\chi \in \mathbb{R}^{n \times 3d}$ is the feature of n joints composed of different feature vectors of 3 d-dimensional lengths.

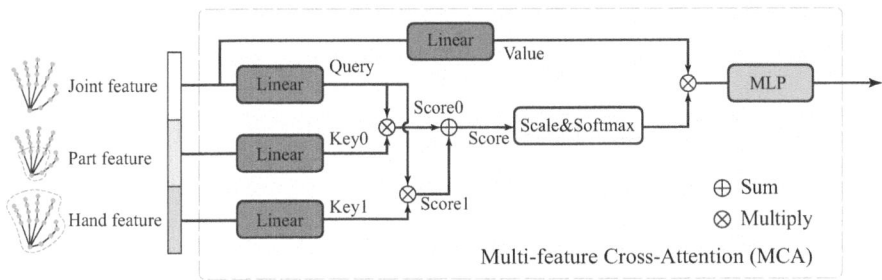

Fig. 2. Overview of the proposed Multi-features Cross-Attention module (MCA).

3.2 Multi-features Cross-Attention Module

The Multi-head Self-Attention in the inner transformer of TNT can only accommodate interactions between two features at most. To allow for effective and convenient interaction of the multi-level features of the joints, we propose a

Multi-features Cross-Attention module (MCA) to improve the inner transformer, as shown in Fig. 2. The MCA has four inputs, namely $Query$, Key_0, Key_1, and $Value$. First, the Query calculates attention scores with Key_0 and Key_1 respectively, then adds the two attention scores to get the final attention score. Finally, the final attention score is calculated with Value to obtain the final output result. This process is formally represented as follows:

$$Score_0 = Linear(Query) * Linear(Key_0^T), \tag{3.5a}$$

$$Score_1 = Linear(Query) * Linear(Key_1^T), \tag{3.5b}$$

$$Scores = Softmax(\frac{Score_0 + Score_1}{\sqrt{d}}), \tag{3.5c}$$

$$X = MLP(Scores * Value). \tag{3.5d}$$

Where $Linear(*)$ is the linear layer.

Taking the calculation of the new joint expression after interaction as an example, the joint feature vector, part feature vector, and hand feature vector that make up the joint point representation are used. The joint feature vector first serves as the $Query$ and $Value$, while the part feature vector and hand feature vector serve as Key_0 and Key_1 respectively. The new joint feature vector is then calculated through the inner transformer with MCA. The other feature vectors are calculated in this way in turn to obtain the corresponding new feature vectors.

3.3 Loss Function

We constrain the predicted 3D hand pose based on the joint 3D positions L_J and finger bone lengths L_B:

$$L = L_J + L_B. \tag{3.6}$$

3D Joint Loss. We calculate the Euclidean distance between the predicted 3D joint coordinates and the ground-truth 3D joint coordinates:

$$L_J = \frac{1}{J} \sum_{i=1}^{J} \|P_i^{pred} - P_i^{gt}\|_1. \tag{3.7}$$

Where J is the number of joints, usually $J = 21$.

Bone Length Loss. The loss is calculated by the predicted bone length B^{pred} and the ground-truth bone length B^{gt}:

$$L_B = \frac{1}{2J} \sum_{i=1}^{J-1} \left(B_i^{pred} - B_i^{gt}\right)^2. \tag{3.8}$$

4 Experiments

In this section, we conduct extensive experiments to demonstrate the effectiveness of our proposed the Multilevel Topology Structure-aware Network (MTS-Net). In Sect. 4.1, we introduce the implementation details of our MTS-Net. We then describe the used datasets for 3D hand pose estimation in Sect. 4.2. We further give the metrics for measuring the estimation performance in Sect. 4.3. Section 4.4 presents both quantitative and qualitative results. We analyze and discuss our MTS-Net in Sect. 4.5.

4.1 Implementation Details

We use Pytorch as the deep learning framework to implement our MTS-Net on a single NVIDIA RTX 2080Ti. We use the Adam as the optimizer [20]. The batch size is 32, and the initial learning rate is set to 0.001 and is decreased at the 140 and 150 epochs. The learning rate decay factor is set to 0.1 and the training is terminated at 160 epochs. For STB [21], RHD [22] and FPHA [23] datasets, we resize all RGB images to 256 × 256 as the input for our MTS-Net. Our model takes 46 h on RHD and STB datasets and 54 h on FPHA dataset. Furthermore, to enhance the resilience of our model, we employ a range of data augmentation strategies, encompassing adjustments in image scale, rotation, translation, brightness, central projection, and color. Our proposed model is trained in an end-to-end manner. This network model we put forward does not necessitate the inclusion of other multimodal data (like depth maps, hand segmentation maps, etc.) as input.

4.2 Datasets

We evaluate our MTS-Net on three publicly available datasets, including the Stereo Hand Pose Benchmark (STB) [21], the Rendered Hand Pose Dataset (RHD) [22] and First-Person Hand Action Benchmark (FPHA) [23]. The RHD is a synthetic dataset, which is constructed with 20 virtual game characters and involves 39 different hand poses. It consists of 4,125 images for training and 2,728 images for testing. The RHD dataset is extremely challenging since the images contain complex backgrounds, rich hand poses, and severe self-occlusion. The STB is a dataset composed of real-world images. STB-SK contains 15,000 images for training and 3000 images for testing, all of which provide accurate hand joint annotations. The FPHA, a public resource, encompasses an extensive collection of 105,459 video frames, each with a high-definition resolution of 1920 × 1080. The FPHA dataset is unique in its inclusion of 45 categories of daily hand actions, involving 26 distinct objects in a variety of hand configurations. A noteworthy feature of the FPHA dataset is its provision of precise labels for both 2D and 3D hand poses, as well as gesture labels.

4.3 Metrics

MPJPE. The Mean Per Joint Position Error (MPJPE) is a commonly used metric to assess the performance of 3D hand pose estimation models. It quantifies the Euclidean distance in millimeters between the predicted joints and the corresponding ground truth joints.

3D PCK. The Percentage of Correct Keypoints (PCK) is a metric, which aims to measure the proportion of correctly located joints in three-dimensional space. It assesses the percentage of estimated joints within a normalized distance to the ground-truth joints with a specified threshold.

AUC. The Area Under the Curve (AUC) is a metric that represents the area under the PCK curve at various error thresholds.

4.4 Quantitative and Qualitative Results

4.4.1 Quantitative Comparisons

We compare our MTS-Net with several state-of-the-art methods [21,24–36] on the STB [21] and RHD [22] benchmarks for the 3D keypoint estimation performance. Table 1 shows that our MTS-Net is able to better estimate the 3D keypoint than existing state-of-the-art methods on the RHD [22] and STB [21] datasets. Specifically, our MTS-Net achieves the AUC [20–50 mm] of 0.998 and the MPJPE of 6.10 mm on the STB dataset. On the RHD dataset, our MTS-Net achieves the AUC [20–50 mm] of 0.954 and the MPJPE of 11.42 mm. These results verify the effectiveness of our method.

In addition, we compare our method with state-of-the-art methods using the 3D PCK curves, as shown in Fig. 3. On the RHD dataset, we compare our work with some state-of-the-art works, including [25,26,29,32,37–39], and [21], with an error threshold range of 20–50 mm. On the STB dataset, we also compare our work with other state-of-the-art works, including [21,25,26,29,40–43], with an error threshold range of 20–50 mm. On the FPHA dataset, we compare our work with [23,44–46], with an error range of 0–50 mm.

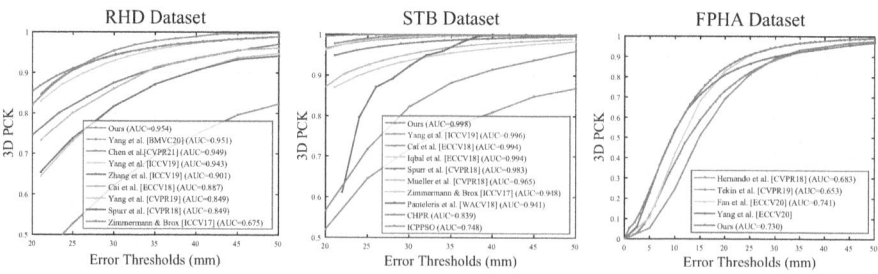

Fig. 3. The 3D PCK curve comparison results with the state-of-the-art methods on the RHD [22], STB [21] and FPHA [23].

Table 1. Comparison of 3D hand pose estimation results with the state-of-the-art methods. "-" denotes the model did not report the results. The best results are marked in **Bold**.

Datasets	STB [21]		RHD [22]		#Params ↓
Method	AUC ↑	MPJPE (mm) ↓	AUC ↑	MPJPE (mm) ↓	
Zimmermann & Brox [21]	0.948	8.68	0.670	30.42	-
Moon et al. [24]	-	7.95	-	20.89	-
Spurr et al. [25]	0.983	8.56	0.849	19.73	-
Cai et al. [26]	0.994	-	0.887	-	-
Ge et al. [27]	**0.998**	6.37	0.920	-	21.76(M)
Boukhayma et al. [28]	-	9.76	-	-	-
Yang et al. [29]	0.996	7.05	0.943	13.14	-
Stergioulas et al. [30]	-	6.71	-	13.88	-
Li et al. [31]	**0.998**	9.43	0.951	11.63	19.60(M)
Yang et al. [32]	0.997	10.05	0.951	12.76	25.36(M)
Zhou et al. [33]	0.898	-	0.856	-	-
Lin et al. [34]	-	16.37	-	-	-
Theodoridis et al. [35]	-	6.93	-	15.61	-
Ivashechkin et al. [36]	-	6.47	-	16.79	-
MTS-Net(Ours)	**0.998**	**6.10**	**0.954**	**11.42**	**14.841(M)**

4.4.2 Qualitative Results

We further present several predicted 3D hand pose estimation examples from STB [21], RHD [22], and FPHA [23] in Fig. 4 for visual evaluation. The first and fourth columns in Fig. 4 display several RGB images under various scenarios. The second and fifth columns in Fig. 4 show the predicted 3D hand pose estimation results, where our MTS-Net generates accurate and plausible poses visually close to the ground truth, as shown in the third and last columns in Fig. 4, under conditions with large self-occlusion, different backgrounds, and large pose variations. As can be seen from Fig. 4, our proposed MTS-Net is capable of effectively handling various scenarios with substantial hand occlusions and complex hand postures. This demonstrates the excellent performance of MTS-Net.

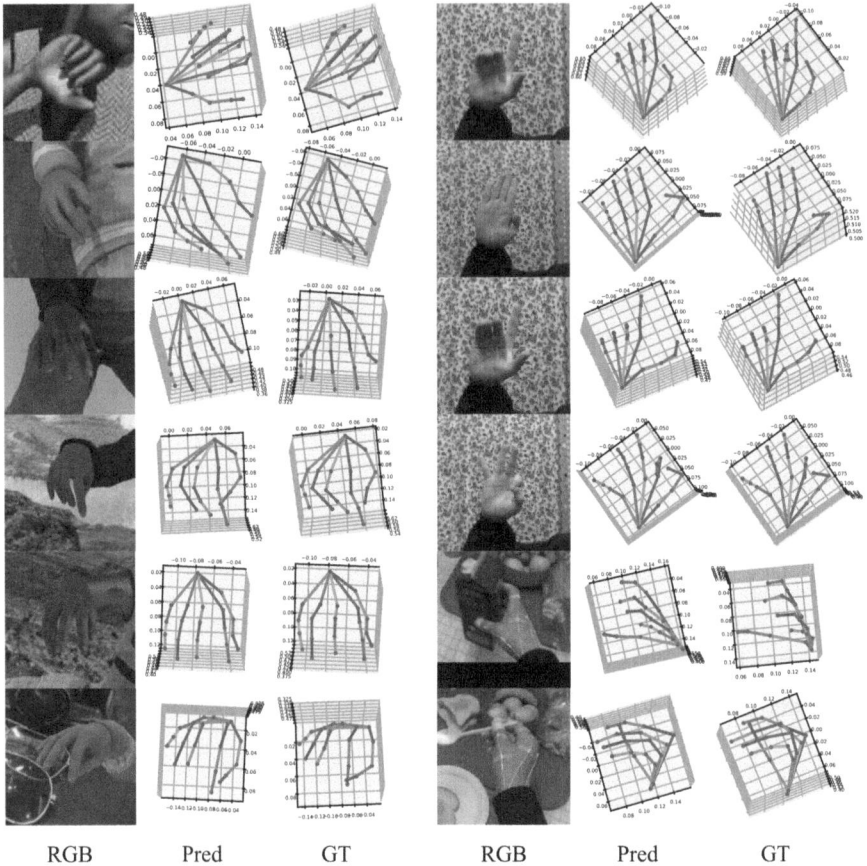

| RGB | Pred | GT | RGB | Pred | GT |

Fig. 4. Qualitative evaluation of the predicted 3D hand pose by our model, with its corresponding ground truth. The testing images are randomly selected from three public benchmarks: RHD [22], STB [21], and FPHA [23].

4.5 Ablation Study

4.5.1 Effect on TNTPose

We need to analyze the positive impact of the TNTPose architecture on the estimation of 3D hand pose. We compare the TNTPose with a model variant that only uses the standard transformer structure in place of the TNTPose, i.e., it only hasthe outer transformer and does not include the inner transformer. As shown in Table 2, our model outperforms the model that only uses the standard transformer.

Table 2. Effect of the TNTPose.

Experiment	AUC ↑	MPJPE ↓
(a) MTS-Net w/ Transformer	0.949	11.83
(b) MTS-Net w/ TNTPose(Ours)	**0.954**	**11.42**

4.5.2 Effect on MCA

To analyze whether our proposed Multiple features Cross-Attention module (MCA) effectively interacts with features and has a positive impact on the model's estimation of 3D hand pose, we design an ablation experiment comparing the use of TNTPose without MCA and the use of MCA in TNTPose, to verify the effectiveness of MCA. As shown in Table 3, Our model, which adopts the MCA structure, surpasses the model that only uses the Transformer. This demonstrates that our proposed MCA can effectively interact with features.

Table 3. Effect of the MCA.

Experiment	AUC ↑	MPJPE ↓
(a) TNTPose w/o MCA	0.935	13.13
(b) TNTPose w/ MCA(Ours)	**0.954**	**11.42**

5 Conclusion

In this paper, we introduce our newly designed MTS-Net, which robustly estimates the 3D hand pose end-to-end from a monocular RGB image. To tackle the challenging topology structure of the hand that is difficult to model, we construct the joint feature, part feature, and hand feature from different levels respectively, and concatenate them into a new joint representation. Specifically, to model both the relationships between joints and the different feature relationships of joints simultaneously, we adopt TNT as the baseline. In this, the inner Transformer and outer Transformer construct different feature relationships of joints and relationships between joints, respectively. At the same time, to enable effective interaction between the multi-level features of the joints, we propose a Multi-features Cross-Attention module (MCA) to effectively complete the interaction between multi-hierarchy features. Finally, the effectiveness of MTS-Net is fully verified through our designed qualitative and quantitative experiments and ablation experiments.

References

1. Chua, S.N.D., Chin, K.Y.R., Lim, S.F., Jain, P.: Hand gesture control for human–computer interaction with deep learning. J. Electr. Eng. Technol. **17**(3), 1961–1970 (2022). https://doi.org/10.1007/s42835-021-00972-6

2. Wu, M.-Y., Ting, P.-W., Tang, Y.-H., Chou, E.-T., Fu, L.-C.: Hand pose estimation in object-interaction based on deep learning for virtual reality applications. J. Vis. Commun. Image Represent. **70**, 102802 (2020). https://doi.org/10.1016/j.jvcir.2020.102802
3. Han, S., et al.: MEgATrack: monochrome egocentric articulated hand-tracking for virtual reality. ACM ToG **39**(4), 87–1 (2020)
4. Chen, X., Wang, B., Shum, H.-Y.: Hand Avatar: free-pose hand animation and rendering from monocular video. In: CVPR, pp. 8683–8693 (2023)
5. Wang, R., Mao, W., Li, H.: Interacting hand-object pose estimation via dense mutual attention. In: WACV, pp. 5724–5734 (2023)
6. Chen, Z., Chen, S., Schmid, C., Laptev, I.: GSDF: geometry-driven signed distance functions for 3D hand-object reconstruction. In: CVPR, pp. 12890–12900 (2023)
7. Köpüklü, O., Kose, N., Rigoll, G.: Motion fused frames: data level fusion strategy for hand gesture recognition. In: CVPR Workshops, pp. 2103–2111 (2018)
8. Azad, R., Asadi-Aghbolaghi, M., Kasaei, S., Escalera, S.: Dynamic 3D hand gesture recognition by learning weighted depth motion maps. IEEE TCSVT **29**(6), 1729–1740 (2019)
9. Zhang, Y., Cao, C., Cheng, J., Hanqing, L.: EgoGesture: a new dataset and benchmark for egocentric hand gesture recognition. IEEE TMM **20**(5), 1038–1050 (2018)
10. Han, S., et al.: UmeTrack: unified multi-view end-to-end hand tracking for VR. In: SIGGRAPH, pp. 50:1–50:9 (2022)
11. He, Y., Hu, W., Yang, S., Qu, X., Wan, P., Guo, Z.: GraphPoseGAN: 3D hand pose estimation from a monocular RGB image via adversarial learning on graphs. CoRR, abs/1912.01875 (2019)
12. Huang, L., Tan, J., Liu, J., Yuan, J.: Hand-Transformer: non-autoregressive structured modeling for 3D hand pose estimation. In: Vedaldi, A., Bischof, H., Brox, T., Frahm, J.-M. (eds.) ECCV 2020. LNCS, vol. 12370, pp. 17–33. Springer, Cham (2020). https://doi.org/10.1007/978-3-030-58595-2_2
13. Wang, Y., Chen, L., Li, J., Zhang, X.: HandGCNFormer: a novel topology-aware transformer network for 3D hand pose estimation. In: WACV, pp. 5664–5673 (2023)
14. Liu, S., Wu, W., Wu, J., Lin, Y.: Spatial-temporal parallel transformer for arm-hand dynamic estimation. In: CVPR, pp. 24091–24100 (2022)
15. Guo, S., Rigall, E., Yakun, J., Dong, J.: 3D hand pose estimation from monocular RGB with feature interaction module. IEEE TCSVT **32**(8), 5293–5306 (2022)
16. Chen, Z., Sun, Y.: Joint-wise 2D to 3D lifting for hand pose estimation from a single RGB image. Appl. Intell. **53**(6), 6421–6431 (2023)
17. Han, K., Xiao, A., Wu, E., Guo, J., Xu, C., Wang, Y.: Transformer in transformer. In: NeurIPS, pp. 15908–15919 (2021)
18. Yin, Q., et al.: 3D hand pose estimation and gesture recognition based on hand-object interaction information. In: ICCC, pp. 1–6 (2023)
19. Newell, A., Yang, K., Deng, J.: Stacked Hourglass networks for human pose estimation. In: Leibe, B., Matas, J., Sebe, N., Welling, M. (eds.) ECCV 2016. LNCS, vol. 9912, pp. 483–499. Springer, Cham (2016). https://doi.org/10.1007/978-3-319-46484-8_29
20. Kingma, D.P., Ba, J.: ADAM: a method for stochastic optimization. In: ICLR (2015)
21. Zimmermann, C., Brox, T.: Learning to estimate 3D hand pose from single RGB images. In: ICCV, pp. 4913–4921 (2017)
22. Zhang, J., Jiao, J., Chen, M., Qu, L., Xu, X., Yang, Q.: 3D hand pose tracking and estimation using stereo matching. CoRR, abs/1610.07214 (2016)

23. Garcia-Hernando, G., Yuan, S., Baek, S., Kim, T.-K.: First-person hand action benchmark with RGB-D videos and 3d hand pose annotations. In: CVPR, pp. 409–419 (2018)
24. Moon, G., Yu, S.-I., Wen, H., Shiratori, T., Lee, K.M.: InterHand2.6M: a dataset and baseline for 3D interacting hand pose estimation from a single RGB image. In: Vedaldi, A., Bischof, H., Brox, T., Frahm, J.-M. (eds.) ECCV 2020. LNCS, vol. 12365, pp. 548–564. Springer, Cham (2020). https://doi.org/10.1007/978-3-030-58565-5_33
25. Spurr, A., Song, J., Park, S., Hilliges, O.: Cross-modal deep variational hand pose estimation. In: CVPR, pp. 89–98 (2018)
26. Cai, Y., Ge, L., Cai, J., Yuan, J.: Weakly-supervised 3D hand pose estimation from monocular RGB images. In: Ferrari, V., Hebert, M., Sminchisescu, C., Weiss, Y. (eds.) ECCV 2018. LNCS, vol. 11210, pp. 678–694. Springer, Cham (2018). https://doi.org/10.1007/978-3-030-01231-1_41
27. Ge, L., et al.: 3D hand shape and pose estimation from a single RGB image. In: CVPR, pp. 10833–10842 (2019)
28. Boukhayma, A., de Bem, R.A., Torr, P.H.S.: 3D hand shape and pose from images in the wild. In: CVPR, pp. 10843–10852 (2019)
29. Yang, L., Li, S., Lee, D., Yao, A.: Aligning latent spaces for 3D hand pose estimation. In: ICCV, pp. 2335–2343 (2019)
30. Stergioulas, A., Chatzis, T., Konstantinidis, D., Dimitropoulos, K., Daras, P.: 3D hand pose estimation via aligned latent space injection and kinematic losses. In: CVPR Workshops, pp. 1730–1739 (2021)
31. Li, M., Wang, J., Sang, N.: Latent distribution-based 3d hand pose estimation from monocular RGB images. IEEE TCSVT 31(12), 4883–4894 (2021)
32. Yang, L., Li, J., Wenqiang, X., Diao, Y., Lu, C.: Recovering hand mesh with multi-stage bisected hourglass networks. In: BMVC, Bihand (2020)
33. Zhou, Y., et al.: Monocular real-time hand shape and motion capture using multi-modal data. In: CVPR, pp. 5345–5354 (2020)
34. Lin, Q., Yang, L., Yao, A.: Cross-domain 3D hand pose estimation with dual modalities. In: CVPR, pp. 17184–17193 (2023)
35. Theodoridis, T., Chatzis, T., Solachidis, V., Dimitropoulos, K., Daras, P.: Cross-modal variational alignment of latent spaces. In: CVPR Workshops, pp. 4127–4136 (2020)
36. Ivashechkin, M., Mendez, O., Bowden, R.: Denoising diffusion for 3D hand pose estimation from images. CoRR, abs/2308.09523 (2023)
37. Chen, X., et al.: Camera-space hand mesh recovery via semantic aggregation and adaptive 2D-1D registration. In: CVPR, pp. 13274–13283 (2021)
38. Zhang, X., Li, Q., Mo, H., Zhang, W., Zheng, W.: End-to-end hand mesh recovery from a monocular RGB image. In: ICCV, pp. 2354–2364 (2019)
39. Yang, L., Yao, A.: Disentangling latent hands for image synthesis and pose estimation. In: CVPR, pp. 9877–9886 (2019)
40. Iqbal, U., Molchanov, P., Breuel, T., Gall, J., Kautz, J.: Hand pose estimation via latent 2.5D heatmap regression. In: Ferrari, V., Hebert, M., Sminchisescu, C., Weiss, Y. (eds.) ECCV 2018. LNCS, vol. 11215, pp. 125–143. Springer, Cham (2018). https://doi.org/10.1007/978-3-030-01252-6_8
41. Mueller, F., et al.: GANerated hands for real-time 3D hand tracking from monocular RGB. In: CVPR, pp. 49–59 (2018)
42. Panteleris, P., Oikonomidis, I., Argyros, A.A.: Using a single RGB frame for real time 3D hand pose estimation in the wild. In: WACV, pp. 436–445 (2018)

43. Sanchez-Riera, J., Srinivasan, K., Hua, K.-L., Cheng, W.-H., Hossain, M.A., Alhamid, M.F.: Robust RGB-D hand tracking using deep learning priors. IEEE TCSVT, **28**(9), 2289–2301 (2018)
44. Tekin, B., Rozantsev, A., Lepetit, V., Fua, P.: Direct prediction of 3D body poses from motion compensated sequences. In: CVPR, pp. 991–1000 (2016)
45. Fan, Z., Liu, J., Wang, Y.: Adaptive computationally efficient network for monocular 3D hand pose estimation. In: Vedaldi, A., Bischof, H., Brox, T., Frahm, J.-M. (eds.) ECCV 2020. LNCS, vol. 12349, pp. 127–144. Springer, Cham (2020). https://doi.org/10.1007/978-3-030-58548-8_8
46. Yang, S., Liu, J., Lu, S., Er, M.H., Kot, A.C.: Collaborative learning of gesture recognition and 3D hand pose estimation with multi-order feature analysis. In: Vedaldi, A., Bischof, H., Brox, T., Frahm, J.-M. (eds.) ECCV 2020. LNCS, vol. 12348, pp. 769–786. Springer, Cham (2020). https://doi.org/10.1007/978-3-030-58580-8_45

Research on Garment Image Retrieval Method Based on Transformer and Multi-layer Feature Fusion

Guangjian Sheng[1,3], Wei Ye[2,3(✉)], Lei Zhang[3], and Zhiran Yu[3]

[1] Hubei Provincial Engineering Research Center for Intelligent Textile and Fashion, Wuhan, China
[2] Engineering Research Center of Hubei Province for Clothing Information, Wuhan, China
61844671@qq.com
[3] School of Computer Science and Artificial Intelligence, Wuhan Textile University, Wuhan, China

Abstract. Image retrieval technology has been increasingly mature. However, the accuracy and robustness of existing methods are still limited when it comes to clothing image retrieval scenarios involving complex visual variations. To address this issue, this paper proposes a multi-level feature fusion framework and introduces multiple feature extraction and fusion modules based on this framework. With this method, we can utilize feature fusion techniques to extract and integrate features at different levels, achieving the acquisition and integration of shallow and deep features of the input image. Additionally, this paper introduces a clustering re-ranking method that combines cosine distance and the k-means ++ algorithm to calculate the spatial similarity of feature vectors and uses this to rank the image similarity. Experimental results demonstrate that the proposed framework exhibits higher accuracy and robustness in clothing image retrieval than existing image retrieval methods. Therefore, this research provides new ideas and methods for further exploration in the field of clothing image retrieval.

Keywords: Multi-layer feature fusion · Feature extraction · Similarity measurement

1 Introduction

The advancement of neural network technology has led to more and more image retrieval methods, but how to achieve efficient image retrieval at low cost is still a challenge. In addition, this technology can also help companies better understand user needs and increase sales and market share. It has an extremely high research value and broad engineering application prospects.

Due to the complexity and diversity of fashion items such as clothing, accessories, and hairstyles, clothing image retrieval is a challenging task. Although traditional content-based image retrieval (CBIR) [1] methods can be used for clothing image retrieval, their effectiveness is not ideal. In recent years, deep learning-based methods have greatly improved retrieval performance. However, considering the unique characteristics and challenges of clothing image retrieval, further improvements are still needed.

To address this issue, researchers have proposed various deep learning-based methods, such as Radenovic´ et al. [2] research on Convolutional Neural Networks and Lu et al. [3] research on Recurrent Neural Networks. In deep learning-based approaches, there are typically two methods that are widely adopted. One is to utilize global features as high-level semantic representations of images, such as DOLG [4], while the other is to use local features to capture discriminative geometric information of specific image regions, such as DELG [5]. Generally, global features can learn invariant characteristics to viewpoints and lighting conditions, while local features are more sensitive to local geometry and texture. The most advanced solutions in the past typically used a two-stage approach. As shown in Fig. 1, the first stage involves locating the candidate object using global features, followed by reordering the results using local features to further improve the accuracy of the retrieval.

In this study, we focused on exploring the methods of using neural networks for image retrieval. Although previous two-stage solutions have achieved state-of-the-art performance, these methods require ranking the images twice, which limits the performance improvements. To overcome these limitations, we abandoned the two-stage framework and sought a one-stage approach to address the image retrieval problem. However, in neural networks, the low-level features of deep neural networks are more focused on capturing local features, while the high-level features are more focused on global features [6]. Therefore, to achieve better results in the field of clothing image retrieval, we propose a new multi-layer feature fusion network method that combines the advantages of low-level features and high-level features.

The multi-level feature fusion network consists of multiple layers, each integrating features from different levels of a pre-trained Transformer model. By combining features from different levels, the multi-level feature fusion network can capture both low-level and high-level features of fashion items and learn their semantic relationships. This fusion can help improve retrieval accuracy and better understand and represent clothing images.

To evaluate the effectiveness of our approach, we conducted experiments on the publicly available clothing image dataset, DeepFashion [7]. The experimental results demonstrate that our method outperforms several state-of-the-art methods in terms of retrieval accuracy and efficiency. Furthermore, we further validate the practicality of our method through the development of a clothing image retrieval system based on our approach. In summary, our work makes the following contributions:

1. We propose a multi-level feature fusion framework that effectively integrates feature information from different levels.
2. Building upon the aforementioned framework, we develop a method for clothing image retrieval using a combination of Transformer networks and a multi-level feature fusion network. This approach leverages the strengths of the Transformer model and the capabilities of the multilevel feature fusion network to enhance retrieval accuracy.
3. We conduct experiments on a publicly available clothing image dataset to validate the effectiveness of our method. The experimental results demonstrate that our approach

significantly outperforms other state-of-the-art methods in terms of both accuracy and efficiency.

2 Related Work

Clothing image retrieval is an emerging field of computer vision research that aims to accurately extract and match fashion items, such as clothing, accessories, and hairstyles, from clothing images to meet the personalized needs of users. With the popularity of e-commerce and social networks, clothing image retrieval has gradually become a popular research direction. This article will introduce the research field of clothing image retrieval and related work, including the application of traditional methods and deep learning methods in clothing image retrieval technology.

2.1 The Traditional Research Field of Clothing Image Retrieval

Before the emergence of deep learning technology, traditional clothing image retrieval research included manual feature extraction and classification algorithms, as well as clothing image retrieval technology based on traditional machine learning algorithms.

Traditional clothing image retrieval methods usually include two stages: feature extraction and classification. In traditional research, manual feature extraction is a tedious task that requires expertise and experience to select appropriate features. After the feature extraction stage, researchers usually use traditional machine learning algorithms, such as support vector machines [8], random forests [9], etc., to classify the extracted features. These algorithms build a classification model by learning and training feature patterns in samples so that new clothing images can be accurately classified and retrieved.

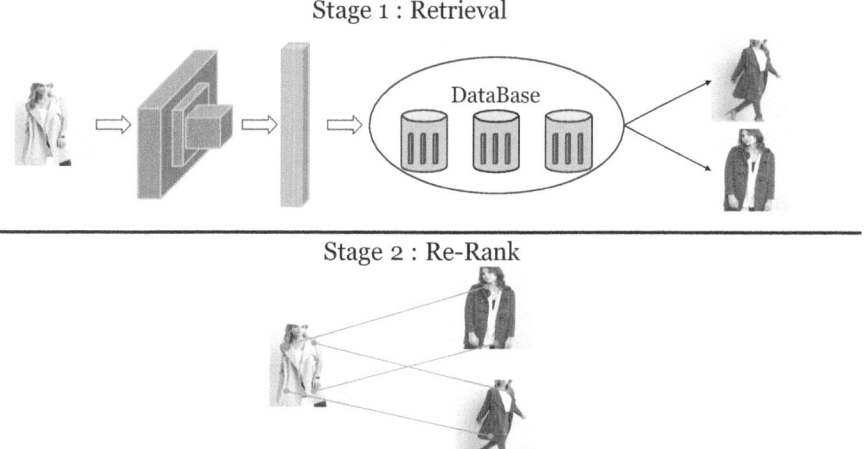

Fig. 1. Two-stage image retrieval method schematic diagram.

Li et al. [10] proposed a hierarchical superpixel merging algorithm to achieve clothing retrieval. Liu et al. [11] applied the Grab Cut automatic segmentation algorithm to segment the clothing image. Liu et al. [12] believed that CNN ignored the global object shape to a large extent and proposed an image retrieval method called sublimated depth feature histogram. Akbacak et al. [13] proposed a novel Multi-Label Multi-Query IR method based on the variance of Hamming distance presented for the query of multiple images having multiple labels.

Traditional methods have limitations such as limited generalization ability of feature extraction and difficulty in coping with the complexity and diversity of fashion items, making it difficult to effectively process the semantic information of clothing images.

2.2 Deep Learning-Based Clothing Image Retrieval Method

With the development of deep learning [14], the image retrieval method has become mainstream in the field of clothing image retrieval. Ko et al. [15] present an image retrieval architecture using specific feature vectors for the fashion domain. Song et al. [16] propose a method to learn multiple latent spaces for attribute-specific fashion image retrieval. Bao et al. [17] propose a novel multi-scale and multi-granularity feature learning network. Chen et al. [18] propose a fashion image retrieval framework based on a dilated convolutional residual network.

In recent years, Transformer has been successful in the visual field, and many Transformer-based image retrieval methods have been widely used. Li et al. [19] utilize the natural language feedback provided by the user to grasp compound and more specific details for clothes attributes. Goenka et al. [20] propose FashionVLP, which brings the prior knowledge contained in large image-text corpora to the domain of fashion image retrieval. Yang et al. [21] put forth a unified solution, namely Hierarchical Aggregation Transformer incorporated with Cross Relation Network. Zhang et al. [22] propose an AABLSTM network, which is based on deep CNN-RNN, to solve the visual fashion analysis of clothing category classification.

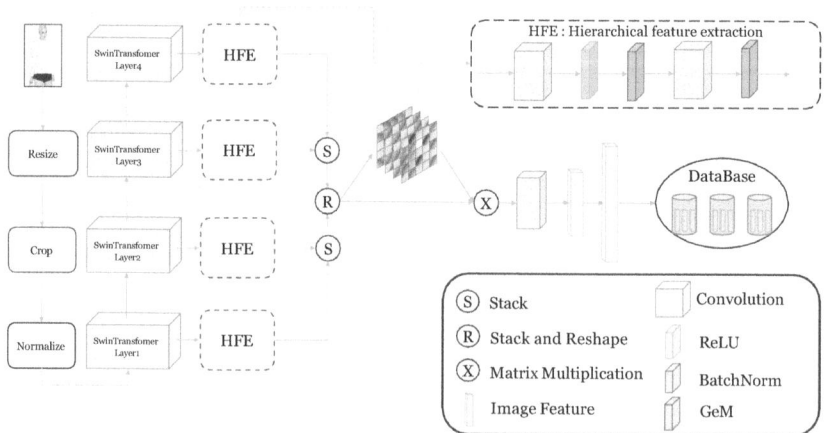

Fig. 2. Multi-layer Feature Fusion Framework.

Transformers have been extensively validated for image retrieval tasks, benefiting from their self-attention mechanism and position encoding capabilities. They enable efficient modeling and information interaction in images. As image retrieval tasks evolve and Transformer models continue to be optimized, the application of Transformer-based methods is expected to expand further.

3 Multi-layer Feature Fusion Method for Image Retrieval

In this section, we introduce our proposed multilayer feature fusion network. Firstly, a multilayer feature fusion framework is proposed. Secondly, two major modules, hierarchical feature extraction, and multi-layer feature fusion, are introduced. Through multi-layer feature fusion, we address the issue of deep neural networks focusing more on local features at lower layers and global features at higher layers, obtaining features with information from multiple dimensions.

3.1 Multi-layer Feature Fusion Framework

Here, we propose a general framework for multi-level feature fusion, as shown in Fig. 2. We use the Swin Transformer with 7 patches in each window to extract multi-level features from the input images. These extracted features are then fed into the level-wise feature extraction module, where different channels and dimensions of features are transformed into onedimensional vectors of the same size. These features are then passed through the feature fusion module, which extracts the overall features of the image.

3.2 Multi-level Feature Extraction

We use the Swin Transformer model as the backbone network and image-net pre-trained weights. The backbone network extracts four layers of features, inputs 3*224*224 size images, and outputs four layers of features. The size of each layer's features is as Table 1. The output features are further extracted through the hierarchical feature extraction module.

Table 1. Swin Transformer feature size.

Layer	Feature shape
1	128x56x56
2	256x28x28
3	512x14x14
4	1024x7x7

3.3 Hierarchical Feature Extraction

The basic hierarchical feature extraction process is shown in Fig. 3. Since the number of channels of the feature output features of each layer of the backbone network is different, we first use 1*1 convolution to adjust the number of channels to 256, then use the ReLU activation function to add nonlinear factors, and use the batch normalization method to normalize the data, and then perform a 1*1 convolution operation to learn the corresponding features, and finally use the geometric mean pooling method to extract hierarchical features with a size of 1*256.

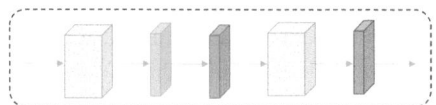

Fig. 3. Hierarchical feature extraction

3.4 Multi-layer Feature Fusion

The basic process of the multi-layer feature fusion method is shown in Fig. 4. First, the input features are stacked to obtain features with a size of 4*256 and then reshaped to obtain features with a size of 4*16*16, and then a 1*1 two-dimensional convolution is used to extract the attention weight. The features and weights are then multiplied to obtain the fused features. After feature flattening and full connection processing, the size of the obtained image feature vector is 1*1024.

4 Experiments

In this section, we will introduce the specific experimental settings in detail to facilitate subsequent researchers to test.

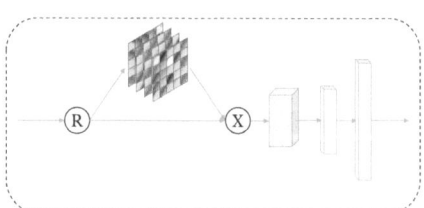

Fig. 4. Multi-layer feature fusion

4.1 Image Filtering and Preprocessing

The initial step involves filtering the images based on a specific rule: if the number of images in a particular category is fewer than 100, that category is excluded. Subsequently, the images were resized to a resolution of 256*256 and cropped at the center to obtain a resolution of 224*224. The standardized process involves using a mean of [0.7773, 0.7435, 0.7320] and a variance of [0.2623, 0.2786, 0.2862]. Finally, the pre-processed image is obtained.

4.2 Backbone

The feature fusion framework presented in this article is compatible with nearly all backbone networks. However, for the purposes of this study, the popular Swin Transformer network has been chosen as the backbone network. Hierarchical features are extracted from each stage layer of the network and subsequently fused using the framework proposed in this article.

4.3 Dataset

All experiments carried out in this article are trained using the DeepFashion dataset. DeepFashion comprises more than 800,000 diverse fashion images, encompassing well-posed shop images as well as unconstrained consumer photos. It is regarded as the largest visual fashion analysis database, as depicted in Fig. 5. The DeepFashion dataset includes comprehensive annotations for clothing items. Each image in the dataset is labeled with 50 categories, 1,000 descriptive attributes, bounding boxes, and clothing landmarks. Additionally, DeepFashion contains over 300,000 image pairs that encompass different poses and domains. Four benchmarks have been developed utilizing the DeepFashion database: Attribute Prediction, Consumer-to-shop Clothes Retrieval, Inshop Clothes Retrieval, and Landmark Detection. The data and annotations from these benchmarks can also be utilized as training and test sets for various computer vision tasks, such as Clothes Detection, Clothes Recognition, and Image Retrieval.

4.4 Evaluation Metrics

4.4.1 Top-K Classification Precision

The calculation of the accuracy of the top k classification is performed using the following formula. As a result of approach 1, the accuracy of the classification increases:

$$P_K = \sum_{i=1}^{k} \frac{R(i)}{k}$$

where $R(i)$ is the correlation between the fashion images q to be retrieved and the ith nearest neighbor image. The retrieval result $R(i) \supset [0, 1]$. Among the labels of the first images of the k nearest neighbor, $R(i) = 1$ as long as one of the labels is the same as the image label retrieved. Conversely, $R(i) = 0$. In the experiments, only category labels are considered to measure relevance.

4.4.2 Mean Average Precision

In the domain of image retrieval, performance metrics consider both the quantity and ordering of the retrieved systems. Mean Average Precision (mAP), built upon precision, incorporates the assessment of location information. mAP serves as a widely adopted and crucial evaluation indicator in engineering. The formula for calculating *mAP* is as follows:

$$R_{mAP} = \frac{P_{avg}}{n}$$

where P_{avg} is the average precision of image retrieval and n means the number if retrieved.

4.5 Loss Function

Following DOLG [4], the training of our method involves only one L2-normalized N class prediction head $\hat{W} \in R^{1024 \times N}$ and only needs image-level labels. ArcFace margin loss is used to train the whole network:

$$L = -\log\left(\frac{exp\left(\gamma \times AF\left(\widehat{\omega_t^T \hat{f_g}}, 1\right)\right)}{\sum_n exp\left(\gamma \times AF\left(\widehat{\omega_n^T \hat{g}}, y_n\right)\right)}\right)$$

where ω_i refers to the i_{th} row of $\hat{\omega}$ and $\hat{f}g$ is the L_2-normalized version of f_g. y is the onehot label vector and t is the groundtruth class index ($y_t = 1$). γ is a scale factor. AF denotes the ArcFace-adjusted cosine similarity and it can be calculated as $AF(s, c)$:

$$AF(s, c) = \begin{cases} cos(acos(s) + m), & c = 1 \\ s, & c = 0 \end{cases}$$

where s is the cosine similarity, m is the ArcFace margin and $c = 1$ means this is the groundtruth truth class.

Fig. 5. DeepFashion dataset sample

4.6 Optimizer

We use the SGD optimizer, with a momentum of 0.9, and a weight decay factor set to 0.0001. To decay the learning rate, the cosine learning rate decay strategy is employed. The initial learning rate is initialized to 0.001.

4.7 Feature Extraction

Regarding feature extraction, based on prior research [4], we employ image pyramids to generate multi-scale representations during inference. More specifically, we utilize three scales, namely 0.8, 1, and 1.2, to extract the ultimate compact feature vector. To fuse these multiscale features, we start by normalizing them, ensuring their L2 norm is equal to 1. Next, we average the normalized features and subsequently apply L2 normalization to obtain the final image features.

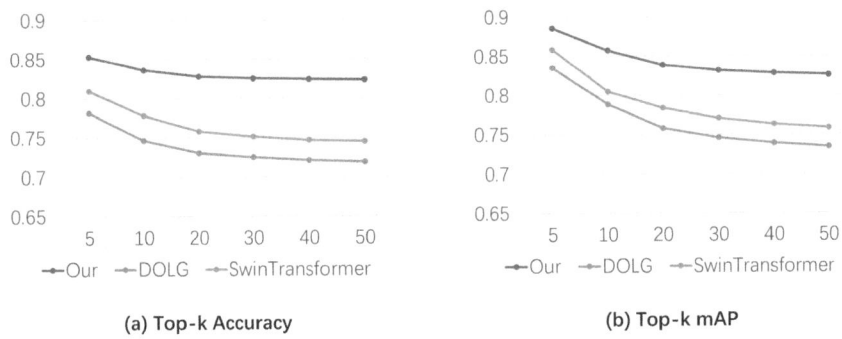

(a) Top-k Accuracy   (b) Top-k mAP

Fig. 6. Comparison and ablation experiment results

4.8 Computer Specifications

To train our model, we utilize a batch size of 64 and perform 200 batches in an experimental environment equipped with an NVIDIA V100 GPU and an Intel(R) Xeon(R) Gold 6240 CPU @ 2.60GHz. The training process is carried out with 32GB of memory. A full training session is completed in approximately 3 days.

5 Experimental Results

5.1 Comparison and Ablation Experiments

We compared our method with several other techniques, namely WTBI, DARN, SOTA, FashionNet, fushioncnn+K-means, and CTL. The comparison was performed using two metrics: Top-10 accuracy and mean average precision (mAP), as illustrated in Table 2.

We reproduce the DOLG image retrieval model for comparative experiments and use the Swin Transformer model for ablation experiments. The Top-k accuracy result is shown in Fig. 6(a), and the mAP result is shown in Fig. 6(b):

5.2 Assisted Retrieval Using Clustering Algorithms

In this case, various clustering methods based on the distance between the center points can be used. The experiments conducted in this article selected K-means++ and K-center as experimental controls. K-means++ accuracy tends to improve when we utilize multi-scale feature fusion techniques, as shown in Fig. 7.

Table 2. Comparison of the effects of different methods.

Method	Accuracy	mAP
WTBI [23]	0.392	0.125
DARN [24]	0.565	0.264
SOTA [25]	0.583	0.468
FashionNet [26]	0.619	0.625
FushionCNN [27]	0.681	0.718
CTL [28]	0.712	0.598
Ours	**0.836**	**0.857**

In regard to accuracy, incorporating the k- means method contributes to a certain extent of improvement. Regarding retrieval time, employing the conventional K-nearest neighbors method yields an average retrieval speed of 110ms, whereas utilizing the k-means method achieves an average retrieval speed of 80ms. Notably, our method demonstrates a more pronounced enhancement in retrieval speed.

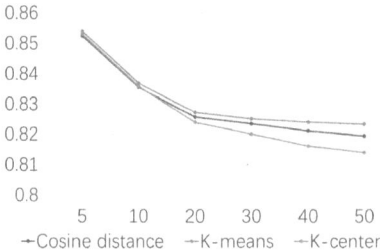

Fig. 7. Comparison of Top-k accuracy

5.3 Top-5 Search Results

We implemented the entire network using Python and visually showcased the top-5 retrieval results. Figure 8 illustrates the visual display of these results.

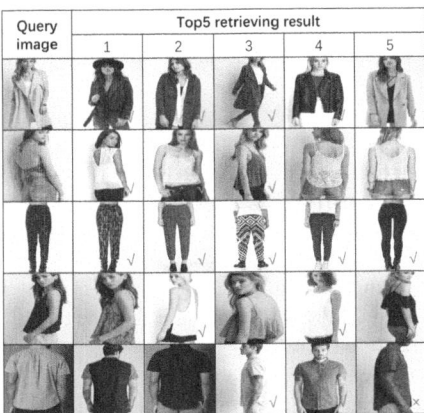

Fig. 8. Top-5 image retrieval results

6 Conclusion

In this article, we try to use a simple method to solve the problem that the low-level features of deep neural networks focus more on local features, while the high-level features focus more on global features. We designed a two-layer structure to extract and fuse multiple-layer characteristics. We also design a scale transformation method that is beneficial for clustering, combining multiple features to enhance each other and generate a representative final descriptor through goal-oriented training. We have demonstrated extensive experimental results for proof-of-concept, and we have significantly improved state-of-the-art performance on DeepFashion.

References

1. Li, X., Yang, J., Ma, J.: Recent developments of content based image retrieval (CBIR). Neurocomputing **452**, 675–689 (2021)
2. Radenovic´, F., Tolias, G., Chum, O.: CNN image retrieval learns from bow: Unsupervised fine-tuning with hard examples. In: Computer Vision–ECCV 2016: 14th European Conference, Amsterdam, The Netherlands, October 11–14, 2016, Proceedings, Part I 14, pp. 3–20. Springer (2016)
3. Xiaoqiang, L., Chen, Y., Li, X.: Hierarchical recurrent neural hashing for image retrieval with hierarchical convolutional features. IEEE Trans. Image Process. **27**(1), 106–120 (2017)
4. Yang, M., et al.: DOLG: singlestage image retrieval with deep orthogonal fusion of local and global features. In: Proceedings of the IEEE/CVF International Conference on Computer Vision, pp. 11772–11781 (2021)
5. Cao, B., Araujo, A., Sim, J.: Unifying deep local and global features for image search. In: Computer Vision–ECCV 2020: 16th European Conference, Glasgow, UK, August 23–28, 2020, Proceedings, Part XX 16, pp. 726–743. Springer (2020)
6. Ng, J.Y.-H., Yang, F., Davis, L.S.: Exploiting local features from deep networks for image retrieval. In: Proceedings of the IEEE Conference on Computer Vision and Pattern Recognition Workshops, pp. 53–61 (2015)

7. Liu, Z., Luo, P., Qiu, S., Wang, X., Tang, X.: DeepFashion: powering robust clothes recognition and retrieval with rich annotations. In: Proceedings of IEEE Conference on Computer Vision and Pattern Recognition (CVPR) (2016)
8. Chen, Y., Zhou, X.S., Huang, T.S.: One-class SVM for learning in image retrieval. In: Proceedings 2001 International Conference on Image Processing (Cat. No. 01CH37205), vol. 1, pp. 34–37. IEEE (2001)
9. Singh, V.P., Srivastava, R.: Improved image retrieval using fast colour-texture features with varying weighted similarity measure and random forests. Multimedia Tools Appl. **77**, 14435–14460 (2018)
10. Li, Z., Li, Y., Tian, W., Pang, Y., Liu, Y.: Crossscenario clothing retrieval and fine-grained style recognition. In: 2016 23rd International Conference on Pattern Recognition (ICPR), pp. 2912–2917. IEEE (2016)
11. Liu, H., Wang, Y., Chen, D., Lv, J., Alshalabi, R.: Garment image retrieval based on grab cut auto segmentation and dominate color method. Appl. Math. Nonlinear Sci. (2022)
12. Liu, G.-H., Li, Z.-Y., Yang, J.-Y., Zhang, D.: Exploiting sublimated deep features for image retrieval. Pattern Recogn. **147**, 110076 (2024)
13. Akbacak, E., Toktas, A., Erkan, U., Gao, S.: MLMQ-IR: multilabel multi-query image retrieval based on the variance of hamming distance. Knowl.-Based Syst. **283**, 111193 (2024)
14. Chen, L.-C., Papandreou, G., Schroff, F., Adam, H.: Rethinking atrous convolution for semantic image segmentation. arXiv preprint arXiv:1706.05587 (2017)
15. Ko, M.S., Lee, Y.H., Cho, C., Song, H.: CoFirNet: conditional feature vector-based fashion image retrieval network. In: 2021 International Conference on Information and Communication Technology Convergence (ICTC), pp. 1659–1661. IEEE (2021)
16. Song, C.H., Han, H.J.: Convolutional attribute mask with two-step attention for fashion image retrieval. In: 2022 26th International Conference on Pattern Recognition (ICPR), pp. 2093–2099. IEEE (2022)
17. Bao, C., Zhang, X., Chen, J., Miao, Y.: MMFL-Net: multi-scale and multi-granularity feature learning for cross-domain fashion retrieval. Multimedia Tools Appl. **82**(24), 37905–37937 (2023)
18. Chen, J., Yuan, H., Zhang, Y., He, R., Liang, J.: DCR-Net: dilated convolutional residual network for fashion image retrieval. Comput. Animation Virtual Worlds **34**(2), e2050 (2023)
19. Li, X., Rong, Y., Zhao, M., Fan, J.: Interactive clothes image retrieval via multi-modal feature fusion of image representation and natural language feedback. In: Neural Computing for Advanced Applications: Second International Conference, NCAA 2021, Guangzhou, China, August 27–30, 2021, Proceedings 2, pp. 578–589. Springer (2021)
20. Goenka, S., et al.: FashionVLP: vision language transformer for fashion retrieval with feedback. In: Proceedings of the IEEE/CVF Conference on Computer Vision and Pattern Recognition, pp. 14105–14115 (2022)
21. Yang, Q., Ye, M., Cai, Z., Su, K., Du, B.: Composed image retrieval via cross relation network with hierarchical aggregation transformer. IEEE Trans. Image Process. (2023)
22. Zhang, X., Shen, M., Li, X., Wang, X.: AABLSTM: a novel multi-task based CNN-RNN deep model for fashion analysis. ACM Trans. Multimed. Comput. Commun. Appl. **19**(1), 1–18 (2023)
23. Quillet, G., Ciobanas, A., Lehmann, P., Fautrelle, Y.: A benchmark solidification experiment on an Sn–10% wtBi Alloy. Int. J. Heat Mass Transf. **50**(3–4), 654–666 (2007)
24. Greenwald, R.A., et al.: Darn/superdarn: a global view of the dynamics of high-latitude convection. Space Sci. Rev. **71**, 761–796 (1995)
25. Wieczorek, M., Michalowski, A., Wroblewska, A., Dabrowski, J.: A strong baseline for fashion retrieval with person re-identification models. In: International Conference on Neural Information Processing, pp. 294–301. Springer (2020)

26. He, T., Hu, Y.: FashionNet: personalized outfit recommendation with deep neural network. arXiv preprint arXiv:1810.02443 (2018)
27. Hou, Y., He, R., Li, M., Chen, J.: Clothing image retrieval method combining convolutional neural network multi-layer feature fusion and k-means clustering. Comput. Sci. **46**(6), 215–224 (2019)
28. Wieczorek, M., Rychalska, B., Dabrowski, J.: On the unreasonable effectiveness of centroids in image retrieval. In: Neural Information Processing: 28th International Conference, ICONIP 2021, Sanur, Bali, Indonesia, December 8–12, 2021, Proceedings, Part IV 28, pp. 212–223. Springer (2021)

Hybrid Attention Mechanism for 3D LIDAR Point Clouds Semantic Segmentation

Yujie Miao, Xiaodong Yi[✉], Naiyang Guan, and Hailun Lu

National Innovation Institute of Defense Technology, Beijing, China
xdong_yi@163.com

Abstract. This study introduces a cutting-edge semantic segmentation framework for LIDAR point cloud data to enhance computer animation and virtual reality applications. Given the inherent challenges of point cloud data such as sparsity, heterogeneity, and multiscale features, our innovative approach incorporates an efficient hybrid attention network focused on significantly improving segmentation accuracy and robustness. The framework comprises an Information Extraction Model (IEM) and an Information Assembly Module (IAM). The IEM utilizes a coordinate-oriented attention mechanism for precise spatial information capture during encoding, effectively handling point cloud sparsity and clutter. During decoding, a depth-separable convolution-based channel attention mechanism optimizes feature channels' importance, addressing category imbalance issues. The IAM is tasked with the deep fusion of global information for refined feature representation, enhancing semantic segmentation performance. Our hybrid attention mechanism improves adaptability to point cloud data complexity and computational efficiency. Experiments demonstrate our method's superiority over current state-of-the-art techniques, marking a significant advancement in point cloud processing for realistic virtual environment construction and interaction.

Keywords: computer animation · point clouds · hybrid attention network · virtual worlds · semantic segmentation

1 Introduction

As computer graphics and virtual reality technologies continue to develop, point clouds data is becoming more and more widely used in computer animation and virtual reality. Computer animation is a kind of dynamic image production technology, which uses the computer as a tool for calculation and processing of graphic images to achieve more vivid and realistic animation effects. Virtual reality, on the other hand, is a technology for interaction between humans and computers. It uses a computer-generated virtual environment to allow users to immerse themselves in and interact with a virtual environment.

In computer animation and virtual reality, point clouds data, as an important form of description of the three-dimensional scene, has rich spatial information and detailed features, which is an important support for the construction of realistic virtual environments. Point clouds data is usually collected by sensors such as LIDAR. It is made up of a large number of discrete points, each of which contains information such as the position and the intensity of the reflection. By processing and analyzing point clouds data, 3D scenes can be modeled, reconstructed, and analyzed.

The semantic segmentation of a point clouds is one of the most important tasks in the processing of point clouds data. Its purpose is to realize the recognition and understanding of various objects and scenes in the environment by assigning each point in the point clouds to the corresponding semantic category. In the field of computer animation and virtual reality, the semantic segmentation of point clouds helps to construct realistic virtual environments and to realize the accurate recognition and interaction of various objects in the environment. Therefore, point clouds semantic segmentation has important application value in computer animation and virtual reality.

However, in contrast to traditional visual data, LIDAR point clouds data presents challenges such as sparsity, heterogeneity, and multi-scale features, which pose difficulties for deep learning-based semantic segmentation. Semantic segmentation accuracy and robustness are often limited by traditional network structure, making it difficult to effectively capture local details and global contextual information in point-clouds data.

In order to address the difficulties in semantic segmentation of point clouds, we propose a new method on the basis of a Hybrid Attention Mechanism. It combines coordinate-based information extraction, channel-based Information Extraction Model, and Information Assembly Module to comprehensively mine the multi-level feature information of point clouds data. We provide new ideas and methods for computer animation and virtual reality applications by accurately extracting and modeling local details and global background information in point clouds data.

The innovative points of this paper are as follows: 1. In this paper, a novel network framework with a hybrid attention mechanism is proposed. It consists of an information extraction module and an information integration module. Through refined feature extraction and comprehensive optimization of computational resources, the quality of semantic segmentation of LIDAR point clouds is significantly improved. 2. An information extraction module (IEM) is proposed. In the information extraction stage, a coordinate-based attention mechanism and a depth-separable convolution-based channel attention mechanism are introduced to effectively capture key spatial location information and overcome the challenges of point clouds data sparsity and disorder. In addition, through the adjustment of the importance of each channel feature, the category imbalance problem can be effectively solved and the model performance can be improved.

3. An information assembly module (IAM) is proposed. This module integrates global information in depth by self-learning, optimizes feature representation, and further improves semantic segmentation accuracy and efficiency.

2 Related Work

In this section, we introduce two categories of largescale point clouds segmentation methods, including the network-based and the attention-based networks.

2.1 Network-Based Methods

One method processes point clouds into pseudo-images, polar coordinates, and voxels before serving as input. In a correlated approach, [1] projects local surface geometry onto tangent planes for 2D convolutional processing. SqueezeSeg methods [2,3] preprocess 3D point clouds data into 2D pseudo-images. RangeNet++ [4] uses a transformative process with 2D convolutions for semantic segmentation on spherical images. SalsaNext [5,6] converts omnidirectional LIDAR-captured 3D point-clouds data into pseudo-images. [7–9] enable an efficient dense semantic segmentation of LIDAR data from a top-view standpoint. Nevertheless, these approaches unavoidably bring about a loss of detailed information, leading to an incomplete utilization of the underlying geometric and structural data.

Another type of network processes point clouds as input without the need for intermediate conversion steps, which is represented by PointNet and PointNet++ [10,11]. They perform segmentation tasks with an STN, classification network, and segmentation network. RandLA-Net [12] introduces an efficient large-scale point clouds segmentation network utilizing random point sampling and a local feature aggregation module for geometric feature preservation. PointCNN [13] rearranges neighboring points into a canonical order, facilitating the conventional convolution to operate in a standard manner. KPConv and DGCNN [14,15] introduce a flexible point convolution for point clouds segmentation, effectively handling density variations and the relationships between a point and its neighbors. RSNet [16] proposes a lightweight local dependency module and incorporates a slice pooling layer.

2.2 Attention-Based Methods

To enhance the accuracy of segmentation, some investigators have integrated the attention mechanism from the Transformer [17] architecture into algorithms dedicated to semantic segmentation. The Transformer model family emerges as especially fitting for the processing of point clouds, attributed to the self-attention operator's ensemble nature at the core of the Transformer network, thereby preserving the positional invariance of input elements. Point Transformer [18,19] first introduced the Transformer mechanism into the 3D point clouds domain. But this approach suffers from the problem of gradient disappearance, when extracting deep point clouds features.

SCAN [20] proposed a sparse cross-scale attention network that aligns multi-scale sparse features using global voxel-encoded attention, which enhances long-range relationship modeling for accurate regression in over-segmented large objects. DLA [21] introduced a trainable attention module, which acquires Dual Local Attention features. The DLA module comprises two components:

the self-attention block and the attentive pooling block, both incorporating an improved position encoding block. MASS [22] introduced a Multi-Attentional Semantic Segmentation model with three attention-based components, resulting in a dense 360° segmentation mask. LPSS Net [23] is a dual-attention mechanism point clouds segmentation algorithm utilizing a transformer mechanism for point clouds feature extraction. Additionally, a novel 3D channel attention mechanism is introduced in the encoding phase to suppress irrelevant information and emphasize essential details. 1D-SalsaSAN [24] employs Scan-Unfolding for projection and integrates a 1D self-attention block derived from the standard self-attention block, enhancing segmentation accuracy, particularly for smaller objects.

However, most of the existing methods are focused on feature channel attention without focusing on spatial coordinate attention that is more suitable to represent spatial information. In addition, for unstructured data such as point clouds, the self-attention mechanism of Transformer is very friendly. Thus, a mechanism for global integration of feature information is adopted for improving segmentation accuracy.

3 Method

The objective of the research is to improve the accuracy and efficiency of semantic segmentation of LiDAR point cloud data to enable the creation of more immersive and interactive experiences in computer animation, VR, and AR. By improving the understanding and processing of complex point cloud data, our approach will provide a more reliable basis for the generation of realistic virtual

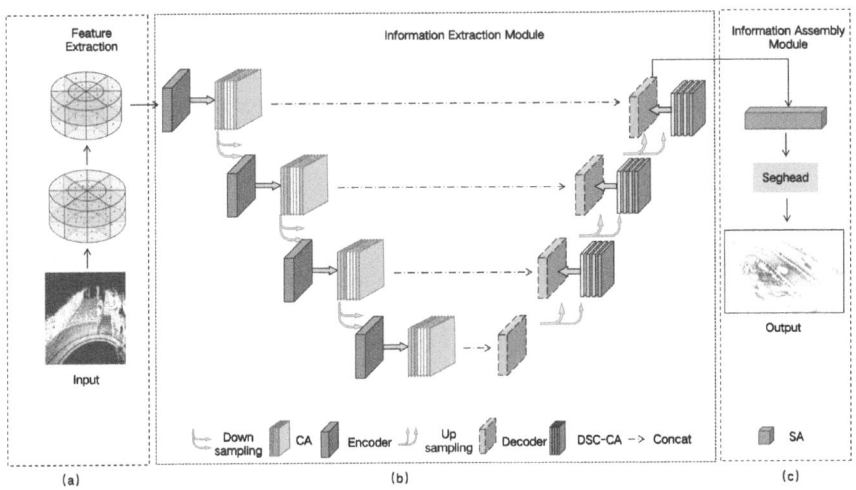

Fig. 1. Model structure of this paper. Where (a) is feature extraction, (b) and (c) are our hybrid attention network. (b) is the information extraction module, and (c) is the information assembly module.

environments and the augmentation of real-world scenes with virtual elements. We propose a network architecture for hybrid attention mechanisms, focusing on features for extracting and integrating information. It contains two modules, one is Information Extraction Model(IEM) and the other is Information Assembly Module(IAM). In the Information Extraction Model(IEM), we first utilize the coordinate-based attention mechanism to capture the most important spatial location information in the encoding phase. In addition, in order to enhance the feature description in the decoding stage, the importance of each channel feature is adjusted to suppress the negative impact of category imbalance on the model performance. Therefore, we propose a channel attention mechanism based on depth-separated convolution. Finally, the Information Assembly Module(IAM) is utilized to further integrate the global information in order to optimize the feature representation. Figure 1 shows the structure of our proposed network.

3.1 Data Representation and Feature Extraction

Given the unique characteristics of LIDAR point clouds data, we initially represent the input point clouds P as an ordered set, $P = \{p_i | i = 1, 2, ..., N\}$, where each point p_i includes its three-dimensional coordinates x_i, y_i, z_i and reflectance r_i. Based on this, we employ the baseline network Cylinder3D [25] for the feature extraction module, effectively processing the spatial structure of point clouds and converting point clouds data into a representation in the high-dimensional feature space $F \in \mathbb{R}^{C \times H \times W \times D}$, where C denotes the number of channels, and H, W, D correspond to the dimensions of height, width, and depth, respectively.

3.2 Information Extraction Module(IEM)

We designed Information Extraction Module(IEM), which includes a coordinate attention mechanism and a channel attention mechanism based on depth-separable convolution, to improve the model's ability to extract information from point clouds features.

3.2.1 Coordinate Attention(CA)

In order to improve the sensitivity of the model to the spatial position of the point clouds, we have developed a 3D point clouds-based Coordinate Attention Module (CA) based on the approach of [26]. This module captures long-range dependencies in one direction while preserving precise positional information in other directions, and refines channel attention by independently aggregating features in three spatial directions. Specifically, coordinate attention is calculated as follows:

For the input feature map x, we utilize one-dimensional global pooling operation to decompose each channel x_c into feature encodings along three spatial dimensions. The one-dimensional feature encoding for the c-th channel with height h is obtained as follows:

$$z_c^D(h,w) = \frac{1}{D}\sum_{i=0}^{D-1} x_c(i,h,w) \tag{1}$$

Where $z_c^D(h,w)$ represents the global contextual features along the depth direction, i is the index along the depth dimension, and h and w are fixed indices along the height and width dimensions, respectively.

By performing global average pooling along the height dimension for each channel, we obtain the global contextual features along the height direction. The formulation is given by:

$$z_c^H(d,w) = \frac{1}{H}\sum_{j=0}^{H-1} x_c(d,j,w) \tag{2}$$

where $z_c^H(d,w)$ represents the global contextual features along the height direction, j is the index along the height dimension, and d and w are fixed indices along the depth and width dimensions, respectively.

By performing global average pooling along the width dimension for each channel, we obtain the global contextual features along the width direction. The formulation is given by:

$$z_c^W(d,h) = \frac{1}{W}\sum_{k=0}^{W-1} x_c(d,h,k) \tag{3}$$

where $z_c^W(d,h)$ represents the global contextual features along the width direction, k is the index along the width dimension, and d and h are fixed indices along the depth and height dimensions, respectively.

These three encoding operations capture the global contextual information along different dimensions for each channel. They can be combined to generate coordinate attention maps, guiding the model to perform spatial weighting on features, thereby enhancing the accuracy of semantic segmentation for LIDAR point clouds.

Subsequently, we encode the features along each dimension using a series of convolutional operations and generate corresponding attention maps using the sigmoid function:

$$f_c^D = \delta(F_{1D}(z_c^D)) \tag{4}$$
$$f_c^H = \delta(F_{1H}(z_c^H)) \tag{5}$$
$$f_c^W = \delta(F_{1W}(z_c^W)) \tag{6}$$
$$g_c^D = \sigma(f_c^D) \tag{7}$$
$$g_c^H = \sigma(f_c^H) \tag{8}$$
$$g_c^W = \sigma(f_c^W) \tag{9}$$

where F_{1D}, F_{1H}, and F_{1W} represent 1×1 convolutional operations along the depth, height, and width dimensions, respectively. δ denotes ReLU or another activation function, and σ represents the sigmoid function.

Finally, utilizing the generated attention maps, we weight the input feature map to enhance spatial sensitivity and fuse the weighted features across the channel dimension:

$$F_{\text{enh}} = (g_c^D \odot F) \oplus (g_c^H \odot F) \oplus (g_c^W \odot F) \tag{10}$$

where $\odot$ denotes element-wise multiplication, and $\oplus$ represents channel-wise fusion operation.

3.2.2 Depth-Separable Convolution Channel Attention(DSC-CA)

Upsampling is usually used to recover the size of the feature map at the decoding stage. After the upsampling, a channel attention mechanism is usually introduced to emphasize the important features and to suppress the unimportant ones in order to improve the feature representation. In contrast to the traditional approaches, we propose a Depth-Separable Convolution and Channel Attention Mechanism (DSC-CA) based module for the processing of the upsampled feature maps. The goal of this module is the reduction of the computational burden and the improvement of the feature representation capability of the model. The specific steps of the implementation of this module are as follows:

The feature representation after upsampling $F_{up} \in \mathbb{R}^{C \times H' \times W' \times D'}$, where C denotes the number of channels, and H', W', and D' denote the height, width, and depth of the feature maps after upsampling, respectively.

In the decoding stage, we first process the upsampled feature map $F_{up} \in \mathbb{R}^{C \times H' \times W' \times D'}$. This is done to improve the feature characterization capability and reduce the computational complexity. Deep convolution and point-by-point convolution are two key steps in this process. The first is deep convolution, where a convolution kernel of $k \times k$ is applied to each channel independently to capture spatial information, denoted as $F_{depth} = \text{depthconv}(F_{up}; K_{depth})$, where $K_{depth} \in \mathbb{R}^{C \times k \times k}$. Then there is a point-by-point convolution: The depth convolution result is fused across channels by a 1×1 convolution kernel, adjusting the channel dimensions, expressed as $F_{dsc} = \text{pointconv}(F_{depth}; K_{point})$, where $K_{point} \in \mathbb{R}^{C' \times C \times 1 \times 1}$, C' is the adjusted channel number.

To obtain global information for each channel, Global Average Pooling (GAP) is performed on the output of the depth-separable convolution (F_{dsc}). The result is a global feature representation at the channel level:

$$G_c = \frac{1}{H' \times W'} \sum_{h=1}^{H'} \sum_{w=1}^{W'} F_{dsc}(:, h, w) \tag{11}$$

Next, the attentional weights for each channel are computed using a two layer fully connected network (FC layer) and a sigmoid activation function. In this process, the weights for each channel are assigned by learning the importance of the different channels in the global feature G_c:

$$A_{ttc} = \sigma(W_2 \cdot \text{ReLU}(W_1 \cdot G_c + b_1) + b_2) \tag{12}$$

where W_1, W_2 is the fully connected layer weight, b_1, b_2 is the bias term, and σ and ReLU are the sigmoid and ReLU activation functions, respectively.

Finally, the computed channel attention weights (A_{ttc}) are applied to the output of the depth-separable convolution (F_{dsc}). The feature maps are recalibrated by elementary multiplication to improve the representation of the important channels. Through the above process, the DSC-CA module in the decoding phase implements depthwise separable convolution and channel attention mechanism, effectively processing the upsampled feature map and enhancing the model's representation capability.

3.3 Information Assembly Module(IAM)

Transformer model in 3D space is suitable for point clouds processing and analysis due to its exchange-invariant deformation and powerful global feature learning. In this paper, we design a global feature integration mechanism for point clouds processing and analysis by exploiting the global feature learning capability of the Transform model. To capture the dependencies between global features, we introduce Self-Attention (SA) after encoding and decoding the network.

3.3.1 Self-attention (SA)

By computing the relationship between features to dynamically adjust the feature representation, SA improves the global information integration capability of the model. To further improve the global information integration capability of the model, we introduce the self-attention mechanism after the encoding and decoding process. First, to compute the query vector, key vector, and value vector, we perform a linear transformation on the decoded feature map F_{decoder}. This is accomplished by the following equation:

$$Q = F_{\text{decoder}} W_Q \tag{13}$$

$$K = F_{\text{decoder}} W_K \tag{14}$$

$$V = F_{\text{decoder}} W_V \tag{15}$$

where F_{decoder} denotes the feature map of the decoder output, and W_Q, W_K, and W_V are the linear transformation matrices of the query, key, and value vectors, respectively. To efficiently transform the input features into different representation spaces, these matrices are obtained by learning.

Next, we compute the dot product between the query vector and the key vector in order to obtain a score of the relationship between the features. This score is then normalized by a scaling factor. Finally, a softmax function is applied to obtain the attention weights:

$$\text{Att}(Q, K, V) = \text{softmax}\left(\frac{QK^T}{\sqrt{d_k}}\right) V \tag{16}$$

where d_k is the dimension of the key vector, this scaling factor helps to avoid obtaining too large values when computing the dot product, which could cause the Softmax function to work in its saturation region, thus affecting the propagation of the gradient. The Softmax function ensures that all weights sum to 1, so that each output element is a weighted sum of the input values, where the weights are determined by the similarity between the features.

Ultimately, the resulting vector of weighted values is a dynamic adaptation of the original features, highlighting important features and suppressing unimportant information, thereby improving the understanding and integration of global information by the model. Thus, self-attention provides an effective means for semantic point clouds segmentation models to capture global dependencies, optimize feature representation, and improve segmentation accuracy and efficiency.

3.4 Loss Function

In this study, we propose a composite loss function that includes cross entropy loss, Lovasz softmax loss, and focal loss to improve the performance of semantic segmentation of LIDAR point clouds. The composite loss function aims to simultaneously solve the category imbalance problem, improve the accuracy of segmentation boundaries, and improve the ability to detect hard-to-recognize samples. The following is a description of the specific composite loss function:

$$L_{total} = L_{ce} + L_{lovasz} + L_{focal} \quad (17)$$

where L_{CE} denotes the cross-entropy loss, which is the underlying loss function used to compute the difference between the model predictions and the true labels, penalizing recognition errors in all categories. The cross-entropy loss formula is as follows:

$$L_{ce} = -\sum_{n=1}^{N}\sum_{c=1}^{C} y_{n,c} \log(\hat{y}_{n,c}) \quad (18)$$

where N is the total number of samples in the batch, C is the number of categories, $y_{n,c}$ is the true label of sample n for category c, and $\hat{y}_{n,c}$ is the probability that the model predicts that sample n belongs to category c.

L_{lovasz} is the Lovasz-Softmax loss, a loss function that focuses on improving the accuracy of the model's segmentation boundaries, which improves the quality of the segmentation by directly optimizing the Jaccard metrics:

$$L_{lovasz} = \frac{1}{|C|}\sum_{c=1}^{|C|} \overline{\Delta J}(m(c), c) \quad (19)$$

With $|C|$ denoting the total number of categories, $\overline{\Delta J}$ is a smoothed approximation of the Jaccard loss for each category c, and $m(c)$ represents the margin of error order for that category.

And L_{focal} is the focal loss, which is a loss function designed to make the model focus more on hard-to-categorize samples by reducing the impact of easy-to-categorize samples on the loss:

$$L_{focal} = -\alpha_t(1 - p_t)^\gamma \log(p_t) \quad (20)$$

where α_t is the weight of category t to balance the contribution of loss across categories; p_t is the predicted probability that a sample belongs to category t; and γ is a moderating factor used to mitigate the effect of easily separable samples on loss and to increase the weight of difficult-to-separate samples in loss.

Thus, our composite loss function can not only effectively deal with the category unbalance problem, but also improve the ability of the model to deal with edge details and hard-to-separate samples, so as to achieve better performance on the task of semantic segmentation of LIDAR point clouds.

4 Experiment and Results

In order to validate the effectiveness of the proposed method, we have conducted experiments on two publicly available LIDAR point clouds data sets, SemanticKITTI [27] and nuScenes [28]. For detailed accuracy evaluation and ablation experiments on each of the proposed modules, the method in this paper is compared with representative methods from recent years.

Table 1. Benchmark of semantic segmentation for LIDAR point clouds. Results are evaluated on SemanticKITTI test set.

Methods	mIoU	car	bicycle	motorcycle	truck	other-vehicle	person	bicyclist	motorcyclist	road	parking	sidewalk	other-ground	building	fence	vegetation	trunk	terrain	pole	traffic
RangeNet++	52.2	91.4	25.7	34.4	25.7	23.0	38.3	38.8	4.8	91.8	65.0	75.2	27.8	87.4	58.6	80.5	55.1	64.6	47.9	55.9
PolarNet	54.3	93.8	40.3	30.1	22.9	28.5	43.2	40.2	5.6	90.8	61.7	74.4	21.7	90.0	61.3	84.0	65.5	67.8	51.8	57.5
SqueezeSegv3	55.9	92.5	38.7	36.5	29.6	33.0	45.6	46.2	20.1	91.7	63.4	74.8	26.4	89.0	59.4	82.0	58.7	65.4	49.6	58.9
Salsanext	59.5	91.9	48.3	38.6	38.9	31.9	60.2	59.0	19.4	91.7	63.7	75.8	29.1	90.2	64.2	81.8	63.6	66.5	54.3	62.1
KPConv	58.8	96.0	32.0	42.5	33.4	44.3	61.5	61.6	11.8	88.8	61.3	72.7	31.6	95.0	64.2	84.8	69.2	69.1	56.4	47.4
FusionNet	61.3	95.3	47.5	37.7	41.8	34.5	59.5	56.8	11.9	91.8	68.8	77.1	30.8	92.5	69.4	84.5	69.8	68.5	60.4	66.5
KPRNet	63.1	95.5	54.1	47.9	23.6	42.6	65.9	65.0	16.5	93.2	73.9	80.6	30.2	91.7	68.4	85.7	69.8	71.2	58.7	64.1
Cylinder3D	67.8	97.1	67.6	64.0	59.0	58.6	73.9	67.9	36.0	91.4	65.1	75.5	32.3	91.0	66.5	85.4	71.8	68.5	62.6	65.6
Ours	70.0	97.8	67.2	64.4	60.3	59.7	74.3	70.4	37.0	92.6	66.8	79.2	33.4	92.5	67.2	87.9	71.3	70.9	65.2	66.8

Table 2. Benchmark of semantic segmentation for LIDAR point clouds. Results are evaluated on nuScenes validation set.

Method	mIoU	bicycle	bus	car	motorcycle	pedestrian	truck	driveable	other-flat	sidewalk	terrain	manmade	vegetation	barrier	construction	traffic-cone	trailer
RangeNet++	65.5	66.0	21.3	77.2	80.9	30.2	66.8	69.6	52.1	54.2	72.3	94.1	66.6	63.5	70.1	83.1	79.8
PolarNet	71.0	74.7	28.2	85.3	90.9	35.1	77.5	71.3	58.8	57.4	76.1	96.5	71.1	74.7	74.0	87.3	85.7
Salsanext	72.2	74.8	34.1	85.9	88.4	42.2	72.4	72.2	63.1	61.3	76.5	96.0	70.8	71.2	71.5	86.7	84.4
Cylinder3D	76.1	76.4	40.3	91.2	93.8	51.3	78.0	78.9	64.9	62.1	84.4	96.8	71.6	76.4	75.4	90.5	87.4
Ours	77.2	77.2	42.7	91.6	95.4	53.8	77.8	79.2	67.3	63.3	84.9	97.5	71.7	78.0	75.7	91.3	87.8

4.1 Dataset and Evaluation

4.1.1 Datasets

Two large datasets, SemanticKITTI and nuScenes, were used to evaluate our proposed method. The nuScenes dataset consists of 1000 driving scenarios, of which 850 scenarios were used for training and validation, and the remaining 150 scenarios were used for testing. For LIDAR semantic segmentation, 16 categories are used after merging similar categories and removing uncommon categories. For SemanticKITTI, it consists of 22 point clouds sequences. Sequences 00 to 10, 08, and 11 to 21 are used for training, validation, and testing, respectively. A total of 19 categories were used for the point clouds semantic segmentation task.

4.1.2 Evaluation

As the primary evaluation metric, we adopted the mean intersection over union (mIoU). The formulas are as follows:

$$\text{mIoU} = \frac{1}{N} \sum_{i=1}^{N} \frac{TP_i}{TP_i + FP_i + FN_i} \qquad (21)$$

where N is the number of classes, TP_i is the number of true instances of class i, FP_i is the number of false positive instances of class i, and FN_i is the number of false negative instances of class i.

4.1.3 Parameter Setting

All comparative experiments in this experiment were run on the same server with an Nvidia RTX 3090Ti GPU. The operating system was Ubuntu 20.0, the experimental parameters were batch size 8, epoch 40, learning rate 0.001, and optimizer was Adam.

4.2 Results on SemanticKITTI Dataset

We report the results of our model on the SemanticKITTI test set in this experiment. As shown in Table 1, compared with the existing methods, including RangeNet++ [4], PolarNet [8], SqueezeSegv3 [3], RandLA-Net [12] etc., our method achieves the state-of-the-art on the SemanticKitti test set. And as far as mIoU is concerned, our proposed method achieves 70.0% in terms of mIoU, which is the best performance among all the compared methods with an improvement of at least 2%. For difficult class like "fence" and "pole", where objects are usually thin and easily confused with background, our method also shows relatively high segmentation accuracy. The visualization of the semantic segmentation of the point cloud on the SemanticKITTI validation set is shown in Fig. 2. Where (a) is the ground truth, (b) is the result predicted by our method. As it can be seen from the detail image, the method proposed in this paper is able to accurately determine the category of the vehicles (red boxes and red circles in the figure).

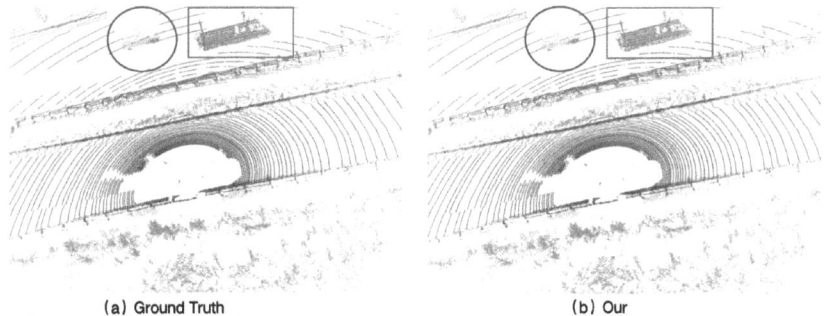

(a) Ground Truth (b) Our

Fig. 2. Visualization of the semantic segmentation of the LIDAR point cloud on the SemanticKITTI validation set. Where (a) is the ground truth, (b) is the result predicted by our method. (Color figure online)

4.3 Results on NuScenes Dataset

We also report our proposed model's results on the nuScenes validation set. As shown in Table 2, our method achieves state-of-the-art performance on the nuScenes validation set compared to existing methods, including RangeNet++, PolarNet, Salsanext [6], Cylinder3D [25]. It can be seen that the method in this paper achieves excellent performance on mIoU, especially in the motorcycle and bicycle categories. The performance of semantic segmentation is significantly improved. This is an indication that our proposed hybrid attention mechanism approach can effectively improve the accuracy of semantic segmentation.

Table 3. Ablation studies for network components on the SemanticKITTI validation set

Baseline	CA	DSC-CA	SA	mIoU
✓				65.9
✓	✓			66.3
✓	✓	✓		66.8
✓	✓	✓	✓	67.9

4.4 Ablation Experiment

To evaluate the impact of the Coordinate Attention Mechanism (CA), Depth Separated Convolution-based Channel Attention Mechanism (DSC-CA), and Self-Attention Mechanism (SA) modules on the network, we performed ablation experiments on the SemanticKITTI validation set. The results are shown in Table 3. It can be seen that embedding CA improves mIoU by 0.4%, CA+DSC-CA improves mIoU by 0.9%, and the combination of the three by 2% in total.

Compared to the baseline, all module combinations are improved. The experimental results show that the accuracy of semantic segmentation of LIDAR point clouds can be improved by the hybrid attention mechanism proposed in this paper.

5 Conclusion

In this study, addressing the challenges of sparsity and complexity in point cloud data, crucial for computer animation and virtual reality applications, we introduce a hybrid attention mechanism network tailored for semantic segmentation of LIDAR point clouds. This method is engineered to enhance the accuracy and efficiency of point cloud processing, thereby facilitating the creation of more realistic and interactive virtual environments. We present two core modules: the Information Extraction Model (IEM) and the Information Integration Model (IAM). Within the IEM, we employ a coordinate attention mechanism to precisely capture and extract critical spatial information, crucial for depicting intricate details in virtual scenes. This module leverages a depth-separable convolutional channel-based attention mechanism, which not only enriches the feature information by focusing on significant spatial locations but also optimizes computational resources by minimizing the processing of irrelevant features.

The IAM incorporates a self-attention mechanism to amalgamate global context information, thereby ensuring the generation of richer and more accurate feature representations. This aspect is particularly important in computer animation and virtual reality, where the detailed and accurate rendering of scenes can significantly enhance user immersion and interaction. Our experimental results demonstrate that the proposed hybrid attention mechanism substantially improves the semantic segmentation accuracy of LIDAR point clouds. This advancement significantly contributes to the development of more accurate and efficient computer animation and virtual reality systems, offering profound implications for the realism and interactivity of virtual environments.

References

1. Tatarchenko, M., Park, J., Koltun, V., Zhou, Q.-Y.: Tangent convolutions for dense prediction in 3D. In: Proceedings of the IEEE Conference on Computer Vision and Pattern Recognition, pp. 3887–3896 (2018)
2. Wu, B., Wan, A., Yue, X., Keutzer, K.: SqueezeSeg: convolutional neural nets with recurrent CRF for real-time road-object segmentation from 3D lidar point cloud. In: 2018 IEEE International Conference on Robotics and Automation (ICRA), pp. 1887–1893. IEEE (2018)
3. Wu, B., Zhou, X., Zhao, S., Yue, X., Keutzer, K.: SqueezeSegV2: improved model structure and unsupervised domain adaptation for road-object segmentation from a lidar point cloud. In: 2019 International Conference on Robotics and Automation (ICRA), pp. 4376–4382. IEEE (2019)
4. Milioto, A., Vizzo, I., Behley, J., Stachniss, C.: RangeNet++: fast and accurate lidar semantic segmentation. In: 2019 IEEE/RSJ International Conference on Intelligent Robots and Systems (IROS), pp. 4213–4220. IEEE (2019)

5. Cortinhal, T., Tzelepis, G., Erdal Aksoy, E.: SalsaNext: fast, uncertainty-aware semantic segmentation of LiDAR point clouds. In: Bebis, G., et al. (eds.) ISVC 2020. LNCS, vol. 12510, pp. 207–222. Springer, Cham (2020). https://doi.org/10.1007/978-3-030-64559-5_16
6. Aksoy, E.E., Baci, S., Cavdar, S.: SalsaNet: fast road and vehicle segmentation in lidar point clouds for autonomous driving. In: 2020 IEEE Intelligent Vehicles Symposium (IV), pp. 926–932. IEEE (2020)
7. Paigwar, A., Erkent, Ö., Sierra-Gonzalez, D., Laugier, C.: GndNet: fast ground plane estimation and point cloud segmentation for autonomous vehicles. In: 2020 IEEE/RSJ International Conference on Intelligent Robots and Systems (IROS), pp. 2150–2156. IEEE (2020)
8. Zhang, Y., et al.: PolarNet: an improved grid representation for online LiDAR point clouds semantic segmentation. In: Proceedings of the IEEE/CVF Conference on Computer Vision and Pattern Recognition, pp. 9601–9610 (2020)
9. Bieder, F., Wirges, S., Janosovits, J., Richter, S., Wang, Z., Stiller, C.: Exploiting multi-layer grid maps for surround-view semantic segmentation of sparse lidar data. In: 2020 IEEE Intelligent Vehicles Symposium (IV), pp. 1892–1898. IEEE (2020)
10. Qi, C.R., Su, H., Mo, K., Guibas, L.J.: PointNet: deep learning on point sets for 3D classification and segmentation. In: Proceedings of the IEEE Conference on Computer Vision and Pattern Recognition, pp. 652–660 (2017)
11. Qi, C.R., Yi, L., Su, H., Guibas, L.J.: PointNet++: deep hierarchical feature learning on point sets in a metric space. In: Advances in Neural Information Processing Systems, vol. 30 (2017)
12. Hu, Q., et al.: RandLA-Net: efficient semantic segmentation of large-scale point clouds. In: Proceedings of the IEEE/CVF Conference on Computer Vision and Pattern Recognition, pp. 11108–11117 (2020)
13. Li, Y., Bu, R., Sun, M., Wu, W., Di, X., Chen, B.: PointCNN: convolution on x-transformed points. In: Advances in Neural Information Processing Systems, vol. 31 (2018)
14. Thomas, H., Qi, C.R., Deschaud, J.-E., Marcotegui, B., Goulette, F., Guibas, L.J.: KPConv: flexible and deformable convolution for point clouds. In: Proceedings of the IEEE/CVF International Conference on Computer Vision, pp. 6411–6420 (2019)
15. Wang, Y., Sun, Y., Liu, Z., Sarma, S.E., Bronstein, M.M., Solomon, J.M.: Dynamic graph CNN for learning on point clouds. ACM Trans. Graph. (TOG) **38**(5), 1–12 (2019)
16. Huang, Q., Wang, W., Neumann, U.: Recurrent slice networks for 3D segmentation of point clouds. In: Proceedings of the IEEE Conference on Computer Vision and Pattern Recognition, pp. 2626–2635 (2018)
17. Vaswani, A., et al.: Attention is all you need. In: Advances in Neural Information Processing Systems, vol. 30 (2017)
18. Engel, N., Belagiannis, V., Dietmayer, K.: Point transformer. IEEE Access **9**, 134826–134840 (2021)
19. Zhao, H., Jiang, L., Jia, J., Torr, P.H.S., Koltun, V.: Point transformer. In: Proceedings of the IEEE/CVF International Conference on Computer Vision, pp. 16259–16268 (2021)
20. Shuangjie, X., Wan, R., Ye, M., Zou, X., Cao, T.: Sparse cross-scale attention network for efficient lidar panoptic segmentation. In: Proceedings of the AAAI Conference on Artificial Intelligence, vol. 36, pp. 2920–2928 (2022)

21. Yanfei, S., Liu, W., Yuan, Z., Cheng, M., Zhang, Z., Shen, X., Wang, C.: DLA-Net: learning dual local attention features for semantic segmentation of large-scale building facade point clouds. Pattern Recogn. **123**, 108372 (2022)
22. Peng, K., et al.: MASS: multi-attentional semantic segmentation of LiDAR data for dense top-view understanding. IEEE Trans. Intell. Transp. Syst. **23**(9), 15824–15840 (2022)
23. Wang, H., et al.: LiDAR point semantic segmentation using dual attention mechanism. J. Russian Laser Res., 1–11 (2023)
24. Suzuki, T., Hirakawa, T., Yamashita, T., Fujiyoshi, H.: 1D-SalsaSAN: semantic segmentation of lidar point cloud with self-attention. In: VISIGRAPP (5: VISAPP), pp. 445–452 (2023)
25. Zhou, H., et al.: Cylinder3D: an effective 3D framework for driving-scene lidar semantic segmentation. arXiv preprint arXiv:2008.01550 (2020)
26. Hou, Q., Zhou, D., Feng, J.: Coordinate attention for efficient mobile network design. In: Proceedings of the IEEE/CVF Conference on Computer Vision and Pattern Recognition, pp. 13713–13722 (2021)
27. Behley, J., et al.: SemanticKITTI: a dataset for semantic scene understanding of lidar sequences. In: Proceedings of the IEEE/CVF International Conference on Computer Vision, pp. 9297–9307 (2019)
28. Caesar, H., et al.: nuscenes: a multimodal dataset for autonomous driving. In: Proceedings of the IEEE/CVF Conference on Computer Vision and Pattern Recognition, pp. 11621–11631 (2020)

Think Twice Before Acting: Efficient Knowledge Distillation for 6-DOF Camera Relocalization

Zhendong Xiao, Junqi Wu, and Wu Wei[✉]

South China University of Technology, Guangzhou, China
{auxiao2022,auwujunqi}@mail.scut.edu.cn, weiwu@scut.edu.cn

Abstract. Knowledge distillation, traditionally used to train compact student networks through deep teacher models, has been successfully applied to many vision tasks. While Convolutional Neural Networks (CNNs) have been extensively studied to enhance the performance of smaller models, this approach remains unexplored for Vision Transformers (ViTs) in camera relocalization tasks. ViTs offer unique architectural benefits for advancing vision-based understanding, but they are challenging to deploy. In this paper, we introduce LocKD, a novel method optimized for integrating compact ViT models into camera relocalization tasks. LocKD innovatively leverages the intrinsic features within ViTs and introduces dual modules: a feature mimicking module for the nuanced capture of shallow layer details, which are crucial for constructing attention maps, and an attention generation module aimed at the deeper layers to ensure a richer assimilation of semantic content. Furthermore, LocKD synergistically combines with logit-based distillation methods to enhance the performance of the student model. Specifically, empirical validations on the Oxford RobotCar dataset demonstrate that our approach yields a 7.14% and 11.1% improvement compared to EffLoc-Small. This shows the potential of our method in improving the efficiency and effectiveness of camera relocalization tasks using compact ViT models.

Keywords: knowledge distillation · camera relocalization · vision transformers · feature mimicking · attention generation

1 Introduction

Camera relocalization plays a crucial role in various computer vision tasks with numerous applications, including augmented reality (AR) [1], delivery drones [2], robotics and autonomous driving [3–6]. Historically, camera localization methods have predominantly utilized indirect structure-based techniques [7–11]. These methods, particularly used in visual Simultaneous Localization and Mapping (SLAM) systems [12], establish dense correlations between 2D pixel arrangements and 3D scene points and compute the 3D position and 3D orientation(6-DoF) of camera pose [13–15]. Subsequently, the camera pose is estimated by employing techniques such as the Perspective-nPoint (PnP) solver [16] or the Kabsch algorithm with RANSAC [17].

Nowadays, the remarkable progress of computer vision has employed deep neural networks to obviate the need for key frame storage and distinct appearance-based mechanisms [18–21]. Kendall's pioneering works illustrate the capability of Convolutional Neural Networks (CNNs) directly regress the camera's 6D pose from RGB image, which facilitate end-to-end approaches to circumvent feature-matching process [22–24]. Atloc [25] employs attention mechanisms and CMRNet [26] combines deep learning [27] with geometric constraints to improve image-based relocalization in LiDAR maps. CFIL [28] proposes a frequency-domain feature extraction module and feature interaction in the frequency domain to enhance salient features. Furthermore, the Vision Transformer (ViT) [29] has significantly advanced many computer vision tasks, but with more parameters compare with CNN-based models [30–33]. EffLoc [34] first adopts efficient Vision Transformers to advance single-image camera pose estimation. Unfortunately, reducing network size by swapping large backbones for smaller ones incurs significant accuracy losses. But, compact distillation models for ViT-based camera relocalization still unexplored. Our research introduces a knowledge distillation approach designed for ViT-based camera relocalization.

Knowledge distillation(KD) demonstrates efficacy in conveying knowledge from an advanced teacher network to a compact student model [35–38]. This approach has been extensively investigated for Convolutional Neural Network (CNN) models, proving successfully across image classification, object detection and semantic segmentation [39–43]. Vision Transformers (ViTs) [29], partition images into patches with embedding positional information, outperform CNN-based models with more parameters. It is impractical to directly transfer knowledge distillation between independent architecture of CNNs and ViTs. In this work, we proposed a innovative knowledge distillation of ViT-based camera relocalization. Figure 1 showcases LocKD's robust generality across weather and time variations because of concentrating on geometrically stable features instead of moving objects.

In summary, our main contributions of this work are three-fold:

- We propose LocKD, a innovative approach to knowledge distillation specifically for 6-Dof single-image Camera relocalization generalize to Vision Transformers.
- Our research introduces a dual-layer distillation strategy for enhanced attention map construction in compact Vision Transformer architectures. This approach ensures comprehensive assimilation of semantic information, enabling superior feature distillation and high-fidelity grasp of intricate spatial details.
- By integrating LocKD with a logit-based knowledge distillation framework, we demonstrate augmented accuracy and robustness to learn camera poses. Empirical validation on the Oxford RobotCar dataset reveals that LocKD outperforms EffLoc-Small 7.14% and 11.1% in terms of precision and relia-

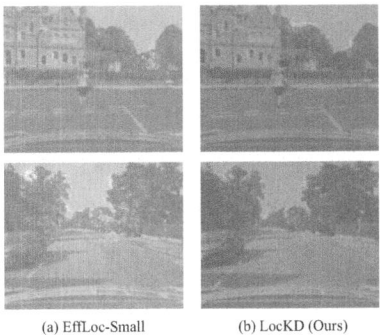

(a) EffLoc-Small (b) LocKD (Ours)

Fig. 1. Saliency maps from two scenes within the Oxford RobotCar dataset highlight the robustness of Effloc-Small and LocKD in camera pose regression. Unlike Effloc-Small, concentrates attention on distant trees and moving vehicles, LocKD prioritizes geometrically stable features, such as the distant skyline and the edges of trees. LocKD enhances global localization robustness compared to Vit-Small.

bility. This advancement underscores the potential of LocKD, offering insights into future directions in knowledge distillation of ViTs.

2 Methodology

We hereby explicate our technique for applying knowledge distillation to ViT-based camera relocalization. Reflecting CNN feature distillation which predicated on L2 distances among feature maps, we formulate a general knowledge distillation loss accordingly:

$$L_{kd}(f_t, f_s) = \sum_{i=1}^{H}\sum_{j=1}^{W}\sum_{k=1}^{C} \left(f_t(x_{i,j,k}) - f_s(x_{i,j,k})\right)^2. \quad (1)$$

wherein f_t and f_s represent the features extracted by the teacher and student models correspondingly. H, W signify the feature dimensions in terms of height and width, while C denotes the number of channels. Subsequently, we transit knowledge distillation applied to efficient ViT.

2.1 Feature Mimicking

For every instance, the student's feature can be represented as $f_s \in \mathcal{R}^{D_s \times N}$ and teacher's feature as $f_t \in \mathcal{R}^{D_t \times N}$. The method employed a linear embedding layer to align the student's D_S and teacher's D_T dimension. The loss of feature mimicking is encapsulated as follows:

$$L_{fm} = \sum_{i=1}^{N}\sum_{j=1}^{D} \left(f_t(x_{i,j}) - \pi_{i,j}\, f_s(x_{i,j})\right)^2, \quad (2)$$

where $\pi_{i,j}$ serves as a linear embedding layer that reshapes f_s to match the dimensionality of f_t. Here, N and D represent the count of patch tokens and the embedding dimension of the teacher's feature respectively.

2.2 Attention Generation

A straightforward linear transformation helps align the feature dimension of both student's and teacher's model. Subsequently, we deploy a randomly attention generated mask $Mask \in \mathcal{R}^{N \times 1}$ obscures original tokens within the student model's input which is written as:

$$\hat{f}_s(x_i) = \begin{cases} \text{Masked Patch Token}, & \text{if } r_i < \eta \\ \text{Initial Patch Token}, & \text{Otherwise,} \end{cases} \quad (3)$$

$$\text{Masked}_i = \begin{cases} 1, & \text{if } r_i < \eta \\ 0, & \text{Otherwise,} \end{cases} \quad (4)$$

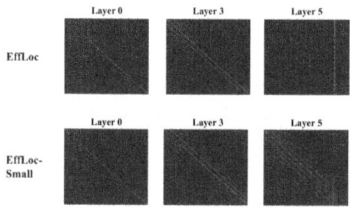

Fig. 2. EffLoc and EffLoc-Small display attention maps across layers 0 to 5, with the initial four layers categorized as shallow for Feature Mimicking, and the last two as deep for attention generation. The X-axis and Y-axis represent the key and query tokens, respectively.

where r_i represents a random variable uniformly distributed within $[0,1]$, and $i \in [0, N-1]$ corresponding to the token dimension's coordinates.

The generation block $Attn$ utilizes the newly masked feature $\hat{f}_s(x_i)$ to generate the teacher's complete feature through attention mechanisms. This process is formally expressed as:

$$Attn(\hat{f}_s(x)) \longrightarrow f_t(x). \quad (5)$$

Concluding the development of the *attention* generation method, we formulate the distillation loss L_{Attn} as

$$L_{attn} = \sum_{i=1}^{N} \sum_{j=1}^{D} \text{Masked}_i (f_t(x_{i,j}) - Attn(f_s(x_{i,j})))^2. \quad (6)$$

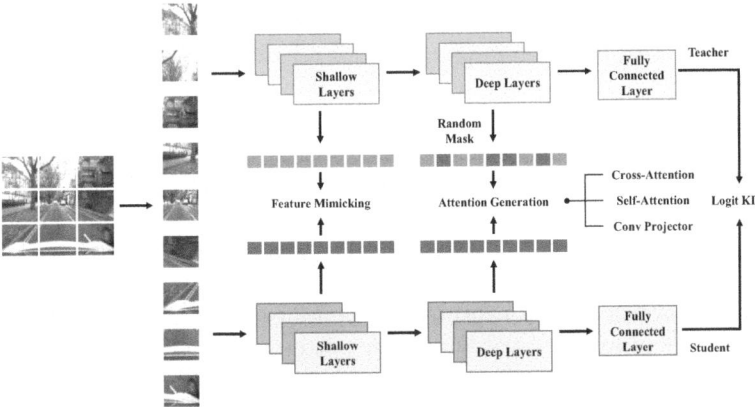

Fig. 3. Overview of our proposed Method. LocKD unites teacher and student under an identical architecture for distillation, integrating feature mimicking for shallow layers. Cross-attention, self-attention, and the convolutional projector are employed in attention Generation module for the distillation of deeper layers. Ultimately, both layers are feature-based and can be seamlessly combined with output logit-based distillation methods to enhanced Vit-based camera relocalization.

2.3 LocKD

In conclusion, the Lockd model we introduced illustrated in Fig. 3, which trains the student model yielding the final loss expression:

$$L = \alpha L_{fm} + \beta L_{attn} + L_{logit}, \tag{7}$$

where L_{logit} denotes the standard logit-based distillation approach, verifies by Touvron [44] to be applicable across both CNNs and smaller ViTs. The hyperparameters α and β serve to balance the loss. We defined the initial four layers as shallow layers, intended for Feature Mimicking, while the final two layers are classified as deep layers, serving attention generation purposes. Attention visualization map in Fig. 2 reveals layers 5 which is deep layer exhibit distinct patterns between EffLoc and Effloc-Small.

3 Experiments

3.1 Experiment Setup

Our research utilizes the ImageNet-1K dataset [45], comprising 1000 categories, to refine pretrained knowledge distillation models for ViT-based camera relocalization. During data preprocessing, image resize to 256 × 256 pixels through both random and center cropping, followed by normalization to scale pixel intensities between -1 and 1. The model development is facilitated using PyTorch 1.11.0 [46] and Timm 0.6.13. To regulate the distillation loss, we employ hyperparameters α and β as outlined in Eq. 7. Hyperparameter η modulates the masking rate for distillation of feature mimicking layers as indicated in Eq. 4. The NKD method [47] is utilized with parameters $\{\alpha = 0.5, temperature = 1\}$ in logit distillation. Experiments are performed on an Nvidia V100 GPU, evaluating models based on the outcomes of the final epoch.

3.2 Oxford RobotCar Datasets

The Oxford Robot-Car dataset [48] provides an wealth of real-world data through more than 100 repetitions of a consistent 10 km route in center Oxford. Gathered biweekly over a year, it captures a wide range of environmental conditions such as changes in weather, varying traffic patterns, pedestrian movement, construction works, and different roadwork situations. It includes recordings from six cameras mounted on the car, along with integrated LIDAR, GPS, INS data, and stereo visual odometry. The dataset is distinguished by its dynamic features, such as moving and stationary vehicles, cyclists, and pedestrians, which introduce complex challenges for vision-based relocalization tasks.

For a fair assessment, we employ the evaluation protocol defined by MapNet [49]. Our empirical analysis concentrates on two specific segments from the dataset: LOOP, spanning 1120 m, and FULL, covering 9562 m, distinguished by their route distances Table 1.

Table 1. Results of EfficientVit backbone on Oxford RobotCar dataset with EffLoc. Average position and rotation errors are assessed relative to the baseline model, alongside general KD, NKD, FKD, and our proposed method for each sequence. Our approach achieves enhanced performance, yielding new benchmarks in the field.

Class	Teacher	EffLoc-Small	KD	NKD	FKD	Ours
Loop1	7.58 m, 3.72°	8.71 m, 4.2°	8.67 m, 4.18°	8.96 m, 4.17°	8.59 m, 4.11°	**8.51 m, 4.04°**
Loop2	7.89 m, 4.19°	8.86 m, 4.7°	8.84 m, 4.59°	8.63 m, 4.45°	8.61 m, 4.45°	**8.60 m, 4.41°**
Full 1	27.23 m, 11.41°	30.59 m, 12.8°	32.43 m, 13.2°	33.16 m, 13.9°	28.79 m, **11.4°**	**28.54 m**, 11.45°
Full 2	44.82 m, 9.87°	53.79 m, 11.15°	52.71 m, 11.07°	57.21 m, 13.4°	49.41 m, 10.8°	**48.41 m, 10.79°**
AVG	21.88 m, 7.40°	25.49 m, 8.21°	25.66 m, 8.26°	26.99 m, 8.98°	23.85 m, 7.69°	**23.51 m, 7.67°**

3.3 Baseline Methods

We benchmark our proposed method LocKD, against three established baselines.

- The traditional approach within knowledge distillation(KD) directly supervise the student's predictions with the teacher's. As delineated in Eq. 1, the objective is to minimize the discrepancy between the local predictions of the teacher model and the student model.
- Normalized Knowledge Distillation (NKD) [50] refines the distillation loss by extracting and addressing the non-target component, thereby aligning the

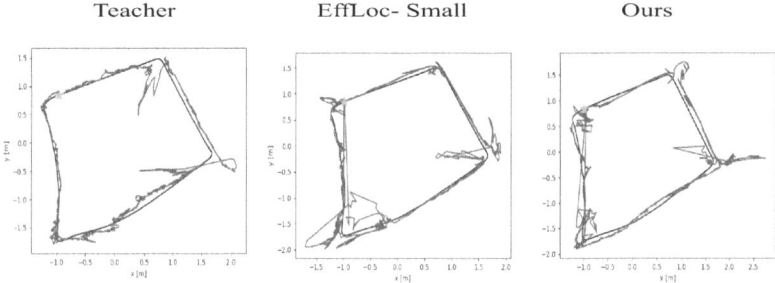

Fig. 4. Trajectories for Teacher (Left), EffLoc-Small (Middle), and LocKD (Right) within the Oxford RobotCar dataset are illustrated. Each path begins with a yellow star and Ground truth paths are outlined in black, while the predicted trajectories are shown in red. The small backbone of the teacher produces numerous outliers particularly in the bottom-left corner compare to our model. (Color figure online)

student's ancillary logits with the teacher's. NKD further employs normalization of these non-target logits to optimally utilize soft labels in computing distillation losses.
- The state-of-the-art feature-based Knowledge Distillation method (FKD) [51] integrates attention-guided and non-local distillation techniques. This dual approach enables the student model to assimilate not only individual pixel features but also the interrelations among various pixels, enhancing its overall predictive capability.

Table 2. The effect of Feature Mimicking on different layers for average position and rotation errors of four sequences.

Layer	EffLoc − LocKD					
0	-	✓	-	-	✓	✓
3	-	-	✓	-	✓	✓
5	-	-	-	✓	-	✓
Avg	25.66 m, 8.26°	25.47 m, 8.17°	25.79 m, 8.51°	25.76 m, 8.41°	24.37 m, 7.98°	24.41 m, 8.05°

3.4 Main Results

The Oxford RobotCar dataset introduces considerable challenges demanding a relocalization model characterized by robustness and versatility. Table I illustrates a comparative evaluation of our novel approaches against EffLoc-Small, conventional Knowledge Distillation (KD), Normalized Knowledge Distillation (NKD), and the feature-focused Knowledge Distillation technique (FKD). While

Table 3. Ablation study of the losses of *Feature Mimicking* and *Attention Generation* for mean position and rotation errors of four sequences.

Losses	EffLoc- Small (Student)			
L_{fm}	-	✓	-	✓
L_{attn}	-	-	✓	✓
EffLoc (Teacher)	25.66 m, 8.26°	24.13 m, 7.99°	25.56 m, 8.14°	**23.64 m, 7.72°**

KD slightly improves training compare to EffLoc-small. As we expected, EffLoc-small degrades the performance with smaller backbone of EffLoc. Both NKD and FKD boost the results from KD model. For the Full 1, FDK with a slight advantage on mean rotational error for our approach. For the challenging sequences Full1 and Full 2, LocKD exhibits impressive 7.14% and 11.1% improvements from the mean position errors respectively. Moreover, Fig. 4 illustrates the relocalization trajectories for loop 2, our model elevates the robustness and accuracy though mimicking texture features in shallow layers(0–4) and preserving more semantic information in deep layers(5,6) with attention generation. As depicted in Fig. 2, the attention distribution across layers 0 and 3 demonstrate notable similarities Table 2.

We further validate the the effects of feature mimicking in either layer 0, 3 and 5 of our approach illustrated in Fig. 2. Broadly speaking, feature mimicking on either the shallow or deep layers can benefit the student model. The initial four layers with feature mimicking significantly propels the student model performance. Besides comparing the improvements at various distillation layers, feature mimicking at the shallow layers yields more advantages than deep layers. Considering the trade-offs between memory-cost and performance, we opt for attention generation in deep layers to enhance the student model's performance Table 3.

3.5 Ablation Study

We conduct an ablation study on the losses of Feature Mimicking and attention generation to investigate their influences on the student with EffLoc-Small. As shown in Fig. 3, both Feature Mimicking and attention generation modules significantly enhance the student model's capabilities. Implementing either module independently reveals that the Feature Mimicking loss notably outperforms the attention generation module. Because the shallow layers emphasizing basic but more crucial features than the high-level information from deep layers. Additionally, we discovered that these two losses offer synergistic benefits. When integrating two losses together, the student achieve optimal prediction with minimal transition and rotation errors of 23.64 m and 7.72° respectively.

4 Conclusion

In this study, we have pioneered a method for applying knowledge distillation to ViT-based camera relocalization. Looking ahead, our future work will concentrate on extending this approach to multiple images within varying and dynamic environments, moving beyond the current single-image framework. Despite the promising performance of LocKD in camera relocalization tasks, our method encompasses certain limitations that warrant further investigation. The adaptability of LocKD to diverse lighting conditions and weather variations has not been fully assessed. As part of our continued efforts, we will investigate adaptive training strategies and domain adaptation methods to ensure consistent performance across a wide range of environmental conditions.

References

1. Klein, G., Murray, D.: Parallel tracking and mapping for small AR workspaces. In:6th IEEE and ACM International Symposium on Mixed and Augmented Reality, pp. 225–234 (2007)
2. Wang, W., Zhao, W., Wang, X., Jin, Z., Li, Y., Runge, T.: A low-cost simultaneous localization and mapping algorithm for last-mile indoor delivery. In: 5th International Conference on Transportation Information and Safety (ICTIS). IEEE (2019)
3. Bresson, G., Alsayed, Z., Yu, L., Glaser, S.: Simultaneous localization and mapping: a survey of current trends in autonomous driving. IEEE Trans. Intell. Veh. **2**(3), 194–220 (2017)
4. Brachmann, E., Rother, C.: Visual camera re-localization from RGB and RGB-d images using DSAC. IEEE Trans. Pattern Anal. Mach. Intell. **44**(9), 5847–5865 (2021)
5. Li, D., Zhang, H., Cheng, J., Liu, B.: Improving efficiency of DNN-based relocalization module for autonomous driving with server-side computing. J. Cloud Comput. **13**(1), 25 (2024)
6. Wang, S., Kang, Q., She, R., Tay, W.P., Hartmannsgruber, A., Navarro. D.N.: Robustloc: robust camera pose regression in challenging driving environments. In: Proceedings of the AAAI Conference on Artificial Intelligence, pp. 6209–6216 (2023)
7. Martinez-Carranza, J., Calway, A., Mayol-Cuevas, W.: Enhancing 6d visual relocalisation with depth cameras. In: 2013 IEEE/RSJ International Conference on Intelligent Robots and Systems, pp. 899–906. IEEE (2013)
8. Xu, R., Shen, F., Wu, H., Zhu, J., Zeng, H.: Dual modal meta metric learning for attribute-image person re-identification. In: 2021 IEEE International Conference on Networking, Sensing and Control (ICNSC), vol 1, pp. 1–6. IEEE (2021)
9. Yao, J.: Ndc-scene: Boost monocular 3D semantic scene completion in normalized devicecoordinates space. In: 2023 IEEE/CVF International Conference on Computer Vision (ICCV), pp. 9421–9431. IEEE Computer Society (2023)
10. Klein, G., Murray, D.: Improving the agility of keyframe-based slam. In:Computer Vision–ECCV 2008: 10th European Conference on Computer Vision, Marseille, France, October 12-18, 2008, Proceedings, Part II 10, pp. 802–815 (2008)
11. Gee, A.P., Mayol-Cuevas, W.W.: 6d relocalisation for RGBD cameras using synthetic view regression. In: *BMVC*, vol. 1, pp. 2 (2012)

12. Elvira, R., Tardós, J.D., Montiel, J.M.: Orbslam-atlas: a robust and accurate multi-map system. In: 2019 IEEE/RSJ International Conference on Intelligent Robots and Systems (IROS), pp. 6253–6259. IEEE (2019)
13. Ke, T., Roumeliotis, S.I.: An efficient algebraic solution to the perspective-three-point problem. In: Conference on Computer Vision and Pattern Recognition (2017)
14. Yao, J., Pan, X., Wu, T., Zhang, X.: Building lane-level maps from aerial images. In: ICASSP 2024-2024 IEEE International Conference on Acoustics, Speech and SignalProcessing (ICASSP), pp. 3890–3894. IEEE (2024)
15. Terzakis, G., Lourakis, M.: A consistently fast and globally optimal solution to the perspective-n-point problem. In: European Conference on Computer Vision (2020)
16. Lepetit, V., Moreno-Noguer, F., Fua, P.: Epnp: an accurate o (n) solution to the PnP problem. Int. J. Comput. Vision (2009)
17. Brachmann, E., et al.: Dsac-differentiable ransac for camera localization. In: Proceedings of the IEEE Conference on Computer Vision and Pattern Recognition, pp. 6684–6692 (2017)
18. Krizhevsky, A., Sutskever, I., Hinton, G.E.: Imagenet classification with deep convolutional neural networks. In: Advances in Neural Information Processing Systems (2012)
19. Liu, W., et al.: SSD: Single shot multibox detector. In: European Conference on Computer Vision (2016)
20. Shen, F., Zhu, J., Zhu, X., Xie, Y., Huang, J.: Exploring spatial significance via hybrid pyramidal graph network for vehicle re-identification. IEEE Trans. Intell. Transp. Syst. **23**(7), 8793–8804 (2021)
21. Yao, J., Wu, T., Zhang, X.: Improving depth gradientcontinuity in transformers: A comparative study on monocular depth estimation with cnn. *arXiv preprint*arXiv:2308.08333 (2023)
22. Kendall, A., Grimes, M., Cipolla, R.: Posenet: a convolutional network for real-time 6-dof camera relocalization. In: International Conference on Computer Vision (2015)
23. Shen, F., Xie, Y., Zhu J, Zhu X, Zeng H.: Graph interactive transformer for vehicle re-identification. IEEE Trans. Image Proce. Git (2023)
24. Kendall, A., Cipolla, R.: Geometric loss functions for camera pose regression with deep learning. In: IEEE Conference on Computer Vision and Pattern Recognition (CVPR) (2017)
25. Wang, B., Chen, C., Lu, C.X., Zhao, P., Trigoni, N., Markham, A.: Atloc: attention guided camera localization. In: AAAI Conference on Artificial Intelligence (AAAI) (2020)
26. Cattaneo, D., Vaghi, M., Ballardini, A.L., Fontana, S., Sorrenti, D.G., Burgard, W.: Cmrnet: camera to lidar-map registration. In: IEEE Intelligent Transportation Systems Conference (ITSC) (2019)
27. Shen, F., Ye, H., Zhang, J., Wang, C., Han, X., Yang, W.: Advancing pose-guided image synthesis with progressive conditional diffusion models. *arXiv preprint*arXiv:2310.06313 (2023)
28. Weng, W., Lin, W., Lin, F., Ren, J., Shen, F.: A novel cross frequency-domain interaction learning for aerial oriented object detection. In: Chinese Conference on Pattern Recognition and Computer Vision (PRCV). Springer (2023)
29. Alexey, D., et al.: An image is worth 16×16 words: transformers for image recognition at scale. In: International Conference on Learning Representations (2021)
30. Shen, F., Du, X., Zhang, L., Tang, J.: Triplet contrastive learning for unsupervised vehicle re-identification. *arXiv preprint*arXiv:2301.09498 (2023)

31. Han, K., Xiao, A., Enhua, W., Guo, J., Chunjing, X., Wang, Y.: Transformer in transformer. Adv. Neural. Inf. Process. Syst. **34**, 15908–15919 (2021)
32. Touvron, H., Cord, M., Sablayrolles, A., Synnaeve, G., Jégou, H.: Going deeper with image transformers. In: Proceedings of the IEEE/CVF International Conference on Computer Vision, pp. 32–42 (2021)
33. Shen, F., Shu, X., Du, X., Tang, J.: Pedestrian-specific bipartite-aware similarity learning for text-based person retrieval. In: Proceedings of the 31th ACM International Conference on Multimedia (2023)
34. Xiao, Z., Chen, C., Yang, S., Wei, W.: Effloc: Lightweight vision transformer for efficient 6-dof camera relocalization. *arXiv Preprint* (2024)
35. Zhou, H., et al.: Rethinking soft labels for knowledge distillation: a bias–variance tradeoff perspective. In: International Conference on Learning Representations (2020)
36. Zhao, B., Cui, Q., Song, R., Qiu, Y., Liang, J.: Decoupled knowledge distillation. In: Proceedings of the IEEE/CVF Conference on Computer Vision and Pattern Recognition, pp. 11953–11962 (2022)
37. Xie, Y., Shen, F., Zhu, J., Zeng, H.: Viewpoint robust knowledge distillation for accelerating vehicle re-identification. EURASIP J. Adv. Signal Process. **1–13**, 2021 (2021)
38. Li, G., Li, X., Wang, Y., Zhang, S., Wu, Y., Liang, D.: Knowledge distillation for object detection via rank mimicking and prediction-guided feature imitation. In: Proceedings of the AAAI Conference on Artificial Intelligence, pp. 1306–1313 (2022)
39. Yang, J., Martinez, B., Bulat, A., Tzimiropoulos, G.: Knowledge distillation via softmax regression representation learning. In: International Conference on Learning Representations (2020)
40. Chen, P., Liu, S., Zhao, H., Jia, J.: Distilling knowledge via knowledge review. In: Proceedings of the IEEE/CVF Conference on Computer Vision and Pattern Recognition, pp. 5008–5017 (2021)
41. Hu, J., Huang, Z., Shen, F., He, D., Xian, Q.: A rubust method for roof extraction and height estimation. In: IGARSS 2023-2023 IEEE International Geoscience and Remote Sensing Symposium. IEEE (2023)
42. Qiao, C., Shen, F., Wang, X., Wang, R., Cao, F., Zhao, S., Li, C.: A novel multi-frequency coordinated module for sar ship detection. In: 2022 IEEE 34th International Conference on Tools with Artificial Intelligence (ICTAI), pp. 804–811. IEEE (2022)
43. Guo, S., Alvarez, J.M., Salzmann, M.: Distilling image classifiers in object detectors. Adv. Neural Inf. Proce. Syst. **34** (2021)
44. Touvron, H., Cord, M., Douze, M., Massa, F., Sablayrolles, A., Jégou, H.: Training data-efficient image transformers & distillation through attention. In: International Conference on Machine Learning, pp. 10347–10357 (2021)
45. Deng, J., Dong, W., Socher, R., Li, L.J., Li, K., Fei-Fei, L.: Imagenet: a large-scale hierarchical image database. In: Proceedings of the IEEE/CVF Conference on Computer Vision and Pattern Recognition, pp. 248–255 (2009)
46. Paszke, A., et al.: Pytorch: an imperative style, high-performance deep learning library. Adv. Neural. Inf. Process. Syst. **32**, 8026–8037 (2019)
47. Yang, Z., et al.: Rethinking knowledge distillation via cross-entropy. *arXiv preprint*arXiv:2208.10139 (2022)
48. Maddern, W., Pascoe, G., Linegar, C., Newman, P.: 1 year, 1000 km: the oxford robotcar dataset. Int. J. Rob. Res. **36**(1), 3–15 (2017)

49. Brahmbhatt, S., Gu, J., Kim, K., Hays, J., Kautz, J.: Geometry-aware learning of maps for camera localization. In: 2018 IEEE/CVF Conference on Computer Vision and Pattern Recognition (2018)
50. Yang, Z., Zeng, A., Li, Z., Zhang, T., Yuan, C., Li, Y.: From knowledge distillation to self-knowledge distillation: a unified approach with normalized loss and customized soft labels. In: IEEE/CVF International Conference on Computer Vision (ICCV) (2023)
51. Zhang, L., Ma, K.: Improve object detection with feature-based knowledge distillation: towards accurate and efficient detectors. In: International Conference on Learning Representations (2021)

A Spatially Enhanced CNN and Multiscale Transformer Fusion Approach for Chest Radiograph Registration

Jia Chen[1], Zeping Lin[1], Fei Fang[1(✉)], Huanrong Jiang[2(✉)], Yajie Meng[1], and Jinlong Qin[1]

[1] Wuhan Textile University, Wuhan, China
fangfei369@163.com, myj@hnu.edu.cn
[2] New H3C Technologies Co., Ltd., Hangzhou, China
18907172836@189.cn

Abstract. Deformable medical image registration research, crucial in image analysis and clinical fields, often relies on ConvNets to create U-shaped networks. However, due to the limited receptive fields of ConvNets, traditional methods may be less effective in aligning images with substantial dissimilarity. This paper presents a hybrid approach merging ConvNet with attention mechanism, leveraging the remote modelling abilities of attention mechanism to address the above challenges. First, we design a multiscale transformer fusion module (MTF) and integrate it into the skip connections of the U-shaped network, enhancing spatial relationship modelling. Second, We propose a plug-and-play registration head for positional reference in deformation field generation. Additionally, to enhance the lung registration accuracy in chest radiographs, we design a new loss function named lung region loss. Compared to current methods, this hybrid approach shows marked improvements in average Dice Similarity Score (DSC), Hausdorff Distance (HD), and Average Symmetric Surface Distance (ASSD) across three benchmark datasets, demonstrating its effectiveness in medical image registration.

Keywords: image registration · multiscale attention fusion · positional reference

1 Introduction

Deformable image registration(DIR) [1] is the basis for many medical image analysis tasks. such as co-registering MRI brain images before neuro-morphometry analysis [2] and segmenting organs at risk in radiotherapy planning [3]. In modern medicine, two images acquired in clinical event tracking usually have some complementary information to exploit. In order to make better use of this information, the two medical images should be spatially aligned. The task of DIR is to minimize the difference between the medical image to be aligned and the fixed medical image by means of spatial deformation.

Traditional image alignment [4,5] usually employs image processing techniques such as key point detection, edge extraction, and region segmentation to maximize the predefined similarity metric between the moving image and the fixed image. However, this approach is computationally expensive and usually slow in practice, as the optimization problem needs to be solved anew for each pair of invisible images.

Recently, convolutional neural networks(CNNs) have achieved advanced performance in many aspects of medical image analysis, including medical image segmentation [6], disease diagnostics [7], image reconstruction [8], and image registration [1] [9]. Compared with traditional medical image registration, methods based on CNNs use a single global function in the training stage to reduce the previous image registration time and increase the accuracy of image registration. The CNNs can learn the alignment representation of the two images from the training image pair so that the spatial position changes of the images can also be quickly captured in the testing phase, thereby achieving the purpose of quickly aligning the images.

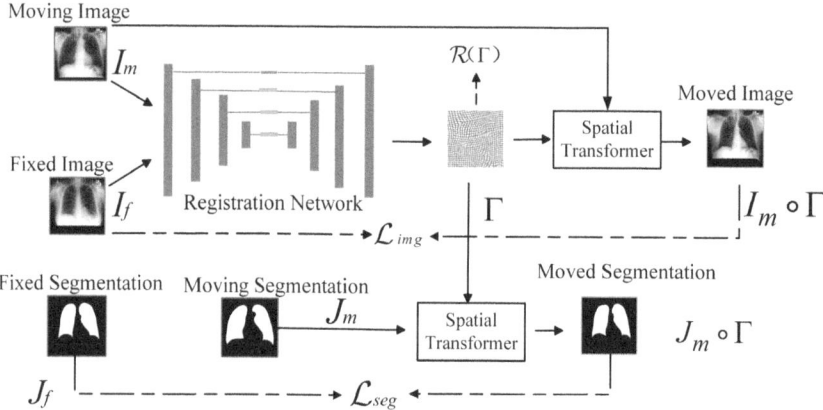

Fig. 1. The proposed hybrid Transformer-ConvNet network takes two inputs: I_m and I_f. The network generates a nonlinear warping function(Γ), which is then applied to $I_m(J_m)$ through a spatial transformation function. The loss term $\mathcal{L}_{img}$ is defined on $I_m \circ \Gamma$ and I_f. The loss term $\mathcal{L}_{seg}$ is defined on $J_m \circ \Gamma$ and J_f.

Most existing medical registration models are based on the U-shaped structure of ConvNet [10,11], derived from partial improvements to U-Net [6]. The U-shaped structure can gradually reduce the scale of features, integrate the structural information of underlying features and the semantic information of deep features, and strengthen the model's feature expression ability of image information. However, when dealing with significantly distinct images, the conventional ConvNet-based registration model struggles to discern positional changes among distant pixels accurately. This limitation arises from the inherent inductive bias of convolution in traditional U-shaped registration quasi-networks, which hinders the original skip connections from effectively capturing global features at each layer. At the same time, in traditional registration network training, the predicted movement position of pixels in the deformation field does not have any specific position reference, and the alignment between spatially adjacent pixels does not provide a movement reference for each other. In fact, spatially adjacent pixels should be adjacent or not far apart after registration.

The advent of the Vision Transformer marked the first incorporation of Transformer architecture from natural language processing tasks [12] into computer vision tasks [13]. Following the success of the Vision Transformer, the Swin Transformer [14] introduced a shifted window mechanism to enhance the capture of long-distance information in images, consequently improving the modelling capability of global features. This feature can alleviate the issue of the limited receptive field present in conventional ConvNet-based registration models.

Simultaneously, we observed that conventional registration encompasses the entire image and assigns equal weight to organ regions and unrelated tissue regions. While skull peeling [15] can mitigate interference in brain registration, challenges persist in lung registration within chest radiographs due to other tissue interference, particularly in addressing notable deformations or differences between input chest radiographs. Meanwhile, In clinical research, generating anatomically credible results is critical for diagnostic studies. Consequently, we propose to learn the accuracy of organ registration from anatomical segmentation.

Based on these observations, we present a hybrid approach merging ConvNet with Transformer. MTF is added to the skip connection in the form of residuals to improve the remote modeling capabilities. Besides, we designed a plug-and-play registration head in which the specific positions of pixels are embedded in the process of predicting the deformation field to provide a position reference for the deformation of adjacent pixels. At the same time, we designed a new loss function to reduce the interference of other tissues during lung registration.

Our contributions can be summarized as follows:

- We present a registration network merging ConvNet with Transformer. Specifically, We designed a multi-scale transformer fusion module (MTF) into the skip connections of the U-shaped network, Our method can improve the modelling ability of global features and the robustness of the mode.
- We propose a new spatially enhanced registration head(SERH) in which we embed the position information of image pixels to improve the sense of spatial position during registration.
- For improving lung registration accuracy in chest radiographs, We design a new loss function named lung region loss.

2 Related Works

2.1 Deformable Image Registration Based on Weakly Supervised Learning

DIR based on weakly supervised learning [1,3] establishes a spatial correspondence between moving image (segmentation) and fixed image (segmentation) by optimizing energy function:

$$\check{\Gamma} = \arg\min_{\Gamma} E_{\text{sim1}}(I_m \circ \Gamma, I_f) + \lambda \mathcal{R}(\Gamma) \\ + E_{\text{sim2}}(J_m \circ \Gamma, J_f). \tag{1}$$

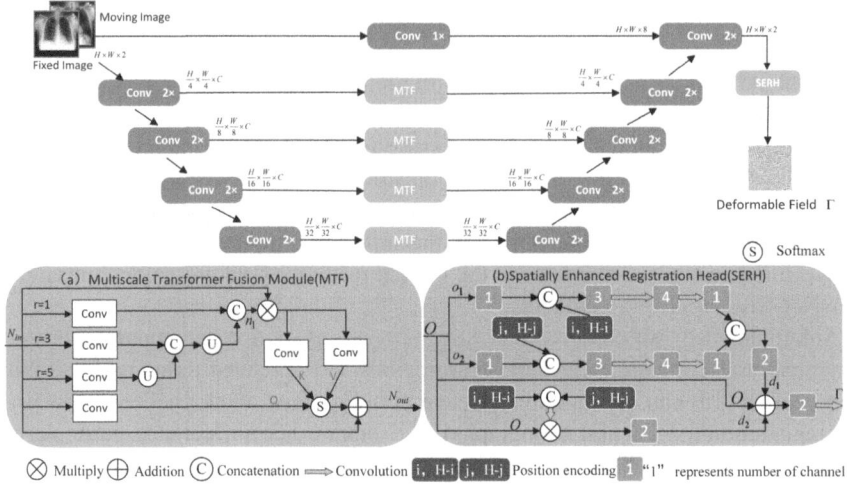

Fig. 2. Architecture of the proposed image registration network.

where I_m is the moving image, I_f is the fixed image, J_m is the moving segmentation, J_f is the fixed segmentation, Γ parametrically transforms the spatial transformation mapping of each point of the image I_m to I_f, $\mathcal{R}(\Gamma)$ imposes smoothness of the deformation field, and λ is the regularization hyper-parameter, E_{sim} measures the level of alignment between the deformed moving image (segmentation) and fixed image (segmentation). $\check{\Gamma}$ is computed by minimizing the above energy function.

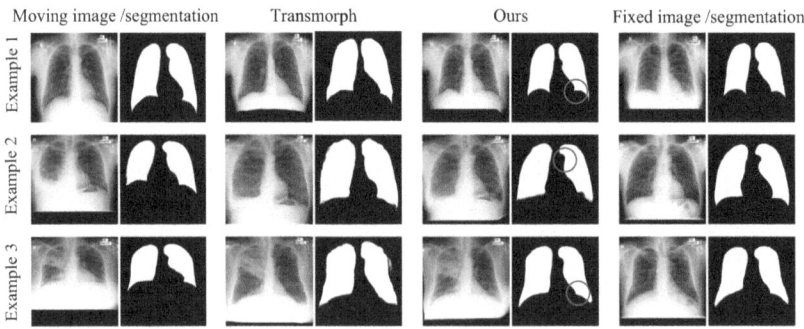

Fig. 3. Visualization of the results after registering a pair of images. The red circle highlights the area of the lung anatomy that is better preserved by our method when compared with Transmorph. (Color figure online)

2.2 Based on CNN-Transformer Hybrid Registration Model

There are two categories of hybrid models here. One is to directly replace the original convolution layer with the classic Transformer block. The most classic example is that [14] directly replaces the entire encoder with the swin transformer. Using successive swin transformer blocks to extract image features, the decoder still uses CNN as the main architecture. The other is that similar modules using similar attention mechanisms are used in CNN-based models. The most common ones are spatial attention and channel attention [16,17] and inter-image co-attention [18] and cross-attention [19] between multi-modal images. These attention mechanisms allow traditional registration networks to capture more comprehensive features. These mechanisms have indeed proven their effectiveness in actual experiments.

3 Method

Based on the above section description, we propose a weakly supervised image registration model using a hybrid approach that combines ConvNet with Transformer, as shown in Fig. 1. Specifically, We add MTF into the skip connections of the U-shaped network. At the end of the decoder, we design a plug-and-play SERH for predicting the deformable field. Figure 2 illustrates the architecture of the registration network. Furthermore, to improve lung registration accuracy in chest radiographs, we design a new loss function, lung region loss.

3.1 Mutiscale Transformer Fusion Module(MTF)

To enhance the U-shaped registration backbone model, we add MTF to the skip connection in the form of residual blocks to extract the global features of each layer. This modification facilitates the provision of pertinent multiscale global information to each layer of the decoder. Consequently, each decoder layer gains access to both global and local features. Our combination strategies then enable the model to easily perceive pixel displacement changes during the registration process, especially when faced with the problem that some corresponding pixels may be spatially far apart. As shown in Fig. 2 (a). It integrates multiscale mechanisms and multi-head self-attention mechanisms.

We place MTF after the output feature $N_{in} \in \mathbb{R}^{C \times H_1 \times W_1}$ of every layer of downsampling, where C denotes the channel dimension, and H_1, and W_1 denote the size of the input tensor. Specifically, first, we input N_{in} into the dilated convolution of three parallel branches to extract multi-scale information, where the convolution kernel size is 1×1. The atrous rate dr_i from top to bottom in Fig. 2(a) and the atrous rate R_i ($i = \{1, 2, 3\}$) is $\{1, 3, 5\}$ corresponding to the MTF. We use this to upsample the output of each branch from bottom to top and splice it with the previous branch. To sum up, the above process can be expressed as:

$$n_i = \text{DWConv2D}_{1 \times 1}^{dr_i}(N_i), \quad (2)$$

$$n_2 = \text{Conc}_{1 \times 1}(n_3, \text{UnS}(n_2)), \quad (3)$$

$$n_1 = \text{Conv2D}_{1 \times 1}(\text{Conc}(n_1, \text{UnS}(n_2))), \quad (4)$$

$$N_{kv} = n_1 \times N_{in}. \tag{5}$$

where Conc represents concatenation, N_i represents the output of three atrous convolutions, $DWConv2D_{1\times1}^{dr_i}$ denotes a 1×1 atrous convolution with an atrous rate of dr_i and N_{kv} denotes the final output. Then, we input the obtained features into two 1*1 convolution blocks to obtain N_K, N_V, which respectively represent K and V in MTF. Both record rich multi-scale contextual information in skip connections. We get N_Q by performing a convolution operation on the initial N_{in}.

$$N_K = \text{Conv2D}_{1\times1}(N_{kv}), \tag{6}$$

$$N_V = \text{Conv2D}_{1\times1}(N_{kv}), \tag{7}$$

$$N_Q = \text{Conv2D}_{1\times1}(N_{in}) \tag{8}$$

The self-attention process can be expressed as follows:

$$Attention = \text{Softmax}\left(\frac{N_Q \times N_K^T}{\sqrt{d_{N_k}}}\right) \times N_V \tag{9}$$

where $d_{(N_K)}$ represents the channel dimension of N_K, and division by $\sqrt{d_{(N_K)}}$ can be considered as an approximate normalization.

Finally, we add the initial N_{in} and Attention to get the MTF output result N_{out}

$$N_{out} = Attention + N_{in} \tag{10}$$

3.2 Spatially Enhanced Registration Head(SERH)

As shown in Fig. 2(b), SERH takes the obtained feature map $O \in \mathbb{R}^{2 \times H \times W}$ from the U-shaped network as input. Our goal is to embed the spatial positional encodings S_{ij} into the feature map O to derive the deformation field Γ. We encode the position at (i,j) of O as follows:

$$S_{ij} = (i, j, H - i, W - j), \tag{11}$$

where S_{ij} represents the position encoding of each pixel in the both I_m and I_f. (i,j,H,W) represent the distance to the left, right, top, and bottom. This approach is employed due to the potential variations in the input size (H, W) of the image across different individuals [20].

As shown in Fig. 2(b), to enhance the influence of pixel position in registration, we employ two different embedding methods at the same time.

Split Embedding. We split the input feature map O based on the number of feature channels, and divide it into two equally sized segments: o_1 and o_2. Simultaneously, we split S_{ij} into two parts based on different orientations: $(I, H - i)$ and $(j, W - j)$. By employing convolutional operations, we embed positional encodings corresponding to different orientations into the split feature maps. Finally, we concatenate the results of these two parts to obtain the deformed feature, d_1:

$$d_1 = Concat(W_1((i, H - i) + o_1), \\ W_2((j, w - j) + o_2)), \quad (12)$$

where W_1 and W_2 represent two convolutional processes with non-shared weights. Specifically, they modify the number of feature channels from 3 to 4 and ultimately to 1.

Direct Embedding. We directly embed the positional encoding S_{ij} into the input feature map O, and ultimately obtain the deformed feature d_2:

$$d_2 = (O \times W_3(S_{ij})), \quad (13)$$

where W_3 represents a convolutional operation intended to change the feature channels of S_{ij} from 4 to 2.

Table 1. Registration performance comparison in terms of mean DSC, HD, ASSD scores on three datasets among traditional SimpleElastic [4] and SyN [5], deep learning methods AC-RegNet [11] and Transmorph [10]. The numbers in the parenthesis are the standard deviation

Dataset	Method	DSC	HD (mm)	ASSD (mm)
JSRT	SimpleElastix	0.871(0.036)	27.110(10.615)	4.814(1.618)
	SyN	0.791(0.184)	30.448(18.560)	1.955(1.800)
	AC-RegNet	0.948(0.059)	24.180(8.990)	2.420(0.795)
	Transmorph	0.960(0.017)	11.428(7.643)	1.574(0.233)
	Ours	**0.969(0.014)**	**9.452(5.956)**	**1.199(0.198)**
MONT	SimpleElastix	0.866(0.053)	27.174(20.304)	4.890(2.488)
	SyN	0.855(0.062)	24.706(11.658)	1.545(0.609)
	AC-RegNet	0.943(0.087)	24.600(14.492)	2.160(0.433)
	Transmorph	0.953(0.024)	14.347(7.297)	1.538(0.265)
	Ours	**0.959(0.238)**	**11.722(5.970)**	**1.456(0.124)**
SHEN	SimpleElastix	0.833(0.042)	34.004(5.458)	5.376(1.581)
	SyN	0.829(0.044)	32.983(7.468)	1.294(0.466)
	AC-RegNet	0.945(0.059)	21.783(6.538)	2.149(0.341)
	Transmorph	0.952(0.027)	15.237(7.893)	1.722(0.240)
	Ours	**0.957(0.029)**	**10.007(6.006)**	**1.538(0.285)**

Finally, we add d_1, d_2 and O together and feed the sum to the next convolution layer, W_4, thereby obtaining the deformable field Γ.

$$\Gamma = W_4(d_1 + d_2 + O) \quad (14)$$

The two encoding methods we employ improve the ability to perceive changes in pixel positions in the presence of large differences in images.

3.3 Objective Function

The entire objective function contains three parts, the segmentation similarity $Ł_{seg}$, the image similarity $Ł_{img}$ and the displacement field smoothness $\mathcal{R}(\Gamma)$.

Our naming of images follows our definitions in the related work section. In order to provide the registration network with a more anatomical background of the lungs during training, we incorporate the segmentation-aware loss $Ł_{seg}(J_m \circ \Gamma, J_f)$ into the loss function. In this loss, we quantify the level of spatial alignment between the fixed label J_f and the warped version of moving segmentation J_m. In our experiments, we set $Ł_{seg}$ to classical categorical cross-entropy:

$$Ł_{seg} = \lambda_{ce} CE(J_m \circ \Gamma, J_f), \tag{15}$$

where λ_{ce} is a weighting factor for the additional term $Ł_{seg}$ and CE() is the cross-entropy function.

In the image registration of chest radiographs, we use $Ł_{er}$ to perform registration constraints on the entire chest radiograph. Meanwhile, since there are other human tissue parts in the image that are not of interest or may interfere with lung registration, we hope to focus on the registration of the lung organs in the image. Therefore, we also design the lung region loss $Ł_{lr}$ to improve the registration of the lungs in the image.

$$Ł_{er} = SIMM(I_m \circ \Gamma, I_f), \tag{16}$$

$$Ł_{lr} = (1+c)SIMM(I_f \times J_f, \\ I_m \circ \Gamma \times J_m), \tag{17}$$

where c represents the lung area as a percentage of the entire image, Structural Similarity Index(SSIM) [21] is a perceptual metric used for measuring the similarity between two images. Through multiplying the distorted image $I_m \circ \Gamma$ by J_f, we separate the lung organs from the moving image and apply a higher weight(1+c) to lung registration than the non-organ tissue areas, which increases the model's registration attention to the lung organs. $I_f \times J_f$ represents the lung area of the fixed image I_f.

Table 2. Ablation study on the testing sets

MTF	SERH	Lung region loss	JSRT	MONT	SHEN
✔	✘	✘	0.966	0.955	0.954
✘	✔	✘	0.956	0.949	0.942
✘	✘	✔	0.944	0.940	0.938

The expression of $Ł_{img}$ is as follows:

$$Ł_{img} = Ł_{lr} + \lambda_{er} Ł_{er}, \tag{18}$$

where λ_{er} is a weighting factor for the additional term $\mathcal{L}_{er}$.

In order to make the deformation field smoother, we introduce a regularizer $\mathcal{R}(\Gamma)$ in the loss function.

$$\mathcal{R}(\Gamma) = \sum_{p \in \Omega} ||\nabla u(p)||^2, \tag{19}$$

where $u(p)$ is the spatial gradients of the displacement field Γ.

In conclusion, the total loss function $\mathcal{L}_{loss}$ is defined as:

$$\mathcal{L}_{loss} = \mathcal{L}_{img} + \mathcal{L}_{seg} + \lambda_r \mathcal{R}(\Gamma), \tag{20}$$

where λ_r is a weighting factor for the additional term $\mathcal{R}(\Gamma)$.

4 Experiments

4.1 Experiment Setup

Datasets. Throughout the complete experiment, we used a total of three public image databases: the Japanese Society of Radiological Technology (JSRT) database [22], the Montgomery County X-ray database (MONT) [23] and the Shenzhen Hospital X-ray database (SHEN) [24].

The JSRT dataset contains 247 images with ground truth segmentation labels. The MONT dataset contains 138 images with real labels. The SHEN dataset contains 550 images with real labels. We randomly select 75% of the images for model training and the rest for testing. We pre-processed these public chest X-ray datasets. Specifically, we unify the images in the dataset to the size of 256×256. We finally obtained 22,358 image pairs by pairing the images in the dataset.

Evaluation Metrics. To evaluate the effectiveness of image registration algorithms, we employ three commonly utilized segmentation evaluation metrics, namely DSC, HD, and ASSD. These metrics measure the concordance between the transformed source segmentation post-registration and the target masks. Dice Similarity Coefficient (DSC) [25] quantifies the degree of overlap between the segmentations. Hausdorff Distance (HD) measures the furthest separation between contours in millimetres. Average Symmetric Surface Distance (ASSD) provides an overall assessment of alignment accuracy. DSC ranges from 0 to 1, with higher values indicating better performance. Conversely, for ASSD and HD, lower values suggest better performance.

Implementation Details. In our experiments, we trained our model and advanced models. Our model is run for 100 epochs with an initial learning rate of 0.001. Simultaneously, we set $\lambda_{ce} = 1$, $\lambda_r = 3$, $\lambda_{er} = 1$. Using Adam as the optimizer, we set the training batch size to 32. For testing, the batch size was set to 1. All our experiments were performed on an NVIDIA 4070Ti, and Pytorch was used as the deep learning framework.

Table 3. Study on the plug-and-play and effectiveness of SERH

Method	JSRT	MONT	SHEN
AC-RegNet	0.948	0.943	0.945
Add SERH in AC-RegNet	**0.955**	**0.950**	**0.949**
Transmorph	0.960	0.953	0.952
Add SERH in Transmorph	**0.962**	**0.954**	**0.954**

4.2 Comparison with Other Methods

We conducted experiments on SHEN, MONT, and JSRT with various partition protocols and compared our proposed approach with traditional methods and state-of-the-art methods. We compare our method with two traditional methods SimpleElastic [4] and SyN [5], a CNN-based method AC-RegNet [11] and a method based on Transformer and CNN, Transmorph(2D) [10]. The comparison results are shown in Table 1. From Table 1, our method is consistently better than the above models. Figure 3 shows several examples for visual comparison with other registration methods, where the first two columns are the moving images and their segmentations, the last two columns are the fixed, and columns 3 and 4 are the warped moving images by Transmorph(2D) [10], and column 5 and 6 are the warped results of our method. We can see that our registration model is more accurate in registering the lung area. At the same time, we can hardly see the edge-blurring effect in the lung area after registration, and the lung segmentation after registration is closer to fixed segmentation.

4.3 Ablation Studies

We perform an ablation study on loss region loss($Ł_{er}$), MTF and SERH to evaluate the effect of the lung segmentation registration performance. Table 2 shows the results of ablation experiments on the test set. We can see from Table 2 that the addition of both lung region loss, MTF and SERH has a positive effect on improving the registration performance, which demonstrates that each added part contributes independently to the final registration results. This is because SERH can provide a position reference for predicting pixel displacement in the deformation field, thus improving the registration accuracy of the lung and MTF provides multi-scale contextual information to the model. Meanwhile, through the separation of lung organs from chest radiographs and the application of a higher registration weight to these organs rather than non-organ tissue areas, the registration attention on lung organs is enhanced.

In order to verify the plug-and-play and effectiveness of SERH, we replaced the final prediction deformable field convolutional layer in AC-RegNet and Transmorph with SERH. The experimental results shown in Table 3 show that the SERH can still play a positive role.

5 Conclusion

In this paper, we propose a novel deformable registration network, merging ConvNets and Transformer. Our approach enhances long-range capabilities using MTF. A specialized registration head guides pixel deformation, while a new loss function improves lung organ registration accuracy. Future work involves exploring spatial relationships between adjacent pixels in deformation.

References

1. Balakrishnan, G., Zhao, A., Sabuncu, M.R., Guttag, J., Dalca, A.V.: Voxelmorph: a learning framework for deformable medical image registration. IEEE Trans. Med. Imaging **38**(8), 1788–1800 (2019)
2. Gaser, C.: Structural mri: morphometry. In: Neuroeconomics, pp. 399–409 (2016)
3. Seungjong, O., Kim, S.: Deformable image registration in radiation therapy. Radiat. Oncol. J. **35**(2), 101 (2017)
4. Avants, B., Tustison, N.J., Song, G.: Advanced normalization tools: V1. 0. Insight J. (2009)
5. Avants, B.B., Epstein, C.L., Grossman, M., Gee, J.C.: Symmetric diffeomorphic image registration with cross-correlation: evaluating automated labeling of elderly and neurodegenerative brain. Med. Image Anal. **12**(1), 26–41 (2008)
6. Ronneberger, O., Fischer, P., Brox, T.: U-net: convolutional networks for biomedical image segmentation. In: Navab, N., Hornegger, J., Wells, W.M., Frangi, A.F. (eds.) MICCAI 2015. LNCS, vol. 9351, pp. 234–241. Springer, Cham (2015). https://doi.org/10.1007/978-3-319-24574-4_28
7. Lian, C., Liu, M., Zhang, J., Shen, D.: Hierarchical fully convolutional network for joint atrophy localization and alzheimer's disease diagnosis using structural mri. IEEE Trans. Pattern Anal. Mach. Intell. (TPAMI) **42**(4), 880–893 (2018)
8. Zhu, B., Liu, J.Z., Cauley, S.F., Rosen, B.R., Rosen, M.S.: Image reconstruction by domain-transform manifold learning. Nature **555**(7697), 487–492 (2018)
9. Huang, W., et al.: A coarse-to-fine deformable transformation framework for unsupervised multi-contrast mr image registration with dual consistency constraint. IEEE Trans. Med. Imaging (TMI) **40**(10), 2589–2599 (2021)
10. Chen, J., Frey, E.C., He, Y., Segars, W.P., Li, Y., Du, Y.: Transmorph: transformer for unsupervised medical image registration. Med. Image Anal. **82**, 102615 (2022)
11. Mansilla, L., Milone, D.H., Ferrante, E.: Learning deformable registration of medical images with anatomical constraints. Neural Netw. **124**, 269–279 (2020)
12. Vaswani, A., et al.: Attention is all you need. In: Advances in Neural Information Processing Systems (NeurIPS), vol. 30 (2017)
13. Dosovitskiy, A., et al.: An image is worth 16×16 words: transformers for image recognition at scale. In: International Conference on Learning Representations (ICLR) (2020)
14. Liu, Z., et al.: Swin transformer: hierarchical vision transformer using shifted windows. In: Proceedings of the IEEE/CVF International Conference on Computer Vision (ICCV), pp. 10012–10022 (2021)
15. Akkus, Z., Galimzianova, A., Hoogi, A., Rubin, D.L., Erickson, B.J.: Deep learning for brain MRI segmentation: state of the art and future directions. J. Digital Imaging **30**, 449–459 (2017)
16. Chen, X., et al.: DuSFE: dual-channel squeeze-fusion-excitation co-attention for cross-modality registration of cardiac SPECT and CT. Med. Image Anal. **88**, 102840 (2023)

17. Zhong, L., et al.: Qacl: quartet attention aware closed-loop learning for abdominal mr-to-ct synthesis via simultaneous registration. Med. Image Anal. **83**, 102692 (2023)
18. Ahn, S.S., et al.: Co-attention spatial transformer network for unsupervised motion tracking and cardiac strain analysis in 3d echocardiography. Med. Image Anal. **84**, 102711 (2023)
19. Khor, H.G., Ning, G., Sun, Y., Lu, X., Zhang, X., Liao, H.: Anatomically constrained and attention-guided deep feature fusion for joint segmentation and deformable medical image registration. Med. Image Anal. **88**, 102811 (2023)
20. Zhang, H., Wang, R., Zhang, J., Liu, D., Li, C., Li, J.: Spatially covariant lesion segmentation. In: Proceedings of the Thirty-Second International Joint Conference on Artificial Intelligence (IJCAI), pp. 1713–1721 (2023)
21. Wang, Z., Bovik, A.C., Sheikh, H.R., Simoncelli, E.P.: Image quality assessment: from error visibility to structural similarity. IEEE Trans. Image Process. (TIP) **13**(4), 600–612 (2004)
22. Shiraishi, J., et al.: Development of a digital image database for chest radiographs with and without a lung nodule: receiver operating characteristic analysis of radiologists' detection of pulmonary nodules. Am. J. Roentgenol. **174**(1), 71–74 (2000)
23. Candemir, S., et al.: Lung segmentation in chest radiographs using anatomical atlases with nonrigid registration. IEEE Trans. Med. Imaging (TMI) **33**(2), 577–590 (2013)
24. Jaeger, S., et al.: Automatic tuberculosis screening using chest radiographs. IEEE Trans. Med. Imaging (TMI) **33**(2), 233–245 (2013)
25. Dice, L.R.: Measures of the amount of ecologic association between species. Ecology **26**(3), 297–302 (1945)

The Phantom Dance: Personalized Anatomical Skeleton Inference from Monocular Views

Boyuan Cheng[1(✉)], Yingjie Xi[1], Jingyao Cai[1], Rupert Page[2], Jian Jun Zhang[1(✉)], and Xiaosong Yang[1(✉)]

[1] Bournemouth University, Poole, UK
{bcheng,yxi,jcai,jzhang,xyang}@bournemouth.ac.uk
[2] University Hospitals Dorset, Bournemouth, UK
rupert.page@uhd.nhs.uk

Abstract. The role of anatomical skeletons in animation production is increasingly important. Crafting a customized anatomical skeleton generally involves detailed manual modeling or depends on high-precision motion capture equipment, both of which can be costly to implement. This paper presents PASI (Personalized Anatomical Skeleton Inference), a novel end-to-end method for estimating anatomical skeletons from monocular inputs. PASI incorporates two modes of pose estimation algorithm to acquire motion data, eliminating the need for special motion capture devices. For bone personalization, we introduce an innovative scaling algorithm to prevent the distortion of bone shape during transformation. Besides, an optimization step is also proposed to minimize motion error, enhancing the fidelity of the inferred skeleton. The method is evaluated for its performance and processing speed, showing promising results in generating personalized skeletons.

Keywords: computer animation · anatomical skeleton · skeleton inference

1 Introduction

In film and game production, character movements are orchestrated by animation system. The fidelity of animations plays a crucial role in conveying the characters' realism, significantly impacting the audience's immersive experience. To animate a character, animators embed a tree-like framework of interconnected joints, known as a skeletal rig, within the character's mesh, simulating the skeletal structures in natural organisms. This approach allows animators to manipulate the rig, thereby driving the character's mesh. However, skeletal rig tends to overlook how changes in a character's pose can affect their body shape, which can result in unrealistic skin deformations during pose transitions. Recent developments in the parametric modeling of human skin (e.g., [1–3]) have demonstrated the potential for more naturally deforming skin that aligns with changes in pose, thereby capturing movements with greater detail than traditional rigging techniques. Nevertheless, the external appearance of human exhibits considerable variation among individuals, which implies that an epidermal model designed for one person cannot be directly applied to another. Hence, it is essential to select a motion representation that offers greater adaptability, while also capturing the intricacies of movements in detail.

Fig. 1. The proposed method is used to infer anatomical skeletons from given images and videos.

In reality, the movements of the human body are governed by its internal anatomy, such as bones and muscles. Instead of directly manipulating a joint skeleton, many animators prefer to first construct a detailed anatomical model of their character's skeleton, then layer on muscles, fat, and additional elements. This approach animate the character's exterior skin based on the underlying structure. By simulating the interactions between bones and skin, anatomical skeleton-driven animation achieves more lifelike and accurate biomechanical movements.

Crafting anatomical skeletons customized to specific individuals involves accommodating the unique shapes, sizes, and interconnections in the human body. This intricate process demands significant time and resources, presenting a formidable obstacle for small studios or independent animators who may lack the necessary hardware and expertise. OpenSim [4] provides a set of pre-constructed and validated anatomical skeletal models that can simulate a wide range of human movements. This enables users to directly employ these ready-made models, bypassing the intricate task of anatomical modeling from scratch. Nonetheless, substantial challenges persist in achieving highly customized skeletal estimations. Existing works [5,6] struggle with adapting to diverse human body shapes, which restrict their usability. Moreover, when converting captured motion data into a skeleton, the resulting movements of the constructed skeleton do not align precisely with the original input.

To address the issues, an end-to-end method PASI (Personalized Anatomical Skeleton Inference) is proposed to estimate anatomical skeletons from monocular inputs (Fig. 1). PASI makes following contributions:

- Two modes of motion data are adopted to accommodate a wide range of human body shapes and poses. Users can select the mode that best aligns with the specific features of their intended character.

- An innovative scaling algorithm is introduced to align the bones with the desired target shape while ensuring that the bones are not distorted and deformed.
- An optimization step is proposed to minimize motion errors resulting from the constraints inherent in OpenSim. Thereby ensuring higher fidelity of the generated skeleton.

2 Related Works

Numerous studies have focused on the challenge of developing a customized anatomical model of an individual based on external observations.

Hamadi et al. [7] proposed a approach that allocate complex internal anatomical structures (e.g., bones, muscles, and nerves) to differently shaped target figures while preserving the features of the transferred anatomical structures. However, apart from the skeletal template, the authors did not provide any other real data to validate the results of the proposed method. Hence, this work lack anatomical constraints.

Living Book of Anatomy (LBA) [8] uses RGB-D cameras (e.g., Kinect) for the extraction of key points and computes a geometric transformation factor for the bones between every two joints in conjunction with the joint points of a standard human skeleton, allowing for the capture of dynamic anatomical skeletons in real-time. Nonetheless, the system demands a substantial level of hardware equipment. As a result, it becomes inaffordable for the majority of users to employ the LBA system for predicting anatomical skeletons.

Zoss et al. [9] propose a method of learning the nonlinear relationship between skin surface deformation and jaw movement from real data. Once the learning is complete, the mapping can be applied to track the motion of the invisible jaw from the visible skin surface. However, the method can only predict the bone movement trajectory from the skin, without accounting for the personalized variations in bone shapes and specific details.

Ichim et al. propose Phace [10], which models the physical interactions between facial muscles and rigid skeletal structures by minimizing nonlinear potential energy, while Wang et al. [11] develop a method to precisely simulate the movement of soft tissues driven by hand bones, using magnetic resonance imaging (MRI) data. Both methods reconstruct the external skin based on the internal skeleton, which is contrary to the objective of this project.

PIANO [12], the first parametric model, learns a set of parameters from medical images to represent hands with various shapes and postures. By fine-tuning its parameters, it becomes capable of covering a significant portion of the diverse hand found in real-life scenarios. NIMBLE [13] represents an enhancement over PIANO when applied to the same dataset, as it parametrically models bones, skin, and even muscles simultaneously. Nevertheless, these methods exclusively concentrate on the hand bone and do not encompass the entire skeleton.

OSSO [5] uses the STAR [3] model to represent the body surface and the PCA technique to construct a skeletal parametric model. The mapping relationship between skin and bone parameters is then learned to enable prediction from skin to skeleton. The researchers evaluate the method on a DXA (dual-energy x-ray absorptiometry) dataset of lying down poses and show that it outperforms other existing methods in terms of accuracy and robustness. However, the method only guarantees the accuracy of the predicted skeleton for lying down poses.

OpenSim [4] is a widely used platform for creating and analyzing anatomical skeletal models, serving not only to capture and process motion data but also to conduct biomechanical analyses and simulations on the input. Its applications are particularly valuable in fields such as medical, sports, and biomechanical engineering. SKEL [6] improves upon the OSSO method by integrating with OpenSim, aiming to enhance bone position accuracy. Despite these advancements, SKEL faces challenges with disconnected or misaligned bones and struggles to adapt to individuals with different body types, such as children, indicating limitations in its generalizability.

In this project, two pose estimation algorithms are integrated, enhancing the adaptability to a wide range of body shapes. Additionally, we introduce an optimization algorithm to make the generated skeleton with high fidelity and a greater level of personalization.

3 Method PASI

Figure 2 presents an overview of PASI. Using monocular input, 3D joint points are obtained through pose estimation algorithms (Sect. 3.1). These points are then inputted to the inverse kinematics module, which is used to compute the transformation of each human bone and generate a prior skeleton with motion (Sect. 3.2). During the optimization phase, the skeleton is refined by aligning it with the previously extracted key points, adjusting both the bone structure and the motion's amplitude (Sect. 3.3). Ultimately, a customized anatomical skeleton is obtained.

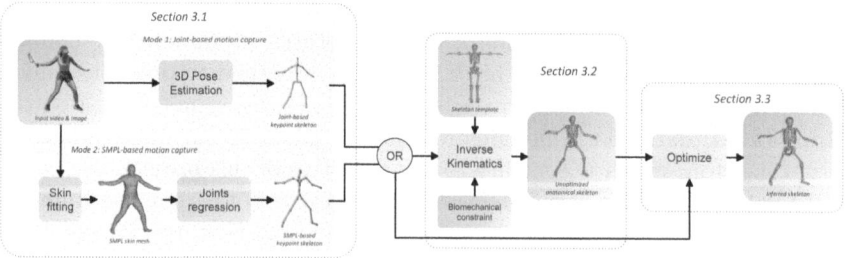

Fig. 2. Overview of PASI.

3.1 Motion Data Acquisition

The acquisition of input motion data typically relies on multi-camera capture systems or specific sensors worn by subjects. This reliance not only imposes demands on specialized hardware but also presents considerable inconvenience for individual users. To address this issue, we adopt pose estimation algorithms to replace physical sensors, which enables the extraction of required motion data solely from monocular videos or images. We also provide pathways for two pose estimation algorithms: joint-based and SMPL-based (left part of Fig. 2).

The joint-based method extracts joints directly from 2D images. We first employ AlphaPose [14] to detect human figures in images or videos and to estimate their 2D poses. These estimated poses are then input into MotionBERT [15], which infers their corresponding 3D representations. This method operates independently of predefined human models, thereby offering enhanced flexibility to adapt extreme shapes of the human body, such as children and the elderly. However, with only a monocular viewpoint, the joint-based approach might struggle to reconstruct the complete 3D pose accurately.

The SMPL-based approach addresses the issue above by leveraging the SMPL [1] skin mesh to fit the target character. The inclusion of SMPL ensures the joint points regressed from the mesh align with the constraints and specifications of the epidermal structure, thereby offering a more precise representation. Nonetheless, SMPL models are trained using specific datasets, which might not encompass certain unique human body shapes and poses. Therefore, the generalization capability of the SMPL-based approach can be limited for samples not covered by the training data, such as those involving children and the elderly.

In this study, integrating two pose estimation algorithms allows the proposed method adapts to a wide range of body shapes simultaneously. Users can select a more compatible mode based on the specific features of the intended character as well as their preferences.

3.2 Inverse Kinematics

A crucial step in this project involves transforming the motion data extracted from images or videos into specific movements of anatomical skeleton. In this stage, an inverse kinematics (IK) problem is solved by calculating the optimal joint angles and movements of the skeleton to closely match the extracted motion data. OpenSim provides a template skeleton model with a set of virtual markers defined on the surface of each bone. The inverse kinematics problem can be formulated as an optimization process, which aims to minimize the weighted squared error between the joint points and their corresponding virtual markers on the skeletal template:

$$E_{IK}(\theta) = w_i E_{markers}(\theta) + \omega_j E_{joints}(\theta)$$

where w_i and ω_j denote the weights of the ith marker point and the jth joint angle, respectively, for which OpenSim sets fixed values based on the constraints of biomechanics[1]. The markers term measures the distance between the ith extracted joint point $\mathbf{x}_i^{\text{exp}}$ and the virtual marker point $\mathbf{x}_i(\theta)$ calculated based on the current joint angle θ:

$$E_{markers}(\theta) = \sum_{i \in \text{markers}} \|\mathbf{x}_i^{\text{exp}} - \mathbf{x}_i(\theta)\|^2$$

The joint term quantifies the disparity between the angle of joint in the skeleton and the angle derived from the pose estimation algorithm.

$$E_{joints}(\theta) = \sum_{j \in \text{joints}} (\theta_j^{\text{exp}} - \theta_j)^2$$

After multiple computational iterations, joint rotation angles that depict the dynamic alterations of the human skeleton in 3D space are obtained. By sequentially applying these rotation angles to each marker on the skeletal template, anatomical skeletal motions are effectively reconstructed. The workflow for this section is illustrated in the middle part of Fig. 2.

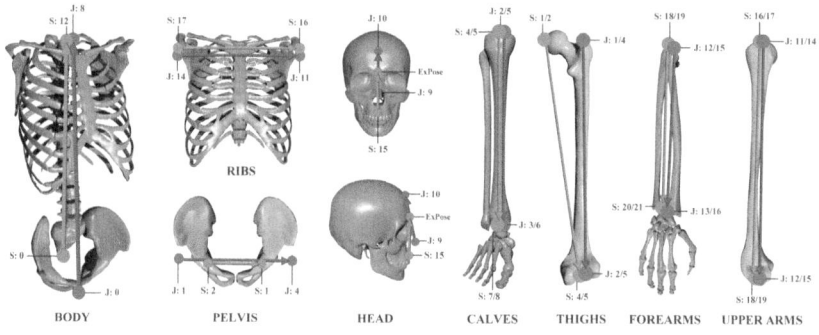

Fig. 3. The schematic of the endpoint selection for bones. In the joint-based method, the vector representation of bones is marked in red, while in the SMPL-based method, it is designated in blue. The index of the key point corresponding to each selected endpoint in motion data is also provided. (The SMPL-based upper endpoint of the head is obtained by averaging some facial key points derived from ExPose [16] (Color figure online).)

3.3 Optimization

Despite the anatomical skeleton being generated utilizing the method above, discrepancies between the animations (pose) and the movements in the given input persist. This divergence primarily stems from two critical factors:

---

[1] Biomechanical constraints refer to the limitations on the movement of body structures imposed by anatomical and physiological factors (e.g., range of motion of joints, controlling muscles, etc.).

Firstly, the key points extracted through pose estimation techniques may not align perfectly with the anatomical positions of the virtual markers defined within the skeletal template (see *Skeleton template* in Fig. 2). Skeletal templates with virtual markers are typically driven by data collected via sensors, which are positioned on the sides of bones rather than at the joints between bones. Consequently, the virtual markers may not fully capture the natural joints of human anatomy.

Secondly, the skeletal template is constructed with bones of fixed lengths, whereas the actual distances between points in motion data are variable. This variability arises from individual differences in body proportions and the inherent discrepancies in data extracted by pose estimation algorithms across different frames. Virtual markers assigned to bones of fixed length in the template may not align well with the motion points.

These deviations in the position of the extracted motion data and the virtual markers on the template may lead to inaccuracies in the representation of the joint movements extracted in Sect. 3.1. To enhance the alignment between the skeleton and the input, an optimization method is introduced, whose core idea involves considering each bone as a vector and calibrating it using the joint skeleton previously extracted (right part of Fig. 2).

Table 1. Subordination of the vector-represented bones and their accompanying small bones.

Vector-represented Bones	Small Bones
Skull	Jaw
Ribs	Clavicle, Scapula, Cervical vertebrae (C1 to C7), Thoracic vertebrae (T1 to T12)
Ulna	Radius, Capotate, Hamate, Trapczium, Trapezoid, Triquetrum, Pisiform, Phalanx
Femur	Patella
Tibia	Fibula, Talus, Metatarsal, Cuneiform, Navicular, Lunate

3.3.1 Bone to Vector

To model each human bone as a vector, it is crucial to appropriately select the locations of the two endpoints of each bone. The connection between these two endpoints should depict the bone's orientation, while the distance between them should correspond to the bone's length. In this paper, we have determined reasonable endpoints for the vector representation of each bone through multiple attempts and adjustments. These endpoint coordinates are calculated based on the relative positions of points on the bone mesh (Fig. 3). Distinct motion representations captured by the two approaches in Sect. 3.1 result in varying endpoint positions relative to each bone.

Furthermore, certain smaller bones can be regarded as components of the vector-represented larger bones, thus requiring the same geometric transformations as these larger bones. Table 1 indicates the correspondence between the vector-represented bones and their respective small bones.

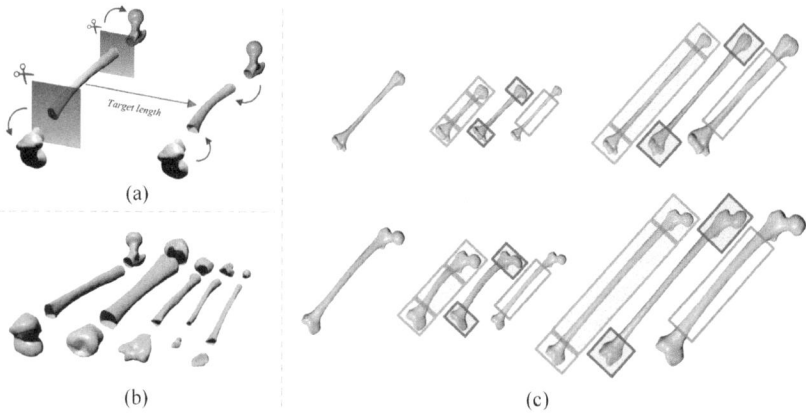

Fig. 4. (a) Diagram of the algorithm: trim the ends off a bone model and scale its intermediate section along its principal axis to match a target length, then re-attach the cut ends. (b) The bone meshes are divided into two ends and an intermediate section (from left to right, femur, tibia, humerus, ulna, radius). (c) Taking femur and humerus as examples, our method is compared to the traditional method. On the left are the generic bone meshes, in the middle are the 0.7× meshes, and on the right are the 1.5× meshes. Bones marked in green have been scaled using our method, while those highlighted in red have been scaled directly along a specific axis. Bones colored in orange have been uniformly scaled across all three dimensions. (Color figure online)

3.3.2 Bone Shape Optimization

This step primarily aims to adjust and optimize the bone's geometry to more accurately align with the individual's body size in the video or image.

The pose estimation algorithm analyzes the video by splitting it into individual frames. The length of the line segment at the same position fluctuates between each frame, leading to uncertainty in the target length of each bone. To address this issue, we employ the average length of segments for each body part across all frames as the target length. Notably, the average of the arm and leg parts should be calculated from both the left and right. This step guarantees the uniformity of target lengths within each frame and maintains the consistency of bone lengths in the body's symmetrical structure.

To adapt a skeletal model to the target length, a prevalent approach involves computing a scaling factor and equally scaling the model in all three dimensions (x, y, and z) or along the primary axis of the bones. However, uniform scaling can lead to discrepancies in the joints between bones and inconsistent thickness throughout the model. On the other hand, scaling along a specific axis might distort and deform the ends of the bones. To simultaneously avoid the aforementioned problems, we introduce an innovative method for scaling bone models (Fig. 4).

The original bone length and the target length are denoted as L_{bone} and L_{target} respectively. Considering the anatomical structure of the bone, the bone model can be divided into three sections along its principal axis (the vector representing the bone). These sections comprise the proximal and distal ends, and the intermediate section that lies between them, whose lengths can be denoted as L_{proximal}, L_{distal} and L_{middle}. The length of the intermediate section can be represented as:

$$L_{\text{middle}} = L_{\text{bone}} - (L_{\text{proximal}} + L_{\text{distal}})$$

To adjust the bone length to L_{target}, the remaining target length after subtracting the length of the ends is first calculated, which can be expressed as:

$$L_{\text{target-middle}} = L_{\text{target}} - (L_{\text{proximal}} + L_{\text{distal}})$$

Following this, the scaling factor k for the intermediate section is calculated by comparing the lengths of $L_{\text{target-middle}}$ and L_{middle}:

$$k = \frac{L_{\text{target-middle}}}{L_{\text{middle}}}$$

Subsequently, the intermediate section of the bone undergoes a scaling transformation along its principal axis, resulting in a modified segment, the length of which can be expressed as:

$$L_{\text{new-middle}} = k \times L_{\text{middle}}$$

Ultimately, the length-adjusted bone model is obtained by reassembling the scaled segment with the two unaltered ends, resulting in a total length of:

$$L_{\text{new-bone}} = L_{\text{proximal}} + L_{\text{new-middle}} + L_{\text{distal}}$$

which matches L_{target}. Since the scaling is exclusively applied along the principal axis of the bone, the size of the cross-section will not change, which facilitates a seamless reintegration. This approach maintains the anatomical structure of the bone while ensuring precise adjustments to its length.

3.3.3 Motion Optimization

To maximize the anatomical skeleton's resemblance to the character in the video or image, we calibrate each bone according to the previously extracted joint skeleton and calculate the corresponding rotation matrix. For each pair of vectors, V_{bone} and V_{target}, we first normalize them to obtain unit vectors a and b, respectively, as follows:

$$a = \frac{V_{bone}}{\|V_{bone}\|} \quad b = \frac{V_{target}}{\|V_{target}\|}$$

Subsequently, the cross product of a and b is computed to determine the rotation axis vector V_{rot}, and their dot product is used to compute the cosine of the rotation angle θ:

$$V_{rot} = a \times b = V_x i + V_y j + V_z k$$

$$\cos(\theta) = \frac{a_x b_x + a_y b_y + a_z b_z}{\|a\| \cdot \|b\|}$$

Here, V_{rot} indicates the rotation axis direction, with i, j, and k representing the unit vectors along the x, y, and z axes, respectively. Utilizing the Rodrigues rotation formula, the rotation matrix R is derived as:

$$R = I_3 + K\sin(\theta) + K^2(1 - \cos(\theta))$$

where R denotes the rotation matrix, I_3 is the identity matrix, and K is the skew-symmetric matrix formed from V_{rot}. The structure of K is given by:

$$K = \begin{bmatrix} 0 & -V_z & V_y \\ V_z & 0 & -V_x \\ -V_y & V_x & 0 \end{bmatrix}$$

During the application of the rotation matrix to the bone mesh, we take into account the parent-child relationships within the skeletal structure. For each bone mesh M, we compute a local rotation matrix, $\mathbf{R}_M^{local}$, which signifies the rotation of M relative to its immediate parent bone. Subsequently, the global rotation matrix $\mathbf{R}_M$ for M is derived by concatenating the local rotation matrix of M with the global rotation matrix $\mathbf{R}_{P(M)}$ of its parent bone $P(M)$. The global rotation matrix $\mathbf{R}_M$ is recursively formulated as follows:

$$\mathbf{R}_M = \mathbf{R}_{P(M)} \cdot \mathbf{R}_M^{local}$$

The scaling and rotation operations are applied independently to each segment of the skeleton, potentially disrupting the cohesive structure of the original anatomical framework. Consequently, it becomes necessary to reconnect the selected endpoints on each bone according to the skeletal architecture. This process finalizes the optimization of the inferred anatomical skeleton.

4 Experiment

4.1 Quantitative Evaluation

The optimized and unoptimized systems were evaluated using a set of 8 images and 8 videos, each showcasing individuals with varied characteristics (such as gender, age, and body shape) and engaging in different activities (basketball, football, Tai Chi, dancing, boxing, and tennis). During the optimization process, the endpoints of the vector-represented bones were aligned with corresponding parts on the previously extracted joint skeleton. In this study, the system's absolute error is determined by calculating the mean Euclidean distance between each skeletal endpoint and its respective key point. Considering the diversity in body sizes among the subjects in the test images and videos, relying solely on the absolute error for analysis lacked intuitive clarity. To address this, we introduce another metric known as relative error, which is the ratio of the absolute error to the total height of the joint skeleton.

Table 2. Absolute and relative errors for the optimized and unoptimized systems tested on images.

Evaluation Method	Man	Woman	Old	Child	Yoga	Sit	Walk	Run
AE (Unoptimized)	**0.0998**	0.3241	0.3461	0.1720	0.1215	0.1940	0.1793	0.1501
AE (Optimized)	0.1299	**0.2898**	**0.3020**	**0.1591**	**0.1192**	**0.1483**	**0.1544**	**0.1356**
RE (Unoptimized)	**0.0504**	0.1637	0.1748	0.0869	0.0614	0.0980	0.0906	0.0758
RE (Optimized)	0.0666	**0.1464**	**0.1518**	**0.0803**	**0.0602**	**0.0749**	**0.0780**	**0.0685**

Table 3. Absolute and relative errors for the optimized and unoptimized systems tested on videos.

Evaluation Method	Ball1	Ball2	TaiChi	Boxing	Tennis	Dance1	Dance2	Dance3
AE (Unoptimized)	0.4331	0.3745	0.2675	**0.5020**	0.4022	**0.3067**	0.3923	0.2455
AE (Optimized)	**0.3670**	**0.3487**	**0.2435**	0.5487	**0.3819**	0.3929	**0.3413**	**0.2337**
RE (Unoptimized)	0.2759	0.2069	0.1820	**0.3061**	0.2612	**0.1800**	0.3138	0.1497
RE (Optimized)	**0.2338**	**0.1927**	**0.1657**	0.3138	**0.2480**	0.2306	**0.2730**	**0.1408**

Tables 2 and 3 show the performance of the systems according to the two evaluation metrics. The accuracy of optimized anatomical skeletons generally surpasses that of unoptimized ones. While there are instances where the optimized skeleton's error marginally exceeds the original (by a maximum relative error of 0.0506), it remains within an acceptable range.

4.2 Qualitative Evaluation

Evaluating the visual performance of the generated skeletons is a crucial metric in this study as well. Figure 6 illustrates the optimized (right) and unoptimized (left) outcomes of inferring skeletons in multiple body shapes and poses. In contrast to the unoptimized skeleton, the optimized one achieves personalized adjustments for each bone, ensuring their movements align well with the target character. Furthermore, PASI demonstrates capacity in dealing with extreme body shapes, as illustrated by the result tested on child sample (the second one in the second row). The last test sample in Fig. 6 presents a comparison between the skeleton inferred by PASI using Biobank [17] epidermal data and the ground truth, demonstrating a similarity in both shape and pose. However, the lack of hand and foot landmark points in the captured motion data led to discrepancies between the intended and actual movements of the hands and feet in the outcomes.

4.3 User Study

We also invited 8 users to compare an optimized system with an unoptimized one by making side-by-side evaluations based on skeletons generated from 16 different samples. Figure 5 demonstrates that, in the majority of instances, users favored our system.

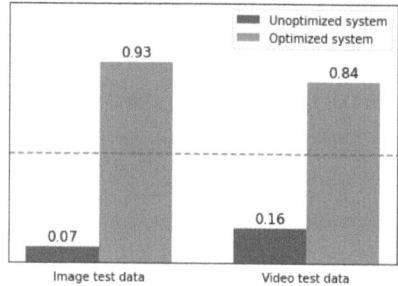

Fig. 5. User study for anatomical skeleton inferring from image and video data.

4.4 Processing Speed

We measured the processing time for reconstructing a skeleton from a single frame. All steps were performed on a desktop machine with an Intel® Core™ i7-8700 processor (6 cores and 12 threads) with a GTX 1080. We used an image of 1000×1000 pixels size as input and measured the running time for each step. The results are shown in Tables 4 and 5. Based on these results, we confirmed that our method can generate skeleton models at a fast rate.

Table 4. Processing time for each procedure (joint-based mode).

Procedure	Time (s)
Motion data acquisition	5.61
Inverse kinematics	0.34
Prior skeleton generation	0.01
Optimization	1.47
Total processing time	7.43

Fig. 6. Qualitative evaluation of anatomical skeleton inferences in multiple body shapes and poses (left: unoptimized skeleton, right: optimized skeleton.)

Table 5. Processing time for each procedure (SMPL-based mode).

Procedure	Time (s)
Motion data acquisition	2.98
Inverse kinematics	0.44
Prior skeleton generation	0.01
Optimization	1.59
Total processing time	5.02

5 Conclusion

In this paper, we propose a pioneering end-to-end method, PASI, which infers anatomical skeletons from monocular inputs. PASI employs two modes of pose estimation algorithms to acquire motion data, offering users the flexibility to select a more fitting mode according to the input and their preference. Through innovative algorithms for scaling and motion optimization, PASI ensures the quality of the generated skeleton. Future work could focus on estimating the movement of hand bones and predicting muscle activity across the entire body. In addition, we also would like to learn the relationship between the epidermis and the skeleton from real medical data, which will increase the anatomical accuracy of the inferred skeleton.

References

1. Loper, M., Mahmood, N., Romero, J., Pons-Moll, G., Black, M.J.: SMPL: a skinned multi-person linear model. ACM Trans. Graphics (Proc. SIGGRAPH Asia) **34**(6), 248:1–248:16 (2015)
2. Romero, J., Tzionas, D., Black, M.J.: Embodied hands: modeling and capturing hands and bodies together. ACM Trans. Graph. (Proc. SIGGRAPH Asia) **36**(6) (2017)
3. Osman, A.A.A., Bolkart, T., Black, M.J.: STAR: sparse trained articulated human body regressor. In: Vedaldi, A., Bischof, H., Brox, T., Frahm, J.-M. (eds.) ECCV 2020. LNCS, vol. 12351, pp. 598–613. Springer, Cham (2020). https://doi.org/10.1007/978-3-030-58539-6_36
4. Delp, S.L., et al.: OpenSim: open-source software to create and analyze dynamic simulations of movement. IEEE Trans. Biomed. Eng. **54**(11), 1940–1950 (2007)
5. Keller, M., Zuffi, S., Black, M.J., Pujades, S.: OSSO: obtaining skeletal shape from outside. In: Proceedings IEEE/CVF Conference on Computer Vision and Pattern Recognition (CVPR), pp. 20492–20501 (2022)
6. Keller, M., et al.: From skin to skeleton: towards biomechanically accurate 3d digital humans. In: ACM ToG, Proc. SIGGRAPH Asia, vol. 42 (2023)
7. Ali-Hamadi, D., et al.: Anatomy transfer. ACM Trans. Graph. (TOG) **32**(6), 1–8 (2013)
8. auer, A.: Modélisation anatomique utilisateur-spécifique et animation temps-réel: Application à l'apprentissage de l'anatomie. PhD thesis, Université Grenoble Alpes (2016)

9. Zoss, G., Beeler, T., Gross, M., Bradley, D.: Accurate markerless jaw tracking for facial performance capture. ACM Trans. Graph. (TOG) **38**(4), 1–8 (2019)
10. Ichim, A.-E., Kadleček, P., Kavan, L., Pauly, M.: Phace: physics-based face modeling and animation. ACM Trans. Graph. (TOG) **36**(4), 1–14 (2017)
11. Wang, B., Matcuk, G., Barbič, J.: Hand modeling and simulation using stabilized magnetic resonance imaging. ACM Trans. Graph. (TOG) **38**(4), 1–14 (2019)
12. Li, Y., Wu, M., Zhang, Y., Xu, L., Yu, J.: Piano: A parametric hand bone model from magnetic resonance imaging. In: Zhou, Z.H. (ed.) Proceedings of the Thirtieth International Joint Conference on Artificial Intelligence, IJCAI-21, pp. 816–822. International Joint Conferences on Artificial Intelligence Organization. Main Track (2021)
13. Li, Y., et al.: Nimble: a non-rigid hand model with bones and muscles. ACM Trans. Graph. **41**(4) (2022)
14. Fang, H.S., et al.: Alphapose: whole-body regional multi-person pose estimation and tracking in real-time. IEEE Trans. Pattern Anal. Mach. Intell. **45**(6), 7157–7173 (2022)
15. Zhu, W., Ma, X., Liu, Z., Liu, L., Wu, W., Wang, Y.: Motionbert: unified pretraining for human motion analysis. arXiv preprint arXiv:2210.06551 (2022)
16. Choutas, V., Pavlakos, G., Bolkart, T., Tzionas, D., Black, M.J.: Monocular expressive body regression through body-driven attention. In: European Conference on Computer Vision (ECCV), pp. 20–40 (2020)
17. Sudlow, C., et al.: UK biobank: an open access resource for identifying the causes of a wide range of complex diseases of middle and old age. PLoS Med. **12**(3), e1001779 (2015)

Research on Human-Robot Collaboration Safety Model and Key Algorithms in Assembly Systems

Weina Li[1,2], Zhiquan Feng[1,2(✉)], Dehui Kong[1,2], and Zishuo Xia[1,2]

[1] School of Information Science and Engineering, University of Jinan, Jinan 250022, China
ise_fengzq@ujn.edu.cn
[2] Shandong Provincial Key Laboratory of Network Based Intelligent Computing, Jinan 250022, China

Abstract. When humans interact with robots at "zero distance", human-robot interaction faces challenging security issues such as the possibility of bodily harm from the robots - a problem that can no longer be solved by traditional safety measures based on human-robot distance or physical parameter space constraints. Therefore, this paper introduces a new security approach, human-robot cooperative safety model, whose main innovations are: designing a human-robot cooperative safety model based on the understanding of the user's intention, and realizing a self-enclosed human-robot cooperative assembly system based on multimodal perception. The experimental results show that the method can effectively avoid the danger of personal safety caused by misrecognition and misinterpretation of the robot in the interaction process, improve the intention understanding ability in the interaction system, reduce the user's fear of the robot, and enable the user to complete the human-robot interaction session more realistically and smoothly.

Keywords: assembly systems · intent comprehension · human-robot collaboration · safety model

1 Introduction

China has entered the stage of aging, and how to solve the problems of daily needs around the elderly will become the focus of social attention. In the later stages of life, individuals often experience cognitive slowing and memory decline, which, if unaddressed, can progress to conditions such as amnesia and dementia. Cognitive degeneration in the elderly not only impacts their quality of life and increases the burden on families but also places greater demands on public social services. Research indicates that engaging elderly individuals in collaborative activities like puzzle assembly games can enhance their reaction times, logical thinking, and manual skills, thereby helping to mitigate the risks associated with cognitive decline. However, due to increasing societal pressures, younger adults often lack the time to engage with the elderly in such activities, and there is also a significant shortage of caregiving personnel. Against this backdrop, the introduction of intelligent service robots and human-robot collaboration technologies represents an innovative and efficient solution.

In the current context of rapid social, economic, and technological development, human-robot collaboration has emerged as a prominent focus in both academic research and practical applications. On the other hand, the complexity and safety challenges associated with human-robot collaboration are increasingly evident. The essence of human-robot interaction is the exchange and sharing of information between humans and machines; however, significant differences in language and thought processes can lead to misrecognition and misunderstanding during these interactions. The traditional human-robot safety and security measures are to completely isolate the robot from people and eliminate any physical collision, which leads to problems such as weak perception of various human behavioural information, poor flexibility, and a single and unnatural interaction mode in the interaction process of the robot. In summary, although intelligent service robots are widely used, existing human-robot collaboration safety algorithms are not specifically applicable to tasks like puzzle assembly, making their practical and safe integration into the daily lives of the elderly challenging.

Based on this, this study starts from the background of the application of companion robots in puzzle assembly systems, analyses the scene comprehension and then understands the intention of the elderly through visual and auditory information, and discusses the human-robot safety collaboration model, aiming to explore a human-robot safety collaboration interaction model.

2 Related Works

In recent years, multimodal fusion methods have made a lot of progress in the fields of computer vision, natural language processing, speech recognition, etc., and multimodal fusion also has a wide range of applications in robot interaction. In the field of multimodal fusion, researchers have focused on large-scale pre-trained language models and visual models, which is undoubtedly a great success. Kawaji et al. [1] and Benjamin et al. [2] have also combined vision and hearing so that robots can interact well with users. Al-Qaderi et al. [3] proposed a solution to the problem of human recognition by social robots using multimodal perception. Song K S et al. [4] used facial expression and speech emotion recognition results as classifiers in the fusion phase of the decision layer using K-NN. Wu et al. [5] proposed an integrated probabilistic decision framework with distance based inference (DBI) and knowledge based inference (KBI). Trick et al. [6] proposed a new multimodal intent recognition method using Bayesian algorithm to outputs user intent. Li et al. [7] proposed an efficient and flexible multimodal fusion method (PMF) specifically for fusing unimodal pre-trained transformers. Sharma et al. [8] proposed Ekman model fusion i.e., visual audio and text to classify emotions into discrete categories. Shi et al. [9] proposed a novel attention-based relevance based relevance framework called MultiEMO perceptual multimodal fusion framework.

In intent understanding, computers identify the user's intentions and needs by analysing the user's diverse modal information and extracting key information from it. Zhou et al. [10] proposed an OOD detection model that utilises simple and efficient KNN discriminative semantic features. Instead of using direct classification, Ouyang et al. [11] proposed to determine whether it is IND or OOD based on the number of detected intents. Mueller et al. [12] proposed a pre-training approach for pre-training model H5, which takes into account the semantic information inherent in the tags during encoding. Zhang et al. [13] first pre-trained using large-scale unlabelled data and then used a contrast learning approach to capture the similarity between intents and finally achieve the discovery of new intents. Sun et al. [14] proposed to solve the problem of insufficient training samples using static augmentation + dynamic augmentation, using task consistency loss and contrast loss to ensure the performance of the meta-learner and the distribution of the samples.

In summary, current human-robot collaboration models fail to fully exploit the potential of complementarities between different modal data when understanding intentions, and most systems have robots autonomously determining and outputting intentions, lacking effective response strategies for scenarios with high naturalness and safety requirements. For the problem of how to guarantee the security in the process of human-robot interaction, the existing methods focus on physical isolation or spatial temporal constraints, and are generally weak in the ability to perceive and understand the user's intention. Different from the existing methods, this paper adopts the human-robot collaboration approach to solve the pain point problems of the robot in the grasping process, especially the safety problems between the robot and the human in the grasping process. To this end, the robot's understanding of the human's operation intention is taken as the entry point, focusing on how to carry out free and safe human-robot collaboration and handover without restricting the robot's behaviour. This paper proposes a deep neural network-based robot optimal grasping position detection method, and incorporates user intent understanding at the final decision-making layer to complete the safety of human-robot collaboration in the assembly process.

3 Method

3.1 Framework

The self-enclosed man-machine coordinated assembly system uses a robotic arm that allows seven degrees of freedom of movement and a mechanical gripper that is an adaptive gripper designed for versatile gripping applications. With the plug-in installed in the TM flow, the user can easily gain full control of the gripper, including position and force control and gripper detection. The acquisition device for image and depth data is kinectv2. For training the neural network, the computer system is windows and the graphics card is RTX3090*2. The structure of the experimental scenario is shown in Fig. 1.

In the entire human-robot collaborative assembly system, the robotic arm initially waits in a pre-defined starting position for user interaction. Once the system confirms the user's intention to interact, it proceeds to recognize and analyze the user's hand posture, making an initial assessment of the user's intent. Kinect v2 captures multimodal information such as user voice, gestures, and target detection to generate information for the user's intent library through recognition and analysis. In this design, the focus is placed on the gripping phase of the robotic arm. Upon entering the interaction phase, the system first evaluates the user's gripping posture. Since the robotic arm operates in a confined space with four accessible sides, if the user's hand moves downward or backward during gripping, the object will be entirely obscured by the hand. After

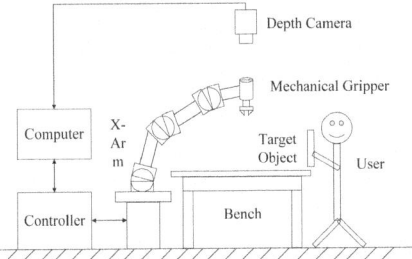

Fig. 1. Hardware architecture diagram of the self-enclosed human-robot cooperative assembly system. The picture shows the key hardware components at the early stage of the system design, including: the motion unit (controller, robotic arm and mechanical gripper), the vision unit (depth camera), and the computation unit (computer).

the initial interaction, the system utilizes Kinect v2 to capture an RGB image of the user holding the object. The improved R-CNN neural network is employed for image segmentation and recognition, effectively separating the user's hand from the target object and outputting an optimal gripping position to ensure the safety of user interaction. Simultaneously, the system incorporates information from the user's intent library to determine the final gripping position (Fig. 2).

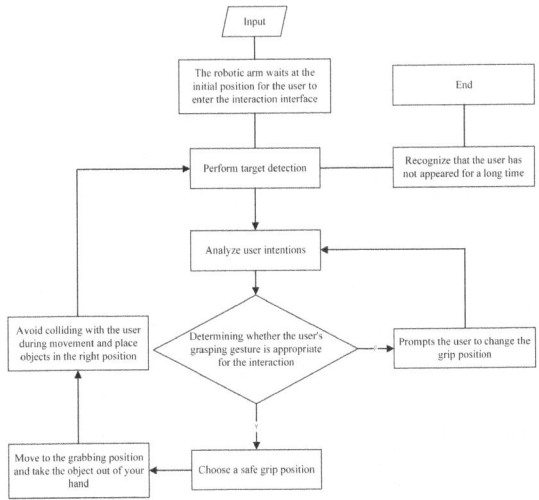

Fig. 2. Human-robot cooperative assembly system interaction flow chart.

3.2 Grab Position Detection

After the recognition of the target object in the environment image through the algorithm, in order to further confirm the location of the target object needs to design an algorithm to frame the target object, which is used to confirm the location of the target object and the current attitude, in order to prepare for the grasping link. In the feature point screening, both the rough and simple BF matching and the later selected FLANN matching are used to judge the feature points by setting the threshold value, and these algorithms are still based on a single judgment, and there will still be unqualified feature points, which will bring trouble when the target object is framed afterward. For optimal position detection, in order to eliminate these redundant feature points, this paper adopts a two-step cascade system consisting of a deep network, where step 1 is used to select a set of candidate grasping regions containing the target object, and step 2 detects and obtains a grasping frame on the candidate regions based on the previous step. The final data used for robotic arm grasping is represented as (u, v, θ) and the position is shown in Fig. 3.

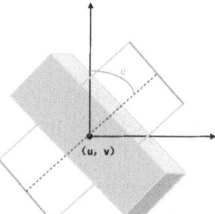

Fig. 3. The grasping position diagram of the target object (the part to be assembled). In the figure, (u, v) is the position of the center of gravity of the grasping frame under the image coordinate system, and θ is the angle between the length of the grasping frame and the longitudinal axis of the image coordinate system; the blue rectangle indicates the target to be grasped; and the rectangular box indicates the position of the gripper, in which the yellow line indicates the opening direction of the gripper. (Color figure online)

Before the system identifies the optimal grasping position, the initial step involves locating the approximate region containing the target in a binary image, where the background is black, and the target object is represented in white. Subsequently, the minimum rectangular image containing the target is extracted from the binary image, the color image, the depth image, and the surface normal vector feature map based on the depth image. After preprocessing, multiple sets of search boxes are generated. Each set of search boxes is transformed into an input feature. These input features are then fed into a neural network with two hidden layers. The two hidden layers are denoted as h [1] and h [2], with each layer having K_1 and K_2 neurons, respectively, and the output of the neurons is modeled by the sigmoid function. At the top of the second hidden layer is a logistic classifier used for prediction. The forward propagation process of the network is as follows:

$$h_j^{[1](t)} = \sigma\left(\sum_{i=1}^{N} x_i^{(t)} W_{i,j}^{[1]}\right) \quad (1)$$

$$h_j^{[2](t)} = \sigma\left(\sum_{i=1}^{K_1} h_i^{[1](t)} W_{i,j}^{[2]}\right) \quad (2)$$

$$P(\hat{y}^{(t)} = 1 | x^{(t)}; \Theta) = \sigma\left(\sum_{i=1}^{K_2} h_i^{[2](t)} W_{i,j}^{[3]}\right) \quad (3)$$

In the given context: N represents the dimensionality of the feature vector. The feature $x^{(t)} \in \mathbb{R}^N$ and the output $\hat{y}^{(t)} \in \{0,1\}$. The sigmoid function $\sigma(a) = 1/(1+\exp(-a))$. $\Theta = (W^{[1]}, W^{[2]}, W^{[3]})$ represents the weight parameters of the neural network, acquired through a deep learning algorithm.

In the context of weight training, the objective is to identify a single grasp configuration that maximizes the probability of the robot successfully grasping the target. This is mathematically represented as follows:

$$G^* = \arg\max_G P(\hat{y}^{(t)} = 1 \mid \phi(G); \Theta) \tag{5}$$

In the given context: G represents the specific grasp configuration, encompassing its position, orientation, and dimensions. G^* denotes the optimal grasp configuration. The function ϕ is employed to extract a suitable input representation of the rectangular frame G.

3.3 Algorithm Overall Framework

The overall block diagram (FRAMEWORK) of the proposed algorithm is shown in Fig. 4. In the input layer, this paper uses kinectv2 to obtain multimodal information such as user's voice, gesture and target object detection, including the user's voice commands, deep gesture images, and the target object coordinates.

In the recognition layer, for speech information, the system passes the information into DFCNN [15], converts the user's speech information into Chinese text, then processes the Chinese text with word splitting as well as de-duplication, and converts it into word vectors by word2vec [16] Chinese word vector model, and finally generates sentence vectors to represent the user's speech information. The cosine similarity between the generated sentence vectors and the sentence vectors of the speech intention set in the speech intention library is calculated, and the results with a similarity greater than 80% are counted as the user's speech sub-intention set; for the gesture information, the system uses AlexNet [17] for the initial segmentation of the RGB images captured by the depth camera. Based on the distribution probability of the image grey values, the gesture category is judged and the corresponding subintent set is output; the target detection is chosen to use the lightweight network R-CNN for the detection, and the anchor frame classification value output from a certain time frame is compared with the target classification value in the database, and the subintent set corresponding to the classification value and the corresponding probability is output.

In the fusion layer, when real-time intent acquisition is performed, the multimodal information input through the three channels is first processed for recognition and then entered into the corresponding recognition information library, respectively, and when real-time intent acquisition is performed, the user subintentions and the probability of each of the corresponding intents are obtained respectively according to the recognition information transmitted from the recognition layer. The probability of each intention corresponding to each modality is normalised as the entropy value of the modality, and the weight of each modality is obtained by normalising the entropy value of each subintention. Next the intentions of each modality are arranged and combined, and the user intention with the highest probability is obtained based on the weights. The system will temporarily output the better intention and conduct real-time interactive evaluation with the user to confirm the user's next real intention.

In the application layer, the system, after real-time interaction with the user, determines the optimal intent that most closely matches the user's real intent for output; the system determines the operation that the user wants to carry out according to the optimal intent and encodes the operation semantics to transmit to the controller of the robotic arm, which sends motion commands after decoding to drive the robotic arm to complete the collaborative interaction between the human-robot.

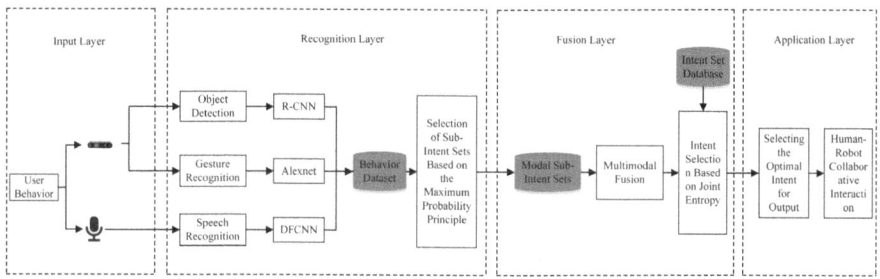

Fig. 4. General framework diagram of the algorithm. The whole system is divided into input, recognition, fusion and application layers according to the temporal logic of the algorithm, and the picture shows in detail the specific work carried out in each layer.

3.4 Optimal Grasp Point Selection Based on Joint Entropy

The joint entropy $H(X, Y)$ of two random variables (X, Y) is defined as the mathematical expectation of the self-information of their joint probabilities, as shown in Eq. (1). In simpler terms, joint entropy $H(X, Y)$ represents the level of uncertainty that arises when random variables X and Y occur together.

$$H(X, Y) = \sum_{x_i \in X} \sum_{y_i \in Y} p(x_i, y_i) I(x_i, y_i) \#$$

$$= \sum_{x_i \in X} \sum_{y_i \in Y} p(x_i, y_i) \log \frac{1}{p(x_i, y_i)} \tag{6}$$

where $p(x_i, y_i)$ represents the probability of events x_i and y_i occurring simultaneously, and $I(x_i, y_i)$ denotes the self-information of x_i and y_i. Here, X represents the set of recognition rates of the robot for the target object, and Y represents the ease of operating that target object. These are determined by three factors: the initial grasp position (g), the relative distance between the item and the robotic arm (s), and the deviation angle (α). It's necessary to transform these three determining factors into a probabilistic form, enabling them to be used as parameters for calculating joint entropy.

The initial grasp position of an item, denoted as $H(g_i)$, is determined through preliminary training of a deep learning neural network, resulting in the grasp point position g_i:

$$H(g_i) = \frac{e^{g_i}}{\sum_j e^{g_j}} \tag{7}$$

The probabilistic factor representing the relative distance between an item and the robotic arm is denoted as $H(s_i)$. The maximum range the robotic arm can reach is defined as the maximum achievable range, ensuring that all areas within the Kinect-captured image can be accessed. To calculate the distance s_i between the robotic gripper and item i at a given moment:

$$H(s_i) = \frac{e^{s_i}}{\sum_j e^{s_j}} \tag{8}$$

The probabilistic factor representing the angle by which an item deviates is denoted as $H(\alpha_i)$. To calculate the deviation angle α_i for item i, we refer to the dimensions (a, b) of the recognition box for item i within the central square. When an item j is identified in real-time recognition, the deviation angle α_i can be determined using the known information and Eq. (1) (Fig. 5):

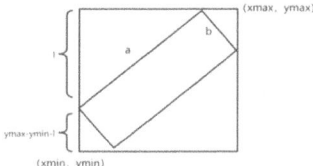

Fig. 5. Block diagram of assembled part recognition. In the figure, (a, b) is the length and width of the assembled part, (x_{min}, y_{min}) is the position information of the lower left corner of the anchor frame returned by the recognition, and (x_{max}, y_{max}) is the position information of the upper right corner of the anchor frame returned by the recognition.

Given that '$y_{max} - y_{min}$' and '$x_{max} - x_{min}$' are known and denoted as 'c' and 'd,' we proceed by squaring them to obtain:

$$\sqrt{(a^2 - l^2)[b^2 - (c - l)^2]} = l^2 - cl + e^2) \tag{9}$$

So, $H(\alpha_i)$ is:

$$H(\alpha_i) = \frac{e^{|\gamma - \alpha_i|}}{\sum_j e^{|\gamma - \alpha_i|}} \tag{10}$$

In these given context: g_i represents the preliminary training results of a deep learning neural network, providing the grasp point location for item i. $H(g_i)$ denotes the probabilistic representation of the positional factor. s_i represents the distance between the robotic gripper and item i at a particular moment. $H(s_i)$ denotes the probabilistic representation of the relative distance factor. α_i represents the deviation angle of item i. $H(\alpha_i)$ signifies the probabilistic representation of the deviation angle factor. a, b represent the length and width of the recognition box for item i centered within the grid. (x_{min}, y_{min}) denotes the lower-left coordinates of the recognition box for item i. (x_{max}, y_{max}) represents the upper-right coordinates of the recognition box for item i.

3.5 HCC

Algorithm Key Algorithm for Multimodal Fusion, Intent Understanding, and Collaboration in Self-contained Assembly Systems
Input: Sets of intent probabilities within the speech channel (***Voice***), gesture channel (***Hand***), and object detection channel (***Target***). Output: The current optimal grasp point, denoted as ***Position***. 1. Based on the extracted intent features from each modality, recognize and obtain sub-intent sets for the three modalities, along with the corresponding probabilities for each sub-intent. Employ the Maximum Probability Principle method to normalize and fuse the three sub-intent sets, resulting in the user's intent; 2. According to the user's intention is transformed into robotic arm commands, when the user's intention is to grasp or take, it is necessary to judge whether the user's gesture is appropriate or not, and then make a decision on the grasping position, and when the user's intention is something else, it is necessary to directly execute the commands; 3. Using a neural network for preliminary grasp point acquisition, we obtain a set of 'G^*'; 4. $X = \{P_x \mid P_x=$ recognition probability vector for item i } ; 5. Calculated using formulas (5), (6), and (8), we obtain: $Y = \{ H(g_i), H(s_i), H(\alpha_i) \}$; 6. Calculated to compute the joint entropy ' H (X, Y) ' using formula (4); 7. If ($\exists$H (X, Y) == 0)   {If the grasp point acquisition fails, return to step3} 8. Else 9. Output the grasp point information '***Position***' corresponding to max (H (X, Y)) 10. ***END***

The whole human-computer cooperative assembly system is divided into waiting, calculating grasping position, implementing grasping and placing. The algorithm proposed in this paper realizes the system to reason the user's interaction intention and realize the human-robot cooperative interaction control based on the three modal data of vision, hearing and target detection, which solves the problems of weak system intention comprehension and wrong intention comprehension that may occur during the use of the human-robot cooperative assembly system by the user. By using the information entropy to calculate the weight of each input modality reduces the influence of behavior unrelated to the intention when performing feature extraction and fusion; multimodal intention fusion according to the principle of maximum probability solves the limitations of the system's monolithic modal inputs and reduces the user's cognitive load, thus ensuring the user's safety in human-robot collaboration, and downplaying the user's fear of interacting with the robot and the sense of sense of resistance. In addition, by selecting the grasping point based on information entropy, the initial position and relative position of the target object are fused, which reduces the possibility of error in intention understanding and improves the reliability of the system. In summary, the algorithm in this paper solves the problems of error-prone, unnatural and unsafe intention understanding in the process of human-robot system.

4 Experimental Results and Analysis

4.1 Experimental Setup

In order to facilitate the experiment, we set the blocks as the assembly parts in the experiment. In this paper, the system completes the hardware design of the human-robot cooperative assembly system on the basis of the existing hardware equipment in the laboratory (Fig. 6). Since there will be many times of grasping, holding and putting and other refined actions in the assembly system, and the interaction object is the elderly who are easy to be injured by the flaccid movements, the humanoid robot which has a friendly appearance but weak grasping ability is discarded in the aspect of hardware, and the robotic arm which has a high control precision and a fast moving speed is chosen to act as the arm of the system with the robotic claw and is responsible for the completion of the collaborative actions. A depth camera is equipped in the system to acquire the multimodal information of the user, which acts as the eyes and ears of the system, and through the computer's training to recognize and analyze the intention, the action sequence is transmitted to the controller to act as the brain of the system. In order to facilitate the experiment, we set the blocks as the assembly parts in the experiment.

Fig. 6. Real experimental scene diagram. The picture shows the key hardware components in the real experimental scenario, where the red box is the motion unit (controller, robotic arm, and robotic gripper), the blue box is the vision unit (depth camera), and the green box is the computation unit (computer). (Color figure online)

4.2 Evaluation Metrics

This paper verifies and analyses the algorithm and the system from three entry points: safety performance, intention understanding and user evaluation, to verify whether the algorithm proposed in this paper has feasibility and whether it meets the design objectives. Based on the analysis of the safety performance of the system, the two aspects that are most likely to cause harm to the user are (1) whether the robotic arm will pinch the hand when it takes the blocks from the user's hand, and (2) whether the robotic arm will collide with the hand in the process of moving. Starting from the entry point, this paper designs four evaluation metrics, which are safety grip reliability, collision possibility, intention understanding accuracy and user usage evaluation. Among them, three more quantitative indicators are designed for safe grip reliability, which are grip success rate, operation execution time and hand pinching possibility. The definitions of each indicator are as follows:

GSR is defined as the number of times a robotic arm was able to successfully grasp an object from a human hand as a percentage of the total number of grasp attempts.

AET is defined as the time taken by the system to complete gripping the object.

GHR is defined as the number of times a robotic arm grips a human hand as a percentage of the total number of grasp attempts.

ACR is defined as the number of times the robotic arm successfully avoided known obstacles and the user's hand as a percentage of the total number of avoidance attempts.

SI is defined as the number of times the system intent was understood correctly as a percentage of the total number of times the user expressed the intent in the experiment.

4.3 Experimental Design

To ensure the accuracy of the experimental results, we invited 20 students who planned to invite 20 students between the ages of 20 and 30 years old and 20 elderly people over the age of 60 years old to participate in the experimental validation work. Different users completed two block assembly tasks with the robot through random, subjective actions, and each experimenter performed 10 experiments, which were 5 experiments for the pick-and-place task (requiring the experimenter to ask the robot to pick up the specified blocks from the table before putting them into his/her own hands) and 5 experiments for the grasping task (requiring the robot to discriminate that there are blocks in the hands of the experimenter that need to be grasped, and then to pick up and place the blocks from the experimenter's hands into a reasonable position on the table). (Requiring the robot to identify the blocks in the experimenter's hand that need to be grasped, pick them up from the experimenter's hand and then place them in a reasonable position on the table). At the beginning of the experiment, the computer communicated with the robot arm's controller to ensure that the robot arm would wait for the user's interaction at the set initial position, and then turned on the infrared camera of the kinectv2 to determine whether the user entered the interaction scene.

Inspired by research on human gripping postures, we discretised the common human gripping postures in human-robot handover tasks into six categories based on the orientation of the palm. If the user is holding an object in his/her hand, the human palm will have six orientations to choose from (Fig. 7), whereas the last three orientations are too heavy for the human wrist and humans will not choose these three intentionally difficult postures when they want to complete a collaboration. Our user survey analysis of the six gripping positions showed that 67.61% of users chose the upward facing direction to complete the collaboration. Therefore, we recommend the experimenter to choose the palm-up position before the experiment starts.

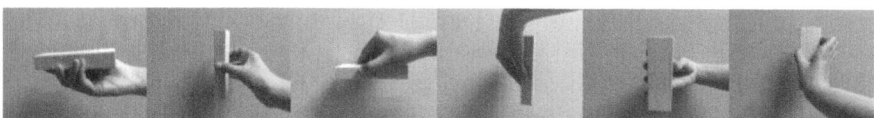

Fig. 7. The various positions in which humans tend to grasp objects, which are upward, forward, downward, backward, leftward and rightward.

4.4 Validation of Experimental Validity

In order to further validate the feasibility and design goals of the algorithm proposed in this paper, we illustrate the different aspects of the final system for the grasp-and-release task experiment (Fig. 8). The system must adapt to as many different grasping styles as possible, choosing in real time the correct way to approach the experimenter and take the object from their hands.

Fig. 8. Example diagrams of the experiment. The first row shows the experimenter holding the assembled part vertically and the second row shows the experimenter holding the assembled part horizontally.

4.5 Safety Grip Reliability Test

In order to further evaluate the safety model, we conduct experiments to assess the risk of the robotic arm pinching the human hand during the human-robot handover, especially in the robotic arm gripping session. In order to better reflect the advantages and persuasiveness of the algorithms in this paper, this subsection does the comparison experiments of three collaborative algorithms in the same experimental environment, which are the human-computer handover model based on classification decision-making (HGC) [18], the human-computer handover model based on visual detection (HVC) [19], and the collaborative algorithm based on joint entropy selection in this paper.

The human-robot handover model based on classification decision-making sets multiple operators and corresponding prerequisite conditions. The system only operates based on whether the prerequisite conditions are met, rather than understanding the user's true intention. The human-robot interaction model based on visual detection uses PointNet++, which was recently developed on point clouds, for human grasping classification, making it difficult for the model to search for nearby points (Table 1).

Table 1. Comparison of Algorithm Performance

	Type	GSR	AET(s)	GHR
HGC	simple	74.7%	13.15	35.9%
HCC	simple	89.3%	15.37	14.1%
HGC	complex	/	/	/
HCC	complex	78.6%	32.77	24.9%

The experimental results show that under simple grasping gestures, the success rate of grasping in this article has been improved, and the possibility of gripping hands has been greatly reduced, ensuring the safety of users; In some complex grasping gestures, HGC is unable to achieve grasping operations. HCC can remind users of the risk of hand gripping and change the gripping gesture to reduce the possibility of hand gripping and safely complete human-robot interaction (Table 2).

Table 2. Comparison of Algorithm Performance

	Type	GSR	AET(s)	GHR
HVC	simple	76.2%	13.95	26.8%
HCC	simple	89.3%	15.37	14.1%
HVC	complex	55.9%	19.83	84.3%
HCC	complex	78.6%	32.77	24.9%

The experimental results show that under some complex grasping gestures, HVC can achieve grasping operations, but the possibility of gripping is relatively high, which basically cannot guarantee user safety. HCC greatly reduces the possibility of gripping while ensuring successful grasping, and improves the safety performance of the system.

4.6 Collision Probability Experiment

In the context of human-robot collaboration, another safety concern may arise from collisions between the robot's arm and the human hand. To address this, we initially employed the Unity3D platform for simulating and predicting the future motion trajectories of the robot's arm and gripper. This simulation allowed us to assess the robot's ability to avoid collisions with known obstacles and the user's hand (Tables 3 and 4).

Table 3. Successful Avoidance Rate in Simulation Experiments

SumNumber	Success Anti-Collision Number	Collisions	ACR
100	82	18	82%
150	128	22	85.33%
200	184	16	92%
300	293	7	97.66%
400	395	5	98.75%

Experiments show that the HCC algorithm has a high probability of successfully avoiding the human hand both in the simulated environment (Fig. 9a) and in the real environment (Fig. 9b), which can well avoid the risk of the robotic arm colliding with the human hand during the moving process and ensure the safety performance of the system.

Table 4. Successful Avoidance Rate in Real Experiments

SumNumber	Success Anti-Collision Number	Collisions	ACR
100	68	32	68%
150	113	37	75.33%
200	165	35	82.1%
300	261	39	87.66%
400	360	40	90%

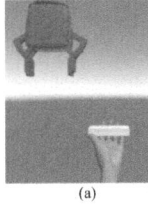

(a)   (b)

Fig. 9. Example diagram of the experiment. (a) shows that the experimenter simulated the trajectory of the mechanical gripper in Unity3D platform, and constructed the mechanical gripper, human hand, and assembled parts in 3D. In (b), it shows that the experimenter collided the mechanical gripper with the human hand in the real scenario, and avoided the damage to the human hand to the greatest extent.

4.7 Intent Understanding Accuracy Experiment

In order to verify the safety performance of the algorithm, whether the robot can safely interact with humans, such as whether it can detect the presence of the user, whether it can correctly understand the user's intention so as to avoid causing injuries or dangers to humans. In this paper, we conducted a large number of experiments, focusing on the grasping link in the scenario where the robot assists the user in completing the assembly to verify and analyse the proposed algorithm. In the process of experimental operation, in order to better improve the user experience and reduce the operational burden, this experiment adopts four commonly used gestures and four commonly used speech to help the experimenter to express their intentions, and their specific definitions are shown in Tables 5 and 6.

For the information input of each single channel, this article collected the command actions of gestures, with 2000 images for each class. The Inception v3 model was used for training, and 600 experiments were conducted for each type of command in the test. Finally, the recognition rate of the four gestures reached 98.9%.

In order to compare with other methods, this paper implements an intention understanding algorithm using the Bayesian classification principle used by Trick et al. [6]. The experimental process uses Bayesian classification to take the intention with the highest probability among all intentions as the final result. Each experimenter performed 10 expressions of intent and a total of 400 tests were performed. The Bayesian classification intent understanding algorithm achieved an average recognition rate of 92.10% and an

Table 5. Gesture

GestureName	GestureDescription
h_1	Five fingers spread forward
h_2	Five fingers clenched into a fist
h_3	Gather the spread-out five fingers into a fist
h_4	Open the fist, spreading out the fingers

Table 6. Speech and Intent Library

VoiceName	VoiceDescription	IntentName	IntentDescription
v_1	start	i_1	start
v_2	stop	i_2	stop
v_3	grab	i_3	grab
v_4	put	i_4	put

intent understanding accuracy of 80.30%. In order for the system to correctly understand the user's real intention in complex application scenarios, we use multimodal fusion to make full use of the information of different modalities, and optimize the fusion algorithm of gesture, speech and target detection to achieve an average recognition rate of 97.24%, and an average intention understanding accuracy of 96.1%. It can be seen that the multimodal intent understanding algorithm reduces the misinterpretation of traditional intent understanding algorithms and improves the intent understanding accuracy of the system.

4.8 User Evaluation

In order to further verify the interaction effect of the algorithms in this paper and whether the user experience is satisfactory, we surveyed the experimenters who participated in the experiment to evaluate this system by NASA. The NASA evaluation metrics are based on a 5-point scale, where higher scores on memory burden, physical burden, and difficulty in expressing intentions indicate a heavier burden. Higher scores for task completion and satisfaction indicate better performance. Figure 10 shows the mean per interaction scores for 40 experimenters.

After comprehensively analyzing the evaluations of all the experimenters, we can see that the collaborative algorithm based on joint entropy selection proposed in this paper has the characteristics of low operation burden and no special memory required. The user cognitive load is low, the interaction process is more fluent, and it also brings a sense of novelty to the user, and the user evaluation is high.

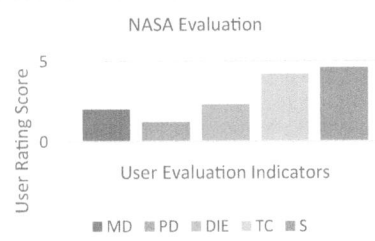

Fig. 10. User Evaluation Results for Intent Understanding and Collaborative Critical Algorithms for Multimodal Fusion Based on NASA Evaluations.

5 Conclusion

This article designs a self enclosed human-robot collaborative assembly system, which can analyze the user's true intention through single or multiple modal inputs, transmit the user's intention to the robot, make the robot understand the user's current intention, and finally use joint entropy to select a relatively safe position for the user to perform grasping, avoiding the harm caused by the robot to humans from the root, Improved the optimization of robot grasping position selection, enhanced the safety guarantee level of robots during human-robot handover process, fully improved the efficiency of collaboration, and provided a foundation for the completion of collaborative tasks.

Although some research results have been achieved in this paper, there are still deficiencies that need to be explored and mapped more deeply in future research. The main research scenario in this paper is to achieve human-robot cooperative grasping in the case of a human grasping an object horizontally, and the number of multimodal channels used and the types of assembly intentions provided are relatively small. In the future, it is hoped that more grasping postures will be explored, extended multi-channels such as emotion recognition and physiological data will be added to the system, and the variety of services for intention understanding will be increased. Future research could also consider introducing more flexible approaches to solving collaboration problems in dynamic scenarios to increase the variety of collaborations and the robustness of the system.

Acknowledgments. The author would like to thank three anonymous reviewers. This research was conducted in collaboration with Kong Xia and Feng. The author would like to express my sincere gratitude to Kong Xia and Feng. The work was supported by University of Jinan and Shandong Provincial Key Laboratory of Network Based Intelligent Computing.

References

1. Kawaji, T., Okada, K., Inaba, M., Inoue, H.: Human robot interaction through integrating visual auditory information with relaxation method. In: Proceedings of IEEE International Conference on Multisensor Fusion and Integration for Intelligent Systems, MFI2003, pp. 323–328. IEEE (2003)

2. Benjamin, C.L., Sylvain, A., Bruno, G.: Multimodal fusion and inference using binaural audition and vision. In: International Congress on Acoustics, pp. 05–09 (2016)
3. Al-Qaderi, M.K., Rad, A.B.: A multi-modal person recognition system for social robots. Appl. Sci. **8**(3), 387 (2018)
4. Song, K.S., Nho, Y.H., Seo, J.H., Kwon, D.S.: Decision-level fusion method for emotion recognition using multimodal emotion recognition information. In: 2018 15th International Conference on Ubiquitous Robots (UR), pp. 472–476. IEEE (2018)
5. Wu, Z., Cai, L., Meng, H.: Multi-level fusion of audio and visual features for speaker identification. In: Advances in Biometrics: International Conference, ICB 2006, Hong Kong, China, January 5--7, 2006. Proceedings, pp. 493-499. Springer, Heidelberg (2005)
6. Trick, S., Koert, D., Peters, J., Rothkopf, C.A.: Multimodal uncertainty reduction for intention recognition in human-robot interaction. In: 2019 IEEE/RSJ International Conference on Intelligent Robots and Systems (IROS), pp. 7009–7016. IEEE (2019)
7. Li, Y., Quan, R., Zhu, L., Yang, Y.: Efficient multimodal fusion via interactive prompting. In: Proceedings of the IEEE/CVF Conference on Computer Vision and Pattern Recognition, pp. 2604–2613 (2023)
8. Sharma, A., Sharma, K., Kumar, A.: Real-time emotional health detection using fine-tuned transfer networks with multimodal fusion. Neural Comput. Appl. **35**(31), 22935–22948 (2023)
9. Shi, T., Huang, S.L.: MultiEMO: an attention-based correlation-aware multimodal fusion framework for emotion recognition in conversations. In: Proceedings of the 61st Annual Meeting of the Association for Computational Linguistics (Volume 1: Long Papers), pp. 14752–14766 (2023)
10. Zhou, Y., Liu, P., Qiu, X.: KNN-contrastive learning for out-of-domain intent classification. In: Proceedings of the 60th Annual Meeting of the Association for Computational Linguistics (Volume 1: Long Papers), pp. 5129–5141 (2022)
11. Ouyang, Y., Wu, Z., Dai, X., Huang, S., Chen, J.: Towards multi-label unknown intent detection. In: Proceedings of the 29th International Conference on Computational Linguistics, pp. 626–635 (2022)
12. Mueller, A., et al.: Label semantic aware pre-training for few-shot text classification. arXiv preprint arXiv:2204.07128 (2022)
13. Zhang, Y., Zhang, H., Zhan, L.M., Wu, X.M., Lam, A.: New intent discovery with pre-training and contrastive learning. arXiv preprint arXiv:2205.12914 (2022)
14. Sun, P.F., Ouyang, Y.W., Song, D.J., Dai, X.Y.: Self-supervised task augmentation for few-shot intent detection. J. Comput. Sci. Technol. **37**(3), 527–538 (2022)
15. Bao, H., Ming, D., Guo, Y., Zhang, K., Zhou, K., Du, S.: DFCNN-based semantic recognition of urban functional zones by integrating remote sensing data and POI data. Remote Sens. **12**(7), 1088 (2020)
16. Johnson, S.J., Murty, M.R., Navakanth, I.: A detailed review on word embedding techniques with emphasis on word2vec. Multimedia Tools Appl. 1–29 (2023)
17. Wu, Z., He, S.: Improvement of the AlexNet networks for large-scale recognition applications. Iranian J. Sci. Technol. Trans. Electr. Eng. **45**(2), 493–503 (2021)
18. Yang, W., Paxton, C., Cakmak, M., Fox, D.: Human grasp classification for reactive human-to-robot handovers. In 2020 IEEE. In: RSJ International Conference on Intelligent Robots and Systems (IROS), pp. 11123–11130 (2020)
19. Yang, W., Paxton, C., Mousavian, A., Chao, Y.W., Cakmak, M., Fox, D.: Reactive human-to-robot handovers of arbitrary objects. In: 2021 IEEE International Conference on Robotics and Automation (ICRA), pp. 3118–3124. IEEE (2021)

Seam Carving Empowered by Reinforcement Learning for Optimal Content Preservation

Muhammad Mujahid[1], Md. Shamim Hossain[1], Asad Khan[2], and Zhangjin Huang[1(✉)]

[1] University of Science and Technology of China (USTC), Hefei, China
{mmajeed,shamim2}@mail.ustc.edu.cn, zhuang@ustc.edu.cn
[2] Metaverse Research Institute, Guangzhou University, Guangzhou, China
asad@gzhu.edu.cn

Abstract. Ensuring the preservation of vital content and maintaining the geometric integrity of an image during resizing is crucial. Seam carving is a powerful technique for achieving this, allowing for image resizing with minimal or no content loss while preserving significant elements. A "seam" in this context is an optimal connected path of pixels within an image, extending either from top to bottom or left to right, with the selection of pixels based on their energy levels. In this paper, we introduce an innovative approach based on Reinforcement Learning, specifically using Q-learning. Unlike traditional dynamic programming-based seam carving algorithms, our method employs Q-learning to make seam removal decisions through learned policies. The Q-learning agent in our approach is trained to identify the lowest energy pixels, creating an optimized seam that minimizes content loss and artifacts. The agent's Q-values are acquired through interactions with the image environment, enabling informed decisions about pixel selection based on energy levels. Our experimental results, conducted across various image types, demonstrate the efficiency and effectiveness of our proposed method. This research makes a significant contribution to the fields of image processing and computer vision by introducing a Reinforcement Learning (Q-learning) based seam carving technique. This innovation holds promise for advancing content-aware image resizing, with applications spanning multimedia content management and beyond.

Keywords: Image Resizing · Reinforcement Learning · Seam Carving · Q-Learning

1 Introduction

The task of image retargeting or resizing while preserving crucial content has always been a challenging endeavor in the field of image processing and manipulation. This challenge has intensified with the proliferation and versatility of contemporary display devices, prompting a shift from conventional resizing methods like scaling and cropping, which often resulted in unwanted distortion and the loss of critical details. The landscape changed significantly when Avidan et al. [1] introduced seam carving as a groundbreaking solution. This innovative approach enabled non-uniform scaling by selectively adding or removing seams, offering a more intelligent and content-aware alternative to traditional resizing techniques. Initially devised for image resizing, seam carving has proven versatile and applicable to various contexts beyond its original scope. The fundamental principle guiding seam carving involves identifying pixels with the lowest energy to form a seam within the image. This allows for alterations in dimensions while minimizing damage and distortion to essential features.

Avidan and Shamir's original seam carving algorithm, rooted in dynamic programming, inspired our efforts to enhance its performance and adapt it to a wider array of visual content [1]. In this paper, we present a novel approach centered around Q-learning [2] introduced by Watkins et al. in 1992, a reinforcement learning [3] technique proposed by the Sutton et al. in 1999, to inform decisions about seam removal. Unlike preceding methods, our Q-learning agent dynamically assesses the importance of each pixel based on learned policies, intelligently selecting low-energy pixels to form a seam. This strategic approach prioritizes the preservation of critical features while minimizing distortions in the resized image. The integration of Q-learning into seam carving represents a compelling opportunity to advance content-aware image resizing. The adaptability and learning capacity of the agent, derived from its interactions with the image environment, present the prospect of achieving an optimal balance between content preservation and resizing quality across diverse image types.

The several notable contributions of this study are summarized below:

- We have introduced an innovative seam calculation method employing Q-learning. The content awareness technique embedded in our approach not only preserves image quality but also ensures reproducibility when necessary.
- Our approach intelligently selects low-energy pixels to create a seam, prioritizing the preservation of essential features while minimizing distortions in the resized image.
- Unlike conventional approaches, our method leverages reward-based reinforcement learning. This technique is beneficial for image resizing in both reduction/re-targeting and enlargement.

This paper is organized as follows: In Sect. 2, we delve into the intricacies of related work. Section 3 discusses reinforcement learning. The Q-learning-based seam carving methodology is detailed in Sect. 4. In Sect. 5, we explain the specifics of our proposed methodology. Section 6 outlines the experimental setup and presents results that underscore the effectiveness and versatility of our approach. Finally, Sect. 7 provides the conclusion.

2 Related Works

In the realm of image processing, significant strides have been made in content-aware image resizing, with the availability of diversified multimedia gadgets in modern era many content aware image resizing algorithms are proposed which can broadly categorized as Cropping and scaling [4], Seam carving [1,5,6], Warping [7] and Machine learning [8].

Suh et al. [4] utilized saliency-based cropping and face detection cropping to generate thumbnails, although originally intended for thumbnail generation, the idea can be readily extended to retargeting. This method first identifies a low-level saliency map independent of semantic information in the image and then determines a cropping rectangle containing the most salient parts. For face detection cropping, it employs a face detector to identify faces in the image and generates thumbnails by encompassing all detected faces within the cropping rectangle. While this method performs better than simple cropping and scaling, it encounters challenges with images featuring multiple important features.

Another approach, presented by Feng Liu et al. they introduced data-dependent scaling, also known as Fisheye view warping [9]. This method relies on low-level saliency and high-level object recognition to discern more important regions from less important ones in the image. It preserves the region of interest while distorting unimportant regions, thereby aiding users in resizing by producing distorted unimportant regions instead of completely removing them through cropping.

Advancements persisted in scaling and cropping-based retargeting, Vidya Setlur et al. proposing a non-photo-realistic algorithm for automatic image retargeting [10]. Their algorithm segments the image into different regions and identifies the regions of interest using an importance map. In the subsequent steps, these important regions are extracted from the source image, leaving holes behind, which are then filled using image interpolation. The resulting background image, devoid of important regions, undergoes resizing to the required dimensions. Finally, the foreground regions or important regions, extracted initially, are reintegrated into the resized image.

We know that cropping based image resizing methods do have their drawbacks so a new method independent of cropping and scaling was proposed by Avidan et al. [1]. The technique used in that proposed method was named as Seam Carving, with seam carving emerging as a pioneering technique. This innovative method uses an energy function to evaluate pixel importance based on their energy values. It enables non-uniform scaling by selectively adding or removing seams, overcoming limitations in conventional resizing methods like scaling and cropping.

In [5] extended the technique to video resizing, incorporating graph cuts and introducing a novel energy criterion called the forward energy cost function which was introduced to cater for the energy added by joining the new pixels in the image.

Subsequent research has expanded the capabilities of seam carving and many authors dried to improve the results of seam carving and solve it's drawbacks by either combining the other image resizing techniques with the seam carving or by adding the other image resizing techniques with it, in the following discussion for example Dong et al. introduced the integrated seam carving with image scaling [11], employing a bidirectional similarity function and dominant color descriptor.

Advancements continued with Seam Carving with Improved Edge Preservation introduced by [12] addressing challenges associated with objects featuring lines by integrating a line detector and an improved energy function, in this method they used the canny edge detector to find the line structures and then look for the seams pass through these line structures once any seam passed through they increased the energy of the surrounding pixels so that no other seam can pass through this area again. Frankovich et al. [6]. Proposed Enhanced Seam Carving via Integration of Energy Gradient Functional in which they introduced a new energy gradient cost function to enhance the seam carving method. The integration of depth information in Depth-aware Image Seam Carving by Shen et al. [13] aimed to address content removal issues caused by low-energy pixels within objects, by introducing the concept of depth authors tried to remove more and more distant pixels which are actually the part of the background of the image.

Zahra Toony et al. proposed Active Contour-Based Seam Carving [14], their approach, rooted in the seam carving scheme, aimed to preserve important objects in an image while adjusting its aspect ratio. Active contour-based estimation of the local energy map facilitated the carving and insertion of connected paths of pixels, or seams, optimizing image resizing. This segmentation into prominent and less important parts allowed for targeted seam carving.

Further contributions to the field included Hybrid Image Retargeting using Optimized Seam Carving and Scaling by Zhang et al. [15], introducing an optimized importance map and combining seam carving and scaling for a balanced approach. In Content-Guided Seam Carving Using Deep Convolution Neural Network by Song et al. [8], leveraged deep energy maps generated by a convolution neural network to guide the seam carving process.

The most recent addition, proposed by Ayubi et al. [16], introduces A New Seam Carving Method for Image Resizing Based on Entropy Energy and Lyapunov Exponent in 2023, utilizing information entropy and Lyapunov exponents for optimal seam selection. This diverse collection of research underscores the continuous innovation and varied applications of seam carving in the dynamic landscape of image processing. The collaborative efforts highlighted in this related work section showcase the evolution of seam carving and its ongoing significance in shaping the future of content-aware image resizing.

Cho et al. proposed "Weakly- and Self-Supervised Learning for Content-Aware Deep Image Retargeting" [17]. In this paper, the authors proposed a content-aware image resizing technique that uses deep learning to obtain high-level semantic information. They added a shift layer that moves each pixel from the source to the target grid to resize input photos within a network. They have shown that the shift layer enables end-to-end training and that input images with the target aspect ratio are used directly to generate retargeted images. Image-level annotations provide the spatial semantic information that is transferred to the shift layer. The content loss of the retargeted images is calculated using the image-level annotations. Additionally, after retargeting, the input images are used for structure loss to reduce unwanted visual effects. Finally, the authors present a method for content-aware deep image retargeting that is weakly and self-supervised. For structure and content loss computations, they have used images and their associated image-level annotations; these computations don't require much human labor for the output labels to supervise the networks. Their proposed network takes an input image and a desired retargeting size and then directly produces the resized image using a shift layer; their method learns semantic information and passes it to the shift map.

Eungyeol Song et al. proposed "CarvingNet: Content-Guided Seam Carving Using Deep Convolution Neural Network" [8]. In this paper, the authors propose a method for creating a deep energy map using an encoder-decoder convolution neural network. A deep energy map preserves important parts or boundaries in an image without distortion. Encoder and decoder structures are used to create a deep convolution neural network (DCNN). A retargeting system is built that takes into account the objects and content of the photos when adjusting the image size. Three key elements can be used to summarize the ultimate objectives of this work. First, a deep energy map construction model using a neural network is proposed. Second, the retargeting system-which has the ability to modify image size-applies the energy map. Third, the improved retargeting system is evaluated using a trustworthy evaluation technique. After creating the deep energy map using a neural network, the authors then used dynamic programming based seam carving to remove low-energy pixels from the image like any other seam carving.

Nobukatsu Kajiura et al. proposed Self-Play Reinforcement Learning for Fast Image Retargeting [18]. In this work, authors proposed a solution in response to MULTIOP. This method was designed to determine the best operator sequence that reduces the difference between the original and retargeted photos. Many retargeting operators were combined, and retargeted images were generated at each stage. Due to its extremely long processing time, the practical application of this method is very limited. So, the authors proposed this work to discover the ideal operator combination in an acceptable amount of processing time. They proposed a technique that uses a reinforcement learning agent to predict the ideal operator for each step. They have proposed a multi-operator image retargeting method that works at high speed by gradually anticipating the best retargeting operator. To do this, the authors used a reinforcement learning agent instead of generating numerous images to search for combinations of retargeting operators.

3 Reinforcement Learning

Reinforcement learning, a domain within the realm of Artificial Intelligence, constitutes a machine learning training method wherein an agent is immersed in an environment to learn through a system of rewards and punishments. This learning process involves the agent navigating the environment to discover the optimal policy through experience. Reinforcement learning algorithms are broadly categorized into two types: model-based and model-free. In the former, the agent possesses prior knowledge of the environment before reinforcement, while in the latter, model-free algorithms involve agents entering an environment without any initial awareness, learning the optimal policy through a feedback loop of rewards and punishments. Further classification of Reinforcement algorithms can be based on whether they are value-based or policy-based. Value-based algorithms employ specific equations to update reward values, refining the agent's understanding of optimal policies. Conversely, policy-based algorithms eschew such equations, relying on a greedy approach to iterative update the value function without explicit mathematical formulations. This dichotomy in models and algorithms showcases the versatility and adaptability of reinforcement learning approaches, allowing agents to navigate and optimize their behavior within dynamic and often unknown environments through a strategic interplay of rewards, punishments, and iterative learning processes. The schematic representation of the reinforcement learning strategy is illustrated in Fig. 1.

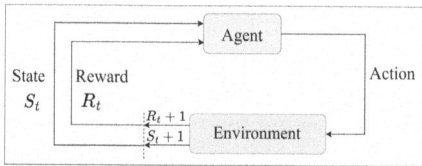

Fig. 1. Illustration of Reinforcement Learning, S represent the state, A is the action, R is reward and t is the timestep.

4 Q Learning Algorithm

The Q-learning algorithm, a model-free and value-based approach within Reinforcement Learning, comprises three key components: the agent's state space, reward matrix, and actions. Each state in the state space may entail multiple actions, each associated with a specific reward value determined by the reward function or equation. As the agent progresses from one state to another by taking actions, it undergoes a dynamic process where rewards are bestowed based on the effectiveness of its chosen actions. Positive or high rewards are assigned when the agent's actions contribute towards reaching the goal state, while negative or low rewards are given for actions that deviate from the intended direction. Given our previous discussion on value-based reinforcement algorithms utilizing equations for reward calculations, we work with two matrices: the reward matrix and the Q matrix. The Q matrix is formed through a specific equation, elucidating the interplay between states, actions, and rewards in the learning process as following.

$$Q(s,a) = r_{i,J} + \gamma * MaxQ(s',a') \tag{1}$$

$Q(s,a)$ is the Q value of the current state and $Q(s',a')$ is the maximum Q value of the next state where γ is the learning rate, in the beginning, Q matrix is initialized to zero and it keeps on updating with new non zero values after every episode or iteration, the agent will keep on exploring the environment and by doing so along with using the reward matrix it will keep on populating the Q table with non zero values according to the Eq. 1 so what will happen that at the end of all iterations for every action at every state, there will be a corresponding value in reward and Q table and, in a result whenever the agent is at a particular state and it wants to move to the next stage then it knows the best cost by just looking at the Q table or Q matrix.

In our case, we have the following assumption in the context of Q learning.

Learning Environment: The comprehensive learning environment for the agent encompasses the entirety of the image, providing a holistic context for its interactions and decision-making processes.

Agent: The focal point of our learning paradigm is represented by the pixel currently undergoing processing, serving as the learning agent within the broader image context.

States S: The various states within the learning framework include all pixels within the image. This diverse set of states forms the backdrop against which the agent makes informed decisions.

Action A: The agent's decision space is defined by a set of three distinct actions: it can move to the pixel located at the top left, top right, or choose to move top up. This dynamic set of actions empowers the agent to navigate and interact within the image environment.

Immediate reward R: The immediate rewards serve as consequential feedback, promptly obtained by the agent upon the execution of an action. These rewards play a crucial role in shaping the learning process and guiding the agent towards optimal decision-making.

5 Methodology

As we already have explained Seam Carving is a technique to remove or add the path of low energy pixels from top to bottom or left to right as they are not as important, the removal of a seam reduces the size of the image by one and insertion of a seam increase the size by one and vertical seam change width while horizontal seam change height. The seam should have one and only one pixel from a row for the vertical seam. The selection of pixels is made by their energy value for which we use the following energy function, this is the same energy function used by Aviden et al. [1], as our method is based on their method so we will use the same energy function in Eq. 2 as they did.

$$e(I) = |\delta I/\delta x| + |\delta I/\delta y| \qquad (2)$$

In the original method, they used dynamic programming to calculate the optimal seam which is a seam with minimum cost based on the energy function e of Eq. 1, for this, they first find the cumulative minimum energy M for all the pixels through traversing the image from the second row to last by using the following formula.

$$M(i,j) = e(i,j) + min(M(i-1,j-1), \\ M(i-1,j), M(i-1,j+1)) \quad (3)$$

This means they selected the three pixels for each current pixel (i,j), one right on top $(i-1,j)$ of it one top right $(i-1,j+1)$, and one top left $(i-1,j-1)$ of the current pixel, they found with the lowest energy pixel out of these three and add its energy value to the current pixel's(i,j) energy value, this process will be repeated for all rows, now the minimum value of M in the last row represents the total cost of a seam with the lowest energy, in the second step we will simply backtracked from this point to found the path of optimal seam. Based on Eq. 3 we have derived our reward function so instead of directly calculating the cumulative minimum energy function from 3 we have used it to derive our reward function to calculate the reward table as we did to find the cumulative minimum energy.

$$r_{i,J} = \gamma_1 * e(i,j) + \gamma_2 * M(i-1,J) \\ where, J = \{j, j+1, j-1\} \quad (4)$$

Here in Eq. 4 the value of γ_1 and γ_2 is selected in such a way that their sum never exceed 1. Figure 2 shows the seam carving approach where the top left figure is in our consideration and the seam is generated based on the calculated cumulative energy.

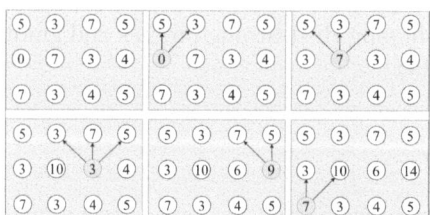

Fig. 2. Illustration of seam carving approach.

As our method is a reinforcement learning (Q learning) based so whole image becomes the learning environment for our agent, every pixel is considered as the state, and at every state agent has three possible actions meaning our agent can move the top up, top right or top left from the current pixel position for exploring the environment and creating the reward and Q table, so like calculating the cumulative minimum energy we have calculated the reward table using Eq. 4, starting from the second row of the imaging agent is at state (i,j) and there are three possible actions $(i-1,j)$ top up, $(i-1,j+1)$ top right and $(i-1,j-1)$ top left that agent can take so in this process agent will take all these three available actions and will get rewarded, that will be the energy value of current pixel (i,j) and add it to the energy values of all three pixels $(i-1,j), (i-1,j+1) and (i-1,j-1)$ for all three actions. This process will be repeated from the first pixel of the second row till the last pixel of the last row to populate the reward table then we will use Bellman's Eq. 1 for Q learning to form our Q table and Eq. 4 to construct the reward table, once we have our Q table then we can go ahead and find the cumulative minimum energy M for all pixels starting from the second row, at every state or pixel agent will have three different Q values of three different actions so we will select the action with the lowest Q value and so did we select pixel with lowest energy suppose the energy of the pixel is e' then function for cumulative minimum energy M for all connected seams will be as following.

$$M(i,j) = e(i,j) + e' \tag{5}$$

We have repeated this process for all rows, now the minimum value of M in the last row represents the total cost of a seam with the lowest energy, in the second step simply backtracked from this point to find the path of the optimal seam. The overall pipeline of the work has been depicted in the Fig. 3. The algorithm of our proposed method has been written in Algorithm 1.

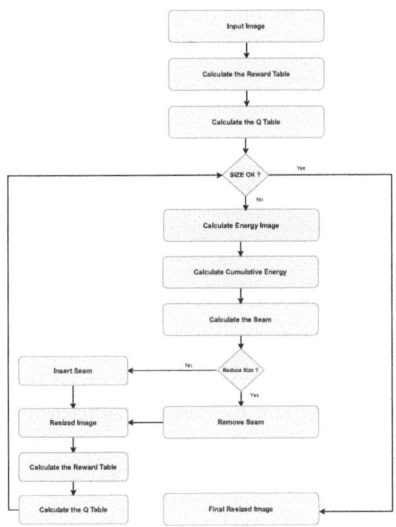

Fig. 3. Flowchart of our proposed method.

6 Experimental Results

The reinforcement learning (Q-learning) based seam carving approach was applied to a series of images to evaluate its performance and practicality for resizing images while preserving important content. Although our proposed method

Algorithm 1. Seam Carving

1: **procedure** SEAMCARVING(image[row][col], N)
2:     Calculate Reward Matrix by 4
3:     Calculate Q Matrix by 1
4:     **for** seam = 0 to $N - 1$ **do**
5:         Calculate the energy of each pixel or energy image by 2
6:         **for** row = 1 to number of rows in energy image **do**
7:             **for** col = 0 to number of columns in energy image **do**
8:                 $a = Q(\text{reward\_row\_count}, \text{reward\_col\_count})$
9:                 reward_col_count += 1
10:                 $b = Q(\text{reward\_row\_count}, \text{reward\_col\_count})$
11:                 reward_col_count += 1
12:                 $c = Q(\text{reward\_row\_count}, \text{reward\_col\_count})$
13:                 reward_col_count = 0
14:                 reward_row_count += 1
15:                 **if** a is minimum among a, b, c **then**
16:                     selected1 = energy_image($row - 1, col - 1$)
17:                 **end if**
18:                 **if** b is minimum among a, b, c **then**
19:                     selected1 = energy_image($row - 1, col$)
20:                 **end if**
21:                 **if** c is minimum among a, b, c or between a and b **then**
22:                     selected1 = energy_image($row - 1, col + 1$)
23:                 **end if**
24:                 cumulative_energy(row, col) = energy_image(row, col) + selected1
25:             **end for**
26:         **end for**
27:         Find the seam using a cumulative energy map and remove it from the image
28:     **end for**
29: **end procedure**

is slower due to the additional steps and computations involved, the visual results are comparable to those of the original dynamic programming-based seam carving method, as demonstrated in the following discussion. The qualitative results for both image reduction and enlargement are presented in Sects. 6.1 and 6.2.

6.1 Image Reduction

In this section, we discuss image reduction using our method in both horizontal and vertical directions, and then compare it with the original seam carving method.

In Fig. 4, we present a sequence of images from left to right, illustrating the original image, the cumulative energy image, and the stepwise reduction in height by 30, 60, 90, and 120 seams. These reductions were achieved using the traditional seam carving dynamic programming-based method. Similarly, in Fig. 5, the left-to-right sequence displays the original image, the cumulative energy image, and the progressive reduction in height by 30, 60, 90, and 120 seams, achieved through our innovative Q-learning-based method.

Figure 6 provides a comprehensive comparison, plotting the average pixel energy of the images against the number of seams removed in both Fig. 4 and Fig. 5. This graph serves as a visual representation of the performance differences or similarities between the original dynamic programming approach and our Q-learning-based method in terms of image resizing and preservation of important content. The juxtaposition of these figures facilitates a nuanced understanding of the efficacy and potential advantages offered by the proposed reinforcement learning approach in seam carving applications.

In Fig. 7, a comprehensive sequence is presented from left to right, starting with the original image, followed by representations of 70 seam positions for both vertical and horizontal seams, and concluding with the image reduced using the original seam carving method. This visual series aims to illustrate the stepwise application and impact of the traditional technique on the image's structure and dimensions.

Contrastingly, Fig. 8 showcases a parallel left-to-right arrangement featuring the original image, 70 seam positions for vertical and horizontal seams, and the subsequent image reduction using our proposed method. This comparative display allows for a direct visual comparison between the outcomes of the traditional approach in Fig. 7 and the innovative seam carving technique introduced in our proposed method in Fig. 8. By scrutinizing these figures side by side, viewers can gain insights into the nuanced differences and potential advantages offered by our novel approach in effectively resizing images while preserving key content.

Upon careful examination of both figures, it becomes apparent that our proposed method yields results congruent with those obtained through the original dynamic programming-based seam carving approach. The alignment in seam positions and the final reduced image between the two methods, as illustrated in Fig. 5 and Fig. 6, provides compelling evidence of the effectiveness and parity of our innovative approach in achieving resizing objectives while maintaining consistency with traditional techniques.

Table 1. Number of Seams VS Average Pixels Energy

Methods	Number of Seams			
	50	100	150	200
Backward Energy [1]	201581	177533	154153	132011
Forward Energy [5]	201509	177549	154270	131994
Enhanced Seam Carving [6]	201322	177150	154043	131521
Ours	200577	175755	152151	130169

Fig. 4. Left to right original image, cumulative energy image, reduce height by 30, 60, 90, and 120 seams when using original seam carving dynamic programming based method.

Fig. 5. Left to right original image, cumulative energy image, reduce height by 30, 60, 90, and 120 seams when using Q learning based method.

6.2 Image Enlarging

To further test our algorithm and prove our point that it produces almost the same results as the original seam carving algorithm, we have arranged another set of experiments where two different images were used and both expanded by 100 seams using the first original seam carving method and then using our proposed algorithm, results of these experiments are represented in Figs. 9 and 10, these two images consists of two sets of images first is made by using the original method and the second is by our algorithm.

It is evident from the original images, seam images, and expanded images from both figures that our proposed method produces the same results as the original seam carving method not only when reducing size but also when it comes to increasing the size.

6.3 Some More Comparison Results

In this subsection, we explore additional findings by comparing the outcomes of our proposed approach with various seam carving techniques, including the original seam carving method [1], which is characterized by a backward cumulative energy technique. Our approach similarly employs a backward cumulative

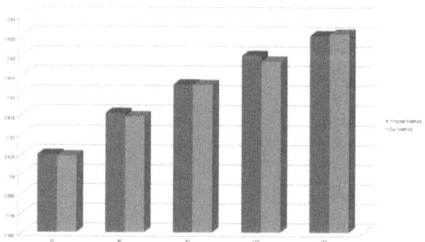

Fig. 6. Figure 3 Average pixel energy of the images VS number of seams removed in Fig. 1 and Fig. 2.

Fig. 7. Left to the right original image, 70 seam positions for vertical and horizontal seam and reduced image respectively using the original method.

Fig. 8. Left to right original image, 70 seam positions for vertical and horizontal seam and reduced image respectively using our proposed method.

energy reinforcement learning implementation. We also consider the forward energy technique [5], designed to address energy changes resulting from pixel removal or addition in the original image, and the approach outlined in [6].

To conduct our experiment, we subjected an image to a sequence of reductions involving 50, 100, 150, and 200 seams using all the aforementioned methods-first employing [6], then [5], followed by [1], and finally, our proposed method. At each step, we meticulously calculated the average pixel energy of the image for each method, providing a detailed analysis of the dynamic changes occurring during the seam carving process. The results of these experiments are presented in Fig. 11 and Table 1.

Both the tabular data and visual results underscore the striking similarity among these methods in terms of image outcomes. Notably, our method aligns closely with the original seam carving method, as indicated by both the tabulated and visual results. It's crucial to clarify that our intention is not to assert that our method produces identical outcomes to the forward energy method [5] and Enhanced Seam Carving [6]. These advanced methods excel in preserving important components compared to the other two methods under discussion. Our research focuses on the Q-learning-based implementation of the original seam carving method, which can be seamlessly extended to incorporate forward energy [5,6] for producing analogous results, thus demonstrating the adaptability and versatility of our proposed approach.

Fig. 9. Left to right, original image, seam image and expanded image using 100 seams, first set using the original method, second set by using our proposed method.

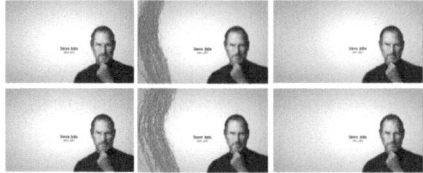

Fig. 10. Left to right, original image, seam image and expanded image using 100 seams, first set using the original method, second set by using our proposed method.

Fig. 11. In each row, the first image is the original, while the subsequent images are progressively reduced using 50, 100, 150, and 200 seams, respectively. The first row is reduced using the Enhanced Seam Carving method [6], the second row uses the Forward Energy method [5], the third row employs the original Seam Carving method [1], and the last row utilizes our reinforcement learning-based method.

7 Conclusion

Based on our discussions and experimental findings, our proposed reinforcement learning (Q-learning) approach to seam carving has proven to be as effective as the traditional dynamic programming method. This innovation aligns with contemporary advancements in machine learning, demonstrating its potential to reshape conventional image processing techniques. The integration of Q-learning into seam carving highlights its adaptability and efficacy in addressing complex optimization challenges. In conclusion, our research affirms that this reinforcement learning approach provides a viable alternative to dynamic programming, offering a promising shift in the way seam carving is approached and executed.

Acknowledgements. This work was supported in part by the National Key Research and Development Program of China (Nos. 2022YFB3303400 and 2021YFF0500900), the Anhui Provincial Major Science and Technology Project (No. 202203a05020016), the "Pioneer" and "Leading Goose" Research and Development Program of Zhejiang (No. 2023C01143), and the National Natural Science Foundation of China (No. 71991464).

References

1. Avidan, S., Shamir, A.: Seam carving for content-aware image resizing. In: Seminal Graphics Papers: Pushing the Boundaries, vol. 2, pp. 609–617 (2023)
2. Watkins, C.J., Dayan, P.: Q-learning. Mach. Learn. **8**(13), 279–92 (1992)
3. Sutton, R.S., Barto, A.G., et al.: Reinforcement learning. J. Cogn. Neurosci. **11**(1), 126–34 (1999)
4. Suh, B., Ling, H., Bederson, B.B., Jacobs, D.W.: Automatic thumbnail cropping and its effectiveness. In: Proceedings of the 16th Annual ACM Symposium on User Interface Software and Technology, pp. 95–104 (2003)
5. Rubinstein, M., Shamir, A., Avidan, S.: Improved seam carving for video retargeting. ACM Trans. Graph. (TOG) **27**(3), 1–9 (2008)
6. Frankovich, M., Wong, A.: Enhanced seam carving via integration of energy gradient functionals. IEEE Sig. Process. Lett. **18**(6), 375–8 (2011)
7. Chen, R., Kzgcll, F.D.: Content-aware image resizing by quadratic programming. In: IEEE Computer Society Conference on Computer Vision and Pattern Recognition Workshops (CVPRW), vol. 13, pp. 1–8 (2010)
8. Song, E., Lee, M., Lee, S.: CarvingNet: content-guided seam carving using deep convolution neural network. IEEE Access **7**, 284–92 (2018)
9. Liu, F., Gleicher, M.: Automatic image retargeting with fisheye-view warping. In: Proceedings of the 18th Annual ACM Symposium on User Interface Software and Technology, pp. 153–162 (2005)
10. Setlur, V., Takagi, S., Raskar, R., Gleicher, M., Gooch, B.: Automatic image retargeting. In: Proceedings of the 4th International Conference on Mobile and Ubiquitous Multimedia, pp. 59–68 (2005)
11. Dong, W., Zhou, N., Paul, J.C., Zhang, X.: Optimized image resizing using seam carving and scaling. ACM Trans. Graph. (TOG) **28**(5), 1–10 (2009)
12. Kiess, J., Kopf, S., Guthier, B., Effelsberg, W.: Seam carving with improved edge preservation. In: Multimedia on Mobile Devices 2010, vol. 7542, pp. 147–157. SPIE (2010)
13. Shen, J., Wang, D., Li, X.: Depth-aware image seam carving. IEEE Trans. Cybern. **43**(5), 1453–61 (2013)
14. Zahra Toony, S.H., Jamzad, M.: Active contour based seam carving forcontent-aware image resizing. In: The 6th Iranian Machine Vision and Image Processing Conference, 27–28 October 2010 (2010)
15. Zhang, Y., Sun, Z., Jiang, P., Huang, Y., Peng, J.: Hybrid image retargeting using optimized seam carving and scaling. Multimedia Tools Appl. **76**, 8067–85 (2017)
16. Ayubi, J., Amirani, M.C., Valizadeh, M.: A new seam carving method for image resizing based on entropy energy and Lyapunov exponent. Multimedia Tools Appl. **82**(13), 19417–40 (2023)
17. Cho, D., Park, J., Oh, T.H., Tai, Y.W., So Kweon, I.: Weakly-and self-supervised learning for content-aware deep image retargeting. In: Proceedings of the IEEE International Conference on Computer Vision, pp. 4558–4567 (2017)
18. Kajiura, N., Kosugi, S., Wang, X., Yamasaki, T.: Self-play reinforcement learning for fast image retargeting. In: Proceedings of the 28th ACM International Conference on Multimedia, pp. 1755–1763 (2020)

Robust Mesh Denoising Based on Weighted Least Squares

Xi Lan[1], Saishang Zhong[2], Jia Chen[2], Zheng Liu[3(✉)], and Xiong Pan[2(✉)]

[1] Geography and Tourism College, Huanggang Normal University,
Huanggang, China
[2] School of Computer Science and Artificial Intelligence, Wuhan Textile University,
Wuhan, China
pxjlh@163.com
[3] School of Computer Science, China University of Geosciences (Wuhan),
Wuhan, China
liu.zheng.jojo@gmail.com

Abstract. Recovering high quality surfaces from noisy meshes is a fundamental problem in geometry processing. The main challenge is to robustly and efficiently handle different kinds of noise including impulsive noise, Gaussian noise while effectively preserving geometric features. In the paper, we first propose a normal filtering model with a novel aggregated fidelity term. The using of the aggregated fidelity term makes the proposed model robust against outliers and comparatively large noise. Then, a patch-aware normal filtering method is presented also based on the weighted least squares framework, which can preserve sharp features. Finally, a folding-free vertex updating scheme is employed to reconstruct the mesh according to the filtered face normals. Intensive experiments on a variety of surfaces demonstrate the superiority of our denoising method visually and quantitatively.

Keywords: Mesh denoising · aggregate fidelity term · weighted least squares · geometric features

1 Introduction

Triangulated meshes are widely used in various fields including computer graphics, computer-aided design, computer vision, and etc. Meshes are usually generated by digital scanner devices or triangulation algorithms. Yet, the scanning process inevitably produce some level of noise due to local measurement errors, which will degrade the quality of meshes and cause troubles in further geometry processing tasks, such as mesh reconstruction, segmentation, and parametrization. Thus, mesh denoising is one of the most fundamental tasks in geometry processing. The main challenge of mesh denoising is to effectively preserve geometric features while removing noise. This problem becomes more challenging for models with different kinds of noise including impulsive noise, large scale noise and irregular surface sampling.

Over the last decade, great efforts have been done on mesh denoising. Recently, state-of-the-art denoising methods, such as bilateral weighting normal filtering [1], TV normal filtering method [2], ℓ_0 minimization [3], guided normal filtering [4], robust and high fidelity denoising method [5], achieve greatly successes. In the following of the paper, these state-of-the-art methods are abbreviated as BF, TV, ℓ_0, GF and RFM, respectively. But in some respects, these methods still have limitations. For example, BF can effectively recover fine details and smooth regions. However, when the noise level increase, BF usually fails to produce satisfactory results, especially for models with sharp features (sharp edges and cornres). TV and ℓ_0 achieve impressive results for preserving sharp features but inevitably suffer staircase effects in smooth regions. This staircase effect is caused by the sparsity regularization of these two methods. Thus, these two methods tend to sharpen fine details and flatten curved regions, especially for ℓ_0 for its high sparsity requirement. GF preserves sharp features well, but it is hard to produce desired results when handling meshes containing narrow structure regions. RFM can recover sharp features well, but it over-smoothes fine details. It seems that all these methods cannot handle impulsive noise well. In other words, none of these methods can remove different kinds of noise robustly. In the presence of large scale noise, most of these state-of-the-art methods cannot preserve geometric features well, except GF. Moreover, GF and RHM cannot produce satisfactory results for meshes with irregular surface sampling. Due to the above limitations of these state-of-the-art methods, it is still quite challenging to preserve geometric features while removing noise, for models corrupted by different kinds of noise including impulsive noise and large scale of noise, and with irregular surface sampling.

In the paper, we first propose a normal filtering model, consisting of a regularization term using the first order difference operator and an aggregated fidelity term. The proposed normal filtering model can preserve geometric features well while removing noise, which is very robust against the different kinds of noise, large scale noise and irregular surface sampling. For surfaces including sharp features, the proposed normal filtering model may blurs sharp features in some extent, when the noise level increases. To overcome this problem, a novel patch-aware normal filtering method is presented to recover the blurred sharp features, which is based on the weighted least squares framework.

To summarize, the contributions of the paper are listed as follows:

- We propose a robust normal filtering model against different kinds of noise, large scale noise and irregular surface sampling. The proposed model includes an aggregated fidelity term. To the best of our knowledge, the aggregated fidelity term is firstly introduced in mesh denoising problem. A fast and efficient iterative solver is adopted in the weighted least squares framework to solve the model.
- We present a novel patch-aware normal filtering method to preserve sharp features, based on the weighted least squares framework.

- We conduct a series of experiments to demonstrate that our method outperforms the state-of-the-art approaches on a variety of meshes, such as CAD, non-CAD, and raw-scanned data.

2 Related Work

Mesh denoising has been widely studied in the last two decades. It is beyond our scope to review all existing mesh denoising methods, and we only review those notable methods that are most relevant to this work. For a comprehensive review on classic mesh denoising methods, interesting readers are referred to [6,7]. Here, we mainly focus on current state-of-the-art denoising methods, which based on optimization and filtering methods.

Filtering methods are widely adopted in mesh noising problem, which are roughly classified into two categories, isotropic and anisotropic methods. The isotropic methods [8,9] are classical and simple. These methods usually smooth the mesh to remove the noise without considering geometric features of the mesh. Indeed, this kind of isotropic method is the processing of reducing area of the mesh, and it evidently blurs geometric features while removing the noise. In order to preserve geometric features, a variety of anisotropic methods [10,11] were presented later on. Compared to the isotropic methods, the anisotropic methods are more robust for preserving geometric features, among which the methods based on bilateral filtering are typical. The bilateral filtering was firstly introduced by Tomasi and Manduchi [12] in image community, and several researchers [13] extend it to mesh denoising. Subsequently, some bilateral normal filtering methods [10,14–17] were proposed, which are highly relevant to this work. Zheng et al. [10] used the bilateral weight functions calculated by the face normal differences and spatial distances between adjacent faces. Solomon et al. [18] presented a general framework to perform feature-preserving smoothing by bilateral filtering. Zhang et al. [4] proposed a guided normal filtering method based on the joint bilateral filtering, which achieves impressive results for preserving sharp features. Wang et al. [19] introduced a data-driven denoising method based on the bilateral normal filtering framework. They proposed to employ multiscale bilateral normal filters to design a geometry descriptor for robustly characterizing the underlying geometry features from the noisy input.

Optimization based methods, another kind of techniques for mesh denoising, which are proposed with priors about underlying surfaces. Generally, to preserve sharp features, the methods usually use a sparsity regularization term. For example, Zhang et al. [2] and Wu et al. [20] used TV (Total Variation) model including a ℓ_1 regularization term to remove noise while preserving sharp features. He and Schaefer [3] extended ℓ_0 minimization [21] to triangulated meshes for preserving sharp features. Lu et al. [22] proposed ℓ_1-median smoothing method, which can effectively handle meshes with different levels and irregular surface sampling.

Recently, data-driven approaches have been applied to mesh denoising [19,23–28]. [19] presents a cascade normal regression method that can learn the mapping from noisy inputs to their corresponding ground truth. [24] proposes a two-step method that avoids blurring fine details. [26] presents a deep neural network for smoothing face normals. Besides, [23,25,27,28] adopt convolutional neural networks for mesh denoising. In short, without any assumptions about underlying features and noise patterns, these methods can remove noise effectively while recovering features well. However, the performance of these data-driven methods relies on the completeness of the training dataset.

3 Normal Filtering Scheme

Similar to most mesh denoising methods based on face normal filtering, our method also has two stages, face normal filtering followed by vertex updating.

3.1 Notations

Let M be a compact triangulated surface of arbitrary topology with no degenerate triangles in $\mathbb{R}^3$. The set of vertices, edges and triangles of M are denoted as $\{v_i : i = 0, 1, \cdots, V-1\}$, $\{e_i : i = 0, 1, \cdots, E-1\}$ and $\{\tau_i : i = 0, 1, \cdots, T-1\}$, respectively. Here V, E and T are the numbers of vertices, edges and triangles of M, respectively. If v is an endpoint of an edge e, then we write it as $v \prec e$. Similarly, $e \prec \tau$ denotes that e is an edge of a triangle τ; $v \prec \tau$ denotes that v is a vertex of a triangle τ.

3.2 Robust Normal Filtering

In this subsection, we will introduce our face normal filtering model, which is robust against different kinds of noise, irregular surface sampling and large scale noise. A fast and iterative solver of our normal filtering model is presented.

3.2.1 Weighted ℓ_2 Norm Normal Filtering Model with Aggregated Fidelity Term

For a given noisy mesh M^{in}, we write face normals of the mesh as N^{in}. To remove noise in N^{in}, our normal pre-filtering model treats face normals N as variable and find them as a solution to the following problem:

$$\min_{\mathrm{N} \in \mathrm{C_N}} \{E(\mathrm{N}) = E_d(\mathrm{N}) + \lambda E_r(\mathrm{N})\}, \qquad (1)$$

where $\mathrm{C_N} = \{\mathrm{N} \in \mathbb{R}^{3 \times \mathrm{T}} : \|\mathrm{N}_\tau\| = 1, \forall \tau\}$. The model (1) consists of the fidelity and regularization term, balanced by the positive regularization parameter λ. The fidelity term is introduced to prevent the solution N deviating from their counterparts of the input N^{in} too much. The regularization term makes the solution N smooth while preserving geometric features.

Fidelity Term:

$$E_d(\mathrm{N}) = \sum_\tau \sum_{\tau_j \in \mathcal{D}_d(\tau)} \mathrm{w}_d(\tau, \tau_j) \|\mathrm{N}_\tau - \mathrm{N}^{in}_{\tau_j}\|^2, \qquad (2)$$

where $\mathcal{D}_d(\tau)$ is the set of triangles consisting of τ and triangles that share common vertices with τ, and $w_d(\tau,\tau_j) = \xi(s_\tau, s_{\tau_j})\omega(N_\tau, N_{\tau_j})$. $\xi(s_\tau, s_{\tau_j})$ is the weight to consider the influence of surface sampling rate, which is defined as

$$\xi(s_\tau, s_{\tau_j}) = s_\tau \frac{s_{\tau_j}}{\sum_{\tau_j \in \mathcal{D}_d(\tau)} s_{\tau_j}}, \tag{3}$$

where s_τ is the area of τ. The design of this weight is based on the fact that, normals of larger triangles are more likely to approximate real normals of the underlying surface. In order to avoid blurring geometric features, the weight $\omega(N_\tau, N_{\tau_j})$ is expected to be small when the sharing edge of faces τ and τ_j is geometric feature, and vice verse. Thus, it can be simply defined as

$$\omega(N_\tau, N_{\tau_j}) = \phi(\|N_\tau - N_{\tau_j}\|, \sigma_d),$$

where $\phi(d, \sigma) = \exp(-d^2/2\sigma^2)$, σ_d is a user-specified parameter.

Note that, $E_d(N)$ is an aggregated fidelity term to penalise the dissimilarity between the normal of one face and the average normal generated by its neighbors, which makes the filtering process be more robust against the impulsive noise (outliers) and large scale noise. In image processing community, the aggregated data term is adopted to handle erroneous input data [29], which leads to a more robust smoothing process. To our best knowledge, this fidelity term is firstly introduced in mesh denoising problem.

Regularization Term:

$$E_r(N) = \sum_\tau \sum_{\tau_j \in \mathcal{D}_r(\tau)} w_r(\tau, \tau_j)\|N_\tau - N_{\tau_j}\|^2, \tag{4}$$

where $\mathcal{D}_r(\tau)$ is the set of triangles sharing common vertices with τ. $w_r(\tau, \tau_j)$ is the weight used to remove noise while keeping geometric features, which also takes into account the surface sampling. To satisfy these requirements, we define $w_r(\tau, \tau_j)$ as

$$w_r(\tau, \tau_j) = \xi(s_\tau, s_{\tau_j})\phi(\angle(N_\tau, N_{\tau_j}), \sigma_r) \tag{5}$$

where $\angle(N_\tau, N_{\tau_j})$ is the angle between two face normals, and σ_r is a user-specified angle threshold.

The regularization term $E_r(N)$ uses the first order difference operator to penalise the dissimilarity between a pair of normals of two adjacent faces. The using of the first order difference operator is more effective than high order operators (e.g., Laplace operator) for recovering the geometric features. We compare our normal filtering model using the first order difference operator with the model proposed by Zheng et al. [1] using Laplace operator in Section xx to show the advantage of the first order operator over the high order operator for preserving geometric features.

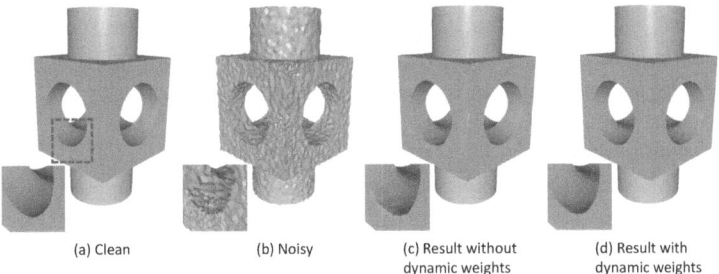

(a) Clean   (b) Noisy   (c) Result without dynamic weights   (d) Result with dynamic weights

Fig. 1. Denoising results of Block (corrupted by Gaussian noise, standard deviation $\sigma = 0.15$ mean edge length). From left to right: (a) clean mesh, (b) noisy mesh, (c) and (d) are results produced by the fixed point iteration (8) without and with dynamically updated weights.

3.2.2 Fixed-Point Iteration Solver

It is challenging to find the exact solution of energy minimization problem (1) due to the nonlinear constraints. Thus, we first ignore the nonlinear constraints of (1). Then, the partial derivatives of (1) with respect to N_τ is as follows

$$\nabla E(N) = \sum_{\tau_j \in \mathcal{D}_d(\tau)} w_d(\tau, \tau_j)(N_\tau - N_{\tau_j}^{in}) + \lambda \sum_{\tau_j \in \mathcal{D}_r(\tau)} w_r(\tau, \tau_j)(N_\tau - N_{\tau_j}).$$

For a critical point N of the energy E we have

$$\nabla E(N) = 0. \quad (6)$$

We define two abbreviations $\tilde{w}_d = w_d(\tau, \tau_j)$ and $\tilde{w}_r = w_r(\tau, \tau_j)$, and rewrite (6) as

$$\sum_{\tau_j \in \mathcal{D}_d(\tau)} \tilde{w}_d(N_\tau - N_{\tau_j}^{in}) + \lambda \sum_{\tau_j \in \mathcal{D}_r(\tau)} \tilde{w}_r(N_\tau - N_{\tau_j}) = 0. \quad (7)$$

The corresponding fixed-point iteration of Eq. (7) can be written as

$$N_\tau^{k+1} = \frac{\overline{N}^{k+1}}{\mathcal{A}}, \quad (8)$$

where $\overline{N}^{k+1} = \sum_{\tau_j \in \mathcal{D}_d(\tau)} \tilde{w}_d^k N_{\tau_j}^{in} + \lambda \sum_{\tau_j \in \mathcal{D}_r(\tau)} \tilde{w}_r^k N_{\tau_j}^k$, $\mathcal{A} = \sum_{\tau_j \in \mathcal{D}_d(\tau)} \tilde{w}_d^k + \lambda \sum_{\tau_j \in \mathcal{D}_r(\tau)} \tilde{w}_r^k$. It is natural to see in (8), the updated face normal N_τ^{k+1} of current iteration is computed as a convex combination of initial normals $N_{\tau_j}^{in}$ of faces in its neighborhood and normals $N_{\tau_j}^k$ of faces in its neighborhood of the last iteration step. We should point out that, if we keep the weights $\tilde{w}_d$ and $\tilde{w}_r$ unchanged during the iteration, the Eq. (8) becomes a single step of Jacobi iteration for solving a linear system constructed by Eq. (7). The convergence of this Jacobi iteration can be guaranteed due to the coefficient matrix of the linear system constructed by Eq. (7) is symmetric positive and diagonally dominant. If the noise level is low, this fixed-weight iteration strategy works well. However, when the noise level increases, our experiments show that this strategy cannot produce satisfactory results, even with fine-tuning parameters. The reason may be as follows. Because both the noise and geometric features belong to high frequency signal, the weights $\tilde{w}_r$ and $\tilde{w}_d$ directly estimated from the noisy mesh can not distinguish them clearly. Some noise will leave in smooth regions and some features will be blurred due to using the inexact weights to filter the face normals. Thus, we dynamically update the weights $\tilde{w}_r$ and $\tilde{w}_d$ with respect to current normals in each iteration. As can be seen in Fig. 1, compared to the fixed-weight iteration strategy, our iteration method (8) with dynamic weights is able to produce much better denoised results.

Here we adopt an approximate strategy to resolve the nonlinear constraints issue of (1). We project the result N_τ^k of each iteration of (8) to an unit sphere. In other words, we simply add a normalization step after each iteration. Thus, we can update N_τ in each iteration as

$$N_\tau^{k+1} = \daleth(\overline{\mathbf{N}}^{k+1}), \qquad (9)$$

where $\daleth(\cdot)$ is a normalize operator. Although we currently cannot give a rigorous proof of convergence of (9), our numerical experiments strongly validate it in practice. A theoretical analysis of it is worthy of the future work.

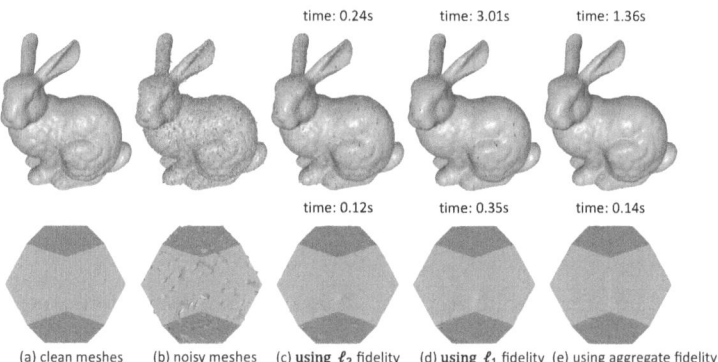

Fig. 2. Comparisons of denoising results produced by using the ℓ_2, ℓ_1 and aggregate fidelity terms. The CPU costs using the ℓ_2, ℓ_1 and aggregate fidelity terms are listed on the top of the first row and second row, respectively.

3.2.3 A Discussion on the Normal Filtering Model (1)

The normal filtering model (1) has an aggregated fidelity term, which makes the model be more robust against different kinds of noise and large noise. In

Fig. 2 we show and compare the denosing results produced by methods using ℓ_2 fidelity term $\|N_\tau - N_\tau^{in}\|^2$, ℓ_1 fidelity term $\|N_\tau - N_\tau^{in}\|$ and our aggregated fidelity term. As we can see from Fig. 2, for handling noisy meshes with different kinds of noise including impulsive noise, the ℓ_1 fidelity method produces better results than the ℓ_2 fidelity method for its sparsity requirement, but worse results than our aggregated fidelity method. Moreover, the CPU costs of these three methods are recorded in Fig. 2. As can be seen, the ℓ_2 fidelity method is fastest, whereas the ℓ_1 fidelity method is slowest due to the time consuming in solving the ℓ_1 norm based problem. In contrast, our method is a little slower than the ℓ_2 fidelity method and is faster than the ℓ_1 fidelity method. However, our method can produce noticeably better results than the other two, even in the presence of large impulsive noise.

3.3 Path-Aware Normal Filtering Method for Recovering Sharp Features

As we known, ℓ_1 based denoising method [2] and ℓ_0 minimization method [3] have crucial advantage in handling meshes consisting of sharp features (such as sharp edges and corners) and flat regions. Compared to these sparse optimization methods, although our ℓ_2 based method proposed above can remove noise without deteriorating sharp features, it may blur sharp features in some extent. Especially, when the noise level increases, this effect will be more severe. To overcome this problem, we further present a patch-aware normal filtering method to better highlight sharp features and smooth flat regions. The method consists of two steps, path generation and path-aware normal filtering, described below.

3.3.1 Patch Generation

With filtered face normals produced by the normal filtering model (1), we can construct a set of patches for our patch-aware normal filtering method. Each patch is a smooth region on the surface, consisting of faces with similar normals. The constructed patches should satisfy the following two conditions: i) Each patch forms a single connected region via shared vertices between neighboring faces; ii) All the patches are non-overlapped, and can cover the whole mesh. In order to construct patches satisfying the above conditions, we design a simple and effective algorithm including three operations, seeding, clustering and merging. The first two operations are iteratively performed, until constructed patches cover the whole mesh. The merging operation is performed only once at last. These operations are detailed as below.

- *Seeding.* We select a face as a seed where the local region including the face is as smooth as possible. To measure the local smoothness of one face τ, we first define a metric function as follows:

$$M_\tau = \sum_{\tau_j \in D_r(\tau)} \|N_\tau - N_{\tau_j}\|^2.$$

Then, we select the face with the minimum value of M_τ as the seed. The selected seed is from the region of the mesh excluding regions of constructed patches.

- *Clustering.* With the selected seed face, we construct a patch P by aggregating faces, which have similar normals to the normal of seed face. To achieve this goal, we first define the dominant orientation N_P for the constructing patch P, which is calculated as follows:

$$\mathrm{N}_P = \daleth(\sum_{\tau \in P} s_\tau \mathrm{N}_\tau),$$

The dominant orientation needs to be dynamically updated during the clustering process. Then, we define two metrics θ_l and θ_p. θ_l represents the angle between the normal of current aggregating face and the normal of its adjacent face in patch P, and θ_p represents the angle between the normal of current face and the dominant orientation of patch P. During the clustering process beginning from the seed face, if both θ_l and θ_p are smaller than a user-specified threshold, the current face will be aggregated into the patch P; otherwise, the face will be ignored. This procedure terminates, when the patch P can not find new face aggregated into it.

- *Merging.* The clustering operation may produce some fragments that, patches include a small number of triangles. This phenomenon may generate unsatisfactory boundaries and cause troubles in the further processing. To tackle this problem, we need merge these fragments into their neighboring patches by using following steps. We first construct a graph by the connectivity of the patches. For each fragment, we then merge it into its neighboring patch whose dominant orientation is most similar to its dominant orientation, if the number of triangles in this fragment is less than $\mathcal{K}$. In this paper, we empirically set $\mathcal{K} = 50$ for all the experiments.

3.3.2 Patch-Aware Normal Filtering

By using the constructed patches from the above step, we can easily extract boundaries from all the paths. The set of edges of all the boundaries is denoted as $\mathcal{C}$. Then, to recover sharp features and flat regions better, we propose a patch-aware normal filtering method by minimizing the following weighted least squares objective function

$$\min_{\mathrm{N} \in \mathcal{C}_\mathrm{N}} \sum_\tau \Big\{ s_\tau \|\mathrm{N}_\tau - \mathrm{N}_\tau^{in}\|^2 + \alpha \sum_{\tau_j \in \mathcal{D}_p(\tau)} \mathrm{w}_{\tau,\tau_j}^p \|\mathrm{N}_\tau - \mathrm{N}_{\tau_j}\|^2 \Big\}, \tag{10}$$

where α is a positive parameter, $\mathcal{D}_p(\tau)$ is the set of triangles sharing common edges with τ, and $\mathrm{w}^p_{\tau,\tau_j}$ is computed as

$$\mathrm{w}^p_{\tau,\tau_j} = s_{\tau_j} \mathcal{H}(\tau,\tau_j) \phi(\angle(\mathrm{N}_\tau, \mathrm{N}_{\tau_j}), \sigma) \cdot \phi(\angle(\mathrm{N}_{P_\tau}, \mathrm{N}_{P_{\tau_j}}), \sigma_P),$$

where $\mathrm{N}_{P_\tau}, \mathrm{N}_{P_{\tau_j}}$ are two dominant orientations of patches P_τ, P_{τ_j}, σ, σ_P are two user-specified angle threshold and $\mathcal{H}(\tau,\tau_j)$ is a function which reads as

$$\mathcal{H}(\tau,\tau_j) = \begin{cases} \epsilon, & \tau \cap \tau_j \in \mathcal{C} \\ 1, & \tau \cap \tau_j \notin \mathcal{C}, \end{cases}$$

where $\epsilon \geq 0$ is a threshold.

The problem (10) is a quadratic minimization with unit normal constraints. We first ignore the unit normal constraints and solve a quadratic programming and then project the minimizer to an unit sphere. Let $\mathrm{w}^p = \mathrm{w}^p_{\tau,\tau_j} + \mathrm{w}^p_{\tau_j,\tau}$. Then, the quadratic problem (without constraints) has the first order optimality condition

$$s_\tau(\mathrm{N}_\tau - \mathrm{N}^{in}_\tau) + \alpha \sum_{\tau_j \in \mathcal{D}_p(\tau)} \mathrm{w}^p(\mathrm{N}_\tau - \mathrm{N}_{\tau_j}) = 0, \forall \tau. \tag{11}$$

The above equations can be reformulated into a sparse and positive semidefinite linear system, which can be solved by various well-developed numerical packages such as Eigen, Taucs and Math Kernel Library (MKL).

4 Vertex Updating

After obtaining the filtered face normals, we need to reconstruct vertex positions for matching them. As we known, there are many approaches for updating vertex positions with new face normals [30,31]. These methods are proposed using the orthogonality between faces and their corresponding normal direction [32]. In this paper, to avoid triangle flipping caused by large scale noise, we adopt the method presented in [31] to update vertex positions.

5 Experimental Results

In this section, we conduct a series of experiments on various CAD, nonCAD, and raw scanned meshes to show the performances of the proposed method. The synthetic noise is generated by a zero-mean Gaussian function with standard deviation proportional to the mean edge length of the ground truth shape, which is denoted as $\bar{l}_e$. We denote this standard deviation as σ. We compare the proposed method with state-of-the-art methods, including bilateral filtering [10], ℓ_0 minimization [3], cascade normal filtering [19], and guided normal filtering [4], which are abbreviated as BFM, L0M, CNR, and GNF. Specially, for methods CNR and GNF, we run the codes provides by their authors; For the other methods, we have implemented them based on their published articles in C++. To show the faceting effect, all the examples are rendered in the flat-shading model.

5.1 Visual Comparisons

To verify the performance of our method, we first compare it with the state-of-the-art approaches on CAD, nonCAD, and raw scanned meshes. For each method, we carefully tune its parameters for generating visually appealing results.

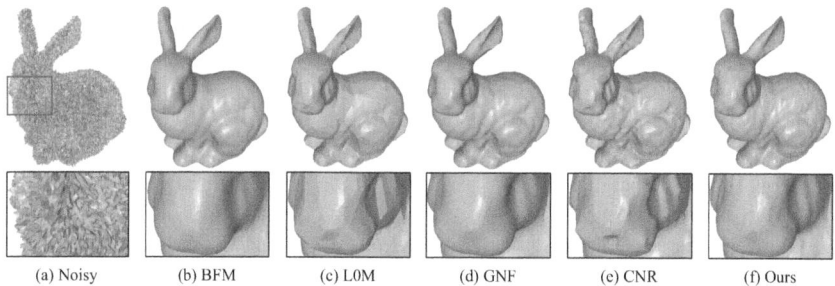

(a) Noisy (b) BFM (c) L0M (d) GNF (e) CNR (f) Ours

Fig. 3. Denoising results of Bunny corrupted by large scale Gaussian noise ($\sigma = 0.8\bar{l}_e$). The zoomed views highlight that our method outperforms the others in preserving geometric details while removing noise effectively.

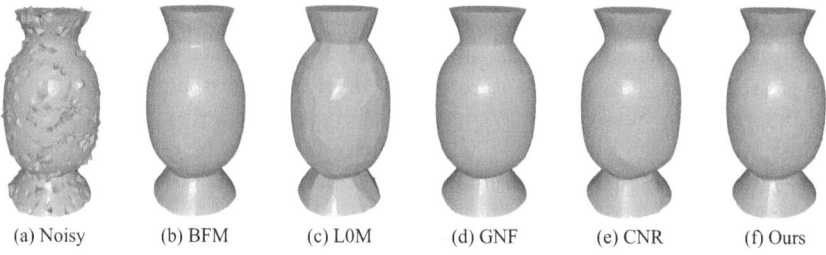

(a) Noisy (b) BFM (c) L0M (d) GNF (e) CNR (f) Ours

Fig. 4. Denoising results of Vase corrupted by impulsive noise ($\sigma = 0.5\bar{l}_e$).

Figure 3 shows the denoising results of Bunny corrupted by large scale Gaussian noise. As can be seen, except method CNR, the other methods can eliminate noise effectively. However, both methods BFM and GNF blur geometric details in varying degrees; see Fig. 3(b) and 3(d). On the contrary, L0M produces lots of staircasing effects in smooth regions; see Fig. 3(c). This is because the ℓ_0 norm requires the highest sparsity requirements. Different from sparisty-based methods, our method employs aggregate fidelity data term, which can preserving geometric details well while removing noise effectively.

Figure 4 shows denoising results of Vase with sharp features. As can be seen, all the methods are able to filter out noise effectively. However, the results of methods BFM, L0M, GNF, and CNR exist relatively large geometric distortions; seen from Fig. 4(b) to 4(e). Besides, method L0M also produces staircasing effects in smooth regions. Different from the above methods, our method can not only suppress noise effectively, but also keep both sharp features and smooth regions well. In addition, due to the aggregate fidelity term, our method does not induce large geometric distortions.

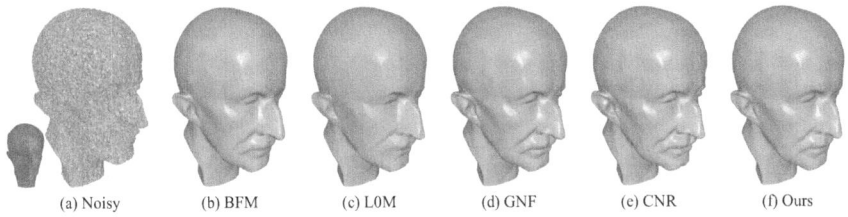

Fig. 5. Denoising results of Max-planck ($\sigma = 0.3\bar{l}_e$).

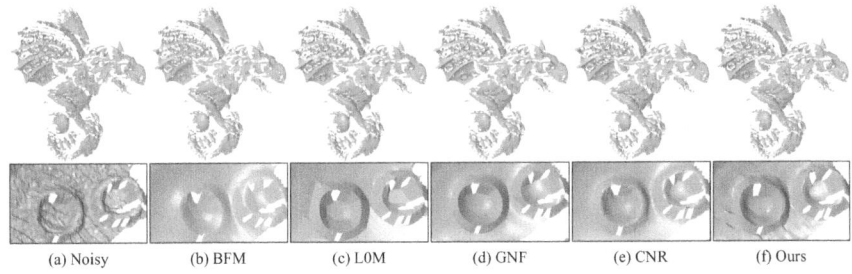

Fig. 6. Denoising results of a real scanned mesh. The zoomed views highlight that our method outperforms the others in recovering geometric features.

Figure 5 shows results of Max-planck with irregular sampling rates. As can be seen, most methods are able to eliminate noise effectively, except the method CNR which remains some noise in the region of forehead; see Fig. 5(e). Besides, methods L0M and GNF over-sharpen some geometric features in vary degrees; see Fig. 5(c) and 5(d). On the contrary, method BFM over-smooths geometric details; see Fig. 5(b). As can be seen in Fig. 5(f), our model can produce satisfactory denoising result, even at regions of highly irregular sampling. This is because our normal filtering model (1) takes the face areas into account in its design, used in both the fidelity and regularization term.

Moveover, we also show denoising results of a real scanned mesh in Fig. 6. Obviously, all the methods can remove noise effectively. Similarly, methods BFM, GNF, and CNR blur geometric features in vary degrees; see Fig. 6(b), 6(d), and 6(e). Besides, method L0M produces staircasing effects on smooth features; see

Fig. 6(c). Different from these methods, our method generates the visually best results with most features preserved; see Fig. 6(f).

5.2 Quantitative Comparisons

For an objective evaluation, we also quantitatively compare our method to the compared methods on synthetic data. To achieve this, the mean square angular error (MSAE) and L_2 vertex-based error ($E_{v,2}$) are employed to measure the fidelity of the denoising result compared to the ground truth. Details about these two metrics can be found in the works [2,10]. We compare our method to the other methods using these two metrics on the comparison examples shown in the previous subsection, except for the real scanned mesh which does not have corresponding ground truth. The comparison results are demonstrated in the Table 1. As we can see, compared to the other methods, our method has the smallest MSAE values and $E_{v,2}$ values. Thus, these quantitative comparisons show that, our method still outperforms the compared state-of-the art methods.

Additionally, we list the mesh sizes and runtime for all the testing methods in Table 1. As can be seen, BFM is always faster than other methods, due to its simplicity. Since our method need to cluster patches, the cost of our method is relatively higher than BFM, but far less than the others.

Table 1. Quantitative evaluation results.

Mesh	Size($|V|$; $|F|$)	MSAE($\times 10^{-3}$), $E_{v,2}(\times 10^{-3})$; Time (in Seconds)				
		BFM	L0M	GNF	CNR	Ours
Bunny	(29.8K; 59.7K)	2405.7, 5.10; 0.28	2401.6, 10.6; 19.2	2656.4, 12.4; 18.5	2652.7, 11.3; 2.56	**2305.8**, **3.34**; 1.68
Vase	(3.8K; 7.7K)	12.3, 5.73; 0.03	30.4, 5.70; 0.75	8.82, 5.1; 0.67	33.2, 4.85; 0.79	**7.45**, **4.19**; 0.08
Max-Planck	(50.0K; 100.0K)	27.7, 1.25; 0.39	36.2, 2.10; 22.3	29.2, 2.02; 13.4	31.6, 1.57; 4.38	**23.7**, **0.83**; 1.78

6 Conclusion

In this paper, we proposed a robust mesh denoising method based on the weighted least square framework. Taking a mesh with considerable amount of noise, outliers and irregular surface sampling, our method can fast and robustly remove noise while preserving geometric features well. The method firstly applies the aggregated fidelity term to the normal vector field, which can remove noise effectively. Then, a novel patch-aware normal filtering scheme is presented to recover sharp features. This scheme can improve the reconstructed mesh quality evidently. We discuss and compare our denoising method with selected state-of-the-art methods in various aspects. The experiments demonstrate that our method can soundly outperform the compared methods for both synthetic and scanned data, in terms of both normal filtering quality and mesh reconstruction accuracy, at reasonable costs.

References

1. Zheng, Y., Fu, H., Au, O.C., Tai, C.: Bilateral normal filtering for mesh denoising. IEEE Trans. Vis. Comput. Graph. **17**(10), 1521 (2011)
2. Zhang, H., Chunlin, W., Zhang, J., Deng, J.: Variational mesh denoising using total variation and piecewise constant function space. IEEE Trans. Vis. Comput. Graph. **21**(7), 873–86 (2015)
3. He, L., Schaefer, S.: Mesh denoising via ℓ_0 minimization. ACM Trans. Graph. **32**(4), 1–8 (2013)
4. Zhang, W., Deng, B., Zhang, J., Bouaziz, S., Liu, L.: Guided mesh normal filtering. Comput. Graph. Forum **34**(7), 23–34 (2015)
5. Yadav, S.K., Reitebuch, U., Polthier, K.: Robust and high fidelity mesh denoising. IEEE Trans. Vis. Comput. Graph. **99**(99), 1–1 (2017)
6. Centin, M., Signoroni, A.: Mesh denoising with (geo) metric fidelity. IEEE Trans. Vis. Comput. Graph. **24**(8), 2380–2396 (2017)
7. Yadav, S.K., Reitebuch, U., Polthier, K.: Mesh denoising based on normal voting tensor and binary optimization. IEEE Trans. Visual. Comput. Graph. **24**(8), 2366–2379 (2017)
8. Taubin, G.: A signal processing approach to fair surface design. In: Proceedings of the 22nd Annual Conference on Computer Graphics and Interactive Techniques, pp. 351–358 (1995)
9. Desbrun, M., Meyer, M., Schröder, P., Barr, A.-H.: Implicit fairing of irregular meshes using diffusion and curvature flow. In: Proceedings of the 26th Annual Conference Computer Graphics and Interactive Techniques, pp. 317–324 (1999)
10. Zheng, Y., Fu, H., Au, O.-C., Tai, C.-L.: Bilateral normal filtering for mesh denoising. IEEE Trans. Vis. Comput. Graph. **17**(10), 1521–1530 (2011)
11. Li, T., Liu, W., Liu, H., Wang, J., Liu, L.: Feature-convinced mesh denoising. Graph. Models **101**, 17–26 (2019)
12. Bilateral filtering for gray and color images. In: Sixth International Conference on Computer Vision (IEEE Cat. No. 98CH36271), pp. 839–846. IEEE (1998)
13. Fleishman, S., Drori, I., Cohen-Or, D.: Bilateral mesh denoising. ACM Trans. Graph. **22**(3), 950–953 (2003)
14. Wang, P.-S., Fu, X.M., Liu, Y., Tong, X., Liu, S.L., Guo, B.: Rolling guidance normal filter for geometric processing. ACM Trans. Graph. **34**(6), 1–9 (2015)
15. Yadav, S.K., Reitebuch, U., Polthier, K.: Robust and high fidelity mesh denoising. IEEE Trans. Vis. Comput. Graph. **PP**(99), 1–1 (2018)
16. Wei, M., Feng, Y., Chen, H.: Selective guidance normal filter for geometric texture removal. IEEE Trans. Vis. Comput. Graph. 1 (2020)
17. Zhong, S., et al.: Shape-aware mesh normal filtering. Comput. Aided Des. **140**, 103088 (2021)
18. Solomon, J., Crane, K., Butscher, A., Wojtan, C.: A general framework for bilateral and mean shift filtering, **1**(2), 3. arXiv preprint arXiv:1405.4734 (2014)
19. Wang, P.-S., Liu, Y., Tong, X.: Mesh denoising via cascaded normal regression. ACM Trans. Graph. **35**(6), 232:1–232:12 (2016)
20. Wu, X., Zheng, J., Cai, Y., Fu, C.-W.: Mesh denoising using extended ROF model with ℓ_1 fidelity. Comput. Graph. Forum **34**(7), 35–45 (2015)
21. Li, X., Cewu, L., Yi, X., Jia, J.: Image smoothing via l0 gradient minimization. ACM Trans. Graph. **30**(6), 1–12 (2011)
22. Lu, X., Chen, W., Schaefer, S.: Robust mesh denoising via vertex pre-filtering and ℓ_1-median normal filtering. Comput. Aided Geom. Des. **54**, 49–60 (2017)

23. Arvanitis, G., Lalos, A., Moustakas, K.: Feature-aware and content-wise denoising of 3D static and dynamic meshes using deep autoencoders. In: 2019 IEEE International Conference on Multimedia and Expo (ICME), pp. 97–102 (2019)
24. Wang, J., Huang, J., Wang, F.L., Wei, M.: Qin, J.: Data-driven geometry-recovering mesh denoising. Comput. Aided Des. **114**, 133–142 (2019)
25. Zhao, W., Liu, X., Zhao, Y., Fan, X., Zhao, D.: Normalnet: learning based guided normal filtering for mesh denoising. arXiv preprint arXiv:1903.04015 (2019)
26. Li, X., Li, R., Zhu, L., Fu, C.-W., Heng, P.-A.: DNF-net: a deep normal filtering network for mesh denoising. IEEE Trans. Vis. Comput. Graph. 1 (2020)
27. Arvanitis, G., Lalos, A.S., Moustakas, K.: Image-based 3D mesh denoising through a block matching 3D convolutional neural network filtering approach. In: 2020 IEEE International Conference on Multimedia and Expo (ICME), pp. 1–6. IEEE (2020)
28. Nousias, S., Arvanitis, G., Lalos, A.S., Moustakas, K.: Fast mesh denoising with data driven normal filtering using deep variational autoencoders. IEEE Trans. Ind. Inform. **17**(2), 980–990 (2021)
29. Pizarro, L., Mrzek, P., Didas, S., Grewenig, S., Weickert, J.: Generalised nonlocal image smoothing. Int. J. Comput. Vision **90**(1), 62–87 (2010)
30. Sun, X., Rosin, P., Martin, R., Langbein, F.: Fast and effective feature-preserving mesh denoising. IEEE Trans. Vis. Comput. Graph. **13**(5), 925–938 (2007)
31. Zhang, J., Deng, B., Hong, Y., Peng, Y., Qin, W., Liu, L.: Static/dynamic filtering for mesh geometry. IEEE Trans. Vis. Comput. Graph. **25**(4), 1774–1787 (2018)
32. Zhong, S., Xie, Z., Wang, W., Liu, Z., Liu, L.: Mesh denoising via total variation and weighted Laplacian regularizations. Comput. Animat. Virt. W. **29**(3–4), e1827 (2018)

Author Index

A
Ai, Menghan I-306, I-350

B
Bi, Huikun I-39

C
Cai, Bosi II-215
Cai, Jingyao II-409
Cao, Junxiang II-181
Chang, Chengjun II-165
Che, Aolin I-336
Chen, Jia I-388, II-397, II-456
Chen, Jianwei I-254
Chen, Jingxue I-375
Chen, Long I-57
Chen, Miaoxia I-336
Chen, Yukun I-72
Chen, Zhaoxiang I-13
Cheng, Boyuan II-409
Cheng, Shiwei II-13
Cui, Hong II-330

D
Dang, Bowen I-207
Ding, Yuhang I-132
Dong, Xiaoju II-181
Du, Lan II-1
Du, Xiaoqin I-105

F
Fan, Wanshu II-342
Fang, Fei I-388, II-397
Fang, Yalan I-28
Fang, Zhijun II-134
Feng, Lincong I-241, I-290
Feng, Yu II-215
Feng, Zhiquan II-330, II-424

G
Gao, Jianyu I-132
Gong, Bencan I-86
Gong, Chenchen II-28
Gou, Jianping II-1
Guan, Naiyang II-370
Guo, Cai I-336

H
Han, Cheng I-366, II-302
Han, Ping I-281
He, Shufan I-118
He, Xiaoqi II-61
Hossain, Md. Shamim II-441
Hu, Wentao II-89
Hu, Xinrong I-57, I-72, I-118, I-193, I-375, II-89, II-280
Hu, Yongli I-241, I-290
Huang, Danming II-28
Huang, Guohang II-46
Huang, Jin I-118
Huang, Junchao II-61
Huang, Tao II-233
Huang, Xiangguo I-193
Huang, Zhangjin II-441
Huang, Zijian I-375
Huang, Zile I-319
Huang, Zixin II-101, II-123
Hung, Cheng-Hao I-160

J
Jiang, Han II-101
Jiang, Huajie I-241, I-290
Jiang, Huanrong I-388, II-397
Jiang, Li II-150
Jiang, Minghua I-13, I-57, I-72, I-146, II-74
Jin, Mingyu I-319
Jin, Xiaobo I-319

© The Editor(s) (if applicable) and The Author(s), under exclusive license to Springer Nature Singapore Pte Ltd. 2025
N. Magnenat Thalmann et al. (Eds.): CASA 2024, CCIS 2375, pp. 471–473, 2025.
https://doi.org/10.1007/978-981-96-2684-7

K

Khan, Asad II-441
Kong, Dehui II-330, II-424
Kuang, Xiaomei II-316

L

Lan, Xi II-456
Li, Cuilan I-28
Li, Hongjun II-165
Li, Junqi I-28
Li, Li I-118, II-89
Li, Lifang I-254
Li, Lin II-1
Li, Min I-306, I-350
Li, Ping I-336
Li, Shuang II-267
Li, Weina II-424
Li, Xiang I-1
Li, Yingjin I-118
Liang, Hui I-268
Liang, Jing II-267
Liang, Jingbin II-267
Lin, Kun I-177
Lin, Mengying II-123
Lin, Zeping II-397
Liu, Chengzhi I-319
Liu, Chun II-150
Liu, Dezhi II-134
Liu, Feng II-112
Liu, Jiajie I-146
Liu, Jingyao I-39
Liu, Li I-13, I-57, I-72, I-146, II-74
Liu, Mengting I-241, I-290
Liu, Shiguang I-177
Liu, Yang II-13
Liu, Yanjun II-342
Liu, Yuan I-254
Liu, Zheng II-456
Liu, Zhicheng I-281
Lu, Hailun II-370
Lu, Shiyu II-302
Luo, Huangqianyu II-197
Luo, Peng I-306, I-350
Luo, Xianzhi II-150
Lv, JiaHui I-1

M

Ma, Hongteng II-123
Mao, Tianlu I-39

Mao, Yu I-28
Meng, Yajie I-388, II-397
Miao, Yujie II-370
Mujahid, Muhammad II-441

P

Page, Rupert II-409
Pan, Junjun I-268
Pan, Xiong II-456
Peng, Tao I-28, I-57, I-72, I-193, II-280

Q

Qin, Jinlong I-388, II-397

R

Rao, Cancan II-165
Ren, Liyu I-13
Ren, Wei I-224
Ren, Ziang II-101

S

Sheng, Guangjian II-357
Shi, Min II-233
Shibghatullah, Abdul Samad I-336
Shu, Zilin II-101
Song, Jinyu II-150
Sun, Shuifa I-254
Sun, Yuxiang II-28
Sun, Zian II-13

T

Tian, Xuefei II-181

W

Wan, Weibing II-134
Wang, Annan I-86
Wang, Cheng II-74
Wang, Chun I-306, I-350
Wang, Jun II-165
Wang, Lei II-249
Wang, Yong I-224
Wang, Zhaojing I-118
Wang, Zhaoqi I-39, II-233
Wang, Zixuan II-165
Wei, Ning I-254
Wei, Wu II-385
Wei, Xiaopeng II-342
Wei, Ziang II-123
Wen, Yi I-193

Author Index

Wen, Zhengke II-123
Wen, Zhicheng II-249
Wong, Sai-Keung I-160
Wu, Fangyu I-319
Wu, Haowen I-224
Wu, Junqi II-385
Wu, Yebo II-61
Wu, Zhiyuan II-181

X

Xi, Yingjie II-409
Xia, Zishuo II-424
Xiao, Zhendong II-385
Xiong, Maolin I-224
Xiong, Mingfu I-193
Xu, Fan I-268
Xu, Jianhua II-1
Xu, Qing II-112
Xu, Qingzhen II-316
Xu, Wei I-28
Xu, Yang I-193

Y

Yan, Xiaoyun II-89
Yang, Bo II-46
Yang, Huamin I-366, II-302
Yang, Jie I-375
Yang, Rui II-89
Yang, Shu-Chi I-160
Yang, Xiaosong II-409
Yao, Xun I-375
Ye, Wei II-357
Yeh, I-Cheng I-160
Yi, Xiaodong II-370
Yin, Aijie II-165
Yin, Baocai I-241, I-290
Yin, Ruhui II-101
Yu, Feng I-13, I-57, I-72, I-146, II-74

Yu, Fudong II-302
Yu, Jiahui II-28
Yu, Zhiran II-357
Yuan, Junbin II-316
Yuan, Zhiyong II-215

Z

Zhan, Yibing II-1
Zhang, Chao I-366
Zhang, Chi II-165
Zhang, Chong I-319
Zhang, Jian Jun II-409
Zhang, Jun II-280
Zhang, Lei II-357
Zhang, Tingbao II-215
Zhang, Tong I-388
Zhang, Xinlei II-28
Zhang, Yan I-224, II-150
Zhang, Yong II-46
Zhang, Yuqiang I-366
Zhang, Zhaolin I-268
Zhang, Zili II-280
Zhao, Jianhui II-215
Zhao, Sheng II-61
Zhao, Xi I-207
Zheng, Qijian II-112
Zheng, Xingwei II-74
zheng, Xiuyuan II-134
Zhong, Saishang II-456
Zhou, Dongsheng II-342
Zhou, Jiashuang I-105
Zhou, Xianzhong II-28
Zhu, Aiqing II-316
Zhu, Dengming II-233
Zhu, Hongyu II-101
Zhu, Jianlin II-46
Zou, Die II-123
Zuo, Huahong I-281

The manufacturer's authorised representative in the EU is Springer Nature Customer Service Centre GmbH, Europaplatz 3, 69115 Heidelberg, Germany. If you have any concerns regarding our products, please contact ProductSafety@springernature.com

Printed and bound by CPI Group (UK) Ltd, Croydon, CR0 4YY

29/04/2026

02099551-0006